International Law and the World War

CONTRIBUTIONS TO INTERNATIONAL LAW
AND DIPLOMACY

EDITED BY L. OPPENHEIM, M. A., LL.D.

*Late Membre de l'Institut de Droit International
Whewell Professor of International Law at the University of Cambridge
Honorary Member of the Royal Academy of Jurisprudence at Madrid
Corresponding Member of the American Institute of International Law*

.

INTERNATIONAL LAW
AND THE WORLD WAR

INTERNATIONAL LAW
AND THE WORLD WAR

BY

JAMES WILFORD GARNER

PROFESSOR OF POLITICAL SCIENCE IN THE
UNIVERSITY OF ILLINOIS

VOLUME II

LONGMANS, GREEN AND CO.
39 PATERNOSTER ROW, LONDON
FOURTH AVENUE & 30TH STREET, NEW YORK
BOMBAY, CALCUTTA, AND MADRAS
1920

THE·PLIMPTON·PRESS·NORWOOD·MASS·U·S·A

CONTENTS

VOLUME II

CHAPTER XXI

TREATMENT OF PRISONERS

SECTION   PAGE

331 Magnitude of the Problem of Caring for Prisoners During the Recent War 1

332 Prisoners of War Information Bureaus............................ 2

333 Inspection of Prison Camps by Neutral Representatives............ 5

334 Character and Methods of Inspection............................ 7

335 Pay of Officers Held as Prisoners.............................. 8

336 Officers' Quarters 12

337 Quarters and Housing Arrangements for Men..................... 13

338 The Ruheleben Prison Camp.................................... 16

339 The Camp at Wittenberg....................................... 18

340 Gardelegen and Other "bad" Camps.............................. 20

341 Mixing of Prisoners of Different Nationalities..................... 23

342 Regulations and Practice as to Clothing.......................... 24

CHAPTER XXII

TREATMENT OF PRISONERS (Continued)

343 Regulations and Practice as to Food and Diet...................... 28

344 The British and French Ration.................................. 29

345 The German Ration.. 30

346 Dependence of British and French Prisoners on Parcels from Home... 32

347 British and French Complaints.................................. 34

348 Regulations and Practice as to Postal Correspondence.............. 36

349 Complaints as to German Policy................................. 37

350 Employment of Prisoners....................................... 40

351 German Practice.. 41

352 Employment of Prisoners Behind the Firing Line................... 44

353 Pay for Prison Labor.. 45

354 Punishment and Discipline...................................... 46

355 Reprisal Measures... 49

356 Differential Treatment of Prisoners Captured on German Submarines. 50

357 Other Reprisals and Threats of Reprisals.......................... 51

358 Exchange of Civilian Prisoners.................................. 53

359 Transfer of Wounded and Invalided Prisoners to Switzerland........ 55

360 Repatriation of Prisoners in Long Captivity....................... 56

CHAPTER XXIII

MILITARY GOVERNMENT IN BELGIUM

SECTION		PAGE
361	General von der Goltz's Appointment as Governor-General	58
362	Revocation of Consular Exequaturs	59
363	Powers of the Governor-General	62
364	Powers of the Local Authorities Taken Over	63
365	German Legislation in Belgium	63
366	Restrictions in Respect to Personal Liberty	68
367	Restrictions in Respect to Patriotic Demonstrations	70
368	German Measures in Respect to Education	72
369	Movement to Detach Flemish Belgium — Transformation of the University of Ghent into a Flemish Institution	74
370	Deportation of Professors Pirenne and Frédéricq	76
371	Right of a Military Occupant to Interfere with Educational Institutions	77
372	Division of Belgium into Two Districts	78

CHAPTER XXIV

MILITARY GOVERNMENT IN BELGIUM (Continued)

373	German Military Courts in Belgium	81
374	Creation of Special Civil Tribunals	83
375	Right of a Military Occupant to Establish Special Tribunals	85
376	German Practice Criticised	88
377	Measures Against the Belgian Judiciary in 1918	89
378	The Germans Take over the Whole Administration of Justice in Belgium	91
379	The German Regime of Criminal Repression in Belgium	92
380	Criticism of the German Theory of War Treason	93
381	Condemnations by the German Tribunals	96
382	Execution of Women — Case of Edith Cavell	97
383	Intervention of the American Legation in Her Behalf	97
384	The German Defence	99
385	Past Practice as to the Execution of Women for War Crimes	102
386	Observations on the Cavell Case	104

CHAPTER XXV

CONTRIBUTIONS, REQUISITIONS, AND FORCED LABOR

387	German Policy in the Wars of 1866 and 1870–71	106
388	German Contributions During the Recent War	108
389	The General Contribution on Belgium	112
390	Provisions of the Hague Convention in Respect to Contributions	113
391	Purposes for which Contributions may be Levied	114
392	The Decuple Tax on Belgian Refugees	116
393	Requisitions of Supplies	117
394	Provisions of the Hague Convention in Respect to Requisitions	122
395	Requisition of Live Stock for Transportation to Germany	123

CONTENTS

SECTION | PAGE
396 Seizure and Transportation of Machinery to Germany.............. 124
397 Requisition of Railway Material................................. 127
398 Cutting of Forests... 128
399 Seizure of Funds of Private Banks and Post-offices 129
400 Requisition of Services for Military Work...................... 132
401 Requisition of Guides... 135
402 Views of the Authorities...................................... 137

CHAPTER XXVI

COLLECTIVE FINES AND COMMUNITY RESPONSIBILITY

403 German Theory and Practice................................... 140
404 German Policy During the War of 1870-71 141
405 Fines Imposed on Belgian Towns and Cities During the Recent War.. 143
406 Proclamations Threatening Collective Punishment.................. 150
407 Fines on French Towns and Cities.............................. 151
408 Views of German Jurists and Military Writers.................... 154
409 The Rule of the Hague Convention............................. 156
410 Interpretation of the Hague Rule.............................. 157
411 German Policy Criticised...................................... 159
412 Concluding Observations...................................... 161

CHAPTER XXVII

DEPORTATION OF THE CIVILIAN POPULATION FROM OCCUPIED TERRITORY

413 Early German Policy.. 163
414 Deportations from France in 1916.............................. 164
415 Manner of Execution of the Measure........................... 166
416 Protests Against the Deportations.............................. 167
417 Treatment of the French Déportés.............................. 168
418 The German Defence.. 169
419 The German Defence Analyzed................................. 170
420 Deportations from Belgium.................................... 171
421 Manner of Execution.. 172
422 Treatment of the Belgian Déportés............................. 175
423 Allied Protests Against the Deportation Measures................ 176
424 Neutral Protests.. 177
425 German Defence of the Policy of Deportation.................... 178
426 Economic Argument and Question of Public Order................ 180
427 The German Defence Analyzed 181
428 Power of a Military Occupant over the Inhabitants of Occupied Territory... 181
429 German Policy Unprecedented in Modern Times.................. 183
430 Conclusion 184

CHAPTER XXVIII

THE GERMAN INVASION OF BELGIUM

SECTION   PAGE
431   The Neutralization of Belgium.................................   186
432   The Treaties of 1870..   187
433   The British Inquiry of Germany and France in 1914.............   187
434   The German Ultimatum to Belgium...............................   188
435   Reply of the Belgian Government and the German Invasion........   189
436   Questions of International Law Involved.......................   190
437   The German Pretext of Military Necessity......................   191
438   The Right of Self-Preservation................................   193
439   The German Theory of Military Necessity — *Kriegsmanier* v. *Kriegs-
        raison*...   195
440   Criticism of the German Theory of *Kriegsraison*..............   196
441   Military Necessity as a Defence for the Invasion of Belgium....   198
442   The German Argument Analyzed..................................   201

CHAPTER XXIX

THE GERMAN INVASION OF BELGIUM (Continued)

443   Alleged French Violations of Belgian Neutrality...............   203
444   German Charges Against Belgium — The Anglo-Belgian "Conversa-
        tions"..   206
445   May a Neutralized State Enter into Alliances?.................   209
446   Effect of the Treaties of 1870 on the Neutralization Treaty...   210
447   Was the Treaty of 1839 Binding on the German Empire in 1914?...   212
448   The Provisions of the Hague Convention in Respect to the Inviola-
        bility of Neutral Territory.................................   214
449   The *Rebus Sic Stantibus* Argument...........................   217
450   Evaluation of the German Arguments............................   220
451   The Right of Passage in Time of War...........................   221
452   Duty of the Guarantors of the Neutralization of Belgium.......   227

CHAPTER XXX

INVASION AND OCCUPATION OF NEUTRAL TERRITORY
(Continued)

I. THE GERMAN INVASION OF LUXEMBURG

453   The Neutralization Convention of 1867.........................   231
454   Invasion of Luxemburg by the Germans in 1914..................   233
455   Germany's Principal Defence...................................   233
456   The German Plea Analyzed......................................   234
457   Invasion of Belgium and Luxemburg Compared....................   235
458   Other German Defences...   235
459   Conclusion...   236

2. JAPANESE VIOLATION OF CHINESE TERRITORY

SECTION		PAGE
460	The Japanese Proceedings..	237
461	Chinese Concession of a "War Zone"............................	238
462	Seizure of Chinese Railways.......................................	239
463	The Japanese Defence Reviewed.................................	240

3. THE OCCUPATION OF GREECE BY ENGLAND AND FRANCE

464 | English and French Troops Occupy Saloniki and Other Places........ | 241
465 | Other Acts of the Entente Powers.................................. | 242
466 | The Greek Protest and the Anglo-French Defence .... | 243
467 | The Conflict Between the King and Parliament...................... | 244
468 | Attitude of the Guaranteeing Powers............................... | 245
469 | The Allied Ultimatum of June, 1916................................ | 246
470 | Other Allied Demands upon Greece .... | 247
471 | The Abdication of the King.. | 249
472 | The Anglo-French Measures Compared with the German Invasion of Belgium. . . .. | 250
473 | The Purpose of the Allied Measures............................... | 253

CHAPTER XXXI

DESTRUCTION OF NEUTRAL MERCHANT VESSELS

474 | Practice of the Past... | 256
475 | Russian Practice in 1904-5.. | 257
476 | Prize Regulations of Other States.................................. | 258
477 | English Opinion as to the Legality of Neutral Prize Destruction.... | 261
478 | English Judicial Authority... | 262
479 | Views of Continental Publicists.................................... | 263
480 | Right of Destruction Affirmed..................................... | 263
481 | Discussion at the Second Hague Conference........................ | 264
482 | Discussion at the International Naval Conference, 1908-9............ | 266
483 | Rules of the Declaration of London................................ | 268
484 | Practice During the Recent War.................................... | 269
485 | Case of the *Frye*.. | 270
486 | Case of the *Maria*... | 271
487 | Case of the *Medea*.. | 271
488 | Losses of the Spanish Merchant Marine............................ | 273
489 | Losses of Denmark and Sweden................................... | 275
490 | Destruction of Norwegian Ships................................... | 276
491 | Total Losses of Neutral Merchant Marines......................... | 277
492 | The German Defence.. | 278
493 | Conclusion.. | 281
494 | Status of Neutral Property Destroyed on Enemy Merchantmen...... | 283

CHAPTER XXXII

CONTRABAND, RIGHT OF SEARCH, AND CONTINUOUS VOYAGE

495 | Importance of the Question During the Recent War................. | 285
496 | British and French Policy.. | 285

SECTION   PAGE
497 Protests Against the Disregard of the Declaration of London........ 288
498 Cotton as Contraband... 289
499 Food Stuffs as Contraband...................................... 291
500 American Complaints Regarding British Detentions................ 291
501 Extension of the Doctrine of Continuous Voyage to the Carriage of
      Conditional Contraband...................................... 295
502 History of the Doctrine of Continuous Voyage.................... 297
503 Neutral Embargoes on Exportations to Belligerent Territory........ 299
504 British and American Practice Compared......................... 300
505 Defense of the Doctrine of Continuous Voyage Under Modern Con-
      ditions... 302
506 The Case of the *Kim* and Others.............................. 303
507 French Cases.. 309
508 German Cases... 311
508a Conclusion.. 313

CHAPTER XXXIII

BLOCKADES

509 The German Submarine "Blockade" of England............. 317
510 Some Examples of Legal Blockades 318
511 The Anglo-French Blockade of Germany.................... 319
512 Criticism of the Proposed Blockade...................... 320
513 The Order in Council of March 11....................... 323
514 Character of the Blockade thus Proclaimed............... 324
515 Neutral Protests...................................... 324
516 The British Defence................................... 325
517 Legality of the Anglo-French Blockade.................. 327
518 Criticism Regarding the Discriminatory Features of the Blockade..... 328
519 Charge that the Blockade Applied to Neutral Ports........ 330
520 Extension of the Doctrine of Continuous Voyage to Blockade Running 331
521 Defence of the Doctrine............................... 333
522 Popular Demand in England for a Real Blockade........... 334
523 German Criticism of the Blockade as a "Starvation" Measure...... 336
524 Attitude of the British and French Governments in Regard to the Ad-
      mission of Hospital Supplies to Germany.................... 339
525 Admission of Food Supplies to the Occupied Districts of Belgium,
      France, and Poland.. 340
526 The Problem of Preventing Commerce with the Enemy.............. 342
527 The Netherlands Over-seas Trust....................... 342
528 The System of "Rationing" Neutrals.................... 344
529 Neutral Protests.................................... 345
530 American Policy.................................... 346
531 Other Expedients................................. 347

CHAPTER XXXIV

INTERFERENCE WITH MAILS AND PERSONS OF ENEMY NATIONALITY ON NEUTRAL VESSELS

532 German Exploitation of the Postal Service for Belligerent Purposes.. 350
533 Early Measures of the British and French Governments........... 352

CONTENTS

SECTION		PAGE
534	Neutral Protests	353
535	Provisions of the Hague Convention Regarding Postal Correspondence.	355
536	Attitude of the American Government	357
537	Views of the British and French Governments	359
538	Removal of Enemy Persons from Neutral Vessels: Case of Piepenbrink.	362
539	Cases of Garde and Others	365
540	Seizures on the *China*	366
541	What Persons are Liable to Seizure on Neutral Vessels?	367
542	Views of the Authorities	368
543	Practice of the Past	370
544	Case of the *Fredrico*	371
545	Status of Despatch Bearers on Neutral Vessels	373

CHAPTER XXXV

THE EXPORTATION OF ARMS AND MUNITIONS TO BELLIGERENTS

546	Policy of the United States	375
547	Are Neutrals Bound to Prohibit Such Traffic?	376
548	Views of German Writers Before the War	378
549	Practice in Former Wars — American Policy	382
550	British and French Practice	385
551	German Practice	389
552	Instances of Embargoes on the Exportation of Arms and Munitions	393
553	Protests of the German and Austrian Governments in 1915	394
554	Their Contentions Analyzed	395
555	The Question of Moral Obligation to Forbid Such Trade	399
556	Analysis of the Arguments	400
557	Practical Difficulties in the Way of Prohibition	402
558	Legality of the Alteration of the Rule During War	405

CHAPTER XXXVI

MISCELLANEOUS QUESTIONS OF NEUTRALITY

559	Loans to Belligerent Governments	408
560	Submarine Cables and Wireless Telegraphy	410
561	Procuring Supplies in Neutral Ports	415
562	Violation of Neutral Waters by Belligerent War Ships	419
563	Internment of Belligerent Warships with their Officers and Crews in Neutral Ports	422
564	Treatment of Submarine in Neutral Waters	430
565	Commercial Submarines, Case of the *Deutschland*	437
566	Taking of Prizes into Neutral Ports	438
567	Case of the *Appam*	439
568	Hovering of Warships off Neutral Ports	443
569	Submarine Operations off the American Coast	445
570	Transit Across Neutral Territory of Materials Susceptible of Military Use	446
571	Navigation of the River Scheldt by Belligerents	450

CHAPTER XXXVII

EFFECT OF THE WAR ON INTERNATIONAL LAW

SECTION		PAGE
572	Imperfections of International Law Revealed by the War............	452
573	Effect of the War on the Laws of Maritime Warfare; Blockade and Contraband	455
574	Other Unsettled Questions of Maritime Law........................	455
575	The Freedom of the Seas...	457
576	The Need of New Regulations.....................................	460
577	Necessity of an International Conference..........................	462

CHAPTER XXXVIII

ENFORCEMENT OF INTERNATIONAL LAW; OUTLOOK FOR THE FUTURE

578 | The Problem Stated.. | 465
579 | Lack of Effective Sanctions...................................... | 467
580 | Indemnity for Damages.. | 469
581 | Penal Clauses of the Treaty of Peace............................. | 471
582 | The Principle of Personal Responsibility of Soldiers for Criminal Acts. | 472
583 | Provisions of Military Manuals................................... | 474
584 | Difficulties of Application.. | 475
585 | Punishment of Crimes Committed in Foreign Territory.............. | 478
586 | Jurisdiction of Crimes on the High Seas........................... | 481
587 | Trial of Offenders in Their Absence............................... | 481
588 | The Plea of Superior Command................................... | 483
589 | Responsibility of Chiefs of States................................. | 488
590 | Decision of the Peace Conference Regarding the Trial of the German Emperor... | 490
591 | Decision of the Peace Conference Considered...................... | 493
592 | Precedents for the Trial of Chiefs of States........................ | 495
593 | Immunity of Chiefs of States..................................... | 497
594 | New Attitude Toward Violations of International Law.............. | 498
595 | Outlook for the Future... | 501

BIBLIOGRAPHY... | 505

INDEX... | 519

INTERNATIONAL LAW
AND THE WORLD WAR

INTERNATIONAL LAW AND THE WORLD WAR

CHAPTER XXI

TREATMENT OF PRISONERS

§ 331. Magnitude of the Problem of Caring for Prisoners during the Recent War; § 332. Prisoners of War Information Bureaus; § 333. Inspection of Prison Camps by Neutral Representatives; § 334. Character and Methods of Inspection; § 335. Pay of Officers Held as Prisoners; § 336. Officers' Quarters; § 337. Quarters and Housing Arrangements for Men; § 338. The Ruhleben Camp; § 339. The Camp at Wittenberg; § 340. Gardelegen and Other "Bad" Camps; § 341. Mixing of Prisoners of Different Nationalities; § 342. Regulations and Practice as to Clothing.

§ 331. **The Magnitude of the Problem of Caring for Prisoners during the Recent War.** The task of caring for the large number of prisoners taken by some of the belligerents during the late war, especially by Germany, exceeded in difficulty and magnitude that of any previous war.[1] The task was further

---

[1] According to an official statement issued by the German government on August 1, 1916, Germany and her allies had captured 2,678,000 prisoners as against 1,695,000 captured by their enemies. Of the former, 1,646,223 were in German prisons. They were distributed by nationalities as follows:

	Officers	Men
French	5947	348,731
Russians	9019	1,202,871
Belgians	656	41,757
British	947	29,950
Servians		22,914
Total	16,569	1,646,223

These figures were increased somewhat, though not considerably, by subsequent captures. According to a statement issued in May, 1917, the Central powers then held nearly 3,000,000, of whom 1,690,730 were in German prisons. In January, 1918, General Friedrich, in charge of prison affairs in Germany, stated to the main committee of the *Reichstag* that 410,000 French captives were then being held in German prisons (New York *Times*, March 11, 1918). Next to Germany, Russia took the largest number of prisoners. In October, 1916, the United States consul-general at Moscow reported that at least 1,000,000 prisoners were being held in

complicated by the internment by most of the belligerents of practically the entire enemy alien population. Manifestly the problem of housing and of adequately feeding, clothing, and guarding so large a number of prisoners for whom no provision had been made in advance, and this at a time when the energies and resources of the nations were being directed toward the destruction of the enemy, was a herculean task. The difficulty was further enhanced, in the case of Germany, by the suddenness with which the problem was thrust upon her, for the greater number of German captives were taken during the early months of the war, and provision for taking care of them was necessarily hasty and inadequate.

§ 332. **Prisoners of War Information Bureaus.** As is well known, the Hague convention of 1899 respecting the laws and customs of war on land [1] made it the duty of belligerents to establish at the outbreak of hostilities a bureau of information charged with answering inquiries about prisoners of war in respect to internments, transfers, releases on parole, exchanges, escapes, admissions to hospitals, deaths, etc.; to collect and preserve all objects of personal use, valuables, letters, etc., found on the battle field or left by prisoners released on parole or exchanged or who had died, and to forward them to the persons interested, etc. The convention of 1907 extended the scope of the bureau to include the furnishing of specific information regarding the regimental number, name, age, place of origin, rank, unit, nature of wounds, date and place of capture, internment, or death, and other information. Shortly after the outbreak of the war the British government took steps toward the putting into effect of the terms of the convention. On August 25, 1914, Sir Edward Grey in a communication to the American ambassador in London announced that His Majesty's government had instituted a prisoners of war information bureau to carry out the obligations which devolved upon them under article 14 of the convention, and he stated that he would be grateful if the ambassador would ascertain

---

Russia. New York *Times*, October 15, 1916. According to an announcement made in the House of Commons on October 28, 1918, British troops had taken since the beginning of the war 327,416 prisoners of whom 264,242 were Germans; of the latter, 97,000 were at the time in prisons in England.

[1] Art. 14.

whether the German and Austro-Hungarian governments were taking steps on their part to carry out the provisions of the article.[1] His Majesty's government, he said, was prepared to communicate periodically to the German and Austro-Hungarian governments lists of prisoners interned in England on the understanding that those governments would send corresponding lists of British prisoners interned in Germany and Austria-Hungary, and that it was likewise prepared, on condition of reciprocity, to forward letters despatched by prisoners in accordance with article 16 of the said convention.[2] In a subsequent communication to Mr. Page, Sir Edward Grey stated that the British prisoners of war information bureau made no distinction between military prisoners of war and civilians interned in the United Kingdom and other parts of the Empire, and that it furnished regular lists of both categories of prisoners.[3] It seems clear that the provisions of the Hague convention in respect to the prisoners of war information bureau were not intended to apply to interned civilians[4] and in charging its bureau with furnishing the enemy governments with information regarding their civilian subjects interned in Great Britain, the British government undoubtedly went further than the Hague convention required.

On August 26 the French government published in the *Journal Officiel* an *avis* announcing that a prisoners of war information bureau had been established in France in conformity with article 14, and that it would furnish the information required by the

---

[1] The organization and activities of the British bureau are fully described by Mr. R. F. Roxburgh in a monograph entitled, *The Prisoners of War Information Bureau in London* (London, 1915).

[2] *Correspondence between His Majesty's Government and the United States Ambassador respecting the Treatment of Prisoners of War and Interned Civilians in the United Kingdom and Germany respectively*, Misc., No. 7 (1915), Cd. 7817, p. 1.

[3] *Ibid.*, p. 53. In a *note verbale* of January 7, 1915, addressed by the German foreign office to the American ambassador, the German government stated that the central committee of the Red Cross society at Berlin had undertaken to furnish information regarding British civil prisoners interned in Germany on condition that a similar institution should be established in England to furnish information regarding German civilians interned in that country, and on condition that the British government would assist it and furnish it with lists of such prisoners and such other information as might be desired. *Ibid.*, p. 50.

[4] Cf. the discussions at the Conference of 1907, *Actes et Docs.*, Vol. III, pp. 9, 10, 109, 114-118.

Hague convention and perform the other obligations imposed by it.[1] The Russian ordinance of October 7/20, 1914, concerning prisoners of war [2] provided for the establishment at Petrograd of a central bureau of information under the direction of the Russian Red Cross society to give information concerning prisoners of war. The Austro-Hungarian ordinance of February, 1915, concerning the treatment of prisoners provided for a *Gemeinsames Zentral Nachweisebureau* at Vienna for furnishing information regarding prisoners.[3]

On September 14 the American ambassador at London received a telegram from the American ambassador at Berlin announcing that the German government had established an inquiry office at Berlin in conformity with article 14 and would collect and forward periodically the information and the objects required by the convention. There was some complaint at first on the part of the British government that the information furnished by the German bureau regarding the condition of English prisoners in Germany was insufficient, but the German government replied that it was doing all in its power to comply with the terms of the convention, and that every effort would be made in the future to furnish the information demanded.[4] The British government further complained because the German bureau declined to answer inquiries addressed to it directly by private persons,[5] although the British bureau was endeavoring to do it and would continue to do so.[6] The German government replied that its bureau could not undertake to answer any but official inquiries, but it added that the task of answering private inquiries had been assumed by the central committee of the Red Cross society, which had an official character. This

---

[1] Text in *Législation de la Guerre de 1914*, Vol. I, p. 85. Cf. also the text of a letter of M. Delcassé of February 28, 1915, in response to a question regarding the treatment of French prisoners in Germany (*Jour. Off.*, February 28, 1915; also *Rev. Gén. de Droit Int. Pub.* (1915), Docs., p. 121).

Cf. also *Régime des Prisonniers*, p. 45, a publication issued by the French government, and Lemoine, *Les Conventions Internationales sur le Régime des Prisonniers de Guerre*, pp. 45, 51.

[2] Text in 22 *Rev. Gén. de Droit Int. Pub.* (1915), Docs., p. 145.

[3] *Ibid.*, p. 152.   [4] *Misc.*, No. 7 (1915), p. 70.

[5] Art. 14 of the convention does not in express terms require the information bureau to answer such inquiries, although Sir Edward Grey so interpreted it, basing his contention on the language of the convention which charges the bureau "to reply to all inquiries about prisoners."

[6] *Ibid.*, p. 18.

duty, it was further added, was being performed by the Red Cross in both Russia and Japan.[1] This attitude of the German government caused some irritation in England and led Sir Edward Grey to accuse it of neglecting the obligations imposed by the Hague convention. He also added that had the German bureau furnished the information in the form required by the Hague convention, there would have been less necessity for special forms of inquiry regarding missing or wounded prisoners in Germany.[2] The German government, however, continued to insist that it had fully complied with all the terms of the convention.[3]

§ 333. **Inspection of Prison Camps by Neutral Representatives.** Shortly after the outbreak of the war the British government gave permission to an attaché of the American embassy in London to visit freely and inspect British prison camps where regular prisoners of war were confined, and on January 29, 1915, a general permit was given to representatives of the American embassy to visit and inspect all places in the United Kingdom where enemy aliens were interned. Every facility was afforded for a full and complete inspection, and the reports made were filed with the embassy at Berlin.[4] In consequence of the numerous reports reaching England that English prisoners held in Germany were being badly treated, Sir Edward Grey in December, 1914, proposed to the German government that an arrangement be entered into between the two governments for a general system of reciprocal inspection of prison camps by representatives of neutral governments.[5] In the meantime the American government expressed its willingness to lend the services of a certain number of officials for the performance of

[1] *Ibid.*, pp. 20-21. [2] *Ibid.*, p. 38.
[3] *Ibid.*, p. 72. The French government complained of the refusal of the German government to furnish information concerning French prisoners held in French and Belgian territory occupied by the German forces, and requested the Spanish ambassador at Paris to protest against this policy as a systematic violation of article 14 of the Hague *règlement*. After two ineffectual protests (March 23 and May 6, 1915) the German government was informed that unless a satisfactory response was made, the French government would be obliged to withhold all information concerning German prisoners held in France. In June, 1915, no reply having been received, the French threat was put into effect. 22 *Rev. Gén. de Droit Int. Pub.* (1915), Docs., p. 135.
[4] McCarthy, *The Prisoner of War in Germany*, p. 4.
[5] *Misc.*, No. 7 (1915), pp. 41-42.

this task. The German government, however, does not appear to have taken much interest in the proposal[1] and several months passed without an answer being returned. The British government, however, continued to press for a reply, and the American government urged the German government to accept the British proposal, pointing out that every facility for the inspection of prison camps in England and Canada was being afforded by the British government, and that Russia had agreed to the inspection of camps in that country by representatives of the American embassy.[2] Finally, on March 17, 1915, more than two months and a half after the British proposal was made, the German government consented to adopt a scheme for the reciprocal inspection of prison camps by representatives of neutral governments.

The French government, which likewise had from the outset permitted representatives of the American government to inspect all prison camps in France,[3] finally succeeded in inducing the German government to agree to permit representatives of the Spanish embassy at Berlin to visit without previous notice all places in Germany where prisoners of war and interned civilians were confined, including also detached labor camps.

[1] McCarthy, *op. cit.*, p. 4.

[2] Mr. Gerard, the American ambassador at Berlin, describes in his book, *My Four Years in Germany*, his own efforts to induce the German government to consent to the inspection of German prison camps. He says: "After vainly endeavoring to get the German government to agree to some definite plan for the inspection of the prisoners; after my notes to the foreign office had remained unanswered for a long period of time, and after sending a personal letter to von Jagow, calling his attention to the fact that the delay was injuring German prisoners in other countries, I finally called on Chancellor von Bethmann-Hollweg and told him that my notes concerning prisoners were sent by the foreign office to the military authorities, and that, while I could talk with officials of the foreign office, I never came into contact with people who really passed upon the notes sent by me and who made the decisions as to the treatment of prisoners of war and inspection of their camps. I begged the Chancellor to break down diplomatic precedent and allow me to speak with the military authorities who decided these questions. And I said, 'If I cannot get an answer to my proposition about prisoners, I will take a chair and sit in front of your palace in the street until I receive an answer.'" As a result of this consultation a meeting was held in the ambassador's office, and an agreement for the reciprocal inspection of prison camps in England and Germany was speedily concluded (pp. 159 ff.).

[3] Cf. a summary of the reports of Mr. Lee Meriwether, a representative of the United States government, who inspected various prison camps in France. New York *Times Magazine*, February 10, 1918.

A similar arrangement was entered into between the Russian X and Austro-Hungarian governments.[1]

§ 334. **Character and Methods of Inspection.** In pursuance of these agreements a staff of inspectors was organized by each of the embassies to whom the permission was thus accorded. The personnel embraced attachés, consuls, specially detailed medical officers, food experts, and the like. In some instances, as in Germany, the ambassador himself conducted some of the inspections. By reason of the large number of detention camps in Germany (the number was approximately two hundred) the task of inspection was very great, and it was further increased by the organization of thousands of working camps which were detached from the parent camps and widely scattered over the country. During the year 1915 more than one hundred and fifty inspections of camps were made in Germany by American officials. The inspectors were generally afforded every facility for conducting their investigations, although complaints were not lacking that German prison commandants in some instances threw obstacles in the way of the inspecting officers.[2] The

[1] On November 11, 1918, shortly before the conclusion of the armistice, an elaborate agreement between the United States and Germany concerning the treatment of prisoners was signed at Berne (text in Supp. to 13 *Amer. Jour. of Int. Law* (January, 1919). Under the agreement diplomatic representatives of the protecting power were to be allowed to designate delegates to inspect prison camps subject to certain conditions. Among other rights the delegates were to be allowed to visit the camps without notice, to converse with the prisoners outside the hearing of the guards, and to present to the camp authorities complaints made by prisoners, together with such suggestions as they might consider advisable.

[2] Dr. D. J. McCarthy, a medical professor in the University of Pennsylvania, who served as an inspector in Germany, refers to a number of such instances in his book, *The Prisoners of War in Germany.* Mr. Gerard in his book, *My Four Years in Germany,* makes frequent complaint of this kind. At Halle he was told that he could not speak to the prisoners out of the hearing of the guard; in consequence he left without making an inspection. At Magdeburg he was told by the authorities that if they had known in advance of his visit, they would not have permitted it. "The German authorities," he says, "in the most petty manner, often concealed from me the presence of British prisoners, especially civilians, in prison camps." (Cf. p. 169.)

The French government made similar complaints. It complained especially of the refusal of the German authorities to permit inspections of detention and prison camps in the regions occupied by the German armies; that special permits were required to visit *chantiers* and hospitals; that prisoners were not freely permitted to formulate their complaints in writing and to send them to the embassy, and that obstacles were placed in the way of inspection of working camps. *Rapports des Délégués du Gouv. Espagnol,* pp. ix-xii. Chas. Hennebois in his book, *In German Hands; the Diary of a Severely Wounded Prisoner,* complained that the

inspection included such matters as housing and equipment, sanitary conditions, employment, the character and quantity of food supplied, kitchen arrangements, cooking, hospital facilities, beds, ventilation, water supply, heat, lighting, etc. The attention of the commandant was frequently called to the existence of conditions which were open to criticism, and suggestions were offered for their improvement, — suggestions which, it may be added, were often adopted. In every case the inspector made a full report to the embassy of the results of his inquiries. These reports appear to be free from prejudice and may be taken as the fairest and most reliable sources of information regarding the treatment of prisoners which we have.[1] Inspections, it may be added, were also made by delegates of the International Red Cross committee at Berne.

§ 335. **Pay of Officers Held as Prisoners.** Soon after the outbreak of the war the governments of Great Britain, Germany, and France and perhaps other belligerent countries issued regulations concerning the treatment which they proposed to accord prisoners held by them.[2]

---

inspections were largely ineffective. The camps, he says, were warned of the intended visit several days in advance, thus offering an opportunity to the camp authorities to conceal anything which they did not wish to be seen; to alter the diet; to increase the amount of heat, and the like (p. 232).

[1] The reports of inspections made in England and Germany by the American representatives were published in a series of parliamentary papers issued by the British government from time to time. A large number of those made of French prison camps in Germany by representatives of the Spanish government have been published in a volume entitled *Rapports des Délégués du Gouvernement Espagnol sur Leurs Visites dans les Camps de Prisonniers Français en Allemagne, 1914-1917* (Librairie Hachette et Cie., Paris, 1918).

[2] The British regulations were embodied in a memorandum of December 14, 1914, on the treatment of interned civilians and prisoners of war in the United Kingdom (text in *Misc.*, No. 7, 1915, pp. 23-24) and a statement of February 3, 1915, regarding the internal management of prisons and the condition under which prisoners were allowed to purchase or receive newspapers (*ibid.*, pp. 54-55). The German regulations were set forth in a " statement [forwarded July 28, 1915] concerning the principles observed in the housing, feeding, and clothing, as well as the postal traffic of men and officers held as prisoners of war " (*ibid.*, pp. 79-81). The French rules were embodied in a series of decrees, circulars, declarations, and letters of the minister of foreign affairs. Cf. the *Rev. Gén. de Droit Int. Pub.* (1915), Docs., pp. 39, 41, 44, 87, 121, and 126. The Russian regulations may be found in a somewhat elaborate *règlement* concerning prisoners of war, bearing the date of October 7/20, 1914 (*ibid.*, pp. 145-151). Those of Austria-Hungary were embodied in an ordinance issued by the ministry of war in February, 1915 (text, *ibid.*, pp. 151-153).

Regarding the pay of officers held as prisoners article 17 of the Hague convention respecting the laws and customs of war on land provides that "officers taken prisoners shall receive the same rate of pay as officers of corresponding rank in the country where they are detained; the amount shall be refunded by their own government." On September 24, 1914, Sir Edward Grey in a communication to Mr. Page [1] requested him to ascertain the intentions of the German government in respect to the observance of article 17. At the same time he stated that the British government was prepared, in case the enemy governments would accord reciprocity of treatment to captured British officers, to allow the same rates in force in the British army to prisoners of war of corresponding rank, whether they belonged to the military or naval forces or whether regular reserve, or territorial. [2] The rates in the infantry of the British army were as follows:

	PER DIEM
	s d
Lieutenant-colonel	23 0
Major	16 0
Captain	11 7
Lieutenant	6 6
2d Lieutenant	5 3
Quartermaster	9 0

Officers receiving these rates would of course be expected to pay for their own food and clothing.

In a communication to Mr. Page of December 2, Sir Edward Grey stated that the British government was in fact allowing German military and naval prisoners half the pay of the corresponding ranks in the British army, and that they were being messed without cost. He also added that if His Majesty's government could receive satisfactory assurance that British officers in German hands were receiving the full pay of corresponding ranks in the German army, Great Britain would accord reciprocity of treatment. [3] After waiting nearly five months and receiving no reply either from Germany or Austria-

---

[1] *Misc.*, No. 7 (1915), Cd. 7817, pp. 4–5.
[2] The Hague convention in respect to the payment of officers does not apply to the naval forces, but the *wish* was expressed by the conference that the principles relating to the laws of war on land should apply as far as possible to maritime war.
[3] *Ibid.*, p. 21.

Hungary to the British proposal of September 24 regarding the mutual observance of article 17, Sir Edward Grey informed Mr. Page that in consequence of the failure of the German and Austro-Hungarian governments to reply to his proposal, the British government had decided to "remodel" the basis on which pay was being allowed officer prisoners held in England. Information being received in the meantime through the Geneva branch of the Red Cross society that British officers held as prisoners in Germany were receiving only sixty marks per month if subalterns, and only 100 marks if of higher rank, from which approximately an amount equal to two-thirds was being deducted for food, the British government reduced the pay of German officers to approximately four shillings a day for subalterns and four shillings six pence per day for captains and all officers of higher rank.[1] Furthermore, officers in receipt of these rates would be expected to defray the cost of their rations and messing. Sir Edward again added that should it be eventually established that either the German, Austro-Hungarian, or Turkish governments were prepared to allow full pay to British officers, an improved treatment would be accorded to the officers of those powers.[2]

In the beginning, the French government likewise adopted the policy of allowing captured German officers the pay allowed French officers of corresponding rank (the amount ranged from 102 to 336 francs per month), but for some months all efforts of the French government to obtain information as to the

---

[1] The American consul-general at Berlin had reported on October 20, 1914, that British officers confined at Tergau were receiving sixty marks per month if lieutenants, all others above that rank one hundred marks, from which the cost of meals and clothing was deducted. *Ibid.*, p. 13. This report was confirmed in December by Major Vandeleer, a British officer who had succeeded in escaping from the prison camp at Crefeld. He added that practically the whole of the pay allowed subalterns was consumed for food and clothing. *Ibid.*, p. 33. Dr. Ohnesorg in June, 1916, reported that British officers interned at Ingolstadt were receiving from sixty to one hundred marks per month according to rank, and that the average cost of their mess was about forty-five marks per month. *Misc.*, No. 19 (1915), p. 7.

[2] *Misc.*, No. 7 (1915), pp. 74–75. McCarthy in his book, *The Prisoner of War in Germany* (p. 199), says British officers with the rank of captain were paid sixty marks per month; others up to and including the rank of colonel were paid salaries up to one hundred marks. This scale was about one-eighth of that which the British government had paid to German officers before the reduction referred to above.

German practice resulted in failure. Finally, it was learned that the German government was allowing French officers sixty marks per month in the case of subalterns, and 100 marks for superior officers, a deduction of 1 mark 80 pfennigs per day from this amount being made for subsistence. So little was left to cover other expenses that the French government was led to protest against the German scale not only because of its insufficiency, but because it was in effect a violation of the Hague convention. Thereupon the French government reduced the scale of pay which it had been allowing German officers to 75 francs and 125 francs per month according to rank. In December, 1915, however, an accord between the two governments was reached by which it was agreed that the officers of each held as prisoners by the other should be paid a monthly allowance equal to that paid its own officers when on leave.[1] The Austro-Hungarian ordinance of February, 1915, concerning the treatment of prisoners promised 16 hellers per day, an amount regarded as sufficient merely to cover the cost of subsistence.[2] The Russian ordinance concerning prisoners of war announced that generals and admirals would receive 1500 rubles per year, officers of the general staff 900 rubles and superior officers 600 rubles.[3] Soon after the entrance of the United States into the war the American government proposed to the German government that officers captured by each side should receive the pay allowed by their own governments in accordance with the Hague convention, and the American government appears to have acted from the outset on this principle. The German government, however, ignored the American proposal and for months did not return an answer, in consequence of which the American government in January, 1918, directed that no further payments be made to German officers held in the United States until information was received from the German government of its willingness to reciprocate. Finally, in November, 1918, an agreement was reached under which officers held by either government were to receive pay at the rate of from 275 marks ($65.50) per month to 400 marks

---

[1] 22 *Rev. Gén. de Droit Int. Pub.* (1915), Docs., pp. 104-121; *Le Régime des Prisonniers de Guerre*, etc., pp. 16, 19, 20, and *Rapports des Délégués Espagnols*, etc., pp. 1-2.

[2] 22 *Rev. Gén. de Droit Int. Pub.* (1915), Docs., p. 152. [3] *Ibid.*, p. 151.

($95.25) per month according to rank. These rates were to apply without regard to whether officers belonged to the active or reserve forces or whether they were regular prisoners of war or interned civilians.

§ 336. **Officers' Quarters.** Regarding the housing and maintenance of prisoners article 7 of the Hague *règlement* provides that

"The government into whose hands prisoners of war have fallen is charged with their maintenance. In default of special agreement between belligerents, prisoners of war shall be treated as regards . . . quarters . . . on the same footing as the troops of the government which captured them."

In a note of December 2, 1914, to Mr. Page Sir Edward Grey stated that the

"accommodation provided for officers in England is entirely apart from soldiers and is either in country houses or officers' quarters in barracks. Their quarters are comfortably furnished, but without luxury. Servants are found for officers from among the prisoners of war." [1]

No complaint appears to have been made by the German government concerning the treatment of officer prisoners held in England, and the reports of the American representatives as well as the testimony of unofficial persons who visited their camps were all in agreement that there was little or nothing to complain of. In France, German officers were housed in some instances in châteaus surrounded by spacious gardens, in old monasteries, or in fortresses, all of which were well lighted and ventilated. In some of the camps where civilians were detained they had their families with them and were provided with German orderlies and cooks.[2] Representatives of the Red Cross and of the American embassy found nothing to criticise and much to praise.

The German memorandum of November, 1914, concerning prisoners of war declared that "as a rule" captured officers and soldiers were not interned in the same place at the same time. Military officers and civil officials of like rank were interned in

---

[1] *Misc.*, No. 7 (1915), p. 21.
[2] Such were the conditions in a camp at LePuy as they were seen by a representative of the associated press in November, 1915. The officers were on parole and were not under guard, although the camp was surrounded by a wall topped by several strands of barbed wire. Cf. also *Régime des Prisonniers*, pp. 16–19.

fortresses. Generals were provided with a living room and a bedroom. Staff officers were each given a single room. Other officers were assigned a small room each, or seevral together in one large room. Officers were allowed to have orderlies of their own nationality for their personal service,[1] one for every five to ten officers. The official statement of February 28, 1915, "concerning the principles observed in the housing, feeding, clothing, etc., of officers and men held as prisoners of war in Germany"[2] declared that the place of internment "must be healthy and absolutely unobjectionable from the hygienic point of view, with at least 15 cubic metres breathing space for each man, one which could be aired, which admitted full daylight and which could be heated and lighted daily." Various charges were made, however, by British officers that the regulations laid down in the German memorandum and statement referred to above were not always observed.

For the most part the American inspectors, however, found little to complain of in regard to the treatment of officers in the German camps. Dr. McCarthy says that in a general way the German government met this problem in a complete and satisfactory manner. With one or two exceptions, he said, "all of these camps are now satisfactory, and considering conditions no reasonable complaint can be found. Fortresses, sanatoria, newly constructed high school buildings, modern barrack buildings and vacated factory buildings have all been utilized for officers' quarters."[3]

§ 337. **Quarters and Housing Arrangements for Men.** The British memorandum respecting the treatment of interned civilians and prisoners of war stated that they were lodged either on board ships,[4] in barracks, in large buildings that had been taken over for the purpose, or in small huts constructed

---

[1] *Misc.*, No. 7 (1915).   [2] Text, *ibid.*, pp. 79-81.

[3] *The Prisoner of War in Germany*, p. 191. All the above-mentioned buildings, he adds, except those at Magdeburg and Ingolstadt, were unobjectionable from the hygienic standpoint. In the other camps the officers were housed in small rooms which were simply but comfortably furnished. Hot and cold water was supplied for bathing purposes; there was sufficient space for field sports and recreations; food arrangements were in the hands of a committee of officers; orderlies were provided to care for their rooms, etc.

[4] In the early days of the war nine ships were taken over by the admiralty and fitted up for the accommodation of interned civilian prisoners, but later the prisoners were removed to camps on land.

for the housing of prisoners. These quarters were, the memorandum added, kept warm and well lighted. Interned civilians
were allowed to choose better accommodations and food at
their own expense. Those who remained in the camps to which
they were assigned were divided into classes according to their
social rank, though all received the same accommodations and
food. Ample hospital and medical facilities were furnished
free of charge.[1] The American representatives who inspected
the prison camps in England found the accommodations quite
up to the standard usually prevailing in prison camps for private
soldiers, and this was the testimony of neutral newspaper
correspondents and other persons who were permitted to visit
them.[2] The only camp in England against which there appears
to have been any serious complaint from Germany was that at
Newbury, which was criticised on the ground that it was "greatly
overcrowded, poorly furnished and generally unfit for human
habitation." [3]

In France prisoners were at first lodged in casernes, but as
the number increased, special buildings were constructed.
Only in North Africa were tents employed. By a circular of
November 27, 1914, commandants were urged to see that

[1] *Misc.*, No. 7 (1915), p. 23.

[2] Cf., e.g., the very favorable report of Chandler Hale concerning the detention
camp in the Isle of Man, *Misc.*, No. 7 (1915), pp. 36-37. Boylston Beal of the
American embassy made a report in the spring of 1916 upon the conditions which
he found in twenty-three prison camps in the United Kingdom. He found that
in every instance the quarters were "clean, neat, well ventilated, heated and
lighted"; that there was no overcrowding; hot and cold water was furnished for
bathing purposes; ample facilities for recreation were provided; concerts, the-
atricals, and libraries were established; the sanitary arrangements were "clean and
neat" and in most cases "odorless"; the hospitals were clean and in good condition; there were few patients then, and the rate of mortality was very low;
the improvements which he suggested were usually made; some of the camps were
models; and he heard no serious complaints and, indeed, few of any kind. His
reports are published in a white paper, *Misc.*, No. 30 (1916), Cd. 8324. Cf. also
an article entitled "Civilians Interned in England" by a London newspaper
correspondent, New York *Times Current History Magazine*, November, 1916, pp.
349 ff.; also despatches in the New York *Times* of June 26 and July 27, 1917.
A correspondent of the New York *Times*, in a despatch of July 8, 1917, from
London, gave a flattering description of the conditions prevailing in the prison
camps of England. He heard only two complaints: (1) No German newspapers
were allowed, and (2) the prisoners were not permitted to sing German patriotic
songs. Cf. also a booklet entitled *German Prisoners in Great Britain*.

[3] This charge was made in November, 1914, by the association of physicians
at Hamburg in an open letter addressed to the physicians of England.

prisoners were not housed in damp or dark places or in hangars not properly covered. By a circular of December 23 directions were given that new camps should be erected only on elevated ground which could be easily drained.[1] Inspections made by representatives of the American embassy and by delegates of the International Red Cross society found nothing to complain of regarding housing facilities in the French prison camps,[2] and no complaints appear to have been made by the German government.

In the United States prisoners were housed in specially constructed wooden huts, well built, heated, lighted and furnished, and surrounded by ample grounds for exercise and recreation.[3] No complaints appear to have been made regarding quarters or treatment generally.[4]

The German regulations of February, 1915, provided that prison camps must be located on healthy sites, that a minimum breathing space of at least five cubic metres for each man (fifteen for officers) must be provided, and that rooms must be well aired, must admit full daylight, and must be heated and supplied with artificial light. They added that "sleeping accommodations consist of cloth sacks (*paillasses*) filled with straw or wood shavings; each prisoner is allowed two woollen blankets, a towel and eating utensils and in each camp provision is made for a bath and wash house."[5] Many complaints were made, however, that the quarters provided in some of the camps were inadequate to accommodate the large numbers of prisoners confined in them, that the blankets and clothing supplied were

---

[1] *Le Régime des Prisonniers, etc.*, p. 29.   [2] *Ibid.*, p. 29.

[3] The number of prisoners held in the United States at any time was hardly more than five thousand, five hundred. They consisted in the main of officers and seamen removed from German merchant ships in American ports, those from German cruisers and "raiders" which came into American ports during the war, and enemy aliens who were interned on account of violation of the laws or who were confined because they were regarded as suspicious or dangerous characters. The camps were located at Fort Oglethorpe, McPherson, Ga., and Fort Douglas, Utah. There was also a small camp at Lancaster, Mass. *Official Bulletin*, June 8, 1918. As to the regulations of the general agreement of November 11, 1918, see Supp. to 13 *Amer. Jour. of Int. Law* (January, 1919).

[4] The treatment of prisoners in the United States is described in detail in articles in the New York *Times Magazine* of July 7, 1918; in the Boston *Herald* of May 4, 1918, and in *Munsey's Magazine*, 1918, pp. 137 ff. As in England, there were complaints in some quarters that German prisoners were too well treated.

[5] Text of the German regulations in McCarthy, *op. cit.*, pp. 271 ff.

insufficient, that the quarters were not well heated and lighted, that they were unsanitary, that the facilities for bathing and exercise were inadequate, and the like. The published reports of the American and Spanish inspectors show that in the majority of camps the quarters provided were fairly satisfactory and perhaps as good as could have been reasonably expected under the conditions, especially during the early months of the war. On account of the large number of prisoners that had to be suddenly provided for, the task of providing adequate accommodations was almost impossible. A few camps — those at Göttingen and Friedrichsfeld, for example — were almost models and afforded examples which should have been followed in every prison camp in Germany.[1] In a good many cases, however, the inspectors found much to be desired, and in some instances the conditions were thoroughly bad. The camps at Ruheleben, Minden, Limburg, Wittenberg, Schneidemühl, Langensalza, and Gardelegen were some of the more notable examples.[2]

§ 338. The Ruheleben Camp. The camp at Ruheleben near Berlin was set apart for the confinement of interned British civilians. There between four and five thousand men of every social rank, degree of education and wealth, occupation and profession, native-born Englishmen and naturalized British subjects of German origin and of pro-German sympathy, were herded together in the filthy stables, box stalls, and hay-lofts of an old race course. Six men were compelled to sleep on a pile of straw, infrequently renewed, in each box, which was

[1] McCarthy, op. cit., p. 73, and Gerard, My Four Years in Germany, p. 165.
[2] McCarthy, p. 74. The shocking conditions prevailing at Minden are detailed by McCarthy, pp. 76-104. Mr. Gerard and Mr. Grew inspected the camp at Döberitz in October, 1914, and reported that the conditions were fairly satisfactory. Misc., No. 7 (1915), pp. 8, 11. But in December "a citizen of the United States living at Havre" found it greatly overcrowded and with insufficient bathing facilities. The men were covered with vermin, the tents were without floors, the straw was sour and of a musty odor, etc. The German government admitted that the charges were not wholly untrue, but stated that the tents had since been replaced with wooden buildings. In any case, it added, the conditions were far better than those prevailing in the internment camp at Newbury, England. Misc., No. 19 (1915), p. 18. Eric Fisher Wood visited the camp during the autumn as a representative of the American embassy and made a most unfavorable report upon the conditions prevailing there. Note Book of an Attaché, p. 296.

But in January, 1915, another representative of the American embassy visited the camp and found conditions much improved, only three tents being left. Misc., No. 16 (1916), p. 48.

about ten feet square. The stables were poorly heated and lighted, and the stench was wellnigh unbearable. The washing arrangements were hopelessly inadequate; toilet facilities were repulsive, and for weeks the prisoners had no place to eat except in the narrow passage ways.[1] The conditions at Ruheleben were the subject of vigorous protest by the British government, and on January 19, 1915, Mr. Acland, parliamentary undersecretary of state for foreign affairs, laid before the American ambassador a memorandum which described in detail the shocking conditions existing there.[2]

The charges set forth in the memorandum were, however, denied by the German foreign office in February.[3] Mr. Gerard interested himself in the matter and urged the German authorities to remedy the conditions complained of. He wrote letters to the various authorities, from the commander of the mark of Brandenburg to the minister of war, but "the only result was that each of the officers addressed claimed that he had been personally insulted by me because I had presumed to call his attention to the inhuman conditions under which the prisoners were compelled to live in the Ruheleben camp."[4] The hopes of the prisoners were raised by the first visit of the ambassador to the camp in March, 1915, when, we are told, he "recoiled with a shudder and denounced the loft as unfit for habitation."[5]

[1] Cf. the very interesting book *"The Ruheleben Prison Camp"* (especially ch. VI) by Israel Cohen, a British subject who spent nineteen months in the camp. The writer says that when he first saw his quarters, he broke down; the air was so thick that one could cut it with a knife; the stench was overpowering, and it was impossible to light a match in the darkness without setting the whole building ablaze (p. 42); the cold was intense; many prisoners had no changes of clothing (p. 73); medical facilities were "shamefully inadequate" (p. 183), and conditions in the hospital were "utterly disgraceful" (p. 185). Cf. also Mahoney, *Sixteen Months in Four German Prisons*, chs. 18–19.

[2] *Misc.*, No. 7 (1915), pp. 46–48.   [3] *Ibid.*, p. 63.

[4] *My Four Years in Germany*, p. 177.

[5] Cohen, *op. cit.*, p. 50. Mr. Gerard in a despatch of June 28, 1916, severely criticised the housing conditions at Ruheleben. The barracks, he said, were overcrowded, notwithstanding that the Imperial authorities had had nearly two years in which to provide ample accommodations. It was unfortunate, he added, that people of education should be herded six together in a horse's stall. In the haylofts above the stables conditions were even worse. In one hay-loft, ten by twelve metres, sixty-four men were confined; beds were so close that they touched; there was little light; the heating system was bad, and no provision was made for the drying of clothes, although the men were often required to answer roll calls in the rain. British white paper respecting conditions at Ruheleben, *Misc.*, No. 25 (1916). Cd. 8296, p. 3.

There was also much criticism of the camp for interned civilians at Holzminden, where there were five thousand prisoners, including a large number of women. The camp was greatly overcrowded; the barracks were small; the beds were arranged in double tiers and consisted of mattresses filled with excelsior; the whole place was infested with vermin, and there was a general atmosphere of depression and uncleanliness.[1]

§ 339. The Camp at Wittenberg. The worst of the German camps was the "plague" camp at Wittenberg, which was the seat of a typhus epidemic in 1915. According to a report made by a government committee under the chairmanship of Mr. Justice Younger of the English High Court,[2] this camp was built on a flat sandy plain devoid of trees or shrubbery. Each barrack was originally intended to accommodate 120 men, but there were before and during the epidemic from 180 to 200 prisoners in each. Between 15,000 and 17,000 prisoners were confined in the camp, although its area was only 10½ acres. The heating arrangements were altogether inadequate, and there was a shortage of coal, although the winter of 1914–1915 was particularly severe in Germany. Added to this, the men were insufficiently clothed, their overcoats having been taken away from them at the time of their capture. What remained in the way of clothing was in rags; many had neither shoes nor socks, their feet being wrapped in straw. No hot water was supplied, and the only facilities for bathing consisted of a trough the water in which was usually frozen during the winter. Normally there was but one mattress for every three prisoners, and every British prisoner was compelled to share his bed with one Russian and one French prisoner. All were covered with vermin, well-known carriers of typhus, and no effort was made to separate those afflicted with the disease from those who were not.

---

[1] McCarthy, op. cit., p. 222. "What possible object," McCarthy adds, "could the Imperial German government have in confining babes in arms, children, young women, middle-aged women and old women tottering to the grave in such a camp?"

[2] Published as a parliamentary paper in April, 1916, Misc., No. 10 (1916), Cd. 8224. Cf. also McCarthy, op. cit., ch. VIII. McCarthy, after reviewing the treatment of interned civilians at Ruheleben and Holzminden, remarks: "After a careful inspection of the Germans interned in England it may be stated that Germany has failed miserably in meeting this problem as compared with the solution of it by the British," p. 225.

Little or nothing was done to prevent the spread of the epidemic, which broke out in December, 1914, although the German officers were urged to take measures to this effect. Upon the outbreak of the epidemic the German military and medical staffs precipitately abandoned the camp, and until August, 1915, with a few rare exceptions, they held no communication with the prisoners or their guards except by means of directions shouted from a distance outside the wire fence. Supplies were pushed in through chutes, and no medical attention whatever was provided by the German staff. At first there were no British medical officers in the camp, although there were a number of Russian and perhaps some French doctors. In February, 1915, however, a number of English doctors, who had been detained at the camp at Halle in violation of the Geneva convention, were transferred to Wittenberg. When they arrived, they found a deplorable condition of affairs. Of these doctors, one only, captain Lauder, survived. He found in one camp fifty hidden cases of typhus, and there were no mattresses at all in the improvised hospital. During the first month of the epidemic the food ration for each patient was half a *petit pain* and half a cup of milk each day. By the first week in March there were one thousand cases of typhus in the camp, and new ones were arriving at the rate of fifty or more a day. There were between two hundred and fifty and three hundred English cases and sixty deaths. The number of deaths among the Russians and French was much larger. In addition to gross neglect and indifference the camp officials were charged with cruelty.

"Incredible as it may seem," says the committee in its report, "the action of the officers and guards in precipitately deserting the camp and thenceforth controlling its caged inmates with loaded rifles from the outside, was only in keeping with the methods and conduct of these men throughout."

"My whole impression of the camp authorities at Wittenberg," says Mr. Osborne of the American embassy, who visited it some months after the epidemic, "was utterly unlike that which I have received in every camp I have visited in Germany. Instead of regarding their charges as honourable prisoners of war, it appeared to me the men were regarded as criminals, for whom a regime of fear alone would suffice to keep in obedience. All evidence of kindly and humane feeling between the authorities and the prisoners was lacking, and in no other camp have I found signs of fear on the part of the prisoners that what they might say to me would result in suffering for them afterwards."

Ambassador Gerard hesitated to make public Mr. Osborne's report until he had visited the camp himself and became satisfied of the truth of his findings. On November 8, after the epidemic had been stamped out, the ambassador inspected the camp and on the same day reported to Mr. Page that he regretted to have to state "that the impression which I gained upon careful examination of the camp and after long conversations with the prisoners, was even more unfavorable than I had been led to expect." [1] Later inspections by representatives of the American embassy found conditions greatly improved, a new commandant having been appointed, an increased supply of clothing having been provided, and the use of police dogs having been abandoned. [2]

§ 340. **Gardelegen and Other "Bad" Camps.** Another "plague" camp was that at Gardelegen. It was greatly overcrowded, there being only six cubic metres of space for each man. The sanitary conditions were "indescribably bad"; bathing facilities were inadequate; there was insufficient clothing; the huts were inadequately heated, and the men, many of whom had no shoes, sat around with their feet tied up in straw and rags. A few had sold their overcoats to obtain food, but their coats had been taken from the great majority of them at the time of their capture and were never returned or replaced. Food rations were reduced by one-half, and while the British and French prisoners received food from home through the parcels post, the Russians were compelled to live on the little furnished by the prison authorities. The men were dirty, infected with vermin, and emaciated; under these circumstances they fell an easy prey to typhus. There was a lack of medicines and food for the sick, the whole equipment of medical supplies being no more than enough to fill a modern sized cupboard. The hospital accommodations were hopelessly inadequate, there

[1] *Ibid.*, p. 9. Mr. Gerard says in his book, *My Four Years in Germany* (p. 173) "The conditions in the camp during the period of the epidemic were frightful." Many complaints, he says, were made by the prisoners against the use of police dogs by which some of the men had been bitten. "It seemed undoubtedly true that the prisoners there had been knocked about and beaten in a terrible manner by their guards, and one guard went so far as to strike one of the British medical officers in the camp." Cf. also McCarthy, pp. 105 ff., and the London weekly *Times* of April 14, 1916. For French testimony as to conditions at Wittenberg and other camps cf. *Régime des Prisonniers*, pp. 57 ff.

[2] Reports of Dr. Ohnesorg, *Misc.*, No. 16 (1916), pp. 24, 85.

being but two hundred beds, although eleven thousand prisoners were confined in the camp. After the epidemic broke out, the sick came in at the rate of fifty per day; the hospital was soon filled and the patients were piled on the floor on bags filled with shavings. As at Wittenberg the guards, the medical staff, and the military authorities fled and left the administration in the hands of the prisoners. Before leaving, the guards unlocked the gates and allowed the prisoners of the various barracks to mix and spread the disease. Near the end of March a German medical officer arrived, but the epidemic was beyond his control. The epidemic lasted four months, and there were over two thousand cases, fifteen per cent of which were fatal. "No excuse," says Dr. Ohnesorg, a representative of the American embassy who inspected the camp, "can be offered for the callousness and cowardice exhibited by the authorities." [1] There were also charges that the authorities were unsympathetic and brutal in their treatment of the prisoners. The whole story is one of shameful neglect, brutality, and callousness.[2]

Conditions at various other camps were reported as bad or unsatisfactory, though none were comparable to those at Wittenberg and Gardelegen. At Schneidemühl conditions were described as deplorable; a typhus epidemic broke out; and there were many charges of cruelty, brutality, and neglect. At the concentration camp at Cassell three thousand seven hundred French and British prisoners and one thousand five hundred Russian prisoners are alleged to have died of typhus.[3]

[1] Quoted by McCarthy, p. 106.
[2] The facts as stated above are taken mainly from Dr. Ohnesorg's report and from the report of a government committee under the chairmanship of Mr. Justice Younger of the English High Court. The report was issued as a white paper in October, 1916. Misc. No. 34 (1916), Cd. 8351. McCarthy says the conduct of the German authorities at Limburg, where there was a large number of cases of tuberculosis among the Irish prisoners, was in a general way similar to that at Wittenberg and Gardelegen. They not only paid no attention to the patients who filled the overcrowded barracks, but denied that the disease existed there. It was at this camp that Sir Roger Casement, with the approval and encouragement of the German authorities, made an unsuccessful attempt to seduce the Irish prisoners from their allegiance to Great Britain. After the failure of the attempt the attitude of the prison officials became unsympathetic and the rigor of the disciplinary régime was increased (pp. 122 ff.).
[3] Statement of an escaped French prisoner, Paris press despatch of September 18, 1917.

Ambassador Gerard found as many as twelve English prisoners occupying a single room in the camp at Castle Celle in November, 1915.[1] Conditions prevailing in the camp at Halle on the Saale were the subject of considerable criticism. It was visited by American representatives some five or six times during 1915 and in the early part of 1916. Ambassador Gerard visited it three times, but on the first two occasions he left without making an inspection, as he was told by the camp authorities that he would not be allowed to converse with the British prisoners in English. He made a third visit in July, 1915, and in a report to Mr. Page stated that "the impressions which I got of the camp on the 30th of July were on the whole far from favorable . . . officers were housed in rooms containing as many as 52 persons and none of the rooms struck me as being particularly clean." Certain minor improvements had taken place, but conditions in general remained much as they were.[2]

In August, 1916, the British government issued a white paper containing the reports of American representatives of some forty prison camps in Germany. So far as housing conditions were concerned, the inspectors found little to complain of in most of them, although in some camps, notably those at Murechberg, Münster, Guben, Minden, and Gnadenfrei, there was either overcrowding, insufficient lighting, or lack of bathing, toilet, or recreation facilities.[3]

The French government complained that French prisoners in Germany were often badly housed in overcrowded, ill-lighted, damp, dingy, and even unsanitary buildings, sometimes on barren sandy plains where the prisoners were exposed to the severity of the winter; that in some cases they were housed in tents in the dead of winter, and that the prisoners were compelled to sleep on piles of damp straw infrequently renewed.[4]

---

[1] *Misc.*, No. 16 (1916), p. 6.

[2] *Misc.*, No. 19 (1915), p. 48. Mr. Gerard says in his book that the camp at Halle was unfit for the confinement of prisoners. They were housed in old factory buildings in the industrial part of the town, and there was no opportunity for games and recreation.

[3] *Misc.*, No. 26 (1916), Cd. 8297.

[4] Report of the Spanish ambassador in *Régime des Prisonniers*, pp. 30–31. The reports of the Spanish representatives, while containing numerous criticisms of conditions prevailing in the German prisons, did not appear to give much attention to housing accommodations. They did complain, however, of the in-

§ 341. **Mixing of Prisoners of Different Nationalities.** A cause of continued complaint among the British prisoners was the German regulation which required prisoners of different nationalities to be housed in the same barracks. As the rule was enforced it not infrequently happened that British, French, Russians, Servians, and even Africans found themselves housed in the same room, and sometimes as many as three prisoners representing as many different nationalities were required to sleep on the same mattress.[1] This rule was enforced against officers and men alike. Aside from their inability to converse with one another, the diverse customs, standards of cleanliness, ideas as to ventilation, and the like caused much friction, which at times led to altercations and fist fights.[2] The refusal of the camp authorities to segregate the Russian prisoners, who were the first and by far the most numerous victims of the typhus epidemic at Wittenberg, was largely responsible for the spread of the disease. At nearly every camp visited by the American inspectors they heard complaints from the English prisoners in regard to this treatment, and from the outset the inspectors insisted that the different races should be housed separately. Representations were even made to the German foreign office but usually without effect, for the Germans took the position that if African and other races were good enough to serve the British as allies, British prisoners could not justly object to being housed with them.[3] At Ruheleben the Jews were separated from other prisoners and segregated in barracks to them-

---

adequacy of the hospital and sanitary arrangements and reproached the German authorities for their neglect of the sick and especially of tubercular patients. Cf. *Rapports des Délégués du Gouv. Espagnol, etc.*, pp. 359 ff. As to the charge of housing the prisoners in tents, it is only just to remark that in time the tents were replaced by wooden structures.

[1] At Wittenberg, for example, there was but one mattress for every three men, and they were so distributed that each was occupied by an Englishman, a Frenchman, and a Russian. Cf. Mr. Justice Younger's report on conditions at Wittenberg, *Misc.*, No. 10 (1916), p. ·.

[2] McCarthy, *op. cit.*, p. 46.

[3] In a *note verbale* of January 11, 1915, regarding the British complaint the German foreign office stated that there was no reason whatever why any separation should be made among captured enemy officers in their quarters. "Since England does not blush to use coloured troops of all races against Germany in the present war, English officers must not be surprised if they are brought into close contact in prison with their comrades in arms of other nationalities." *Misc.*, No. 19 (1915), pp. 18, 29.

selves.[1] A frequent complaint which the inspectors heard
from British prisoners was that they were systematically dis-
criminated against, and that they were less favorably treated
than French prisoners in respect to food, work, discipline, and
the like. Similar complaints were made by the Russian
prisoners.

§ 342. **Regulations and Practice as to Clothing.** Article 7
of the Hague *réglement* imposes on belligerents into whose
hands prisoners of war have fallen an obligation, in the absence
of a special agreement, to treat them as regards clothing as they
treat their own soldiers. The British memorandum concerning
the treatment of interned civilians and prisoners of war announced that

"An ample supply of first class clothing including overcoats, boots, shirts
and underclothing, as well as towels, soap, etc., is kept in each camp, and
is supplied to those who may have need of it, free of charge. Several
cases have been brought to notice where prisoners have gambled away the
garments given to them, and have accordingly suffered from want of clothing until this has been supplied for a second time."[2]

The German statement of principles observed in the housing,
feeding, and clothing of prisoners, of July, 1915, declared that

"In the beginning, non-commissioned officers and men who are prisoners
of war remain in the uniform which they brought with them. If the thin
clothing needs replacing, the prisoners will at first be provided with proper
articles of clothing from the booty of war. When the latter is used up,
new suitable clothing is purchased. The kind of clothing is dependent
upon the season, the climate and the weather. The clothing generally
consists of a suit, necktie and cap; besides shirts, socks, warm underwear
and good shoes are given, as well as overcoats and woollen blankets to protect against the cold. Male civilian prisoners of war will be fitted out in
the same way as military prisoners of war after their present clothing can
no longer be used."[3]

[1] Cohen, *op. cit.*, p. 40. Irish prisoners were segregated at Limburg, one of the
best prison camps in Germany, this with a view to inducing them to desert their
British allegiance. After the failure of Sir Roger Casement's efforts to persuade
them to go over to the side of Germany, they were treated with less consideration.
McCarthy, *op. cit.*, p. 22.

[2] *Misc.*, No. 7 (1915), p. 24.

[3] *Misc.*, No. 7 (1915), p. 80. Mr. Balfour in a communication of February 8,
1917, to Mr. Townsley stated that German prisoners in England were warmly
clad, were furnished with overcoats, and were given the same kind and amount
of underclothing as were furnished British troops. "They not infrequently,"
he added, "urged their friends not to send food or clothing, as everything is provided
for them." *Misc.*, No. 7 (1918), p. 13.

Both the British and German regulations required officers
to provide their own clothing. Under article 4 of the Hague
convention prisoners are entitled to retain possession of their
clothing and other personal effects, but as stated above, charges
were made that the Germans frequently took away the overcoats from their prisoners at the time of capture, and the truth
of the charges was substantiated in some instances by the reports of neutral inspectors. The German authorities, however,
denied the charges and suggested that the prisoners may have
lost their overcoats, sold them, or gambled them away. They
also declared that English prisoners were supplied with captured Belgian and French uniforms when their own uniforms
were worn out; that they were provided with underwear as
needed, and that they were furnished at first with wooden
sabots, it being impossible by reason of the large number of
prisoners to supply them at once with shoes.[1]

The reports of the representatives of the American embassy
substantiate in a number of instances the charges made against
the Germans in respect to the insufficient supply of clothing
provided for the prisoners. Thus Mr. Gerard, who visited
the camp at Döberitz in October, 1915, reported to Mr. Page
that "the prisoners have only one blanket (the German regulations, as announced, provided for two woollen blankets for
each man) and are without overcoats.[2] They therefore suffer
from cold as well as from the condition brought about by
having no change of underwear."

[1] *Ibid.*, pp. 16, 17. The German denial added: "The idea of supplying
articles of clothing to the generality of prisoners of war cannot therefore be enter-
tained." But the Hague convention, as stated above, requires it. Dr. McCarthy,
discussing the working camps in Germany, says: "Practically all the British
prisoners were supplied with clothes from England" (*op. cit.*, p. 165). Cohen
says that many of the prisoners at Ruhleben had no change of clothing, and that
their plight was sad until the American embassy sent a supply. These were
purchased for those who received none from home, partly through a fund raised
by voluntary subscription, and partly with money supplied by the British government. *The Ruhleben Prison Camp*, p. 73.

[2] *Ibid.*, p. 80. In his book, *My Four Years in Germany*, Mr. Gerard says:
"At a time when the British prisoners were without proper clothing, overcoats
and the like, the British government sent me uniforms, overcoats and so on, and I
hired a warehouse in Berlin as a distributing point, but after some months the
German authorities refused to allow me to continue this method of distribution
on the ground that it was the duty of Germany to provide the prisoners with clothes.
But Germany was not performing this duty, and the British prisoners had to suffer
because of this German official woodenheadedness," p. 195.

"I have asked the German government," he added, "whether they are going to give the men another blanket but so far have had no answer." [1] An American citizen residing at Havre gave similar information.[2] The American consul-general at Berlin, however, reported on October 17 that the men were receiving two blankets, but they complained that they were not thick enough.[3] Messrs. Ohnesorg and Pyne reported in June, 1915, that all the men at Würzburg were "badly in need of uniforms";[4] in the same month Mr. Jackson found a few of the men at Stendal in need of shoes and underclothing.[5] Mr. Osborne reported that when he visited the camp at Wittenberg on October 29, 1915, he was told by the commandant that every English prisoner had been provided with an overcoat; but when he investigated the matter he found that practically no overcoats had been given out by the authorities. On the contrary, ten overcoats which had been sent from England had been taken from their owners and given to other British prisoners who were going to work in the camps.[6] Mr. Gerard visited the camp on November 8 and found the situation as described by Mr. Osborne, there being but sixteen overcoats for the 278 men in the barracks which he inspected. While each man had two blankets, "on the whole they were insufficiently clothed." Moreover, Mr. Gerard says he was told by the men and also by the British medical officers that upon their first arrival at the camp the men had been compelled to sell their clothing to their fellow prisoners in order to procure sufficient food to live on.[7]

The French authorities made many complaints that French prisoners in Germany were insufficiently clothed, in consequence of which they suffered severely during the winter season. Large quantities of clothing were sent to the prisoners by the French government, but it was charged that the German government refused to allow shipments of uniforms to French prisoners. However, in May, 1916, an agreement was reached between the two governments by which this restriction was removed.[8]

The French government, on its part, claims to have com-

[1] Ibid., p. 8. [2] Ibid., p. 34. [3] Ibid., p. 11.
[4] Misc., No. 19 (1915), p. 6. [5] Ibid., p. 10.
[6] Misc., No. 14 (1916), p. 5. [7] Ibid., p. 10.
[8] As to the French charges cf. Le Régime des Prisonniers, etc., pp. 42–44. The Rapports des Délégués du Gouv. Espagnol contain little information regarding the German treatment of French prisoners in respect to clothing.

plied fully with the Hague regulations in respect to clothing, and the reports of the American representatives and the delegates of the International Red Cross committee contain no complaints against the French government on this score. Likewise no charges appear to have been made against the British authorities in respect to the clothing of German prisoners. A representative of the American embassy inspected the prison camps in the United Kingdom in the spring of 1916, but he heard no complaints on this score, and he made no criticism in his reports.[1]

[1] Reports of Mr. Beal, *Misc.*, No. 30 (1916), Cd. 8324. The London editor of the *Amsterdam Telegraaf*, John C. Van der Leer, who inspected the British prison camp at Dorchester in December, 1915, reported that every prisoner had three blankets, as the British regulations provided. Every one was given a warm over-coat, two flannel shirts, two pairs of woollen under-garments; also handkerchiefs, a tooth brush, a hair brush, a comb, and a pair of good shoes upon his arrival at the camp. When their uniforms were worn out, they were replaced by new suits furnished by the British government. London weekly *Times*, December 24, 1915.

CHAPTER XXII

TREATMENT OF PRISONERS (Continued)

§ 343. Regulations and Practice as to Food and Diet; § 344. The British and French Rations; § 345. The German Ration; § 346. Dependence of British and French Prisoners on Parcels from Home; § 347. British and French Complaints; § 348. Regulations and Practice as to Postal Correspondence; § 349. Complaints as to German Policy; § 350. Employment of Prisoners; § 351. German Practice; § 352. Employment of Prisoners behind the Firing Line; § 353. Pay for Prison Labor; § 354. Punishment and Discipline; § 355. Reprisal Measures; § 356. Differential Treatment of Prisoners Captured on German Submarines; § 357. Other Reprisals and Threats of Reprisals; § 358. Exchange of Civilian Prisoners; § 359. Transfer of Wounded and Invalided Prisoners to Switzerland; § 360. Repatriation of Prisoners in Long Captivity.

§ 343. **Regulations and Practice as to Food and Diet.** Article 7 of the Hague regulations provides that

"The government into whose hands prisoners of war have fallen is charged with their maintenance. In default of special agreement between the belligerents, prisoners of war shall be treated as regards rations . . . on the same footing as the troops of the government which captured them."

‗ As stated in the preceding chapter, the British practice up to March 16, 1915, when its policy was altered in consequence of the failure of the German government to accord reciprocity of treatment to British officers in respect to pay, was to allow German officers to mess free of cost and to purchase such liquors as they wished.[1] After the adoption of the new scale of payment conformably to the German scale, German officers were required to defray the cost of their subsistence, but the privilege of purchasing liquors, tobacco, chocolate, etc., was left untouched.[2] From the outset, however, British officers held in Germany were required to pay for their food,[3] the cost of which generally consumed about two-thirds of their pay.[4] According to the German memorandum, officers were allowed to "partake moderately" of beer and light wines, but the purchase of cigars, tobacco, and chocolate from German stocks was not allowed.[5]

[1] *Misc.*, No. 7 (1915), p. 21.   [2] *Ibid.*, p. 75.   [3] *Ibid.*, pp. 26, 32.
[4] *Ibid.*, p. 13.   [5] *Ibid.*, p. 80.

Regarding the quantity and quality of food served to officers,
the German memorandum stated that inasmuch as they were
required to defray the cost of their subsistence, "they should
receive each day a sufficient and nutritious fare which would be
varied as often as possible and would be furnished at a moderate
price, so that the means for their small daily wants such as
laundry, etc., would still remain at their disposal." [1] There
were, of course, numerous complaints that the food was poor
in quality, insufficient in quantity, and high-priced.[2]

§ 344. The British and French Rations. Regarding the
rations for private soldiers the British regulations stated that the
daily ration should consist of the following:

Bread, 1 lb. 8 oz., or biscuits, 1 lb.
Meat, fresh or frozen, 8 oz., or pressed, 4 oz.
Tea, ½ oz., or coffee, 1 oz.
Salt, ½ oz.
Sugar, 2 oz.
Condensed milk, $\frac{1}{12}$ tin (1 lb.).
Fresh vegetables, 8 oz.
Pepper, $\frac{1}{72}$ oz.
2 oz. cheese to be allowed as an alternative for 1 oz. butter or
    margarine.
2 oz. of pears, beans, lentils, or rice.

In addition, canteens were provided from which prisoners were
allowed to purchase tobacco, small luxuries, and other things
which they might need,[3] and interned civilians approved by the
military authorities who were able and willing to pay for a
superior diet were allowed a diet and accommodations on a
scale somewhat similar to that provided for officers.[4] The
published reports of the American representatives indicate that
German prisoners in England were well fed, and there were few
complaints.[5]

At the Isle of Man camp the food was pronounced abundant
and excellent, the prisoners being fed in a large glass-roofed
electric-lighted, steam-heated dining hall.[6] Mr. Beal, who

---

[1] *Ibid.*, p. 79.
[2] Cf., e.g., the English complaints, *ibid.*, pp. 26, 29, 32, and 33. As to French
complaints cf. *Régime des Prisonniers*, p. 23.
[3] *Misc.*, No. 7 (1915), p. 23.   [4] *Ibid.*, p. 6.
[5] McCarthy, *op. cit.*, p. 139, says German prisoners in England and France
were well fed and cared for.
[6] Report of Chandler Hale, *ibid.*, p. 36.

inspected all the prison camps in England in 1916, reported that he heard no complaints as to food, that in every camp the kitchens were neat and clean, that many of the cooks were Germans, and that in most cases the food was "excellent." [1]

The French government at first gave German prisoners the same rations of bread, meat, and vegetables that French soldiers received, but in consequence of the reduction by the German government of the daily meat ration from 350 to 125 grams, the French government in December, 1915, correspondingly reduced the meat ration hitherto served to German prisoners inside the camps, but not that served to those who were at work outside or who were sick or wounded. The bread ration was likewise reduced from 700 grams per day to 300 grams. [2] In many camps the food was delivered in bulk to the camp steward, and it was prepared and cooked by German cooks. [3]

§ 345. The. German Ration. The German memorandum of October, 1914, stated that non-commissioned officers and soldiers would receive the same ration as German non-commissioned officers and soldiers received, and that it would be "simple but sufficient." The "statement of principles observed in the housing, feeding and clothing of prisoners" issued in February, 1915, announced that the daily diet was as follows:

"In the morning: coffee, tea or soup.
"At noon: a plentiful fare consisting of meat and vegetables. The meat may be replaced by a correspondingly larger portion of fish.
"At night: a substantial and plentiful meal." [4]

Comparison of this ration, so far as comparison is possible, with that announced by the British government shows that it was decidedly inferior. Thus it does not appear whether prison-

[1] The only serious German complaint against the English in respect to the food of prisoners that I have found was that contained in the "open letter addressed by the association of physicians of Hamburg to the physicians of England" referred to above, which charged that the food served in the camp at Newbury was insufficient in quantity and that the potatoes were not well cooked.

[2] *Régime des Prisonniers*, p. 35, and Lemoine, p. 29. In consequence, however, of an agreement between the two governments in April, 1916, the daily bread ration served in French prisons was increased to 600 grams. Reports made by American inspectors described the *cuisine* in the camp at Tours as of "good quality"; that at Poitiers as "very good," and that at Castelnaudary as "excellent."

[3] This last statement is made on the basis of the author's personal observations during a visit to France in the summer of 1918.

[4] *Ibid.*, p. 14.

ers in Germany received sirup, milk, butter, sugar, or even bread for breakfast, as prisoners in England did. The statement that "a plentiful" meal was served in the evening indicated little as to quantity or quality. As stated above, prisoners in Germany were not allowed to purchase cigars, tobacco, or chocolate from the canteens, though they might receive them from home through the mails.

It appears from the reports of the American inspectors and from numerous published statements of prisoners that the usual diet in the German prisons was: for breakfast, a cup of "coffee" usually made of acorns or chicory, without sugar or milk; for the noon meal, a bowl of soup in which there were vegetables and generally, though not always, a bit of meat or dried fish, and for supper, tea, cocoa, or "coffee," supplemented usually by boiled potatoes or sausage. A piece of black bread, frequently described as "absolutely uneatable," the amount of which was successively reduced from one-third to one-fifth and finally to one-sixth of a loaf, was served with each meal.[1] No knives, forks, or spoons were furnished by the camp authorities. Often the prisoners never saw a piece of meat for an entire week. The menu was hardly ever varied from, except as to the composition of the soup.[2] This diet was obviously insufficient, and both the American and Spanish inspectors complained of

[1] Cf. the report of the commandant of the Ruheleben camp in a *note verbale* communicated by the German foreign office to Mr. Page on February 23, 1915; cf. also reports of American inspectors in *Misc.*, No. 7 (1915), pp. 8, 20, 47; in *Misc.*, No. 26 (1916), pp. 22, 35, 43; also reports of Spanish inspectors in *Le Régime des Prisonniers*, p. 37, and in *Rapports des Délégués du Gouv. Espagnol*, pp. 66, 68, 69; McCarthy, *op. cit.*, p. 165; Cohen, *op. cit.*, pp. 34, 66, 178; Mahoney, *Interned in Germany*, pp. 31, 33, 337, 341; Aubry, *Ma Captivité en Allemagne*, p. 105; Wood, *Note Book of an Attaché*, p. 297. Mr. Wood says the soup served to the prisoners at Döberitz was a concoction chiefly of barley and potatoes. He was told that there was meat in it, but he could find no evidence of it. Breakfast consisted of black bread with a slice of cheese or sausage and either tea or coffee. The diet, he added, was "evidently insufficient"; "I should say it was calculated with German accuracy to just keep body and soul together." Mr. Gerard, who visited the camp in October, 1914, made a similar report. *Misc.*, No. 7 (1915), p. 8. The German authorities, however, denied the charges as to the insufficiency of the diet. *Misc.*, No. 19 (1915), p. 20. The American consul-general at Leipzig found a similar diet at Merseberg in November, 1915. *Misc.*, No. 7 (1915), p. 20. A month later the camp was visited by Messrs. Jackson and Osborne who reported that the diet there as elsewhere was of a "monotonous character," and that the British prisoners depended largely upon parcels from home. *Misc.*, No. 16 (1916), p. 29.

[2] Mahoney, *op. cit.*, p. 33.

it. Mr. Gerard, who visited Ruheleben before the reduced scale of rations was put into effect, informed ambassador Page (January 23, 1915) that there were a "good many cases of destitution among the British civil prisoners and they are increasing weekly. The authorities do not provide the men with margarine or sugar, both of which are necessary for their proper nourishment." [1] A month later he informed Mr. Page that of the 4273 men at that time interned at Ruheleben, approximately 2000 "are in the greatest destitution." [2] Dr. E. A. Taylor, a nutrition expert and representative of the American embassy, made two elaborate reports on food conditions at Ruheleben, [3] in the latter of which he stated that after the putting into effect of the new and reduced scale, prisoners were receiving only a little more than one-third of the protein-carrying foods allowed to regular prisoners of war in the military camps, while the potato rations were less than half the amount allowed the latter class of prisoners. In a letter of June 14, 1916, to Mr. Gerard, Dr. Taylor submitted dietary statistics which indicated, he said, that the food supplied to the interned civilians at Ruheleben during the previous week represented less than half of the requisite food units. [4] A notable feature of the diet for that week, he said, was the absence of vegetables, except one serving of rhubarb without sugar, against which the camp as a unit protested. [5]

§ 346. Dependence of British and French Prisoners on Parcels from Home. Taking advantage of the increasing number of parcels of food which the men were receiving from abroad, [6] the German camp authorities successively reduced the quantity of food served to the prisoners. Many lived wholly on what they

[1] *Misc.*, No. 7 (1915), p. 50.   [2] *Ibid.*, p. 65.
[3] *Misc.*, No. 18 (1916), Cd. 8259, and *Misc.*, No. 21 (1916), Cd. 8262.
[4] *Misc.*, No. 21 (1916), p. 5.   Mr. Gerard states that Dr. Taylor's report showing that the official diet of the prisoners at Ruheleben was a "starvation diet" so incensed the German authorities that they forbade him to revisit Ruheleben. *My Four Years in Germany*, p. 184.
[5] The agreement concerning the treatment of prisoners between Germany and the United States of November 11, 1918, fixed the minimum food value of the daily ration at 2000 calories for non-workers and 2850 for heavy workers. The minimum daily ration of bread for ordinary workers was fixed at 250 grams.
[6] Thirty-nine thousand, five hundred and forty-seven packages during the month of May, 90 per cent of which were estimated to contain food. Twenty-five organizations were sending food to Ruheleben.

received from their governments or from what was sent them through the parcels post by friends or relatives, although much of this food was unfit to eat, because it required from two to five weeks to reach the camp from England. Dr. Taylor states that the German authorities seemed to regard the food sent from abroad as "the regular diet and the camp allotments as the addenda." [1] He further added that the parcels post food consisted mainly of biscuits, cake, jam, tea, honey, and the like, with almost no fats, such as the prisoners most needed and which the German authorities seemed least inclined to provide. The inspectors throughout the year 1916 reported that at most of the camps visited by them, British prisoners were living almost entirely on the contents of their packages, and in some camps they ate none of the food supplied by the German authorities, either because it was unfit, or because it was not prepared or cooked according to English tastes. [2] Thus it came to pass that Germany was largely relieved of the burden of feeding English prisoners. French prisoners likewise relied largely on food sent them from home. The Russian prisoners, however, received little from this source [3] and were compelled

[1] *Ibid.*, p. 7.

[2] Cf., e.g., reports in *Misc.*, No. 26 (1916), pp. 15, 22, 29, 47, and *Misc.*, No. 19 (1915), p. 52. Dr. McCarthy says British women interned at Holzminden were unable to eat the camp diet and were in 1916 subsisting entirely on food sent through the parcels post. *Op. cit.*, p. 221. Speaking generally of food served in the German camps, he says: "The British prisoner takes one look at it, sniffs, 'not fit for a dog to eat,' he says, and turns to a can of beef or ham which has been sent him" (p. 60). The camp at Friedrichsfeld, he says, was "one of the few camps in Germany where the prison food was taken by practically all the British prisoners" (p. 72). At Minden one-fourth of the English prisoners took the noonday meal served by the Germans, and one-fourth to one-third took the bread ration only (p. 79). Mr. Gerard says, "British officers in Germany virtually subsisted on their parcels received from home." Mahoney (*Interned in Germany*, pp. 343, 347) says that had it not been for the parcels received at Ruheleben, few of the prisoners would have survived. At the Sennelager camp fifty-eight thousand packages were received by the British prisoners alone in January, 1916. *Misc.*, No. 26 (1916), p. 15. At Ruheleben from twelve to fifteen thousand parcels were received each day. Mahoney, p. 149.

[3] According to a statement given to the Associated Press by the Copenhagen office of the Moscow prisoners' war relief committee in October, 1918, two million Russian prisoners in Germany and Austria-Hungary were in a "starving condition," large numbers were ill, and other large numbers were dying every day. *New York Times*, October 29, 1918. According to a semi-official statement from Havre on June 12, 1918, five hundred Belgians interned in a German prison camp at Lübeck had died of starvation during the three months preceding.

to rely upon the prison fare which, in consequence of the successive reductions due to the increasing quantities received through the mails by British and French prisoners, was entirely inadequate.

§ 347. **British and French Complaints.** The treatment of interned civilian prisoners in particular caused the British government great concern, and Sir Edward Grey pressed upon the German government a proposal for the exchange of such prisoners, adding that if Germany was not in a position to feed them properly, it was her duty to release them. This proposal was again and again renewed, and in a communication of June 23, 1916, to Mr. Page he asked the American ambassador to inform the German government that if the proposal were not accepted within a week, the British government would be obliged to consider what course it should take with reference to the rations then being supplied German civilians interned in England.[1] But the German government for a long time refused to take action, and it was believed in England that the starvation scale of rations introduced at Ruheleben was intended as a measure of retaliation against Great Britain for interning German civilians.[2]

The Spanish inspectors of prison camps in which French captives were confined, likewise found the food in some camps to be entirely insufficient in quantity or inferior in quality.[3] The French government complained that the scale of diet announced by the German government was not only insufficient in respect to albuminous products, but that the quantity actually served

[1] *Misc.*, No. 7 (1915), p. 9.

[2] The *Tageszeitung* in an editorial attacking the British proposal for a wholesale exchange of civilian prisoners and referring to the British blockade reminded the English that Germany did not begin the interning of civilians nor the hunger war, and it added: "Perhaps we have gone too far in permitting these food packages to reach the prisoners since England bars us from private mail communication with America and stops even milk from America." The *Kölnische Zeitung* remarked that "if it comes to starving, the British prisoners should starve first." It does not appear, however, that the British government resorted to measures of retaliation, and German prisoners continued to receive rations in accordance with the scale announced at the outset. There was some popular demand for retaliation in kind, but the London *Times* expressed the view of the majority of the nation when it declared that the slow starvation of German prisoners in England was "utterly abhorrent to the humanity and the self-respect of the nation."

[3] Cf. *Rapports des Délégués du Gouv. Espagnol sur leurs Visites dans les Camps de Prisonniers Français en Allemagne*, pp. 37, 66, 68, 69.

was below the scale announced in the regulations. It also complained of the lack of variety, that the bulk of the food served was largely liquid, and that the cooking was absolutely unsuited to French tastes.[1] In England and France the cooking was done mainly by German cooks, whereas in the German prison camps the cooks were almost invariably Germans or Russians. This was the cause of much complaint on the part of British and French prisoners who asserted that they could not eat German cooking. The British and French charges were, of course, denied by the German government.[2] It is only fair to state also that the American inspectors found the food in many camps to be "sufficient" in quantity and "satisfactory" in quality, and in some camps they heard no complaints from the prisoners. Likewise the Spanish inspectors limited their criticisms to certain camps. But it is quite clear that even in the camps where the scale of diet announced by the German government was adhered to, the amount and quality of food served were considerably below the English ration. It is obvious that a ration consisting of a concoction called "coffee," with a small piece of bread for breakfast, a bowl of soup for dinner, and a cup of tea with a piece of bread and sausage for supper, is not a sufficient diet to support a normal man for any great length of time. Mr. Gerard states that the amount allowed by the German government to the camp commanders for the feeding of prisoners was only sixty pfennigs (between twelve and fifteen cents) per day. It is, therefore, hard to avoid the conclusion that the German government fell far short of performing the humane obligation which the laws of war impose upon belligerents in respect to the feeding of prisoners. It showed an indifference to the welfare of the prisoners which was inexcusable and indefensible.[3] Had it not been for the enormous quantities of food that were sent

[[1] *Le Régime des Prisonniers*, pp. 38-39.
[2] In a *note verbale* of January 11, 1915, the foreign office stated that a thorough investigation had been made of the various British charges, and that as to food "the English rank and file are sufficiently fed, and none of them are in a half-starved condition." It added: "It may well happen that the English do not find new dishes so palatable as the extravagant fare which England provides for her mercenaries" and that dishes "which English soldiers are reported to have spoken of as too bad for pigs are readily eaten by many Germans and are even a favorite dish in certain parts of England." *Misc.*, No. 19 (1915), pp. 17 and 19.
[3] Cf. Mahoney, *Interned in Germany*, p. 86.

from England and France through the medium of the postal
service, it is not improbable that many prisoners would have
died of starvation. The policy of the German government in
thus throwing upon the enemy the burden of feeding to a large
extent its own nationals held by Germany was unprecedented,
and its conduct in successively reducing the ration, apparently
with a view to shifting this duty from its own shoulders, was
neither honorable nor creditable.

§ 348. **Regulations and Practice as to Postal Correspondence.**
Article 16 of the Hague *règlement* provides that

"letters, money orders, and valuables, as well as postal parcels intended
for prisoners of war, or despatched by them, shall be exempt from all postal
charges in the countries of origin and destination as well as in the countries which they pass through."

In a communication of September 24, 1914, to the American
ambassador in London, Sir Edward Grey stated that letters
written by prisoners of war, whether addressed to persons in the
United Kingdom, allied, neutral, or enemy States, would be
free of postal charges. Those addressed to prisoners of war,
whether posted at home or abroad would be similarly exempt.
The same rule would apply to parcels, which, moreover, would
be insured and registered without cost.[1] As to the privilege
of writing letters, the British memorandum on the treatment of
prisoners stated that every interned prisoner would be allowed
to write two letters a week, each consisting of two ordinary
pages; that they would be posted twice a week; that in special
cases the number and length of letters which might be written
would be unlimited; that there would be no limit to the number
of letters which a prisoner might receive, and that letters to or
from prisoners might be written in either German or English.[2]
Newspapers, however, were not allowed to be sent or received
by post, but prisoners were allowed to purchase English papers
from news agents.[3]

The French government adopted an even more liberal policy
in respect to prisoners' correspondence. At first no restrictions
were placed upon the number or length of letters which they
might write; money orders were allowed to be sent and received,
and so were parcels weighing not more than five kilos. All
parcels were exempt from the payment of postage charges,

[1] *Misc.*, No. 7 (1915), p. 5.   [2] *Ibid.*, p. 24.   [3] *Ibid.*, p. 55.

except a stamp of ten centimes.[1] The unrestricted privilege of letter-writing, however, was so abused that in November following, the privilege was limited to one letter per week of two pages, or two letters of one page, or two postal cards.[2] In consequence of the restrictions which the German government placed on the privilege of French prisoners, the French government in March, 1915, still further reduced the privilege hitherto accorded to German prisoners to make it correspond with the German regulations, i.e., one postal card per week and two letters not exceeding four pages for men, and six pages for officers, per month, except in special cases.[3]

§ 349. Complaints as to German Policy. The German regulations at the outset limited the number of letters which prisoners might write to two each month (one-fourth the number allowed by the British regulations) and the number of postal cards to one per week.[4] Prisoners were allowed to receive and send parcels not exceeding five kilos in weight,[5] but it was not expressly stated whether the privilege applied to interned civilians. Books and periodicals were permitted under censorship.[6] Nothing was said as to the admission of newspapers. In fact, none were admitted to the German prison camps, not even German papers, before the end of March, 1915.[7]

---

[1] Circular of the minister of war of October 14, 1914. Text in 22 *Rev. Gén. de Droit Int. Pub.* (1915), Docs., p. 67.

[2] *Le Régime des Prisonniers*, p. 46. The commander of the seventeenth region reported that each of the forty-five thousand prisoners interned in his district wrote four or five letters a week from six to eight pages in length. The commander of the eighteenth region made a similar complaint. The American regulations allowed each prisoner to write two letters and four postal cards per month and to receive letters without limit.

[3] *Rev. Gén. de Droit Int. Pub.*, October, 1915, pp. 104, 134; also *Rapports des Délégués Espagnols*, p. 62.

[4] *Misc.*, No. 7 (1915), pp. 63, 81.   [5] *Ibid.*, p. 39.

[6] *Ibid.*, p. 80. The agreement of November 11, 1918, between Germany and the United States allowed prisoners to send two letters and four post cards each month and to receive an unlimited number of parcels, provided they did not weigh over seven kilograms each. The length of letters, however, was limited, and the privilege of correspondence was restricted in other particulars. Supp. to 13 *Amer. Jour. of Inter. Law*, pp. 30–32.

[7] Statement of the American consul-general at Berlin. At the Ruheleben camp, however, the sale of certain German newspapers was permitted with the beginning of the summer of 1915, and prisoners of German nativity were allowed to receive local newspapers from home. The pro-German *Continental Times* was also allowed to be sold. All papers, however, were rigidly censored, and those which contained news regarding allied successes were excluded. Cohen, p. 211, and Mahoney, p. 127.

In other respects the German regulations were much less specific than those of Great Britain and were far less liberal. By an ordinance of the Prussian minister of war of February 3, 1915, prisoners were forbidden to use ink in writing their letters, and they were advised "in their own interest" to request their families not to write too often and to keep their letters within the limits prescribed for prisoners. Exchange of correspondence between prisoners of different camps, except when it related to family matters, was not allowed.[1] Charges were also made that in some camps prisoners were not allowed to write letters at all; [2] that they were required to write in German,[3] and the like. Until September, 1915, correspondence with prisoners of war in the occupied regions of Belgium and France was not permitted, nor could parcels containing food or other articles be sent to French prisoners held in those regions.[4] Prior to that date letters and parcels addressed to prisoners there were returned to the senders. This appears to have been contrary to the assurances of the Imperial government, which had in the beginning declared that prisoners interned in the invaded regions would be allowed the same privileges in respect to correspondence that were enjoyed by their comrades who were interned in Germany.[5]

Against this harsh restriction, as against the restrictions imposed on prisoners held in Germany, in respect to letter-writing, the French government protested and abandoned its own early liberal policy only after the refusal of the German government to promise reciprocity of treatment. It also protested against the "long and unjustifiable delays" in the delivery of letters and parcels addressed to prisoners in Germany

[1] Text in 22 *Rev. Gén. de Droit Int. Pub.* (1915), Docs., p. 153.
[2] *Misc.*, No. 7 (1918), p. 13.   [3] *Rapports des Délégués Espagnols*, p. 201.
[4] In September, 1915, an agreement was reached between the French and German governments under which correspondence with French prisoners in the invaded regions was permitted. *Rapports des Délégués Espagnols*, p. 72. Lemoine, *Conventions Internationales sur le Régime des Prisonniers de Guerre*, p. 52.
[5] *Ibid.*, p. 75. In consequence of this attitude of the German government the French government by way of reprisal refused to permit correspondence with German prisoners captured in Africa, and who were interned for the most part in Algeria and Morocco, and later extended the prohibition to correspondence with German prisoners interned in hospitals in the French war zone. *Régime des Prisonniers*, pp. 48, 53. These measures appear to have caused the German government to remove in September, 1915, the restrictions referred to above and to allow correspondence with prisoners held by the Germans in the occupied regions.

(they were sometimes held more than a month, it was alleged), and on July 4, 1915, the minister of foreign affairs caused the German authorities to be informed that unless steps were taken to remedy the abuse, the French government would feel obliged to impose by way of reprisal a systematic delay in a certain number of camps in the delivery of letters to German prisoners,[1] and this appears to have been done. There was also much dissatisfaction with the policy of the German authorities in delaying for a period of ten days all letters before despatching them,[2] and by way of reprisal the French government in March, 1915, adopted this rule.[3] It was even complained that the detention often exceeded the ten-day period prescribed by the regulations.[4] There were likewise complaints relative to long delays in the delivery of letters addressed to prisoners.[5] Complaints regarding the delivery of parcels were even more numerous and frequent. Ordinarily it required from two to six weeks for a parcel posted in England to reach a prison camp in Germany, in consequence of which the food which it contained was often unfit for eating when it was received. The enormous number of parcels, however, imposed a heavy burden upon the camp postal service and made delays in many cases unavoidable.[6]

The French government also complained that the German government by an order of January 3, 1915, forbade the use of the telegraph as a means of communication with prisoners;

---

[1] *Rapports*, p. 136; also *Le Régime des Prisonniers*, p. 50.

[2] *Rapports des Délégués Espagnols*, p. 75.   [3] *Ibid.*, p. 62; Lemoine, p. 52.

[4] Mr. Gerard in a report of November 6, 1915, on the conditions prevailing in the camp at Stendal states that the head of the camp admitted that in some cases letters were detained beyond the ten-day period, the excuse being the lack of a sufficient staff of censors who could read English and French. *Misc.*, No. 16 (1916), p. 15.

[5] The French minister of war stated on March 10, 1915, that the delivery of letters to French prisoners was often delayed from one month to six weeks. *22 Rev. Gén. de Droit Int. Pub.* (1915), p. 126. Cf. also the report of the American consul-general on conditions at the Torgau camp. *Misc.*, No. 7 (1915), p. 13. Cohen (p. 62) says that after April, 1916, letters from England to prisoners in the Ruhleben camp were held for ten days before delivery, for "military" reasons, so that on an average a prisoner had to wait for six or eight weeks for a reply to his letters.

[6] At the Stendal camp, for example, thirty-two thousand packages are said to have been received by the prisoners in a single month. The British government complained that as late as November, 1917, there were from eighteen thousand to twenty thousand undelivered parcels at Limburg-am-Lahn, addressed to British prisoners. *Misc.*, No. 7 (1918), p. 8.

that in violation of the Hague convention it collected customs duties on parcels addressed to prisoners; that it refused to cash money orders, and that it declined to undertake the delivery of letters which did not contain the exact address and place of internment of the addressee, although the writers often did not know where the prisoners were confined.[1]

Regarding the complaints as to delays and losses of letters and parcels addressed to prisoners in Germany, it should be remarked that the problem which confronted the German government was very great in consequence of the fact that there were nearly two million prisoners in Germany distributed among some two hundred parent camps, to say nothing of the thousands of working camps. The task was also increased by the policy of the German government in throwing upon England and France the burden of feeding and clothing to a large extent their own nationals held in Germany. The sending of enormous numbers of parcels which this entailed overwhelmed the camp officials and the postal service.[2]

§ 350. **Employment of Prisoners.** Regarding the employment of prisoners article 6 of the Hague regulations provides that

"The State may employ the labour of prisoners of war, other than officers, according to their rank and capacity. The work shall not be excessive, and shall have no connection with the operations of the war. Prisoners may be authorised to work for the public service, for private persons, or

---

[1] *Régime des Prisonniers*, p. 49. The charge was made in the United States that the letters of American prisoners in Germany were in effect dictated by the German camp authorities. Prisoners, it was charged, were required to state in their letters that they were well treated and well fed. Letters which contained statements to the contrary were not forwarded. Statement of the chief of the intelligence branch of the general staff in the *Official Bulletin* of August 19, 1918.

[2] At the beginning of the year 1916 it was estimated that the German post-office, exclusive of Bavaria and Würtemberg, was handling daily four and a half million letters and cards for prisoners in Germany. This task, it may be added, imposed heavy burdens upon the postal service of Switzerland, Holland, and Sweden, through which countries the mails were despatched. During the month of April, 1918, the Swiss postal authorities received and forwarded 12,441,211 letters and postal cards, 3,549,523 parcels, and 133,852 money orders for prisoners in the several belligerent countries. From September, 1914, to the end of April, 1918, it had received and forwarded 413,952,089 letters and small packages, 76,037,427 registered packages, and 9,340,836 money orders. In addition 6,244,577 bread parcels were forwarded to prisoners in Germany and Austria. The Swiss government bore the expense of this service. It also waived the collection of all postal dues and customs duties on parcels passing through the country.

on their own account. Work done for the State is paid for at rates proportional to the work of a similar kind executed by soldiers of the national army, or, if there are no such rates in force, at rates proportional to the work executed. When the work is for other branches of the public service, or for private persons, the conditions are settled in agreement with the military authorities. The wages of the prisoners shall go towards improving their position, and the balance shall be paid them on their release, deductions on account of the cost of maintenance excepted."

The British memorandum on the treatment of prisoners stated that everything possible would be done to find employment for prisoners who desired to work. In certain cases they were employed in building roads and huts and in levelling and clearing ground. Civilian prisoners, however, were not required to perform work of this kind. Mr. Beal of the American embassy reported in 1916 that prisoners in England were doing a great variety of work in and about the camps. Some were working in railroad quarries, some at road making, others were working in the neighboring fields, etc. None, however, were compelled to work.[1] In England no elaborate system of compulsory labor as in Germany was ever adopted, and no prisoners were employed in mines, factories, the draining of swamps, and the like.

In France prisoners were employed in agricultural work, in quarries, in the construction and repair of roads and bridges, the unloading of ships, the cutting of timber, and the like. In some cases prisoners were put at the disposal of the departmental and communal authorities, but they were never leased out to private contractors, as was done in Germany, nor were they ever employed in dangerous or unhealthy occupations such as the draining of swamps, or in work which had any relation to military operations.[2] As in England no elaborate system of compulsory labor was organized. The work of the prisoners does not appear to have been excessive, and the representatives of the American embassy and of the Red Cross heard no complaints and found nothing themselves to criticise.[3]

§ 351. **German Practice.** The German statement of principles to be observed in the housing, clothing, and feeding of

[1] *Misc.*, No. 3 (1916).

[2] It appears, however, that in September, 1915, a representative of the American embassy found German prisoners at Caen engaged in making shoes for French soldiers; but when he called the attention of the French authorities to the fact, instructions were given to discontinue it. *Régime des Prisonniers*, p. 78.

[3] Cf. the summary of their reports, *ibid.*, p. 76.

prisoners was silent regarding their employment as laborers. In fact, however, prisoners were worked in Germany on an extensive scale, it being estimated that at least eighty per cent of all those held were so employed.[1] Labor was generally compulsory, and those who refused were punished by isolation and deprivation of privileges.[2] They were employed in nearly all the industries of Germany, agricultural, manufacturing, mining, and others, on so large a scale that it may be said that German industry was kept going during the war mainly by prison labor. Several thousand working camps, situated at varying distances from the parent camps to which they were attached, were organized,[3] and to these the prisoners were taken in squads daily or weekly. There were many complaints on the part of the prisoners of being compelled to rise at early hours and travel long distances to the working camp.[4] There were also many complaints that the hours of labor were long, sometimes as many as twelve and even fifteen hours; that prisoners were required to work on Sundays and holidays; that the tasks were unsuited to many of them; that large numbers were set to draining swamps in northern Germany, where they were exposed to the rigors of winter weather, and where they were compelled to work in the water up to their knees;[5] that they were sometimes re-

[1] McCarthy, p. 22.

[2] *Rapports des Délégués Espagnols*, p. 83. Non-commissioned officers were not compelled to work, but they were frequently asked to do so, and if they refused they were sent to reprisal camps. McCarthy, p. 90.

[3] One hundred and fifty such camps are said to have been organized in the neighborhood of the parent camp of Giessen alone. McCarthy (p. 175) says that in the sixth army corps alone there were eighteen thousand working camps. Mr. Gerard says by the summer of 1916 virtually all prisoners were being forced to work in such camps. He states that at many of these camps the inspectors were refused admission on the ground that they might learn the trade secrets. Where prisoners were leased out to contractors for work in mines and industrial establishments, they were worked like convicts at the point of the bayonet and were often badly treated, but where they were employed at farm labor, they lived with their employers and were generally well treated. Such is the opinion of McCarthy, ch. X. The physical impossibility of inspecting all the working camps, even if inspection had been permitted, which it often was not, had the effect of depriving large numbers of prisoners of the benefits that frequently resulted from inspection of the parent camps.

[4] *Misc.*, No. 19 (1915), p. 25. Dr. Ohnesorg and Mr. Osborne reported that the prisoners at Amberg left the camp at 5 o'clock in the morning and travelled seven kilometres to their place of work. *Misc.*, No. 19 (1915), p. 49. Cf. also Mr. Jackson's report, *ibid.*, p. 59.

[5] The French government protested that fifteen thousand French prisoners were sent to drain the swamps of Hanover, Westphalia, and Schleswig, for which

quired to work in cement factories, nitrate plants, and even ammunition plants, and the like.[1]

Among the more serious charges of this kind was that some one thousand five hundred French prisoners were forced to work in a Krupp cannon factory. In April, 1916, the French government requested representatives of the Red Cross society to investigate the charges, but the German authorities refused to allow them to visit plants of a military character.[2] They were,

they were paid thirty pfennigs a day, apparently as an act of reprisal for the internment of German civilians in Dahomey and Morocco. Representatives of the Spanish embassy found French prisoners working in the water eight hours a day. *Régime des Prisonniers*, pp. 80–82. The French government also protested against the working of French prisoners in coal, salt, and potash mines under conditions that were unhygienic and otherwise objectionable. Delegates of the International Red Cross committee investigated the charges at the request of the French government and found them in the main true. Prisoners of every social status and rank were found working in some of the mines. *Ibid.*, pp. 82–83, 173, 252. Strong protests were made that the sickness, accident, and death rate among prisoners in the mines was distressingly large. In some instances French prisoners who were employed in coal mines went on a strike because they regarded such work as contrary to the Hague convention, since the products of their labor were used for military purposes. Mr. Gerard says some of the British prisoners were put to work on the sewage farms of Berlin, but upon his remonstrance they were withdrawn.

[1] Representatives of the Spanish embassy heard many complaints from the prisoners that they were required to do war work. Cf. *Rapports des Délégués Espagnols*, pp. 86, 90, 101, 313. Representatives of the Red Cross committee found notices posted at several camps, notably at Friedrichsfeld and Sennelager notifying prisoners that they must work in cannon and munitions factories, that every means would be employed to compel them to work, and that excuses based on the laws and regulations of their own country would not be accepted. *Ibid.*, pp. 266–267. Sir Edward Grey in a communication to Mr. Page dated January 20, 1916, stated that he had learned with "great concern" that at Friedrichsfeld British prisoners were being compelled to work in ammunition factories. *Misc.*, No. 16 (1916), p. 44. Drs. McCarthy, Taylor, and others heard complaints of this kind. In some cases they found the charges not well founded, as to others they expressed no opinion. McCarthy (p. 162) says that only in rare instances were prisoners found at work directly in munitions and similar plants. But they appear to have been frequently employed at labor which was "preparatory" to such work. Is such labor forbidden by the Hague convention? Art. 6 forbids labor which has "any relation with the operations of war." Strupp (*Internationales Land Kriegsrecht*, p. 48) interprets this provision to exclude all work which serves the military purposes of the enemy, but a German jurist in an article published in the *Berliner Tageblatt* of September 21, 1916, argues otherwise. A French translation of his article may be found in 44 Clunet, pp. 505 ff.

[2] Neutral inspectors, both American and Spanish, reported that it was the general policy of the German authorities not to permit inspection of industrial establishments, apparently because it might result in the revelation of trade secrets. It was difficult, therefore, to verify the charges as to the employment of prisoners in war work.

however, permitted to visit the Krupp plant at Rheinhausen where railway rails, but apparently no munitions or arms, were being manufactured, and there they found large numbers of prisoners at work. They were also told that French prisoners were being worked from four o'clock in the morning until eight in the evening in a munitions plant at Bremen.[1] The evidence is fairly abundant that in not a few cases prisoners were employed at work forbidden by the Hague convention, if the convention be interpreted to exclude forced labor which indirectly serves the military operations of the enemy, such as hauling coal, transportation of munitions, construction of military railroads, and the like.

§ 352. Employment of Prisoners behind the Firing Line. Strong protests were made by the British and French governments against the conduct of the German government in employing its prisoners at forced labor close behind the firing line, with the deliberate intention, it was alleged, of exposing them to the fire of the guns of their own soldiers and of their allies. As early as August, 1916, it was charged that the Germans were systematically employing prisoners in this way, a fact which the German government carefully concealed. When the facts became known to the British government, the German authorities admitted it, but pleaded the excuse of retaliation for similar conduct by the British. French prisoners were similarly exposed for the same reason. In April, 1917, an agreement between the British and German governments had been reached under which prisoners of war were not to be employed by either belligerent within thirty kilometres of the firing line. Nevertheless, it was charged by the British government, the German authorities continued to employ prisoners close to the firing line in violation of the agreement. A British government committee under the chairmanship of Mr. Justice Younger in March, 1918, made a report in which a large amount of evidence was presented, showing that the Germans had long before the conclusion of the agreement referred to above, systematically employed British prisoners within the range of the artillery of their own soldiers; that it had continued to do so since the conclusion of the agreement; that the work required of prisoners was forbidden by the laws of war; that the hours of labor and

[1] *La Régime des Prisonniers*, p. 84.

the tasks were excessive; that prisoners were maltreated and half-starved; that many of them were walking skeletons; that the refusal of the German government to permit neutral inspections of prisoners in occupied territory made it difficult to obtain trustworthy information concerning their whereabouts, etc.[1] Both the British and French governments emphatically denied the German charge regarding the employment of German prisoners behind the firing lines.

§ 353. **Pay for Prison Labor.** All the belligerents appear to have paid their prisoners a small amount for work done, especially that done outside the camps. In Germany there was no fixed scale. The usual compensation for farm labor was from sixteen to thirty pfennigs (3 to 5 cents) per day, in the larger technical industries 75 to 100 pfennigs, and in rare instances skilled laborers received as much as 2 and even 3 marks per day.[2] The French authorities stated that French prisoners received only 30 pfennigs per day for draining marshes, that for work in mines they received up to 90 pfennigs, and that in munitions establishments, where they were compelled to work in violation of the Hague convention, they were paid as much as 2 marks 75.[3]

In England prisoners appear to have been paid a somewhat larger amount. In one camp at least they received as much as 15 shillings per week for work.[4] In France the usual rate of pay was 1 franc per day, but those working in mines received 1 franc 60 centimes (about 32 cents). The Austrian regulations stated that no prisoner should be paid less than 15 hellers (about 3 cents) per day, with extra pay for overtime and for special

---

[1] The report of the committee with accompanying documents was issued as a white paper by the British government in April, 1918. *Misc.*, No. 7 (1918), Cd. 8988.

[2] McCarthy, *op. cit.*, p. 167. At Hakemoor prisoners received at least 30 pfennigs per day for their labor; at Treuenbreitzen, 65; at Crassen, from 30 to 60; at Spandau, 90 with extra pay for overtime; at Tegel, from 50 to 125, etc. Cf. reports of American representatives in *Misc.*, No. 16 (1916), pp. 32, 56, 59, 67; *Misc.*, No. 26 (1916), p. 52; *Misc.*, No. 19 (1915), p. 29; *Rapports des Délégués Espagnols*, pp. 71, 99, 110.

[3] *Régime des Prisonniers*, pp. 76, 80, 81.

[4] Report of Mr. Beal on the camp at Cornwallis Road, *Misc.*, No. 3 (1916), p. 5. The British memorandum stated that prisoners would be paid the same rates for labor that were paid English soldiers in the country for similar work. John C. Van der Leer says prisoners at Dorchester earned about six shillings per week. London weekly *Times*, December 24, 1915.

tasks.[1] German prisoners in the United States were paid 20 dollars per month for work actually performed, with an additional allowance of 5 dollars per month for those who acted in the capacity of foremen.[2]

§ 354. **Punishment and Discipline.** Article 4 of the Hague convention declares that prisoners must be "humanely treated." They may, of course, be punished according to military law for misconduct and for violation of the camp regulations, but the punishment should not be brutal or beyond what measures of safety may require.[3] Mr. Beal in his reports of inspections of the British camps in 1916 stated that in almost every case the camp was managed by a committee chosen by and from among the prisoners themselves, and that everywhere he found a spirit of good feeling between the camp authorities and the prisoners. He heard no complaints of brutality or of excessive punishment.[4] The inspectors of the French prison camps also reported that the discipline was not over severe; their reports uniformly spoke of the good relations between the prisoners and the authorities; they heard of no instances of collective punishments for individual offences or of the tying of prisoners to posts or other forms of brutality; the only punishments inflicted were imprisonment and reduction of rations, the same punishment that was inflicted on French soldiers, and the like.[5]

The disciplinary regime in the German prison camps was more severe, and the complaints of brutality and harsh treat-

[1] New York *Times*, August 5, 1916.

[2] Statement of the department of labor, New York *Times*, November 30, 1918. This statement, however, applied only to men taken from German merchant vessels in American ports and not to those from German war-ships and other interned Germans. According to a press despatch enemy aliens interned at Ft. Oglethorpe were paid at the rate of twenty-five cents a day for camp work (foremen thirty-five cents).

The agreement of November 11, 1918, provided that prisoners should be paid for work done outside the camp at the rate of not less than fifty pfennigs or twelve and a half cents per day, nor more than two marks, or fifty cents. For work done for private individuals or concerns they were to receive the same pay as industrial workers in the locality. A certain portion of the wages earned was to be credited to the prisoner, the remainder to be retained by the captor State.

[3] Cf. Spaight, *War Rights on Land*, p. 280.

[4] *Misc.*, No. 30 (1916), Cd. 8324.

[5] *Régime des Prisonniers*, pp. 65–67. For attempts to escape, offenders were confined for thirty days in a cell, after which they were sent to a camp at Grenoble where the surveillance was more strict, but where otherwise they were treated like other prisoners.

ment were numerous and frequent. The expedient of collective punishment appears to have been frequently resorted to, especially for attempts to escape, the entire camp being deprived of its privilege of exercising in the open, of writing letters, receiving parcels, or participating in games; sometimes the entire camp was deprived of food for a period of twenty-four hours, etc.[1] Many such instances were brought to the attention of the Spanish inspectors during their rounds of the German camps. The individual offender, when caught, was placed in solitary confinement for a certain period.[2] The forms of individual punishment were various, and some of them not without an element of brutality. The most criticised of these was the practice of tying the prisoner to a post with his hands behind him, where he was compelled to stand for some hours in the heat of the sun or in the cold. Sometimes he was suspended with his feet dangling above the ground; sometimes he was compelled to stand for hours with a heavy load on his back or walk to and fro with a heavy sack of bricks on his back.[3] At Ruheleben offenders against the regulations were confined in small, ill-lighted cells for periods ranging from twenty-four to seventy-two hours. Their ration was war bread and cold water. Prisoners who succeeded in escaping, but who were subsequently retaken before reaching the frontier, were placed

[1] *Ibid.*, p. 71. The French government protested against the German practice of collective punishment as being contrary not only to the principles of justice but also to a formal engagement of the German government embodied in a note of December 30, 1915. *Rapports des Délégués Espagnols*, pp. 15, 100.

[2] Mr. Jackson reported that the punishment at Dulmen for attempt to escape was fourteen days (increased to twenty-four for a second offence) solitary confinement, during which the fare for three days out of four was bread (900 grams or three times the usual allowance) and water. On the third day the prisoner received the ordinary evening meal, and the next day he had the usual morning and midday meals, so that he was actually on bread and water only two days out of four. *Misc.*, No. 19 (1915), p. 59. Mr. Jackson was told by the commandant at Zerbst that the regulation punishment for breaches of discipline at camps where there were no cells was tying to a stake, usually for two hours a day. *Misc.*, No. 19 (1915), p. 11.

[3] *Régime des Prisonniers*, pp. 70–71; *Rapports des Délégués Espagnols*, p. 93; Hennebois, *In German Hands*, p. 229; and Mahoney, *Sixteen Months in Four German Prisons*, ch. X. The French authorities frequently protested against these forms of punishment as brutal and contrary to the law of nations. In May, 1918, an agreement was reached between the German and French governments regarding the punishment of prisoners. Among other stipulations agreed upon was one which forbade solitary confinement for the same punishment for a longer duration than thirty days. Text in 45 Clunet, 846 ff.

in solitary confinement until the end of the war.[1] Punishment
for refusal to work was very common, and the offences were
numerous, since British prisoners, in particular, could not be
induced to work at tasks which had any connection with the
war. The punishment was usually severe and consisted of
long terms in a military jail, especially where the refusal was
general and indicated a "conspiracy." Not infrequently the
prosecution demanded terms varying from five to twenty years,
and sometimes even capital punishment was insisted upon,
but this extreme punishment does not appear to have ever been
inflicted.[2]

There were, of course, charges of brutality and cruelty in
some of the camps. German officers were accused of striking,
beating, and handling roughly prisoners in some cases, and the
employment of vicious dogs in some of the camps like Wittenberg was a source of special complaint. The American embassy
protested against this practice.[3] An Irish prisoner was shot by
one of the guards at Limburg,[4] and a young Russian prisoner
at Ruheleben who was mentally deranged in consequence of his
long confinement, was shot and killed by a guard while attempting to escape. He failed to obey a summons to stop, which he
did not understand.[5] The British government in March,
1918, issued a white paper charging the German prison authorities at Brandenburg camp with responsibility for burning to
death eight prisoners.[6] The French government made a number of charges that prisoners were thrust with bayonets and
sometimes seriously wounded for trivial offences, in some cases
for disregard of orders which the prisoners did not understand.[7]

Punishments were generally inflicted without trial. When

[1] Cohen, pp. 56–59, 75.   [2] McCarthy, p. 181.
[3] *Misc.*, No. 16 (1916), pp. 3, 22; *Misc.*, No. 17 (1915), p. 43; *Misc.*, No. 19
(1915), p. 23; McCarthy, pp. 83, 202.
[4] McCarthy, p. 25. When the American embassy learned of the affair at
Limburg, which the military authorities had endeavored to conceal, it undertook
to make an investigation, but the authorities placed all manner of obstacles in the
way of the investigation. *Ibid.*, p. 25.
[5] Mahoney, *Interned in Germany*, p. 239.
[6] *Misc.*, No. 6 (1918), Cd. 8987. The prisoners in question were confined in
a dungeon and were undergoing punishment for certain offences. The hut having
taken fire, the prisoners endeavored to escape, but were thrust back with a bayonet
in the hands of the guard who was waiting orders from his superiors. All eight
were burned to death.
[7] Instances are given in the *Rapports des Délégués Espagnols*, p. 69.

trials for capital offences took place, the American ambassador endeavored to see that prisoners were represented by counsel, but representatives of the embassy were often refused permission to see the accused before trial and even before execution.[1]

§ 355. **Reprisal Measures.** The alleged mistreatment of prisoners led to numerous reprisals and threats of reprisals by belligerents on each side. Reference has already been made to various instances in which the British and French governments altered their policy in respect to the treatment of German prisoners in consequence of the refusal of the German government to accord reciprocity of treatment. From time to time there was wide-spread popular demand in England for the adoption of measures of retaliation against German prisoners for the mistreatment of English prisoners held in Germany. In April, 1915, the subject was discussed at length in both houses of Parliament, and the strongest condemnation was pronounced against the conduct of the German authorities. In the course of the debate in the House of Commons Prime Minister Asquith said: "When we come to the end of this war we shall not forget this horrible record of calculated cruelty and crime; we shall hold it to be our duty to exact such reparation against those who are proved to have been the guilty agents and actors in the matter as it may be possible for us to do." He added that a careful record was being kept of evidence which could be obtained in order that when the proper hour came, proper punishment might be meted out. Lord Kitchener, in the House of Lords, denounced the "barbarous conduct of the enemy toward those who had fallen into their hands."[2] The evidence, he said, clearly showed that articles 4 and 7 of the Hague con-

---

[1] Gerard, *My Four Years in Germany*, p. 192. McCarthy (p. 100) says the whole procedure of the trial of prisoners was more like that of a legal persecution than of a prosecution

The agreement of November 11, 1918, between Germany and the United States contained detailed provisions regarding the trial of prisoners. The protecting power was to be notified of the trial, the nature of the offence, etc., and was to be allowed to appoint counsel to defend the accused and to send a representative to attend the trial. Supp. to 13 *Amer. Jour. of Int. Law*, pp. 22–23.

[2] In January, 1919, a British committee of inquiry into breaches of the laws of war made a report in which it stated that "some 100,000 cases of ill treatment of prisoners of war have already been investigated, and it is estimated that at least 150,000 still remain to be sent in." London weekly *Times*, January 17, 1919.

vention respecting the laws and customs of war on land had been flagrantly violated by Germany. "Our prisoners," he added, "have been stripped and maltreated in various ways and in some cases the evidence goes to prove that they have been shot in cold blood." Lord Kitchener admitted, however, that there had recently been some improvement, and he thought it was only fair to say that the German hospitals should be exempted from any charges of deliberate inhumanity.[1] None of the speakers, however, demanded reprisals against German prisoners, for as Lord Newton put it, "in a competition of brutality, we should be outdistanced immediately." But public opinion outside Parliament was more divided, some of the newspapers like the *Morning Post*, the *Nation*, and the *News* insisting upon measures of reprisal.[2]

§ 356. **Differential Treatment of Prisoners Captured on German Submarines.** While the British government declined to resort to general measures of reprisal against Germany, it did adopt a system of differential treatment for thirty-nine officers and men captured on two submarines which were engaged in sinking British and neutral merchant vessels. There was some demand that men who were engaged in sinking unarmed merchant vessels with their crews and passengers should not be treated as prisoners of war, but should be tried as common murderers, as the Germans later treated Captain Fryatt. It was highly creditable to the government, however, that it declined to go to such extreme lengths. What the admiralty actually did was to segregate the submarine captives in naval detention barracks, but otherwise they were treated virtually as other prisoners, except that some of them were held in solitary confinement.[3] The English policy of differential treatment in respect to submarine prisoners, however, aroused strong indignation in Germany and was denounced as a shameful and degrading procedure against which the German government announced that it would retaliate. The German threat was promptly put into execution by the seizure of an equal number

---

[1] London weekly *Times*, April 30, 1915.

[2] The London *Times*, however, opposed retaliation, because England, it said, could not compete with a nation whose people had no scruples.

[3] Ambassador Page, under whose directions the place where they were detained was inspected, reported that their treatment was virtually the same as that accorded other prisoners.

of British officers — belonging for the most part to the most
distinguished families and regiments — who were confined at
Halle-on-the-Saale, and the placing of them in solitary confinement at Burg and Magdeburg.[1]

There was considerable doubt in England at the outset regarding the wisdom of introducing a distinction between the
treatment of submarine captives and other prisoners, first,
because the better opinion in England was opposed in principle
to the policy of reprisal and, second, because it was foreseen
that Germany would retaliate in kind. The responsibility of
the policy adopted rested largely with Mr. Churchill, first lord
of the admiralty. Mr. Balfour, who succeeded him early in
June, realized the futility of the policy and caused it to be
abandoned.

In consequence of an announcement in the German press that
two captured English aviators had been sentenced to long
terms of imprisonment on the charge of having dropped pamphlets over the German lines, the British government caused the
German authorities to be informed that it would resort to
measures of reprisal against certain captured German aviators
for similar activities in case the two English airmen were not
released. The threat was effective, and they were released.[2]

§ 357. **Other Reprisals and Threats of Reprisal.** In the
summer of 1915 the German government threatened to adopt
retaliatory measures against Canadian prisoners in consequence
of the alleged bad treatment of German civilian prisoners in the
internment camp at Amherst, Nova Scotia. The Dominion
government expressed surprise at the complaint and declared
the charges to be absolutely without foundation. Threats of
reprisal were also made by the German government against
French prisoners in consequence of the alleged brutal treatment
of German military and civilian prisoners in Africa, and the

---

[1] Mr. Gerard in a communication of May 1 to Mr. Page reported that he had
personally visited each of twenty-two of the thirty-nine British officers then subjected to retaliatory treatment. Each occupied a clean cell, was allowed books
and parcels, allowed to smoke, to exercise in the prison yards, etc.

[2] London weekly *Times*, March 15, 1918. It was reported that the Austrian
government had given orders that captured aviators known to have distributed
proclamations within the enemy lines would be given the death penalty. New
York *Times*, September 27, 1918. The French government promptly warned the
Austrian government that it would resort to retaliatory measures if the Austrian
threat were carried out.

transfer of a large number of French prisoners to northern Germany for work in draining marshes and swamps appears to have been intended as a measure of reprisal for the treatment complained of. In April, 1916, the German government, in consequence of the alleged bad treatment of German prisoners in the camp at Saint Angean, sent 250 French officers to a reprisal camp at Voehrenbach.[1] At various other times French prisoners were transferred to other "reprisal" camps upon similar pretexts.

In May and June, 1916, some thirty thousand French prisoners belonging to the upper classes were withdrawn from various camps and transferred to the Baltic and Polish provinces of Russia where they were alleged to have been put on greatly reduced rations, deprived of the privilege of receiving parcels post packages, and set to hard work in the construction of railroads. Representatives of the Spanish embassy were forbidden to visit the camps where they were confined. The pretext for the measure was the internment and alleged bad treatment by the French authorities of German civilians in Morocco.[2] Some two thousand British prisoners also appear to have been transferred to the occupied regions of Russia where they were set to work, in consequence of the action of the British government in sending an equal number of German prisoners from the internment camps in England to work at unloading ships in French ports. Sir Edward Grey stated that the work did not consist in the unloading of munitions cargoes, and he gave assurances that facilities would be afforded for inspection by representatives of the American embassy of the prisoners so transferred. In the autumn of 1916 the German government in retaliation for the alleged failure of the French government to fulfil the terms of an agreement regarding the release of civilian prisoners seized some two hundred French men and women in the occupied region of France and deported them to Germany.[3] Transfers to "reprisal" camps were the most common form of retaliation adopted by the German govern-

---

[1] *Rapports des Délégués Espagnols*, p. 20.

[2] *Rapports des Délégués Espagnols*, pp. 95–96. The alleged mistreatment of German prisoners in Africa and the brutality of the German reprisal measures are the subject of a volume entitled *Les Prisonniers Allemands au Maroc* (Hachette et Cie., Paris, 1917).

[3] *Misc.*, No. 19 (1916), Cd. 8260.

ment, but reduction of rations, deprivation of postal privileges, employment behind the firing line, and other measures were frequently resorted to. Neither the British nor the French government appears to have resorted to the practice of reprisals, although threats were occasionally made, and on several occasions readjustments were made in their regulations concerning the privileges of prisoners so as to bring them into conformity with those of Germany. Aside from the brief segregation of the German submarine crews no reprisal camps were organized either in England or France.

The practice of resorting to reprisal measures against prisoners who are innocent of any offence is a detestable one and cannot be too strongly condemned, although it must be said that the threat to resort to it, in many cases had the effect of securing better treatment of prisoners by the enemy. In July, 1916, the International Red Cross committee in a statement addressed to both belligerent and neutral governments "energetically protested against the practice of reprisals against prisoners as a return to the most barbarous times, one which was unworthy of nations which had given the Red Cross the place which it occupied in their armies and one which put a premium on barbarism for the purpose of vengeance." It appealed to the several belligerents which had resorted to the practice to discontinue it in the future.[1]

§ 358. **Exchange of Civilian Prisoners.** As is well known, the Hague convention respecting the laws and customs of war on land, although containing detailed provisions regarding the treatment of prisoners, is silent on the subject of exchange. In fact, during recent wars exchanges have been rare, and not since the American Civil war has any considerable number of prisoners been released in this way. It is somewhat regrettable that this policy of dealing with prisoners has not found more

[1] The British government in reply to the appeal of the Red Cross committee expressed its regret that the belligerents had been compelled to resort to reprisals and stated that it had discountenanced the policy from the outset. After advertising to a long list of German barbarities in respect to the treatment of prisoners, it added: "His Majesty's government readily respond to that appeal being confident that the neutral powers and the international committee will recognize that the demand for reprisals grows in volume and urgency with the recurrence of abuses, and that the surest means of avoiding reprisals is to promote the abandonment of the policy which inspires them." London weekly *Times*, September 8, 1916.

favor with belligerents, since it not only affords a means of lightening their own heavy burden of taking care of large numbers of prisoners, but it would spare unfortunate captives months and years of confinement, deprivation, and mental torture.

At the beginning of the late war the French government adopted the practice of releasing captured enemy officers on parole, but this policy was soon abandoned in consequence of the refusal of the German government to accord reciprocity of treatment to captured French officers.[1] As has been pointed out in an earlier chapter, an arrangement was entered into between the French and German governments in January, 1916, for the reciprocal repatriation of civilian prisoners. The category of beneficiaries included women and all men under seventeen years of age and over fifty-five as well as those unfit for military service.[2] A somewhat similar agreement was reached after protracted negotiations between the British and German governments in April, 1916, under which some six hundred British civilian prisoners in Germany were released, and about seven thousand German prisoners in England were returned to Germany.[3] A like agreement was also concluded in December, 1917, between the British and Turkish governments.[4] On December 31, 1915, the Pope despatched a telegram to the German and Austrian Emperors, the President of the French Republic, the King of England, the King of the Belgians, the Czar of Russia, the Sultan of Turkey, and the Mikado of Japan appealing to their sentiments of Christian charity to begin the new year by an act of generosity in accepting a proposal to exchange prisoners of war who were incapable of military service. All of them replied expressing their sympathy for the proposal and announcing their willingness to enter into such an arrangement with the enemy governments.[5]

---

[1] Cf. the declaration of the French minister of war, February 16, 1916. *Rev. Gén. de Droit Int. Pub.*, 1915, Docs., pp. 119–120.

[2] As stated above, the German government alleged that the terms of the agreement were not performed in good faith by the French government, in consequence of which the German government adopted measures of reprisal in October, 1916, by arresting two hundred French men and women and deporting them to Germany.

[3] For the terms cf. *supra*, Vol. I, Sec. 46; also British White Paper, *Misc.*, No. 17 (1916), Cd. 8236.

[4] British White Paper, *Misc.*, No. 10 (1918), Cd. 9024.

[5] The text of the papal telegram and the responses may be found in the *Rev. Gén. de Droit Int. Pub.*, 1915, Docs., pp. 99–100.

§ 359. **Transfer of Wounded and Invalided Prisoners to Switzerland.** In April, 1916, agreements between Germany and Great Britain and between France and Germany were reached under which each government agreed to transfer to Switzerland all wounded prisoners held by it as well as all prisoners suffering from any one of twenty specified diseases or infirmities. In order to determine who were eligible to transfer it was agreed that the prison camps and hospitals in both countries should be inspected by Swiss medical men. Prisoners designated by the medical commission were to be assembled at some convenient place for final examination by a commission of which two-thirds of the members were to be Swiss. Finally, it was agreed that each government should defray the cost of the internment of its nationals in Switzerland.[1] After long negotiations an agreement was reached between Germany and Russia, largely through the efforts of Mr. Gerard, for the exchange of incapacitated prisoners of war. The selection of those entitled to the benefit of the arrangement was to be made by members of the Danish Red Cross society, who were authorized to visit prisoners' camps in both countries. Instead of being transferred to Switzerland, however, they were to be returned by way of Sweden to their own countries, the transfer through Sweden being placed entirely in the hands of the Swedish Red Cross society.[2]

Under these arrangements many thousands of wounded and otherwise incapacitated soldiers were either repatriated or transferred to Switzerland where, although still held as prisoners,

---

[1] The correspondence relating to the Anglo-German agreement was published as a parliamentary white paper. *Misc.*, No. 17 (1916), Cd. 8236. The arrival of the first contingent of French prisoners from Germany took place on May 25, 1916, and called forth an enthusiastic welcome from the Swiss population. Cf. the description of the reception in the New York *Times* of June 18, 1916. The first British contingent arrived on May 30. The extraordinary reception which they were accorded by the Swiss is described by the British minister at Berne in a despatch of June 2, 1916, to Sir Edward Grey. Cf. a pamphlet entitled *The Reception of Wounded Prisoner Soldiers of Great Britain in Switzerland*, London, 1916. Cf. also *Régime des Prisonniers*, pp. 91–93.

[2] The agreement of November 11, 1918, between the United States and Germany contained detailed provisions for the repatriation of certain classes of prisoners, notably those who had been in captivity for one year, while those not eligible for repatriation, but who had attained the age of forty years, were to be transferred for internment in a neutral country. The end of the war came, however, before the terms of the agreement could be put into effect.

their lot was materially improved; they were no longer confined
in enemy camps, but were among friends and could breathe the
air of a neutral and friendly country.[1] Those who were entitled
to the benefit of these liberal arrangements, however, constituted
a very small proportion of the total number of prisoners, for the
terms of the agreement were strictly construed, and no prisoner
who did not clearly come within the category of wounded, in-
firm, or incapacitated was transferred or repatriated.

§ 360. Repatriation of Prisoners in Long Captivity. In
April, 1918, an agreement was reached between the German
and French governments under which all non-commissioned
officers and soldiers (with certain exceptions), held by either
side, who had been in captivity not less than eighteen months,
who were between forty and forty-five years of age and fathers
of at least three living children, or who were between forty-five
and forty-eight years of age, should be reciprocally repatriated.
Those not belonging to these classes should be repatriated on
the basis of man for man exchange. All officers belonging to
the above-mentioned classes were to be interned in Switzerland.
The terms of the agreement were also made applicable to Belgian prisoners of war held by Germany and to German prisoners
held by Belgium. Civilian prisoners held in internment camps
by either side, whatever their age or sex, with a few exceptions,
were to be allowed to leave the country in which they were
held, and those interned in Switzerland before November, 1916,
on the ground of ill health were likewise to be liberated. In
July, 1918, a somewhat similar agreement was reached after
five weeks of negotiations between representatives of the British
and German governments at The Hague. In general, the
agreement provided for the exchange on a man for man basis of
captives who had been in prison at least eighteen months, and
for a general exchange of civilians. The German government,
however, raised various questions concerning German prisoners
in China and the release of U-boat crews, whom the British
government declined to liberate, in consequence of which the

[1] In March, 1918, it was stated that 26,000 prisoners of the several belligerents
were being cared for in Switzerland. Of these, 16,000 were English, French,
and Belgian, while 10,000 were German. Besides, some 500,000 invalid and sick
prisoners of various nationalities had been exchanged and repatriated through
Switzerland since the beginning of the war.

above-mentioned agreement appears not to have been ratified by the German government before the conclusion of the armistice.[1]

[1] From first to last the German delegates at the Conference raised numerous objections and did not regard with favor the proposal of the British delegates looking toward a general exchange of combatant prisoners and of interned civilians. There were roughly four thousand British civilian prisoners in Germany and twenty thousand German civilian prisoners in England. The German delegates were willing to agree to an "all for all" exchange; but as in 1915, this solution was not acceptable to the British government, which insisted on a man for man basis.

CHAPTER XXIII

MILITARY GOVERNMENT IN BELGIUM [1]

§ 361. General von der Goltz's Appointment as Governor-general; § 362. Revocation of Consular Exequaturs; § 363. Powers of the Governor-general; § 364. Powers of the Local Authorities Taken over; § 365. German Legislation in Belgium; § 366. Restrictions in Respect to Personal Liberty; § 367. Restrictions in Respect to Patriotic Demonstrations; § 368. German Measures in Respect to Education; § 369. Movement to Detach Flemish Belgium; Transformation of the University of Ghent into a Flemish Institution; § 370. Deportation of Professors Pirenne and Frédéricq; § 371. Right of Military Occupants to Interfere with Educational Institutions; § 372. Division of Belgium into two Districts.

§ 361. General von der Goltz's Appointment as Governor-general. By the end of August, 1915, the greater part of

[1] I have limited the treatment of the subject of military government in occupied territory to German policy in Belgium, partly because of limitations of space and partly because sufficient trustworthy information regarding the government of other occupied territories is not yet available. My chief source of information regarding German military government in Belgium is Huberich and Nicol-Speyer's *German Legislation for the Occupied Territories of Belgium* in fourteen volumes (The Hague, Nijhoff, 1915–1918). This collection contains the texts in French, German, and Flemish of the laws, ordinances, proclamations, and notices as published in the *Gesets- und Verordnungs-Blatt für die Okkupierten Gebiete Belgiens* between September 5, 1914, and the withdrawal of the German armies in the autumn of 1918. I have also used a publication entitled *Arrêtés et Proclamations de Guerre Allemandes*, published by Allen and Unwin, London, 1915. This collection contains the French texts of the proclamations issued by the German authorities at Brussels between August 20, 1914, and January 25, 1915. Many official documents and reports, such as the Bryce Report on alleged German atrocities in Belgium, the reports of the Belgian commission of inquiry, the *Cahiers Documentaires* issued by the Belgian government, and others have also been used. In addition to press despatches published in the London *Times* and the New York *Times* and various articles in the law reviews, I have made use of many books and brochures, of which the following are the more important: Massart, *Belgians under the German Eagle;* Waxweiler, *Belgium, Neutral and Loyal;* Waxweiler, *Belgium and the Great Powers;* Saint Yves, *Les Responsabilités de l'Allemagne dans la Guerre de 1914;* Langenhove, *The Growth of a Legend;* Morgan, *German Atrocities;* Verhaeren, *Belgium's Agony;* Nothomb, *Les Barbares en Belgique;* Williams, *In the Claws of the German Eagle;* Gibson, *Journal from our Legation in Belgium;* Cammaerts, *Through the Iron Bars;* Passalecq, *Les Déportations Belges;* Passalecq, *La Magistrature Belge contre le Despotisme Allemand;* Passalecq, *La Question Flamande et l'Allemagne;* Beck, *The Evidence in the Case;* also his *The War and Humanity;* Mokveld, *The German Fury in Belgium;* de Gerlache de Gomery, *Belgium during the War;* Nyrop, *L'Arrestation des Professeurs Belges et l'Université de Gand,* and Whitlock, *Belgium* (2 vols., New York, 1919).

Belgium had been overrun by the German armies and was under their effective occupation. By a decree of August 26, Field-marshal Baron von der Goltz was appointed governor-general of Belgium, and on the same date Herr von Sandt was made chief of the civil administration near the governor-general.[1]

On September 2, General von der Goltz issued a proclamation notifying the people of Belgium of his appointment, directing their attention to the "victorious advance" of the German army in France, and announcing that his task would be the "preservation of the tranquillity and public order in Belgian territory."

"Every act of hostility by the inhabitants against the German military forces," he added, "every attempt to interfere with their communications with Germany, to injure or interrupt the railway, telegraph, or telephone connections will be punished very severely and every act of resistance or revolt against the German administration would be repressed without pardon." "It is the hard necessity of war," he further added, "that the punishment of hostile acts fall, in the absence of the guilty, upon the innocent. It is the duty of the thinking citizens to exert pressure upon the turbulent elements to restrain them from committing acts against the public order. Belgian citizens desiring to pursue peaceably their occupations will have nothing to fear from the German troops or the military authorities."

Concluding his address, he said:

"Citizens of Belgium, I do not ask anyone to renounce his patriotic sentiments, but I expect from you all reasonable submission and absolute obedience to the orders of the general government. I invite you to give it your confidence and your coöperation. I address this invitation especially to the public officials of the State and of the communes who have remained at their posts. The more you respond to this appeal, the more you will serve your country."[2]

§ 362. Revocation of Consular Exequaturs. Toward the end of November, 1914, the German government informed neutral powers having consular representatives in Belgium that in view of the fact that the German army had occupied various

---

[1] The jurisdiction of the governor-general included not only the occupied territory of Belgium, but also the French district of Givet-Fumay, which was attached to the territory of the governor-generalcy.

By an order of December 3, 1914, General von der Goltz was superseded by General von Bissing, who served until his death in 1916, when he was succeeded by General Falkenhausen, who filled the position until the withdrawal of the German armies in the autumn of 1918.

[2] Text in *Arrêtés et Proclamations de Guerre Allemandes*, pp. 8–9.

portions of the country, the Imperial government "considered the exequaturs of consuls formerly permitted to act in such districts to have expired." The communication stated however, that the German government would be disposed to consider favorably any wishes of allied or neutral countries respecting the establishment of consular offices in the occupied districts, aside from those in which military operations were in progress. The provinces of East and West Flanders were in the latter category, and accordingly the exercise of consular activities therein would not for the present be permitted. As to the other parts of Belgium, consular officers would be permitted in Brussels, Antwerp, and Liège, but not at other places. The issuance of formal exequaturs, however, was not deemed advisable in any case, but temporary recognition of consuls to act would be granted "under reserve of the usual investigations respecting their records." In view of the peculiar circumstances contingent on military occupation, the Imperial government, it was added, would be grateful if "only such persons would be appointed as are assuredly friendly to Germany or at least have neutral connections." [1] The Belgian government promptly entered a protest against the decision of the Imperial government on the ground that article 42 of the fourth Hague convention of 1907 confers only the right of de facto possession upon military occupants, from which no right to cancel exequaturs issued by the government of the country occupied could be derived. Military and administrative considerations, it was said, might justify the withdrawal of the exequatur of a consul who should engage in hostile acts or behave in a manner inconsistent with the duties of his office, but they did not warrant a general cancellation of exequaturs, the upsetting of the whole consular organization, and the exclusion of Belgians who had committed no act of hostility against the authority of the occupant. The German decision, it was added, would involve "disastrous uncertainty," owing to the fact that consulates established today might be displaced to-

[1] The correspondence relating to the treatment of Consuls in Belgium may be found in the American white paper, European War, No. 3, Department of State, Diplomatic Correspondence with Belligerent Governments Relating to Neutral Rights (Washington, 1916), pp. 359 ff.; also in the *Amer. Jour. of Int. Law*, Supp., October, 1916, pp. 445 ff. Cf. also 22 *Rev. Gén. de Droit. Int. Pub.* (1915), Docs., pp. 114–115.

morrow through the retaking of occupied territory.[1] The Belgian government considered that the action of the German government was equivalent to serving notice on the world that the sovereignty of Belgium had been extinguished by German occupation, and that its territory had in effect become a part of the German possessions.

The German government in a *note verbale* of January 13, 1915, replied to the Belgian protest, dissenting from the view therein expressed. Article 42 of the Hague convention, according to its view, imposed on military occupants the obligation to maintain public order in the districts occupied, but it did not require them to permit "enemy" officials to remain in office. Consuls of neutral powers were in an analogous position, and exequaturs granted by an enemy government were not binding upon a military occupant. Attention was also called to the fact that of the more than three hundred consular representatives in Belgium at the outbreak of the war the majority were honorary consuls of Belgian nationality, a large number of whom had left the country. In the interest of neutrals, therefore, whose interests were thus left unprotected, it was the duty of the Imperial government to see that their "consular protection is established securely and effectively," and as a first step allied and neutral governments had been invited to express their wishes. The American government replied that it was not inclined at that time to question the right of the Imperial government to revoke the exequaturs of American consuls in the occupied districts, in view of the fact that consular officers are commercial and not political representatives, and that permission for them to act within defined districts is dependent upon the authority which is in actual control of such districts, irrespective of the question of legal right.[2]

---

[1] The Belgian minister at Washington issued a public statement in which he said: "The issue, as well as the cancellation of an exequatur, are acts which imply the sovereignty of the State from which they emanate. Now, a Power in military occupation of a territory only enjoys a de facto possession which cannot be transformed, in so far as its relations with neutral States are concerned, into a state of sovereignty. Such a change could only become lawful by the consummation of a treaty of peace determining definitely the status of the occupied territory."

[2] During the American Civil war the government of the United States recognized consuls of foreign governments residing in the States of the confederacy. The Confederate government likewise recognized their exequaturs as valid, as

§ 363. **Powers of the Governor-general.** Upon the governor-general was conferred not only the executive but also the legislative power. By a proclamation of General von der Goltz, dated January 4, 1915, the people were reminded that in those parts of Belgium subject to the authority of the German government from the date of his appointment the ordinances issued by him and by the authorities subordinate to him, alone had the force of law. Orders emanating from the king of the Belgians or from his ministers were of no force.

"I am determined," he said, "to employ every power at my disposal to see that all governmental powers are exercised exclusively by the German authorities that have been instituted in Belgium. I expect that Belgian functionaries, in the common interest of the country, will not refuse to continue to exercise their functions, especially as I do not ask of them the performance of services in the direct interest of the German army."[1]

---

long as the consuls treated the Confederate authority with proper respect. But new appointees were required to obtain permits from the Confederate government in order to exercise their functions.

The *Instructions for the Government of the United States Armies* (art. 9) state that "the functions of ambassadors, ministers, and other diplomatic agents accredited by neutral powers to the hostile government, cease, so far as regards the displaced government. But the conquering or occupying power usually recognizes them as temporarily accredited to itself." Article 8 adds that "consuls will be subjected to martial law only in case of urgent necessity." But these provisions appear not to have been retained in the *Rules of Land Warfare* of 1914.

[1] With the establishment of German authority in Belgium, many Belgian officials refused to continue at their posts, although there was no such general exodus as took place in France in 1870–1871. As will be pointed out later, the judges of the courts in 1918 refused to continue the exercise of their functions, although they did not resign.

The governmental organization set up in Belgium was divided into two sections, the military section and the civil section, both located at Brussels. The military section was under the direction of the chief of the general staff and had charge of all matters concerning the army and the national safety, including police, which embraced such matters as communications, surveillance of the Dutch frontier, measures against espionage, passports, military courts, and many others. The civil section was under the direction of a *Verwaltungschef*. Its relations were mainly with the civil authorities of the Belgian government. It exercised a certain supervision over matters of justice, public works, agriculture, finance, and the like. Belgian functionaries who continued in the exercise of their functions were largely under the direction of the chief of the civil section. A multiplicity of new administrative agencies and territorial circumscriptions were created alongside those which the Germans found already in existence. It may also be remarked that by the side of the two sections just mentioned there was created a political section (*Politische Abtheilung*) which occupied itself with the "Belgian problem" in its external and internal bearings. It dealt with matters of foreign affairs, the press, importation and exportation, etc.

Salaries unknown to or contrary to the will of the German government, and which were paid by the former Belgian authorities to Belgian officials, were liable to confiscation.[1]

§ 364. **Powers of the Local Authorities Taken over.** By an ordinance of December 3, 1914, the powers of the provincial governors were transferred to the military governors of the German Empire. All resolutions of the permanent deputations, the provincial councils, and the communal councils, taken since the Belgian law of August 4, 1914, relative to the delegation of powers in case of invasion, in order to be valid required the approval of the German authorities.[2] The provincial councils were allowed to meet only with the permission of the governor-general; their sessions were to be opened and closed in his name; they were limited to such duration as he might fix, and their acts required his approval, to be valid. All powers belonging to the commissioners of arrondissements were transferred to the German military chiefs (*Kreischefs*) of the arrondissements. The German civil commissioners attached to the military chiefs were given the powers of surveillance over the administration of the communes.

§ 365. **German Legislation in Belgium.** In accordance with a well-established principle of international law, Belgian legislation remained in force so long as it was not inconsistent with the conditions of the new régime and until expressly abrogated or modified by the German authorities. The instances in which such legislation was directly abrogated were not numerous. Such an example was the abrogation of article 261 of the Belgian

---

Finally, among the central agencies was one which had jurisdiction of the business of banking (*Bank Abtheilung*). Likewise in the provinces and arrondissements the existing Belgian administrative organization was paralleled by a complex German military and civil organization. In each province was a military governor with the rank of general and a *President der Zivilverwaltung* who was at the head of the civil administration. At the head of each arrondissement was placed a military functionary called a *Kreischef*, civil affairs being under the administration of a *Zivilkommissar* who took the place of the Belgian commissioner. The local Belgian authorities continued to exercise their functions under the control of the two German chiefs. The territory under German occupation was divided into two grand districts, the territory of the government-general and the zone of the armies (*Etappengebiet*), the latter having a military administration distinct from the former. Cf. the sketch in Van der Essen, *Petite Histoire de l'Invasion*, pp. 49 ff., and Whitlock, *Belgium*, Vol. I, Ch. LXI.

[1] Text in Huberich and Speyer, 2d Series, pp. 13–14.   [2] Text, *ibid.*, I, p. 62.

penal code,[1] the abrogation of the Belgian law of August 4, 1914, relative to the delegation of power in the case of invasion,[2] and the laws relating to the militia and the *garde civique*.[3]

Existing laws were, however, frequently modified to bring them into harmony with the conditions of the German occupation. Thus articles 113 and following of the Belgian penal code and the law of August 4, 1914, relating to crimes and offences against the external security of the State were modified so that the German Empire, Austria-Hungary, and Turkey should not be considered as foreign powers in respect to the occupied territory of Belgium.[4]

The unusual conditions resulting from the occupation of the country, and particularly those of an economic and industrial character, made necessary, at least in the judgment of the Germans, a vast amount of new legislation. This legislation covered a wide field and dealt with almost every phase of the economic and industrial life of the Belgian people. The ouput was so extensive that only a brief summary is possible here.[5]

[1] Text, *ibid.*, 2d Series, p. 155.   [2] *Arrêtés et Proclamations*, p. 47.

[3] Huberich and Speyer, I, p. 91. The question as to whether decrees of the king of the Belgians issued after the German occupation were valid was presented to the civil tribunal of Tournai, which rendered a decision holding that inasmuch as the sovereignty in Belgium was "one and indivisible" and could not be exercised simultaneously by the Belgian government and the military occupant, and since the power of legislation had been taken over by the latter, the decrees of the king could have no force. But the court of cassation overruled this decision on July 5, 1917. It rejected the view of divided or substituted sovereignty in occupied territory as "superannuated" and held that the sovereignty remained in the Belgian nation "juridically unaltered," although by *force majeure* the lawful sovereign was temporarily deprived from exercising its powers. The king's ordinance power, therefore, remained intact, and in so far as his decrees were not expressly forbidden by the military occupant, they were valid and must be applied. Text of the decisions in *International Law Notes*, September–December, 1917, pp. 169–171. This decision of the court of cassation is discussed and approved by the Belgian jurist De Visscher in an article entitled *L'Occupation de Guerre*, in the *Law Quar. Review* for January, 1918, pp. 72 ff. A similar question was presented to a Dutch court in connection with a suit brought by a German firm against a Belgian refugee in Holland. It was held that German legislation in Belgium had the force of law, and if the German authorities had not observed the limitations and restrictions imposed by art. 43 of the Hague convention on military occupants in respect to legislation, it was not within the power of a Dutch court to inquire into the matter. Whatever the military occupant, therefore, enacted must be treated by foreign courts as valid legislation. Text of the decision in *International Law Notes*, August, 1917, pp. 127–128.

[4] Text in Huberich and Speyer, I, p. 58.

[5] Hugh Gibson, secretary of the American legation in Belgium, says the German proclamations were so numerous and stupid as to excite ridicule and laughter

Decrees were issued from time to time requiring detailed declarations of stocks of raw materials, food stuffs, farm produce, crops, and even trees.[1] These were followed in many cases by orders to seize such stocks by way of requisition. Other decrees forbade the exportation (except to Germany) of Belgian produce or permitted exportation only upon payment of duties. In no case could merchandise be exported without the authorization of the German authorities.[2] Commerce, trade, agriculture, and the conduct of business generally were subjected to a régime of strict control and supervision, and the operation of various industries (e.g., the brewing of beer) was taken over directly by the German administration. By a decree of February 17, 1917, the exploitation of all industrial enterprises of whatsoever character, and notably manufacturing, was forbidden without the consent of the German authorities, this subject to a penalty of not more than two year's imprisonment or a fine of not more than 100,000 marks.[3] Farmers were forbidden to sell their crops before harvesting, under heavy penalties.[4] The selling of meat without a permit from the German authorities was punishable by a year's imprisonment and a fine of 10,000 marks.[5] The transportation of merchandise from one place to another within the occupied territory was punishable by three years' imprisonment and a fine of 30,000 marks.[6] Importing goods from abroad was punishable by a year's imprisonment or a fine not exceeding 10,000 marks.[7] The feeding of potatoes to animals was punishable by a year's imprisonment and a fine not exceeding 10,000 marks.[8] The maximum prices of many commodities were fixed by the German authorities, and heavy penalties were prescribed for violations thereof. Thus by a decree of September 18, 1915, whoever was found guilty of violating the price regulations or who offered or demanded a price in excess of that fixed by the German

---

by the crowds who daily gathered around the bulletin boards on which they were posted. Cf. his address in the New York *Times* of January 6, 1918.

[1] Cf., for example, a decree of October 17, 1916, requiring a declaration of the trunks of poplar trees, under a penalty of three years imprisonment and a fine of 10,000 marks in addition to the confiscation of the trees. Text in Huberich and Speyer, IX, p. 144.

[2] Decree of February 25, 1915, *ibid.*, I, p. 109.

[3] Text, *ibid.*, X, pp. 135–137.

[4] *Ibid.*, V, pp. 122, 145; VII, p. 403.   [5] *Ibid.*, VII, p. 392.

[6] *Ibid.*, VII, p. 160.   [7] *Ibid.*, V, p. 39.   [8] *Ibid.*, IX, p. 215.

administration was liable to a year's imprisonment and a fine of 10,000 marks, in addition to the confiscation of the merchandise.[1] The same penalty was prescribed for violation of the regulations regarding the economical use of fuel and light.[2] Violation of the decree of December 13, 1916, regulating the production of brandy was punishable by imprisonment for three years or a fine not exceeding 100,000 marks, or both.[3] By a decree of January 5, 1917, a fine not exceeding 10,000 marks or imprisonment for a year, or both, was prescribed for violation of the regulations relating to the breeding of mares and the castration of stallions.[4] A penalty of imprisonment for one year and a fine not exceeding 10,000 marks were prescribed for violation of the regulations concerning the consumption of cream.[5] The display of fireworks was punishable by one year's imprisonment, or more, or a fine not exceeding 5000 marks, or both.[6] These are a few typical examples of German legislation. The number might be multiplied almost indefinitely.

In accordance with article 48 of the Hague convention of October 18, 1907, the occupying authorities continued to collect all State taxes, imposts, and tolls in the territory occupied, to meet the expenses of administration. The assessment and collection were made in conformity with the Belgian laws in force and through the agency of Belgian officials who were competent to exercise their functions.[7] A measure which evoked vigorous protest and complaint was the ordinance of January 16, 1915, levying an additional tax equal to ten times the regular tax on all Belgians who had voluntarily left their domicile and had sojourned more than two months outside Belgium, unless they should return before March 1, 1915. Absence from home was to be considered as conclusive proof of absence from Belgium.

All banks were placed under the control and supervision of a commissioner-general of banking, this as a retaliatory measure against a similar measure of Great Britain and France. Commissioners of surveillance were appointed with power to prohibit certain transactions, examine books, take inventories of funds and other property, and require reports concerning

---

[1] *Ibid.*, IX, p. 319.   [2] *Ibid.*, IX, p. 324.   [3] *Ibid.*, IX, p. 361.
[4] *Ibid.*, X, p. 17.   [5] *Ibid.*, IX, p. 254.   [6] *Ibid.*, X, p. 207.
[7] Ordinance of November 12, 1914, *Arrêtés et Proclamations*, p. 39.

all matters of interest to the occupying authorities. The commissioner-general was empowered to fill vacancies in the boards of directors and the administrative personnel caused by the refusal or legal incapacity of directors, officers, or employés to perform their duties.

Naturally, there was much legislation designed to stimulate crop production and the conservation of food stuffs and raw materials. By an ordinance of December 31, 1914, military governors were given power to fix the maximum price of food stuffs within the territory under their command,[1] and this power was frequently exercised.[2] Other ordinances were issued regulating the planting of potatoes;[3] forbidding the serving of potatoes with the skin removed, at hotels and restaurants;[4] prohibiting the use of animal and vegetable oils and greases for other than human consumption;[5] regulating the slaughter of animals; prohibiting the feeding of potatoes to other animals than hogs and regulating the amount that might be so fed;[6] forbidding tanneries to purchase hides, skins, or other tanning material;[7] forbidding the baking of cakes except on Wednesdays and Saturdays, etc.[8]

Labor and industry were subjected to an elaborate régime of regulation and supervision. By an ordinance of December 15, 1914, a somewhat elaborate code regulating the labor of women and children was put into effect;[9] in some industries the hours of labor were regulated; various ordinances were promulgated for the purpose of coercing the Belgians to perform labor which they regarded as having a military character, and which they refused to perform; other ordinances were issued for the deportation of unemployed laborers to Germany, etc.

[1] *Ibid.*, II, p. 12.
[2] Cf., e.g., an ordinance fixing the price of potatoes, *ibid.*, VII, p. 365. Violation of the ordinance was punishable by imprisonment up to one year and a fine not exceeding 10,000 marks.
[3] *Ibid.*, VI, p. 80.
[4] *Ibid.*, VI, p. 151. The penalty for violation of this decree was not more than six months' imprisonment and a fine not exceeding 5000 marks.
[5] *Ibid.*, VI, p. 90. Penalty for violation, three months' imprisonment and a fine of 5000 marks.
[6] *Ibid.*, VI, p. 80. Giving potatoes to other animals than swine or giving swine more potatoes than the amount specified in the ordinance was punishable by a fine up to 10,000 marks.
[7] *Ibid.*, V, p. 163. The penalty for violation of this decree was imprisonment for one year and a fine equal to fifty times the value of the materials purchased.
[8] *Ibid.*, II, p. 39.   [9] *Ibid.*, I, pp. 75–82.

§ 366. **Restrictions in Respect to Personal Liberty.** .Not only were the industrial and economic activities of the Belgian population subjected to an almost infinite variety of regulations, but their personal liberty was restricted to an even greater degree. By an ordinance of January 16, 1915, all open air assemblies and all political meetings behind closed doors were forbidden. For every other meeting, public or private, a permit was required, for which application had to be made five days in advance to the military commander in the locality. Purely religious, social, scientific, and professional assemblies were excepted from this requirement. All clubs and societies "having a political tendency" or whose object was the discussion of political matters were declared to be dissolved, and the organization of new clubs of this character was forbidden. Violation of this decree was punishable by imprisonment for one year or a fine of 5000 francs. As in the case of most other ordinances issued by the German authorities, the military courts were given jurisdiction of offences arising thereunder.[1]

A variety of petty police regulations was issued from time to time in every town or city occupied by the Germans. Many of these related to the movement of the inhabitants by foot, by carriage, and by automobile. Generally, the inhabitants were required to be in their homes after a certain early hour in the evening, sometimes as early as 7 o'clock.[2] At Brussels civilians were required to show their deference to German officers by taking off their hats or by saluting with the hand. In case of doubt as to whether the soldier were an officer, he should be saluted. Those who failed to do so "must expect the German soldiers to make themselves respected by any and all means."[3] By a decree of November 6, 1914, all clocks in Belgium were required to be set forward fifty-six minutes (Ger-

[1] *Ibid.*, II, pp. 44-45. Cf. also Massart, *Belgians under the German Eagle*, p. 314.

[2] Cf. text of a proclamation issued at Brussels. Gomery, p. 173. In some cases the inhabitants were forbidden to leave their houses except when absolutely necessary, this under penalty of being shot.

[3] Text, Gomery, p. 174. At Noyon on May 15, 1916, the commandant issued a proclamation reminding all male inhabitants over twelve years of age that they must "salute politely" all German officers by uncovering their heads. Facsimile reproduction of the proclamation in New York *Times*, July 22, 1917. Text of this proclamation and a similar one issued at Nesle, July 2, 1915, in Saint-Aymour, *Autour de Noyon*, pp. 287-288.

man time).[1] Another species of petty tyranny of the kind was the removal of French and Flemish names from the railway stations and the substitution of German names. Many towns in both Belgium and France were rechristened and given German names.[2]

By an ordinance of October 13, 1914, all printed matter issued in Belgium, including musical compositions, and all theatrical representations, moving pictures, recitals, and the like were declared to be subject to the censorship of the German authorities; and by an ordinance of February 5, 1916, printers who failed to submit their publications to the censor for his examination were subjected to a penalty of imprisonment for three years or more or a fine not exceeding 5000 marks, or both, and confiscation of the printing press.[3] The sale or distribution of newspapers, except with the express permission of the military authorities, was forbidden.[4] The German authorities had some difficulty in enforcing this ordinance on account of the surreptitious printing of newspapers that had been suppressed and the smuggling in of papers from Holland, and on November 4, 1914, Governor-general von der Goltz issued a proclamation

[1] *Arrêtés et Procs.*, p. 39.

[2] In Belgium and French Flanders, Flemish designations, which before the war had been used alternately with the French, were made official, while in France German names were substituted. Thus Louvain became Löwen, Malines became Mechlin, Ypres, Ypern; Namur, Namen, etc.

[3] Huberich and Speyer, VI, p. 90. Rather than submit to German censorship most of the Brussels papers ceased publication. The sale of foreign newspapers in Belgium was rigorously prohibited, but some were smuggled in. Many of the offenders were detected and heavily fined. The Germans themselves published two journals at Brussels, the *Deutsche Soldaten Post* and the *Réveil*. In spite of the most vigorous efforts and the offer of large rewards, the German authorities were unable to prevent the printing and distribution of forbidden newspapers. Journals like the *Echo de Belge*, *La Libre Belgique*, and the *Courière de la Meuse* appeared at irregular intervals. The last-mentioned journal was published by Belgian refugees in Holland and smuggled into Belgium in spite of the vigilance of the German authorities. *La Libre Belgique* was issued from a portable press which the Germans never succeeded in locating, although a reward of 50,000 francs was offered for information leading to the discovery of the plant and the publishers. New York *Times*, January 28, 1917. The story of *La Libre Belgique* is told in the New York *Times Magazine* of March 10, 1918. Hugh Gibson, secretary of the American legation at Brussels, states that the governor-general regularly received a copy through one channel or another (New York *Times*, January 6, 1918).

[4] *Arrêtés et Procs.*, p. 13. It was in consequence of an altercation between a German officer and a Brussels policeman regarding the sale of forbidden newspapers that the city of Brussels was fined 5,000,000 francs.

warning the inhabitants that the sale and distribution of newspapers or printed matter of every kind, which had not been
expressly authorized by the German censor, was strictly prohibited, and that all persons offending against the ordinance
would be arrested and imprisoned for a long period of time.[1]

The posting of notices either by the municipal authorities or
by private individuals without authority was strictly forbidden.[2]
The taking of photographs of any kind within the occupied
territory of Belgium without the permission of the military
authorities was punishable by a fine of 3000 marks,[3] and the
taking of photographs of destroyed buildings was forbidden
under a penalty of three months' imprisonment or a fine of 2000
marks.[4] The taking out of Belgium of written or printed matter
of whatever character, except identity papers and passports,
without the special and written authorization of the superior
military authorities, was punishable by one year's imprisonment or a fine of 4000 marks.[5]

§ 367. **Restrictions in Respect to Patriotic Demonstrations.**
There were frequent complaints and loud protests against the
German measures prohibiting patriotic demonstrations and the
display of the Belgian flag, the purpose of which, the Belgians
alleged, was to repress their sentiments of loyalty and patriotism, this notwithstanding that Governor-general von der Goltz
had assured the inhabitants in his proclamation of September 2,
1914, that he would "ask no one to renounce his patriotic sentiments." In spite of this assurance a notice was issued on
September 16, 1914, by the military governor of Brussels, von
Leutwitz, informing the inhabitants that the exhibition of the
Belgian national flag would be "regarded by the German troops
as a provocation." Nevertheless, the notice added, this was
not intended to wound the dignity or the feelings of the inhabitants, its sole purpose being to avoid subjecting the citizens
to annoyance. Householders were therefore requested to
remove Belgian flags from their housetops.[6] This notice was
understood to be an order to the burgomaster of Brussels (M.
Max), and he accordingly issued a proclamation to the people
of the city urging them to accept *provisionally* the sacrifice this
required of them.

[1] *Ibid.*, p. 38.   [2] *Ibid.*, p. 7.   [3] *Ibid.*, p. 13.
[4] Huberich and Speyer, V, p. 23.
[5] Ordinance of April 1, 1916. *Ibid.*, VII, p. 20.   [6] *Arrêtés et Procs.*, p. 13.

This proclamation offended the military governor who thereupon issued the following order: "Burgomaster Max, having failed to fulfil the engagements entered into with the German government, has forced me to suspend him from his position. M. Max will find himself under honourable detention in a fortress." The burgomaster was at first imprisoned in a fortress at Namur, but was later deported to Germany and confined in a fortress at Glatz, from which he appears to have been subsequently transferred to Switzerland, where he remained until the end of the war.[1]

Flags used by the inhabitants to decorate their shop windows were torn down by the military authorities and in some cases towns and individuals were fined for displaying the national emblem.[2] By an order of November 14, 1914, Lieutenant-general Hirschberg at Namur charged that the greater part of the population, including the school children, were "manifesting their patriotic feelings by wearing in an open manner the Belgian colors under different forms" with the purpose of "making a public demonstration against the present state of affairs and against the German authority." It was, therefore ordered that this practice should be discontinued, and that the display of Belgian colors, whether on one's person or any object whatsoever, should be forbidden.[3]

The inhabitants of Brussels, who adopted the custom of wearing a tricolor rosette to the great annoyance of the Germans, were forbidden under penalty of fine and imprisonment by an order of July 1, 1915, to wear or exhibit Belgian insignia in a "provocative manner" or to wear or exhibit under any circumstances the insignia of nations with which Germany was at war.[4] Thereupon they substituted an ivy leaf, but this

---

[1] The treatment of M. Max is discussed by Davignon, *Belgium and Germany*, p. 31; Gomery, *op. cit.*, p. 173; Gibson, *Journal from Our Legation in Belgium*, pp. 241, 252.

[2] Brussels was subsequently fined 5,000,000 francs in consequence of a "patriotic demonstration" on July 21, 1915, the national holiday, in violation of the regulations, and Lierre was fined 176,000 francs because a flag was found flying from the top of a tree in the town.

[3] Text in Massart, p. 267.

[4] Maître Gaston de Laval, counsellor of the American legation at Brussels, in an address before the American Bar Association in 1917 (52 *Amer. Law Review*, pp. 259–260) described at length the German measures against the display of the Belgian flag and the celebration of the national holiday, and how the efforts of the Germans were outwitted by the Belgians through various ingenious devices.

likewise was forbidden, whereupon a green ribbon was substituted. The Belgians allege that even the celebration of the
Te Deum in the churches was forbidden and, of course, the singing of the *Brabançonne* and the *Marseillaise*.[1]

§ 368. **German Measures in Respect to Education.** A considerable amount of German legislation and administration in
Belgium was concerned with education, its chief objects being
to prevent anti-German teaching in the schools, to suppress
patriotic exercises and demonstrations by school children, and
to insure a larger recognition of the Flemish and even of the
German language as the vehicles of instruction in the schools.
At the outset the schools were placed under the control of the
German authorities and subjected to a régime of supervision
and inspection. A year's imprisonment was prescribed as the
penalty against school teachers, directors, and inspectors who
permitted teaching, activities, or statements calculated to
excite hatred of the Germans or opposition to the authority of
the military occupant. The singing of the *Brabançonne*, and
other patriotic songs, or the holding of exercises the effect of
which was to inculcate anti-German feeling, or the use of text-
books which contained statements offensive to the Germans
were forbidden, and the military tribunals were given jurisdiction
of all such offences.[2] Dismissal of the schools in honor of the
king and other patriotic manifestations of the sort were rigorously interdicted.

A succession of ordinances were promulgated relative to the
language to be employed in the primary and secondary schools,
the general purpose of which was to insure that the Flemish
language instead of French should be employed in the instruction

---

[1] Massart, pp. 269–271. Cf. Massart, p. 271, for the text of such an order
issued at Ghent. Cf. also Cammaerts, *Through the Iron Bars*, pp. 19 ff. The
practice of singing the *Brabançonne* in the schools, an old custom which had been
followed long before the outbreak of the war, was forbidden under heavy penalties
by a decree of von Bissing on June 26, 1915. Text in Massart, p. 280.

[2] By an ordinance of June 26, 1915, issued by Governor-general von Bissing,
it was provided that "The members of the teaching staff, school managers, and
inspectors, who during the period of occupation, tolerate, favor, provoke, or organize Germanophobe manifestations or secret practices will be punished by imprisonment for a maximum term of one year"; that "the German authorities have the
right to enter all classes and rooms of all schools existing in Belgium and to super-
vise the teaching and all the manifestations of school life with a view to preventing
secret practices and intrigues directed against Germany." Text in Massart, p. 280.

of children whose maternal language was Flemish.[1] This measure, the Belgians allege, was designed to set the Flemish population against the Walloon element and, if possible, to attract their support to the German regime. An effort also appears to have been made to force the German language into the schools of certain parts of Belgium. Thus by an ordinance of April 22, 1916, German was declared to be the maternal language in the "German part" of Belgium, which embraced some twelve districts in the province of Liège and some twenty-two towns and communes in the Belgian province of Luxemburg, unless the head of the family made a declaration to the effect that some other language was the maternal or usual language of the family. Schoolmasters were charged with verifying the truth of the declaration and were empowered to examine the children with a view to ascertaining whether they were qualified to pursue their studies in the language so declared.[2] At Liège and Namur the inhabitants are said to have been required to use the German language in their correspondence.[3]

It would seem to be within the lawful rights of a military occupant to exercise supervision over the schools within the territory occupied, so far as it may be necessary to prevent seditious teaching calculated to provoke and incite hostility to his authority,[4] but it may be doubted whether he has any lawful right to forbid such exercises, as the singing of national anthems, or whether he may justly abrogate the laws of the country which prescribe the language to be employed in the schools, except on the inadmissible assumption that the temporary right of occupation is assimilable to the right of sovereignty. In the present case no considerations of public order or security re-

[1] Cf. the texts of these ordinances in Huberich and Speyer, VI, pp. 177 ff., 243 ff. and VII, pp. 446 ff. By a decree of November 2, 1916, Belgian postal officials in the Flemish part of Belgium were required to employ the Flemish language in all their official correspondence with the communal or other local authorities. Text, ibid., IX, p. 167.

[2] Text in Huberich and Speyer, VII, pp. 120 ff.; cf. also a decree of March 18, 1917, ibid., X, p. 197, and a decree of March 24, 1917, ibid., X, p. 210.

[3] Massart, p. 272. Some instances of German interference with schools in France are detailed in Calippe, La Somme sous l'Occupation Allemande, pp. 166 ff.

[4] The British manual of military law (sec. 379) says that "schools and educational establishments must be permitted to continue their ordinary activity, provided that the teachers refrain from reference to politics and submit to inspection and control by the authorities appointed." In 1870-1871 the Germans closed three lycées in France, the heads of which refused to permit inspection.

quired the forcing of the Flemish or German languages into the
schools; its evident purpose was to "Flemishize" or Germanize
a portion of the country occupied by the enemy. It is very
doubtful whether a reasonable interpretation of the temporary
and limited rights of a military occupant, as they are set forth
in the Hague convention, authorizes him to interfere in any
such manner with the elementary and secondary schools in the
territory under his occupation. It was a species of petty tyranny
more calculated to provoke the hatred and opposition of the
inhabitants than to strengthen the hold of the occupant or to
subserve any considerations of public order or national defence.
It was, therefore, as inexpedient as it was arbitrary and unjustified.

§ 369. **Movement to Detach Flemish Belgium; Transformation of the University of Ghent into a Flemish Institution.**
The attempt of the Germans to win over the Flemish population
and to drive a wedge between the two races with a view to
making the Flemish part of the country a dependency of Germany was not confined to the school and language measures
referred to above. The hands of the Germans were also laid
upon one of the four universities of Belgium as a means of
further promoting their policy of detachment.[1] Accordingly
the University of Ghent was "reorganized" and transformed
by General von Bissing into a Flemish institution. The courses
of instruction were required to be given in the Flemish language,
subject to the condition that the chief of the civil administration

[1] Soon after the occupation of Belgium the Germans entered upon a policy
the purpose of which was to widen the cleft which had long existed between the
Flemish and Walloon elements of the population and to win over to their own
support the sympathy of the former. Advances of various kinds were made toward
Flemish leaders of thought and public opinion; promises of autonomy for Flanders were held out to the Flemings, and a policy of conciliation and leniency toward
them was adopted. Flemish students who had taken refuge in England, Holland,
and other neutral countries were offered inducements to return to Belgium, and
Belgian prisoners of Flemish extraction held by the Germans are said to have been
treated with more leniency and consideration than their Walloon compatriots and
were even permitted to return to Belgium under certain conditions. Cf. an article
by a "Flemish Belgian" entitled "Vain Attempts to Divide the Belgians" in the
New York *Times* of August 2, 1916; also Massart, *op. cit.*, pp. 284 ff. German
proclamations were printed in Flemish; theatres and moving-picture shows in
certain towns were required to print their programmes in Flemish; shopkeepers in
Bruges and Ostend were ordered to replace their French signs with Flemish signs;
Flemish offenders were let off with lighter punishments than those imposed on
Walloons, and the like.

of the governor-generalcy might, by way of exception, permit the employment of "another language" (presumably German) in certain branches of instruction.[1]   The pretext for this measure was the desire to meet the demand of the Flemish population for the establishment of a Flemish university.   It is true that long before the war the Flemish population had desired the establishment of a university in which instruction should be given in their own language.   They felt that the exclusive employment of French in the universities was not only an injustice to themselves, but it compelled Flemish students to master the French language.   They had therefore more than once addressed petitions to the government urging it to provide an institution in which instruction should be given in their own language, and it is said that their demands were on the point of being conceded by the government when the war broke out.[2] But the very evident purpose which the Germans had in view in "Flemishizing" the University of Ghent caused the overwhelming majority of the Flemish population to spurn the German offer, which they well knew was not made in the interest of those whom they professed to regard as an oppressed race, and was, moreover, quite inconsistent with their treatment of the inhabitants of Alsace-Lorraine in this respect. Protests were accordingly addressed to the governor-general by the leading Flemish members of Parliament and scholars, and on July 21, 1915 (the Belgian national holiday), a "manifesto" was issued by the leaders of the Flemish movement then in Holland who, while avowing their devotion to the Flemish cause, "affirmed with like energy that they would remain irreducibly adverse to any idea of reconciliation with the enemy, and that they rejected with indignation any and all his favors." In spite of these protests, however, the German authorities maintained that it was their duty to come to the relief of the long oppressed Flemish race, "liberate them from the Walloon yoke," and provide them with a medium for the development of their culture, whether they desired it or not.

[1] Text of the ordinance in Huberich and Speyer, VI, p. 228.   By a decree of September 30, 1916, professors in the university who refused to give instruction in the Flemish language were deprived of their positions.   *Ibid.*, IX, p. 10.

[2] In November, 1912, the chamber of deputies had voted to transform the University of Ghent into a Flemish institution, but before the details had been agreed upon, the war broke out.

§ 370. **Deportations of Professors Pirenne and Frédéricq.**
The German authorities were highly offended at the refusal
of those professors who could not be induced to continue their
teaching after the reorganization of the university, and especially at the conduct of Professor Pirenne in refusing the rector-
ship and of Professor Frédéricq, one of the leaders of the Flemish
movement, in refusing to retain his professorship under the new
régime.[1] Shortly afterwards (April, 1915), both men were
arrested and deported without trial to Germany where they
were confined in a prison camp. According to the testimony
of their colleagues the two professors were deported on account
of their opposition to the "Flemishization" of the university
and for their unwillingness to be the instruments of the Germans
in the execution of a policy designed to introduce discord and
division among the two racial elements of the nation.[2]

Appeals and petitions were addressed to the governor-general
by Dutch scientists, by the American historical association,
and by other academic and scientific bodies in neutral countries
in behalf of the two exiled professors, and even the government
of the Netherlands is reported to have requested the German
government to permit them to reside in some neutral country
where they might continue their scientific researches; but the
appeals and remonstrances appear to have made no impression
on the German authorities. Naturally the Germans encountered considerable difficulty in finding the requisite staff of
professors who were qualified and willing to give instruction in
the Flemish language, and every species of persuasion, cajolery,

[1] Cf. a letter by Jules Duesberg, professor in the University of Liége, New
York *Times*, September 20, 1916.

[2] The *Hamburger Fremdenblatt* in an editorial reproduced in the New York
Times of August 18, 1916, charged that the two professors were guilty of manifesting their hostile opposition through secret agitation and plots which constituted
a danger to the military administration. Cf. also a letter of J. Mattern entitled
Belgian Libraries in German Hands, New York *Times*, September 22, 1916, and a
statement of the German legation in Stockholm (German text, in Nyrop, *L'Arrestation des Professeurs Belges et l'Université de Gand*, pp. 73 ff.) denying that
General von Bissing had ever requested either one of the professors to continue
in the service of the university and asserting that they were deported because of
their agitation among their colleagues with a view to inducing them to oppose the
German measure of reorganization. This book by a Danish professor contains
a detailed account of the proceedings by which the University of Ghent was transformed and the treatment of the professors. Cf. also 43 Clunet, 893, and the
Revue Gén. de Droit Int. Pub., 1917, p. 111.

and even compulsion is said to have been exercised to obtain the services of qualified professors. The "bait" held out to Flemish scholars proved too attractive to a few of them, and very much to the disgust of their countrymen they accepted chairs in the reorganized institution and gave their coöperation.[1] The great majority of them, however, refused to associate themselves in any way with the new enterprise.

§ 371. **Right of a Military Occupant to Interfere with Educational Institutions.** It is not easy to justify this interference with the University of Ghent upon any other principle than that the occupation of the country had ripened into sovereignty, an assumption which cannot be admitted. The authorities on international law are in substantial agreement that occupied territory is not to be regarded as having passed under the sovereignty of the conqueror until the end of the war, that the power of the military occupant is only de facto and provisional in character, and that he should respect the existing laws and institutions except where their modification or abolition is absolutely necessary.[2] Neither considerations of public order nor military

[1] Cf. an article by a Dutch writer, A. J. Barnouw, in the *Nation* of October 19, 1916. By one means or another a faculty of forty-six persons, recruited partly from the university staff and partly from foreign countries, more than half of whom according to Belgian accounts were without qualification, was finally constituted, and the university as reorganized was opened in the autumn of 1916.

[2] Cf. art. 6 of the Oxford manual of the laws of war adopted by the Institute of International Law and article 43 of the Hague convention of 1907 respecting the laws and customs of war on land. The rule of the Oxford manual declares that "no invaded territory is to be regarded as conquered until the end of the war. Until that time, the invader exercises in such territory only a defacto power essentially provisional in character." Referring to the duty of the occupying authority to take the necessary measures to assure order and public tranquillity, it added: "To that end the invader should maintain the laws in force in the territory in time of peace and should not modify, suspend or replace them unless it becomes absolutely necessary to do so" (art. 44). Pillet expresses the view generally accepted when he says the "institutions of the country [occupied by the enemy] remain the same and continue to function so far as the state of war permits" (*Les Lois Actuelles de la Guerre*, p. 243). Prior to the middle of the eighteenth century no distinction was made in theory or practice between occupation and conquest. The sovereignty of the State occupied ceased with the establishment of the authority of the occupying army, and the inhabitants were required to take an oath of fidelity and sometimes of allegiance. But this view was long ago abandoned, and it is now held by all writers on international law that the power of the occupant is only temporary and founded on military necessity; that the rights of sovereignty remain intact, and that although the inhabitants owe the occupying authority a temporary allegiance and must submit to his authority, he may rightfully exercise only such control as is necessary for the maintenance of his security and the

security required the transformation of the University of Ghent
into a Flemish institution. It belonged to the Belgian people,
it was established for their benefit, and it was supported by their
contributions. Its courses of instruction, the language in which
they were given, and the selection of its professors were matters
of no legitimate concern to the military occupant so long as the
conduct of the university and the character of its teaching were
not such as to endanger the military interests of the occupant
or threaten the public order. The pretext that the measure
was in the interest of an oppressed race ceased to have any
weight as soon as the leaders, as well as the great majority of
those in whose interest it was alleged to have been undertaken,
united in protest against it.

§ 372. **Division of Belgium into Two Districts.** The vigorous
protests against the German movement, which looked ultimately to the detachment of the Flemish part of Belgium from
the rest of the country and of which the transformation of the
University of Ghent into a Flemish institution was the chief
preparatory measure, had no effect upon the German government, and other acts followed in quick succession. Speaking
in the *Reichstag* on the "Flemish Question" on April 5, 1916,
the Imperial Chancellor said:

---

preservation of public order. Departures from the existing law should, therefore,
be confined to such regulations as may be absolutely necessary to accomplish
these purposes; they should for the most part be confined to the determination
of relations between the inhabitants and the occupying power and not to relations
between the inhabitants. The committee of the Brussels Conference that
drafted art. 2, which is substantially the same as art. 43 of the Hague Convention, explained that its purpose was to allow an occupant to change or abrogate
political or administrative laws but not criminal or civil laws dealing with the relations between the inhabitants. Cf. on these points Hall, pt. III, ch. 4; Westlake,
II, 94; Hershey, p. 408; Lawrence, sec. 176; Heffter, sec. 131; Birkhimer, *Military.
Law*, p. 22; Magoon, *Law of Civil Government under Military Occupation in Time
of War*, p. 247. This theory is generally admitted by German writers. Cf.
Stier-Somlo in the *Zeitschrift für Völkerrecht*, Bd. 8, pp. 568–608. Birkhimer
(p. 79) rejects the theory of temporary allegiance held by most writers, but it is
ably defended by Oppenheim in an article entitled "The Legal Relations between
an Occupying Power and the Inhabitants" (*Law Quar. Review*, October, 1917).
Professor Oppenheim, however, argues that the duty of obedience is one not of
international law, but is rather one of martial law of the occupying power. That
is to say, the inhabitants owe him obedience because they are within his power
and will be crushed if they disobey. This view is adopted by a Belgian jurist, Prof.
Chas. de Visscher of the University of Ghent, in an article entitled *L'Occupation
de Guerre* in the *Law Quar. Review*, January, 1918, and by the Belgian Court of
cassation in a decision of May 20, 1916, and in two decisions of June 14 and July
5, 1917, which are analyzed by M. de Visscher.

"Here, too, fate takes no step backward.   Here, too, Germany cannot allow the long suppressed Flemish race'again to be exposed to efforts to make Frenchmen of them.   Germany will secure for them a sound development which does justice to their rich gifts and which is based on their Dutch speech and characteristics.   We do not want neighbors who will again combine against us to throttle us.   We want neighbors who will coöperate with us and with whom we can coöperate for mutual benefit."

Again, early in 1917 the Imperial Chancellor in an address to a deputation which styled itself the "Council of Flanders" and which was composed of a group of "active Flemings" of evident pro-German sympathies, went further and definitely promised them the aid of the German government in making Flanders an autonomous province, if not an independent nation, under German protection.   Finally, by a decree of March 3, 1917,[1] Belgium was divided into two administrative districts, one embracing the Flemish part (the provinces of Antwerp, Limburg, East and West Flanders, and the districts of Brussels and Louvain), the other the more distinctly Walloon portions (the provinces of Hainaut, Liège, Luxemburg, Namur, and the district of Nivelles).   The former district was to be administered from Brussels, the latter from Namur, and over each a German director was appointed.   This measure provoked a storm of protest throughout Belgium; it was denounced as an attempt to divide the Belgian people and to seduce the Flemish population from their natural allegiance and attract it to the support of the Germans.   Such a measure, it was said, was beyond the lawful rights of a military occupant as they are laid down in article 43 of the Hague convention, since it was not founded on considerations of public order or the maintenance of the security of the occupying forces.   Many Belgian officials resigned their posts to avoid giving their support to and rendering coöperation in the execution of the measure.[2]   A number of them were thereupon arrested and deported to Germany.   Against this proceeding the Belgian government addressed a long and spirited protest to the governments of the allied and neutral powers. Protests were also made by the senators and deputies of the national parliament, by many communal councils, by Cardinal Mercier, by various learned societies, commercial and industrial

[1] Huberich and Speyer, 10th Series, pp. 201-202; Passalecq, p. 5.
[2] Van der Essen, *Petite Histoire de l'Invasion*, p. 119.

bodies, universities, the courts, members of the bar, and others.[1] The protests, it may be added, emanated from Flemish persons and bodies as well as from those of Walloon nationality. It is certain that the voice of the overwhelming majority of the population representing both races was raised in opposition, but without effect. The German authorities also went to the length of attempting to suppress all manifestations of opposition to the measure. Thus the city of Antwerp was fined 1,000,000 francs because of rough treatment inflicted by the populace upon a group of Flemish "activists" who were engaged in a agitation in favor of the separation of Flanders from the rest of Belgium.[2] It was also alleged that meetings of Flemish agitators were protected by the German authorities, while those of loyalists were not permitted.[3] In March, 1918, the German authorities issued orders forbidding the provincial and communal councils to discuss the Flemish question, and notice was served upon them that such discussion would be repressed with the greatest severity. Henceforth protests against the dismemberment policy of the German government would not be tolerated.

[1] The texts of these protests may be found in a book by M. Fernand Passalecq entitled *La Magistrature Belge contre le Despotisme Allemand* (1915), pp. 89 ff. The whole "Flemish Question," including German policy in respect to the division of Belgium, is treated more in detail by the same author in a book entitled *La Question Flamande et l'Allemagne* (Paris and Nancy, 1917). Cf. also a brochure entitled *Ce que les Belges de la Belgique Envahie Pensent de la Séparation Administrative*, with a preface by M. de Wiart, minister of justice. See also an article by de Visscher in 25 *Revue Gén.*, 92 ff. where the German measure is criticised as being in violation of the fundamental rules of international law relative to the rights of military occupants. The real purpose, says de Visscher, was to conserve in Belgium a future sphere of influence for Germany.

[2] The mayor of Antwerp was at the same time dismissed, and a Flemish alderman of the city and a deputy in parliament named Francke was fined 1000 francs by a German military tribunal and threatened with deportation for a speech in which he denounced the intrigues of the Flemish "activists."

[3] Cf. the texts of a decree of October 25, 1917, in Passelecq's *La Magistrature Belge*, p. 19, which insured immunity to Flemish activists for forbidding the courts to take jurisdiction of conspiracy charges against them.

CHAPTER XXIV

MILITARY GOVERNMENT IN BELGIUM
(Continued)

§ 373. German Military Courts in Belgium; § 374. Creation of Special Civil Tribunals; § 375. Right of a Military Occupant to Establish Special Tribunals; § 376. German Practice Criticized; § 377. Measures against the Belgian Judiciary in 1918; § 378. The Germans Take over the Whole Administration of Justice in Belgium; § 379. The German Régime of Criminal Repression in Belgium; § 380. Criticism of the German Theory of War Treason; § 381. Condemnations by the German Tribunals; § 382. Execution of Women; Case of Edith Cavell; § 383. Intervention of the American Legation in her Behalf; § 384. The German Defense; § 385. Past Practice as to the Execution of Women for War Crimes; § 386. Observations on the Cavell Case.

§ 373. German Military Courts in Belgium. Upon their occupation of Belgium the German authorities invited the Belgian judges to remain at their posts, and promises were given that they would not be interfered with in the discharge of their functions. This invitation was accepted upon the advice of the minister of justice [1] out of a sense of duty toward the Belgian people, and the courts continued to administer "ordinary" criminal and civil justice in the name of the king and in accordance with the laws of the country. Aside from an occasional interference with the execution of judgments when the rights of Germans were involved, there were no serious encroachments during the early years of the war upon the jurisdiction of the courts in the performance of their functions. From the outset, however, the administration of what the Germans regarded as "extraordinary" justice was withdrawn from the Belgian courts and conferred upon special tribunals organized by the German authorities.

[1] 44 Clunet, 1000. No oath of obedience was required of the judges, and it is quite certain in view of their subsequent attitude toward the German measures respecting the courts that they would not have taken such an oath. Cf. M. Gaston de Laval's address on *Prussian Law as Applied in Belgium*, delivered before the American Bar Association in 1917 (Reports of the Amer. Bar. Assoc., 1917; reprinted in 52 *American Law Review*, 235 ff.). It will be recalled that during their occupation of France in 1870-1871 the German authorities refused to allow the French courts to render their decisions in the name of the French Republic.

Soon after the arrival of the Germans in Belgium they proceeded to establish in the larger towns military tribunals (*Kriegsgerichte*), the judges of which were generally persons who had held the position of public prosecutor (*Staatsanwalt*) to the military courts in Germany. Gradually the system of military courts was extended to all the occupied territory, a chief military prosecutor (*Ober Kriegsgerichtsrat*) being placed at the head of the organization.[1] In theory their jurisdiction was limited to offences against the safety of the military occupant and the security of the German forces, but in fact they were given jurisdiction of practically all cases arising under the numerous ordinances, decrees, and police regulations issued by the governor-general and his subordinates. Their jurisdiction was in consequence of the large number of such acts very extensive and in effect embraced a large field of ordinary criminal justice.

By an ordinance of April 26, 1916, the Belgian courts were prohibited from taking jurisdiction of actions against persons belonging to the armed forces of Germany or of her allies, or against the German civil authorities in Belgium. By the same ordinance they were prohibited from rendering judgments or decrees against foreigners (except subjects of powers at war with Germany) who in consequence of the war were prevented from safeguarding their rights.[2] The result of these and other ordinances was to give to the German military tribunals jurisdiction of all cases in which Germans were parties and of all offences committed by Belgians which had any political or military character, or which were forbidden by the German military penal code or by the ordinances and proclamations issued by the military authorities. According to the imperial ordinance of August 2, 1914, the accused was allowed to defend himself before the military court or to be defended by a third

---

[1] As to the German judicial system established in Belgium cf. Brand Whitlock's *Belgium*, Vol. I, ch. 61. Cf. also De Laval, "German Law in the Occupied Territory of Belgium," *International Law Notes*, February, 1916, p. 20; likewise his address referred to above, p. 253. It may further be remarked that the power to inflict penalties was not limited to the courts, but military governors and commandants had by virtue of their police power a considerable jurisdiction in this respect. They were, in fact, empowered to impose penalties up to three months' imprisonment and fines amounting to 1000 marks. 44 Clunet, 1369.

[2] Text in Huberich and Speyer, VIII, pp. 214 ff.

party. Trials, however, appear to have been secret, and counsel were not allowed to see the accused prior to his arraignment. The accused was permitted the last word, although he was allowed no right of appeal.

§ 374. **Creation of Special Civil Tribunals.** By an ordinance of February 3, 1915, provision was made for the creation in each province of exceptional tribunals to determine the amount of damages for which communes should be held responsible in case of violence, theft, and outbreaks on the part of the inhabitants.[1] By another decree of February 10, provision was made for the creation of a new set of tribunals of exception to judge cases between landlords and tenants.[2] These two decrees, constituting as they did a serious inroad upon the ordinary jurisdiction of the Belgian courts, evoked a spirited protest on the part of the Belgian bar and the public generally. On February 17, the council of the order of advocates of the Brussels court of appeal, headed by the *bâtonnier*, M. Théodor, addressed a protest to Governor-general von Bissing, in which it attacked the whole régime of exceptional courts established by the Germans, as illegal, contrary to the constitution of Belgium, and in violation of the Hague convention. The address further denounced the severity and arbitrariness of the newly established tribunals and protested against the occupation of the *Palais de Justice* by the German troops, who were using it as a caserne. The procedure of the tribunals, it was complained, did not permit the accused the right of public defence nor to have a copy of the charges or to consult his counsel prior to the arraignment. This, the protest went on to say, was "justice without control; the judge was left to himself, to his prejudices and his surroundings; the accused was abandoned to his fate alone, to grapple with his all-powerful adversary." This régime, it added, might be excusable for armies in the field, but the Belgian army was far away, and such a régime was intolerable for civilians whose conduct was peaceable and

[1] Huberich and Speyer, II, pp. 57–59. These courts were to be composed of a president appointed by the governor-general, one assessor appointed by the chief of the German civil administration in Belgium, and one appointed by the Belgian permanent deputation of the provincial council. The latter refused to serve, so that in fact the court consisted of two German members. 44 Clunet, 1003.

[2] Text in Huberich and Speyer, II, pp. 82–86.

irreproachable.[1] The Belgian bar, regarding the whole judicial establishment set up by the Germans as illegal, refused to "associate itself in the illegality of the régime" and on February 19, 1915, the council of the order of advocates of the Brussels court of appeal adopted a resolution forbidding members of the bar to take cases which were to be tried before the German tribunals of exception. In transmitting the text of this resolution to General von Bissing, M. Théodor took occasion to say that the bar was not animated by any spirit of hostility toward the occupying power, but only by a desire to avoid the violation of their oaths of fidelity and obedience to the constitution and the laws of Belgium.[2] The bars of other towns and cities adopted a similar attitude. For addressing this protest to the governor-general, M. Théodor was deported to Germany, where he was detained during the remainder of the war.[3]

The charges of the Belgians in respect to the procedure of the German special tribunals, and particularly as regards the right of defence, appear to have been well founded.[4] It would also seem that the establishment of exceptional tribunals and the withdrawal from the Belgian courts of a large portion of their ordinary jurisdiction were not in accord with the rule of the Hague convention.

[1] The French text of this protest may be found in the *Journal de Droit International*, Vol. 42, p. 288; and in *Cahiers Documentaires*, No. 68 (March 30, 1915). An English translation is printed in Beck's *The War and Humanity*, pp. 121-123.

[2] Text in *Cahiers Docs.*, No. 78 (April 12, 1915).

[3] The case of M. Théodor is discussed in the London *Solicitors' Journal and Weekly* of December 4, 1915, pp. 99 and 110, and in the *Journal de Droit Int.*, Vol. 42, pp. 1085-1087. Cf. also Whitlock, *Belgium*, Vol. I, ch. 63, and Vol. II, ch. 5.

[4] Cf., for example, the procedure followed at the trial of Miss Cavell, *infra*, Sec. 382. Cf. also the description of the procedure followed in the trial of espionage cases in Williams, *In the Claws of the German Eagle*, chs. 2 and 9, and in Van der Essen, *Petite Histoire*, pp. 79 ff. Maître de Laval, in the address referred to above, describes the procedure of the German courts in Belgium. While the right of defence was allowed, it was, he says, little more than a farce. No one but a German-speaking barrister could plead, and counsel was not permitted to see the accused before arraignment nor was he allowed to see a copy of the charges before the beginning of the trial. Under such circumstances Belgian members of the bar, he says, hesitated to defend the cases of Belgians, and in fact a goodly number declined to do it on the ground that it would have amounted to "taking part in the injustice meted out to the accused." "Prussian Law as Applied in Belgium," 52 *Amer. Law Review*, 255. Cf. also an article by a Swiss writer, Dumont-Wilden, entitled *Du Terrorisme Judiciaire en Pays d'Occupation Allemande*, 44 Clunet, 516 ff.

§ 375. **Right of a Military Occupant to Establish Special Tribunals.** The right of a military occupant to deprive the existing courts of their jurisdiction of offences against the authority of the occupying power as well as of offences against persons belonging to his armed forces is recognized by most writers on international law, and in practice military occupants have usually acted in accordance with this theory.[1] Writers on international law are in substantial agreement, however, that the existing body of civil and criminal law ought in the main to be respected by military occupants and should not be altered or abrogated except in so far as their military security or interests require.[2] Article 43 of the Hague convention of 1907 respecting the laws and customs of war on land thus states the rule:

"The authority of the legitimate power having in fact passed into the hands of the occupant, the latter shall take all measures in his power to restore and insure as far as possible public order and safety (*vie publique*) while respecting, unless absolutely prevented, the laws in force in the country."

[1] For example, during the war between the United States and Mexico (1846–1848) General Scott organized special tribunals called "military commissions" in the territory under his occupation and gave them jurisdiction of cases in which the parties were Americans and Mexicans only. Cf. General Scott's *Autobiography*, Vol. II, pp. 393, 541. Similar tribunals were organized by the Federal authorities in the Southern States during the Civil war. Cf. Birkhimer, *Military Government and Martial Law*, pp. 138, 147; also ch. 9. Cf. also Winthrop, *Military Law*, Vol. I, p. 961, and Dunning, *Essays on the Civil War and Reconstruction*. As to the practice in Mississippi cf. my *Reconstruction in Mississippi*, pp. 169, 184.

[2] Holland (*Laws of War on Land*, p. 53) remarks that a military occupant will hardly be justified in changing the rules of private law, e.g., those relating to property, contract, and domestic relations. Cf. also Geffcken's *Heffter*, sec. 131, where it is said that the existing laws remain in force, except where the necessities of war make changes imperative. Cf. also Spaight, *War Rights on Land*, pp. 355–356; Westlake, *Int. Law*, Vol. II, p. 96, and Hall, *Int. Law*, p. 465, who says an invader is forbidden as a general rule to vary or suspend laws affecting property and private personal relations or to regulate the moral order of the community. Some French writers appear to allow military occupants very little discretion. Cf., e.g., Pillet, *Les Lois Actuelles de la Guerre*, p. 241, who says, "All the laws remain intact"; but it is not clear that he denies the right of the military occupant to alter them to meet the new situation caused by the occupation. Bonfils (*Droit Int. Pub.*, sec. 1166) contends that the inhabitants of the territory occupied cannot be subjected to the criminal laws of the occupying State, except in so far as it concerns crimes and misdemeanors against the occupying army, its soldiers, and officers. The existing courts, he says, remain, and they continue to render justice in the name of the government which established them. The attempt of the Germans in 1870 to compel the French courts to render their judgments in the name of the military occupant was an abuse of power and was a confusion of military occupation with sovereignty. *Ibid.*, sec. 1169; cf. also Calvo, Vol. IV, sec. 2186, and Pillet, p. 248.

This principle is laid down in many military codes. Thus the British manual of military law affirms that neither the ordinary civil nor the ordinary criminal jurisdiction in force in the home territory of the military occupant is considered to extend over occupied territory; therefore the civil and penal laws of the occupied country continue as a rule to be valid, the courts which administer them are permitted to sit, and all crimes of the inhabitants, not of a military nature or not affecting the safety of the army, are left to their jurisdiction. If, it adds, the exigencies of the war demand, it is within the power of the occupant to alter or suspend any of the existing laws (such e.g., as are detrimental to his military interests) or to promulgate new ones; but important changes can seldom be necessary and should be avoided as far as possible.[1] The American *Rules of Land Warfare* lay down the same rule regarding respect for the ordinary civil and criminal laws, and as to the courts it declares that "all crimes not of a military nature and which do not affect the safety of the invading army are left to the jurisdiction of the local courts."[2]

The French manual adopts substantially the same view.

"The existing laws," it says, "shall be respected in their totality, save those which relate to recruiting, the liberty of the press and the right of assembly."[3] The existing tribunals of the occupied territory," it adds, "shall continue to exercise their functions and judge all *délits* committed by the inhabitants, save those which involve injury (*atteinte*) to the security of the occupying army. No derogations from this principle are allowable, except those imposed by the necessities of war."[4]

Even the manual of the German general staff admits that the promulgation of new laws or the abolition or modification of existing laws is to be avoided except when imperatively demanded by military necessity, such, for example, as in the case of the press, assembly, elections, etc. The civil and criminal courts, it adds, remain in force; martial law and exceptional

---

[1] Secs. 363, 364, 366. Sec. 368 says: "The ordinary courts of justice and the laws they administer should be suspended only when the refusal of the judges and magistrates to act make it necessary. In such cases the occupant must establish courts of his own and make this measure known to the inhabitants."

[2] Art. 299.

[3] The British manual adds to these exceptions, laws relating to the suffrage and the right to bear arms.

[4] *Les Lois de la Guerre Continentale*, p. 121 (ed. by Jacomet).

tribunals are permissible only when the behavior of the inhabitants make it necessary.[1] This is the doctrine and practice of the United States.[2]

It would seem, therefore, from the opinions of the text writers, the provisions of the military codes, and the practice in recent wars that a military occupant may not alter the existing body of law except in so far as its provisions are incompatible with the new order of things resulting from the occupation and except in so far as modification may be necessary for the maintenance of the public order and the protection of the safety and security of the occupying authorities.[3] In short, the modifications introduced must be founded on consideration of military necessity. In the second place, he may not lawfully set aside the ordinary jurisdiction of the existing courts and establish special military tribunals except for the trial of offences committed against the authority of the occupant and such offences as involve his safety and respect for his authority. In short, the jurisdiction of such tribunals must be limited to crimes of a "military nature." [4]

[1] French trans. by Carpentier, pp. 144-146. Loening, a well-known German authority, remarks that the existing tribunals cannot be displaced so long as the rights of the occupant are not violated by them. *Rev. de Droit Int. et de Lég. Comp.*, Vol. V, p. 94.

[2] Cf. Birkhimer, *Military Government and Martial Law*, ch. VI, who says the United States during the Civil war and the Spanish-American war acted on the principle that the existing laws in occupied territory remained in full force so far as not incompatible with the objects and conduct of the war. During the Russo-Japanese war the Chinese tribunals were as a general rule allowed by the Japanese authorities to administer justice, except in the case of offences against the Japanese army. Ariga, *La Guerre Russo-Japonaise*, p. 410. Likewise during the Chino-Japanese war the Japanese authorities permitted the existing tribunals to try offences in the territory occupied and according to Chinese law, except those against the Japanese army. Ariga, *La Guerre Sino-Japonaise*, ch. 13, and Pillet, *op. cit.*, p. 242, note 1. During the South African war the British authorities applied the law of the Transvaal in the occupied territories, and offences affecting the army or its interests were dealt with under that law. On account of the lack of local judges it became necessary to establish certain special courts to deal with offences under the law thus applied. Spaight, pp. 357-358.

[3] Professor Oppenheim states the generally accepted view when he says that the military occupant "must not alter the local laws according to discretion; he must respect them and leave them in force unless absolutely prevented by military necessity"; and he points out that military occupants are limited in this matter not only by the express prohibitions of the Hague convention, but by the "usages established between civilized nations," by the "laws of humanity," and by the "requirements of the public conscience." "Legal Relations between an Occupying Power and the Inhabitants," *Law. Quar. Review*, October, 1917, p. 5.

[4] Cf. the American *Rules of Land Warfare*, art. 299.

§ 376. **German Practice Criticised.** But the Germans in Belgium unquestionably went further than this. They not only altered various provisions of the Belgian criminal code and introduced new laws in respect to the press and assembly, which was quite within their legal rights, but they also introduced a new code of labor legislation and promulgated a large number of new laws in respect to trade, education, health, language, business, and ordinary industrial pursuits, such as agriculture, stock breeding, the slaughtering of animals for food, the muzzling of dogs, the feeding of animals, the planting and harvesting of crops, the sale of produce, the tanning of hides, the conservation of foods, and hundreds of other matters which had little or no connection with the maintenance of the public order or the protection and security of the occupying forces. As stated above, heavy penalties were prescribed for violation of these ordinances, and the newly established military courts were given jurisdiction of offences against them, almost without exception. The net result was, as the Belgians charged, to supersede the great body of existing legislation of the country and to hand over to the German military courts the larger part of the ordinary jurisdiction of the Belgian tribunals. They even went, as has been said, to the length of altering the law of tenancy and of depriving the ordinary courts of jurisdiction over disputes between renters and landlords and conferring it upon special tribunals organized by the German authorities.[1] Fin-

---

[1] The question of the legal right of the military occupant to promulgate an ordinance of this kind which had no connection with the maintenance of public order or the security of the occupying forces, and whether the courts of Belgium might before applying it inquire into its validity, was presented to the courts of appeal of Brussels and Liège, and conflicting decisions were rendered. The decision of the court of appeal of Brussels was then taken to the court of cassation for final determination. The court of cassation, relying upon the terms of art. 43 of the Hague convention of 1907 respecting the laws and customs of war on land, which imposes upon belligerents an obligation to respect the laws in force and not to depart from them except in case of absolute necessity, reached the conclusion, that an ordinance relating to contracts for hire could not be justified by "absolute necessity," and that consequently the German ordinance in question was not within the lawful right of the belligerent promulgating it. Nevertheless, it concluded the ordinance was obligatory on all persons subject to the jurisdiction of the occupying power, and it must be applied by the national tribunals. This, because the refusal of the judicial authorities to give effect to it would only precipitate a conflict between them and the military occupant, which would of course end in the triumph of the latter. In short, derogations from the existing laws are binding upon the inhabitants and should be obeyed whether they are justifiable or not.

ally, it may be added, the German military criminal code was applied in Belgium in all cases involving offences against the German troops or against German authority.[1]

§ 377. **Measures against the Belgian Judiciary in 1918.** The last year of the German occupation of Belgium brought still more serious encroachments upon the rights of the Belgian magistrature in consequence of its attitude toward the Flemish question. In January, 1918, a group of Belgian senators and deputies addressed a letter to the court of appeals of Brussels in which they denounced the activities of the so-called "Council of Flanders" as revolutionary and treasonable and demanded that its members be prosecuted for violation of certain articles of the Belgian criminal code.[2] The court after considering the request decided that the offences charged constituted crimes and *délits* punishable under the criminal code, and it directed the State's attorney to institute an examination with a view to the prosecution of the members of the "Council."[3] Thereupon several of the "activists" were arrested, and the examination was begun. At this juncture the German authorities inter-

---

This is the view of the authorities generally. Cf. Westlake, Vol. II, p. 97. The text of this decision may be found in *International Law Notes* for September, 1916, pp. 136–138. Text of the decision of the Court of Appeal of Liége which was affirmed by the Court of Cassation in the above mentioned case, 44 Clunet, pp. 1809 ff. See also the Comment of de Visscher in 45 Clunet, pp. 1090, ff. In May 1919 the French Court of Douai rendered a decision holding that the action of the German military governor at Maubeuge (Nov. 1914) in creating a tribunal charged with applying French law in civil and correctional matters was contrary to Article 43 of the Hague Convention and consequently the judgments of such a tribunal were invalid. Text of the decision in 46 Clunet (1919) p. 770.

[1] Par. 161 of the German military criminal code provides that "a foreigner or a German who in territory occupied by German troops, commits an act punishable under the laws of the Empire against troops or against any authority established by order of the Emperor shall be punished exactly as if he committed it in Federal territory." This extension of the German criminal law to foreign territory temporarily under German occupation is criticised by a Swiss jurist in 44 Clunet, 518. Cf. also De Laval's address on *Prussian Law as Applied in Belgium, loc. cit.* But the criticism is not entirely convincing.

[2] Among other things the "council of Flanders" openly proclaimed its sympathy with the German separatist designs and sent a deputation to Berlin to concert with the German authorities for the detachment of Flanders from the rest of Belgium. At the same time they proclaimed the "autonomy" of Flanders and invited the German government to recognize them as the body entitled to speak for the Flemish population.

[3] It may be remarked in this connection that the great majority of the forty-eight members of the court were of Flemish nationality. Passalecq, *La Magistrature Belge contre le Despotisme Allemand*, p. 44.

vened and required the immediate release of the accused, and
the judges were ordered to discontinue all proceedings against
them. Persisting in their course, several judges of the court
were arrested and deported to Germany where they were confined in the same prison with Burgomaster Max, who had been
deported some two years earlier. A few days later (February
10) the chief of the German administration for the district of
Flanders sent each member of the court of appeal a notice to the
effect that in consequence of their participation in the proceedings referred to above, they had "associated themselves in a
political manifestation," and that henceforth they would be
prohibited from exercising their functions.[1] On February 11,
the court of cassation met and after listening to an address of
the procurator-general in which he reviewed the conduct of the
Flemish "activists" and the proceedings of the German authorities in respect to the attitude of the court of appeals, adopted
a resolution declaring that the interference of the German
authorities with the administration of justice was incompatible
with the independence of the judiciary and with the laws which
governed them, and that the arrest of the judges and the sup-
pension of the counsellors of the court of appeal was contrary
to the law of nations and to the solemn promises made by the
German authorities. The court thereupon announced that
without abdicating its functions, it would suspend its sittings
for the present.[2] On the following day the civil tribunal and

---

[1] Text in Passalecq, p. 50. On February 19, the governor-general addressed
a letter to the procurator-general in which he defended the dismissal of the judges
of the court of appeal. "It is contrary to all reason," he said, "that in occupied
country the courts, which are under the authority of the occupying power, should
be allowed to take jurisdiction of offences against the dispossessed power with
which the occupying power finds itself at war. The attitude of the court of
appeal constitutes a wilful political demonstration, and it compelled me to inter-
dict the exercise of their functions to these judges who misunderstand to such
a point the conditions to which the regular performance of their duties were subject during the period of occupation." As to the conduct of the court of cassation
"it was regrettable that it had failed to recognize legally *les faits accomplis* and the
consequences which result therefrom from the point of view of international law,
and instead of abstaining from every attitude of hostile manifestation, had joined
with the court of appeals and sacrificed their duty toward the Belgian people —
a duty which required them to continue in the exercise of their functions." Text
of the letter in Passalecq, pp. 67–69.

[2] On February 25, 1918, the court of cassation met again and unanimously
adopted an *arrêt* in which it defended at length its decision of February 10, again
affirmed that the Belgian courts were within their rights in taking jurisdiction

the tribunal of commerce of Brussels decided unanimously to follow the action of the supreme court. Other courts quickly followed their example and with them the members of the bar until eventually practically the entire magistrature of the country had ceased to function.

§ 378. **The Germans Take over the Administration of Justice in Belgium.** Against this "strike" of the judges the German authorities took quick and heroic action. On March 26, governor-general Falkenhausen issued a notice in which, adverting to the action of the courts throughout Belgium in suspending their functions, he informed the people that they would have "to bear the consequences." The notice added:

"Conformably to article 43 of the Hague convention concerning the laws and customs of war on land I have ordered the organization of German tribunals which shall be charged with the maintenance of order and public safety. Until the entry into activity of these tribunals the military commandants will be charged with the repression of crimes and misdemeanors in pursuance of Par. 18, line 3, of the *Kaiserliche Verordnung* of December 28, 1899." [1]

On April 19 appeared two decrees providing for the establishment of new tribunals to take the places of those which had declined to continue their functions.[2] The first decree provided that repressive justice in Belgium should be administered by Imperial German tribunals; that the language employed should be German; that they should apply the law as laid down in the Belgian criminal code, but that they should pronounce only penalties prescribed by the German Imperial criminal code; that the procedure followed should be that of the German Imperial code of criminal procedure, and that no appeal would be allowed from their decisions. The second decree provided for the creation of a set of tribunals for the administration of justice in civil matters, likewise in accordance with German procedure and in the German language.

These measures stirred the popular indignation to a high pitch, and on June 5 the Belgian government addressed a long

of plots and conspiracies directed against the integrity of the country by Belgian citizens, denied that it was a matter which concerned the German authorities, and denounced the conduct of the German administration as an attack upon the dignity and independence of the Belgian courts. Text in Passalecq, pp. 71-74.

[1] Text in Passalecq, p. 76   [2] Texts, *ibid.*, pp. 125-132

protest to the governments of the allied and neutral powers, in which it denounced the action of the German authorities as being not only contrary to the constitution and laws of Belgium, but in violation of article 43 of the Hague convention and destructive of the rights and independence of the Belgian people.[1] The protest, however, was without result, and the judicial régime thus set up in Belgium continued until the end of the war.

§ 379. **The German Régime of Criminal Repression in Belgium.** The system of criminal repression established in Belgium by the Germans was one of great rigor and severity, being quite in accord with their traditional theory of military necessity. As has been said, the German Imperial military criminal code was introduced into Belgium and applied with rigor.[2] Article 57 creates the crime of war treason (*Kriegs-verrath*) and enacts that all persons who on the field are guilty of this crime shall be condemned to imprisonment for not less than 10 years or for life. Article 58 enumerates twelve separate offences which shall be regarded as war treason if done with the object of helping the enemy or prejudicing the German or allied troops.[3] Article 160 provides that foreigners who commit these acts within the theatre of war or in territory occupied by the German troops shall be punished equally with Germans who commit them. In Belgium, therefore, all persons, Belgians as well as Germans, were liable to the penalties of war treason. In short, what was war treason for a German was war treason for foreigners. May a military occupant apply his

---

[1] Text in Passalecq, pp. 79–84. Cf. also 45 Clunet, 1122, 1132 ff., where the German treatment of the Belgian magistrature is criticised by two Swiss writers. Cf. also Van der Essen, *Petite Histoire de l'Invasion*, pp. 75 ff.; the numerous protests in Passalecq, *op. cit.*, pp. 89 ff., and Whitlock, *Belgium*, Vol. I, ch. 62.

[2] The right of the German government to apply its own criminal code in foreign territory under the occupation of its armies has been attacked by various writers. Cf., e.g., M. de Laval's address entitled *Prussian Law as Applied in Belgium* referred to above. Cf. also an article by a Swiss jurist in 44 Clunet, 518 ff. The question, however, is debatable.

[3] The offences enumerated include those punishable by art. 90 of the German criminal code: the destruction of railways and telegraphs; betraying the secrets of the password; falsification of service orders or communications; serving as guides to the enemy or deceiving the Germans when serving as guides for them; causing trouble to or deceiving the German troops in the presence of the enemy; entering into communication with the enemy concerning military matters; spreading hostile information in the army; failing to give legitimate help to the German troops; allowing prisoners to escape, and furnishing the enemy with signals.

own law respecting war treason to the inhabitants of occupied territory? May a foreigner commit war treason against the authority of a military occupant?

§ 380. **Criticism of the German Theory of War Treason.** Professor J. H. Morgan in a paper read before the Grotius Society of London in 1916 criticised the term "war treason" as a "hybrid," a "bastard," and an "intellectual outrage" of German invention, "one hardly recognized by English and French jurists and one embodying a conception based on the assumption that the effect of occupation is to transfer the allegiance of the inhabitants to the occupying power — a conception which is contrary to the fundamental notion of treason." A military occupant, he argued, has no lawful right to extend the law of treason to the inhabitants of occupied territory, and he added, that it is unjust to punish as a traitor such an inhabitant who misguides an enemy whom he is forced to serve, or who gives his own army information or assistance.[1] The injustice of so treating the inhabitants of occupied territory may readily be admitted, but the weight of authority and practice do not justify the view adopted by Professor Morgan. On the contrary, the great majority of writers on international law, as well as the military manuals, generally recognize the crime of war treason, an offence that may be committed by the inhabitants of occupied territory equally with the subjects of the occupying power, this on the theory that occupation creates a status of temporary allegiance which the inhabitants owe the occupying power so long as the period of effective occupation continues.[2] The British manual of military law states that the

---

[1] *Procs. of the Grotius Society*, Vol. II, pp. 161 ff. Westlake, *International Law*, Pt. II, p. 100, likewise criticises the term "war treason" as applied to acts committed by the inhabitants of occupied territory as an exceptional relic of the time when occupation meant conquest and transfer of allegiance. Such acts, he says, cannot be regarded as treason without violating the modern view of the nature of military occupation, and without introducing the notion of moral fault into an invader's view of what is detrimental to him.

[2] The doctrine of temporary allegiance is well established. Cf. Dana's *Wheaton*, p. 436; Halleck, *Int. Law*, ch. 32, sec. 14; Taylor, *Int. Pub. Law*, sec. 569; Spaight, *War Rights on Land*, pp. 333–335, and various other authorities cited by Oppenheim in an article on "War Treason" in the *Law Qu. Review*, July, 1917, where the matter is fully considered. Cf. also his article entitled, "The Legal Relations between an Occupying Power and the Inhabitants," in the same *Review* for October, 1917, and an article by a Belgian jurist, Chas. de Visscher, entitled *L'Occupation de Guerre*, in the same *Review* for January, 1918. Among French writers who

inhabitants of occupied territory who give information to the enemy may be punished for war treason. Even other offences committed by private individuals, such as damaging railways, telegraphs, allowing prisoners to escape, conspiracy against the occupying forces, intentional misleading of enemy troops, voluntarily assisting the enemy, fouling the sources of the water supply, damage or alteration of military notices and sign posts, concealing animals, vehicles, supplies, and fuel in the interest of the enemy, circulating proclamations in the interest of the enemy, and the like, are also classed as war treason.[1] The American *Rules of Land Warfare* (1914) reproduce almost identically the above article from the British manual.[2] The French manual, however, condemns the doctrine of war treason. It recognizes that hostile acts committed by the inhabitants of occupied territory against the authority of the occupant may be severely punished, but it adds that such acts may not be qualified as treason, treason being exclusively restricted to acts committed by individuals against their own country in the interest of the enemy.[3] It is quite evident from this review of the authorities and of the law as embodied in the military manuals that the doctrine of war treason as applied to hostile acts committed by the inhabitants of occupied territory is well established in England and the United States, and that it is not without recognition in France. It is an error, therefore, to stigmatize it as a German doctrine, although it will readily be admitted that the severity, not to say brutality, with which the theory was applied in Belgium was peculiarly German.

recognize the doctrine of war treason as applied to the inhabitants of occupied territory may be mentioned Bonfils (*Manuel de Droit Int. Pub.*, sec. 1154), Despagnet (*Cours de Droit Int. Pub.*, sec. 538), Longuet (*Le Droit Actuel de la Guerre Terrestre*, p. 122), Merignhac (*Traité du Droit Int. Pub.*, Vol. III, p. 290), and Guelle (*Précis des Lois de la Guerre*, Vol. I, pp. 129-130). Pillet, however, criticises the whole notion of war treason as a German doctrine based on the assumption that the population of occupied territory is bound by the same fidelity towards the enemy which it owes to its own country. Acts qualified by the Germans as war treason, he says, may be severely punished, but it is wrong to regard them as treason. *Les Lois Actuelles de la Guerre*, p. 208.

[1] Sec. 445.

[2] Art. 372. Cf. also the elaborate provisions in respect to war traitors in the Instructions for the Government of the United States Armies in the Field (1863), secs. 90–102.

[3] *Les Lois de la Guerre Continentale*, ed. by Jacomet, art. 71.

In addition to the formidable list of capital offences introduced into Belgium through the extension thereto of the German Imperial criminal code, a host of new ones was created through decrees of the governor-general, to say nothing of scores of others which were punishable by terms of imprisonment or heavy fines. By a decree of February 5, 1915, military governors of provinces, chiefs of arrondissements, and commandants of troops were empowered to issue police regulations and to prescribe penalties for violation of the same. In the case of provincial governors the punishments which they were authorized to prescribe were unlimited; those which chiefs of arrondissements could impose were limited to three weeks' imprisonment and fines not exceeding 300 francs; those of local military commanders, to two weeks' imprisonment and a fine of 200 francs. Appeals were allowed from sentences imposed by the two last-mentioned authorities, to the governor, whose decision was final. Appeals from sentences imposed by the provincial governors could be taken to the governor-general.[1] The power thus conferred was frequently exercised, e.g., to prohibit the sale of newspapers, to restrict the movement of the inhabitants, to close certain houses, and the like. To the military courts was given jurisdiction not only of all offences which were punishable according to the German military criminal code, but also (by a decree of June 19, 1915) of all offences against German troops or against the authority of the Empire and of every infraction of the regulations established by the military authorities for guaranteeing the security of the German troops.[2] The jurisdiction of the military tribunals was extended from time to time until it embraced nearly every offence committed by Belgians which had any military or political character or which affected in any degree German interests in the country.[3] The German decrees were so multifarious and dealt with so many petty matters that the dockets of the military courts were always crowded; at times the jail accommodations for the condemned were quite insufficient, and hotels and other buildings had to be requisitioned for the purpose.[4]

[1] Huberich and Speyer, II, pp. 64-66.   [2] Ibid., III, pp. 121 ff.
[3] Cf. De Laval, *Prussian Law as Applied in Belgium*, loc. cit., 252.
[4] If, e.g., a Belgian was charged with frying potatoes instead of boiling them, as the German regulations required, or if he was accused of feeding good potatoes to hogs in violation of the regulations, he was tried by the military courts.

§ 381. **Condemnations by the German Tribunals.** According to German statistics 103,356 persons were convicted by the German courts in the occupied territory of Belgium during the year from October 1, 1915, to September 20, 1916. Of these, 100 were condemned to death, 491 to the penalty of *réclusion* (imprisonment at hard labor with loss of civil rights), 11,001 to ordinary imprisonment, 591 to deportation to Germany,[1] and 88,226 to pay fines. The condemned included 19,857 women. The offences for which they were convicted included violations of pass regulations, violations of police and economic measures, of regulations concerning declarations, the despatch of letters, offences against the security of the German troops, violations of the laws of the Empire, violations of the regulations in respect to carrier pigeons, attempts to cross the Dutch frontier, press offences, keeping arms and munitons, war treason, and many others.[2] Other thousands were convicted during the later years of the war not included in the above-mentioned report. The total number was probably several hundred thousand. The crimes of "war treason" and "espionage" in particular appear to have been construed in somewhat the same fashion as the Germans interpreted the term *franc-tireur*, and large numbers of Belgians were condemned to death for acts which the criminal code treats as ordinary crimes.[3] During the early years of the war hardly a week passed in which the press despatches did not contain reports of the shooting of batches of Belgians for the offences of "treason," "war treason," or "espionage."[4] Large numbers were heavily fined, sentenced to long terms of imprisonment, or deported to Germany for what would

[1] This was prior to the inauguration of the wholesale system of deportation to Germany in the autumn of 1916. Whitlock in his book on *Belgium* (Vol. I, p. 463) declares that in one year over six hundred thousand persons were fined, imprisoned, deported, or condemned to death by the German military courts in Belgium. He cites many instances of severe, not to say cruel, punishments inflicted for trivial offences.

[2] Cf. an article by Oberkriegsgerichtrat Willeke, adjoint to the governor-general of Belgium, *Deutsche Juristen Zeitung* February 1, 1917, p. 218; French trans. by E. Dreyfus, vice-president of the tribunal of the Seine, in 44 Clunet, 1369–1371.

[3] During the year covered by the statistics referred to above the number of persons reported as having been convicted of war treason was 505.

[4] I have collected a large number of such instances, but for want of space they cannot be detailed here. Many instances are cited by Whitlock in his book on *Belgium*.

seem to have been trivial offences. During the last three months of 1916, forty-two death sentences were reported to have been imposed by one court alone.[1] As late as the beginning of the year 1918 the Belgian legation at Washington made public a statement in which it asserted that Belgian patriots were being shot every day, that the average number of death sentences amounted to thirty a month, and that the more notable victims of the German regime of repression were ten deputies and senators, not less than fifteen burgomasters and aldermen, a number of judges, and several eminent professors who had been imprisoned or deported to Germany.

§ 382. **Execution of Women; Case of Edith Cavell.** As stated above, a large number of the victims were women, for the German military authorities showed little or no disposition to make any distinction between male and female offenders. Of these, one in particular attracted widespread attention by reason of the prominence of the victim, the character of her offence, and the efforts of the American minister to save her life. It was the case of Miss Edith Cavell, a British subject who for many years had been the head of a nurses' training school in Brussels. With five other persons, two of whom were also women, she was condemned to death on the charge of concealing in her house British and French soldiers, with furnishing them money and clothing, and with aiding them and Belgians of military age to escape from the country, thus enabling them to rejoin the ranks of Germany's enemies.[2] At the trial she admitted her guilt and when asked for a statement of her motive, replied that she considered it to be her duty to aid her countrymen to escape from Belgium where they were liable to be shot by the Germans. Her purpose, she added, was not to conduct them to the lines of Germany's enemies, but to save their lives by assisting them to get out of Belgium.

§ 383. **Intervention of the American Legation in Her Behalf.** The American minister interested himself in her case, partly

---

[1] London weekly *Times*, June 1, 1917.

[2] At the same sitting the court condemned four other persons, one of whom was a woman, to a term of fifteen years imprisonment at hard labor for the same offence, and still seventeen others to sentences of penal servitude ranging from two to eight years on the charge of war treason. Cf. governor-general von Bissing's proclamation of October 12, 1915, announcing the verdict of the court, facsimile in Gibson's *Journal from our Legation in Belgium*, p. 348.

because she was under the protection of his legation, and partly because of the character of the work in which she was engaged. He succeeded in obtaining a promise from the military authorities that they would keep him informed as to the developments in the case, a promise, however, which he says was not kept, for in fact he never learned officially of the trial until after its conclusion. Upon learning through unofficial sources of her conviction, he wrote from his sick-bed to Baron von der Lancken, head of the political section of the governor-generalcy of Belgium, urging him to suspend the execution of the sentence. "I am too ill," said the minister, "to present my request to you in person, but I appeal to the generosity of your heart to support it and to save this unfortunate woman from death." This appeal was shortly followed by another communication in which he called the attention of the Baron to the fact that Miss Cavell had spent her life in alleviating the sufferings of others; that she had trained many nurses, some of whom were at that time ministering to the wounded in Germany, and that at the beginning of the war she had given her services as freely to German soldiers as to those of Germany's enemies. With commendable straightforwardness she had admitted her guilt, and because the sentence imposed upon her was more severe than had been imposed by the same court in similar cases, the Baron was urged to defer execution until his request for a pardon could be submitted to the governor-general.

Hugh Gibson, secretary of the American legation, in a report to Mr. Whitlock states that early on the evening of October 11, after the conclusion of the trial, he inquired at the office of the Political Direction and was informed that the sentence had not been imposed, and that as soon as a decision was reached, the American legation would be fully informed. Later in the evening he learned through outside sources that the sentence of death had been passed at 5 o'clock in the afternoon; and that it would be *carried out during the night*. Accompanied by M. de Laval, counsellor to the legation, and the Spanish minister, he sought out Baron von der Lancken and inquired whether the report that sentence had been passed was really true. The Baron expressed disbelief in the truth of the report, but telephoned to the presiding judge of the court, by whom he was informed that the report was true, and that the sentence would be carried out

at 2 o'clock in the morning. Von der Lancken was then urged
as an act of courtesy to stay the execution in order that an
appeal could be taken from the decision of the military court.
He replied that the military governor was the supreme authority
in matters of this kind, and that an appeal co ld be taken only
to the Emperor, the governor-general having no authority to
intervene in the case. He consented, however, to telephone
the military governor and inquire whether there were any
chance for clemency. The governor replied that he had approved the sentence of the court only after mature deliberation,
that the circumstances of Miss Cavell's case were such that he
considered the infliction of the death penalty imperative, and
he must therefore decline to hear the plea of clemency or receive
any representation in regard to the matter.[1] The execution
of the sentence was duly carried out secretly at 2 o'clock in the
morning of October 12.

The execution of Miss Cavell aroused a feeling akin to horror
in neutral countries, and the American press in particular,
almost without exception, denounced the act as shocking and
brutal. In London a great memorial service in her honor,
attended by representatives of the king and queen, was held at
St. Paul's, and the horror which the act aroused led to the
enlistment within three days of more than ten thousand recruits
in the British army.

§ 384. The German Defence. The Germans defended the
execution of Miss Cavell, as they defended other acts of severity,
on the ground of military necessity. She was, it was said, the
head of a vast underground system which had been the means
of aiding hundreds of English, French, and Belgians to escape
from Belgium, some of whom had rejoined the armies of Germany's enemies; she had been repeatedly warned of the grave
character of the offence, and she knew well the penalty which
German military law prescribed for such acts. Herr Zimmermann, German undersecretary of State for foreign affairs, in
an interview given to a representative of the newspaper press,
thus defended the act:

[1] This report of Mr. Gibson, together with all the correspondence between the
American minister and Baron von der Lancken, between Ambassador Page and Mr.
Whitlock, and between Mr. Page and Sir Edward Grey, is contained in a White
Book issued by the British government, *Misc.*, No. 17 (1915), Cd. 8013. Cf. also
Mr. Gibson's book *Journal from Our Legation in Belgium*, pp. 345 ff., and Whitlock's
Belgium, Vol. II, chs. 7–9, where the Cavell case is discussed in great detail.

"It is undoubtedly a terrible thing that the woman has been executed; but consider what would happen to a State, particularly in war—if it left crimes aimed at the safety of its armies to go unpunished because committed by women. No criminal code in the world — least of all the laws of war — makes such a distinction; the feminine sex has but one preference according to legal usages namely, that women in a delicate condition may not be executed. Otherwise man and woman are equal before the law, and only the degree of guilt makes a difference in the sentence for the crime and its consequences. I have before me the court's decision in the Cavell case, and can assure you that it was gone into with the utmost thoroughness, and was investigated and cleared up to the smallest details. . . . Only the utmost sternness could do away with such activities under the very nose of our authorities, and a government which in such case does not resort to the sternest measures, sins against its most elementary duties toward the safety of its own army."

She may have had a "fair trial" so far as the procedure of the German military tribunals may be said to have been "fair." The proceedings, however, being secret, the world has no information as to this further than what her judges and executioners have seen fit to disclose. In accordance with German military court procedure she was denied all information concerning the charges against her before she was arraigned at the bar. Until that moment she was allowed no opportunity to consult with her counsel in order to prepare her defence. Her attorney, in fact, did not see her until she was brought into the courtroom.[1] To an American or English lawyer this procedure sounds like a mockery of justice, for the right of defence under such conditions can have only a very limited value.

Aside from the character of the trial, the interpretation which the court placed upon the provision of the German military penal code (article 58) which she was charged with violating, hardly seems warranted. This article reads as follows: "All persons will be sentenced to death for military treason, who with the object of helping a hostile power, or prejudicing the German

[1] This was the statement of her attorney, Kirscheim, a Belgian subject of Roumanian origin, who had been legal adviser to the German legation at Brussels. "Lawyers defending prisoners before a German military court," he said, "are not allowed to see their clients before trial and are not permitted to see any document of the prosecution." When M. de Laval suggested his intention of attending the trial as a spectator, Miss Cavell's attorney dissuaded him from doing so for the reason that it "would cause great prejudice to the prisoner, because the German judges would resent it." Gibson, *op. cit.*, p. 349. Cf. the observations on this indictment against the impartiality of the German military judges by a well-known American lawyer, James M. Beck, in his *The War and Humanity*, p. 136.

or allied troops by committing any one of the following acts: . . .
(5) guiding soldiers to the enemy (*dem Feinde Mannschaf-
ten zuführt*)." Miss Cavell's offence did not, it was pointed out,
consist in "guiding soldiers to the enemy," nor was her object
to help Germany's enemies or to injure her troops or those of her
allies. What she did was to aid persons of enemy nationality
to escape from occupied territory to a neutral country, whose
duty it was to intern them upon their arrival and thus prevent
them from going on to England or any other belligerent country.
If the Dutch government permitted them to escape to a belligerent country, the accused could not be said to have been
guilty of "guiding" them to the enemy, for the provision of the
military code which she was charged with violating probably
had reference to the act of personally guiding or directing enemy
fugitives, stragglers, or detached soldiers back to their own lines.[1]
The German military court, however, took a different view and
held that the accused was guilty of guiding soldiers to the enemy
with the object of aiding the latter.

The conduct of the German military authorities in keeping
the American legation, under whose protection the accused had
been placed by her own government in accordance with a well-
established practice, entirely ignorant of the trial after they had
promised to keep the legation informed of all steps in the development of the case was widely criticised in the United States
as being not only an act of discourtesy, ingratitude, and bad
faith, but a policy of deliberate subterfuge and prevarication
for the purpose of hastening the trial to a conclusion, forestalling
the intervention of the American legation in behalf of the accused, and sending her to her death before a pardon could be
obtained. It was well known to the military authorities in
Belgium that the Emperor had recently granted pardons to the
Countess de Bellville and to Miss Thuliez for identical offences,[2]
and there was good reason to believe that the imperial clemency
would have been extended to Miss Cavell. The military
authorities in Belgium, however, appear to have determined

---

[1] Cf. Beck, *The War and Humanity*, p. 138; Gibson, *op. cit.*, p. 350, and Whitlock,
Belgium, Vol. II, p. 96.

[2] The story of the condemnation of Mlle. Thuliez and the commutation of her
sentence, which was brought about by the intervention of the Spanish minister,
is told by her in the *Revue des Deux Mondes* (reproduced in New York *Times
Magazine*, May 11, 1919).

that the "Cavell woman," as she was characterized by Herr Zimmermann, should not be afforded this opportunity to escape, and her trial and execution were therefore kept from the American legation and hastened with almost cruel indecency in order to prevent an appeal from reaching the Emperor.

§ 385. Past Practice as to the Execution of Women. In reply to the criticism that the putting to death of women for offences such as that for which Miss Cavell was condemned was almost if not entirely without precedent in modern wars, German apologists retorted by charging the French with having executed in March and May, 1915, two German women, Margaret Schmidt and Ottilie Moss, and in August, 1916, one Mrs. Phaad; the Belgians with having condemned a woman named Julia Van Wartinghem at Antwerp in August, 1914; the British with having put Alice Lisle to death in 1685; the Russians with having hanged two women on the charge of being accomplices in the plot to assassinate Alexander II, and the Americans with having hanged Mrs. Surratt for complicity in the assassination of President Lincoln. Even admitting the truth of the charges made by Germany against her adversaries in respect to the execution of women, there is an important difference between the Cavell case and the others referred to above. The German women whom the Belgian and French governments are said to have executed were convicted of spying, an offence which by the military codes of all nations is punishable with death. Miss Cavell, on the contrary, was not charged with being a spy;[1] her offence was merely helping individuals to escape from territory then in the occupation of the enemy. She had done nothing to reveal German military movements, nor had she furnished the enemy with any information of military value.

The same difference exists between the Cavell offence and

---

[1] The proclamation of October 12, 1915, posted by General von Bissing announcing the condemnation of Miss Cavell and various other persons, stated that they had been sentenced to death "for conspiring to commit treason." He, of course, had reference to war treason (*Kriegsverrath*) which is the offence referred to in art. 58 of the German Imperial military criminal code, for the violation of which she was tried and executed. She was not tried for the offence of treason as that term is ordinarily understood. No charges were made that she was guilty of "espionage" until after her execution when the public opinion of the world had been aroused. Then it was that the German press frequently referred to her as the "spy Cavell." By no interpretation could her offence be regarded as "espionage."

complicity in the assassination of the head of the State such as Mrs. Surratt was charged with. In the case of Mrs. Surratt it may also be remarked that the trial was public; she was allowed the fullest right of defence; the right of appeal was allowed, and the military commission which found her guilty accompanied its verdict with a recommendation for clemency.[1] There was no attempt to conceal the fact of the trial from the public, nor was she hurried to her death within a few hours after the trial in order to forestall an appeal and a possible pardon.

It is true that article 102 of the instructions for the government of the United States armies (of 1863) declared that "The law of war, like the criminal law regarding other offences, makes no distinction on account of the difference of sex concerning the spy, the war traitor, or the war rebel," but it will be observed that the offences here referred to are spying, treason, and rebellion and not such offences as that for which Miss Cavell was executed. It has been stated that hundreds of women during the American Civil war were guilty of such offences as that of Miss Cavell, but no one ever appears to have been shot or hanged.

The English case referred to by the Germans, that of Alice Lisle, who was executed for giving shelter to a non-conformist clergyman, was not a happy one. It occurred more than two hundred and thirty years ago in an age when cruelties and barbarities were common in warfare, when there were several hundred capital offences in the criminal code, and it may be added, the judgment was pronounced by a judge (Jeffrys) whose name even among Englishmen has long been regarded with infamy. So far as is known, no Englishman of respectability has ever been found to defend the crime of Jeffrys, although the charge against his victim was very similar to that for which Miss Cavell was shot.[2]

---

[1] President Johnson refused to pardon her or commute her sentence, and she was hanged; but the feeling against hanging women was so general in the United States that the President's action was widely criticised even in the North.

[2] Concerning the execution of Alice Lisle, Lord Macaulay said: "And it is just to say that during many generations, no English government save one, has treated with rigor persons guilty merely of harboring defeated and flying insurgents. To women especially has been granted, by a kind of tacit prescription, the right of indulging in the midst of havoc and vengeance, that compassion which is the

The execution of Miss Cavell, it may be remarked, formed a striking contrast to the treatment which the English accorded to a German woman (Mrs. Louise Herbert) during the recent war. At the trial she admitted that she had sought information regarding the location of munitions depots in England with a view to transmitting it to Germany. Although the offence was far more serious than Miss Cavell's, she was let off with a punishment of six months' imprisonment.[1] Again in February, 1916, a woman was convicted of espionage by a criminal court in England. Her activities were discovered six days after her arrival in England, and her correspondence was intercepted in the interval between her arrival and her arrest. The jury found her guilty, and the court was therefore compelled to sentence her to death, but the sentence was commuted to life imprisonment.[2] Whether the execution of Miss Cavell was justifiable or not, the English cannot therefore be reproached with hypocrisy in respect to the infliction of the death penalty on women.

§ 386. Observations on the Cavell Case. The execution of Miss Cavell revealed Prussian militarism in a very bad light, and while there may be differences of opinion regarding the legal right of a military occupant to execute a woman for such an offence as that which she committed, most fair-minded persons will agree that it was a case of extreme severity accompanied by elements of brutality such as the best sentiment of the civilized world condemns. It was a case in which the rigor of military law might well have been tempered by mercy, as was done by the English in similar cases. It is certain that

---

most endearing of all their charms. Since the beginning of the great Civil war, numerous rebels, some of them far more important than Hickes or Nelthorpe, have been protected from severity of victorious governments by female adroitness and generosity. But no English ruler who has been thus baffled, the savage and implacable James alone excepted, has had the barbarity even to think of putting a lady to a cruel and shameful death for so venial and amiable a transgression." History of England (Hurst edition), Vol. I, p. 414.

[1] Press despatches of October 21, 1915. Several women were fined or imprisoned by English courts during the Boer war, but none were executed. Spaight, *op. cit.*, p. 343.

[2] Statement of Herbert Samuel, secretary of state for home affairs in the House of Commons, February 17, 1916. Another woman, together with a male confederate, was convicted by an English court of spying, and although the male offender was executed, the sentence of the woman was commuted to a term of imprisonment. New York *Times*, December 12, 1918.

the execution injured rather than benefited the German cause. It aroused the undying hatred of the English, powerfully stimulated recruiting, and intensified the national determination to avenge what was regarded as a shocking and brutal judicial murder of an unfortunate woman whose devotion to her own country had caused her to overstep the hard limits set by a military conqueror. What Thomas Carlyle said of the execution by Napoleon of an old German bookseller may be equally said of the execution of nurse Cavell:

"I am not sure but he had better have lost his best park of artillery, or had his best regiment drowned in the sea, than shot that poor German bookseller, Palm. It was palpable, murderous injustice which no man, let him paint an inch thick, could make out to be other. It burnt deep into the hearts of men, it and the like of it, suppressed fire flashed in the eyes of men as they thought of it waiting their day, which day came."

CHAPTER XXV

CONTRIBUTIONS, REQUISITIONS, AND FORCED LABOR

§ 387. German Policy in the Wars of 1866 and 1870–1871; § 388. German Contributions during the Recent War; § 389. The General Contribution on Belgium; § 390. Provisions of the Hague Convention in Respect to Contributions; § 391. Purposes for which Contributions may be Levied; § 392. The Decuple Tax on Belgian Refugees; § 393. Requisition of Supplies; § 394. Provisions of the Hague Convention in Respect to Requisitions; § 395. Requisition of Live Stock for Transportation to Germany; § 396. Seizure and Transportation of Machinery to Germany; § 397. Requisition of Railway Material; § 398. Cutting of Forests; § 399. Seizure of Funds of Private Banks and Post-offices; § 400. Requisition of Services for Military Work; § 401. Requisition of Guides; § 402. Views of the Authorities.

§ 387. **German Policy in the Wars of 1866 and 1870–1871.** In all the wars in which Germany has been a belligerent her policy in respect to the exaction of pecuniary contributions, the imposition of fines on communities, and the requisition of supplies and services of the inhabitants of occupied territory has been especially rigorous and in accord with the extreme views which her military writers and publicists have always held in regard to the rights of a military occupant. Bluntschli charged the Prussians with having levied without sufficient reason excessive contributions during the war of 1866 on various towns and cities which took sides with Austria, and he adds that such methods of warfare were not civilized, and at the time Europe did not recognize them as such.[1]

During the Franco-German war of 1870–1871 the Germans, as is well known, not only resorted to the power of requisition on an unprecedented scale, but in addition levied heavy contributions on many towns and districts which they occupied. In December, 1870, a per capita assessment of twenty-five francs was levied on the inhabitants of all the occupied districts of France for the avowed purpose of breaking the resistance of the population and of exerting pressure against

[1] *Droit International Codifié* (Fr. trans. by Lardy), sec. 654.

106

the people to turn them against Gambetta and induce the election of an assembly in favor of ending the war. This latter expedient, says Loening, "was extraordinary, but the situation was none the less so."[1]

In nearly all the cities occupied, says Calvo, the inhabitants were compelled to raise within short periods of time enormous sums, exceeding many times the resources of their municipal treasuries, and necessitating recourse to forced loans or appeals to the generosity of the inhabitants.[2] The French minister of the interior in an official report estimated that in the thirty-four departments invaded the contributions of war levied amounted to 39,000,000 francs, the taxes collected by the German authorities aggregated 49,000,000, and the supplies requisitioned totaled 327,000,000.[3] Many of the contributions thus levied did not differ from pillage except in name.[4]

While a few German writers, like Bluntschli,[5] Geffcken,[6] and Wehberg,[7] think the German authorities went too far, the vast majority of them have defended the conduct of the Germans even when it was resorted to avowedly for the purpose of breaking the resistance of the French and of compelling them to sue for peace.[8]

The German general staff in the *Kriegsbrauch im Landkriege* asserts, however, that the power of requisition was resorted to by the Germans during the Franco-German war "with the utmost tenderness for the inhabitants even if in isolated cases excesses occurred." It justifies the severity in respect to the

---

[1] *Rev. de Droit Int. et de Lég. Comp.*, Vol. V, p. 108

[2] *Op. cit.*, Vol. IV, sec. 2254.

[3] As to the German policy in 1870–1871 cf. Despagnet, *Droit Int. Public*, secs. 588 ff.; also Bonfils, secs. 1219, 1226, n. 3; Pont, *Les Réquisitions Militaires*, ch. III; Kluber, p. 359, and Rouard de Card, *Droit Int.*, pp. 178 ff. Excellent reviews of the law and practice in respect to requisitions and contributions may be found in two articles by Ernest Nys in the *Rev. de Droit et de Lég. Comp.*, Vol. 38 (1906), pp. 274 ff. and 406 ff.; in an article by C. N. Gregory in the *Columbia Law Review* for March, 1915, pp. 1–21; in Bordwell, *Law of War*, see Index; Halleck, *Int. Law*, Vol. II, see index; Calvo, *Droit Int.*, Vol. IV, secs. 2235 ff.; Spaight, pp. 395 ff.; Thomas, *Réquisitions Militaires*, and Ferrand, *Des Réquisitions*.

[4] Cf. Latifi, *Effects of War on Private Property*, p. 34, and Bluntschli, *op. cit.*, sec. 654.

[5] *Op. cit.*, sec. 654.   [6] Heffter, p. 30, n. 4.

[7] *Capture in War*, ch. IV (English trans. by Robertson).

[8] Cf. for example, two articles by Loening entitled *L'Administration du Gouvernement-Général de l'Alsace durant la Guerre de 1870-1871*, in the *Revue de Droit Int.*, 1872-1873 (Vols. IV-V), pp. 692 ff. and 69 ff.

imposition of fines, on the ground of the "embittered character which the war took on in its latest stage and the lively participation of the population which necessitated the sternest measures."[1]

§ 388. German Contributions during the Recent War. As has been said, German writers have attempted to justify German policy during the war of 1870–1871, partly on the ground that the war was forced on Germany, and consequently it was legitimate to resort to heavy pecuniary levies to make those who had brought on the war bear a portion of the cost and also to break their spirit of resistance and to induce them to sue for peace.

In the recent war, however, no such excuse could be pleaded, because Germany was herself the aggressor, at least against Belgium. Moreover, the impoverished condition to which Belgium was reduced in consequence of the German invasion made the imposition of heavy pecuniary exactions a peculiar hardship for those who were compelled to raise the large sums demanded. But this extenuating circumstance does not appear to have been taken into consideration, and no sooner had the German military forces established themselves in Belgium than they proceeded to levy pecuniary impositions of various kinds on the towns, cities, and districts which fell under their occupation, to say nothing of the enormous community fines, which are considered in the following chapter of this work. During the early months of the war the following "contributions" are known to have been levied by the Germans upon Belgian and French cities and districts:

Brussels	40,000,000 francs [2]
Antwerp	50,000,000 francs
City of Liège	20,000,000 francs
Province of Liège	50,000,000 francs
Namur	32,000,000 francs [3]
Courtrai	10,000,000 francs

[1] Carpentier's French trans. of the *Kriegsbrauch*, p. 136.

[2] Some accounts say 50,000,000 (e.g., Cammaerts, *Through the Iron Bars*, p. 38). The Germans originally demanded 200,000,000 of Brussels, but after "protracted negotiations" with the local authorities they reduced the amount to 40,000,000. The city was given three days in which to raise the sum exacted. Gibson, *Journal from Our Legation in Belgium*, p. 115.

[3] The original demand upon Namur was for 50,000,000, but the amount was reduced to 32,000,000 on condition that the first million should be paid within twenty-four hours. Massart, *Belgians under the German Eagle*, p. 156, and Cammaerts, *op. cit.*, p. 37.

Tournai.....................2,000,000 francs
Roulers....................1,500,000 francs
Lille.......................7,000,000 francs [1]
Roubaix and Tourcoing ......1,000,000 francs [2]
Valenciennes................3,000,000 francs
Lens........................700,000 francs
Armentières.................500,000 francs
Louvain.....................100,000 francs [3]
Coulommiers.................100,000 francs [4]
Mancourt (Fr. village)....10 francs per capita [5]
Charleroi..................10,000,000 francs [6]
Beaumont.....................8,000 francs [7]
Givet (December, 1916).......625,000 francs [8]

[1] Proclamation of General Graevenitz, November 4, 1914, text in Fage, *Lille sous la Griffe Allemande*, p. 46. Payment of the first million was required to be made on November 10; two millions on November 17; three millions on November 24; and the remainder on December 1. In default of payment on the dates mentioned the city would be fined. The city treasury being empty the mayor addressed an appeal to the citizens who responded to the extent of raising 5,400,000 francs. The mayor then addressed a letter to the military governor in which he referred to the impoverished condition of the inhabitants, reminded him that they had already raised 1,500,000 francs toward the revictualment of the German troops and that 1200 houses in the city had been destroyed by bombardment and burning, with a loss of 300,000,000 francs. He therefore appealed to the governor to take pity on the inhabitants and reduce the amount of the contribution demanded. The governor replied on November 22 consenting to defer until December 1 the payment due on November 24, but refusing to reduce the amount and threatening to resort to measures of coercion in case the full amount was not paid on the dates fixed. On December 8, the mayor was requested to raise an additional 800,000 francs toward the payment of the expenses of the German troops. Text of the correspondence between the mayor and the German military governor in Fage, *op. cit.*, pp. 47–56.

[2] Maccas puts the amount at 10,000,000.

[3] The civil authorities of Louvain notified the German authorities that it was impossible to pay this contribution, as the city treasury was empty. The officer who demanded it thereupon agreed to accept 3080 francs. See an official publication of the Belgian government entitled *L'Armée à Louvain en Août 1914 et le Livre Blanc Allemand*, p. 17.

[4] The German officer who demanded the contribution threatened to shoot the state's attorney and burn the town in case the amount was not handed over by 8 o'clock on the following day. *Rapports et Procès-Verbaux d'Enquête de la Commission Instituée en Vue de Constater les Actes Commis par l'Ennemi en Violation du Droit des Gens*, Vol. I, pp. 30–32.

[5] *Ibid.*, Vol. V, pp. 114–121. One hour was given in which to raise the amount, in default of which the inhabitants would be searched, any one found with money in his possession would be shot, hostages would also be taken, and the village burned.

[6] Toynbee, *The German Terror in France*, p. 74. It is not clear whether this exaction was intended to be a "contribution" or a "fine."

[7] *Rapports et Procès-Verbaux*, Vol. II, p. 52. The mayor being able to raise only 1800 francs, the Germans obtained the rest by "robbing private individuals."

[8] Huberich and Speyer, *German Legislation in Belgium*, 10th Ser., p. 2.

A demand for 450,000,000 francs was made upon the province of Brabant, but the amount was so excessive and the protests of the local authorities so strong that the Germans were finally induced to cancel it.[1]

On September 6, 1914, a contribution of 30,000,000 francs was levied on the department of the Marne. In the absence of the prefect the German officer in command addressed his demand to the mayor of Châlons. The mayor protested that it was impossible to raise so large a sum, but the German commander persisted in his demand and required a reply by 9 o'clock the following day. Of the total amount, 22,000,000 was required to be raised by the city of Rheims and the remaining 8,000,000 by the city of Châlons. After some *pourparlers* the German officer agreed to accept the sum of 500,000 francs with the understanding, however, that it should be regarded as only the initial payment, and that the remainder would have to be paid later. He thereupon handed the mayor the following receipt:

"I certify that I have this day received from the city of Châlons-sur-Marne on the part of the representative of the city the sum of 500,000 francs in notes. This sum represents a part of the contribution of war of 30,000,000 which the General-in-chief of the German army in the department of the Marne has imposed on the department.
Châlons-sur-Marne. September 8, 1914.

Signed: FREIHERR VON SECKENDORFF
Intendant of the Army."[2]

On account of the early evacuation of this region, however, the Germans were unable to collect the remainder of the contribution.

A contribution of 15,000,000 francs was levied on the department of the Nord in addition to a monthly contribution of 2,000,000 francs.[3] The town of Laon appears to have been systematically exploited. In 1914 it was required to raise 500,-000 francs; in 1915, 1,000,000; in 1916, 1,800,000, and in 1917, 3,000,000.[4] The city of Lille also appears to have been fre-

---

[1] Passalecq, *Les Déportations Belges,* p. 176; Massart, p. 156, and Gomery, *Belgium in War Time,* p. 181. Hugh Gibson, secretary of the American legation in Belgium, adverting to the amount of the demand, remarks that it was equal to nearly one-tenth of the total indemnity imposed on France at the close of the war of 1870–1871. *Journal from Our Legation in Belgium,* p. 115.

[2] Text in Matot, *Reims et la Marne, Almanach de la Guerre* (1916), pp. 146–150.

[3] *Lille sous le Joug Allemand,* p. 4.

[4] Press despatch from Laon, October 14, 1918.

quently and heavily mulcted by exactions of one kind or another, the exact nature of which is not clear.   In a letter dated July 17, 1917, the mayor protested to the military governor, General Graevenitz, in the following words:

"Scarcely have we paid over the money for a forced levy of 24,000,000 francs, when you demand the payment of a new sum of 33,000,000.   During the first year of occupation when the city of Lille still possessed a large proportion of its resources, you demanded from it, in various forms, the sum of 28,000,000 francs.   During the second year a total of 30,000,000. And during the third year, when the city is in the deepest distress, when its trade is annihilated, its stores closed, its industries destroyed, you double the tribute and raise it to the sum of 60,000,000 francs."

Denouncing such exactions as contrary to the Hague convention and adverting to the threat of the German commander that in case the amount were not promptly raised, the city would be fined 1,000,000 francs for each day of arrears, the mayor concluded:

"Consequently I come to declare to you, in the name of the city council, whose spokesman I am, that the city of Lille, bowed under oppression, isolated from the outer world, powerless to appeal to any tribunal from the arbitrary tyranny to which it is subjected, will pay the new tribute on the dates indicated, but it will pay with the knife at its throat."[1]

These are some examples of contributions levied upon particular communities, the facts as to which seem to be authentic enough.[2] The instances referred to above by no means exhaust the list. It may be safely assumed that few towns or cities escaped either a fine or a contribution, and many were subjected to both.[3]

[1] Text of the letter in the *Figaro* of October 13, 1917. An official despatch from Paris, published in the New York *Times* of October 19, 1918, stated that 500,000,000 francs had been levied on Lille, Roubaix, and Tourcoing under the form of contributions by the Germans since the beginning of the war, and that of this amount 250,000,000 had been extorted from Lille. This city, it is said, was compelled to pay rent for the use of the German Emperor's castle on the island of Corfu, which was occupied as a military hospital by the allies. New York *Times*, November 18, 1918. See also Fage, *op. cit.*, ch. IV.

[2] The facts as to the exactions referred to above have in the main been gathered from official reports issued by the Belgian and French governments. In addition to the reports cited in the preceding footnotes, the Belgian government issued a series entitled *Cahiers Documentaires*, from which I have derived much information. There is also much documentary information in M. Passalecq's work *Les Déportations Belges* (Paris and Nancy, 1917).

[3] Cf., for example, various instances mentioned by the abbé Charles Calippe in his book, *La Somme sous l'Occupation Allemande*, especially pp. 25, 29, 45, 102,

§ 389. **The General Contribution on Belgium.** In addition to the special contributions levied upon particular cities, towns, and villages, a general contribution of 480,000,000 francs was imposed by General von Bissing on the nine occupied provinces of Belgium by a decree of December 10, 1914.[1] The contribution was to be paid in monthly instalments of 40,000,000 francs on the tenth of each month. It appears that the monthly amount at first demanded by General von Bissing was 35,000,000 francs, but that in consideration of an undertaking on the part of the German authorities that they would pay cash for the supplies requisitioned by them, that the levy would be limited to one year, and that no additional contributions would be exacted, the Belgian authorities agreed that the contribution should be fixed at 40,000,000 francs per month. This appears from an *avis* published by General von Bissing on January 9, 1915.[2]

With this understanding the instalments were promptly paid each month through the agency of an association of banks at the head of which was the *Société Générale* to which the German authorities had granted the exclusive privilege of issuing bank notes.

The Belgians contend that the understanding was violated by the Germans when they renewed in November, 1915, for an indefinite term, the contribution of 40,000,000 francs, whose duration had been limited to one year, and by their refusal to make prompt payments for goods and services requisitioned.[3] In November, 1916, the monthly contribution was increased from 40,000,000 to 50,000,000 francs, and in May, 1917, it was raised to 60,000,000 francs, the reason alleged by the German authorities being the increased cost of provisioning the army in the occupied region.[4]

---

and 104. Péronne, he says, was required in September, 1915, to raise 1,860,000 francs per month, beginning retroactively on July 1, making a total of 3,720,000 (p. 102). Cf. also De Saint-Aymour, *Autour de Noyon*, a book which contains much information regarding German practices in the region of which Noyon is the chief town. Cf. especially his account of how Nesle was bled by contributions (p. 187).

[1] Text in *Arrêtés et Proclamations de Guerre Allemandes*, p. 49; in Huberich and Speyer, *German Legislation in Belgium*, 2d Series, p. 11, and Passalecq, *op. cit.*, p. 396.

[2] Text in *Arrêtés et Procs.*, pp. 72-74.

[3] Brand Whitlock in *Everybody's Magazine*, August, 1918, p. 82, says the Germans violated the above-mentioned undertaking four different times.

[4] *Cahiers Documentaires*, No. 84 (September 20, 1917), p. 3.

The Belgian government protested against the continuation of the levy, not only as a violation of an agreement entered into by the Belgian authorities and the governor-general, but also on the ground that it was excessive, being between two-thirds and three-fourths of the total budget of the State. The amount of the contribution, it was complained, would be burdensome under normal conditions when the country was prosperous, but in view of the fact that a large part of Belgium had been laid waste, the people impoverished and their industries to a considerable extent paralyzed, the contribution amounted to confiscation.[1]

It is impossible to determine from the information now available the total amount of money that was exacted by the Germans under the form of contributions from the regions occupied by them. The Belgian government estimated that down to August 10, 1917, the total amount of the general contribution paid over aggregated 1,440,000,000 francs. To this had to be added 200,000,000 francs levied on the communes[2] and, of course, many other millions levied under the form of community fines, to say nothing of the enormous exactions in the form of requisitions.[3] No statistics are available to the author as to the total exactions in the occupied regions of France or in the other territories which fell under German occupation.

§ 390. Provisions of the Hague Convention in Respect to Contributions. Article 49 of the Hague convention of 1907 respecting the laws and customs of war declares that if an

---

[1] Cf. also a protest of the Belgian Senators and Deputies, text in the United States *Official Bulletin* of January 5, 1918.

[2] *Cahiers Documentaires*, No. 84 (September 20, 1917), p. 3. Cf. also Passalecq, p. 176.

[3] In the autumn of 1918, after the conclusion of the armistice, the Belgian government, in preparing its bill of reparations to be presented to the German government, estimated that the total amount of contributions and fines that had been extorted from Belgium was 2,575,000,000 francs (New York *Times*, October 22 and November 8, 1918). Lord Robert Cecil, speaking in the House of Commons on August 6, 1918, said the Germans had levied contributions upon Belgium amounting to 2,280,000,000, and that these "monstrous exactions" must certainly be taken into account when the peace terms were being arranged. Among the categories of "damages" enumerated in the treaty of peace which the reparations commission is authorized to take into consideration in determining the amount of the indemnity to be paid by Germany is "damage in the form of levies, fines and other similar exactions imposed by Germany or her allies upon the civil population." Art. 244, annex 1, par. 10.

occupant levies in addition to the regular taxes "other money contributions . . . this shall be only for the needs of the army or for the administration of the territory in question." The phrase "needs of the army" is very elastic [1] and might be interpreted to cover almost unlimited exactions, but it was clearly not the intention of the conference to authorize military commanders to exact contributions for the enrichment of the occupying belligerent, for the purpose of meeting the expenses of the war, or to lay contributions under the disguise of fines. Bluntschli justly remarks that international law forbids a military occupant from exacting any other contributions than those which are absolutely indispensable for the administration of the territory and the needs of the army.[2] Spaight holds a similar view, and he adds that even under the restrictions imposed by international law they strike one as being peculiarly unjust and are in fact a relic of the theory that an invader has a vested right to the private property of those who fall within his power.[3] The committee of the first Hague conference which considered the article relating to contributions reported that its effect was to prohibit military occupants from enriching themselves, and this was the general understanding.[4] Nevertheless, Loening and other German writers hold that it is legitimate for a military occupant to exact money contributions for the purpose of forcing an enemy to submit,[5] and Lammasch defended this proposition at the Hague in 1899, but it found no favor.

§ 391. Purposes for which Contributions may be Levied. Likewise the theory held by some writers, such as Massé and Vedari, that the power of a belligerent to levy contributions on

---

[1] At the Second Hague Conference an effort was made to substitute for the vague term "needs of the army" a more precise one (e.g., "absolute necessity"), but the proposal was rejected through fear of compromising the success of the convention. Several delegates, notably Lansberge, Odier, and Karnebeek, advocated the abolition of contributions, but this proposal was defeated. *Actes et Documents*, III, p. 134.

[2] *Op. cit.*, sec. 654.   [3] *Op. cit.*, p. 383.

[4] Cf. Rolin's Report, 2d commission, July 5, 1899. The Institute of International Law considered the matter at its session of 1880 and adopted the following rule, which is incorporated in art. 58 of its manual of the laws of war: "The occupant may levy extraordinary money contributions only as an equivalent for fines or taxes, or of supplies in kind not delivered." Cf. on this point an article entitled *Contributions de Guerre Imposées par l'Allemagne*, by M. Clunet in Clunet's *Journal*, 43: 48 ff.

[5] *Rev. de Droit Int.*, Vol. V, p. 107.

the inhabitants may be used as a means of indemnifying himself
for the expense of the war is no longer admitted.   Such a contention, as Calvo remarks, is in flagrant contradiction with
the principle that war is a contest between States and not between peoples.   A belligerent, therefore, has no more right
to compel the inhabitants to supply him with money for carrying
on the war than he has to compel them to enlist in his armies.[1]
The old maxim that "war must support war" (*la guerre nourrit
la guerre*) is repudiated by the Hague conventions and by practically all the text writers.[2]

A few German writers like Loening, however, still maintain,
as stated above, that the power to levy contributions may be
employed for the purpose of breaking the spirit of resistance of
the enemy and thus compelling him to submit, and this seems
to be the view laid down in the *Kriegsbrauch im Landkriege*,
where it is said that "experience has shown that pecuniary
exactions produce the greatest effect on the civil population." [3]
But, as Bonfils remarks, if it is permissible to bring pressure on
the inhabitants to sue for peace by imposing money exactions
on them, why not admit the right of pillage, incendiarism,
murder, robbery, etc.?

What appears to have been an innovation in the practice
of levying pecuniary exactions on the people of occupied territory was the imposition by the Germans of special contributions
on particular individuals of wealth.[4]   Such a procedure would
seem to be nothing more than a form of confiscation in violation

---

[1] *Droit Int. Pub.*, Vol. IV, sec. 2231.

[2] Cf. Bentwich, *War and the Private Citizen*, p. 62; Nys in the *Rev. de Droit Int.*,
Vol. 38, p. 429, and Wehberg, *op. cit.*, p. 41.

[3] But cf. the French manual, art. 107, and The British manual, arts. 423-424.
Clunet (44: 1728) reproduces an editorial from the Rhenish and Westphalian
Zeitung which defends the levying of contributions for this purpose.   Among
other things it said: "Every billion, whether in gold or in kind we extract from
Belgium, France or Servia strengthens us and weakens our enemies.   We have
endured such sacrifices that we do not have a right to neglect any of our
opportunities.   To be sure, it is necessary to avoid useless brutality.   But an
iron law makes it our duty to be more severe wherever this severity may bring
some relief to our people."

[4] Sarolea in his *How Belgium Saved Europe*, p. 140, referring to this practice
by the Germans in 1914-1915, states that a contribution of 1,000,000 francs was
imposed on Baron Lambert de Rothschild, and a contribution of 30,000,000 francs
on M. Solvay, the well-known manufacturer.   This charge seems to be admitted
by Muerer, *Die Völkerrechtliche Stellung der vom Feinde Besetzten Gebiete* (1915),
p. 71.

CHAPTER XXV

CONTRIBUTIONS, REQUISITIONS, AND FORCED LABOR

§ 387. German Policy in the Wars of 1866 and 1870–1871; § 388. German Contributions during the Recent War; § 389. The General Contribution on Belgium; § 390. Provisions of the Hague Convention in Respect to Contributions; § 391. Purposes for which Contributions may be Levied; § 392. The Decuple Tax on Belgian Refugees; § 393. Requisition of Supplies; § 394. Provisions of the Hague Convention in Respect to Requisitions; § 395. Requisition of Live Stock for Transportation to Germany; § 396. Seizure and Transportation of Machinery to Germany; § 397. Requisition of Railway Material; § 398. Cutting of Forests; § 399. Seizure of Funds of Private Banks and Post-offices; § 400. Requisition of Services for Military Work; § 401. Requisition of Guides; § 402. Views of the Authorities.

§ 387. German Policy in the Wars of 1866 and 1870–1871. In all the wars in which Germany has been a belligerent her policy in respect to the exaction of pecuniary contributions, the imposition of fines on communities, and the requisition of supplies and services of the inhabitants of occupied territory has been especially rigorous and in accord with the extreme views which her military writers and publicists have always held in regard to the rights of a military occupant. Bluntschli charged the Prussians with having levied without sufficient reason excessive contributions during the war of 1866 on various towns and cities which took sides with Austria, and he adds that such methods of warfare were not civilized, and at the time Europe did not recognize them as such.[1]

During the Franco-German war of 1870–1871 the Germans, as is well known, not only resorted to the power of requisition on an unprecedented scale, but in addition levied heavy contributions on many towns and districts which they occupied. In December, 1870, a per capita assessment of twenty-five francs was levied on the inhabitants of all the occupied districts of France for the avowed purpose of breaking the resistance of the population and of exerting pressure against

---

[1] *Droit International Codifié* (Fr. trans. by Lardy), sec. 654.

the people to turn them against Gambetta and induce the election of an assembly in favor of ending the war. This latter expedient, says Loening, "was extraordinary, but the situation was none the less so."[1]

In nearly all the cities occupied, says Calvo, the inhabitants were compelled to raise within short periods of time enormous sums, exceeding many times the resources of their municipal treasuries, and necessitating recourse to forced loans or appeals to the generosity of the inhabitants.[2] The French minister of the interior in an official report estimated that in the thirty-four departments invaded the contributions of war levied amounted to 39,000,000 francs, the taxes collected by the German authorities aggregated 49,000,000, and the supplies requisitioned totaled 327,000,000.[3] Many of the contributions thus levied did not differ from pillage except in name.[4]

While a few German writers, like Bluntschli,[5] Geffcken,[6] and Wehberg,[7] think the German authorities went too far, the vast majority of them have defended the conduct of the Germans even when it was resorted to avowedly for the purpose of breaking the resistance of the French and of compelling them to sue for peace.[8]

The German general staff in the *Kriegsbrauch im Landkriege* asserts, however, that the power of requisition was resorted to by the Germans during the Franco-German war "with the utmost tenderness for the inhabitants even if in isolated cases excesses occurred." It justifies the severity in respect to the

---

[1] *Rev. de Droit Int. et de Lég. Comp.*, Vol. V, p. 108

[2] *Op. cit.*, Vol. IV, sec. 2254.

[3] As to the German policy in 1870–1871 cf. Despagnet, *Droit Int. Public*, secs. 588 ff.; also Bonfils, secs. 1219, 1226, n. 3; Pont, *Les Réquisitions Militaires*, ch. III; Kluber, p. 359, and Rouard de Card, *Droit Int.*, pp. 178 ff. Excellent reviews of the law and practice in respect to requisitions and contributions may be found in two articles by Ernest Nys in the *Rev. de Droit et de Lég. Comp.*, Vol. 38 (1906), pp. 274 ff. and 406 ff.; in an article by C. N. Gregory in the *Columbia Law Review* for March, 1915, pp. 1–21; in Bordwell, *Law of War*, see Index; Halleck, *Int. Law*, Vol. II, see index; Calvo, *Droit Int.*, Vol. IV, secs. 2235 ff.; Spaight, pp. 395 ff.; Thomas, *Réquisitions Militaires*, and Ferrand, *Des Réquisitions*.

[4] Cf. Latifi, *Effects of War on Private Property*, p. 34, and Bluntschli, *op. cit.*, sec. 654.

[5] *Op. cit.*, sec. 654.   [6] Heffter, p. 30, n. 4.

[7] *Capture in War*, ch. IV (English trans. by Robertson).

[8] Cf. for example, two articles by Loening entitled *L'Administration du Gouvernement-Général de l'Alsace durant la Guerre de 1870–1871*, in the *Revue de Droit Int.*, 1872–1873 (Vols. IV–V), pp. 692 ff. and 69 ff.

imposition of fines, on the ground of the "embittered character which the war took on in its latest stage and the lively participation of the population which necessitated the sternest measures."[1]

§ 388. German Contributions during the Recent War. As has been said, German writers have attempted to justify German policy during the war of 1870–1871, partly on the ground that the war was forced on Germany, and consequently it was legitimate to resort to heavy pecuniary levies to make those who had brought on the war bear a portion of the cost and also to break their spirit of resistance and to induce them to sue for peace.

In the recent war, however, no such excuse could be pleaded, because Germany was herself the aggressor, at least against Belgium. Moreover, the impoverished condition to which Belgium was reduced in consequence of the German invasion made the imposition of heavy pecuniary exactions a peculiar hardship for those who were compelled to raise the large sums demanded. But this extenuating circumstance does not appear to have been taken into consideration, and no sooner had the German military forces established themselves in Belgium than they proceeded to levy pecuniary impositions of various kinds on the towns, cities, and districts which fell under their occupation, to say nothing of the enormous community fines, which are considered in the following chapter of this work. During the early months of the war the following "contributions" are known to have been levied by the Germans upon Belgian and French cities and districts:

Brussels	40,000,000	francs [2]
Antwerp	50,000,000	francs
City of Liège	20,000,000	francs
Province of Liège	50,000,000	francs
Namur	32,000,000	francs [3]
Courtrai	10,000,000	francs

[1] Carpentier's French trans. of the *Kriegsbrauch*, p. 136.

[2] Some accounts say 50,000,000 (e.g., Cammaerts, *Through the Iron Bars*, p. 38). The Germans originally demanded 200,000,000 of Brussels, but after "protracted negotiations" with the local authorities they reduced the amount to 40,000,000. The city was given three days in which to raise the sum exacted. Gibson, *Journal from Our Legation in Belgium*, p. 115.

[3] The original demand upon Namur was for 50,000,000, but the amount was reduced to 32,000,000 on condition that the first million should be paid within twenty-four hours. Massart, *Belgians under the German Eagle*, p. 156, and Cammaerts, *op. cit.*, p. 37.

Tournai	2,000,000 francs
Roulers	1,500,000 francs
Lille	7,000,000 francs [1]
Roubaix and Tourcoing	1,000,000 francs [2]
Valenciennes	3,000,000 francs
Lens	700,000 francs
Armentières	500,000 francs
Louvain	100,000 francs [3]
Coulommiers	100,000 francs [4]
Mancourt (Fr. village)	10 francs per capita [5]
Charleroi	10,000,000 francs [6]
Beaumont	8,000 francs [7]
Givet (December, 1916)	625,000 francs [8]

[1] Proclamation of General Graevenitz, November 4, 1914, text in Fage, *Lille sous la Griffe Allemande*, p. 46. Payment of the first million was required to be made on November 10; two millions on November 17; three millions on November 24; and the remainder on December 1. In default of payment on the dates mentioned the city would be fined. The city treasury being empty the mayor addressed an appeal to the citizens who responded to the extent of raising 5,400,000 francs. The mayor then addressed a letter to the military governor in which he referred to the impoverished condition of the inhabitants, reminded him that they had already raised 1,500,000 francs toward the revictualment of the German troops and that 1200 houses in the city had been destroyed by bombardment and burning, with a loss of 300,000,000 francs. He therefore appealed to the governor to take pity on the inhabitants and reduce the amount of the contribution demanded. The governor replied on November 22 consenting to defer until December 1 the payment due on November 24, but refusing to reduce the amount and threatening to resort to measures of coercion in case the full amount was not paid on the dates fixed. On December 8, the mayor was requested to raise an additional 800,000 francs toward the payment of the expenses of the German troops. Text of the correspondence between the mayor and the German military governor in Fage, *op. cit.*, pp. 47–56.

[2] Maccas puts the amount at 10,000,000.

[3] The civil authorities of Louvain notified the German authorities that it was impossible to pay this contribution, as the city treasury was empty. The officer who demanded it thereupon agreed to accept 3080 francs. See an official publication of the Belgian government entitled *L'Armée à Louvain en Août 1914 et le Livre Blanc Allemand*, p. 17.

[4] The German officer who demanded the contribution threatened to shoot the state's attorney and burn the town in case the amount was not handed over by 8 o'clock on the following day. *Rapports et Procès-Verbaux d'Enquête de la Commission Instituée en Vue de Constater les Actes Commis par l'Ennemi en Violation du Droit des Gens*, Vol. I, pp. 30–32.

[5] *Ibid.*, Vol. V, pp. 114–121. One hour was given in which to raise the amount, in default of which the inhabitants would be searched, any one found with money in his possession would be shot, hostages would also be taken, and the village burned.

[6] Toynbee, *The German Terror in France*, p. 74. It is not clear whether this exaction was intended to be a "contribution" or a "fine."

[7] *Rapports et Procès-Verbaux*, Vol. II, p. 52. The mayor being able to raise only 1800 francs, the Germans obtained the rest by "robbing private individuals."

[8] Huberich and Speyer, *German Legislation in Belgium*, 10th Ser., p. 2.

berg (population 850), after furnishing 50 cows, 35 pigs, and 1600 kilos of oats, was forced to deliver in January and February, 1915, 100 pigs, 100,000 kilos of wheat, 50,000 kilos of beans or peas, 50,000 of oats, and 150,000 of straw.[1]

The city of Lille was systematically exploited. In addition to the war contributions already referred to and the imposition of a fine of 5,000,000 francs, it was compelled to furnish supplies in such quantities as to reduce the inhabitants to the verge of starvation.[2]

As the blockade of Germany became more effective and her own domestic stocks of raw materials were reduced, the policy of requisition in the occupied territories was pushed to the extreme limit. By the spring of 1918 it appears to have degenerated into a system of indiscriminate pillage. Factories were dismantled, growing crops in the fields were requisitioned, nearly all the live stock in the occupied regions was carried off, farm implements, household furniture and utensils, especially those of brass and copper,[3] were seized by officers who are said

[1] Cf. also Gomery, *op. cit.*, p. 192, for this and other similar cases. At Tournai 110,000 bottles of wine had to be found for the Germans.

[2] The Paris correspondent of the London *Times* (weekly ed., December 25, 1914) thus described the condition of Lille at the end of the year 1914. "It has been bombarded; it has been fined; it has been squeezed of money as an orange is emptied of juice; hunger and misery steal through its charred and ruined streets." For the details as to how Lille was bled by requisitions, together with the documentary evidence, see Fage, *op. cit.*, ch. V.

[3] The town of Bruges, in addition to having been heavily fined, was searched four times for copper; every bit of metal was carried away and every workshop was robbed of its machinery. The manufacturing industries in many towns and cities were destroyed by the spoliation of machinery and raw materials which were taken to Germany. In many towns and cities articles of household furniture, sewing machines, pianos, silver plate, and works of art were loaded on trucks and shipped to Germany. Everywhere wine cellars were emptied, and there appears to have been a great amount of drunkenness among the soldiers and this was responsible for some of the worst outrages committed against the civilian population. There is an abundance of evidence to establish the charges in respect to pillage and drunkenness in the diaries found on captured or dead German soldiers. Many such diaries are printed in the original language in which they were written, in Bedier's *German Atrocities from German Evidence*, pp. 22–23, and in Dampierre's *German Imperialism and International Law*, Eng. Trans., ch. 3. Some of the diaries frankly admit that the Germans pillaged and plundered like vandals, carried off everything they could, and indulged in drunken and disgraceful orgies. Eric Fisher Wood (*Note Book of an Attaché*, p. 189), describing his visit to the château at Chantilly, says that the Germans "took away pretty much everything of value." Cf. also Appendix B of the Bryce Report. Gibson in his *Journal from Our Legation in Belgium* (p. 196) says "that the way the Germans cleared out the wine of the country was a revelation to everybody. They would

to have made house to house visits for the purpose; even clocks and jewellery, doorplates, ornaments, and all personal objects containing metal, and finally the churches were despoiled of their organs, bells, and ornaments.[1] Mr. Whitlock, the American minister, declared that the only establishments which the Germans respected in Belgium were the breweries.

The Germans appear to have considered their policy of exploitation as the lawful right of a military occupant, this on the principle of the ancient maxim that "war must support war." The German press defended the policy of the military authorities and even boasted that it had been the means of assuring the preservation of the economic life of Germany. At the same time the press and the government were daily asserting that the German authorities had done and were doing everything in their power to keep Belgian industries going and to provide the people with employment and the means of subsistence.[2] The same policy in respect to requisitions is alleged to have been carried out in Servia, Roumania, Poland, northern Italy, and other territories occupied by the armies of the Central powers.[3]

---

not take what they needed for the day's drinking, but would clear out whole cellars at a time and load what was not drunk into carts to be carried away." German policy in respect to requisition in the country around Noyon is described by the Abbé Calippe in his book, *La Somme sous l'Occupation Allemande* (1918). Cf. especially pp. 60, 77, and 85. See also Fauchille, *Les Allemands en Ter. Occupé*, 24 *Rev. Gén.*, 316 ff. and 44 Clunet, 949 ff. Nevertheless Dr. Noldecke in an article in the *Deutsche Juristen Zeitung* of April 1, 1917 (reproduced in 44 Clunet, 1354 ff.) asserted that Germany was not making war on peaceful inhabitants and that "our soldiers are careful to respect their honor and their property."

[1] Cf. the protest of Cardinal Mercier in the New York *Times* of April 26, 1918. In December, 1918, the archbishop of Cologne sent to the archbishop of Berne twenty cases of religious ornaments that had been carried away by the Germans from the diocese of Rheims. New York *Times* Paris despatch, December 19, 1918.

[2] This assertion is made by the *Nord Deutsche Zeitung* in its issue of December 29, 1914. Adverting to this claim, Mr. Vernon Kellog, an American official in the Belgian relief service, remarks that "The bald truth is governor von Bissing's repeated declarations of rehabilitating industries in Belgium, and the similar statements of the general staff of northern France, are equivocations. What has been strongly attempted has been a forced exploitation of the people for German military advantage." See his article in the *Atlantic Monthly*, August, 1917, p. 152.

[3] Poland was stripped of food supplies; in northern Italy even the church bells and kitchen utensils were seized, and Servia was "plundered and ruined." Cf. New York *Times*, June 10, 1918; London weekly *Times*, November 25, 1915, July 25, 1917, and February 9, 1917; Toynbee, *op. cit.*, ch. 3; also his brochure,

§ 394. **Provisions of the Hague Convention in Respect to Requisitions.** The rules governing the right of requisition are found in article 52 of the Hague convention of 1907 respecting the laws and customs of war on land. They are as follows:

> Neither requisitions in kind nor services can be demanded from communes nor inhabitants, except for the needs of the army of occupation. They shall be in proportion to the resources of the country . . . contributions in kind shall, as far as possible, be paid for in cash; if not, a receipt shall be given, and the payment of the amount due shall be made as soon as possible."

These rules, the Belgian commission of inquiry alleges were systematically violated.[1]

The Destruction of Poland; a Study in German Efficiency, which contains an almost unbelievable account of German exploitation and plunder in Poland.

In August, 1919, the Roumanian delegation at the Peace Conference made public a report of the former Austro-Hungarian minister of war which had fallen into the hands of the Roumanian authorities, showing how the Central powers had "pillaged" Roumania by means of requisitions. According to the report they took from the country 291,000 carloads of wheat, 163,000 carloads of corn, 77,000 carloads of barley and oats, 19,000 carloads of dry vegetables, 86,000 carloads of fodder, 8500 carloads of oleaginous grains, 3,000,000 hectolitres of wine, 550,000 hectolitres of brandy, 1,000,000 cows and oxen, 400,000 calves, 4,400,000 sheep, 2,000,000 lambs and 1,000,000 hogs. In addition enormous quantities of petrol, benzine, and mineral oils as well as locomotives, cars, machines, and agricultural implements were taken.

[1] Report on the Violations of the Laws of Nations (Eng. trans.), p. xvi. Some German writers still maintain, or did recently, that requisition of supplies, or services without payment is lawful. Cf. Leuder in Holtzendorff, Vol. IV, p. 502, and Loening in the *Rev. de Droit Int.*, Vol. IV, p. 645. It is the duty of the State, says Loening, from which the supplies are taken, to indemnify the owners; it is wholly a question of municipal not of international law. In case the State is victorious, it will exact an indemnity from its adversary sufficient in amount to cover the value of the supplies taken. This seems to be the view of the *Kriegsbrauch* (Carpentier, p. 136). But Bluntschli (sec. 655) and practically all English and French writers adopt the contrary view. The obligation of the occupying army to pay for supplies taken is fully discussed by Ferrand in his *Des Réquisitions*, pp. 210 ff., and his conclusion is that the Hague convention left no doubt as to the obligation.

Regarding the rule that requisitions shall be in proportion to the resources of the country, Moltke in his well-known letter to Bluntschli of December 11, 1880, observed that "the soldier who endures suffering, privation, fatigue, and danger cannot be content to take only in proportion to the resources of the country. It is necessary for him to take all that is necessary to his subsistence." French text in *Revue de Droit Int.*, 13: 80-82; German text in von Moltke's *Gesammelte Schriften und Denkwürdig Keiten*, Vol. 5, p. 95. This is also the view laid down in the *Kriegsbrauch im Landkriege*, Part II, ch. 4. The right of requisition without payment, it says, exists as much as ever, and will certainly be claimed in the future by armies in the field, and considering the size of modern armies, must be claimed.

There were many complaints that the rule of the Hague convention in respect to payment for goods requisitioned was not observed, and there is considerable evidence in support of the charges.[1]

§ 395. **Requisition of Live Stock for Transportation to Germany.** The seizure and transportation to Germany on an extensive scale of live stock, particularly horses and cattle, from the occupied districts was the subject of strong complaint both in Belgium and France. Soon after the occupation of Belgium the governor-general issued an order forbidding the exportation of horses from the occupied districts; an exception being made, however, in the case of exportation to Germany.[2]

Early in October, 1914, the German minister of agriculture sent a commission to Belgium, the Belgians allege, to organize a systematic spoliation of Belgian horse breeders. Notices were placarded throughout the occupied districts announcing that on specified days the commission would sit in a particular town or village for the purpose of purchasing horses for which cash prices would be paid.[3] These notices directed the owners of horses to bring them in at the places and times mentioned, warning them that those who refused would be liable to have their horses confiscated, or that the commune would be punished by a fine of 10,000 francs and the owner by a fine of 2500 francs.[4]

As to the rule that requisitions must be in proportion to the resources of the country, it will never be observed in practice, we are told, for the needs of the army must determine the amount (Carpentier, p. 138). But Strupp, *op. cit.*, p. 111, condemns this view, and so does Stier-Somlo in the *Zeitschrift für Völkerrecht*, 8: 568. The French manual (art. 103), the British *Manual* (sec. 417), and the American *Rules* (art. 345) adopt the rule of the Hague convention. Requisitions, they declare, can be made only for the indispensable needs of the army, and they must be in proportion to the resources of the country.

[1] Bryce Report: Evidence and Documents on Alleged German Atrocities, Appendix, p. 288; Passalecq, p. 389; Gibson, *op. cit.*, pp. 115 and 252, and Gomery, p. 194.

[2] By a decree of October 24, 1916, even the sale of horses by one Belgian to another or their removal from one commune to another was forbidden. Huberich and Speyer, Ser. IX, p. 152.

[3] Cf. the text of various notices of this character in the Belgian report on the Violations of the Law of Nations, p. 12, and in Davignon, *Belgium and Germany*, p. 119.

[4] Professor Van der Essen of the University of Louvain asserts that more than 90 per cent of the horses in Belgium were requisitioned, thus reducing the inhabitants to the necessity of employing oxen for drawing their wagons and carts. *Petite Histoire de l'Invasion*, p. 95.

The horses thus seized were transported to Germany where they were sold at public auction by the minister of agriculture, by chambers of commerce, or by designated individuals, official notices being published in the newspapers informing the farmers of the community of the intended sales.

A large number of cattle, and especially milch cows, was also seized in the occupied districts of both Belgium and France and transported to Germany. Lord Robert Cecil, on March 19, 1918, referring to the German charge that Great Britain was endeavoring to starve the civil population of Germany by means of an unlawful blockade, stated that in the occupied area of northern France there were at the time of the arrival of the German armies half a million cattle, whereas " hardly one is left today. Belgium had 1,500,000 cattle; we know that practically half of these have gone to Germany." [1]

Article 52 of the Hague convention respecting the laws and customs of war expressly forbids requisitions in kind except " for the needs of the army of occupation." It was clearly not the intention of the conference to authorize the taking away by a military occupant of live stock for the maintenance of his own industries at home or for the support of the civil population of his country. By no process of reasoning can requisitions for such purposes be construed to be for the " needs of the army of occupation."

§ 396. Seizure and Transportation of Machinery to Germany. A similar charge against the Germans was that of committing spoliations upon Belgian manufacturing industries by dismantling factories and workshops and carrying away their machinery and tools to Germany. In the district of Charleroi machinery to the value of twelve million francs is alleged to have been taken.[2]

[1] Representative Hicks of the United States in a speech in Congress on April 4, 1918, *Cong. Record*, p. 4971, stated that since the occupation of northern France and Belgium by the Germans 2,700,000 head of cattle had been seized in France and 1,800,000 head in Belgium. The sources of his information are not given.

[2] Preface to the Belgian report on Violations of the Laws of Nations in Belgium, p. 15. Mr. Langhorne, charge d'affaires of the American legation in Belgium, in a report to the department of state under date of September 29, 1917, stated that he had received information that the looms and machinery in the textile mills of Roubaix and Tourcoing had been removed and sent to Germany, and that such as could not be removed and transferred had in some instances been dynamited or destroyed with hammers. He also added that in the neighborhood of Courtrai

In the reparation account prepared by the Belgian government in 1919 for the information of the Peace Conference it was stated that the value of machinery and materials carried away by the Germans amounted to two billion francs.

The Belgian government addressed a protest to the governments of neutral countries against these acts as being contrary to article 53 of the Hague convention respecting the laws and customs of war, which, although it allows, subject to restoration and indemnity for its use, the seizure of war material belonging to private persons, does not authorize the seizure and exportation by the occupying belligerent of machinery and implements used in the industrial arts.[1] The industrial establishments of northern France were similarly despoiled of their machinery much of it being systematically destroyed.[2]

---

the owners of all mills had been ordered by the military authorities to furnish a list of their machinery; that all textile fabrics had been requisitioned even in small retail stores; that woollen blankets had been taken from private houses, and that there were extensive requisitions of wine. Text in pamphlet entitled *Treatment of Conquered Territory*, issued by the United States Committee on Public Information, p. 31. In March, 1917, a decree was issued by governor-general von Bissing ordering the seizure throughout Belgium of certain articles for removal to Germany when the quantities held by any owner exceeded certain specified amounts. There were sixty articles on the list, including table-cloths, napkins, silks, manufactured or raw, waterproof stuffs and garments, oil-cloths, woollen yarns, tarpaulin, leggings, knee bandages, and other sanitary articles (New York *Times*, March 9, 1917). Mr. Herbert Hoover in a cablegram to the American government in January, 1918 (New York *Times*, January 1), stated that the " entire industrial life of northern France had been destroyed by the Germans. There is scarcely a single factory that can be operated without a very large portion of equipment." Some details concerning the systematic destruction of industrial plants in France and the spoliation of the machinery may be found in a Paris despatch published in the New York *Times* of November 29, 1918.

[1] Par. 2 of art. 53 reads as follows: " All appliances whether on land, or sea, or in the air, adapted for the transmission of news or for the transport of persons or goods, apart from cases governed by maritime law, depots of arms, and generally, all kinds of war material may be seized, even though belonging to private persons, but they must be restored and compensation for them arranged for at the peace." The authority to requisition here conferred is clearly limited to " war materials" and is conditioned upon the obligation to restore the same at the end of the war and to indemnify the owners for their use.

[2] Many details of the systematic methods by which the Germans despoiled the French factories of their machinery or destroyed it are given in an article by a correspondent of the London *Morning Post* who visited the devastated region in December, 1918. The article is reproduced in the New York *Times Current History Magazine* for March, 1919, pp. 504 ff. The great cotton factories of Lille, Roubaix, and Tourcoing especially, were completely stripped of their machinery. Much of it was carried to Germany and installed in German establishments;

What was said above in regard to the illegality of the requisition of live stock and its transportation to Germany for the benefit of German industry and for the support of the civil population at home must be said of the seizure and transportation for similar purposes of the machinery and equipment of Belgian and French factories and other manufacturing establishments. The materials thus taken were not for the needs of the army of occupation, and the carrying of them away was nothing more than pillage and spoliation under the disguise of requisitions.[1] The treaty of peace stipulated that among the damages for which Germany should be required to pay an indemnity was " the carrying away, seizure, injuring or destruction of all property belonging to the allies, wherever situated, with the exception of naval and military works or materials." Art. 244, annex I.

---

the copper and brass were taken for military uses; the rest was destroyed. The correspondent estimates that the tools and machinery taken from Lille or destroyed were worth at pre-war prices about forty million francs. From the factories of Tourcoing over one million kilos of copper and brass are alleged to have been taken. Representatives of German establishments visited the French factories and selected such machinery as could be used and transported by them to their own plants in Germany. See also 42 Clunet, p. 117 ff.

[1] The authorities are all in agreement that the right of requisition as recognized by the Hague convention is understood to embrace only such supplies as are needed by the army within the territory occupied and does not include the spoliation of the country and the transportation to the occupant's own country of raw materials and machinery for use in his home industries. " To be legitimate," says Bluntschli (op. cit., sec. 654), " requisitions must be limited to objects absolutely indispensable to the maintenance of the army." Stier-Somlo, in the article cited above, says that only things " required by military necessity " may be taken. Cf. also Ferrand, Des Réquisitions, p. 50, and Passalecq, op. cit., p. 174. The British Manual (sec. 416) and the French Manual (sec. 104) say that only things " indispensable or necessary to the army of occupation " may be requisitioned. Nevertheless the Germans contended that the spoliation of Belgian and French industrial establishments and the transportation of their machinery to Germany was a lawful act of war under article 23 (g) of the Hague Convention which allows a military occupant to appropriate enemy private property whenever it is " imperatively demanded by the necessities of war." In consequence of the Anglo-French blockade which threatened the very existence of Germany it was a military necessity that she should draw in part on the supply of raw materials and machinery available in occupied enemy territory. But it is quite clear from the language and context of art. 23 (g) as well as the discussions on it in the Conference that it was never intended to authorize a military occupant to despoil on an extensive scale the industrial establishments of occupied territory or to transfer their machinery to his own country for use in his home industries. What was intended merely was to authorize the seizure or destruction of private property only in exceptional cases when it was an imperative necessity for the con-

§ 397. **Requisition of Railway Material.** Hardly less justifiable than the carrying away of machinery and raw materials
was the tearing up of the tracks of various Belgian railroads,
especially of interurban roads (*les chemins de fer vicinaux*),
which are owned not by the State but by private individuals,
and the transportation of the rails to Poland and elsewhere for
the construction of military railways.[1] The Belgian government protested to the governments of neutral powers against
this form of spoliation, not only because it deprived the Belgians
of the only means of commercial transportation which remained
under their control,[2] but also because it was in violation of the
Hague convention respecting the laws and customs of war on
land.   Article 53 of the convention, as stated above, authorizes
the seizure of "appliances for the transport of persons or things,"[3]
even when they belong to private individuals, upon condition
that they be restored and compensation made at the conclusion
of peace.

Manifestly, this stipulation had reference only to the *use* or
exploitation of such "appliances" by the occupying belligerent
and can hardly be construed to authorize the tearing up of
railway tracks and their removal to a foreign country, for in
such a case the probability of their restoration intact at the
end of the war would be very remote.   It might be otherwise
with rolling stock, which could be easily removed from the
territory occupied and returned at the end of the war without

---

duct of his military operations in the territory under occupation.   This view is
further strengthened by art. 46 which requires belligerents to respect enemy
private property and which forbids confiscation and by art. 47 which prohibits
pillage.   Compare the observations of Professor Nast of the University of Nancy
in 26 *Rev. Gén.* (1919), pp. 111 ff.

[1] Van der Essen, *Petite Histoire de l'Invasion*, p. 96.   In 1916 a neutral traveller
in Turkey saw quantities of Belgian rolling stock in use on the Bagdad Railway.
London *Times*, September, 1916, p. 7.

[2] The main railway lines, which in Belgium are owned and operated by the
State, were taken over and operated by the German military administration,
mainly for military purposes.   So were those of northern France.   Much of the
rolling stock is said to have been carried away to Germany.

[3] The act of the Brussels Congress of 1874 had expressly enumerated among
the "appliances" referred to in art. 53 of the Hague convention, "railway plant,
land telegraphs, steamers and other ships."   The Hague Conference, however,
deemed it wise not to enumerate specifically the objects the seizure of which it
intended to authorize.   But there can be no doubt that railway lines come within
the scope of the paragraph quoted.

necessary injury to the plant. The right of a belligerent to seize and operate railways belonging to the State is conditioned upon the same obligation. Article 55 of the above-mentioned convention lays down the rule that the occupying belligerent shall be regarded only as the usufructuary of public property situated in the territory occupied, and that he must safeguard the substance (*le fond*) of such property and administer it in accordance with the rules of usufruct. It is very doubtful whether the tearing up of a railway track and the transportation of the rails to a distant country under the occupation of the belligerent, to be used by him for the purpose of building new lines, can be regarded as "administration" according to the rules of usufruct.[1]

§ 398. **Cutting of Forests.** A somewhat similar complaint made against the Germans was the cutting without discrimination of large numbers of trees from the State and communal forests to be sent to Germany for use in the manufacture of

---

[1] "The rules of usufruct," says Holland (*Law of War on Land*, par. 115), "may be shortly stated to be that the property subject to the right must be so used that its substance sustains no injury." The authorities who have considered the rights of belligerents over railroads in occupied territory, so far as I am aware, have not pronounced an opinion on the question of their right to tear up the tracks and take the rails out of the country for use elsewhere. They are all in agreement, however, in holding that a belligerent has no lawful right to damage or destroy a railway line further than to cut it in order to prevent the enemy from drawing supplies over it or from maintaining communications. They all seem to be agreed, likewise, that the occupying belligerent is bound to restore the road at the end of the war in the same condition in which he found it. This rule was approved by the Institute of International Law in 1883. *Annuaire*, Vol. VIII. The question is discussed at length by Ferrand, *Des Réquisitions*, pp. 144 ff., who holds that rolling stock may not be transported by a belligerent to his own country, because it would interfere with commerce in the country occupied and is, moreover, not a military necessity.

Cf. on this point the views of Stein, a professor in the University of Vienna, in an article entitled *Le Droit International des Chemins de Fer en Cas de Guerre*, *Rev. de Droit Int. et de Lég. Comp.*, Vol. XVII, especially p. 350; of Moynier, *ibid.*, Vol. XX, p. 365; of Buzzati, *Les Chemins de Fer en Temps de Guerre*, *ibid.*, Vol. XX, p. 388, and of Nowacki, *Die Eisenbahnen im Kriege* (1906), p. 31. Stein, whose views are attacked by Moynier and Buzzati, holds that a belligerent may destroy the tracks in certain cases where military necessity requires it; but even he does not admit that they may be taken up and transported by a belligerent to a distant country for use in the construction of new lines. Cf. also Ferrand, *op. cit.*, pp. 65–66, for a discussion of Buzzati's and Stein's views. The *Kriegsbrauch im Landkriege* allows a belligerent the right only to use the railways of the enemy State, and these, it says, must be returned at the end of the war. French trans. by Carpentier, p. 148.

rifle stocks. There were also extensive cuttings to secure material for trench shelters, for corduroying roads, and for fuel,
cooking and heating. Some of the forests thus denuded were
as ancient as the cathedrals which likewise suffered from the
hands of the Germans. In France, especially in the region of
the Argonne, trees in large numbers are alleged to have been
cut and transported to Germany for use as timber.[1] A similar
charge, it will be remembered, was made by the French against
the Germans in 1870.[2] The right of an occupying belligerent
in respect to the lopping of forests is thus stated by Westlake:
"In the case of forests, the right of a usufructuary is to cut the
trees which regularly come to cutting during his tenancy."[3]
The German *Kriegsbrauch im Landkriege* admits that, although
a military occupant is not bound to follow the enemy's mode of
administration in respect to State forests, he must not damage
the woods by excessive cutting; still less may he cut them
down altogether.[4]

§ 399. **Seizure of Funds of Private Banks and Post-offices.**
Another serious charge against the Germans was that in many
instances they seized and confiscated the deposits of private
banks. Thus on August 12, 1914, the funds of a branch of
the national bank of Belgium at Hasselt, amounting to 2,075,000
francs, were appropriated by order of the military authorities.
Likewise at Liège the Germans upon their entrance into the
city seized the funds of the local branch of the national bank,
amounting to 4,000,000 francs.[5] Two million nine hundred
thousand francs are also alleged to have been taken from other
private banks at Liège; 20,000 francs from a bank at Huy;
975,000 from a bank at Verviers, and "all the cash" in a bank
at Brussels. At Noyon the safes of the bank Société Générale

---

[1] Not a tree is said to have been left standing in the famous Belgian forest of
Houthulst, which dated from the ninth century and which covered an area of
two hundred square miles.

[2] See the case of the fifteen thousand oaks cut by the Germans in the French
state forests, the unperformed contracts for the sale of which the French government refused to enforce after the return of peace. Cobbett's *Leading Cases
and Opinions on International Law*, Vol. I, p. 226; Bordwell, *Law of War*, pp.
96, 329, and Spaight, *War Rights on Land*, p. 367.

[3] *Int. Law*, Pt. II, p. 106. [4] Carpentier, p. 168.

[5] *The Case of Belgium*, pp. 16-17; also the seventeenth report of the Belgian
commission of inquiry. Massart, p. 133, charges that 43,000 francs were seized
from the People's Bank at Auvelois. Cf. also Van der Essen, *Petite Histoire*, p. 40.

were broken open by means of a blowpipe, and 2,000,000 francs in securities and cash were seized.[1]   The same thing was done at Péronne.   The deposits of the *Banque Générale Belge*, a private institution at Namur, were likewise confiscated, but on petition of the directors the German authorities agreed to allow the money to be applied towards the contribution of 50,000,000 francs which had been levied on the town.[2]   At Louvain the Germans are alleged to have seized the available cash assets of various private banks.[3]   Private banks in other towns and cities appear to have been similarly treated.[4]

In September, 1916, the Belgian government filed a protest with the department of state at Washington against what it described as an enforced loan of 1,000,000,000 francs said to have been imposed by the German military authorities upon the banks of Belgium.   According to a statement of the Belgian minister of finance of September 19, this was accomplished by the compulsory transfer of the funds of the *Banque Nationale* of Belgium and the *Société Générale de Belgique*, both of which are private institutions, to the German Imperial bank.   M. Carlier, director of the national bank of Belgium, was deported to Germany on account of his opposition to the proposed transfer. The German authorities denied that the funds thus transferred were to be used for subscriptions to the fifth German war loan, but the Belgian government asserted that inasmuch as the transfer took place at the time the German loan was being put through, it was evident that the purpose was to furnish the Imperial bank with a fresh supply of cash with which to swell its subscriptions to the loan.   The protest of the Belgian government denounced the measure as an "outrage against private property and a violation of international laws and conventions."[5]

---

[1] Some of the details are given by Saint-Aymour in his book, *Autour de Noyon*, p. 96.

[2] *Martyrdom of Belgium*, p. 7.

[3] Fifth Belgian report; Maccas, *op. cit.*, p. 212, and the Belgian document *L'Armée Allemande à Louvain*, p. 11.

[4] Notably at Ath, Dinant, Mons, Charleroi, Nivelles and Ghent.   Fauchille in 26 *Rev. Gén. de Dr. Int.* (1919), p. 313.

[5] Despatch in the New York *Times* of September 10, 1916, which contains a summary of a protest filed with the department of state by the Belgian government. Cf. also Passalecq, *Les Déportations Belges*, pp. 158-159. Passalecq states that on September 12, 1916, a German military automobile drew up in front of the *Banque Nationale* and demanded its funds.   The governor of the bank protested, but without avail.   Four hundred and thirty million marks were seized

The French government in a protest addressed in March, 1917, to the neutral powers against various acts of German barbarism and vandalism referred to the pillage of various French banks and urged them to warn their banks against dealing in securities taken from such banks.[1]

Regarding the right of a military occupant to seize the funds of banks, article 53 of the Hague convention respecting the laws and customs of war declares that

"An army of occupation can only take possession of cash, funds and realizable securities which are strictly the property of the State, depots of arms, means of transport, stores and supplies, and, generally, all movable property of the State which may be used for operations of war."

Clearly the authority here conferred in respect to the seizure of funds and securities is limited to those not belonging to municipalities, communes, or private individuals. This is admitted by the *Kriegsbrauch im Landkriege*.[2]

The national bank of Belgium, like the national banks of the United States, was a private institution, and its funds were the property of private individuals. The seizure of the funds of its branches was, therefore, plainly an act of confiscation of private property in violation of the express terms of the Hague convention and contrary, it appears, to German practice during the Franco-German[3] war of 1870–1871.[4]

---

and taken away. The funds seized appear to have been German bank notes, but they were the property of the banks from which they were seized. According to M. Passalecq, the excuse advanced by the German authorities was that the money was lying idle, and the amount was larger than was necessary to meet the local needs. The funds seized were apparently credited to the banks from which they were taken, and according to the press despatches they were replaced by an equivalent of forced currency without any effective guarantee. The treatment which the *Banque Nationale* received at the hands of the Germans is described at length by Brand Whitlock in his *Belgium*, Vol. II, pp. 343 ff. and 401 ff.

[1] In December, 1918, after the conclusion of the armistice, agents of the paymaster-general of the French army found in various banks of Brussels large numbers of chests placed there by the German military authorities and containing strong boxes filled with securities taken from various towns and cities in northern France. According to a press despatch from Paris on December 25, 1918, the Germans had returned stocks taken from the banks of northern France amounting approximately to six billion francs.

[2] The public funds referred to in art. 53 "must be entirely distinguished from municipal funds which are regarded as private property." Morgan's Eng. trans., p. 160.

[3] Compare the observations of M. Fauchille in 26 *Rev. Gén.*, p. 311.

[4] When the Prussians entered Rheims on September 4, 1870, they desired to seize the funds of the local branch of the *Banque Nationale de France*, but being

Charges were also made against the Germans for having seized and confiscated the funds of the post-offices in many of the towns and cities which they occupied.   So far as these funds belonged to the State, it was, of course, allowable to seize them, but the Belgian post-offices are also savings banks as well as the custodians of old-age and other pension funds which could not have been lawfully seized.[1]   It does not appear, however, that the Germans made any distinction between the funds which belonged to the State and those which were the property of private individuals.

§ 400.   **Requisition of Services for Military Work.**   A very serious charge against the Germans was that they habitually forced the inhabitants of occupied territory to perform labor which directly or indirectly served to facilitate their military operations.   As is well known, during the war of 1870–1871 they compelled French civilians to work on roads, dig trenches, remove embankments which the French troops had thrown up to oppose the advance of the enemy, and even to drive carts laden with shells and ammunition.[2]   During the recent war they pursued the same policy on a larger and even more ruthless scale.   The reports of the Belgian commission of inquiry charge that at various places the inhabitants were compelled to dig trenches for the Germans, sometimes even when they were

---

informed that the bank was a private institution, Crown Prince Frederick decided that they should not be molested so long as they "were not used for the maintenance of the French army."   Schiemann, *Rechtslage der öffentlichen Banken im Kriegsfalle* (Greifswald, 1902), p. 76.

[1] Cf. Holland, sec. 113, and Spaight, p. 411.

[2] Sutherland Edwards, *The Germans in France*, p. 295, quoted by Spaight. pp. 150, 151.   Nys, *Réquisitions et Contributions, Rev. de Droit Int.*, Vol. 38, p. 415. When in January, 1871, a German commander in the department of the Meurthe requisitioned the services of 500 French laborers to repair a bridge and they refused to comply with his demand, he ordered all public works in the department to be closed and prohibited all work in factories, on roads, streets, railway lines, and other public utilities.   Likewise all private *ateliers* employing more than ten laborers and every private factory were ordered to be closed.   Violation of the order was punishable by a fine of from 10,000 to 50,000 francs for each day and for each day's delay in the payment.   The order was to remain in force until 350 laborers responded to the call of the commander.   Text of the order in the *Rev. de Droit Int.*, Vol. III (1871), p. 315.   At Nancy on January 23, 1871, at 4 P.M. the same military commander addressed a communication to the mayor demanding the services of 500 laborers and warning him that if they failed to appear by noon of the following day, the overseers and a certain number of laborers would be seized and shot.   Text, *ibid.*, p. 315; cf. also Ferrand, *op. cit.*, p. 64; Bonfils, sec. 1150, and Geffcken on Heffter, sec. 131, n. 4.

exposed to the fire of the enemy; that they were forced to erect defensive works, and that they were compelled to work on German fortifications.[1]

Persistent attempts were made by means of threats, confinement, and other forms of systematic intimidation of both individuals and towns, to force the Belgian railway employés to work for the enemy. For refusing to do so, they were in some cases subjected to imprisonment or deportation.[2]

The refusal of the Belgian railway employés to perform the labor demanded was based on the ground that the effect would be to liberate the services of an equivalent number of Germans who, after the desertion of the Belgian employés, had been compelled to take their places in order to keep the railway lines in operation. Moreover, their labor would facilitate the transportation of German troops and military supplies, to which, naturally, no patriotic Belgian desired to contribute. Neither the distress which they suffered from unemployment nor the promise of high wages was sufficient inducement to make them resume their labors.

Lieutenant-general von Westarp undertook to hold the community responsible for the refusal of the inhabitants to comply with his demand for laborers. The pretext of patriotism and the provisions of the Hague convention, he said, could not be invoked as an excuse.[3]

At Malines all vehicular traffic was stopped for ten days as a punishment for the refusal of the laboring population to work for the Germans, and a number of workmen were finally seized

---

[1] Violations of the Laws of Nations in Belgium, pp. 53-55. Cf. also Prof. Van der Essen's brochure entitled, *A Statement about the Destruction of Louvain*, pp. 17-18. Massart, *Belgians under the German Eagle*, p. 113, cites various instances in which Belgians were compelled to dig trenches for the Germans, prepare ground for the landing of aeroplanes, build huts, employ their own horses and wagons in the hauling of munitions, and the like. A Dutch newspaper correspondent, writing in *Les Nouvelles* of Maastricht in December, 1916, stated that a thousand Belgians were at the time being compelled to perform military work on the Somme front, and that four thousand others were about to be sent there. New York *Times*, December 21, 1916.

[2] Report of the Belgian minister of railways, posts, telegraphs, and marine regarding the affair at Luttre; French edition of the Belgian report on Violations of the Laws of Nations in Belgium, pp. 77, 81-84; Passalecq, *Les Déportations Belges*, pp. 393 ff.; Toynbee, *The Belgian Deportations*, ch. IV; Gomery, *Belgium in War Time*, pp. 235 ff., and Cammaerts, *Through the Iron Bars*, ch. V.

[3] Notice posted at Ghent, June 10, 1915. German, French, and Flemish texts in the Belgian official report (French ed.), p. 80; also Passalecq, p. 14.

and taken by force to the arsenal, where they were compelled to work against their will.[1]

At Sweveghem-les-Courtrai in West Flanders, where the military authorities undertook to compel the employés of a wire factory to manufacture barbed wire, the town was "isolated" by surrounding it with troops, and the inhabitants were forbidden to enter or leave.[2]

The town of Harlebeke near Courtrai was punished by an order prohibiting the Belgian food committee from supplying the town with food, by the closing of all cafés, and the keeping of the people indoors between the hours of 4 P.M. and 7 A.M., because the women of the town refused to do "military work" for the Germans. Twenty-nine of the female offenders were deported to Germany as prisoners.

The village of Lokeren near Liège was "isolated" because the working population refused to assist the Germans in the construction of military works. At Tournai the railway employés were at first imprisoned for four months for refusing to work; still persisting in their refusal, they were sentenced to a year's imprisonment, and certain of the railway officials were deported to Germany.

Because the quarrymen at Lessines refused to work, on the ground that the stone produced by them would be used by the Germans in the construction of military trenches, ninety-six leading citizens of the town are alleged to have been taken before a military court, which imposed fines upon them varying in amount. At Hainaut ninety-four persons are alleged to have been sentenced to prison for terms varying from two months to five years each for similar conduct. Throughout the years 1916, 1917, and 1918 the Germans, it was charged, continued to force Belgian and French civilians to work at tasks which related directly or indirectly to military operations.[3]

---

[1] The attempt of the Germans to compel Belgian railway employés to work is detailed in Massart, pp. 300 ff.; in Passalecq, pp. 17 ff. and 390 ff., and Gomery, pp. 235 ff. Cf. also a communication of Sir Edward Grey to the ministers of The Netherlands, Spain, and the United States protesting against the German policy of compelling Belgians to work in munitions factories. New York *Times*, July 4, 1916.

[2] Eighteenth and nineteenth reports of the Belgian commission of inquiry; Passalecq, pp. 17 ff. and 390 ff., and Toynbee, *The Belgian Deportations*, ch. IV.

[3] These charges were so numerous and frequent that it is impossible to consider all of them here. Hardly a week passed in which charges of this kind were not

The treaty of peace required Germany to pay an indemnity on account of damages caused to civilians by being forced to labor "without remuneration" but nothing was said in regard to damages on account of being forced to do work forbidden by the Hague Convention.

§ 401. **Requisition of Guides.** Frequent charges were also made against the Germans for having forced enemy civilians to serve them as guides. This practice in former times was common,[1] but it appears to have been condemned by the first Hague conference, and the condemnation was renewed by the Conference of 1907. Article 44 of the convention of 1907 respecting the laws and customs of war on land is as follows:

"A belligerent is forbidden to force the inhabitants to furnish information about the army of the other belligerent or about its means of defence."

Professors Holland and Oppenheim are among the few authorities of repute who entertain doubt that this article forbids the employment of forced guides, and their explanation is that a proposal to insert an express provision forbidding the impressing of guides was opposed by Germany, Austria-Hungary, Russia, and Japan.[2] But most of the other authorities hold the contrary view, and it seems quite certain that the committee which approved the article at The Hague in 1907 intended that it should forbid the compulsory employment of guides.[3] Japan, Germany, Austria-Hungary, Montenegro, and

---

made in the press despatches. Young Belgians, Frenchmen, and Russians were said to have been dragooned and forced to perform military labor, such as digging trenches, working in munitions factories, sometimes immediately behind the lines, where they were exposed to the fire of their own troops. In some instances charges were made that Belgians of military age were even conscripted and forced to serve in the German army. In January, 1918, the Belgian legation at Washington made public an official communication of the Belgian government charging that Belgian women, many of them between the ages of seventeen and thirty-five, were being compelled to dig trenches, and that boys were being forced to work under fire. Text, New York *Times*, January 2. Cf. also Saint-Aymour, *Autour de Noyon*, pp. 272 ff., for the copy of an order of July 20, 1915, issued at Holnon, requiring women and children fifteen years of age and over to work in the fields from 4 o'clock in the morning until 8 o'clock in the evening.

[1] Westlake, *Int. Law*, Pt. II, p. 101, and Pillet, *op. cit.*, p. 99.

[2] Holland, *Laws of War on Land*, p. 53; Oppenheim, *Int. Law*, Vol. II, p. 121.

[3] Spaight, p. 369; Westlake, Vol. II, pp. 101-102; Hershey, p. 411; Lawrence, p. 418. The whole matter is discussed by Higgins, *The Hague Peace Conferences*, pp. 267-269, and by Ferrand *Des Réquisitions*, pp. 18 ff. and 70 ff. Ferrand

Russia, however, reserved their ratifications to article 44, and it was not, therefore, technically binding on any of the belligerents in the recent war. Nevertheless, they all accepted article 23, which forbids compulsory service in the "operations of war," an expression which would seem quite broad enough to exclude the taking of guides.

The German general staff in the *Kriegsbrauch im Landkriege*, however, refused to accept this view. "Whatever," it says, "may be the horror aroused by the sentiments of humanity in requiring a man to commit an injury to his own country and directly to fight against his own troops, no belligerent operating in an enemy country can entirely renounce this expedient." It even upholds the right of a belligerent to compel the inhabitants to furnish information about their own army, its strategy, its resources, and its military secrets. It admits that the majority of writers of all nations condemn the practice, but nevertheless it cannot be entirely dispensed with; " *Kriegsraison* will make it necessary."[1]

It is difficult to see how the practice can be defended on any other theory than that a belligerent has a moral and lawful right to force the inhabitants to take part in the military operations of the enemy, for such it amounts to in effect. A competent guide, as Spaight very properly remarks, "may be of far more value to a general operating in a strange country than very many troops, and it is quite illogical to forbid him to impress soldiers if you permit him to impress a guide whose employment may be more militarily important and infinitely more damaging to the enemy than a thousand men in the ranks."[2] It is a cruel measure, says Bonfils, for he who guides an army of invasion commits an act more injurious to his own country than if he fought in the ranks of his enemy. Pillet expresses substantially the same opinion.[3] The French official *manuel*

---

reviews at length the arguments for and against the practice of taking guides. Like most writers, he thinks it was clearly the intention of the Conference to condemn the impressment of guides, although he admits that the language employed in art. 44 is unfortunately not clear, and that it should be revised by the next conference, so as to remove all doubt as to its meaning.

[1] Morgan, *The War Book of the German General Staff*, p. 153, and Carpentier, p. 110. See the criticism of this doctrine by Merignhac, *Les Lois de la Guerre Continentale suivant le Grand Etat-Major Allemand*, p. 33.

[2] *War Rights on Land*, p. 370.   [3] *Lois Actuelles*, p. 144.

for the use of army officers condemns it as irreconcilable with the rights of persons. "It is evident," says the French *manuel*, "that the person who is forced to guide or facilitate the expeditions of the enemy finds his patriotism cruelly undermined."[1] The British *manual* likewise pronounces it as contrary to Article 44 of the Hague convention.[2] Even some German writers condemn it as illegitimate.[3]

§ 402. Views of the Authorities. The Germans during the late war, of course, proceeded on their traditional theory as to the rights of a military occupant, and it must be admitted that the writers on international law recognize a fairly wide latitude to belligerents in respect to requisitions of labor and services of the inhabitants of occupied territory. Even Bonfils holds that "the inhabitants may be required by the enemy to transport by means of their own horses and vehicles necessary supplies for the army, the wounded, prisoners, and troops." Although of great use to the enemy who requires these services, he continues, they do not constitute direct and immediate participation in the operations of the war. And, he concludes, if a belligerent has a right to exact certain personal services, it must be admitted that he has a right to punish the inhabitants for refusing them.[4]

Lawrence likewise calls attention to the obvious fact that the line of demarcation between permissible and forbidden services is shadowy, "but," he adds, "the underlying principle is clear. To drive a herd of bullocks to a slaughter pen is a very different thing from driving an ammunition wagon into a field of conflict."[5] Holland points out that the substitution of the phrase *any operations of war* in article 23*h* of the convention of 1907 in the place of *military operations*, the language employed in the convention of 1899, increases the immunity of the inhabitants against the right of a belligerent to exact services of them,

[1] Art. 95.   [2] Art. 382, n. *d*.
[3] E.g., Loening, Strupp, Huber, Meurer, and Albert Zorn.
[4] *Droit Int. Pub.*, secs. 1147–1148 and 1150. Bonfils, however, strongly condemns the act of Count Renard, German prefect at Nancy, who in 1871 threatened to shoot a number of laborers in case his demand for 500 workmen to reconstruct a bridge was not complied with. But the *Kriegsbrauch im Landkriege* attempts to justify the threat on the ground that it accomplished the purpose desired without it being necessary to carry it out. Morgan, pp. 144–145. It is also defended by Strupp, *op. cit.*, p. 113.
[5] *Principles of Int. Law*, p. 419 (4th ed.).

since the former term includes many acts not amounting to what would be described as *military operations*. He adds, however, that the language is still ambiguous, and he raises, without answering, the query whether it would be lawful for a belligerent to compel hostile nationals to aid in the construction of urgent public works, such as the repair of roads and bridges.

The great majority of jurists and writers deny the right of a belligerent to compel persons of hostile nationality to work on the fortifications of the enemy.[1] For the same reason the compulsory digging of trenches must be condemned; so must the driving of ammunition wagons, the cutting of stone for trench supports, and the production of barbed wire for the erection of military defences. For still stronger reasons forced work in arsenals for the production of arms and munitions to be used against their own countrymen is forbidden. It may also be doubted whether forced labor in railway shops and in the operation of railway trains which are used by the enemy for the transportation of troops and military supplies is permissible. The line of demarcation between such services and work on fortifications is at best very shadowy, and there is no principle of logic or reason why a belligerent should be allowed to require the one and forbidden to exact the other. Indeed, under the conditions of modern warfare, work in wire and munition factories, in stone quarries, and in the railway service may be of infinitely greater value to a belligerent than the services which are expressly forbidden by the Hague con-

[1] Ferrand, p. 60. As is well known, charges were made against the Germans in 1870–1871 for compelling the French to work on fortifications and the care which Loening, the authors of the *Kriegsbrauch*, and others have taken to deny the charge shows that they did not recognize such acts as legitimate. Oppenheim holds that a belligerent may not only requisition drivers, guides, farriers, etc., but he may require "the execution of public works *necessary for military operations*, such as the building of *fortifications*, roads, bridges, soldiers' quarters, and the like." *International Law*, Vol. II, pp. 121–122. The British *Manual* (secs. 388 and 391), it may be remarked, recognizes a rather large right of requisition in respect to personal services, much larger in fact than that recognized by the French *Manuel*. Professional men and tradesmen, it says, such as surgeons, pharmacists, electricians, carpenters, butchers, bakers, etc., may be requisitioned for the needs of the army. Railway, telegraph, steamship employés, and the like, whether employed by the State or by private companies, it says, may be similarly requisitioned, provided the services required do not directly concern the operations of war against their own country. Likewise they may be requisitioned to repair roads, bridges, and railways in the interest of the general safety of the country, but not with the object of facilitating military operations.

vention. The services of the Belgian railway employés in particular were of great military value to the Germans, not only because they released an equivalent number of Germans and left them available for service in the army, but because, owing to the different construction of Belgian railway locomotives and railway machinery as compared with those in use in Germany, the operation of the Belgian lines by Germans was carried on with difficulty and resulted in numerous accidents. The service of Belgian engineers, machinists, and trainmen was, therefore, as necessary to the Germans as soldiers in the field. If this be true, on what principle could the Germans be allowed to requisition the services of the former and yet forbidden to impress the inhabitants to act as guides or to serve in their ranks? [1]

---

[1] The question of the right of a military occupant to compel railway employés to continue their work has been the subject of some discussion by writers on international law, but it appears to be still unsettled. Stein, an Austrian professor, submitted to the Institute of International Law in 1885 a proposed *règlement* dealing with railroads in time of war (*Annuaire*, Vol. VIII), Art. 9 of the proposed *règlement* affirmed that an occupant may force the officials and employés of state railroads to serve him and may punish them for disobeying. At the session of the Institute in 1888, M. Moynier presented a report on the matter which was adverse to Stein's conclusions. A new committee was appointed to consider the matter, but apparently nothing has come of it. M. Buzzati in a critical study of this report rejects the distinction between the employés of state railways and of private railways, but he is in accord with Stein in holding that they may be forced to obey the military occupant, though only *in case of emergency* (*Rev. de Droit Int. et de Lég. Comp.*, 1888, pp. 402–403). Ferrand, *Des Réquisitions*, p. 66, however, takes a contrary view. In consequence of the extensive use which is made by military occupants of railways to facilitate their operations, the exercise of compulsion upon the employés to assist in the movement of trains cannot, M. Ferrand thinks, be regarded as a simple measure of local administration. Pillet (*Les Lois Actuelles de la Guerre*, sec. 181) holds that an occupant is not bound to retain employés whom he finds in the railway service, but on the other hand, they ought to be allowed to abandon their employment whenever it is repugnant to their sentiments of patriotism to continue to serve an administration directed by the enemy.

CHAPTER XXVI

COLLECTIVE FINES AND COMMUNITY RESPONSIBILITY

§ 403. German Theory and Practice; § 404. German Policy during the War of 1870–1871; § 405. Fines Imposed on Belgian Towns and Cities during the Recent War; § 406. Proclamations Threatening Collective Punishment; § 407. Fines on French Towns and Cities; § 408. Views of German Jurists and Military Writers; § 409. The Rule of the Hague Convention; § 410. Interpretation of the Hague Rule; § 411. German Policy Criticised; § 412. Concluding Observations.

§ **403. German Theory and Practice.** The theory of collective responsibility for offences committed by the civilian population of occupied districts against the authority of the occupying belligerent was interpreted in a wider sense and applied on a more extensive scale by German military commanders during the recent war than was ever done in any war of the past. The punishments imposed in the application of the theory were unprecedented in number, sometimes novel in form, and often excessive in character. They consisted of pecuniary fines, the seizure and shooting of hostages, the burning of towns and villages, the destruction of private houses, the deportation of the civilian population, the commercial isolation of refractory towns, the interdiction of public charitable relief to the unemployed, the confinement of the inhabitants within doors for certain periods, and the like.[1]

As a general principle, the right of a military occupant to impose, under certain conditions, fines and other punishments upon communities for acts committed by the civilian population against his authority has long been recognized and acted upon in practice. Among the earlier instances of resort to such measures was the action of Napoleon who, during his occupation of Lombardy in 1796, announced that any district under his occupation in which fire-arms were found in possession of the inhabitants should be liable to a fine equal to one-third its

[1] Some of these measures are described in other chapters of this treatise. In the present chapter I have dealt mainly with the imposition of fines.

140

revenue. A like penalty was threatened against any village in which a French soldier had been killed, unless the individual perpetrator of the crime was arrested and delivered up to the local authorities.[1]

§ 404. German Policy during the War of 1870–1871. It was not until the Franco-German war of 1870–1871, however, that the theory of collective responsibility was applied on an extensive scale and interpreted to cover offences for which the population punished could not have been justly held responsible. In August, 1870, a general order was issued by the Prussian military authorities decreeing that French communes in which hostile acts were committed against their authority by persons not belonging to the French army should be liable to a fine equal to the amount of the local land tax, and that those communes from which individual offenders came should be liable to the same punishment.[2] In October of the same year it was announced that communes in which damage was done to railways, bridges, canals, and telegraph lines, even when the mischief was wrought by others than the local inhabitants and without their knowledge and connivance, should be held responsible for such acts.[3]

Those announcements turned out to be more than empty threats, for in fact huge fines were imposed and collected in many instances. Thus Lorraine, in addition to other penalties, was fined 10,000,000 francs for the destruction of a bridge with the alleged connivance of the inhabitants.[4] In June, 1871, the village of Bray was fined 37,500 francs, and hostages were taken to insure the payment of the fine.[5] Combles was required to pay 325,000 francs for a certain offence, and Driencourt was assessed 1000 francs because a stranger was found in the village.[6] The commune of Launois was forced to pay 10,000 francs to

---

[1] Hall, *Int. Law*, 4th ed., pp. 491 and 492.

[2] Concerning this order cf. Bonfils, *Droit Int.*, sec. 1219; Calvo, *Droit Int.*, sec. 2236; Spaight, *War Rights on Land*, pp. 408–409; Merignhac, *Lois et Coutumes de la Guerre sur Terre*, sec. 106; Nys, *Droit Int.*, Vol. III, p. 429; Despagnet, *Cours de Droit Int.*, sec. 589; Bluntschli, *Droit Int. Cod.*, sec. 643 bis. The text of the above-mentioned order may be found in the *Rev. de Droit Int. et de Lég. Comp.*, Vol. II, p. 666; cf. the defence of this order, by Loening, *ibid.*, Vol. V, p. 77.

[3] Edwards, *The Germans in France*, pp. 76, 211.

[4] Edmonds and Oppenheim, "The Laws and Usages of War" in the British *Manual of Military Law* (ed. of 1914), p. 305.

[5] Pradier-Fodéré, *Traité de Droit Int.*, Vol. VII, p. 281.   [6] *Ibid.*, p. 279.

the families of two Prussian dragoons who were alleged to have been killed by *francs-tireurs*.[1] Châtillon was fined 1,000,000 francs for the destruction of a bridge;[2] Etamps, 40,000 francs for the cutting of a telegraph wire,[3] and Orléans, 600,000 francs on account of the killing of a Prussian soldier by an unknown person during an altercation between himself and the soldier.[4] St. Germain was given the option of paying a fine of 100,000 francs or of being burned because three German dragoons had disappeared from the community.

In some instances exactions were levied which in form and pretext were fines, but which in reality were nothing else than contributions in disguise. The enormity of the amounts and their disproportion to the offences alleged would seem to leave no doubt as to this.[5] Thus the department of the Seine was assessed 24,000,000 francs, and Rouen was required to raise 6,500,000 francs within five days.[6] The departments of Aisne, Ardennes, and Aube were compelled to pay 3,000,000 francs as a punishment for the action of the French in taking as prisoners of war the crews of captured German merchant vessels and for expelling Germans from France. The departments of Meurthe, Meuse, and Seine-et-Marne were assessed 2,755,253 francs on the same account.[7] A contribution, which was intended as a punitive measure, was the levy in December, 1870, of twenty-five francs per capita on the inhabitants of all the occupied districts of France with the avowed purpose of breaking the resistance of the French people and of inducing them to sue for peace.[8]

[1] Spaight, *op. cit.*, p. 409.
[2] Bonfils, *op. cit.*, sec. 1219; Ferrand, *Des Réquisitions*, p. 239, and Guelle, *Précis des Lois de la Guerre*, Vol. II, p. 221. Guelle states that the village of Ham was fined 25,000 francs because the fortress was retaken from the Germans by a detachment of regular French troops. See also Latifi, *Effects of War on Private Property*, p. 34, and Rouard de Card, *La Guerre Continentale*, p. 178.
[3] Guelle, p. 221.
[4] Bonfils, *op. cit.*, sec. 1219, and Depambour, *L'Occupation en Temps de Guerre*, p. 119.
[5] Compare Guelle, Vol. II, p. 221.
[6] Depambour, p. 119, and Rouard de Card, p. 178.
[7] Calvo, *op. cit.*, Vol. IV, sec. 2236. Bismarck considered the action of the French to be a violation of international law, but as the law then stood, the crews of merchant vessels were liable to be treated as prisoners. Compare Edmonds and Oppenheim, in the British *Manual*, sec. 459, note *b*.
[8] Bonfils, sec. 1222, and Ferrand, *Des Réquisitions en Matière de Droit Int.*, p. 221.

Punishments other than fines were laid in some instances. Thus when the railroad bridge over the Moselle between Nancy and Toul was blown up, whether by civilian inhabitants or French troops is not clear, the town of Fontenoy was burned by the Germans.[1] At Charmes the town casino was burned as a punishment for the act of the inhabitants in firing upon the escort of a convoy of prisoners.[2]

The German theory of collective responsibility was applied by Lord Roberts and General Kitchener in the South African war, when communities were held responsible and were punished not only by heavy fines, but by wholesale burning of farms, the destruction of private houses, and the imprisonment of the leading inhabitants for damages committed upon railway and telegraph lines by "small parties of raiders." It is not clear whether the offenders were lawful belligerents or non-combatants; in the former case their acts were not violations of the laws of war, and therefore they were not legally punishable.[3] In any case, the measures resorted to were extremely severe and of very doubtful expediency, as such measures always are, because they tend to drive the enemy to desperation, embitter the whole population, and thus retard rather than hasten the termination of the war. Such measures were not resorted to during the Chino-Japanese, the Spanish-American, or the Russo-Japanese wars, and apparently not during the more recent Turco-Italian and Balkan wars.

§ 405. Fines Imposed on Belgian Towns and Cities during the Recent War. During the recent war the Germans, as already stated, extended the theory of collective responsibility and applied it on a larger scale and under a greater variety of forms than was ever done in any previous war.

The following instances, the facts regarding which seem to be sufficiently established, illustrate fairly well the German theory and practice.

[1] Spaight, p. 122, and Guelle, p. 221. Pillet (Le Droit de la Guerre, p. 236) declares that the bridge was destroyed, not by civilians, but by French troops; consequently, it was a legitimate act of warfare.

[2] Edmonds and Oppenheim, op. cit., p. 305, note b.

[3] Spaight, p. 124; Bordwell, p. 150. Cf. especially the proclamation of Lord Roberts of June 14, 1900, announcing that houses and farms in the vicinity of places where damage was done would be burned; and that of General Maxwell of June 15, 1900, declaring that in case telegraph wires were cut or railway bridges destroyed, the farm nearest the place where the act was committed would be burned.

In November, 1914, the city of Brussels was fined 5,000,000 francs by General von Leutwitz for the act of a policeman in attacking a German officer during the course of a dispute between the two, and for facilitating the escape of a prisoner.[1]

According to Belgian accounts the affair which led to the imposition of the fine grew out of the attempt of the German military authorities to prevent the sale of "contraband" newspapers. A German secret service agent, it appears, undertook to arrest certain Belgians for selling Dutch newspapers contrary to the regulations; the latter resisted arrest and were supported by the policeman in question who, it is alleged, attacked the German officer.

In April, 1915, Brussels was again fined 500,000 marks in consequence of the refusal of the municipal authorities to repair a road between Brussels and Malines. The municipal authorities protested that the road in question was outside the city limits, and that the funds of the city could not be spent on public works not within its jurisdiction. They also protested that the exaction was in reality a contribution, and that the military authorities had earlier engaged not to levy any further special contributions on the city. The general in command, however, maintained that the levy in question was a "fine" and not a "contribution," and therefore the pledge regarding contributions was inapplicable.[2] In July, 1915, Brussels was fined 5,000,000 marks in consequence of a "patriotic demonstration" by the inhabitants on July 21, the national holiday, the "moderate size of the fine imposed being due to the loyal coöperation of the municipal authorities in preserving order."[3] The mayor

---

[1] The notice imposing the fine was posted at Brussels, November 1, 1914. The text may be found in various collections of proclamations issued in Belgium, among others the report of the Belgian commission of inquiry. The notice states that the policeman in question was sentenced to imprisonment for a term of five years and that "The city of Brussels, excluding suburbs, has been punished for the crime committed by its policeman De Ryckere against a German soldier, by an additional fine of five million francs." Gibson, *Journal from Our Legation in Belgium*, p. 302.

[2] Brand Whitlock in *Everybody's Magazine*, August, 1918, p. 81.

[3] Lieutenant-General Hut, German governor of Brussels, in a letter to the mayor stated that the municipal authorities had given their approval to the regulations prohibiting all public demonstrations, meetings, processions, and display of flags on the fête day of July 21, but that in spite of this agreement, late in the evening disturbances were created by the distribution of tracts urging the people to disregard the regulations. During the evening Cardinal Mercier drove through the

addressed a protest to the governor-general, von Bissing, in which he denied the right of a military occupant to punish the civil population for manifesting their sentiments of patriotism on the occasion of the celebration of their national independence, but it had no effect.[1]

Early in 1916 Brussels was fined 500,000 marks and the suburb of Schaerbeek 50,000 marks in consequence of the murder by an unknown person of a young Belgian in the latter commune on the night of January 6. Brussels was held partly responsible, because the crime was alleged to have been committed with a revolver obtained in that city, notwithstanding the fact that the German authorities had, on January 1, issued a proclamation requiring all persons to deliver up their firearms and munitions at the city hall and threatening with the death penalty those found with arms in their possessions after a fixed date. Finally, in March, 1918, Brussels was reported to have again been fined 2,000,000 marks on account of a demonstration of certain anti-Flemish agitators.[2]

Numerous towns and cities were fined for the alleged firing by *francs-tireurs* and civilians upon German troops and for other offences against the occupying authorities. Thus Louvain was fined 20,000,000 francs in consequence of shots alleged to have been fired by civilians.[3]

---

streets, and his appearance led to demonstrations "which were contrary to the German regulations and which had the effect of inciting the people to rebellion or foolish deeds." "No occupying power," said General Hut in his letter to the mayor, "would bear a similar challenge. I therefore proposed to the governor-general to fine the community. The governor accepted the proposal and imposed a fine of 5,000,000 marks. The governor remarked: 'It is only in consideration of the loyal coöperation of the municipal authorities in preserving order that the fine is laid so moderate.'" Massart (*Belgians under the German Eagle*, p. 275) says the Germans even went to the length of announcing that the closing of stores on the national holiday would be regarded as a forbidden "demonstration," but this portion of the order they were unable to enforce in Brussels or elsewhere.

[1] The town of Lierre was fined 57,500 francs for a similar "demonstration" on the same day, the chief offence, it is alleged, being the raising of a Belgian tricolor on the top of an oak tree.

[2] Amsterdam despatch of March 23 (New York *Times*, March 24, 1918). In August, 1918, the bodies of two German soldiers who had been assassinated in the woods near Brussels were found, whereupon the German authorities notified the municipal authorities that the city would be fined unless the murderers were arrested.

[3] The German white book, *Die Völkerrechtswidrige Führung des Belgischen Volkskriegs*, p. 241, says, however, that it was impossible to collect this fine.

A levy of 60,000,000 francs was made upon the province of Liège shortly after it fell under the occupation of the Germans, but it is not quite clear whether it was intended as a fine or a contribution.[1] Subsequently a levy of 10,000,000 francs was imposed on the city of Liège in consequence of the alleged firing of shots from private houses upon German troops. In August, 1918, Liège was again fined 500,000 francs for the refusal of the municipal authorities to obey a German order directing the demolition of certain buildings that had been damaged by fire.[2] Mons was compelled to pay 100,000 francs for the firing by an unknown person upon a German soldier, and the town was threatened with another fine in case a certain Englishman should be found within its limits.[3] In April, 1917, Mons was ordered to furnish 600 young Belgians for compulsory labor, and the city was notified that it would be fined 300 marks for every man not furnished. In June, 1917, Mons, according to the press despatches, was fined 500,000 francs because a Belgian paper published in Holland stated that the crown prince Rupprecht of Bavaria was in Mons when the city was bombarded by allied airmen.[4]

Tournai is said to have been fined 3,000,000 francs for the killing of an Uhlan.[5] Merris and La Gorgue were each fined 50,000 francs for the firing of shots at German troops; the village of Marson (population 300), 3000 francs, and the commune of Warnelon, 10,000 francs for similar offences.[6] The commune of Cortemarck was fined 5000 marks on the pretext that one of the inhabitants had committed espionage by making signals to the enemy.[7]

[1] It is variously described in the press despatches as a "fine," a "contribution," and a "war levy." It makes little difference whether technically it was a fine or a contribution, for, as stated above, many of the "fines" imposed by the Germans were in fact "contributions" in disguise.

[2] New York *Times*, August 4, 1918, on the authority of the *Echo de Belge*.

[3] Massart, *Belgians under the German Eagle*, p. 147.

[4] New York *Times*, June 8, 1917, despatch from Amsterdam. Were there not clearly established instances of the imposition of fines by the Germans in other cases where the element of community guilt was totally lacking, one would be inclined to regard this allegation as a joke.

[5] London *Times*, September 25, 1914.

[6] Ferrand, *Des Réquisitions en Matière de Droit Int.* (1917), p. 41, and Morgan, *German Atrocities*, p. 85.

[7] Text of the notice in Massart, p. 153. The curé and the vicar of the commune were held "responsible for the members of the parish" and were punished by deportation to Germany.

On January 16, 1915, the Belgian legation at Washington issued a public statement charging the Germans with having imposed a fine of 10,000,000 francs on the city of Courtrai, not for the disobedience of the inhabitants, but for obeying the orders of the military commander.[1]

For the cutting of a telephone wire by an unknown person at Arlon, the town was fined 100,000 francs and given four hours in which to raise the amount, in default of which 100 houses were to be pillaged. Before the sum was raised 47 houses are alleged to have been sacked.[2] The commune of Puers was fined 3000 francs for a similar offence. Other towns fined on the charge that the telegraph or telephone systems "did not work properly" were Ghent, 100,000 marks; Ledebourg, 5000 marks; Selzaete, 150,000 francs; Destelbergen, 30,000 marks; Schellebelle, 50,000 marks; Sweveghem, 4900 marks; Winckel Sainte-Croix, 300 marks, and Wachtebeke, 3000 marks.[3] Seraing was fined because a bomb had burst within the limits of the commune, and Eppeghem was fined 10,000 francs on the charge that a peasant had fired a shot at a hare or a pigeon.[4]

A fine of 20,000 marks was imposed on the town of Malines for the neglect of the mayor to notify the military authorities of a journey which Cardinal Mercier had made in violation of the German regulations concerning the circulation of automobiles.[5] The same town was threatened with a fine in case

[1] Gomery, *op. cit.*, p. 201. According to the Belgian version, the inhabitants had been ordered by two German officers shortly after the occupation of the city to deliver up their arms in the tower of Broel. Subsequently a new commander arrived who charged that the arms had been clandestinely deposited at the tower without instructions from the military authorities. The city was thereupon fined 10,000,000 francs. Von Mach (*Germany's Point of View*, p. 195) ridicules the Belgian explanation and defends the imposition of the fine as a legitimate and humane punishment.

[2] Reports on Violations of the Laws and Customs of War in Belgium, preface by J. Van den Heuvel, p. 24; also p. 58; cf. also Saint Yves, *Les Responsabilités de l'Allemagne dans la Guerre de 1914*, p. 385.

[3] Massart, p. 146, quoting the *Nieuwe Rotterdamsche Courant* of January 30, 1915, and Gomery, *op. cit.*, p. 200. The hamlet of Hornbeck, near Malines, was twice fined 3000 marks on account of the cutting of a telephone wire. The Belgians claim that the burgomaster organized a night watch which caught a German soldier attempting to cut the wire, and when the return of the fine was demanded, the German commander imposed a third fine of 3000 marks for the act of the mayor in organizing a night watch without the permission of the German authorities.

[4] Massart, pp. 147-148.

[5] Annex IV to Cardinal Mercier's address to the cardinals, archbishops, and bishops of Germany, Bavaria, and Austria-Hungary, published in a brochure entitled *An Appeal to Truth*, p. 26.

the authorities did not furnish the Germans within 24 hours with a list of the employés of the railway administration in order that they might be requisitioned for labor.[1]

Antwerp is said to have been fined 50,000 francs because an unknown person altered the letters in a public notice posted by the Germans announcing the capture of 52,000 Russians and 400 guns, so as to make it read "52,000 sparrows and 400 nuns."[2] Tilsbury was fined for a somewhat similar offence alleged to have been committed by street gamins. Antwerp was later fined 120,000 marks for refusing to assist in the reconstruction of certain buildings destroyed by the Germans. In July, 1918, Antwerp is said to have been fined 1,000,000 francs and the burgomaster was deported in consequence of certain anti-German activities in the city. The village of Wellen was fined 120,000 marks for having failed to furnish its quota of requisitioned wheat; Zele in East Flanders was fined 80,000 marks for giving food and cigarettes to English prisoners who were passing through the town; Ghent and Ledeberg were fined each 10,000 marks in August, 1918, on account of alleged damages done to the railroads.

The village of Grenbergen was assessed 5000 francs because an inhabitant allowed his pigeons to fly in violation of the military regulations.[3] Ostend was fined 1,000,000 marks on the pretext that a pigeon shot by the Germans had on it a letter which was being despatched from Ostend.[4] Assche, Battice, Aeltre, and Wynghone were fined for various offences.

On August 22, 1914, General von Neiber imposed a fine of 3,000,000 francs on the town of Wavre (population 8500) for the "unqualified behavior, contrary to the law of nations and the usages of war, of the inhabitants in making a surprise attack on the German troops." The town was given a week in which to raise the amount. In a letter of August 27, General von Neiber informed the mayor as follows:

"I draw the attention of the town to the fact that in no case can it count on further delay, as the civil population has put itself outside the law of nations by firing on the German troops. The city will be burned and

[1] The mayor replied that the local authorities, not being charged with the administration of the railways, did not possess the information demanded.
[2] Massart, p. 148; Gomery, p. 200; *Cahiers Documentaires*, 2d Ser., No. 33 (March 19, 1915).
[3] Massart, p. 147.   [4] Gomery, p. 200.

destroyed if the fine is not paid in due time, without regard for any one; the innocent will suffer with the guilty." [1]

The Belgian accounts state that in consequence of the inability of the town to raise the amount a large number of houses were burnt.[2] Professor Waxweiler affirms that the civilian population took no part in the hostilities, and that a medical inquiry established the fact that the German soldier who had been wounded during the course of the affair received his wound from a German bullet.[3]

Lessines is alleged to have been subjected to a "heavy fine" because the women of the town declined to do military work for the Germans. Other towns were fined or otherwise punished for the refusal of the inhabitants to perform what the Belgians regarded as military work or for attempting to dissuade their fellow citizens from performing such labor. In November, 1917, a fine of 10,000 francs is alleged to have been imposed by the German authorities on the province of East Flanders for its failure to furnish 40,000 laborers whose services had been requisitioned.[4] Communal fines (10,000 francs in each case) were also threatened for the failure of the owners of horses to bring in their animals at the direction of German agents who were sent to Belgium to requisition horses for transportation to Germany. Besides, an individual fine of 500 francs was to be imposed upon each owner who refused to comply with the order.[5]

During the autumn of 1916 many towns and communes were fined in consequence of the refusal of the civil authorities to furnish the Germans with lists of the "unemployed" whom the military authorities were then deporting in large numbers to Germany for compulsory labor. Bruges was threatened with a fine of 150,000 marks for each day's delay in furnishing such a list. The authorities refused to furnish the list, and

---

[1] Text in Belgian reports on Violations, etc., p. 37. Cf. also Dampierre, *L'Allemagne et le Droit des Gens*, p. 148, and Saint Yves, *op. cit.*, p. 385. Some of the accounts say that the fine was imposed by General von Bülow.

[2] *Facts about Belgium*, p. 7; Gomery, p. 199. Grasshoff, a German writer (*The Tragedy of Belgium*, p. 173), alleges, however, that the threat was not executed, and that the city was spared from burning.

[3] *Belgium, Neutral and Loyal*, p. 281.

[4] Amsterdam despatch, New York *Times*, November 6, 1917.

[5] Ferrand, *Des Réquisitions*, p. 437.

the fine was imposed and paid.[1] Bruges was later fined 500,000 francs on account of the soiling of the German flag by two children [2] and on another occasion 100,000 marks in consequence of a demonstration at the railway station where some Belgian prisoners were waiting. Tournai, which had already in 1914 been fined 3,000,000 francs for the alleged killing of a German Uhlan, was now assessed 200,000 marks for the refusal of the civil authorities to furnish the Germans with a list of all male inhabitants of the town, and a further fine of 20,000 marks was threatened for each day's delay in the furnishing of the information demanded.[3]

§ 406. **Proclamations Threatening Collective Punishment.** Many proclamations were issued by the German military authorities announcing that communities would be held responsible for acts of hostility committed by individual Belgians. Thus on September 25, 1914, General von der Goltz issued a proclamation at Brussels in which, adverting to certain alleged surprise attacks by the inhabitants upon German convoys and patrols, he gave warning that a register was being kept of the localities in the neighborhood of which such attacks had taken place, and that they might expect their punishment as soon as the German troops arrived.[4]

On October 5 the general issued another proclamation in which, referring to the cutting of the railway and telegraph line between Lovenjoul and Vertryck, both of which towns had been compelled to "give an account," he announced that in the future the places nearest the spot where such acts had taken place, whether the inhabitants were accomplices or not, would be punished without pity.[5] Other proclamations were issued from time to time announcing that villages in which hostile acts were committed would be burned; that they would be held responsible for the destruction of railways, bridges, etc.; that collective punishments would be inflicted without mercy, and the like. On August 17, 1914, the mayor of Hasselt was compelled to post a proclamation warning the inhabitants against acts of hostility and notifying them that "in case of the

---

[1] London *Times* (weekly ed.), November 3, 1916.   [2] Gomery, p. 200.
[3] New York *Times*, November 18, 1916.
[4] Text in reports on the Violations of the Rights of Nations in Belgium, p. 41; also Waxweiler, *Belgium, Neutral and Loyal*, p. 282.
[5] Text in Waxweiler, p. 282; also in *Arrêtés et Procs.*, pp. 21-22.

inhabitants' firing on the soldiers of the German army one-third of the male population will be shot." [1]

On October 15, 1914, Colonel Schmidhuber issued a proclamation at Lille threatening with the penalty of death all persons guilty of destroying or damaging bridges, canals, railroads, telegraphs, etc., and announcing that the communes in which such acts were committed, *as well as those to which the guilty parties belonged* would be punished in each case by a fine equal to the amount of their annual land tax.[2]

On December 23, 1914, a proclamation was posted at Brussels announcing that "in case the graves of dead soldiers are damaged or violated, not only will the perpetrator be punished but the commune will be held responsible." Many other similar proclamations might be quoted. Those mentioned illustrate fairly enough the German theory and practice in respect to collective responsibility.

By a notice posted on October 7, 1914,[3] the principle of collective responsibility was applied to the family. After calling attention to an alleged order of the Belgian government summoning the militia to join the army, the notice declared that "all those who receive these orders are strictly forbidden to obey them. . . . In case of disobedience the families of the militiamen will be held responsible." A somewhat similar notice was issued on June 26, 1915, giving warning that families would be held responsible in case any member between the ages of sixteen and forty, fit for military service, should be found guilty of joining the Belgian army.[4]

§ 407. **Fines on French Towns and Cities.** In the occupied districts of France the same policy was followed by the Germans, and many towns and communes were fined for acts alleged to have been committed by the inhabitants against the authority of the occupying forces. Thus in August, 1914, the commune of Lunéville was fined 650,000 francs for an alleged attack by

---

[1] Text in Dampierre, *German Imperialism and International Law*, p. 229.

[2] Text in Fage, *Lille sous la Griffe Allemande*, p. 33. See also a proclamation of General Heinrich of Oct. 29, 1914, threatening to hold the city of Lille responsible for various acts committed by individuals, *Ibid.*, p. 35.

[3] Text in *Arrêtés et Procs.*, pp. 22–23.

[4] Massart, pp. 315 ff., calls attention to various instances in which Belgian mothers were imprisoned for the acts of their sons in joining the army or for refusing to inform upon them.

certain of the inhabitants on the German troops.[1] The French
authorities, however, emphatically denied the truth of the charge
and accused the Germans not only of having themselves fired
the shots complained of, but also of having massacred 18 inhabitants of the town and burned 70 houses.

Upon the occupation of Rheims the Germans levied an "exorbitant indemnity" on the city, but it is not clear whether it
was intended as a fine or a contribution. The amount was
finally cut down to 150,000 francs in gold and a quantity
of supplies to the value of 800,000 francs. Hostages were
taken to insure the payment within four days of the sum
required.[2]

The commune of Sissonne (population 1500) was fined 500,000
francs in September, 1914, on the charge that the road between
Sissonne and Montaigu had been strewn with broken glass for
the purpose of impeding automobile traffic.[3] The town being
unable to raise the full amount, General von Bülow sent messen-
gers to the Prince of Monaco, who owned a château near by
filled with valuable works of art and family heirlooms, to notify
him that unless he paid the fine, the château and the adjoining
village, as well as Sissonne, would be destroyed on November 1.
The Prince replied that he was unwilling to pay the fine, but
would pledge his word to the German Emperor that in case no
intentional damage were done to the château or the two communes, he would remit to the Emperor the unpaid balance at
the end of the war. It appears that through the good offices
of the American and Spanish ambassadors at Paris the matter
was adjusted, and the château and villages were saved.[4]

Lille was fined 500,000 francs because the inhabitants made

[1] The text of notice imposing the fine may be found in the Report of the French
official commission of inquiry on violations of international law in French territory
occupied by the enemy, *Journal Officiel*, January 8, 1915. A facsimile reproduction in French may be found in a collection entitled *Scraps of Paper: German
Proclamations in Belgium and France* (p. 11), published by Hodder and Stoughton,
London, 1917; in Dampierre, *L'Allemagne et le Droit des Gens*, p. 149, and in various
other publications.

[2] Wood, *The Note Book of an Attaché*, p. 168.

[3] Text of the order imposing the fine in the pamphlet *German War Practices*
(p. 45), issued by the United States Committee on Public Information.

[4] See the text of ambassador Herrick's despatch of October 27, 1914, to the
secretary of state and the texts of two letters of October 22 to the German Emperor and General von Bülow in *German War Practices* (pp. 45–47), referred to in
the preceding footnote.

a demonstration of sympathy for a detachment of French prisoners who were being escorted through the streets by a German military guard. The city was allowed one week in which to raise the amount of the fine.[1] Valenciennes was reported to have been fined 3,000,000 francs, two-thirds of which were imposed in consequence of the seizure of a song entitled "William's Last Will and Testament," which was considered as disrespectful to the Emperor; the remainder, because of the failure of the town to deliver a quantity of flour requisitioned by the military authorities.[2]

The town of Epernay was fined 176,560 francs in September, 1914, for not having delivered within the time specified certain supplies which the German military authorities had requisitioned for the use of their troops. The notice of the fine was accompanied by a threat to "take the most rigorous proceedings against the population itself and to conduct forcible requisitions in the houses of the inhabitants" in case the amount was not paid on the following day. The mayor protested against the fine on the ground that certain supplies requisitioned (notably 12,000 kilograms of salted bacon) were not to be found in the town, although he had used all his endeavors to procure them. The German authorities could not, however, be induced to relinquish the fine or reduce the amount, and an appeal was made by the mayor to the inhabitants to raise the sum demanded.[3] The amount was collected and turned over to the German authorities at 5 o'clock on the day fixed. Erbéviller and other places were fined on the charge that shots were fired by civilians at German soldiers.[4] As in Belgium, punishments other than pecuniary fines were laid upon French towns in various in-

---

[1] Press despatches of March 12, 1915. The department of the Nord had already been subjected to a contribution of 15,000,000 francs, in addition to a monthly contribution of 2,000,000 francs. About half of the burden fell upon Lille. See a book entitled *Lille sous le Joug Allemand* (Paris, 1916), p. 4. The text of General von Heinrich's proclamation imposing the fine of 500,000 francs on Lille may be found in Fage, *op. cit.*, p. 270. The Commune of Rouchin, near Lille, was fined 10,000 marks by von Heinrich because a crime had been committed within its territory and the offender had not been apprehended. *Ibid.*, p. 98.

[2] Maccas, *op. cit.*, p. 208. Large sums were also exacted of Tourcoing, Roubaix, and Armentières, but they appear to have been regarded by the Germans as contributions rather than fines.

[3] Facsimile reproduction of the order in *Scraps of Paper*, etc., p. 23; cf. also Matot, *Reims et la Marne, Almanach de la Guerre*, p. 169.

[4] Saint Yves, *op. cit.*, p. 387.

stances.[1] The theory of collective responsibility for individual offences was frequently enunciated in public proclamations. Thus by a proclamation of General von Bülow, issued at Noyon in the spring of 1916, mayors and magistrates were notified that towns and villages would be held responsible and would be heavily fined in case fire-arms were found after a certain date in the possession of any inhabitant.[2]

In other territories occupied by the Germans, notably Russia and Roumania, the policy of collective responsibility and punishment was applied as in Belgium and France.[3]

§ 408. **Views of German Jurists and Military Writers.** The great majority of American, English, and French writers on international law have condemned as arbitrary and contrary to the elementary principles of justice the theory of collective responsibility as it was applied by the Germans in many instances during the war of 1870-1871, particularly where it was applied to districts other than those in which the offence was committed, where the amount of the fine was out of all proportion to the gravity of the offence, where the acts complained of were committed not by the civilian population but by the regular troops of the enemy, as appears to have sometimes been the case, and where the fines levied were imposed for the psychological purpose of inducing the population to cease their resistance and sue for peace.[4]

---

[1] Thus the entire population of Roulers was compelled to remain indoors from 2 P.M. until 8 P.M. every day for three weeks, because one of the inhabitants was found guilty of giving food to Russian prisoners employed by the Germans at work in the vicinity of the town. London *Times* (weekly ed.), June 23, 1916, quoting from the Amsterdam *Telegraf*.

[2] Text in New York *Times Magazine*, July 22, 1917.

[3] Thus Windau was fined 50,000 rubles, Vilna 75,000 marks, Craiova 50,000,000 francs, Bucharest 50,000,000 francs, Warsaw 250,000 marks, Libau 500,000 rubles, etc. London *Times* (weekly ed.), December 15, 1916; New York *Times*, June 26, 1917; 42 Clunet, 277.

[4] Cf., for example, Bordwell, *Law of War*, p. 317; Lawrence, *Principles*, p. 448; Spaight, *op. cit.*, p. 408; Westlake, *Int. Law*, Vol. II, p. 96; Bonfils, *op. cit.*, sec. 1219; Despagnet, *op. cit.*, sec. 589; Ferrand, *Des Réquisitions*, pp. 239 ff.; Feraud-Giraud, *Des Réquisitions Militaires*, p. 17; Merignhac, *Les Lois et Coutumes*, sec. 106; Nys, *Droit Int.*, Vol. III, p. 429; Guelle, *Précis*, Vol. II, p. 219; Latifi, *op. cit.*, p. 34; Pillet, *Le Droit de la Guerre*, pp. 234 ff. Cf. also Calvo, *op. cit.*, Vol. IV, sec. 2172, and G. F. de Martens, *Traité*, Vol. III, p. 265. Rolin Jacquemyns, a Belgian jurist, defends in general the German policy of 1870-1871, although he condemns as unjustifiable the punishment of communes other than those in which offences were committed. *Rev. de Droit Int. et de Lég. Comp.*, Vol. II, pp. 666 ff., and Vol. III, pp. 311 ff.

Even a few German writers, such as Bluntschli,[1] Gefficken,[2] Loening,[3] and apparently Albert Zorn, admit that in some instances the German commanders pushed the theory of collective responsibility too far. The majority of German writers, however, have attempted to justify without exception the punitive measures resorted to by the German commanders in 1870–1871. Leuder found a justification in the embittered character which the war took on in its later stages and in the determined resistance of the French people after it had become evident that their success was hopeless,[4] and this defence is relied upon by the *Kriegsbrauch im Landkriege*, which adds that experience shows pecuniary penalties to be the most effective means of insuring the obedience of the civil population.[5] Regarding the charge that the amount of the fines levied was excessive in many instances, Leuder remarks that the promptness with which they were paid is evidence enough that they were "in truth not too exorbitant."[6] He even goes to the length of holding that communities may be fined for the continued persistence of the inhabitants in keeping up a struggle in which there is no hope of success (*durch frivol fortgesetze Kriege*).[7] The 25-franc per capita levy for breaking the resistance of the French was therefore a justifiable measure.[8]

[1] *Droit Int. Cod.* (Fr. trans. by Lardy), sec. 643 bis.

[2] See his note (No. 7) to sec. 126 of Heffter.

[3] See his article *L'Administration du Gouvernement-Général de l'Alsace durant la Guerre de 1870–71* in the *Rev. de Droit Int. et de Lég. Comp.*, Vol. V (1873), p. 77. Loening defends the action of the Germans in imposing a fine equal to the amount of the local land tax on districts in which offences were committed against the safety of the German army by persons not belonging to the French army. The effect, he says, was "remarkable" and was the means of preventing many wrongs. "It therefore marked a great progress in the penal law of war." He also defends the 25-franc per capita levy for the purpose of breaking the resistance of the French and bringing pressure on them to sue for peace. But the Germans went too far, he says, when they extended the principle of collective responsibility to communes from which the offenders came, because in most cases there was no relation between the offence and the commune punished.

[4] Holtzendorff, *Handbuch des Völkerrechts*, Vol. IV, p. 508; cf. also sec. 112, n. 14 (p. 473).

[5] Morgan, *The War Book of the German General Staff*, p. 178. Both Leuder and the general staff assert that the fines levied by the Germans were small in comparison with the contributions extorted by Napoleon.

[6] *Op. cit.*, p. 509.

[7] *Ibid.*, p. 505. See Westlake's comment on this doctrine in his *Collected Papers on International Law*, p. 251.

[8] *Ibid.*, p. 510. Lammasch at the First Hague Conference likewise defended the theory that money contributions may be levied for the purpose of exercising pressure upon the inhabitants to sue for peace. Ferrand, *Des Réquisitions*, p. 229.

Finally, Leuder, Loening, and the *Kriegsbrauch im Landkriege* defend the policy of pecuniary penalties as applied in 1870–1871 on the ground that it was successful in deterring the civil population from persisting in their resistance to the authority of the enemy — a very doubtful justification, because if the test of the legitimacy of an instrument or a measure be merely its success, few instrumentalities or methods would be unlawful. But Bluntschli,[1] Von Liszt,[2] Albert Zorn,[3] Meurer,[4] and Wehberg[5] very properly, it would seem, limit the right of collective punishment to communities and individuals who facilitate the commission of crimes against the authority of the occupying belligerent, or who fail to prevent them when it is possible to do so.

§ 409. The Rule of the Hague Convention. The right of a military occupant to the unqualified obedience of the inhabitants over whom his authority has been effectively established is recognized by all writers on international law, and it is clearly affirmed by the Hague convention respecting the laws and customs of war. The principle has also long been recognized, and it is affirmed inferentially by the above-mentioned Hague convention (article 50) that he may hold the entire population responsible under certain conditions for acts committed against his authority[6] by persons not belonging to the armed forces of the enemy and may punish the community by fines or otherwise for such acts. This right, however, is not unlimited. It is subject to certain well-recognized limitations and restrictions and cannot be exercised arbitrarily at the will of the commander. Article 50 of the Hague convention referred to above declares that "no general penalty (*peine*), pecuniary or other, shall be inflicted upon the population on account of acts of individuals

---

[1] *Op. cit.*, sec. 643 bis.

[2] *Das Völkerrecht*, p. 340.

[3] *Das Kriegsrecht zu Land*, p. 242. Zorn, like Loening, apparently disapproves the punishment of communes other than those in which the offence was actually committed.

[4] *Das Kriegsrecht der Zweiter Haager Konferenz*, p. 286.

[5] *Capture in War*, p. 48.

[6] There is a difference of opinion as to whether the right of punishment is limited to offences in violation of the laws and customs of war. Bordwell (p. 316) thinks it is so limited, but Spaight (p. 408) holds otherwise and affirms that it extends to all acts forbidden by the occupying authorities, whether they are infractions of war law or not.

for which they cannot be regarded as jointly and severally responsible (*solidairement responsables*)." [1]

§ 410. **Interpretation of the Hague Rules.** This rule is incorporated in the war manuals of the United States, Great Britain, and France in the identical language in which it was formulated by the Hague conference.[2] Unfortunately the convention does not define the elements of responsibility, and military commanders, therefore, are left to judge for themselves in each specific case whether the act is or is not one for which the community can be properly held responsible. But the determination of the fact of responsibility is obviously governed by certain well-established principles, one of which, it would seem, is that the community is not really responsible unless the population as a whole is a party to the offence, either actively or passively. The American *Rules* interpret the provision to forbid collective punishments, except for such offences "as the community has committed or permitted to be committed," the inference being that the community cannot be punished for individual acts for which it was not actually responsible. If the offence has been committed by isolated individuals in remote parts of the community, without the knowledge or approval of the public authorities or of the population, and which therefore the authorities could not have prevented, it would seem unreasonable and contrary to one of the oldest rules of the criminal law to impute guilt or responsibility to the whole population.[3] Likewise, if the authorities have exercised

---

[1] The word *amende* employed in the Brussels Declaration was rejected by the Hague conference for the term *peine* on the ground that the use of the former term involved a confusion of ideas of the criminal law with those of international law. Cf. Albert Zorn, *op. cit.*, p. 240, and Meurer, *op. cit.*, p. 287. The change, however, has been criticised by some writers because the word *amende*, it is said, has a clear and definite meaning in international law. Cf. Pont, *Les Réquisitions*, p. 92, and Merignhac, *Les Lois et Coutumes de la Guerre sur Terre*, p. 290.

[2] United States *Rules of Land Warfare*, art. 354; British *Manual*, art. 385; French *Manual*, art. 109.

[3] Commenting on art. 50, Lawrence (*Principles of International Law*, p. 447) remarks that it allows inferentially pecuniary penalties upon communities when the responsibility can be brought home. "If a detachment occupying a village," he says, "were slaughtered in the night while asleep, few would argue that the community had no collective responsibility if a conspiracy of silence should baffle all attempts to discover the real perpetrators. On the other hand, if a train were derailed in the night while passing through a wild ravine far from human habitation, it would be wrong to hold that the population for miles around could have known of the deed and have assisted in it directly or indirectly."

reasonable diligence to prevent the act, and if they have exerted themselves to discover and punish the actual perpetrators, it hardly seems reasonable or just to say that the community is really responsible. To so hold is to insist that the public authorities are obliged to guarantee the perfect enforcement of the law, something which no community has ever in fact been able to do.

Nys remarks that collective responsibility exists only when the offence is imputable to all the inhabitants, as in the case of public injuries to the occupying force, manifestations of revolt, and the like, or when the population by its attitude and will opposes an investigation.[1] Nys even contends that community fines may not be justly levied for the acts of a few isolated individuals. Such fines, he says, may be imposed only where the whole population is guilty, and this guilt must be proven by the military authorities. He repudiates Loening's view that no obligation rests upon the military authorities to establish the guilt of the inhabitants, and also the doctrine of Loening, Leuder, and others that the effectiveness of pecuniary punishment in preventing a repetition of the acts is a sufficient justification for the resort to collective penalties.[2] The purpose of article 50, as Spaight remarks, was to confine collective punishment to such offences as the community has either committed or has allowed to be committed.[3] Bonfils interprets the meaning of the article in a similar sense. A fine, he says, must be in its *quantum* proportionate to the gravity of the offence; it must bear only upon the offender and his accomplices; it is iniquitous when it falls upon the innocent who were not able to foresee the act, nor to prevent it, nor to discover the offender.[4]

---

[1] *Le Droit International*, Vol. III, p. 429. Cf. also Brenet, *La France et Allemagne devant le Droit International pendant leurs Opérations de la Guerre 1870-71*, p. 197, and Westlake (*op. cit.*, Vol. II, p. 106), who remarks that no fine is justifiable except where the responsibility can "justly be imputed to the inhabitants."

[2] Cf. his article on *Contributions et Réquisitions* in the *Revue de Droit Int. et de Lég. Comp.*, Vol. 38 (1906), p. 430. Cf. also Merignhac (*op. cit.*, p. 282), who contends that contributions under the form of fines can be levied only on offenders and their accomplices, and that they are illegal when they fall upon innocent persons, whatever the motive for which they are levied.

[3] *Op. cit.*, p. 408.

[4] *Op. cit.*, sec. 1218. To the same effect cf. also Despagnet, *op. cit.*, secs. 587-588; Feraud-Giraud, *op. cit.*, p. 17, and Bordwell, *op. cit.*, p. 317, who remarks that collective punishment is permissible only when the community could and should have prevented the act.

§ 411. **German Policy Criticised.** If, in the main, the principles thus laid down regarding the nature and limits of collective responsibility be admitted as sound, it is difficult to justify many of the impositions levied by German military commanders during the late war. Again and again they imposed fines which would seem to have been out of proportion to the gravity of the offences alleged and in some cases quite beyond the ability of the impoverished inhabitants to pay. It has been asserted that this was true of the levy of 60,000,000 francs on Liège (it matters little whether it was technically a contribution or a fine), a sum which amounted to about 300 francs per capita of the population; of the levy of 50,000,000 francs on Craiova, a town of only 52,000 inhabitants; of the fine of 10,000,000 francs on Courtrai; of the 100,000-franc fine on Mons; of the fine of 3,000,000 francs on Tournai; of the fine of 3,000,000 francs on the village of Wavre, and various others. It must also be remembered that in a number of instances these impositions were in addition to other heavy exactions in the form of requisitions, contributions, and tax levies. Sometimes the offences alleged were inconsequential acts committed by isolated individuals and involved no military injury or evidence of organized hostility to the authority of the occupying forces. Some of them, indeed, were so obviously mere pretexts that the exactions imposed were, as has been said, nothing more than contributions under the guise of fines. Some writers hold, and very properly, that such impositions do not differ from pillage except in name, and are therefore forbidden by international law.[1]

In other cases the fines imposed can be justified only on a theory of collective responsibility which is rejected by the great majority of writers, and which hardly seems in accord with reason or justice. Such a case was the fine of 5,000,000 francs on Brussels for the act of a police constable. The affair was one of which the population had no knowledge; they were neither active nor passive accomplices; nor was the act one which the authorities could have prevented, because they could not have foreseen it. It was an isolated individual offence, and the offender was promptly arrested by the German authorities

---

[1] Cf. Latifi, *Effects of War on Property*, p. 34, and Bluntschli, *Droit Int. Cod.*, sec. 654.

and punished by a term of imprisonment. It is difficult to understand the process of reasoning by which responsibility for an act of this kind could be imputed to the whole population. The fine was, therefore, nothing more than a contribution in disguise and involved no question of community responsibility.

The legality of the fine of 5,000,000 francs laid on Brussels in consequence of the popular demonstration on the national holiday and the subsequent fine of 2,000,000 francs on account of an anti-Flemish demonstration has been denied by the Belgian writers on the ground that a military occupant has no lawful right to repress by huge fines the manifestation by the inhabitants of their patriotic sentiments. It can hardly be contended, however, that if acts of this kind amount in fact to open manifestations of hostility toward the occupying power, or if they are accompanied by public disorders, they may not be repressed or punished by means of fines.

The 500,000-franc fine levied on Brussels in consequence of the crime of murder by an unknown person in the suburb of Schaerbeek — this on the assumption that the weapon used had been procured in Brussels, where the possession of fire-arms by the inhabitants had been forbidden by the military authorities certainly involved a wide extension of the theory of collective responsibility. The local civil authorities had issued a proclamation directing the people to bring in their fire-arms and deposit them at the city hall and warning them of the severe penalties to which they were liable in case of non-compliance with the orders of the military authorities. If the civil authorities did all in their power to insure compliance with the German military regulations and also exerted themselves to discover the offender, as they claim to have done, it may be seriously doubted whether under any reasonable or just interpretation of the rule as to collective responsibility either guilt or responsibility could be imputed to the whole population.

The imposition by the German officers in numerous instances of fines for the acts of unknown individuals for cutting telegraph and telephone wires, for firing upon German troops, for committing injury to bridges and lines of communications, for defacing public notices, tearing down the German flag, strewing glass on the highways, and other similar acts would seem to be defensible only on the assumption that the mass of the population were accomplices, or at least approved the acts, and that the civil authorities could have prevented them had they desired to do so, an assumption which in the majority of cases was probably unwarranted.

Both the Belgian and French authorities charge the Germans with imposing community fines in various instances for acts which were committed, not by the civil population, but by persons belonging to the regular armed forces, and which were, therefore, legitimate acts of war for which the community was not liable to punishment. There can be little doubt that the German *franc-tireur* doctrine was over-exploited and often invoked as a justification for severities against the civil population for acts which were committed by persons belonging to the regularly organized armed forces.

§ 412. Concluding Observations. On the whole, the evidence regarding German practice in respect to the imposition of pecuniary penalties on the civil population of occupied districts during the recent war justifies the conclusion that their policy was based on a theory of collective responsibility which is neither in accord with the well-established principles of modern criminal law nor with the interpretation of article 50 of the Hague convention which has been given it by the great majority of recent writers on international law, including even many of those of German nationality. Unfortunately, the theory of collective responsibility, even when applied in its mildest form, necessarily involves the punishment of innocent persons, and for this reason it ought never be resorted to when other more just measures would accomplish the same end, and in no case unless an active or passive responsibility can really be imputed to the mass of the population, or where the civil authorities have failed to exercise reasonable diligence to prevent infractions or to discover and punish the actual offender in case they have been unable to prevent the offences. Some writers hold that collective punishments ought never be resorted to except as a measure of reprisal, while others, like Bonfils and G. F. de Martens, condemn the whole theory and express the hope that it will ultimately disappear entirely from warfare.[1]

[1] Bonfils, *Droit Int. Pub.*, sec. 1224, and G. F. de Martens, *Traité de Droit Int.*, Vol. III, p. 265. Cf. also Rouard de Card, p. 178.

As the Germans had already learned in 1870–1871, however, it is a measure which is both easy of enforcement and generally effective in deterring the civil population from committing infractions against the authority of the occupying forces, and these circumstances have accentuated the temptation to abuse the right and to extend it to cases to which it cannot be applied, except upon an interpretation which can hardly be reconciled with reason or the generally recognized principles of criminal justice. It was just because of its effectiveness that Leuder, Loening, and other German writers sought to justify the wide extension of the theory and its use on a large scale in the war of 1870–1871. There is no difficulty in justifying such a policy if one only accepts the German doctrine that the test of the legitimacy of an instrument or a measure is its effectiveness, i.e., that its employment contributes to the attainment of the object of the war.[1]

[1] Cf., for example, the introduction to the *Kriegsbrauch in Landkriege;* Leuder in Holtzendorff, Vol. IV, sec. 96; von Hartmann, *Militärische Nothwendigkeit und Humanität* in the *Deutsche Rundschau*, Vol. XIII, pp. 119 ff., and Vol. XIV, pp. 117 ff., and von Clausewitz on *War* (Eng. trans. by Graham, ch. II). Cf. also the views of Field-marshal Prince Schwarzenberg quoted in the *Continental Times* of September 17, 1915. There is little German literature dealing with the levying of collective penalties during the recent war which is yet available in America. Meurer's monograph entitled *Die Völkerrechtliche Stellung der vom Feind Besetzten Gebiete* (1915) contains a brief general defence of the German policy, and Albert Zorn in his *Kriegsrecht zu Land* (1915) apparently finds nothing for which the Germans may justly be reproached.

CHAPTER XXVII

DEPORTATION OF THE CIVILIAN POPULATION FROM OCCUPIED TERRITORY

§ 413. Early German Policy; § 414. Deportations from France in 1916; § 415. Manner of Execution of the Measure; § 416. Protests against the Deportations; § 417. Treatment of the French *Déportés;* § 418. The German Defence; § 419. The German Defence Analyzed; § 420. Deportations from Belgium; § 421. Manner of Execution; § 422. Treatment of the Belgian *Déportés:* § 423. Allied Protests against the Deportation Measures; § 424. Neutral Protests; § 425. German Defence of the Policy of Deportation; § 426. Economic Argument and Question of Public Order; § 427. The German Defence Analyzed; § 428. Power of a Military Occupant over the Inhabitants of Occupied Territory; § 429. The German Policy Unprecedented in Modern Times; § 430. Conclusion.

§ 413. **Early German Policy.** A practice resorted to on a large scale during the recent war, and which aroused strong indignation throughout the world and called forth spirited protests from various neutral governments, was the policy of the German military authorities of deporting large numbers of the civilian population from certain districts occupied by their armies. From the very outset the German commanders adopted the practice of arresting and sending to Germany as a punitive measure Belgian civilians who were charged with having committed acts of hostility against their authority, those suspected of participation in the "unorganized Belgian people's war," and large numbers of hostages taken from various communities for the purpose of insuring the good behavior and obedience of the civil population. During the early months of the war large numbers of Belgians were deported for refusing to work for the Germans in railway shops, barbed-wire factories, ammunition plants, and other manufacturing establishments.[1] Upon their occupation of French territory extensive deportations from those regions also took place. The French official commission

---

[1] M. Van den Heuvel, Belgian minister of state, estimated that down to October 1, 1915, between thirteen and fourteen thousand Belgian civilians had been deported to Germany as prisoners, and that of these about three thousand had been returned. See his article *De la Déportation des Belges en Allemagne, Rev. Gén. de Droit Int. Pub.*, Vol. 24, p. 262.

163

of inquiry in a report made in March, 1915, stated that ten thousand persons, including men, women, and children of all ages, had been carried off to Germany, only to be repatriated after months of captivity and harsh treatment. Further than that their compatriots had been charged with having fired upon German troops no reason was assigned for deporting them.[1] Upon their occupation of Poland the same policy was carried out on an even more extensive scale, many thousands of Polish workingmen being conscripted or cajoled into entering into voluntary agreements and being carried away for compulsory labor to Germany or to other parts of the occupied territory.[2] The policy of deportation is also alleged to have been adopted in Roumania by the military authorities of the Central powers.[3]

§ 414. Deportations from France in 1916. At first the German policy of deportation was, as said, resorted to mainly as a punitive measure against the inhabitants for alleged acts

---

[1] The second volume of the Reports of the French commission is devoted entirely to these early deportations. Its findings were based on the depositions of some three hundred *déportés* who were repatriated prior to February 28, 1915. The depositions are printed in the Report, pp. 19-72. There is in the *Rev. Gén. de Droit Int. Pub.* for July-October, 1915 (Docs., p. 99), a protest of the French government against the deportation to Germany of fourteen hundred French civilians from the departments of Meurthe-et-Moselle, Ardennes, and Vosges during the first months of the war. M. Delcassé stated on December 30, 1914, that some of these persons had been released and returned to France, but that the greater number still remained in captivity. Some details regarding the deportations from various French towns may be found in the Abbé Calippe's book, *La Somme sous l'Occupation Allemande*, pp. 199 ff., and in Saint-Aymour, *Autour de Noyon*, ch. XV. The last-mentioned writer gives the names of fifteen communes near Noyon with the number of persons deported from each. Not less than 30 per cent of the inhabitants, he says, were carried away by the Germans (p. 305). Eight hundred persons were deported from Noyon alone.

[2] According to a press despatch of January 3, 1918, from Petrograd the number of Poles and Lithuanians who were reported to have been forcibly "transferred" to Germany was three hundred thousand. New York *Times*, January 4, 1918. Cf. also the charges of a Polish member of the *Reichstag* in the New York *Times* of November 7, 1916; also the issues of the *Times* of December 8, 1916, and June 20, 1917, and a statement issued by the United States Food Administration containing the testimony of F. C. Walcott, *Official Bulletin*, November 7, 1917, p. 5.

[3] The Roumanian minister of foreign affairs in a telegram of February 7, 1917, to the Roumanian legation in Paris charged that the Germans had begun to transport for internment in Germany all Roumanian males between sixteen and sixty-seven years of age. Apparently this measure was in retaliation for the alleged action of the Roumanian government in handing over German prisoners to Russia for transportation to Siberia. The Roumanian government denied the German charge and protested against the deportation of its civil population. New York *Times*, February 8, 1917; also London weekly *Times*, April 20, 1917.

of hostility, and it attracted little attention outside the countries from which they were deported. It was not until the summer of 1915, when some twenty-five thousand of the inhabitants of Lille, Roubaix, Tourcoing, and other French cities were suddenly arrested and deported by the Germans to other occupied regions of France, where they were dispersed throughout the rural districts, principally in the departments of the Aisne and the Ardennes, that the voice of the neutral world was raised in protest.[1]

It appears that in the early days of April notices were placarded by the German military authorities in the cities mentioned offering to settle unemployed families, the number of which according to the German version was very large, in the occupied departments of the North of France where they would be given work, for which they would be paid regular wages. The response to this invitation for volunteers not being satisfactory to the German military authorities, they decided upon the drastic remedy of forcible deportation and compulsory labor with a view to reducing the number of unemployed and to diminishing the alleged heavy burden of feeding the civil population, a burden which, it was asserted, had been greatly increased through the operation of Great Britain's "starvation blockade."[2] Thereupon notices were posted requiring all the

[1] My principal sources of information regarding the French deportations are a French yellow book dealing with the conduct of the Germans toward the inhabitants of the invaded districts, issued in the summer of 1916. It contains the texts of the various German orders, notices, and proclamations posted in the three cities mentioned above together with M. Briand's communication of July 25, 1916, addressed to the powers, and various other documents. It also contains the sworn depositions of some two hundred inhabitants, most of whom were victims or eye-witnesses. Much of this material may be found in English in a book entitled *The Deportation of Women and Girls from Lille*. (Geo. H. Doran and Co., New York, 1916.) I have also made use of numerous press despatches published in the New York *Times* and the London *Times*; the New York *Times Current History Magazine* for October, 1916; a brochure by M. Basdevant entitled *Les Déportations du Nord de la France et de la Belgique en Vue du Travail Forcé et le Droit International* (Paris, 1917), and various articles in Clunet's *Journal* and in the *Rev. Gén. de Droit Int. Public.*

[2] The German pretext was thus stated in a proclamation posted at Lille on April 29, 1916, by the German military governor, von Graevenitz: "The attitude of England renders it increasingly difficult to feed the population. To lessen misery, the German authority has recently asked volunteers to work in the country. This offer has not had the success which was expected. Consequently the inhabitants will be removed by compulsion and transported to the country. Those removed will be sent into the interior of French occupied territory far behind the

inhabitants, except children under fourteen years of age, their mothers, and elderly persons, to prepare to be immediately deported, in some cases within an hour and a half.

§ 415. Manner of Execution of the Measure. Members of families were directed to assemble in front of their houses, and all were forbidden to be absent from their homes between 9 o'clock at night and 6 o'clock in the morning (German time) without a permit. An officer would designate the particular members of each family to be deported. Each person designated was advised "in his own interest" to provide himself with utensils for eating and drinking, a woollen blanket, good shoes, and a supply of linen. The people were advised to "remain calm and obedient," and they were informed that any attempt to evade removal would be "pitilessly punished."

The execution of these measures began during Easter week. Officers accompanied by detachments of troops went around during the night or early morning hours from house to house in certain quarters of each of the three cities mentioned and picked out certain members of each family for deportation.[1] Their orders were to select males of military age, able-bodied males not of military age who were not engaged in any permanent trade or occupation, families entire who were without employment or means of support, and unemployed females. Special effort was to be made to select individuals who were either familiar with farm work or suited to the performance of such labor. Women were to be selected to do the cooking for the men or to work in French families who might be in need of domestic servants. The result of this mode of selection was to dismember many families, and its execution led to many pathetic scenes. Husbands and fathers were torn away from their homes, young girls were mixed promiscuously with persons of varying social ranks and moral character, and all were herded into railway coaches and carried away to destinations of which they and their relatives were ignorant. Here they were held

---

front, where they will be employed in agriculture and in no way in military work. By this measure the opportunity will be given them to better provide for their support."

[1] The "raids" on Lille took place at about 3 o'clock in the morning. The streets were guarded at both ends by troops and defended by machine guns.

in a virtual state of slavery and compelled to work under the supervision of the military authorities at such tasks as they designated and subject to such conditions as they chose to prescribe.[1]

§ 416. **Protests against the Deportations.** Shortly after the posting of the notices at Lille, the mayor from his sick-bed addressed a protest to the military governor calling his attention to official declarations which had been earlier posted by the military authorities on the walls of the city to the effect that Germany was not making war upon the civilian inhabitants and promising to respect their rights of person and property, so long as they should conduct themselves peaceably and commit no acts of hostility against the German military authority. "To destroy and break up families," the mayor concluded, "to tear from their homes thousands of peaceable citizens, to force them to abandon their goods without protection would be an act of a nature to arouse general reprobation."

Mgr. Charost, the bishop of Lille, likewise addressed a protest to the governor in which he described the German deportation proceedings as " a policy of wholesale kidnapping of women and young girls and the carrying of them away to unknown places without judicial inquiry and without cause. This was not war, but the worst of torture and a violation of the most sacred rights of family among a people who cherish intensely the sacred-

---

[1] The scenes in some instances were so heart-rending that officers of humane feeling are said to have broken down and refused to carry out their orders, for which a number of them were imprisoned in fortresses for disobedience. See an article by Cyril Brown in the New York *Times* of August 19, 1916, where the "press-gang" methods of the Germans are described. Women and girls of all ranks, he says, were seized in the dead of night and herded together with roughs and prostitutes. Ambassador Gerard in his book *My Four Years in Germany* (p. 335) states that he was told by Americans who were familiar with the facts that the deportation order was carried out "with the greatest barbarity"; that a man would come home at night and find that his wife or children had disappeared, and no one could tell him where they had gone, except that the neighbors would relate that German non-commissioned officers and a file of soldiers had carried them off. "That night at dinner," he adds, "I spoke to the Chancellor about this and told him that it seemed to be absolutely outrageous; and that without consulting with my government I was prepared to protest in the name of humanity against a continuance of this treatment of the civil population of France. The Chancellor told me that he had not known of it, that it was the result of orders given by the military, that he would speak to the Emperor about it and that he hoped to be able to stop further deportations. I believe that they were stopped but twenty thousand or more who had been taken from their homes were not returned until months afterwards."

ness of the family-relation." [1] The minister of foreign affairs on
June 27 requested the French ambassador to Switzerland to
acquaint the Spanish ambassador at Berlin with these facts
and to urge him to intercede "with all possible energy" with the
German government to induce it "to put an end to this state of
things and return to their homes the victims of these arbitrary
acts." These and other protests, however, appear to have had
no effect, and the deportations proceeded until, as stated above,
some twenty-five thousand inhabitants were removed. On
July 25, 1916, M. Briand, president of the council of ministers,
requested the diplomatic representatives of France abroad to
call the attention of the governments to which they were accredited to the treatment to which the German authorities had
subjected the inhabitants of the three cities mentioned and to
lay before them a note which contained a large amount of documentary evidence (much of which was German) concerning the
details with which the deportation measures had been carried
into execution.

§ 417. Treatment of the French Déportés. Regarding the
treatment which the *déportés* received at the hands of the
Germans in the localities to which they were taken and the character of the work they were required to perform, the French
Yellow Book makes many serious charges. It contains hundreds of depositions made before justices of the peace, besides
letters and other documents, alleging that they were compelled
to perform work which was directly or indirectly connected
with military operations. Thus in the department of the Aisne
each female *déportée* was required to make twenty-five sand
bags a day for use in the trenches. Other deponents alleged
that they were forced to make barrows for breaking the force
of cavalry charges, to work in munitions factories, to drive
artillery wagons, and the like. The larger number, however,
were set at work in the fields, orchards, and gardens. Many
women were employed as domestic servants and were required
to milk cows, clean the streets, cook and wash for the soldiers,
or serve as orderlies for German officers. There were, of course,
many complaints of brutal treatment, insufficient feeding, long
hours, excessive tasks, assignments to work to which the *déportés* were unsuited, work under degrading conditions, the

[1] *Annexe* 11 to the French Yellow Book.

lodging of women promiscuously with men, and the like. The Germans, of course, denied most of the charges regarding the ill treatment of the *déportés*.[1]

§ 418. **The German Defence.** As has been said, the German government defended its policy of deportation in this particular instance as a legitimate military measure adopted mainly in the interest of the inhabitants themselves, for whom it desired to find employment, and with a view to reducing the burden of providing food for those who had no means of support. The argument also appears to have been put forward that it was essential to relieve the pressure on the military railways by reducing the amount of food which it was necessary to ship into the three cities mentioned. It would perhaps be going too far to say that the German authorities were not animated to some extent by the desire to ameliorate the condition of the unemployed population, but there can be little doubt that the chief reason was the desire to find farm laborers to harvest the bountiful crops in the occupied rural districts, upon which the occupying forces were largely dependent for their subsistence. In an official statement published in the *Norddeutsche Zeitung*[2] the policy of the German government was declared to be entirely in accord with the rules of international law. Reference was made to article 43 of the Hague convention respecting the laws and customs of war which declares that "After the legal authority has actually passed into the hands of those occupying the country, the latter are under obligation to take all the measures possible to restore public order and safety."

"There is no doubt," the statement continued, "that provision for the insuring of the feeding of the population belongs to the work of maintaining public order and public life. But owing to the circumstances prevailing this could only be done through the agricultural output of the occupying territory itself. In the case at hand, the only way to do away with a state of distress was to compel a part of the population to work in their own interest. Appeals having been made to the inhabitants to volunteer for work in the regions where their services were needed, without satisfactory re-

[1] The *Norddeutsche Zeitung* declared that the persons "transplanted," in so far as they were families, women, and children, were quartered with the inhabitants of the districts to which they were taken and set to work under the supervision of the local authorities and in pursuance of an understanding with them, while single men were brought together in labor colonies. Quoted in New York *Times*, November 9, 1916.

[2] English text in the New York *Times* of November 9, 1916.

sponse, the German authorities were justified in resorting to compulsion, and in view of the fact that the harvesting season was rapidly advancing and in view of the increasing shortage created by the internationally illegal English blockade it was necessary to act energetically and quickly."

§ 419. The German Defence Analyzed. The German defence is based on two assumptions neither of which appears to have been in accordance with the facts: (1) that the deportations were necessary to the maintenance of the public order, and (2) that it was a necessary measure to reduce the German burden of supporting the civilian population of the territory occupied by their forces. It does not appear that the Germans ever in fact made any charge that the alleged lack of employment had endangered the public order or threatened its security. At the time, the inhabitants were demeaning themselves peaceably, and no considerations of public order required their deportation. In the second place, the German excuse that the lack of employment in the cities mentioned entailed a burden upon the treasury of the occupying belligerent had no foundation in fact, since it is well known not only that the German authorities did not bear the cost of providing for the relief of the destitute among the civil population, but that by means of a system of requisitions which in many instances did not differ in principle from pillage, by means of huge collective fines and contributions, and by the spoliation of the occupied regions and the exportation to Germany of the available stock of raw materials, machinery, and live stock, the Germans themselves were mainly responsible for the conditions upon which they sought to justify the policy of deportation. Moreover, the burden of providing for their relief was borne not by the German government but by the charity and generosity of neutral agencies. The harsh and cruel manner in which the measure was carried out, even if it had been legally justified in principle, made it wholly indefensible.

The policy of deporting French civilians appears to have been resorted to by the German military authorities from time to time throughout the succeeding years of the war, though not on any such extensive scale as that described above.[1]

---

[1] Before the evacuation of the Somme region in the spring of 1917 many of the inhabitants are said to have been carried away by the Germans. From Nesle more than four hundred women and girls and all able-bodied men over sixteen years of age are alleged to have been deported into the interior (London *Times*,

§ 420. Deportations from Belgium. That the German government was not moved by the almost universal denunciation of its deportation policy in the spring of 1916 in France may be assumed from the fact that in the autumn of the same year it proceeded to resort on a still more extensive scale to the policy of deportation of the civilian population from various districts of Belgium. The attempt of the Germans to induce the inhabitants to work voluntarily having for the most part failed, they decided upon the more drastic expedient of deporting them to Germany and compelling them to work there. Accordingly, on October 3, 1916, the general headquarters issued a decree "establishing a regime of forced labor with deportation," article 1 of which provided that "persons capable of working may be constrained by force to work *even away from their domicile*, whenever on account of gambling, drunkenness, lack of employment, or laziness they are compelled to rely upon the assistance of others for their support." Article 3 declared that every such inhabitant called upon to work and who should refuse to perform the task assigned to him would be punished by a term of imprisonment not exceeding three years and a fine not exceeding 10,000 marks, or one of these penalties.[1] The publi-

---

March 23 and 26, 1917). From Noyon fifty girls between the ages of fifteen and twenty-five are alleged to have been carried off to act as officer's servants. (Statement of a French official in pamphlet entitled *Frightfulness in Retreat*, p. 17.) As to the deportations from the region around Noyon cf. the details and statistics in Saint-Aymour, *Autour de Noyon*, ch. XV. Senator Chéron, describing the retreat of the Germans, stated that "in all the villages they carried away as captives the inhabitants between the ages of fifteen and sixty, excepting women who had very young children dependent upon them." French Yellow Book, p. 146. Prior to their retreat from northern France in the autumn of 1918 the Germans are alleged to have carried off large numbers of the civilian population from various towns and villages. During the last fifteen days of their occupation of Lille they were charged with taking away as captives some fifteen thousand of the inhabitants.

[1] Text in Passalecq, *Les Déportations Belges à la Lumière des Documents Allemands*, p. 3. This elaborate collection of documentary material compiled by the director of the Belgian bureau of documents is my main source of information on the subject of the Belgian deportations. An abridgment of this work was printed under the title *La Vérité sur les Déportations Belges* with a preface by M. Vandervelde, Belgian minister (Paris and Nancy, 1917). Cf. also Toynbee, *The Belgian Deportations*, an English publication which contains some of the documentary material found in Passalecq; an article by M. Van den Heuvel, Belgian minister of state, entitled *De la Déportation des Belges en Allemagne*, *Rev. Gén. de Droit Int. Pub.*, Vol. 24, pp. 261 ff.; Basdevant, *La Déportation des Habitants de la Belgique et du Nord de la France* (Paris, 1917), and Whitlock, *Belgium*, Vol. II, ch. 35–40.

cation of this decree was immediately followed by a campaign inaugurated by the German press with a view to mollifying public opinion in Belgium and especially in neutral countries and preparing it for the favorable reception of a measure which it was foreseen was certain to evoke bitter protest.[1] The first step in the execution of the measure was to obtain lists of the unemployed who refused to work and of all persons who were receiving charitable relief. To this end the local civil authorities were "invited" to furnish the German military authorities with the names of all such persons within their jurisdictions, together with other information, on blanks provided for this purpose.[2] These requests were accompanied by threats of fines, imprisonment, and of deportation in case of non-compliance with the German demands. For the most part, the local officials refused to furnish the lists. Thereupon the military authorities seized the records of the communal administration, removed the recalcitrant magistrates from office, in some cases imprisoned them, and in a number of instances imposed heavy fines on the communities whose magistrates declined to comply with the German demands.[3]

§ 421. **Manner of Execution.** Having obtained in one way or another what purported to be a list of the unemployed and dependent population in each commune, the military authorities thereupon addressed orders, either individual or collective, to all such persons directing them to assemble at a fixed hour and place on the following day prepared to be "transferred" to Germany.[4] They were advised to bring with them certain

---

[1] The views of the German press are set forth in Passalecq, ch. II. The leading journals discoursed upon the great amount of idleness in Belgium; they reviewed the efforts of the German military authorities to induce by promises of high wages the Belgians to work at home or in Germany, painted glowing pictures of the opportunities which would be afforded those who voluntarily consented to be "transplanted" to Germany, and the like.

[2] It is apparent from the evidence that the lists demanded were those drawn up by the Belgian relief commission and the national committee for relief in Belgium, and this was admitted by the Germans.

[3] Thus Bruges was fined 400,000 marks and threatened with an additional fine of 100,000 marks for each day's delay in furnishing the list requested. The town of Tournai was similarly fined 200,000 marks and threatened with a further fine of 20,000 marks for each day's delay. See the New York *Times* of November 18, 1916, for the text of the resolution of the municipal council of Tournai refusing to furnish the list.

[4] The selection of the cities and towns from which the deportations were made appears to have been largely arbitrary. Among those upon which the heaviest "raids" were made were Alost, Antwerp, Bruges, Brussels, Charleroi, Coutrai,

specified articles of apparel, and warning was given that those who refused to appear at the time and places designated would be heavily fined or imprisoned. Notwithstanding the threat, large numbers in fact refused to obey the order to assemble and were rounded up by the soldiers and forcibly conducted to the places of assembly designated.[1] Naturally many mistakes were made, and large numbers of persons who belonged neither to the indigent nor to the idle class were brought in. The Germans admitted that this happened in many instances, but blamed the local civil authorities for their refusal to coöperate by themselves furnishing *bona fide* lists of persons liable to deportation. The Belgians, on their part, charge that the Germans made no real effort to separate the indigent and unemployed from the rest of the inhabitants; that in some communities practically the entire adult male population was assembled for deportation,[2] and that thousands of persons who were not subjects of charitable relief and many of whom were regularly employed were carried away.[3] When the inhabitants were assembled, a military officer accompanied by a physician passed down the lines and designated those who were excused. Unmarried able-bodied men capable of work were preferred,[4] and the Belgians charge that little time was spent investigating the cases of workmen who claimed to be employed, the doubt in such cases usually being resolved against those who had the appearance of being good laborers.[5]

Ghent, Liège, Nivelles, Termonde, and Tournai. Twenty-five thousand persons are alleged to have been deported from Antwerp alone.

[1] In many communities the inhabitants fled to the forests and concealed themselves, and not a few appear to have succeeded in getting past the heavily charged stockade on the Dutch frontier and escaping into Holland.

[2] E.g., at Nivelles and Borinage, where the entire male population without any age limit was summoned; at Wavre, where all males between the ages of seventeen and fifty-six years of age were summoned; at Mons, where all males of military age (about ten thousand altogether) were called.

[3] Many instances are cited by Passalecq. Cf. also Toynbee, *The Belgian Deportations* (p. 50), and Cammaerts, *Through the Iron Bars*, p. 63. Cf. also the article by M. Van den Heuvel cited above, p. 276, and the New York *Times* of December 23, 1916.

[4] But married men were frequently selected, and so were women in some cases. Thus two hundred female textile laborers are alleged to have been deported from Ghent.

[5] General von Bissing says in his defence, referred to below, that strict orders were given that the procedure of selection should be painstaking, and that each case should be investigated in the presence of the mayor, a local physician, and a representative of the German administration.

When the selections had been made, the victims were offered the alternative of going voluntarily to Germany or of being taken by force. Those who were willing to go voluntarily were requested to sign a contract to work for a period of six months at designated rates of wages, and they were to be allowed ample time to make the necessary preparations for their departure. To induce them to enter into such agreements promises of higher wages than would be paid those who refused were made. In addition, a sum of money would be paid them in advance, and they were promised a larger degree of liberty and more favorable treatment. The Belgians allege that in some instances the pressure to induce laborers to sign contracts took the form of threats of imprisonment and deprivation of food.

Naturally, under these circumstances a goodly number of the victims were induced to sign contracts, a circumstance which afforded the German authorities an opportunity later, when the voice of the civilized world had been raised in protest, to assert that large numbers had consented voluntarily to be "transferred" and had even gone "cheerfully." The great majority, however, refused to be cajoled by threats or induced by promises of high wages to enter into agreements and had to be deported by force. No reliable statistics are available as to the number of Belgians deported. It was estimated that during the first month following the inauguration of the policy of deportation one hundred thousand persons were carried away. Others place the number between two and three hundred thousand.[1] Naturally the German estimates were lower.

The German policy of deportation did not end with the year 1916, notwithstanding the strong protests of various neutral governments and the denunciation of public opinion in the greater part of the neutral world, to say nothing of the promises which the Emperor is said to have made in February, 1917, to the Pope

---

[1] Cf. Passalecq, *op. cit.*, p. viii; Basdevant, *op. cit.*, p. 21, and Clunet's *Journal*, 45: 1321. M. Vandervelde, Belgian minister of munitions, in a statement given out on November 24, 1916, at Havre stated that the Belgian minister at The Hague had telegraphed on November 17 that "more than 200,000 had already been deported." M. Van den Heuvel in the article cited above estimated the number at about one hundred and twenty-five thousand; Cammaerts, *Through the Iron Bars* (p. 61), places the number at two hundred thousand; Cardinal Mercier in his letter of November 10, 1916, to governor-general von Bissing (text in Toynbee, pp. 81 ff.) estimated the number of *deportés* at four hundred thousand.

that there would be no further deportations.[1] Nevertheless, the scale upon which it was resorted to during the succeeding years of the war was far less extensive.

§ 422. **Treatment of the Belgian Déportés.** The great majority of the *déportés* were sent to Germany, but a considerable number were taken to the occupied regions of France, where they were compelled to work at such tasks and under such conditions as the German authorities prescribed. The proclamations calling up the inhabitants usually stated that they would be "transferred" to Germany for forced labor, but generally no details as to the character of the labor or the wages to be paid were given. Many harrowing tales were told by the victims who were subsequently released of the cruel treatment they received at the hands of German authorities; of long journeys in overcrowded, filthy cattle trucks without food or drink; of how they were mocked and jeered at by the populace of German towns through which they passed; of how they were compelled to work at degrading tasks and in munitions factories and other establishments for the manufacture of war materials; of how they were overworked, starved, tortured, and denied the wages which had been promised them, and the like.[2] In January,

[1] Thus a despatch from Havre on May 23, 1917, stated that three thousand persons had been deported from Brussels since the first of the month. On May 14, it was announced that all men in the province of Luxemburg were being deported, and that a census of the female population was being taken with a view to replacing male farm laborers with women (New York *Times*, May 30, 1917). As late as February 14, 1918, a Havre despatch stated that the deportations were continuing, two thousand seven hundred persons from Lokeren having been carried off "within the last few weeks" and put to work at military tasks. See the Memorandum presented to Secretary Lansing by the Belgian minister and published in the New York *Times* of June 15, 1918. A Havre despatch of March 6, 1918, again stated that the deportations were continuing, and that in some cases children thirteen years of age were being carried away. In October, 1918, the Belgian government issued a statement that "from the coast to beyond Bruges the male population from fifteen to forty-five years of age is being torn from their homes and subjected to the most brutal treatment. These men are compelled to work at forced labor for the military needs of the enemy."

[2] Cf. the report of Brand Whitlock, American minister to Belgium, made public at Washington on April 21, 1917. Cf. also a conversation between Mr. F. C. Walcott, an American citizen who was in the service of the Belgian relief commission, and governor general von Bissing, *National Geographic Magazine*, May, 1917; also an article by Vernon Kellogg, *Atlantic Monthly*, October, 1917. James W. Gerard, American ambassador to Germany, in his *My Four Years in Germany* (pp. 351-352), referring to the treatment of the Belgian *déportés*, says "Several of these Belgians who were put to work in Berlin managed to get away

1917, the German government consented to allow representatives of the American embassy to make an investigation of the conditions prevailing in the working camps of the *déportés*, but before the investigation was made, war broke out between the United States and Germany, and the American diplomatic staff was withdrawn.

§ 423. Allied Protests against the Deportation Measures. The German deportations evoked bitter protest not only in Belgium, Great Britain, and France, but in many neutral countries. In Belgium formal protests were addressed to the governor-general by ministers of State, senators and deputies, judges, municipal councils, labor organizations, scientific bodies, the bar, Cardinal Mercier, and others.[1] All of them denied the German charge that the Belgian workingmen were voluntarily idle; all absolved Great Britain from responsibility for the paralyzed condition of Belgian industry, and all placed it upon the German authorities. They denounced the harsh and cruel manner in which the deportation measures were carried out and charged that in fact the German authorities made little or no distinction between the employed and the unemployed. Cardinal Mercier in three letters addressed to General von Bissing attacked his "physical and moral welfare" argument and denounced the deportations as a crime against civilization and one for which there was no excuse. The Belgian government addressed a protest to the neutral powers denouncing "to all civilized nations these unworthy proceedings which shamelessly ignore the laws of humanity as well as the rules and conventions of war." The Belgians complained that not only were the deportations contrary to the laws and usages of war, but they were also in violation of repeated pledges given by the German military authorities. Cardinal Mercier

---

and come to see me. They gave me a harrowing account of how they had been seized in Belgium and made to work in Germany at making munitions to be used probably against their own friends. I said to the Chancellor, 'There are Belgians employed in making shells contrary to all rules of war and the Hague convention. He said, 'I do not believe it.' I said, 'My automobile is at the door. I can take you in four minutes to where thirty Belgians are working on the manufacture of shells.' But he did not find time to go."

[1] The texts of many of these protests may be found in Passalecq, pp. 296 ff. The protest of the governments of Great Britain and France is printed in the New York *Times* of December 6, 1916.

in his letters of October 19 and November 10, 1916, to Governor-general von Bissing reminded him of the assurances which had been given him by General von Huhne, military governor of Antwerp, after the fall of that city, that if the Belgians who had taken refuge in Holland and England would return to Belgium, they would not be carried away to Germany for forced labor or military service. This promise, he pointed out, had been renewed by General von der Goltz. The governor-general even issued an address to the people of Belgium confirming these assurances. Similar assurances had been made to the Dutch legation in Brussels and to the Dutch consul-general at Antwerp.[1] Relying upon the good faith of the German promises, thousands of the exiles returned to Belgium. This pledge, said Cardinal Mercier in his letter of November 10 to von Bissing, "has been violated during the last fortnight thousands of times over every day."

The German government admitted that such assurances had been given, but claimed that they were made "under very different circumstances and under the expectation that the war would be a matter of only a few months."[2] Moreover, the promises referred to applied only to *repatriés* who had employment and not to those without employment.

§ 424. **Neutral Protests.** Various neutral governments likewise addressed representations to the German government remonstrating against the deportations and calling attention to the painful impression which the German policy had made on neutral public opinion.[3] The fact is, the voice of almost the

---

[1] The texts of the German pledges may be found in Passalecq, pp. 236 ff. Cf. also a statement of M. Vandervelde, New York *Times*, November 25, 1916; likewise Cammaerts, *Through the Iron Bars*, pp. 48–49, and Basdevant, *op. cit.*, p. 34.

[2] The action of the German authorities in disregarding the assurances thus given was the subject of much criticism in the Netherlands, whose government had on the strength of the German promises advised and encouraged the Belgian refugees to return to their country. The Dutch government protested, and in January, 1917, the German government agreed to repatriate Belgian refugees from Holland who had returned to Belgium and were subsequently deported to Germany. Text of Dutch protest in *Grotius, Annuaire International pour l'Année, 1916*, p. 113.

[3] Remonstrances are known to have been made by the governments of the United States, Holland, Switzerland, Brazil, and Spain. Text of the American protest in the New York *Times*, December 9, 1916. The Swiss Federal Council protested not only on the ground of the inhumanity of the German policy, but also because it was contrary to the Hague convention. Great mass meetings were

entire neutral world was raised in protest against a policy which was regarded as differing but little from slavery, but strong and impressive as it was, it appears to have made little impression on the German government, and the policy of deportation was, as has been said, continued at intervals, although on a less extensive scale, throughout the remaining years of the war.[1]

§ 425. **German Defence of the Policy of Deportation.** The reasons given by the German authorities in justification of the Belgian deportations were somewhat different from those put forward in defence of the deportations from France. In the latter case the principal object avowed was to procure agricultural laborers to harvest the crops in the occupied country districts of France, and considerations of social and moral necessity were less emphasized. In the case of the Belgian deportations, however, the need of laborers in Germany, where most of the *déportés* were taken, was not put forward as the dominating consideration, but it was rather the German solicitude for the health, good order, morals, and social benefit to the working people of Belgium that moved Germany to "transfer" them to a country where they would not be exposed to the demoralizing influences under which they were living, and where in addition they would be assured of remunerative employment. These considerations were set forth in a letter of governor-general von Bissing on November 3, 1916, to the syndical

---

held in Boston, New York, Philadelphia, Baltimore, Chicago, and many other cities, at which the German policy of deportation was denounced as a system of slavery. Many protests were addressed to the President of the United States by various public associations and other bodies, urging the American government to use its influence to stop the deportations. The American press was practically unanimous in its condemnation. Even the Pope, who in his endeavor to be absolutely neutral had abstained from intervening by protests or remonstrances against the conduct of any of the belligerents, now broke his silence and made representations to the German government with a view to bringing about a discontinuance of the policy of deportation and the repatriation of those who had been carried away. New York *Times*, January 18, 1917, and Van den Heuvel, article cited, p. 294.

[1] Protests in Germany, indeed, were not lacking, and on December 2, 1916, a number of socialist deputies in the *Reichstag* severely arraigned the government for its treatment of the Belgians and demanded that its policy should be stopped. In reply to this criticism Dr. Helfferich said: "The setting of the unemployed Belgians to work is thoroughly consistent with international law. They are not given work which, according to international law, they should not perform. We are only making use of our undoubted rights."

commission of Brussels in reply to an appeal addressed on November 9, 1916, to the governor-general urging him to put a stop to the continued deportation of the Belgian population. Declining to comply with the request, the governor-general went on to say:

> Clearsighted Belgians in the spring of 1915 drew my attention to the dangers of idleness and distaste for work. They showed that assistance, from whatever direction it came, constituted, finally, an economic burden upon Belgium and brought with it also idleness. The result was that the working people deteriorated physically and morally and that especially skilled laborers lost their capacity and could not be employed in time of peace in Belgian industry."

Then adverting to his decrees of August, 1915, and May, 1916, relating to compulsory labor of the unemployed, he stated that "these decrees were founded on considerations of health" and were necessary "to avoid public calamity." [1] Again in a letter, dated November 23, 1916, to Cardinal Mercier who had addressed a protest to him against the deportations, the governor-general declined to modify his policy and reasserted that "the extensive unemployment which prevails in Belgium is a great social evil" that had been removed by the transportation of the idle to Germany. [2]

Again in an interview of November 11, 1916, with Cyril Brown, correspondent of the New York *Times*, he defended the policy of "transplantation" as a necessary measure against an intolerable social evil. It was not only, he said, no hardship for the unemployed or the population as a whole, but was "at bottom a blessing both for the workers and the nation." "Nothing," he added, "so demoralizes a man as idleness, and nothing tends more to weaken a nation than the fact that a large part of it is compelled for years to do nothing." [3] In a

---

[1] Text in Passalecq, pp. 346–348. The same defence was put forward in a letter of November 16 to M. Favereau, President of the Belgian senate. Passalecq, p. 301.

[2] Text of his letter in the New York *Times* of January 14, 1917; also in Passalecq, pp. 335 ff.

[3] This interview is published in the New York *Times* of November 12, 1916. "Our military security and the interests of the Belgian population demand the removal of the Belgian workingmen to Germany. No matter what impression the incident may make, our security comes first. It is the duty of the German administration to see that the people who have been confided to it do not relapse into a condition of enervation." Again: "We are responsible for the situation in

memorial concerning the employment of Belgian workmen in Germany issued by the German government and widely distributed in the United States, with a view to "preventing a one-sided judgment on the question by those far removed from the war theatre and who therefore can form only a superficial opinion of the conditions obtaining in the occupied territories," the "social necessity" argument was elaborated, and the great benefit which deportation had brought to the working population of Belgium in contrast to their "previous lamentable condition" was set forth in glowing terms.

§ 426. The Economic Argument and Question of Public Order. While the principal motive alleged by the German authorities was humanitarian and altruistic — the desire to preserve the working population of Belgian from relapsing into a condition which constituted a danger to their physical and moral welfare — there were also economic reasons and considerations of public order which made necessary the deportation of the unemployed population. The burden of supporting nearly a half million idle men was intolerable, and while it was admitted that this expenditure was being met largely through the benevolence of neutral agencies, there was always the danger that it might ultimately become unbearable. Moreover, this source of relief might be cut off at any time, leaving a large portion of the population without means of subsistence. But even if this eventuality should not come to pass, the presence of so large an idle class constituted a danger to the public order the maintenance of which was an obligation imposed on Germany by the Hague convention. True, no serious disorders had as yet taken place, but the danger existed and would increase with the multiplication of the number of the unemployed. It was, therefore, not only the right but the duty of the Germans to take necessary precautions against the possibility of disorders which might endanger the security of the military occupant as well as that of the civil population itself.[1]

Belgium; it is our duty to maintain order and prevent the country from falling into a state of marasmus and to develop it." The social welfare argument is also developed in the *Berliner Lokalanzeiger* of October 27, 1916; in the *Frankfurter Zeitung* of October 28, and in the *Kölnische Volkszeitung* of October 28 and November 5.

[1] This argument is elaborated in the German "memorial" referred to above and in the German reply to the protest of the American government.

§ 427. **The German Defence Analyzed.** Somewhat inconsistently, the Belgian workingmen were charged with laziness and reproached for their unwillingness to work, and yet it was admitted that opportunities in Belgium for employment were to a large degree lacking. The industries of the country, governor-general von Bissing told a correspondent of the New York *Times*, had been reduced to a state of paralysis by the "illegal" blockade of the British government, which refused to permit the importation of raw materials into Belgium.[1] Notwithstanding this, the German government had done everything in its power to obtain from the British government a relaxation from its policy. "I did everything possible," he said, "to revive Belgian industries, but because of the lack of raw materials it was impossible to bring the Belgian factories to their height of production." The result was "to reduce nearly 500,000 Belgian laborers to a chronic state of demoralizing idleness."[2] The Belgians pointed out that the German solicitude for the amelioration of the economic conditions of Belgium was hardly reconcilable with the harsh, not to say ruthless, manner in which they themselves had exploited the resources of the country by means of requisitions and fines. Many of the communes undertook to provide employment for the idle by constructing public improvements of one kind or another. It was a matter of local concern, and as the expenditures involved were borne by the inhabitants and not by the military occupant, they considered that it was within their rights. Governor von Bissing's approval was necessary, and at first authorizations were given for such undertakings, but subsequently, on the ground that they were entailing excessive financial burdens on the communes and that the undertakings were not productive, he put a stop to it.[3]

§ 428. **Power of a Military Occupant over the Inhabitants of Occupied Territory.** Article 43 of the Hague convention of

[1] This assertion was reiterated in the German "memorial" referred to above and in the reply to the protest of the American government. "This prevalence of unemployment has been caused by the English policy of isolation, which has cut off Belgian industry from the importation of raw material and the exportation of manufactured goods and has thus brought the greater part of Belgian industry to a standstill."

[2] New York *Times*, November 12, 1916.

[3] See his explanation in an interview in the New York *Times*, November 12, 1916.

1907 respecting the laws and customs of war on land imposes upon military occupants the duty of taking measures for the maintenance of public order and security in the territory occupied. Unquestionably, if the presence of large numbers of idle and unemployed persons really constitutes imminent danger to the public order or gravely threatens the security of the occupying forces, the occupying belligerent would be fully warranted in taking reasonable measures to remove the danger, even if it necessitated the deportation of the idle population. The danger, however, must be real and not merely imaginary to justify so extreme a measure. In the present case there is no reason to believe that such a danger actually existed. The Belgian protests affirmed that the unemployed workingmen conducted themselves in a peaceable and orderly manner, and the governor-general in his defence made no charges to the contrary, but merely alleged that the presence of so large an idle class constituted a danger which might at any moment threaten the public order. The Germans also proceeded on the theory that the idleness of which they complained was due to the unwillingness of the Belgian workingmen to labor. It is true that for the most part they refused to work in industries the products of which were intended by the Germans to be used for military purposes, as they had a right to do. They did not, however, refuse to work in other industries, although in consequence of the economic measures referred to above, there were few opportunities for such work. For this, Germany and not they were responsible. In any case, the burden of feeding them did not fall upon the German treasury, as one might infer from reading the arguments put forward b the Germans. In fact, they were fed by the charity of neutral agencies and by contributions of their own compatriots, and so long as their own countrymen and their friends in other countries were willing to provide for their relief, Germany had no just cause for complaint on the score of expense.

The assertion of General von Bissing that he was animated by a desire to remove a great social evil and to ameliorate the condition of the laboring classes has generally been regarded as a mere pretext. The Germans had shown no real consideration for the social or economic welfare of the Belgian population; on the contrary, they had exploited the country for their own purposes in every possible way, and by paralyzing its industries through requisitions, pecuniary exactions, economic restrictions, the carrying away of its live stock, raw materials, farm implements, factory machinery, and the like, they had reduced the population to idleness and impoverishment. The neutral world, therefore, has regarded the professed German solicitude for the welfare of the Belgian people as sheer hypocrisy, and that the real motive back of the policy of deportation was the desire to find workers for their own industries. As stated above, no conscientious effort appears to have been made to confine the deportations to the unemployed, but in general able-bodied working-men, employed and unemployed alike, were carried away without distinction. At the time the deportation policy was inaugurated the German government was pushing its "man power mobilization scheme" to the limit and was bending its energies to replace its own men who were being killed, captured, or disabled. The supply of laboring men in Belgium afforded a tempting recruiting ground, and pretexts for impressing them were easily found. Every able-bodied workman, therefore, taken from Belgium and put to work in the industries of Germany released a German for service in the army or for work in munitions plants or other industries the output of which was devoted directly or indirectly to military purposes.[1]

§ 429. **The German Policy Unprecedented in Modern Times.** Whatever may be the technical merits of the German case, the enormous scale on which the policy of deportation was carried out and the harsh and indiscriminate, not to say cruel, way in which it was executed, makes it comparable to the slave raids on the Gold Coast of Africa in the seventeenth century. It appears to be without precedent in modern wars. In ancient times it was the practice of the Roman conquerors to carry back to Italy a portion of the inhabitants and hold them in captivity, and it is said to have been the practice of Attila to force the conquered tribes into his army, but not since the beginning of the modern age — not even during the Thirty

---

[1] Among the "damages" enumerated in the treaty of peace for which Germany was required to pay an indemnity were "acts of cruelty, violence, or maltreatment (including injuries to life or health as a consequence of imprisonment, deportation, internment, or evacuation, of exposure at sea or of being forced to labor), wherever arising." Art. 244, Annex. I, Par. 2.

Years' war — has any invader seized and virtually enslaved a large part of the civil population in order to carry on his own industries at home and to release his own able-bodied men for military service. The international conventions are silent on the question of the right of an invader to subject the conquered population to such treatment, for the reason, no doubt, that it was not considered necessary in this age to prohibit formally a belligerent from resorting to a measure which the humane conscience of the civilized world had so long condemned. But the Hague convention expressly imposes upon belligerents the obligation to "respect family honor and rights" and to respect, unless absolutely prevented, the laws in force in the country. It likewise forbids the requisition of services except for the needs of the army of occupation. Manifestly, an interpretation of the letter, to say nothing of the spirit, of these rules which would justify such a policy is wholly inadmissible. Indeed, it seems difficult to reconcile so harsh a measure even with the doctrines of the German *Kriegsbrauch im Landkriege*, which certainly goes farther than most military manuals in recognizing the largest latitude to military occupants.[1]

§ 430. **Conclusion.** When everything is said in defence of the German policy that can be said, it has little left to stand on and it is hard to see how any humane voice can be raised in defence of it. It was of very doubtful expediency, even if it were legal, since it only served to turn the public opinion of the rest of the civilized world against Germany and aroused a hatred among the Belgian people that will require many generations to efface.[2]

---

[1] Morgan, *War Book of the German General Staff*, p. 148; also Carpentier's trans., p. 103. Article 23 of the Instructions for the Government of the United States Armies (1863) declared that "private citizens are no longer enslaved or carried off to distant parts." The incorporation in a military manual of a prohibition which seemed so obviously unnecessary in the twentieth century caused the authors of the revised instructions (*Rules of Land Warfare*) issued by the United States government in 1914 to omit it entirely from the new code. The distinguished German writer Stier-Somlo in an article dealing with the provisions of the Hague convention referred to above points out that they protect the honor of the family, and that they prohibit the separation of members of families. *Zeitschrift für Völkerrecht* (1914), Bd. VIII, pp. 581–608.

[2] Cf. the following opinion of the American minister to Belgium, in a report to the department of state in April, 1917: "They have dealt a mortal blow to any prospect they may ever have had of being tolerated by the population of Flanders; in tearing away from nearly every humble home in the land a husband and a

father or a son and brother, they have lighted a fire of hatred that will never go out. They have brought home to every heart in the land in a way that will impress its horror indelibly on the memory of three generations, a realization of what German methods mean, not as with the early atrocities in the heat of passion and the first lust of war, but by one of those deeds that make one despair of the future of the human race, a deed coldly planned, studiously matured, and deliberately and systematically executed, a deed so cruel that German soldiers are said to have wept in its execution and so monstrous that even German officers are now said to be ashamed. The rage, the terror, and despair excited by this measure all over Belgium were beyond anything we had witnessed since the day the Germans poured into Brussels." New York *Times*, April 22, 1917. Cf. also a communication of Viscount Grey dated November 22, 1916, to M. Hymans, the Belgian minister to England (British White Paper relating to the deportations of Belgians to Germany, *Misc.*, No. 37 (1916), Cd. 8404, p. 5.

CHAPTER XXVIII

THE GERMAN INVASION OF BELGIUM

§ 431. The Neutralization of Belgium; § 432. The Treaties of 1870; § 433. The British Inquiry of Germany and France in 1914; § 434. The German Ultimatum to Belgium; § 435. Reply of the Belgian Government and the German Invasion; § 436. Questions of International Law Involved; § 437. The German Pretext of Military Necessity; § 438. The Right of Self-Preservation; § 439. The German Theory of Military Necessity; *Kriegsmanier* v. *Kriegsraison;* § 440. Criticism of the German Theory of *Kriegsraison;* § 441. Military Necessity as a Defence for the Invasion of Belgium; § 442. The German Argument Analyzed.

§ 431. **The Neutralization of Belgium.** As is well known, Belgium in 1914 was a permanently neutralized State under the collective guarantee of a group of European powers: Austria, France, Great Britain, Germany, and Russia. That neutrality was proclaimed and guaranteed in the general interest of Europe and was imposed upon Belgium without her solicitation, if not without her consent.[1]

By article VII of the treaty of November 15, 1831, concluded between the above-mentioned five powers, it was declared that "Belgium within the limits specified in articles I, II and IV shall form an independent and perpetually neutral State. It shall be bound to observe such neutrality towards other States." :

By another article the signatory powers engaged to guarantee that perpetual neutrality as well as the integrity and inviolability of the territory of Belgium. By a treaty of April 19, 1839, between the same powers, the treaty of 1831 was replaced by a new agreement the seventh article of which was identical with the corresponding article of the earlier treaty. Article II

---

[1] Concerning the purposes of the neutralization treaty see Stowell, *The Diplomacy of the War of 1914*, p. 380. For the history of the events leading up to the conclusion of the treaty cf. Deschamps, *La Neutralité de la Belgique*, ch. III; Kleen, *Les Lois et Usages de la Neutralité*, Vol. I, p. 91; Rivier, *Principes du Droit des Gens*, Vol. I, p. 110; Nys, *Notes sur la Neutralité, Rev. de Droit Int. et de Lég. Comp.*, Vol. 32, pp. 603 ff.; Piccioni, *Essai sur la Neutralité Perpétuelle*, pp. 38 ff., and Renault, *Les Premières Violations du Droit des Gens par l'Allemagne*, pp. 19 ff.

placed the execution of the treaty under the guarantee of the signatory powers.[1]

§ 432. The Treaties of 1870. When the outbreak of war between France and the North German Confederation in 1870 became imminent, the British government, apprehensive that one or the other of the belligerents might violate the treaty by marching its armies through Belgium in order to attack the other, sought and obtained from both prospective belligerents renewed assurances that they would respect the neutrality which they had in agreement with the other powers guaranteed in 1839. These assurances were embodied in identical treaties concluded between Great Britain and Prussia on August 9, 1870, and between Great Britain and France on August 11 of the same year. In both treaties the British government pledged itself to employ its forces against either belligerent which should violate the neutrality so guaranteed.[2] Throughout the war of 1870–1871 both belligerents scrupulously respected the neutrality of Belgium, and Belgium on her part performed her obligations of neutrality in the strictest manner, going even to the length of forbidding the transportation of German wounded across her territory.[3]

During the period between the war of 1870–1871 and the outbreak of the late war there were no occasions in which the question of the observance of the neutralization treaty was raised either by the guaranteeing powers or by Belgium.

§ 433. The British Inquiry of Germany and France in 1914. On July 31, 1914, when war between Germany and France seemed imminent, Sir Edward Grey, evidently apprehensive that Germany would, in spite of the treaty of 1839, march her troops through Belgium, adopted the identical course which the British government followed in 1870 and instructed the British ambassadors at Berlin and Paris that it was essential in view of the existing treaties that the British government should know whether the German and French governments were prepared to under-

---

[1] The text of the treaty may be found in Hertslet, *The Map of Europe by Treaty*, Vol. II, pp. 994 and 997; in Deschamps, *op. cit.*, pp. 287–288, and in Fuehr, *Neutrality of Belgium*, pp. 199 ff.

[2] Texts in Hertslet, *op. cit.*, Vol. III, pp. 1803–1835 and 1886–1888, and Fuehr, *op. cit.*, pp. 210 ff.

[3] Dumas, *Droit de Passage en Temps de Guerre, Revue Gén. de Droit Int. Pub.*, 1909, p. 25.

take an engagement to respect the neutrality of Belgium so long as no other power violated it. On the evening of the same day the French government replied to the British inquiry saying that it was "resolved to respect the neutrality of Belgium, and it would only be in the event of some other power violating that neutrality that France might find herself under the necessity in order to assure the defence of her security to act otherwise." The reply also added that "this assurance has been given several times." The reply of the German secretary of state for foreign affairs was that he could not possibly give an answer before consulting the Emperor and the Chancellor. At the same time he added that it was very doubtful whether they could return any answer at all. In a despatch of August 1, Sir Edward Grey again insisted on an answer, saying that the neutrality of Belgium was a matter of very great interest to England.

"If Germany could see her way clear," he said, "to give the same assurance as that which had been given by France, it would materially contribute to relieve anxiety and tension here. On the other hand, if there were a violation of the neutrality of Belgium by one combatant while the other respected it, it would be extremely difficult to restrain public feeling in this country."

§ 434. The German Ultimatum to Belgium. On August 2, the German government in a note alleging that "reliable information" having been received that French forces "intended to march on the line of the Meuse by way of Givet and Namur," leaving no doubt as to the intention of France to march through Belgian territory against Germany and fearing that Belgium in spite of the utmost good will would be unable to repel so considerable a French invasion, proposed to Belgium that permission be granted to German troops to march through her territory. Germany promised in return that when peace was concluded, the kingdom of Belgium and all its possessions should be protected to the fullest extent; that its territory should be evacuated, and that if Belgium would preserve an attitude of friendly neutrality towards Germany, the German government would engage to pay cash for all supplies needed by the German troops and would indemnify her for all damage caused. "It is essential for the self-defence of Germany," the note added, "that she should anticipate any such hostile attack; Germany had in view no hostile act against Belgium, and she would feel the deepest regret if Belgium should so regard her intentions." The character of an ultimatum was given to the proposal by the threat that "should Belgium behave in a hostile manner toward German troops . . . Germany will be obliged to consider Belgium as an enemy," in which case Germany "will make no promises to the kingdom, but will leave to the decision of arms the regulation of the ultimate relations of the two States toward each other." Finally it added that "the German government is justified in hoping that this eventuality will not arise and that the Belgian government will take appropriate steps to prevent its arising."[1] A reply within twelve hours was requested to this ultimatum.

§ 435. Reply of the Belgian Government and the German Invasion. On the following day at 7 o'clock in the morning the Belgian government delivered a reply to the German proposal for "friendly neutrality," in which it declared that it was "profoundly and painfully astonished" at the demand; that Belgium had always faithfully observed her international obligations and performed her duties in a spirit of loyal impartiality; that the attack upon her independence with which Germany threatened her was a flagrant violation of the law of nations which no strategic interest could justify; that the intentions attributed to France were in contradiction to the formal assurances made by the French government on August 1, and that if the Belgian government accepted the proposal, it would sacrifice its national honor and betray, at the same time, its duty toward Europe. In conclusion, the reply stated that "if the Belgian government, conscious of the part that Belgium has played for more than 80 years in the civilization of the world, be disappointed in its expectations, it is resolved to repel by every means in its power any attack upon its rights."[2] On August 4 the Belgian minister of foreign affairs was informed by the German government that, as Belgium had declined its "well-intentioned" proposals, it deeply regretted the necessity of carrying out by force of arms, if necessary, the measures

[1] The text of this proposal is printed in *The Case of Belgium*, p. 5; also in *Diplomatic Correspondence Respecting the War* published by the Belgian government, presented to both houses of the British parliament in October, 1914, *Misc.*, No. 12, pp. 18–19.

[2] Text in *The Case of Belgium*, p. 7, and *Dip. Cor.* cited above, pp. 21–22.

considered indispensable in view of the French menaces. Thereupon German troops marched into Belgium. The Belgian government then addressed an appeal to Great Britain, France, and Russia to coöperate with it as guaranteeing powers in the defence of Belgian territory, and the same day the Belgian government was informed by the government of Great Britain that it expected Belgium to resist with all the means at her disposal, and that the British government was prepared to join Russia and France, *should Belgium so desire*, in resisting the German violation of her territory. On the same day Sir E. Goschen was informed by Sir Edward Grey that "in view of the refusal of the German government to give the same assurance respecting Belgium that France had given, and in view of the violation of Belgian territory, he must repeat the request referred to above and ask that a satisfactory reply be received in London by twelve o'clock that night." If not, the ambassador was to ask for his passports and to say that His Majesty's government "felt bound to take all steps to uphold the neutrality of Belgium and the observance of a treaty to which Germany is as much a party as ourselves." [1] Sir E. Goschen states that upon receipt of this telegram he called on the German secretary of state for foreign affairs and inquired in the name of His Majesty's government whether the Imperial government would refrain from violating Belgian neutrality. Herr von Jagow at once replied that he was sorry to say that his answer must be no, as in consequence of the German troops having crossed the frontier that morning, Belgian neutrality had already been violated. [2]

§ 436. Questions of International Law Involved. The questions of international law involved in the violation of the neutrality of Belgium may be reduced to three: (1) Is the violation of the territory of a neutral by a belligerent ever justifiable, and if so, was it justifiable in the present case? (2) Is it permissible to a neutral to grant the right of passage through its territory of the troops of one of the belligerents for the purpose of attacking its adversary? (3) Where two or more States have by treaty guaranteed the permanent neutrality of another State, is it the right or duty of one of the guaranteeing powers to intervene, independently of the other co-guarantors, for the

---

[1] English White Book, despatch No. 159.
[2] Despatch of Sir E. Goschen to Sir Edward Grey, August 8.

purpose of preventing the violation of the guarantee by one of the parties?

Acts in violation of the territory of neutral States by belligerents may, for the purpose of the present discussion, be grouped into two classes: (1) the use of neutral territory as a theatre of hostilities, a base of operations, or a place for recruiting their forces or for fitting out or increasing their armaments; (2) as a right of way for the passage of troops. The law of neutrality as it is understood today does not recognize any distinction between the two classes of acts; both are forbidden to belligerents, one quite as much as the other. But intrinsically there is an important distinction between them, for the injury sustained by the neutral in the two cases may be very different. Where opposing belligerents fight their battles upon the territory of a neutral or use it as a base of operations or for recruiting their forces or for fitting out their armaments, not only the honor and dignity of the nation are outraged, but it may suffer material injury from the inevitable destruction of property and interference with the occupations and normal life of the inhabitants. On the contrary, the use of neutral territory merely for the passage of troops does not necessarily produce such results. It would be quite possible for a belligerent to march an army across a small State without interfering in any considerable degree with the lives, property, or daily pursuits of the inhabitants. Indeed, if he should purchase his supplies from the local inhabitants, it might be a source of actual advantage to them. In the present case Germany asked only for the right of passage for her troops; she declared that she contemplated no hostile act against Belgium; she promised to protect the kingdom in all its possessions, to indemnify it for all damage done, and to buy and pay cash for all supplies needed for the troops during their passage through the country.

§ 437. The German Pretext of Military Necessity. The German government readily admitted that its act was a violation of a treaty to which it was a party and a violation of a long-established principle of international law, but justified the act as one of military necessity. It was "a question of life and death"; the duty of self-preservation required Germany "to forestall the French advance," [1] and this duty must override

---

[1] Despatch of the German foreign secretary to Prince Lichnowsky, August 4, 1914, English White Book, No. 157.

treaties and rules of international law when they stand in the way. Sir E. Goschen thus stated the reasons which the Imperial secretary of state gave in defence of Germany's action.

"Herr von Jagow again went into the reasons why the imperial government had been obliged to take this step — namely, that they had to advance into France by the quickest and easiest way, so as to be able to get well ahead with their operations and endeavour to strike some decisive blow as early as possible. It was a matter of life and death for them, for if they had gone by the more southern route they could not have hoped, in view of the paucity of roads and the strength of the fortresses to have got through without formidable opposition entailing great loss of time. This loss of time would have meant time gained by the Russians for bringing up their troops to the German frontier. Rapidity of action was the great German asset, while that of Russia was an inexhaustible supply of troops."

Sir E. Goschen then said, "I should like to go and see the Chancellor, as it might be, perhaps, the last time I should have an opportunity of seeing him. He begged me to do so. I found the Chancellor very agitated. His excellency at once began a harangue which lasted for about twenty minutes. He said that the step taken by His Majesty's government was terrible to a degree; just for a word — 'neutrality,' a word which in war time had so often been disregarded — just for a scrap of paper, Great Britain was going to make war on a kindred nation who desired nothing better than to be friends with her." [1]

In a speech in the *Reichstag* of August 4, the German Chancellor stated the case of Germany as follows:

"We are in a state of legitimate defence (*wir sind jetz in der Notwehr*). Necessity knows no law. Our troops have occupied Luxemburg and have

---

[1] The Chancellor's reference to the treaty of 1839 as a "scrap of paper" was the subject of severe criticism. In an interview with a representative of the Associated Press on January 24, 1915 (text in *Amer. Jour. of Int. Law*, July, 1915, p. 717), Chancellor von Bethmann-Hollweg asserted that the phrase had been misunderstood and a wrong meaning given to his words. "When I spoke," he said, "I already had certain indications, but no absolute proof on which to base a public accusation that Belgium had long before abandoned its neutrality in its relations with England. England drew the sword only because she believed her own interests demanded it. Just for Belgian neutrality she never would have entered the war. That is what I meant when I told Sir E. Goshen, in that last interview when we sat down to talk the matter over privately man to man, that among the reasons which had impelled England into war the Belgian neutrality treaty had for her only the value of a scrap of paper. I may have been a bit excited and aroused. Who would not have been at seeing the hopes and work of the whole period of my chancellorship going for naught? I recalled to the ambassador my efforts for years to bring about an understanding between England and Germany, an understanding which, I reminded him, would have made a general European war impossible, and have absolutely guaranteed the peace of Europe. In comparison with such momentous consequences, was the treaty not a scrap of paper?" Cf. also Schoenborn's explanation in *Deutschland und der Weltkrieg* (Eng. trans.), p. 532.

perhaps already penetrated into Belgium. This is against the law of nations (*das widerspricht, den Geboten des Völkerrechts*). France, it is true, has declared to Brussels that it is determined to respect the neutrality of Belgium as long as its adversary respects it, but we know that France was ready to invade Belgium. France can afford to wait; we cannot. A French attack on our flank in the region of the lower Rhine might have been fatal. It is for that reason that we have been compelled to ignore the just protests of the governments of Luxemburg and Belgium. The injustice which we thus commit we will repair as soon as our military object has been attained.[1] Anybody who is threatened as we are threatened and is fighting for its highest possessions can have only one thought — how he is to hack his way through (*wie er sich durchhaut*)."

§ 438. **The Right of Self-preservation.** The authorities on international law are generally agreed that there are conceivable circumstances under which the violation of neutral territory by a belligerent is justifiable. The necessity of self-preservation is certainly such a case. Rivier states the rule as follows: "When a conflict arises between the right of self-preservation of a State and the duty of that State to respect the rights of another, the right of self-preservation overrides the duty." "In certain cases," he adds, "a government is bound to violate the rights of another country for the safety of its own. That is the excuse of necessity, an application of the reason of State. It is a legitimate excuse."[2] "In certain cases," says Oppenheim, "it is a fact that violations committed in self-preservation are not prohibited by the law of nations; they are justified in cases of necessity and of this, every State must be the judge."[3]

[1] The text in *Deutschland und der Weltkrieg* is slightly different from the above, but in substance it is the same. Baron Beyens, Belgian minister at Berlin, relates that on August 4 he had an interview with Herr von Jagow, during the course of which the latter said: "We have been obliged by *absolute necessity* to address to your government the request of which you are aware. For Germany it is a matter of life and death. In order not to be crushed, she has first to crush France and then turn against Russia. We have learnt that the French army was preparing to pass through Belgium in order to attack our flank. We are bound to forestall it." Second Belgian Grey Book, Nos. 25 and 51.

[2] *Principes du Droit des Gens*, Vol. I, p. 277.

[3] *Int. Law*, Vol. I, p. 178. On the question of the right of a State to violate the neutrality of another State on the ground of self-preservation cf. Grotius, *de Jure Belli ac Pacis*, Bk. II, ch. 2, par. 7; Vattel, *Droit des Gens*, Bk. II, ch. 7; Kluber, *Droit des Gens*, sec. 44; Twiss, *Law of Nations*, Vol. I, sec. 102; Halleck, *Int. Law*, Vol. I, p. 95; Rivier, *Principes*, Vol. I, sec. 20; Bonfils, *Droit Int. Pub.*, secs. 242 *et seq.*; Despagnet, *Droit Int. Pub.*, secs. 172–175; Pradier-Fodéré, *Droit Int. Pub.*, Vol. I, secs. 211–286; Calvo, *Droit Int. Pub.*, Vol. I, secs. 208–209; Hall, *Int. Law*, 4th ed., pp. 57, 281; Phillimore, Vol. I, secs. 210–220; Pomeroy, *Int. Law*, p. 351, and Lawrence, *Principles*, p. 501.

Westlake approves the destruction by the English of the Danish fleet in 1807 to prevent its falling into the hands of Napoleon, and apparently he justifies such acts as the seizure of Amelia Island by the United States in 1817, the invasion of West Florida by General Jackson in 1818, and the destruction in American waters of the *Caroline* by the British in 1837.[1] The violation of Korean territory by the Japanese in 1904 was defended by the Japanese on the ground that the maintenance of the independence and territorial integrity of Korea was one of the objects of the war, and that Japan was justified in landing troops there to prevent its occupation by the Russians. Lawrence, who has attempted to justify the conduct of the Japanese, although he admits that technically there was a violation of international law, points out that Korea's position was "curious and anomalous"; that "theoretically it had long been within Japan's sphere of political influence," and that "practically it never had been and was never meant to be fully independent."[2] But this justification has not commended itself to all writers. The Japanese act, says Spaight,[3] was based on the extremely dubious assumption that Russia would land there if the Japanese did not forestall them.[4] In this respect the Japanese case was analogous to that of Germany in the recent war, although in other respects they were very different. The law of self-preservation was not involved in the Japanese case, but, on the other

[1] *Int. Law*, Pt. I, p. 315. The destruction of the Danish fleet, says Westlake, is essentially similar to that of a belligerent having sure information that his enemy, in order to obtain a strategic advantage, is about to march an army across the territory of a neutral clearly too weak to resist, in which circumstances it would be impossible to deny him the right of anticipating the blow in the neutral territory.

There is no doubt, he says (*Collected Papers on Int. Law*, p. 120), that a belligerent may violate the territory of a neutral State on the ground of self-preservation, e.g., where one belligerent has sure information that a corps of the other, quite beyond the ability of the neutral to resist, is on the march to obtain a strategic advantage by violating the territory of the latter.

[2] *War and Neutrality in the Far East*, pp. 208 et seq. The British Manual of Military Law (sec. 468, n. d) remarks that "the circumstances under which Manchuria and Korea became the theatre of war were peculiar and exceptional arising out of the inability of China and Korea to free themselves from Russian occupation and influence. The very purpose of the war was the expulsion of the Russians from Manchuria and Korea."

[3] *War Rights on Land*, p. 481.

[4] Cf. also Hershey, *Int. Law* and *Diplomacy of the Russo-Japanese War*, pp. 70 et seq., and Smith and Sibley, *Int. Law as Interpreted during the Russo-Japanese War*, pp. 22–23.

hand, the obligation to protect a weaker neighbor from aggression by a third State was assigned as the principal justification for the violation.

In its "proposal" to the Belgian government of August 2, the German government stated that it had received "positive information" that French troops intended to march upon the Meuse by way of Givet and Namur, thus leaving no doubt of France's intention to disregard the neutrality of Belgium, and consequently the German government could not help fearing that Belgium, in spite of her willingness to prevent it, was not in a position to do so. It was, therefore, Germany's "imperative duty of self-preservation to forestall the attack of the enemy." The note did not state the source or nature of the information, and the assertion was supported by no proof. It was contrary to the written assurance that the French government had given the British government on August 1, which assurance had been communicated to the German government.[1] It is clear that the German government did not place any reliance upon the assurance given by France to England of her intention to respect the treaty of neutralization, nor upon the assurance given by England to Germany that her own course would be the same irrespective of whichever belligerent should violate the treaty.

§439. The German Theory of Military Necessity: *Kriegsmanier* v. *Kriegsraison*. As is well known, the German doctrine of military necessity embraces more than the right of self-preservation and includes acts of mere military interest, utility, and convenience. According to their view any act without which the object of the war cannot be attained is legally justifiable on the ground of military necessity. They distinguish between *Kriegsraison*, which some writers translate as the "law of necessity in warfare" or the "reason of war," and *Kriegsmanier*, the "usages of war." The latter are the normal rules of war

---

[1] In a letter of August 10, 1914, to President Wilson the Emperor said: "Belgium had to be violated on strategical grounds, news having been received that France was already preparing to enter Belgium and the King having refused my petition for a free passage under guarantee of the country's freedom." Mr. Gerard (*My Four Years in Germany*) says the original draft of the Emperor's letter spoke of "knowledge" having been received, but that the word "knowledge" was struck out and the word "news" substituted, thus indicating that there was doubt in the Emperor's mind as to his position.

which are binding upon a belligerent under ordinary circumstances; the former are the exceptional rules which a belligerent may apply in case of urgent necessity.[1] But some German writers seem to interpret the distinction to mean that the ordinary laws of war cease to be binding upon a belligerent whenever their observance would defeat the attainment of the object of the war. *Kriegsraison geht vor Kriegsmanier* is an old German maxim.[2] This doctrine has long been a leading tenet of the laws of war as expounded by the German military writers and jurists,[3] and it is given great emphasis in the *Kriegsbrauch im Landkriege*, which lays down the proposition that *Kriegsraison* allows a belligerent to have recourse to all means which enable him to attain the object of the war.

§ 440. **Criticism of the German Theory of *Kriegsraison*.** It must be admitted that within reasonable limits this much

[1] Westlake, *Collected Papers on Int. Law*, p. 243.

[2] Cf. Oppenheim, *Int. Law*, Vol. II, sec. 67, where the origin of the maxim is explained. According to Professor Oppenheim the distinction between *Kriegsraison* and *Kriegsmanier* is merely that between the laws of war and the usages of war; the maxim referred to above means simply that the reason of war takes precedence over the *usages* of war, not over the *laws* of war. Cf. also De Visscher, *Les Lois de la Guerre et la Théorie de la Nécessité*, *Rev. Gén. de Droit Int. Pub.*, Vol. 24 (1917), p. 99. The distinction is fully explained by Leuder in Holtzendorff's *Handbuch des Völkerrechts*, secs. 65–66. *Kriegsraison*, says Leuder, allows a belligerent to disregard the ordinary laws of war in cases of extreme necessity when the object of the war can be attained only by their non-observance and also as a measure of retortion or retaliation for unjustifiable non-conformity by the adversary. "When therefore," he says, "the circumstances are such that the attainment of the object of the war and the escape from extreme danger would be hindered by observing the limitations imposed by the laws of war and can only be accomplished by breaking through those limitations, the latter is what ought to be done, because it must be done in order to avoid defeat and perhaps ruin." Nevertheless, Leuder adds that this doctrine does not imply that there are no binding laws of war; that would be "shooting quite beyond the mark."

[3] Cf. Ullmann, *Völkerrecht*, sec. 144; Zitelmann, *Haben wir noch ein Völkerrecht?*, *Preussische Jahrbücher*, October–December, 1914; Liszt, *Das Völkerrecht*, sec. 39; Kluber, *Droit des Gens*, sec. 245; and Meurer (*Die Haager Friedens Konferens*, Vol. II, p. 14), who says there is no violation of the laws of war when an act of war is necessary for the maintenance of the troops or for their defence against a danger which cannot be avoided by other means or to attain or consolidate the success of a military operation not in itself prohibited. *Kriegsraison*, says Strupp (*Das Internationale Landkriegsrecht*, p. 5), is founded on the supreme duty which is laid on the military command to assure the successful issue of the war. Again he says: "The provisions of the laws of war can be disregarded whenever a violation appears to be the only means of carrying out an operation of war or assuring its success or even of preserving the armed forces, even if only a single soldier is concerned" (*Zeitschrift für Völkerrecht*, Bd. VII, p. 363). Cf. the comment of De Visscher, *La Belgique et les Juristes Allemands*, p. 33.

criticised theory is legally defensible; that is to say, a belligerent is justified in disregarding a rule of war law whenever conformity to the rule would involve his destruction; but the German writers have exalted the distinction between what they call *Kriegsmanier* and *Kriegsraison* into a system and converted the exception into a general rule. They have confused self-preservation with mere strategical interest or convenience and have laid down the broad and unwarranted doctrine that observance of the laws of war is not required if conformity thereto interferes with the attainment of the object of war. The question raised by the term *Kriegsraison*, says Westlake, is not whether the code of war is defective or badly conceived in such and such of its provisions, but rather whether a necessity, a necessity not of war but of success, may deprive it of its authority.[1] Manifestly, such a theory when carried out to its logical conclusion leads to the absolute supremacy of the strategical or military interest as formulated in the ancient maxim *omnia licere quae necessaria ad finem belli;* that is, it would lead to the very negation of international law.[2] As De Visscher very properly remarks, the unlimited application of *Kriegsraison* is not only in direct opposition to the general spirit which animated the Hague Conference, but it is formally condemned by article 22 of the convention respecting the laws and customs of war on land, which declares that belligerents are not unlimited in the choice of their means.[3]

---

[1] *Int. Law*, Vol. II, p. 116.

[2] The German distinction in criminal law between the right of legitimate defence (*Notwehr*) and the state or law of necessity (*Notstand, Notrecht*) has been carried over by their jurists into international law. Self-defence involves the exercise of a right against aggression, while the "law of necessity" allows a belligerent to violate the right of innocent third parties whenever it is necessary to safeguard his own interests. Cf. Kohler, *Notwehr und Neutralität*, in the *Zeitschrift für Völkerrecht*, Bd. VII (1914), p. 577; Strupp, *ibid.*, p. 733; also his *Das Internationale Landkriegsrecht*, pp. 5 ff., and Heinscheimer in the *Juristische Wochenschrift*, 1916, pp. 244 ff. Cf. also Meurer, *Kriegsrecht*, p. 14, and Wehberg, *Capture in War* (Eng. trans.), p. 4. The German distinction beween the terms *Notstand, Notwendigkeit*, and *Notrecht* is examined at length by Max Huber in an article in the *Zeitschrift für Völkerrecht*, Bd. VII. It is examined and criticised by De Visscher in his book *Belgium's Case: A Juridical Inquiry*, pp. 20-21; in his book *La Belgique et les Juristes Allemands*, pp. 32 ff., and in an article entitled *Les Lois de la Guerre et la Théorie de la Nécessité*, in the *Rev. Gén. de Droit Int.*, 1917, pp. 74 ff. Cf. also an article by E. L. in Clunet's *Journal*, 1917, pp. 471 ff., entitled *Théories Allemandes pour la Légitimation Juridique de la Maxime "Not kennt kein Gebot"*; and an article by G. F., *ibid.*, pp. 61 ff.

[3] Article cited, p. 101.

Such a view of military necessity has been almost unanimously condemned by writers outside Germany. The excuse of necessity as a justification for violating the law, says Rivier, is legitimate only when the violation is necessary, not when it is a simple matter of utility or interest.[1] Westlake likewise points out that the doctrine of necessity is applicable only in cases of self-preservation and where the threatened injury or danger will not admit of the delay which the normal course of action would involve.[2]

The rule laid down by Daniel Webster in the case of the *Caroline* was that in order to justify the violation of neutral territory the violating government must show "a necessity of self-defence, instant and overwhelming, leaving no choice of means and no moment for deliberation."[3] German writers also are not lacking who reject the theory of military necessity enunciated above. Bluntschli, for example, says: "One may do in time of war whatever is required in military operations, that is to say, whatever is necessary for the attainment of the object of war so long as it does not violate the laws of humanity and the accepted usages of civilized nations."[4] Again he lays down the principle that the rules of international law in respect to the rights and obligations of belligerents must be respected even in an unjust war.[5]

§ 441. **Military Necessity as a Defence for the Invasion of Belgium.** As has been pointed out, both von Bethmann-Hollweg and von Jagow defended the invasion of Belgium almost entirely on the ground of military necessity, and it was not until the public opinion of the neutral world had condemned this defence as a hollow pretext that other reasons were advanced. Even after other alleged reasons were discovered, the plea of military necessity continued to be the chief defence upon which the Germans rested their case. Professor Niemeyer of Kiel in an article published in the *Juristische Wochenschrift*[6] thus stated the necessity argument:

---

[1] *Principes du Droit de Gens*, Vol. I, p. 278.
[2] *Int. Law*, Vol. II, p. 114. Cf. the similar views of Hall, 6th ed., p. 264; Hershey, *Essentials*, p. 144, and Oppenheim, Vol. II, p. 177.
[3] Moore, *Digest of Int. Law*, Vol. II, sec. 217.
[4] *Droit Int. Cod.*, sec. 549.   [5] *Ibid.*, sec. 519.
[6] No. 16, 1914, translated and published in the *Michigan Law Review* for Jan., 1915, with comment and criticism by Prof. J. S. Reeves.

"We have experienced that the neutrality of Belgium was made impossible by the Belgian-French, French-English and Belgian-English understandings and military measures that preceded the German invasion because the necessity of war demanded these measures and movements. And no one dare place blame upon these nations because they carried out a march through Belgium. *Omnia licere in bello quae necessaria sunt ad finem belli* — this statement (from Grotius) of the necessity of war covers the conduct of both sides."

The late Professor Joseph Kohler of the University of Berlin made a similar defence.

"Germany," he said, "could appeal to the law of necessity; France was on the point of marching against Germany through Belgium; it was therefore necessary for Germany to forestall the attack by herself marching into Belgium. In doing this she acted in self-defence and was not therefore restricted by treaties or consideration for the rights of Belgium; she was not even bound to pay for the damages committed in consequence of the passage of the German troops; for this Belgium must look to France because France had shifted the war to Belgium in order to overcome Germany. Moreover, Belgium herself was to blame in consequence of her hostile attitude toward Germany in refusing to her the right of passage to ward off the French attack; indeed Belgium should have helped Germany to repulse the French violation of Belgian neutrality. Instead, Belgium herself agreed to the French violation of her neutrality; she conspired with France with a view to assisting her to invade Germany; she was therefore an aggressor and forfeited her neutral immunity through her own folly. Of this understanding with France there were the most obvious proofs. Even before the outbreak of the war French officers had arrived at Belgian fortresses in order to facilitate French operations against Germany, Belgian soldiers were instructed to fire upon German soldiers but not upon those of France, and when French aviators flew over Belgium the Belgian government made no protest." [1]

Professor Schoenborn of the University of Heidelberg likewise finds in the plea of necessity a complete justification of the invasion of Belgium. "The march through Belgium," he says, "was *absolutely imperative* in the interest of self-preservation by the German Empire; only in this way did it seem possible to resist successfully the efforts of Germany's enemies to crush her." Germany, he says, was in the position of a forester who is attacked by a poacher and who sees an armed companion approaching under cover of another man's house and on the point of entering it for the purpose of obtaining a favorable

[1] *Notwehr und Neutralität, Zeitschrift für Völkerrecht*, Bd. VIII (1914), pp. 576 ff.

aim; the forester thereupon bursts open the door and enters the house himself in order to take the second poacher by surprise and overpower him.[1]

Then turning to the question as to whether Germany was really in a position of urgent necessity, Professor Schoenborn proceeds to argue that it was Germany who was attacked, the proof of which is to be found in the history of the events preceding the war. This proof, according to him, consisted in the undisputed determination of Germany's enemies to annihilate her, or at least to destroy her position as a world power. Thus

"Germany was in a most difficult strategic position from the very beginning; she was involved in a war on two fronts with two of the most powerful military States of Europe, which had in recent years made tremendous preparations for war; she was deprived of her freedom of action at sea owing to England's highly threatening attitude, even in the last days of July; and in the beginning, furthermore, forced to rely mainly on her own military resources because it was no longer possible to hope for armed assistance from Italy, and because her ally Austria, also immediately involved in a war on two fronts, could employ only a part of her forces against Russia, whose army alone was estimated to be numerically equal to the combined forces of the central powers. There was but one advantage on Germany's side to counterbalance all this; the prospect that the great numerical superiority of her enemies could be effectively developed only after the lapse of time, whereas the rapidity of the German mobilization was regarded as unparalleled."

That France "intended" to take advantage of this circumstance the German government had received "reliable information."

---

[1] The analogy is false; presumably the "poacher" was France, and his armed companion was England. But France had not attacked Germany. Germany herself was the "poacher," for it was she who first declared war against France. Furthermore, Great Britain had not come to the aid of France, nor did she declare war against Germany until the German troops had entered Belgium. A more exact analogy would be to say that the German "forester" forced his way through the house of an innocent neighbor to attack one whom the "forester" professed to believe was an enemy, this not because there was no other way of getting at him, but because it was the shortest way of approach and was beset by fewer obstacles. Professor Kohler in the article referred to above attempted to defend the action of Germany by recourse to a somewhat similar analogy. "If I am attacked by an enemy," he said, "who has stationed himself in the house of a neighbor, I am justified in shooting into the house in order to defend myself and to prevent a continuation of the attack." *Zeitschrift für Völkerrecht*, Bd. VIII, p. 577. The same is true, he said, "when the aggressor has not yet entered the house of the third party, but is on the point of rushing in in order to fire at me from within the house. In that case I have the right to get ahead of him by forcing myself into the house and if I injure the house I am acting in self-defence." The conclusion is warranted, but the premise is false, for no enemy had attacked Germany within the territory of Belgium, and there is no evidence that one was preparing to do so.

True, France had given assurances that she would respect the neutrality of Belgium, but those assurances were conditioned on the contingency that Belgium's neutrality must be "respected" by other powers, an assurance, he says, that amounted to little, because it left France full liberty of action in case a German patrol should stray by mistake across the Belgian frontier or a German aviator should fly over some projection of Belgium. "After considering all these points," Schoenborn concluded, "no unbiassed judge will deny that Germany was in a position of extreme necessity." [1]

§ 442. **The German Argument Analyzed.** The conclusion of Schoenborn and the other German apologists would be entitled to some weight if their assumptions had any foundation in fact. The burden of their argument, when stripped of its subtleties, was that Germany, finding herself involved in a war in which her adversaries had the advantage of numbers and of geographical situation, was justified on grounds of military necessity in marching her armies through the territory of a neutral State — a State, too, whose inviolability Germany had solemnly pledged herself to respect and guarantee — in order to offset the disadvantage to which she would have been exposed by attacking her enemies by way of her own frontier. The shortest distance between Germany and her chief adversary and the best roads lay through the territory of Belgium, and, besides, this route was beset by no such military defences as she would be compelled to face by taking the more southerly route around Belgium. It was, therefore, purely considerations of strategical interest and of military convenience which actuated the German government and in no sense a case of necessity.[2] It was to the interest of Germany that she should strike France quickly before Russia could bring her armies into full action; this could be done only by sending her forces through Belgium.[3] The plea that it was necessary to forestall the threatened action

---

[1] See his chapter entitled *Belgium's Neutrality* in *Modern Germany* (Eng. trans. of *Deutschland und der Weltkrieg*), p. 545. The argument of military necessity is relied upon by many other German jurists. Cf. among others Zitelmann, *Haben wir noch ein Völkerrecht?* in the *Preussische Jahrbücher* for October–December, 1914, p. 472; von Liszt, *Das Völkerrecht*, 10th ed. (1915), p. 202, and a propagandist brochure entitled, *Die Wahrheit über den Krieg.*

[2] Cf. Renault, *Les Premières Violations*, p. 62.

[3] Cf. the views of Fuehr, an apologist of Germany's action, in his book *The Neutrality of Belgium*, p. 185.

of France is without weight, for France had given her solemn assurances that she would respect the neutrality of Belgium, provided her adversaries would do likewise, and there is no evidence to justify the German assumption that the assurances were made in bad faith. The insincerity imputed to the French government was merely a pretext, and it is clear from the German correspondence with the Belgian and English governments that it was the intention of the German government from the outset to send its armies through Belgium. At the time of the delivery of the German ultimatum to Belgium, France had not violated the neutrality of Belgium; even according to the admission of the German government there existed only "reliable information" of an *intention* to do so.[1] The only possible conclusion is that if the plea of military necessity be admitted as a justifiable defence for the invasion of Belgium, any belligerent act which subserves a military interest may be defended on the same ground, and in that case it is quite useless for States to enter into engagements to respect the rights of one another, for treaties will in truth be but "scraps of paper" and international guarantees what Frederick the Great conceived them to be, namely, "works of filigree more satisfying to the eye than of any utility."

[1] The formal declaration of war delivered to the Belgian government stated that Germany had been compelled to take this action in view of French *menaces*. Mr. James M. Beck, in his *Evidence in the Case* (p. 229), aptly remarks that if it were really true that the German government had evidence of the intention of France to invade Belgium, it was the greatest tactical blunder that it did not permit France to carry out her intention, because it would have furnished Germany with a justification of her own conduct which could never have been questioned.

CHAPTER XXIX

THE GERMAN INVASION OF BELGIUM
(Continued)

§ 443. Alleged French Violations of Belgian Neutrality; § 444. German Charges against Belgium; the Anglo-Belgian "Conversations"; § 445. May a Neutralized State Enter into Alliances? § 446. Effect of the Treaties of 1870 on the Neutralization Treaty; § 447. Was the Treaty of 1839 Binding on the German Empire? § 448. The Provisions of the Hague Convention in Respect to the Inviolability of Neutral Territory; § 449. The *Rebus sic Stantibus* Argument; § 450. Evaluation of the German Arguments; § 451. The Right of Passage in Time of War; § 452. Duty of the Guarantors of the Neutralization of Belgium.

§ 443. Alleged French Violations of Belgian Neutrality. After the German armies had crossed the Belgian frontier and the public opinion of the world had been aroused by the act, the Germans promptly set about to discover other pretexts than that of military necessity to justify their conduct. The charge was now put forward that France had already before the delivery of the ultimatum actually violated the neutrality of Belgium and this with the consent of the Belgian government.[1] The charges of French violations of Belgian territory took various forms. Baron von Schoen, German ambassador at Paris, in the declaration of war which he handed to the French government on August 3 charged that "several French airmen had already violated the neutrality of Belgium by

---

[1] Cf. the following from a proclamation issued on August 4, 1914, by General von Emmich after his troops had entered Belgium: "It is my greatest regret that the German troops find themselves obliged to cross the frontier of Belgium. They are acting under inevitable necessity, as the neutrality of Belgium has already been violated by French officers who under disguise have crossed the Belgian territory in motor cars to enter Germany." On August 9 General von Bülow issued a proclamation to the Belgian people in which he said: "We are fighting the Belgian army solely to force a passage towards France which your government has wrongfully refused to us, although they have allowed the French to make a military reconnaissance, a fact which your papers have concealed from you."

flying over Belgian territory." [1] M. Viviani promptly denied the charge as being without foundation. [2]

After the delivery of the ultimatum of August 2 the German minister to Belgium informed the Belgian government that "French dirigibles had thrown bombs and that a French cavalry patrol had crossed the frontier in violation of international law." Upon being asked where the bomb-throwing had taken place, he replied, "in Germany."

Richard Grasshoff, a German writer, [3] charges that Belgium had before August 4 "opened her frontiers to the French." The proof which he submits in support of the charge consists mainly of the testimony of certain persons, mostly Germans, who claimed to have seen French soldiers at Liège and Namur between July 26 and July 29. One witness claimed to have seen a French aeroplane over Brussels. Two others claimed to have seen, or to have been told by others who had seen, French patrols in Belgium. These charges are characterized by extreme vagueness, no names are given and some of them are based on hearsay evidence. It is not probable that the nationality of an aeroplane seen flying high in the air over Belgium could have been distinguished by a man on the earth far below. It is not improbable also that the persons taken for French soldiers were in fact Belgians, for there is a striking similarity between their uniforms. [4] The French government investigated the charges, and on August 4 the French minister of war declared that "our soldiers are rigorously and in the most formal manner forbidden even as patrols to enter Belgian territory." [5] Most if not all of the acts charged took place in

---

[1] Dr. Ernest Müller-Meiningen in his *Der Weltkrieg und der Zusammenbruch des Völkerrechts*, ch. 1, charges that it was established by the declarations of French prisoners that French officers were "professionally active" in Liège and Brussels some weeks before the outbreak of the war. He also quotes from the *Norddeutsche Zeitung* of January 18, 1915, a statement based on sworn testimony that as early as July 24 two companies of French infantry were detrained at Erqueline in Belgium. The statement referred to was made on December 22, nearly five months after the incident alleged.

[2] French Yellow Book, No. 148.

[3] The *Tragedy of Belgium*, pp. 23-40 (Eng. trans. of a book entitled *Belgiens Schuld*).

[4] These various charges are examined and refuted by Waxweiler in his book, *Belgium and the Great Powers*, pp. 158 ff.: by Saint Yves, *Les Responsabilités de l'Allemagne dans la Guerre de 1914*, pp. 299 ff.; and in a Belgian official document entitled *Cahiers Documentaires*, No. 35, January 27, 1917.

[5] The French instructions relative to the violation of neutral territory may be found in a publication of the ministry of foreign affairs entitled *Les Violations des*

fact before the outbreak of war between Germany and France and between Belgium and Germany, so that it is not clear how the presence of a few French soldiers or patrols in Belgium or the passing of aeroplanes over Belgium constituted a violation of Belgian neutrality, for violations of neutrality cannot take place anterior to the existence of a state of war. The charges that French officers were permitted to inspect the fortifications of Liège in July, and that French officers were employed to train Belgian soldiers — if they were true, which the Belgians emphatically deny — can hardly be regarded as a violation by Belgium of her neutral obligations or a justification for the German invasion of the country. As is well known, German officers had for years been employed by the Turkish government for similar purposes, but it was never contended that this was a violation of the neutrality of the Ottoman Empire. Charges were even made that French soldiers constituted a part of the garrison at Liège, but it is somewhat singular that when the place fell into the hands of the German army, no Frenchmen were found among the garrison. The charge made in General von Emmich's proclamation of August 4 that French officers in motor cars had crossed Belgian territory and entered Germany is surrounded with the same mystery, for they appear never to have been captured,[1] and it is difficult to see what object they could have had in view in penetrating the interior of Germany before the outbreak of the war. It may be safely assumed that the airmen, the French soldiers at Liège, and the disguised motorists whom the Germans claim to have seen in Belgium were phantom men who belonged to the class of legendary aviators who are alleged to have flown far into the interior of

---

Lois de la Guerre par l'Allemagne, pp. 24 ff. The New York *Times* of August 12, 1917, printed a despatch from Copenhagen quoting from an article written by Lieutenant-general Baron Freytag-Loringhoven of the German general staff in which the author admitted that the charges against the French were without foundation. The German charge that French soldiers penetrated German territory before the outbreak of the war is analyzed by Professor Allier of the University of Paris in his book *Les Allemands à Saint-Dié* (Paris, 1918), ch. 1. He points out that French soldiers had strict orders not to approach within ten kilometres of the German frontier, and he reproduces the text of a telephone message sent by General Joffre to the commanders of the frontier sections at 5:30 o'clock on August 2, directing them to abstain scrupulously from violating these instructions, because it was important that France should not have to bear the responsibility of first having violated German territory. He also produces considerable evidence that the Germans themselves violated French territory at various points on August 2 and 3.   [1] Cf. Saint Yves, *op. cit.*, p. 302.

Germany several days before the outbreak of the war and
dropped bombs on Nuremberg, a charge which the Germans
themselves now admit to have been without foundation.[1]

§ 444. German Charges against Belgium; the Anglo-Belgian
"Conversations."   More serious charges were now to be
made against Belgium, namely, that she had years before the
outbreak of the war deliberately repudiated the obligations
imposed upon her by the neutralization treaty and had virtually
become a vassal of Great Britain.   It was frequently asserted
by German writers at the time of the ultimatum of August 2,
that they were convinced that this situation had come to pass,
but they were unable to produce the proof.[2]   This proof they
claim to have discovered in the archives of Brussels after the
German occupation of that city in October, 1914.   The alleged
evidence is contained in three documents, the first of which
was a report of the chief of staff of the Belgian army containing
a record of a series of "conversations" between him and Colonel
Barnardiston, the British military attaché at Brussels, disclosing that as early as 1906 the Belgian government was consulting
the British government in regard to steps to be taken by Belgium, Great Britain, and France against Germany and particularly with a view to the admission of British troops into Belgium
for operations against Germany.   The second document contained a report of similar conversations in 1912, and a third was
a report made in 1911 by Baron Greindl, Belgian minister at
Berlin, to the Belgian minister of foreign affairs disclosing that
the former official was familiar with the above-mentioned plans
and designs, against the expediency of which he took occasion
to protest.   Facsimiles of these documents with appropriate
comment by Dr. Dernburg were published by the German
government and widely circulated in neutral countries.[3]

---

[1] A German professor named Schwalbe investigated this charge and published
an article in the *Deutsche Medizinische Wochenschrift* of May 18, 1916, in which he
declared that the charge was entirely without foundation.

[2] Cf. Zitelmann, *Haben wir noch ein Völkerrecht, Preussische Jahrbücher*,
October–December, 1914, p. 472. "Germany does not need to have recourse
to the plea of necessity," says professor Schoenborn, "to justify her act, for long
before the German ultimatum the Belgian government had already violated its
own neutral obligations most seriously to Germany's disadvantage and thereby
torn down the barriers raised by the treaty and given Germany the right to defend
herself by all means." *Modern Germany*, p. 546.

[3] The title of the document is *The Case of Belgium in the Light of Official Reports
Found in the Secret Archives of the Belgian Government after the Occupation of Brus-*

"Taken together, these documents show," says Dr. Dernburg of this publication, "that the British government had the intention, in case of a Franco-German war, of sending troops into Belgium immediately — that is, of doing the very thing which, done by Germany, was used by England as a pretext for declaring war on Germany.

"They show also that the Belgian government took, in agreement with the English General Staff, military precautions against a hypothetical German invasion of Belgium and that the Belgian government was determined from the outset to join Germany's enemies." [1]

But a careful examination of these documents, published in the German official reports, affords no basis for the conclusion which the Germans drew therefrom. The text of the "conversations" both of 1906 and 1912 show clearly that the proposed entry of British troops into Belgium was entirely contingent upon the violation of the neutrality of Belgium by Germany in case of war between her and France, and it is stated in at least two places in the conversations that the admission of British troops could take place only with the consent of the Belgian government and then only for the purpose of enabling Belgium to defend her neutrality against violation by Germany.[2] The

---

sels. The Germans also made much of certain alleged "secret military manuals" discovered at Brussels containing detailed information concerning Belgian roads, rivers, etc. This information, it is alleged, had been obtained between the years 1908 and 1914 by British agents through the assistance of Belgian officials, and it had been published by the British general staff. The importance which the Germans attributed to these "discoveries" is somewhat singular in view of their own practice. It is said that the Germans were in possession of every item of information regarding the roads, rivers, canals, and topography of the country that could be of the least military value to their government. It has been stated that when the German armies entered Belgium, they had copies of the Belgian general staff map, which had been reprinted in Germany with marginal notes in German. Some of these were found in the camps which had been evacuated by the German troops. Waxweiler, *Belgium, Neutral and Loyal*, p. 198. The conduct of the Belgian government in permitting the Germans to obtain this information was not reprehensible in German eyes, but it was a violation of the neutralization treaty to have allowed the British to secure it in the same way.

[1] This strange and curious contention is equivalent to arguing that Belgium should have consulted with and sought the coöperation of the very power which she had reason to believe would be the first to violate her neutrality and against which the Belgians were seeking to protect themselves. Subsequent events fully justified their suspicions and fears. A grievance which Professor Hampe (*Belgium and the Great Powers*, in *Modern Germany*, pp. 340 ff.) seems to have had against Belgium was that she "preferred the friendship of France and England to that of Germany, and thereby ceased to be neutral."

[2] The original document recording the conversations of 1906 contains a marginal entry which reads as follows: *L'entrée des Anglais en Belgique après la violation*

assertion of the German Chancellor that the evidence contained
in the documents showed that Great Britain was determined
to throw troops into Belgium without the consent of the Belgian
government is not, therefore, well founded.   German apologists
have frequently referred to the "conversations" as if they
embodied the terms of an agreement or convention.[1]   But the
documents show unmistakably that there was no agreement or
arrangement of any kind.   They were merely the minutes of a
conversation between the chief of the Belgian general staff and
the British military attaché both of whom suspected as future
events justified them in suspecting, that in the event of war
between Germany and France, Germany would show no respect
for the neutrality of Belgium.   They were simply informal
consultations, such as frequently take place between representatives of foreign officers, and they related only to the coöperation
of Great Britain as one of the guarantors of Belgian neutrality,
in enforcing the observance by Germany of her own treaty
obligations, in case she should disregard them.   Not only is
there no evidence that the matter ever went any farther, but
Sir Edward Grey publicly declared that there was not even
any note of them at the foreign office.   On the basis of these
discoveries the Chancellor in his address to the *Reichstag* on
December 2, 1914, was able to say that "when our troops entered
Belgian territory during the night of the 3d and 4th of August
they were in the confines of a State which had long since riddled
its neutrality."   Professor Schoenborn even goes to the length

---

de neutralité par l'Allemagne.   The *Norddeutsche Zeitung* of November 25, 1914,
in publishing these documents detached the above entry from the context of which
it formed an integral part for the purpose of creating the impression that it had been
added by some one else than those who took part in the conversations.   It also
neglected to translate the entry, as was done in the case of the rest of the document.
De Visscher, *The Case of Belgium,* p. 119, and Waxweiler, *Belgium, Neutral and
Loyal,* pp. 186, 189.   The full text of the conversations may be found in Waxweiler, p. 283, and in a brochure by M. Brunet entitled *Calomnies Allemandes,
les Conventions Anglo-Belges.*

[1] For example Professor Jastrow of the University of Pennsylvania who in the
New York *Nation* of March 4, 1916, variously referred to them as an "agreement,"
an "arrangement," etc.   They are referred to in similar terms by General von
Bernhardi in an article published in the Chicago *Tribune* and other American papers
of March 14, 1916.   The *Norddeutsche Allgemeine Zeitung* of November 24,
1914, in which the documents were first printed, translated the word "conversation" as "convention" (*Abkommen*), concluded (*abgeschlossen*) in September,
1906, for the purpose, it appears, of misleading the German public into believing
that a *convention* had actually been concluded between Belgium and England.

of asserting that the conversations amounted virtually to an offensive alliance between Belgium and Great Britain.[1] They were, he asserts, practically a surrender by Belgium of her liberty of action in favor of England, thus making her a vassal of the latter power. It was "an unconditional and one-sided adherence to an aggressive group of powers to whom Belgium agreed to join her forces. It was therefore Belgium herself who, from within, broke down the protecting rampart which treaty and international law had erected around her territory . . . and replaced it by military agreements with one of the two groups of the European powers."[2]

By this and similar lines of reasoning the responsibility for the German invasion of Belgium was thus thrown back upon Belgium herself.

§ 445. **May a Neutralized State Enter into Alliances?** But admitting that the effect of the conversations of 1906 and 1911 was to establish in effect an alliance between Belgium and Great Britain, does it follow that such a situation was inconsistent with the obligations of Belgium under the neutralization treaty? If such an alliance can by any process of reasoning be construed to have resulted from the conversations referred to above, it was purely defensive in character, having in view the protection of the very neutrality which the treaty of 1839 was designed to establish and perpetuate. It would seem that an alliance with such an object in view is entirely consistent

---

[1] See his chapter in *Modern Germany*, p. 551. Professor Kuno Franke asserts that Belgium had become a vassal of France. "There can be no doubt," he says, "that France, while not openly violating international agreements, has gradually succeeded in circumventing them by making Belgian territory to all intents and purposes a part of the French line of defence against Germany. The Belgian fortresses covering the main passages from Germany into France were strongly fortified; the Belgian army, under French supervision, was brought up to the highest point of efficiency; all Belgium was systematically imbued with French sympathies and ideals and strong dislike and fear of Germany, so that in reality it has been for the last twenty-five years not a neutral State, but a vassal State of France." *Germany's Fateful Hour*, p. 13.

[2] *Ibid.*, p. 553. For similar reasoning cf. Kuno Franke, *Germany's Fateful Hour*, Pubs. of the Germanistic Society of Chicago, pp. 13–14; Grasshoff, *The Tragedy of Belgium*, ch. I; Franke, *Die Belgische Neutralität*; Fuehr, *The Neutrality of Belgium*, pp. 174–175; Hampe, *Belgium and the Great Powers*, in *Modern Germany*, pp. 340 ff.; Dernberg, *Germany and the Real Issue*, Pubs. of the Germanistic Society, No. 10, p. 11; also his *Searchlights on the War*, p. 9; Burgess, *The European War*, p. 171; Niemeyer, *Die Juristische Wochenschrift*, 1914, No. 16; and Schulte, *Von der Neutralität Belgiens*.

with the status of neutralization,[1] and this view is held by many writers.[2] Some writers, indeed, maintain that a neutralized State is especially bound to take all steps, including defensive alliances, which may be necessary to protect its neutrality against violations by other states. The purpose and effect of neutralization is not to destroy the sovereignty of the State neutralized or to deprive it of the right of defence. That the Belgians would have been fully justified in entering into an alliance with friendly powers for the purpose of obtaining their assistance for the protection of their neutrality against the designs of Germany was abundantly established by subsequent events.[3]

§ 446. Effect of the Treaties of 1870 on the Neutralization Treaty. Finally, the Germans sought to justify their invasion of Belgium by contending that the neutralization treaty of 1839 was no longer binding when the invasion took place. Three lines of argument were put forward in support of this contention: (1) That the treaty was superseded by the Anglo-German and Anglo-French conventions of 1870,[4] (2) that the German Empire was not a party to the treaty of 1839, and (3) that the treaty had lapsed under the operation of the doctrine of *rebus sic stantibus.*

The first argument can easily be answered. The diplomatic

---

[1] Some German writers, however, contend that the alleged alliance was in fact offensive in purpose. Cf., e.g., Schoenborn, *op. cit.*, p. 551.

[2] E.g., by Arendt, *Essai sur la Neutralité de la Belgique*, p. 92; Nys, *Rev. de Droit Int. et de Lég. Comp.*, 1901, p. 27; Rivier, *Principes du Droit des Gens*, Vol. II, p. 60; Deschamps, *op. cit.*, pp. 366 ff.; De Visscher, *op. cit.*, pp. 130 ff.; Hagerup, *La Neutralité Permanente*, in the *Rev. Gén. de Droit Int.*, 1905; Piccioni, *Essai sur la Neutralité Perpetuelle*, p. 100, and Hilty, *Die Neutralität der Schweiz.*

[3] "If the German Chancellor desires to know why conversations relative to military matters took place between Belgian and English officers he may find one reason for these interviews in a fact well known to him, namely that Germany had built a complete network of railways for strategical purposes extending from the Rhine to the frontier of Belgium across a barren and sparsely populated region. These railways were constructed to facilitate a sudden attack against Belgium such as was made in August last; this fact was sufficient to justify *pourparlers* between Belgium and other States, the basis of which was that the neutrality of Belgium would not be violated by them, unless it was first violated by another power." Declaration of the Belgian foreign office, quoted by Saint Yves, p. 327.

[4] The first argument was advanced by Burgess (*European War*, p. 170), by Geo. Bernard Shaw, by Dr. Dernburg, by Edmund von Mach, by Fuehr (*op. cit.*, chs. 3 and 8), and other German apologists. Fuehr (p. 150) asserts that the treaties of 1870 "constitute the strongest evidence that the treaty of 1839 was not considered by England as binding on the signatories."

history of the treaties of 1870 and even the express language
of both show clearly that it was not the intention or understanding of the parties that they were to supersede the treaty of
1839.[1] They were entered into upon the initiative of the
British government with a view to securing a definite assurance
from Germany and France that during the war then imminent
neither belligerent would violate the neutrality of Belgium.
The British government never assumed for a moment that the
treaty of 1839 had lapsed; on the contrary, the debates in
Parliament at the time showed that Parliament and public
opinion regarded the treaty as still in force, and that it was the
duty of the British government as one of the guaranteeing
powers to see that it was observed by both Germany and France.
In demanding and obtaining fresh assurances from both belligerents that they would respect the treaty, Great Britain was
only adopting a precautionary measure intended to place both
governments on record and to remove all possibility of doubt
as to her own position in respect to her obligation to guarantee
the observance of the treaty, as well as the duty of France and
Germany to respect it. If there were any doubt as to the
intention of the parties, it is removed by the language of the
treaties, which conclude as follows:

"And on the expiration of that time (twelve months after the conclusion
of peace) the independence and neutrality of Belgium will, so far as the
high contracting parties are respectively concerned, *continue to rest as heretofore* on the *1st article of the quintuple treaty of the 19th of April 1839.*"

Furthermore, in the preamble to each of the treaties of 1870
it is declared that "their said Majesties have determined to
conclude between themselves a separate treaty, which, *without
impairing or invalidating the conditions of the said quintuple
treaty* [of 1839] *shall be subsidiary and accessory to it.*" Therefore

[1] Cf. Morley, *Life of Gladstone*, Vol. II, pp. 340-341. During the debates in
Parliament at the time, objection being raised that the treaties of 1870 might be
construed as weakening the force of the treaty of 1839, Lord Granville stated on
August 8 that "as to this instrument weakening in the slightest degree the effect
of the previous treaty of 1839 I entirely deny it. There is an express reservation
of that treaty." Cf. Hansard, *Parliamentary Debates*, Vol. CCIII, pp. 1675,
1757, quoted by E. R. Turner in the *Nation*, December 24, 1914, p. 744. Mr.
Gladstone expressed a similar view (*ibid.*, pp. 1784 and 1789) on August 10. He
said: "The treaty of 1839 loses nothing of its force even during the existence of
this present treaty." Cf. also Saint Yves, *op. cit.*, p. 322, and Renault, *Les Premières Violations*, pp. 23-24.

when the treaties of 1870 expired, as they did in 1872, the status of Belgium remained as it had been fixed by the treaty of 1839. Furthermore, it should be remarked that Austria and Russia (the other co-guarantors under the treaty of 1839) were not parties to the treaties of 1870; consequently, to contend that the latter treaties superseded the treaty of 1839 is to affirm that three of the parties to the latter treaty could set it aside without the consent of the other two. It is somewhat singular also that if it was the intention. of the parties to the treaties of 1870 to set aside the treaty of 1839 and to extinguish the status of neutralization, that purpose was never affirmed by any writer or maintained by any government at the time. Not until after Germany had deliberately violated the treaty in 1914 and the public opinion of the world had been turned against her did her apologists in their search for pretexts put forward the contention that the treaty of 1839 had been terminated by the dual conventions of 1870. Until then no German, English, or French publicist ever once asserted that the treaties of 1870 had had any such effect.[1]

§ 447. **Was the Treaty of 1839 Binding on the German Empire in 1914?** The argument that the neutralization treaty was not binding on the Empire, since the German party was Prussia only,[2] is equally untenable. It is of course true that the treaty of 1839 was signed by Prussia and not by the German Empire, for the Empire had not yet been formed. But there is an abundance of authority among German text writers themselves in favor of the view that the German Empire succeeded to the treaty rights and obligations of Prussia. Moreover, the Imperial government had uniformly acted in practice in accord-

[1] Geffcken, a German publicist, for example, says of the treaties of 1870, "far from impairing the treaty of 1839 they only aimed at regulating the observance of it in a given case." Holtzendorff, *Handbuch des Völkerrechts*, Vol. IV, p. 642. Cf. also De Visscher, *Belgium's Case*, pp. 81 ff.

[2] This argument is developed at length by Burgess (*The European War*, pp. 169–170). His principal contention is that the British government in 1870 did not regard the treaty of 1839 as binding on the North German Confederation, because it demanded and procured from the German government in 1870 a new treaty, which lapsed in 1872. Therefore, "the present German Empire has never signed any treaty guaranteeing the neutrality of Belgium." Cf. also Schulte, *Von der Neutralität Belgiens*, in *Deutsche Kriegsschriften*, No. 3 (1915); von Mach, *Germany's Point of View*, ch. XIII; Fuehr, *op. cit.*, ch. 8; Dernburg, *Germany and England, the Real Issue*, No. 10, and his *Searchlights on the War*, p. 8, and Schoenborn, in *Modern Germany*, p. 539.

ance with this view, and it does not appear that the German government after the outbreak of the recent war ever formally took the position that the treaty of 1839 was terminated by the conventions of 1870. It remained for the apologists of the German invasion of Belgium to invent and exploit this contention. As early as July 22, 1870, before the conclusion of the dual conventions of that year, Bismarck wrote to the Belgian minister at Berlin as follows:

"In confirmation of my verbal assurance I have the honor to give you in writing a declaration which in the presence of the treaties now in force [this could only have referred to the treaty of 1839] is quite superfluous, that the North-German Confederation and its allies will respect the neutrality of Belgium on the understanding, of course, that it is respected by the other belligerent party."[1]

In 1911, at the time of the controversy respecting the Dutch project for fortifying Flushing when certain newspapers had asserted that, in case of a war between Germany and France, Germany would violate the neutrality of Belgium, the Belgian foreign office suggested that a declaration by the German government would serve to calm public opinion and dispel suspicion. Herr von Bethmann-Hollweg, then chancellor, replied that he fully appreciated the feelings of the Belgian government, and he added that Germany had no intention of violating Belgian neutrality, although he considered that by making a public declaration, Germany would weaken her military position in regard to France.[2]

Again on April 29, 1913, the following declarations were made during the course of a debate in the *Reichstag:* A member of the Social Democratic party having said: "The approach of a war between Germany and France is viewed with apprehension in Belgium, for it is feared that Germany will not respect the neutrality of Belgium," Herr von Jagow, secretary of state, replied: "Belgian neutrality is provided for by international conventions, and Germany is determined to respect those conventions." In answer to fresh inquiries by a member of the Social Democratic party Herr von Heeringen, minister of war,

[1] *Archives Diplomatiques*, 1871–1872, Vol. I, p. 244, quoted by Turner in the *Nation* of December 24, 1914, p. 744, and by De Visscher, *op. cit.*, p. 86.
[2] Note of M. Davignon, Belgian minister of foreign affairs, to the Belgian ministers at Berlin, London, and Paris. *Diplomatic Correspondence of the Belgian Government respecting the War*, No. 12.

replied: "Germany will not lose sight of the fact that the neutrality of Belgium is guaranteed by international treaty."[1] On July 31, 1914, three days before the German ultimatum to Belgium, Herr von Bülow, the German minister at Brussels, told M. Davignon, the Belgian minister of foreign affairs, that he was certain that the sentiments expressed by the German Chancellor in 1911 and 1913 "had not changed."

As stated above, the German Imperial government had uniformly recognized in practice that treaties concluded between the individual States and foreign powers prior to the creation of the Empire were binding upon the Empire. Among such treaties may be mentioned that of 1828 between Prussia and the United States. The courts of the United States have always regarded this treaty as binding upon the German Empire,[2] and it does not appear that the Imperial government ever sought to avoid its obligations under the treaty on the ground that having been entered into between Prussia and the United States, it was not binding upon the Empire.

Throughout the long controversy concerning the sinking of the *William P. Frye* during the recent war the German government never once contended that the treaty of 1828 was not binding upon the Empire. On the contrary, the validity of the treaty was admitted, and the Imperial government agreed to compensate the owners of the vessel for the act of the commander of the *Eitel Friedrich* in sinking the vessel contrary to the provisions of the treaty.[3]

It is impossible to avoid the conclusion, therefore, that if this and other treaties concluded by Prussia and other German States before the founding of the Empire remained in effect and were binding on the imperial government, as they were admitted to be, the treaty of 1839 for the neutralization of Belgium was likewise in force in 1914 and was equally binding upon the Empire.

§ 448. The Provisions of the Hague Convention in Respect to the Inviolability of Neutral Territory. Finally, if we admit,

---

[1] *Ibid.*, inclosure in No. 12; also Davignon, *Belgium and Germany*, p. 7.

[2] Some of the cases involving the application of the provisions of this treaty are examined in an editorial in the *Amer. Jour. of Int. Law* for October, 1915, pp. 952 ff.

[3] Similarly in the case of the *Appam* (§ 567 *infra*) the German government based its claim to a right of asylum for the vessel on the Prussian-American treaties of 1799 and 1828, which it considered to be still in force.

arguendo, that the merging of Prussia into the Empire operated to terminate the treaty of 1839, Germany's offence in forcing a passage through Belgian territory was none the less a violation of the law of nations, for the German Imperial government was a party to convention No. V unanimously adopted by the Second Hague Conference, which contains the following provisions:

> The territory of neutral Powers is inviolable. (Art. 1.)
> Belligerents are forbidden to move troops or convoys of either munitions of war or supplies across the territory of a neutral Power. (Art. 2.)
> A neutral Power must not allow any of the acts referred to in Articles 2 to 4 to occur on its territory. (Art. 5.)
> The fact of a neutral Power resisting, even by force, attempts to violate its neutrality cannot be regarded as a hostile act. (Art. 10.)

It was argued, however, that this convention was not binding upon Germany, because it had not been ratified by all the belligerents in accordance with the "general participation" clause.[1] This argument is purely technical and is hardly creditable to the distinguished jurists who were reduced to the necessity of relying upon refinements, subtle distinctions, and technicalities to justify an act which is incapable of justification upon grounds of law or necessity. But even this argument broke down for the reason that at the time the convention was violated by Germany, none of the non-signatory powers were at war with Germany. At that moment all the belligerents were parties to the convention, and it was, therefore, in accordance with the general participation clause binding upon all of them.[2] In any case, whether the convention as such was technically binding or not, the above-mentioned provisions respecting the inviolability of neutral territory are merely declaratory of a long-established and universally admitted rule of the existing customary law, and as such their validity was not dependent upon formal convention.[3] It was therefore as binding upon

---

[1] E.g. by von Liszt in the *Dresdener Anzeiger*, September 23, 1914, and the *Berliner Tageblatt* of February 10, 1915, and by von Mach in the New York *Times* of November 1, 1914. Cf. also the *Norddeutsche Zeitung* of November 14, 1914, and the *Kölnische Zeitung* of December 14, 1914, quoted by De Visscher, p. 62; Burgess, New York *Times*, October 28, 1914, and Peters, in the *Preussische Jahrbücher* for January, 1915.

[2] Cf. De Visscher, *La Belgique et les Juristes Allemands*, pp. 54 ff.

[3] On this point cf. Scott, *The Hague Conventions and Declarations of 1899 and 1907*, p. 11, and Renault, *Les Premières Violations*, p. 45. The view that the pro-

Germany as any other existing customary rule of the law of nations. But even if the convention had been ratified by all the belligerents, it was not according to German logic applicable, because when the invasion took place, Belgium was not "neutral" in the sense of the convention, but was already in a state of war with Germany; consequently it was the territory of a belligerent power which the German armies entered and not that of a neutral. Professor Schoenborn goes the full length in maintaining that from the moment the Belgian government refused to comply with the German ultimatum of August 2, Belgium was in a conditional state of war in spite of herself; therefore the provisions of the Hague convention respecting the inviolability of neutral territory ceased automatically to apply, and the invasion of Belgium was no breach of the convention.[1] This line of argument reduces the convention to a nullity. In its final analysis it amounts to this: If State A demands of State B permission to commit an act in violation of the latter's neutrality and State B refuses, a condition of war supervenes between the two powers, and no question of neutrality is involved. State A, therefore, has violated no law or obligation.[2] It follows from this reasoning that the formality of a declaration of war suffices to render inapplicable all the provisions of Hague convention No. V; in short, an invasion of neutral territory constitutes no violation of neutrality when the invasion is preceded by a declaration of war.[3] This reasoning is pure sophistry. If war had any such effect on treaties of this kind, it is quite useless for the powers to undertake by international

visions of international conventions which are merely declaratory of an existing law are binding whether the conventions as such have been ratified is upheld by all writers. This is admitted by Zitelmann, *The War and International Law*, in *Modern Germany*, pp. 665-666, and by Strupp, *Zeitschrift für Internationales Recht*, 1915, pp. 342-343.

[1] *Deutschland und der Weltkrieg*, pp. 570-572.

[2] Cf. Renault, *Les Premières Violations*, p. 66.

[3] Cf. on this point the searching criticism of a distinguished Belgian jurist, De Visscher, in an article entitled *Les Lois de la Guerre et la Théorie de la Nécessité* in the *Rev. Gén. de Droit Int. Pub.*, 1917, pp. 74 ff. Cf. also the views of the Swiss jurist M. Huber in the *Zeitschrift für Völkerrecht*, Bd. VII (1915), pp. 357-358. M. Renault (*op. cit.*, p. 66) points out that the Germans did not take the pains to address an ultimatum to the government of Luxemburg. Therefore, in accordance with the above line of reasoning, Luxemburg was not a belligerent, and consequently Germany violated her neutrality, whereas that of Belgium was never violated!

convention to safeguard the neutrality of States against violations of their territory.

§ 449. The *rebus sic stantibus* Argument. Finally, the defenders of Germany's conduct argued that even if it be admitted that the neutralization treaty was not terminated in 1872 upon the expiration of the treaties of 1870, it had ceased to be binding by the year 1914 under the operation of the doctrine of *rebus sic stantibus*, which by implication is a part of every treaty. The conditions which prevailed at the time of the neutralization of Belgium in 1831 had, it was asserted, totally changed by 1914, and the position of Belgium as a European power had been entirely transformed. Belgium had become a strong military State; powerful fortifications had been erected at Antwerp, Liège, and Namur, and as a result of the annexation of the Congo, Belgium had become a colonial power.[1]

"The Belgium of 1908," says Professor Karl Hampe of Heidelberg, "ruled over an immense colonial empire eighty times as large as herself; she was no longer that little State which had once been created as a European bulwark against France and which later, in the system of the balance of power, with difficulty maintained her place in the scale. . . . Able to maintain herself only by the guarantee of her creators, not by her own strength, she had adopted in Africa the imperialistic policy of a Great Power, in the last analysis at the expense of others. Her neutrality, which was always a delicate fragile thing, through the connection with the vast African empire, was subjected to a test of strength to which, in the long run, it was scarcely likely to prove equal." [2]

Professor Schoenborn puts forward a similar argument. A permanently neutralized State, he says, must abstain from every policy that might possibly draw it into war waged by others and must avoid actions that might force participation in it. The acquisition of the Congo, he holds, was open to question, because it "changed the whole basis of the Belgian State and involved it in difficult political problems." In consequence of

[1] Fuehr even thinks it important to add that there had been a marked increase in the revenues, the foreign trade, and the wealth of Belgium! (*Neutrality of Belgium*, ch. 7.)

[2] *Belgium and the Great Powers*, in *Modern Germany*, p. 363. Professor John W. Burgess in his apology for the invasion of Belgium (*The European War of 1914 —Its Causes, Purposes and Probable Results*, p. 171) likewise draws upon the doctrine of *rebus sic stantibus* for support of the proposition that in August, 1914, Belgium "possessed no other neutrality than the ordinary neutrality enjoyed by all States not at war, when some States are at war."

the changed situation thereby created, the treaty of 1839 became obsolete by the acts of Belgium herself.[1]

Writers on international law are generally agreed that treaties become obsolete through the operation of the rule of *rebus sic stantibus*.[2] But when they speak of treaties ceasing to be binding by virtue of the operation of this rule, they have reference to a complete change in the state of things which was the basis of the treaty and one of its tacit conditions.   The change of circumstances must be such as either to render the execution of the treaty difficult or impossible, or to entail the performance of obligations which were not foreseen by the contracting parties and which, had they been foreseen, would never have been assumed.   It is difficult to see how the above-mentioned changes which Belgium underwent between 1831 and 1914 were of this character, at least so far as they involved the validity of the treaty of neutralization.   There is no evidence that the powers which guaranteed the neutralization of Belgium intended to impose on her the status of unarmed neutrality, as was done in the case of Luxemburg, whose fortresses were required to be dismantled.   The treaty of neutralization did not require Belgium to disband her army or to dismantle her fortresses, nor did it prohibit the strengthening of them in the future.   Moreover, not one of the guaranteeing powers ever entered a protest against the Belgian policy of increasing and perfecting the organization of her military force, although that policy had been carried on systematically many years before the outbreak of the recent war and with the full knowledge of Germany and other guaranteeing powers.   The diplomatic documents relating to the neutralization of Belgium show unmistakably that it was the intention of the powers to impose upon Belgium the status of permanent neutrality, a neutrality which would not be impaired by any changes in the political or military

[1] *Belgium's Neutrality*, in *Modern Germany*, pp. 539–547. Fuehr (*op. cit.*, ch. 4) adopts the same view.

[2] Cf. Wharton, *International Law Digest*, Vol. II, p. 58; Phillimore, *Int. Law*, Vol. II, pp. 58–59; Taylor, *Int. Pub. Law*, secs. 394–395; Pomeroy, *Lectures on International Law*, p. 352; and Hershey, *Essentials of Int. Pub. Law*, pp. 319–320. For German interpretations of the rule see Schmidt, *Ueber die Völkerrechtliche Clausula "rebus sic stantibus"*; Liszt, *Das Völkerrecht*, p. 186; Kaufmann *Das Wesen des Völkerrechts und die Clausula "rebus sic stantibus"*; and Trietschke, *Politics*, Eng. trans., Vol. I, pp. 28, 96.

constitution of the country.[1] There is no necessary incompatibility between the erection of fortifications for purpose of defence and the maintenance of a status of neutralization, and as is well known, this principle has recently been acted upon by the United States in the erection of fortifications in the Panama canal zone. With the exception of Luxemburg, neutralized States have generally been allowed to maintain standing armies and to erect fortifications on their exposed frontiers, and it has not heretofore been assumed that in consenting to be neutralized, they surrendered their right to take such measures of defence to protect their neutrality as they might deem proper. Both Belgium and Switzerland have acted on this assumption, and until the apologists of the German invasion of Belgium set out to find excuses for Germany's conduct, the contrary assumption was never put forward.

Regarding the contention that the acquisition of the Congo by Belgium completely altered her position as a European power and thereby impaired, if it did not terminate, the treaty of neutralization, it is sufficient to say that no such contention was ever put forward before the outbreak of the recent war, and it is not probable that it would have ever been advanced had not German apologists been reduced to the necessity of finding excuses for Germany's unlawful invasion of Belgium. If the annexation of the Congo rendered the treaty obsolete, why should its validity have been affirmed and reaffirmed by Germany's statesmen during all these years? As is well known, the European powers gave their consent in 1908 without reserve to the annexation by Belgium of the Congo, and Germany displayed a particular cordiality in her recognition of the annexation, she being the first to act.[2] If the acquisition of the Congo was incompatible with the status of neutralization, the guarantors should have warned Belgium in regard to the matter. But neither Germany nor any of the other co-guarantors raised any objection.

Finally, it is well known that the status of neutralization was imposed upon Belgium because of her geographical situation in respect to the powers of Europe. That situation was not

---

[1] Cf. the protocol of January 27, 1831, in Martens, *Nouveau Recueil*, Vol. X, p. 170, and De Visscher, p. 92.

[2] Cf. De Visscher, p. 102, and Waxweiler, p. 134.

altered in the slightest by the annexation of African territory. European Belgium remained exactly as it was in 1839, with her territorial boundaries unaltered, and the reasons which led to her neutralization existed in 1914 as they existed then. As a European power Belgium's position, geographically and politically, remained the same, and to argue that the acquisition of African territory so completely altered the conditions which existed at the time the neutralization status was imposed, as to destroy the binding effect of the treaty, is to subject the rule of *rebus sic stantibus* to an interpretation which is wholly unwarranted. Under such an interpretation treaties between the United States and foreign powers entered into before the acquisition of Porto Rico and the Philippines could easily be argued out of existence.

Even admitting that the rule was applicable in the present case, the invasion of Belgium was legally indefensible, because it is generally agreed that the reservation *rebus sic stantibus* does not authorize one of the parties to a treaty to repudiate its obligations whenever in its judgment its own interests require a termination of the treaty. It only allows the complaining party to insist upon a revision of the treaty, its replacement by another treaty, or its abrogation.[1] In the present case Germany made no effort to have the treaty modified or abrogated through negotiation with the other parties, but instead proceeded to repudiate it, after which the doctrine of *rebus sic stantibus* was invoked in justification of an act already committed. Clearly, the case was not one in which the application of the rule was permissible.

The Belgian treaty, says Schoenborn, was "incompatible with the vital interests of Germany; consequently it ceased to have any binding force for her."[2] We may readily admit the soundness of this proposition, but the inference that the observance of the Belgian neutralization treaty by Germany would have jeopardized the existence of the Empire or imperilled its vital interests, the impartial judgment of history will probably never accept.

§ 450. **Evaluation of the German Arguments.** Such are the reasons that were put forward in justification of the invasion

---

[1] Cf. Westlake in the *Rev. de Droit Int. et de Lég. Comp.*, 1901, p. 394.
[2] *Modern Germany*, p. 545.

of Belgium. It is probably safe to affirm that never before have technicalities and legal subtleties been exploited with so much ability to justify an act for which there was no moral or legal justification. A regrettable feature of the controversy is that among those who gave the great weight of their opinion in support of such arguments are to be found the greater number of Germany's most honored and distinguished jurists, from whom the world had a right to expect some impartiality and judicial poise in the consideration of the legal questions involved in the Belgian invasion.[1] The more honorable course, it would seem, would have been to admit the validity of treaties and conventions whose validity had never before been questioned, to have invoked solely the plea of military necessity, and to have stood by the declaration of the Chancellor in his address of August 4, 1914, that the invasion was contrary to the law of nations, and that it was a wrong for which Germany would make reparation. The attempt to argue out of existence those treaties by appeals to technicalities and legal refinements and to place the responsibility on France and Belgium by means of unfounded charges, is evidence that Germany had a very poor case. That her leading jurists should have prostituted their talents in support of such reasoning was highly discreditable to German legal scholarship.[2]

§ 451. The Right of Passage in Time of War. We now come to another question raised in connection with the violation of Belgium, namely, whether Belgium could have granted the

---

[1] It is refreshing to be able to record that a few distinguished German scholars had the courage to oppose the views of Schoenborn, Zitelmann, Liszt, Kohler, Hamper, Niemeyer, and others. Among them may be mentioned Dr. Hans Wehberg, who resigned in disgust from the board of editors of the *Zeitschrift für Völkerrecht* because he did not sympathize with the extreme views expressed through the columns of its managing editor, Professor Kohler. See his letter addressed to the German press in the *Berliner Tageblatt* of September 24, 1915 (English trans. in the *Amer. Jour. of Int. Law*, October, 1916, p. 925). Professor Lammasch, one of the leading Austrian jurists and publicists, also criticized the grounds alleged in justification of the invasion of Belgium. See his article entitled *Vertragstreue in Völkerrecht, Österreichische Zeitschrift für Öffentliches Recht*, 1915, No. 1; also the brochure of Professor Walther Schückung of the University of Marburg, entitled *Die Deutschen Professoren und der Weltkrieg*, in which he laments that the propaganda of the German professors was conducted with so little tact that the effect was contrary to the results expected.

[2] The logic of the German professors is luminously analyzed and dissected by the Belgian jurist De Visscher in his book *La Belgique et les Juristes Allemands* (Paris, 1916).

German demand for "friendly neutrality, entailing free passage of German troops through her territory," without herself violating a well-settled rule of international law and thereby rendering herself liable to attack by France for the advantage thus given to her enemy. The ancient publicists generally held that the troops of one belligerent had an absolute right of passage through neutral territory, and that this right could not be refused without injustice. Even Grotius in his day maintained that neutral nations ought to allow the right of passage to an army seeking to maintain its rights in a just war, and that in such cases it might be taken by force.[1] Vattel held that the right of free passage might be granted so long as the privilege was accorded to both or all belligerents equally.[2] Wheaton affirmed that it could be granted or withheld at the discretion of the neutral, and that its being granted or withheld constituted no ground of complaint on the part of the other belligerent, provided the same privilege was granted to him, unless there were sufficient reasons for withholding it.[3] Phillimore,[4] Kent,[5] Manning, Sir William Scott,[6] Twiss,[7] Martens,[8] and many others pronounced in favor of substantially the same view. Baty, who has made a careful study of the subject, states that the jurists of the first half of the nineteenth century, with the possible exception of Kluber (who recognized the right of passage where it had been granted by treaty before the outbreak of war), were unanimous in following Grotius and Vattel in their view that neutrals might permit the right of passage so long as the permission was granted impartially.[9] But since the middle of the nineteenth century opinion has been practi-

---

[1] *De Jure Belli ac Pacis*, Liv. II, secs. 12–13.
[2] *Droit des Gens*, Bk. II, ch. VII, secs. 119–121.
[3] Lawrence's *Wheaton*, Part IV, ch. III, sec. 8.
[4] *International Law*, Vol. III, sec. CLIX.   [5] Abdy's Kent, p. 328.
[6] Case of the *Twee Gebroeders*.
[7] *Law of Nations*, sec. 218.
[8] *Précis*, Vol. II, sec. 310.
[9] *International Law in South Africa*, p. 73. But in fact, the right thus granted can rarely be of equal advantage to both belligerents. For example, during the South African war the right of passage through Portuguese territory would have been of immense benefit to the Boers, since they had no access to the sea through their own territory, whereas it would have been of far less benefit to the British who could reach the Transvaal through their own territory of Cape Colony. Cf. Dumas, *Du Droit de Passage en Temps de Guerre*, *Rev. Gén. de Droit Int. Pub.*, 1909, pp. 7 ff. (p. 289).

cally unanimous against this view.[1] Hautefeuille in 1848 was the first writer to adopt the view that a neutral State is bound to refuse the right of passage to any and all belligerents, even where the right has been promised by treaty. This rule, observes Halleck, is most consonant with the general principles of neutrality. "The passage of troops," says Hall, "for the sole and obvious purpose of attack, is clearly forbidden."[2] "It is now generally recognized," says Oppenheim, "that a violation of the duty of impartiality is involved when a neutral allows a belligerent the passage of troops or the transport of war material over its territory. And it matters not whether neutral gives such permission to one of the belligerents or to both alike."[3] "No State," says Twiss, speaking of the neutralization of Belgium and Switzerland, "is entitled to demand of either of these States, under the general law of nations, that it should allow a free passage to its troops for belligerent purposes through its territory."[4] Heffter, Funck-Brentano, and Sorel, Bonfils, Guelle, and Heffcken express emphatic opinions that neutrals have no such right.[5]

A few modern writers, among them Calvo and Bluntschli, allow neutrals to grant the right of passage in pursuance of treaty stipulations, if the treaty has been made prior to the outbreak of the war. "The fulfilment of such an obligation," says Bluntschli, "could not be regarded as assistance to the belligerent and therefore as a violation of neutrality."[6] It was in pursuance of a treaty (signed June 11, 1891) that Portugal granted permission to the English government to transport

---

[1] As early as the middle of the eighteenth century the right of passage was sometimes refused. In 1744 Marshal Maillebois appeared at the frontier of the electorate of Cologne with an army and demanded of the elector the right of passage. He offered to pay for the supplies taken for his troops and to cause as little damage as possible. But the request was refused, and the marshal desisted from forcing a passage. Arendt, *Essai sur la Neutralité de la Belgique*, p. 127.

[2] *Int. Law*, p. 624.   [3] *Int. Law*, Vol. II, p. 345.   [4] *Law of Nations*, sec. 250.

[5] Geffcken remarks that the conduct of the Swiss government in 1870 in refusing to allow troops of Baden to cross Swiss territory in trains over the most direct route was more in harmony with the modern idea of neutrality. Geffcken also approves the conduct of the Belgian government in refusing to allow wounded German soldiers to be transported across Belgian territory, because it would have facilitated the military operations of Germany by allowing her the use of the Belgian railways. See his note to Heffter, secs. 147–150. During the same war, Bismarck protested against the conduct of the government of Luxemburg in allowing French troops to traverse the Duchy in order to reënter France.

[6] *Droit Int. Cod.*, trans. by Lardy, sec. 771.

troops through Portuguese East Africa during the Boer war. The Portuguese government claimed that the grant of passage was in fulfilment of a convention concluded long before the war and could not be regarded as a "superfluous support of one of the belligerent parties or as a violation of the duties imposed by neutrality." The English government on its part contended that in this particular case it was only availing itself of existing treaty rights which the neutral cheerfully granted. English writers at the time had much to say in defence of the policy of "benevolent neutrality" — exactly the same thing as the "friendly neutrality" which the Germans demanded of Belgium in 1914 — and they cited the authority of such precedents as that of 1877, when Roumania, in pursuance of a treaty, granted the right of passage to Russian troops in their war against Turkey.[1] The Transvaal government protested and, clearly, with justice.[2] Spaight, an English writer, affirms that the procedure of Portugal "was hardly conformable with the strict canon of the law of neutrality."[3] Baty points out that the treaty of 1891 contemplated only the right of commercial passage, and it was by a forced interpretation that it could be construed to cover the transportation of troops and military supplies.[4] There can be little doubt that the law of neutrality as then generally recognized not merely required of Portugal equal treatment of both belligerents, but also imposed upon her the duty of absolute prohibition in respect to the use of her territory by either belligerent, and her conduct, as well as that of England, has been almost universally condemned.[5]

If any doubt existed at the time in regard to the rights of belligerents and neutrals in such cases, it was removed by the Hague convention respecting the rights and duties of neutral powers and persons in case of war on land, article 2 of which forbids belligerents to move troops or convoys of either munitions of war or supplies across the territory of a neutral power, and article 5 of which forbids neutrals to allow such acts to occur in their territory. It is one of the elementary principles

[1] Cf. Campbell, *Neutral Rights and Obligations in the Anglo-Boer War*, p. 67, where the whole question of the right of Portugal to grant free passage to the British troops is fully examined.

[2] Amery, *Times History of the War in South Africa*, Vol. IV, p. 367.

[3] *War Rights on Land*, p. 485.   [4] *Int. Law in South Africa*, pp. 76–77.

[5] Cf. Campbell, *op. cit.*, pp. 66–70.

of international law that a neutral cannot allow its territory
to be made a base of operations by one of the belligerents in
his war against the other. As Renault justly remarks, it is
difficult to imagine assistance more direct or more dangerous
to the adversary than to permit his opponent to attack him on
a point where normally he could only await attack.[1] In return
for a concession which would have made Belgium an ally of
Germany, the German government offered nothing more than
a promise to guarantee the possessions and independence of
Belgium and to evacuate her territory upon the conclusion of
peace. In view of the subsequent record of the German government in respect to its international engagements, it may be
seriously doubted whether the promise would have been fulfilled. In any case, Germany's ability to do so would have
been entirely contingent upon the triumph of her arms, an
eventuality of which the Belgians were by no means certain.

It seems impossible to reach any other conclusion than that
the German demand upon Belgium was one which the Belgian
government had no lawful right to grant. It was both the legal
and moral duty of Belgium to refuse the demand, and it was
to her everlasting honor that she resisted to the utmost of her
power the German attempt to force a passage. ·The German
contention that Belgium could have granted the right of passage for German troops without violating her obligations as
a neutral,[2] is based on a view of the law of neutrality which is
entirely inconsistent with the very nature of neutrality. Schoenborn's argument that after the delivery of the ultimatum to
Belgium she was in a conditional state of war and could therefore have granted the right without violating the law of neutrality is but one of many lamentable specimens of German
logic by which treaties were argued out of existence and international engagements reduced to a nullity. Other German
writers less specious in their reasoning asserted that in view of
the circumstances it was both the duty and interest of Belgium
to accede to the German request. In view of the overwhelming
odds against her, she should have yielded to *force majeure* and,

---

[1] *Les Premières Violations*, p. 49. M. Renault asks, "What would have been
said in Germany if Belgium had granted to France such a concession as that which
Germany demanded?" and he adds, "There is no need to answer the question."

[2] This contention is made by Schulte, *Von der Neutralität Belgiens* (*Deutsche
Kriegsschriften*), No. 3, 1914, p. 68, and by Hampe, *Modern Germany*, p. 379.

like Luxemburg, contented herself with a formal diplomatic protest, in which case she would have been indemnified at the conclusion of peace for any losses sustained on account of the passage of German troops.[1] This line of argument is based on the assumption that considerations of national honor, of self-respect, and of international duty meant nothing to Belgium. Professor Kohler even went to the length of referring contemptuously to the Belgian pretence that the national honor and international obligations of the country forbade compliance with the terms of the German ultimatum, and he contrasted Belgium's conduct with that of Luxemburg, which yielded "without resistance and without loss of honor."[2] But the Belgian sense of national honor and of international duty was different, and the heroic resistance of the Belgian people in its defence must always constitute one of the bright pages in the history of the war.[3]

---

[1] Such is the argument of Fuehr, *op. cit.*, p. 190; Müller, *Der Weltkrieg, etc.*, p. 28; De Welck, *Die Schuld von Belgien (Jahrbücher für die Deutsche Armee und Marine,* 1915), and Hampe, *op. cit.*, p. 379. It was to the interest of Belgium, says Hampe, that she should have complied with the German demand. "Germany only asked for benevolent neutrality and the German ultimatum pledged to guarantee her territory and independence and to withdraw from the country at the conclusion of peace." The right of passage, he adds, was not plainly forbidden by Belgian neutrality. Belgium refused because she was bound by "inclination, agreements and one-sided military subservience to England."

[2] Renault, *op. cit.*, p. 33. Grasshoff, *Belgiens Schuld*, p. 6, tells us that "the resistance of Belgium was incomprehensible, it was a political mistake." Fuehr (*op. cit.*, p. 191) thus states the political philosophy of his country: "For the statesman who renders full account of his responsibility to his people, not the honor, but the welfare of the country is and must be the guiding principle of his decisions." This view of national honor may be contrasted with a passage in Cardinal Mercier's pastoral letter of Christmas 1914: "We may now say, my brethren, without unworthy pride, that our little Belgium has taken a foremost place in the esteem of nations. I am aware that certain onlookers, notably in Italy and in Holland, have asked how it could be necessary to expose this country to so immense a loss of wealth and of life, and whether a verbal manifesto against hostile aggression, or a single cannon shot on the frontier would not have served the purpose of protest. But assuredly all men of good feeling will be with us in our rejection of these paltry counsels. Mere utilitarianism is no sufficient rule of Christian citizenship."

[3] Labberton, a Dutch professor of moral philosophy at the University of Ghent and one of von Bissing's appointees after the transformation of that institution into a Flemish-German university, in his book *Belgium and Germany* (Eng. trans. by Leonard) tells us that Germany was justified in violating the neutrality of Belgium by a "high moral duty" (p. 33); that when Belgium rejected the German ultimatum, she ceased to be neutral and became an active participant on the side of the allies (p. 43), and that the violation of Belgian neutrality was a "new,

§ 452. **Duty of the Guarantors of the Neutralization of Belgium.** We come now to the final question raised in connection with the violation of Belgian neutrality, namely, whether it was the legal right and duty of Great Britain alone and without the consent and coöperation of the other guarantors to intervene for the purpose of preventing the violation of the neutralization treaty by one of the parties thereto. This question was first raised in 1867 in a debate in the House of Lords regarding the nature of the obligations assumed by the British government as a party to the Luxemburg convention, which expressly declared the guarantee to be "collective." In the course of the debate Lord Derby affirmed that in the event of the violation of the convention, no single signatory was bound to intervene to prevent its violation. The guarantee, he maintained, being joint and collective, the obligation to enforce the observance of the treaty rested upon the guarantors collectively. But this view provoked a vigorous protest in Parliament, Lord John Russell, among others, declaring that the guarantee was directed especially against possible aggressions of the co-guarantors themselves, and, that in consequence, each party was under an individual obligation to guarantee the territory in question against violation by any and all powers. Among the writers on international law there is little difference of opinion in regard to the nature of the obligation. Bluntschli holds that if the neutralization treaty expressly stipulates that the guarantee shall be common and collective, and not individual, intervention for the purpose of enforcing the guarantee must be collective. In such case the guaranteeing powers must examine the question together and must intervene in common if they judge intervention necessary. If they cannot agree, each is authorized and bound, *bona fide*, to execute the treaty conformably to the interpretation which it places on the treaty.[1] Pradier-Fodéré takes substantially the same position,[2] and so do Rivier,[3] Calvo,[4] and Nys.[5] The language of the Belgian neutralization treaty,

ethical creation" and a "proof of ethical genius" (p. 93)! The Chancellor's speech of August 4, frankly admitting that Germany was committing a wrong against Belgium, was, he says, a most admirable act. "If this is not the height of moral earnestness," he adds, "then I know not where to seek it" (p. 81)!

[1] *Droit Int. Cod.*, tr. by Lardy, sec. 440.   [2] *Droit Int. Pub.*, sec. 1010.
[3] *Op. cit.*, Vol. II, p. 104.   [4] *Op. cit.*, sec. 2611.
[5] *Droit International*, Vol. III, p. 40.

unlike that by which the neutralization of Luxemburg was guaranteed, does not expressly state whether the obligation of intervention is individual or collective; it merely declares that "the five powers . . . guarantee her that perpetual neutrality, etc." But as Hall points out,[1] such a guarantee would be meaningless if it did no more than provide for common action under circumstances in which the guaranteeing powers would act together. Oppenheim, speaking of Lord Derby's interpretation of the nature of the guarantee, says, "I do not know of any publicist who would or could approve it."[2] Piccioni, who has made a thorough study of the matter, says it was clearly the intention of the Conference of 1867 to assimilate the guarantee in respect to the neutralization of Luxemburg to that of Belgium, and that there was no intention to introduce any distinction between them, although the word "collective" was not employed in the Belgian treaty. This, he adds, was the opinion expressed by Bismarck in the German parliament on September 24, 1887.[3] We are certainly safe in saying that the overwhelming, if not the entire, weight of present-day authority is in favor of the right, if not the duty, of individual intervention on the part of each guaranteeing power for the purpose of preventing the violation of the treaty. To have required England in the present case to summon the other guaranteeing powers for common counsel would have rendered the treaty illusory. The violation of the treaty was too sudden to permit of common counsel; moreover, the violator in the present case was one of the guarantors, and her ally was another: the other two guarantors were allies of England, and therefore their consent and approval could be presumed. Under the circumstances it can hardly be denied that England's right to intervene singly to prevent the violation of the treaty was clear and undoubted. Was it also her legal duty? Let Bluntschli answer the question. "The States which have guaranteed the neutrality of Belgium," he says, "and which do not defend her against an aggressor do not keep their engagements and are themselves guilty of a violation of law."[4] "The violation of permanent neutrality by a belligerent," says von Liszt, "is an infraction of the law of nations, and it makes legal the inter-

---

[1] *Op. cit.*, p. 345. [2] *International Law*, Vol. I, p. 575.
[3] *Essai sur la Neutralité*, pp. 21, 53. [4] *Op. cit.*, sec. 440, n. 1.

vention of the other powers against the State which has disturbed the reign of peace." [1] From the very first the English government proceeded on this theory. Mr. Disraeli in the House of Commons in 1870 affirmed that the treaty of guarantee had embodied a rule of modern international law which should be vigorously maintained. Lord John Russell, speaking in the House of Lords at the time, said: "Our obligations to Belgium are the most sacred. We have assumed these obligations separately as well as jointly with other powers. We do not have to choose from among several ways; we have to follow only one path and that is the path of honor. We are bound to defend Belgium." [2] Lord Granville expressed substantially the same opinion in the House of Lords on August 8, 1870. Mr. Gladstone has been quoted as expressing a contrary opinion, [3] but this is an error. It is true he stated in the House of Commons on August 10 that he could not subscribe to the doctrine of those who held that there was an obligation on each of the guaranteeing powers, individually, to insure the observance of the treaty irrespectively of the particular position in which it might find itself at the time when the occasion for acting on the guarantee arises. [4] It is clear from the context that what he denied was the obligation of Great Britain alone to defend the neutrality of Belgium under circumstances which might imperil the existence of Great Britain herself. What he evidently had in mind was the conceivable inability of one of the guaranteeing powers at a given moment, resulting from exceptional circumstances, to fulfil the obligations imposed by the treaty. In any case, the *right* of Great Britain to intervene if she was willing to undertake alone the enforcement of the treaty was beyond all question. Regarding her interest in the enforcement of the treaty, Mr. Gladstone said:

[1] *Das Völkerrecht*, p. 63.

[2] Quoted in Deschamps, *La Neutralité de la Belgique*, p. 295. See Stowell, *op. cit.*, pp. 615 ff. for various extracts from the parliamentary debates of 1870 regarding the nature of the guarantee and the obligations imposed by the treaty.

[3] *Hampe*, e.g., in *Modern Germany*, p. 355, attributes to Gladstone the statement that he denied expressly England's duty to intervene alone for the protection of Belgian neutrality. Cf. also Schulte, *op. cit.*, p. 75, Dernburg in the *North American Review* for December, 1914, and Jastrow, *Germany's Just Cause*, p. 14.

[4] Hansard, *Parl. Debates*, Vol. CCIII, p. 1787. Cf. also Stowell, *op. cit.*, p. 390, and De Visscher, *Belgium's Case*, p. 56.

"We have an interest in the independence of Belgium which is wider than that which we may have in the literal operation of the guarantee. It is found in the answer to the question whether under the circumstances of the case, this country endowed as it is with influence and power, would quietly stand by and witness the perpetration of the direst crime that ever stained the pages of history, and thus become participators in the sin."

The position of England in regard to her obligations under the treaty was no different in 1914 from what it was in 1870, when neither belligerent was her ally and neither her enemy. In a statement furnished the press by Sir Edward Grey on September 16, 1914, he said, in answer to a criticism of the German Chancellor that England would not have intervened had France instead of Germany been the violator of Belgian neutrality:

"The German chancellor entirely ignores the fact that England took the same position in 1870 in regard to the neutrality of Belgium that she has taken now. In 1870 Prince Bismarck, when approached by England, admitted and respected the treaty obligations in respect to Belgium. The British government stands in 1914 as it stood in 1870. It is Herr von Bethmann-Hollweg who refuses to meet us in 1914 as Prince Bismarck met us in 1870."[1]

Any other course than that which Great Britain adopted would have been in the face of a long-established construction of the nation's obligations as a party to the treaty, and one that had been reaffirmed by every government that had had occasion to pass upon the question since the treaty was concluded.

[1] London *Times*, September 16, 1914.

CHAPTER XXX

INVASION AND OCCUPATION OF NEUTRAL TERRITORY (Continued)

I

THE GERMAN INVASION OF LUXEMBURG

§ 453. The Neutralization Convention of 1867; § 454. Invasion of Luxemburg by the Germans in 1914; § 455. Germany's Principal Defense; § 456. The German Plea Analyzed; § 457. Invasion of Belgium and Luxemburg Compared; § 458. Other German Defences; § 459. Conclusion.

II

JAPANESE VIOLATION OF CHINESE TERRITORY

§ 460. The Japanese Proceedings; § 461. Chinese Concession of a "War Zone"; § 462. Seizure of Chinese Railways; § 463. The Japanese Defence Analyzed.

III

THE OCCUPATION OF GREECE BY ENGLAND AND FRANCE

§ 464. English and French Troops Occupy Saloniki and Other Places; § 465. Other Acts of the Entente Powers; § 466. The Greek Protest and the Anglo-French Defence; § 467. The Conflict between the King and Parliament; § 468. Attitude of the Guaranteeing Powers; § 469. The Allied Ultimatum of June, 1916; § 470. Other Allied Demands upon Greece; § 471. The Abdication of the King; § 472. The Anglo-French Measures Compared with the German Invasion of Belgium; § 473. The Purpose of the Allied Measures.

I

THE GERMAN INVASION OF LUXEMBURG

§ 453. **The Neutralization Convention of 1867.** Like Belgium, the Grand Duchy of Luxemburg was an independent State whose permanent neutrality was declared and guaranteed by a group of European powers of which Prussia was one.

While the status of both States was identical in that their neutrality had been placed under the guarantee of the great powers, there was one difference in the nature of the guarantees, namely, Luxemburg was declared to be under the *collective*

guarantee of the signatory governments, whereas the word
"collective" is not found in the Belgian neutralization treaty.
The original proposal of Bismarck was that the guarantee
should be *individual*. This phraseology was altered at the
request of the British secretary of state for foreign affairs, Lord
Stanley, and the guarantee made "collective" for the reason
that the British government was disinclined to undertake an
obligation to guarantee the neutrality of Luxemburg, single-
handed and without the coöperation of the other guaranteeing
powers. Great Britain had been willing in 1839 to become a
guarantor of the neutralization of Belgium, without a stipulation
that the obligation should be collective, because the maintenance
of the neutrality of Belgium was of more vital interest to her
than that of Luxemburg. Consequently she did not object to
entering into a treaty for the neutralization of Belgium which
might impose on her alone an obligation to guarantee the enforcement of the treaty.[1] Thus while the treaty of 1839 left
each of the contracting powers free to undertake to guarantee
single-handed the observance of its provisions, the treaty of
1867 seems to have contemplated the concurrent action of all
the guarantors.[2]

A second difference between the treaties of 1839 and 1867
is to be found in the fact that the status of neutralization imposed on Luxemburg was, unlike that of Belgium, an unarmed
neutrality. The government of Luxemburg was required to
demolish its existing fortifications and was forbidden to erect
new ones. Aside from the maintenance of a small body of

[1] For the details regarding the neutralization of Luxemburg see Stowell, *The Diplomacy of the War of 1914*, pp. 425–427; see also pp. 606 ff. for the texts of various extracts from the parliamentary debates of 1867 on the subject. See also Piccioni, *Essai sur la Neutralité*, pp. 49 ff.; Weiss, *The Violation by Germany of the Neutrality of Belgium and Luxemburg*, pp. 6 ff.; Saint Yves, *Les Responsabilités de l'Allemagne dans la Guerre de 1914*, pp. 284 ff.; *Amer. Jour. of Int. Law*, Vol. IX, pp. 948 ff., and an official publication of the Luxemburg government entitled *Neutralité du Grand-Duché pendant la Guerre de 1914–18, Attitude des Pouvoirs Publics* (Luxemburg, 1919).

[2] On August 2, 1914, the day on which German troops entered Luxemburg, Sir Edward Grey in a conversation with the French ambassador at London re-
minded him that the treaty of 1867 differed from that of 1839 in that England was *bound* to interfere for the purpose of enforcing the observance of the latter treaty without necessarily obtaining the coöperation (*concours*) of the other guaranteeing powers, whereas in the case of Luxemburg the concurrence of all the guaran-
tors was considered necessary. French Yellow Book, No. 137.

troops for the preservation of order, the Grand Duchy was also forbidden to keep a standing army, this on the principle that the powers having solemnly pledged themselves to respect its neutrality, it would have no need of armies and fortifications for defence against attack from without.

During the war of 1870–1871 Bismarck charged that France violated the neutrality of the Grand Duchy, and that the Luxemburg government was a party to the violation in that it offered facilities to French troops to return to France by way of Luxemburg.[1] The Prussian government appears to have respected the treaty, and as steps were taken to prevent further violations by the French, the neutral co-guarantors did not find it necessary to protest or intervene.

§ 454. **Invasion of Luxemburg by the Germans in 1914.** On July 31, 1914, when war between Germany and France seemed imminent, M. Eyschen, minister of state and President of the government of Luxemburg, made inquiries of the French and German ministers whether, in the event of war between their countries, their governments would respect the neutrality of the Duchy. The German minister replied in substance that Germany would do so, provided France would make a similar promise.[2] On the following day M. Viviani, President of the French council of ministers, gave assurances that the government of the Republic intended to respect the neutrality of Luxemburg in conformity with the treaty of 1867, unless a violation by Germany should compel it to do otherwise in order to safeguard its own interests.[3] On the afternoon of this same day (August 1) a detachment of German troops seized the railway station of the *Trois Vierges*, and during the course of the night, before Germany had declared war against France, German troops entered the territory of the Grand Duchy.[4]

§ 455. **Germany's Principal Defence.** On the following day M. Eyschen received a telegram from Herr von Jagow, saying:

"to our great regret, the military measures which have been taken have become indispensable by the fact that we have received sure information that the French military were marching against Luxemburg (*im Vormarsch auf Luxemburg sind*). We were forced to take measures for the protection of our army and the security of our railway lines.

[1] Piccioni, *op. cit.*, p. 53.   [2] French Yellow Book, No. 11.
[3] *Ibid.*, No. 129.   [4] Renault, *Les Premières Violations*, p. 13.

We do not intend any hostile act against Luxemburg, and Luxemburg will be fully indemnified for any damage caused by the use of railways leased to the Empire."

The German military commander thereupon issued a proclamation in which it was stated that "all the efforts of our Emperor and King to maintain peace have failed. The enemy has forced Germany to draw the sword. France has violated the neutrality of Luxemburg and has commenced hostilities on the soil of Luxemburg against German troops, as has been established without a doubt." The occupation of Luxemburg, he added, was for the sole purpose of opening the way for future operations; the liberty and property of the inhabitants would be guaranteed and respected; the occupying troops would observe an "iron discipline," and all requisitions would be paid for in cash. The proclamation concluded: "I count upon the spirit of justice of the people of Luxemburg not to lose sight of the view that His Majesty decided to order troops into Luxemburg only in obedience to stern necessity due to the violation of Luxemburg by France."[1]

On August 4 the Chancellor in his address to the *Reichstag* defended the violation of both Belgium and Luxemburg on the ground of military necessity and reiterated the charge that France had already violated the neutrality of both countries.

§ 456. The German Plea Analyzed. As in the case of Belgium, no proof was submitted in support of the charge against France. Only "reliable information" had been received that French troops were marching upon the Grand Duchy, and neither the source nor the nature of this information was ever disclosed. M. Eyschen promptly protested against the German invasion and denied that a single French soldier was in Luxemburg, or that there was any indication whatever of any intention on the part of France to violate the neutrality of the country.[2] In view of the solemn assurances of M. Viviani, the emphatic denial of M. Eyschen, and the failure of the German government to furnish any evidence whatever in support of its charges against France, it is safe to assume that they

---

[1] Text in Renault, p. 14.
[2] French Yellow Book, No. 131. Cf. also Saint Yves, *op. cit.*, p. 298; Van den Heuvel, *De la Violation de la Neutralité Belgique*, pp. 12, 13, and Henckel, *Germany's Violation of Luxemburg*, New York *Times*, July 26, 1916.

were without foundation. The alleged intentions of France were merely a pretext, and the violation of Luxemburg was committed by Germany solely in her military interest and in no sense on the ground of military necessity.

§ 457. **Invasion of Belgium and Luxemburg Compared.** Several differences between the procedure by which the neutrality of Luxemburg and that of Belgium was violated may be noted. In the first place, no ultimatum was addressed to the Luxemburg government demanding the right of "friendly passage" as was done in the case of Belgium. Luxemburg had no army, and her frontiers were undefended by fortresses, thanks to the treaty of 1867. Being therefore without means of resistance, the German government apparently did not consider it worth while to go through the formality of asking for permission to march its troops through the country.[1] In accordance with the reasoning of the German jurists explained in the preceding chapter, namely, that an ultimatum addressed to a neutral State automatically places it in a conditional state of belligerency, and consequently a subsequent invasion of its territory constitutes no infraction of the law of neutrality, the failure to address an ultimatum to Luxemburg or to follow it with a formal declaration of war made the invasion of the Duchy a violation of the law of neutrality, whereas the invasion of Belgium was not.

§ 458. **Other German Defences.** Nevertheless, German jurists attempted to justify the invasion on the ground that the government of Luxemburg tacitly consented to the entrance of the German troops, in the first place, by refraining from offering resistance, unlike the Belgian government, and in the second place, by subsequently accepting an indemnity for the damages committed by the invading army and for the use of the local railways.[2] This argument is without weight. In the first place, the government of Luxemburg protested "energetically"

[1] Herr von Jagow in his telegram to M. Eyschen of August 2, referred to above, stated that "in the presence of imminent danger it was unfortunately impossible to enter into preliminary *pourparlers* with the Luxemburg government" with a view to obtaining consent for the passage of German troops.

[2] Renault, *Les Premières Violations*, p. 16. The German brochure, *Die Wahrheit über den Krieg*, asserts that "the people of Luxemburg even yielded reasonably to military necessity, and that although at first they were not friendly toward the Germans, they became so as shown by their irreproachable demeanor toward the German troops."

not only to Germany, but to the other signatory powers of the neutralization treaty, and denounced the invasion as the repudiation of a solemn engagement and a violation of international law. It offered no resistance for the obvious reason that it had no means of resistance, and because under the circumstances resistance would have been quite useless.[1] Even had the Luxemburg government consented, tacitly or otherwise, to the invasion, it would have afforded no legal justification for Germany's act, because the territory of the Grand Duchy had been neutralized in the general European interest, by an international convention, and the consent of the other parties thereto would have been necessary to release Germany from her obligations as a party. As to the acceptance of the indemnity by Luxemburg, it is sufficient to say that a violation of an international neutralization convention to which a number of States are parties cannot be subsequently legalized by the payment of an indemnity to and the acceptance of it by the State thus neutralized.

In the second place, no charge was ever made against Luxemburg for having violated its own obligations under the neutralization treaty, so that one of the principal excuses put forward by the German government in defence of the invasion of Belgium did not exist here. Again, no contention was ever advanced by the German jurists that the treaty of 1867 was not binding either because the German Empire was not a party to it, or because it had become obsolete through the operation of the rule of *rebus sic stantibus*.

§ 459. Conclusion. These and other circumstances aggravate the German offence, since most of the excuses put forward in

---

[1] The argument also appears to have been put forward in Germany that the occupation of Luxemburg was a justifiable act, because the grand duchy was not in a position to defend its neutrality. Cf. Henckel, *Germany's Violation of Luxemburg*, New York *Times*, July 26, 1916. This argument impresses one very much like the reasoning of Treitschke and others that small States have no right to an independent existence, because they are incapable of defending their independence. If Luxemburg was powerless to protect her own neutrality, it was partly because the European powers had placed her in that situation by requiring her to dismantle her fortresses and by prohibiting her from maintaining an army. Cf. Servais, *The Grand Duchy of Luxemburg and the Treaty of London of May 11, 1867* (p. 175), who justly remarks that "No responsibility can be held to be incurred by the Grand Duchy, if it does not repel an attack directed against it, since it has been left powerless to do so; what can alone be demanded, is that it should not connive with an aggressor, and that, should an aggression arise, it should denounce and protest against the same."

justification of the invasion of Belgium were wholly lacking.[1] Of all the pleas put forward in defence of the invasion of Luxemburg, that of military necessity is the only one which is entitled to consideration, and unless military necessity is interpreted to include whatever subserves a strategical interest, that plea is without weight. Since no declaration of war was ever made against Luxemburg, technically the situation of the country differed from that of Belgium. Nevertheless, in fact it was put under a regime of military occupation;[2] the French and Belgian ministers were required to leave,[3] and neutral diplomatic representatives were permitted to exercise their functions subject to such conditions as the German authorities saw fit to impose. The sovereignty of the State was by these and other acts in effect displaced for that of Germany.[4]

II

JAPANESE VIOLATION OF CHINESE TERRITORY

§ 460. **The Japanese Proceedings.** Another example of the violation of neutral territory by a belligerent, and one which has been regarded by some as analogous to the German invasion of Belgium, was the marching of Japanese troops in September, 1915, across a portion of the territory of China in order to facilitate the military operations of Japan against the German leased

---

[1] Cf. an article of Colonel Feyler in the *Journal de Genève* of January 27, 1915. The author remarks that "of the three possible violations of perpetual neutrality, that of Luxemburg was the gravest and least justifiable."

[2] In June, 1917, a strike of miners was suppressed by the German authorities. The leaders were arrested and tried by court-martial; the places of the strikers were filled by Belgian *déportés*, and meetings and demonstrations on the part of the miners were suppressed by German troops. The government of Luxemburg protested vigorously against this infringement upon the sovereignty of the Grand Duchy. New York *Times*, June 30, 1917.

[3] French Yellow Book, No. 156.

[4] After the withdrawal of the Germans in November, 1918, following the conclusion of the armistice, American soldiers passed through the grand duchy on their way to Germany. General Pershing issued a proclamation to the inhabitants notifying them that it had become necessary for the American troops to pass through and to establish and maintain there for a certain time their lines of communication. The proclamation declared that the presence of the Americans would not be prolonged beyond what was strictly necessary, and that the authority, rights, and institutions of the country would be fully respected. Since the Americans came as friends and liberators, they were welcomed by the inhabitants, and no complaint was made that they were guilty of violating the sovereignty of the country.

territory of Kiau-Chau. Upon the outbreak of the war in 1914 the Chinese government issued a neutrality proclamation announcing its intention of treating all belligerents impartially. The German government is said to have indicated its willingness to keep its naval squadron away from Tsing-tau and to place Tsing-tau with the Shantung railway under the jurisdiction of the Chinese government or to allow it to be neutralized. The Chinese government, however, agreed not to oppose belligerent action within the territory leased to Germany and to consider hostilities carried on therein as not taking place within Chinese territory.[1]

Tsing-tau, embracing the larger part of the leased territory of Kiau-Chau, lies on the south side of the Shantung promontory, the German sphere of influence running westward. On the north side of the promontory, about seventy miles from Tsing-tau, is Lung-Kau, a Chinese harbor, in which Japanese troops were landed against the protest of Chinese officials, and from which place they later marched across Chinese territory to the rear of Tsing-tau. They also seized the custom-house and post-office and stretched a railway and telegraph line across the country in disregard of the rights of China and despite the protests of Chinese authorities.

§ 461. Chinese Concession of a "War Zone." It being apparent that the Japanese forces were indisposed to respect the neutrality of China in the region of Tsing-tau and being unable to compel respect for its sovereignty, the Chinese government thereupon, following the advice of its Japanese legal adviser, Professor Ariga, consented to recognize the existence of a "war zone" embracing an area of Chinese territory with a radius extending thirty miles from Tsing-tau. Within this region hostilities would be permitted, the concession being made with a view to limiting the sphere of Japanese activities in northern Shantung. The proposal recited that the allied forces of Great Britain and Japan had, to the regret of China, begun operations at Lung-Kau and other places outside the German leased territory, although both powers were in friendly relations with the Chinese government. Therefore China, following the precedent of the Russo-Japanese war of 1904 when the area of

[1] Gilbert Reid, "The Neutrality of China," *Yale Law Journal*, December, 1915, p. 122.

operations in the Liao-Tung peninsula was limited, proposed a similar restriction on the area of operations of the Japanese forces. The Chinese government would accordingly "not accept responsibility" for the passing of troops through or the conduct of operations at Lung-Kau, Kiau-Chau, and the adjacent districts, but in other portions of China strict neutrality would be enforced.[1] It was charged that Japan showed no respect for the zone thus defined by the Chinese government.[2]

The German minister at Peking protested against the Chinese concession thus granted to Japan as a violation of neutrality and informed the Chinese government that it would be held responsible for all injuries sustained by Germany in consequence of the Japanese invasion of Chinese territory. The Chinese government in its reply pleaded its inability to oppose an effective resistance to the action of the Japanese forces and charged Germany with having first violated the neutrality of China by fortifying Tsing-tau. Finally the Chinese government called the attention of the German government to the fact that Tsing-tau had never been ceded to Germany, but only leased to her, in consequence of which the territory was still under the legal sovereignty of China.

§ 462. **Seizure of Chinese Railways.** A second violation of Chinese territory by the Japanese consisted in the seizure of the railway station at Weihsien, west of Tsing-tau, and the

---

[1] Text of the proposal in Jones, *The Fall of Tsing-tau*, p. 46. Manchuria was recognized as a war zone in 1904, because the district had been occupied by Russian troops for years; but the area recognized by China in the recent war had never been occupied by German troops. Moreover, in 1904 both belligerents agreed to the recognition of the war zone; in 1915 Germany's consent to the limitation of the area of operations was not obtained. Finally, the arrangement of 1904 was of equal benefit to both belligerents; that of 1915 was entirely for the benefit of Japan and virtually made China her ally, although against her will.

[2] "They landed their troops at Lung-Kau, marched into the hinterland, and instead of working toward Tsing-tau, the Japanese army turned its back on the German garrison and marched westward, thus violating the neutrality of China. Though the latter protested vehemently, Japan went ahead and marched her troops still farther westward, out of the war zone, to Tsinanfu, the capital of Shantung. . . . China in deadly fear of a revolutionary uprising against the invader and with the one object of saving, if possible, her people of Shantung from the horrors of war, declared a war zone. To this zone Japan paid not the least attention, but marched her troops about as if Shantung was in reality Japanese territory. She seized the Shantung railway, a Chino-German enterprise, the valuable coal mines belonging to the company and committed many acts of violence and force upon the once peaceful Shantung communities." Jones, *The Fall of Tsing-tau*, pp. 173-174.

subsequent occupation of the railway line from Tsing-tau as far west as Tsinanfu, including the coal mines worked by the Germans. The Japanese government justified its act, in the first place, on the ground of military necessity. Japan was planning the destruction of the German base of Tsing-tau, and it was therefore imperative that the line should be occupied and used for the purpose of accomplishing this object. Moreover, it would be dangerous from the Japanese point of view to leave a section of railway to the rear of the Japanese forces, in the hands of the enemy. It was also asserted that the railway was German-owned and German-controlled and could not therefore be considered as neutral property.

Again it was argued that the Chinese government had shown its unwillingness or inability to restrain the Germans from using the railway for military purposes, to the detriment of Japan. Finally, it was alleged that Japan and Great Britain were coöperating in the attack upon Tsing-tau with a view to taking the place from Germany and returning it to China, its rightful owner. Consequently, China should welcome their coöperation and adopt an attitude of benevolent neutrality toward Japan with a view to facilitating an object that would result in the restoration to China of what rightfully belonged to her.[1]

§ 463. **The Japanese Defence Reviewed.** Regarding the merits of the contention thus put forward in defence of the Japanese measures there is naturally a difference of opinion. As in the case of the Anglo-French occupation of Greece to be described hereafter, it is hardly fair to judge such acts on the basis of the ordinary normal rules of international law governing the rights of neutrals. It must be admitted that the situation which confronted the Japanese was anomalous, as it was in the cases of Korea in 1904 and of Greece in 1915. The Chinese government in its note of September 3, 1914, readily acknowledged that an "extraordinary situation" had been created in Shantung in virtue of the German lease. It was also true, as the Japanese contended, that the railway from Tsing-tau to Tsinanfu was built by the Germans, that it was largely, if not entirely owned by them and that therefore when the Japanese

---

[1] The correspondence between the Chinese and Japanese governments regarding the Japanese violation of Chinese sovereignty may be found in a memorandum laid before the Peace Conference in February, 1919, by the Chinese delegation.

seized it they were taking possession not of Chinese but of German private property and property which was being used by the enemy for military purposes. Whatever may be the differences of opinion regarding the necessity of the measures adopted by the Japanese all will agree that they were wholly different in spirit and purpose from the German violation of Belgian neutrality.

III

THE OCCUPATION OF GREECE BY ENGLAND AND FRANCE

§ 464. **English and French Troops Occupy Saloniki and Other Places.** A case of occupation of neutral territory by belligerents which was *sui generis* in character, and concerning the legitimacy of which there has been much discussion, was the occupation of a portion of the territory of Greece by the Anglo-French forces during the late war. In October, 1915, British and French troops landed at Saloniki, took possession of the custom-houses, arrested the consuls of Austria-Hungary, Bulgaria, Germany, and Turkey at Saloniki and Mytilene and transported them to France where they were detained for a time on board a French war ship at Toulon. Subsequently various other cities in Greece were occupied by the forces of the Entente powers, notably Milos, Lemnos, Cephalonia, Corinth, Imbros, Mytilene, Castelloriza, the Chalcidice peninsula, and a large part of Macedonia.

In January, 1916, French troops landed on the Greek island of Corfu and occupied the castle of Achillein owned by the German Emperor, hoisted the French flag over it, and made it the headquarters of the Servian army, which had been transported to the island. At the same time the Austrian and German consuls in the island were arrested. These latter acts aroused much indignation in the Central Empires both of whose governments protested to the government of Greece, which in turn addressed a protest to the governments of Great Britain and France, on the ground that Corfu was neutralized territory.[1] The governments of Great Britain and France defended their occupation of Corfu on the ground that it was necessary to

[1] The permanent neutrality of the island of Corfu had been guaranteed by a treaty of March 29, 1864, signed by the governments of Great Britain, France, and Russia.

transfer thereto a portion of the Servian army which was in dire need of rest and recuperation. It was a clear duty of humanity, they asserted, to transport the remnant of the Servian army to some neutral place where sanitary facilities, an adequate food supply, and opportunities for recuperation could be found, and Corfu had been selected for this purpose "in order to save these heroic soldiers from famine and destruction." [1] There was no intention of occupying the island for the purpose of military operations, and guarantees were given the Greek government that it would be used only for the purpose mentioned.[2] It was also alleged by the English and French governments that the island had become a base of operations for Austrian and German submarines and could not therefore be considered strictly as neutral territory.[3]

§ 465. Other Acts of the Entente Powers. After the occupation of Saloniki a regime of martial law appears to have been established by the commanders of the allied forces; the town was made a fortified naval base; British and French warships filled the harbors; the railway, telegraph, postal, and customs administration was taken over; the Greek army, which had been mobilized, was required to evacuate the territory between Saloniki and Dorian, and what was in effect a blockade of Greece was established by the occupying Anglo-French forces.[4] Against the occupation of Greece by the Anglo-

---

[1] The Greek government in its protest asserted that the territory of Italy, an ally of Great Britain and France, could have been utilized for this purpose, thus avoiding the violation of Greek neutrality.

[2] This explanation is contained in a note handed to the Greek government by the ministers of the Entente allies in January, 1916. The note added that they did not suppose Greece would object to the proposed transfer of the Servians to Corfu, since they were allies of Greece and would remain in the island but a short time. In February it was announced that 75,000 Servian troops had been transferred to the island and that 2500 others were shortly expected.

[3] The occupation of a Greek fort on the Karaburum peninsula by the allied troops in January, 1916, was also defended on the alleged ground that a German submarine had torpedoed a British transport within the territorial waters of the peninsula, and it was necessary, therefore, to take precautionary measures against similar violations of Greek neutrality in the future.

[4] In June, 1916, the Greek government addressed a formal protest to neutral powers against the allied blockade as a violation of international law. Since June 6, the protest declared, the Greek coast had been subjected to a limited blockade, ships being held up and searched and taken to naval bases established by the allied forces. Various vessels flying the Greek flag had been taken to Bizerta, Tunis, and there converted into transports by the allies. As a result, it was de-

French forces the governments of the Central powers protested, and the Greek government was informed that it would be held responsible for permitting its neutrality to be thus violated.

§ 466. **The Greek Protest and the Anglo-French Defence.** On October 2, 1915, the French minister at Athens had informed the prime minister of Greece of the intention of French and British troops to land at Saloniki and explained the reasons which impelled the allied governments to adopt this measure. The communication was as follows:

"By order of my government I have the honor to announce to your Excellency the arrival at Saloniki of the first detachment of French troops, and to declare at the same time that France and England, allied to Servia, send their troops to help the latter, as well as maintain their communications with her, and that the two powers count upon Greece, who already has given them so many proofs of friendship, not to oppose measures taken in the interests of Servia, of whom she also is the ally."

To this communication premier Venizelos replied:

"In answer to your letter I have the honor to declare to your Excellency that, being neutral in the European war, the royal government could not possibly authorize the proceeding in question, for it constitutes a breach of Greece's neutrality, the more manifest since it comes from two great belligerent powers. It is, therefore, the duty of the royal government to protest against the passage of foreign troops across Greek territory. The circumstance that these troops are destined solely to aid Servia, Greece's ally, in no way modifies the legal position of the King's government; for even from a Balkan point of view, Greece's neutrality could not be affected before an actual *casus foederis* was committed, by the danger now threatening Servia, which caused the despatch of international troops to her help."

By a vote of 257 to 40 the Greek chamber of deputies approved this protest, but at the same time it approved the declaration of premier Venizelos that Greece was bound by treaty as well as higher vital interests to come to the aid of her ally Servia.

---

clared, Greece's food supplies had been cut off and her maritime commerce, "the essential of her national economy," stopped.

"The intentions of the Entente allies with respect to Greece," the British foreign office declared, "have been entirely misinterpreted by the press and government of Greece. There never was any intention to declare a blockade. What the Entente allies had in view was the cancellation of special privileges enjoyed by Greek shipping, such as permission to load at British, French and other belligerent ports goods which were not allowed to be exported except under special licenses, which heretofore have been granted Greek ships." Later, however, the measure undoubtedly became a blockade in the strict sense of the word and was maintained until after the abdication of King Constantine in June, 1917.

No attempt was made by the government to oppose the landing of the troops; indeed, it is stated that the protest was made merely as a formal and perfunctory compliance with the technical requirements of the law of neutrality; [1] that in fact the landing of the troops was with the tacit approval, if not upon the invitation, of the government; that they were enthusiastically welcomed by the mass of the population, and that they were acclaimed by the people as they marched through the streets.

The king of Greece, however, who was known to be strongly under German influence, did not share the views of his prime minister, Venizelos, whose reply to the French communication voiced the views of the king rather than those of the Venizelos government, and he protested vigorously against the landing of the allied troops at Saloniki as well as against the other measures adopted by the allies, as being contrary to international law and no different in principle from the German invasion of Belgium.[2]

§ 467. **The Conflict between the King and Parliament.** The king therefore dismissed the Venizelos ministry despite the fact that it had the confidence of the Greek parliament and the overwhelming support of public opinion and ordered new elections when a large number of the electors were under arms and disqualified from voting. At the elections the new government which had in the meantime been constituted by the king was condemned by a large majority of the voters who demanded the recall of Venizelos. Instead of resigning in obedience to the clearly pronounced will of the people, the old cabinet remained in power. The government was, therefore, carried on in contravention of the constitution, which provided for a system of parliamentary government, that is, government by ministers under the control of and responsible to parliament. In the face of a threatened uprising of the people the ministry finally resigned, and Venizelos was recalled to power. Again he insisted that Greece should fulfil her obligations under the treaty with Servia, and that the king should, in accordance with the letter and spirit of the constitution, bow to the national will and not insist upon the enforcement of his own personal

[1] Cf. De Visscher, *La Belgique et les Juristes Allemands*, p. 10.
[2] See his interview with a representative of the Associated Press (New York *Times*, January 21, 1916).

views. To this the king replied that he was ready to admit that in respect to questions of domestic policy the will of parliament was supreme, but that so far as the conduct of foreign affairs was concerned the will of the king must prevail, and that he was responsible to God alone for the manner in which he conducted the foreign policy of the State.[1] Venizelos thereupon again resigned, although still possessing the confidence of the Greek parliament, and two short-lived ministries representing the royal will followed. The king then dissolved the chamber and ordered new elections, in which the liberal party by way of protest refused to take part. A "fiction of a chamber" was elected, and the arbitrary unconstitutional regime continued.[2] Greece had now ceased to be a constitutional monarchy, and the country was governed personally by the king with the aid of a small group which disclaimed all responsibility to the parliament, and which appears to have been strongly condemned by the country.

§ 468. Attitude of the Guaranteeing Powers. The situation had now reached a point where the allied governments felt that further measures were justified with a view to reëstablishing the constitutional government which they had many years before guaranteed to maintain. Greece, it was said, in fact owed her liberty and free constitution to the intervention of Great Britain, France, and Russia. They were the sole signatories to the treaties of 1827 and 1832, by which the kingdom had been brought into existence, and of the treaty of 1863, which guaranteed its independence and the maintenance of its constitutional institutions; they were, therefore, in a sense its guardians and protectors. That the three guaranteeing powers never intended that an absolute monarchy under the leadership of a prince who claimed to rule by divine right should be set up in Greece was evident, they contended, from the utterances of British and French statesmen before and after the election of Otho as king

[1] Ion, "The Hellenic Crisis," *Amer. Jour. of Int. Law*, January, 1917, p. 70. When Venizelos waited on the king and urged him to come to the aid of Servia in accordance with the treaty, and when the king returned the above quoted reply, Venizelos is reported to have answered: "You are enunciating the doctrine of the divine right of kings, with which we have nothing to do in Greece. Your father was freely elected by the Greek people to be their king and you are his successor. There is no divine right in that title; it is based on the mandate of the people."

[2] Cf. the letters of John A. Huybers in the *Nation*, Vol. 103, Nos. 2664 and 2667.

in 1832.[1] The father of Constantine owed his election not only to the will of the people of Greece, but to the choice and suggestion of the protecting powers. One of the conditions under which he was placed on the throne was that the kingdom should be a constitutional monarchy. The guarantee clause (article 3) described the kingdom as a "monarchical, independent and constitutional State."[2]

§ 469. **The Allied Ultimatum of June, 1916.** On June 21, 1916, an ultimatum was addressed by the ministers of the three protecting powers to the government of Greece demanding the immediate demobilization of the Greek army; the substitution of a new cabinet "devoid of any political prejudice and presenting all the necessary guarantees for the application of the benevolent neutrality toward the allied powers to which Greece was pledged"; the dissolution of the chamber and the holding of new elections, and the dismissal of certain police officials who had permitted, if they had not encouraged, insults to the allied legations and assaults upon Greek sympathizers with the allied policy.[3]

The ultimatum declared that the protecting powers would "continue to be inspired with the utmost friendliness and benevolence toward Greece" and that they did not ask her to abandon her neutrality, as proof of which they placed foremost among their demands the complete demobilization of the Greek army in order to insure to the Greek people tranquillity and peace. They charged that the attitude of the Greek government had not been in conformity with repeated engagements, nor even with the principles of a legal neutrality; that it had fomented the activities of certain foreigners who had striven

[1] Extracts from a number of utterances to this effect by Lord John Russell, Sir Robert Peel, Lord Palmerston, M. Guizot, and others may be found in Mr. Ion's article cited above, pp. 52 ff.

[2] It is evident from the history of the Greek constitution and the related diplomatic instruments, says Professor Ion (p. 65), that the Greek nation and her protectors aimed at establishing and maintaining on the classical soil of ancient Hellas, not an absolute monarchy but a constitutional kingdom, and one of the most liberal type; and while living under the rules of such a regime, "the people expect to derive all the benefits accruing from such liberal institutions, the most important of them being the free choice of their governing body to carry out the national will without any obstruction or arbitrary interference."

[3] Text in London weekly *Times*, June 30, 1916, and in a British white paper, *Misc.*, No. 27 (1916), Cd. 8298. Italy signified her assent to the demands.

to lead Greek public opinion astray, to distort the national feeling, and to create hostile organizations which were contrary to the neutrality of the country; that the entrance of Bulgarian forces into Greece and the occupation of Fort Rupel and other strategic points with the connivance of the Greek government [1] constituted a new menace for the allied troops and made new guarantees necessary, and finally that

"universal suffrage had been impeded, the chamber had been dissolved a second time within a period of less than a year against the clearly expressed will of the people, the electorate had been summoned to the polls during a period of mobilization with the result that the present chamber only represented an insignificant portion of the electoral college, that the whole country had been subjected to a system of oppression and of political tyranny, and had been kept in leading strings without regard for the legitimate representations of the Powers."

To this ultimatum the king yielded and shortly afterwards signed an order for the demobilization of the Greek army. By a note dated June 23, M. Zaimis, prime minister, gave an undertaking to carry out the terms of the ultimatum in their entirety.

§ 470. Other Allied Demands upon Greece. Other demands upon Greece, equally extraordinary in character, soon followed. In September, 1916, an ultimatum containing the following recital and demands was addressed by the allied governments to the government of Greece.

1. The two allied governments, hearing from a sure source that their enemies receive information in divers ways, and notably through the agency of the Greek telegraphs, demand the control of the posts and of the telegraphs including the wireless system.

[1] Fort Rupel, said to be one of the strongest fortifications in the world and dominating the valley of the Struma, was surrendered to the Bulgarians by the Greek garrison practically without resistance, and later in the year the Bulgarians occupied the Greek seaport of Kavala, and the garrison of 10,000 Greek soldiers was handed over to the Germans with its provisions and munitions of war. The surrender of Fort Rupel the Entente powers regarded as evidence of a deliberate agreement by the Greek government with the Central powers to shut up the allied troops in Saloniki. They must, therefore, take precautionary measures. The facts regarding the surrender of Fort Rupel I have obtained from *Le Messager* of Athens, especially the issues for June 23/5, 1916, and June 24/6, 1916. This journal charges that the fort was delivered over to the Bulgarians without resistance and upon the order of the Greek government. Cf. also Ion, 12 *Amer. Jour. of Int. Law*, 796, who remarks that the surrender of Fort Rupel was "rightly considered by the guardians of Greece as a hostile act directed against them and demanding the adoption of appropriate measures for the security of their armies on the Balkan front."

2. Enemy agents employed in corruption and espionage must immediately leave Greece and not return until the conclusion of hostilities.[1]

3. The necessary measures must be taken against such Greek subjects as have rendered themselves guilty of complicity in the above-mentioned corruption and espionage.

These demands were promptly complied with. In October, 1916, the admiral of the allied fleet in the Mediterranean demanded that the Greek fleet, with the exception of three vessels, be handed over to the keeping of the Entente powers. He further demanded that the three warships to be retained by Greece should be disarmed; that the forts on the sea-coast should be dismantled, and that the Piraeus-Larissa railroad should be placed under the control of the Anglo-French authorities. These demands, like the others mentioned above, were promptly complied with, although the Greek government addressed a protest to the government of the United States and presumably to the governments of other neutral powers.[2]

In the following month, November, 1916, the French admiral demanded of the Greek government that it surrender to the allies 18 batteries of field artillery and 16 batteries of mountain artillery with 1000 shells for each battery; 40,000 Mannlicher rifles with 220 cartridges for each rifle; 140 machine guns with ammunition, and 50 motor vans, — this for the purpose of restoring the equilibrium which had been disturbed by the cession of war material to the German and Bulgarian authorities and in order to maintain the system of benevolent neutrality which the Greek government had promised.[3] The Greek government protested that the amount and character of war materials thus demanded were in excess of that taken by Germany and Bulgaria, but nevertheless it yielded and complied with the admiral's demands.

In the following month another note was presented to the Greek government demanding the removal of all troops in continental Greece and all armament and munitions to the Peloponnesus except such as were absolutely necessary to maintain order;

[1] This demand was aimed specifically at Baron von Schenck, the head of the German propaganda in Greece since the outbreak of the war. Von Schenck's activities in Greece had been carried out on an extensive scale, his expenditures in the interest of the German propaganda having assumed lavish proportions.

[2] Text in New York *Times*, December 3, 1916.

[3] London weekly *Times*, December 1, 1916.

a prohibition of all meetings and all assemblies of reservists in Greece north of the Isthmus of Corinth; the vigorous enforcement of the measures prohibiting all civilians from carrying arms; reëstablishment of allied control of Greek public services; the immediate release of all prisoners held for political reasons or on charges of high treason, sedition, or similar offences;[1] the removal of the commander of the first army corps, and the presentation by the Greek government of apologies to the ministers of the allied powers which should include a formal salute of the British, French, Italian, and Russian flags on a public square of Athens in the presence of the minister of war and the assembled garrison. At the same time the Greek government was informed that military necessity might lead the protecting powers shortly to land troops at Itea, on the gulf of Corinth, and take them to Saloniki by the Larissa railroad, and it was likewise informed that the blockade of the Greek coasts would be maintained, "until satisfaction has been accorded on all the points indicated above."[2] After some hesitation the government of Greece agreed to comply with the demands, its decision having been hastened by an ultimatum on January 9 giving it forty-eight hours in which to return a reply.[3]

§ 471. **The Abdication of the King.**   The last of the measures of the allied governments was a demand in June, 1917, for the abdication of King Constantine, this on the ground that he had practically overthrown the system of constitutional government which the guaranteeing powers had pledged themselves by the treaty of 1863 to maintain; that he had acted against the liberties of the people of Greece, and that in the face of the popular will he had prevented the country from fulfilling its treaty obligations to Servia and had aided and encouraged Bulgaria and Germany in violation of the pledge of benevolent neutrality. The demand was presented to the Greek premier by M. Jonnart, a special commissioner selected for the purpose, and like the other demands it was promptly complied with.[4]

[1] These prisoners were the supporters of Venizelos who, it was alleged, were being persecuted by the government then in power.

[2] Text in London weekly *Times*, January 5, 1917, and New York *Times*, January 20, 1917.

[3] Text of the reply to the allied note, New York *Times*, January 21, 1917.

[4] Cf. a book by M. Recouly entitled *M. Jonnart en Grèce et l'Abdication de Constantin* (Paris, 1918).

On June 12, 1917, the king abdicated. He left the country with some thirty of his political followers who were expelled, and his younger brother Alexander succeeded him.[1] Venizelos returned to power, the Anglo-French blockade was raised, and "the constitutional rights and unity of Greece were reëstablished." Subsequently Greece formally entered the war on the side of the Entente allies.

§ 472. The Anglo-French Measures Compared with the German Invasion of Belgium. Such were some of the measures carried out on the territory of Greece by the governments of the contending belligerents. It would be hard to justify on strict legal principles these grave infringements upon the sovereignty of a neutral State. The whole situation, however, was anomalous and, it is believed, without precedent.[2] It was frequently asserted by German sympathizers that the Anglo-French occupation of Greece and the other measures which followed were no different in principle from the German occupation of Belgium.[3] Those whose sympathies were on the side of the Entente powers, however, contended that while technically there was a similarity between the acts, there were points where the analogy broke down, the circumstances under which the occupation of Belgium and Greece took place as well as the purposes which the occupying belligerents had in view being entirely different. In the first place, the neutrality of Greece, unlike that of Belgium, had not been placed under the special guarantee of the powers, and consequently the occupation of a portion of its territory by France and England did not involve the repudiation by one of the parties of a special treaty, as did

[1] M. Jonnart issued a proclamation regarding the measures of the allies in which he said: "They have no intention of tampering with the constitutional prerogatives; they have other aims, namely, to assure the regular and constitutional progress of the country, to which the late King George of glorious memory has always been scrupulously faithful but which King Constantine has ceased to respect."

[2] The London *Law Times* of January 15, 1916 (p. 224), compared the allied occupation of Greece with the occupation of Mexico in 1862 by the English, French, and Spanish forces; the occupation of Crete by various powers in 1897; the occupation of Syria in 1860–1861, and the occupation of Mexico by France in 1864. The analogy, however, is not very striking. Cf. also the London *Law Times* of October 23, 1915, p. 523.

[3] The German Chancellor in a speech in the *Reichstag* on December 9, 1915, referred to the parallelism between the Anglo-French occupation of Saloniki and the German invasion of Belgium.

the German invasion of Belgium.[1] To this argument, however, it will be replied that the immunity of a neutral State from occupation by a belligerent is not dependent upon special treaties, but is guaranteed by the Hague convention as well as the customary law of nations. While, therefore, the Anglo-French measures may have been less flagrant in degree, they were none the less a violation of the law of nations. In the second place, the Entente governments argued that since Greece was bound by a treaty with Servia to come to the latter's aid, and since Servia was an ally of Great Britain and France, the refusal of the Greek government, on account of the unconstitutional attitude of the king, to fulfil its obligations under the treaty justified Servia's allies in occupying the territory of Greece for the purpose of defending a common ally.[2] The Venizelos ministry, a large majority of the Greek parliament, and apparently a majority also of the people of Greece were in favor of coming to the aid of Servia in fulfilment of the obligations of the treaty. The king, however, maintained that the obligation to defend Servia applied only in case of a Balkan war and not in case of a general European war in which Servia's adversaries included non-Balkan States. Specifically, the king admitted that the *casus foederis* would arise if Bulgaria attacked Servia when the latter power was at war with Austria-Hungary and Germany, but he denied that Greece was bound to assist Servia in a war with two great powers unless she was attacked by Bulgaria acting alone and not in combination with those powers.[3]

[1] Cf. Headlam, *Belgium and Greece*, p. 4; also a statement handed by Sir Edward Grey on December 9, 1917, to the Associated Press, and De Visscher, *La Belgique et les Juristes Allemands*, pp. 9–10.

[2] The terms of the treaty between Greece and Servia appear never to have been officially made public. They are, however, generally known. The Paris *Temps* claims to have obtained a copy which was subsequently published in its columns. According to the published version, the provision which imposed on Greece an obligation to come to the aid of Servia reads as follows: "In the event of war between one of the contracting parties and a third power, or in the event of important Bulgarian forces — at least two divisions — attacking the Greek army or the Servian army, Greece and Servia engage themselves reciprocally that Servia will assist Greece with all her armed forces, and that Greece will assist Servia with all her forces on land and sea."

[3] Professor S. P. Duggan in an article entitled "Balkan Diplomacy" in the *Political Science Quarterly* (Vol. 32, pp. 240 ff.) expresses the view that it was not considerations of neutrality that really moved Constantine and his adherents in taking the attitude which they did, but rather the prestige and power of the Central Empires, for they sincerely believed that Greek intervention in behalf of Servia

If the published version of the treaty is correct, the king's interpretation of the treaty hardly seems justified. In any case, the Entente protagonists argue, it was the interpretation of the ministry and of parliament which should have prevailed. Thus the action of the king in preventing the government from fulfilling the treaty obligations of the country as they were interpreted by the parliament and the ministry was contrary to the constitution, and the intervention of the protecting powers was merely to "neutralize" the effect of the unconstitutional action of the king.[1]

In the third place, the occupation of Greece differed from the invasion of Belgium in that the sympathies of a large majority of the people of Greece, at least 80 per cent of them according to the admission of the king himself, were from the outset on the side of the Entente powers,[2] and that the allied troops landed at Saloniki with the permission, if not at the invitation, of the Venizelos ministry, notwithstanding the fact that it went through the formality of addressing a protest to the British and French governments.[3] The ministry, it is

---

would result not only in the rapid overrunning of Servia by the Central powers, but in the occupation of Greece by their armies. The facts regarding the treaty and the controversy over its meaning are explained admirably and in detail by Mr. Theodore Ion in an article entitled "The Hellenic Crisis from the Point of View of Constitutional and International Law," in the *Amer. Jour. of Int. Law*, Vol. 12, pp. 312 ff. Mr. Ion shows quite conclusively that the interpretation placed upon the treaty by the king was not well founded, and that Greece was legally bound to come to the aid of Servia in the recent war. Cf. also an article by L. Maccas entitled *La Grèce et l'Entente* in 25 *Rev. Gén. de Droit Int. Pub.* (1918), pp. 29 ff. and 154 ff.

[1] On this point Sir Edward Grey said in his statement to the Associated Press on December 9, 1917: "The unconstitutional behavior of King Constantine, his refusal to abide by the terms of the Greek treaty with Servia, and the flouting of the decisions of M. Venizelos and his parliamentary majority hardly admit of denial, even by the Germans themselves, who content themselves with saying that he acted for what he believed to be the best interests of his country. As Great Britain, France, and Russia have uniformly acted together, the whole matter of their landing troops to neutralize the king's unconstitutional action was both their right and duty." Cf. also Headlam's brochure *Belgium and Greece*, pp. 7–11.

[2] Cf. Ion, *Amer. Jour. of Int. Law*, January, 1917, p. 66.

[3] Sir Edward Grey in his statement to the Associated Press on December 9, 1917, referred to above, thus stated the Anglo-French case: "Objection may possibly be brought that the arguments up to this point rest on technicalities in old treaties, and in order to justify our action, at any rate morally, we must show that we were not acting against the wishes of the Greek people. To this may be replied absolutely, without the possibility of controversy, that our troops went to Saloniki with the express approval of the then head of the Greek government,

alleged, even fixed the number of troops which was considered necessary for the protection of Greece and to enable her to fulfil her obligation under the treaty with Servia.[1]

If Greece was a constitutional monarchy with a system of government by ministers responsible to the legislature, as the treaty of 1863 was intended to establish and guarantee, the ministry was undoubtedly within its constitutional rights in granting permission to the Anglo-French troops to land. The effect of the opposition of the king to the fulfilment by Greece of her obligations under the treaty with Servia and of his attempt to control personally the foreign policy of the country in defiance of the will of parliament and the nation was to subvert the constitutional arrangements of 1863 and to convert the constitutional monarchy into an autocracy. The intervention of the guaranteeing powers, so far at least as it was necessary to restore the constitution and reëstablish the supremacy of parliament, would appear, therefore, to have been defensible.

§ 473. The Purpose of the Allied Measures. The Entente powers never demanded of Greece that she should fulfil her obligations under the treaty with Servia. Although they would have been entirely justified in doing so, they never attempted to force her to abandon her neutrality. What they did ask was that they should be allowed to use the port of Salonîki and the

---

and that he had himself suggested the stipulation in the Greek-Servian treaty for a provision by which the Servian government's needs could, in view of the default of Greece on this point, be fulfilled by the despatch into Greek territory of an equivalent force by Great Britain and France." Professor Ion, who has made a careful study of the Anglo-French occupation of Greece, says, after a detailed consideration of the facts, that the Entente powers did not obtain the actual consent of the Greek government, nor were the troops landed at the invitation, properly speaking, of the Greek authorities. Nevertheless, he adds that the British and French governments believed that their proceeding, although irregular in form, had the tacit approval of both the Greek cabinet and legislature at the time. It is also probable, he further adds, that Great Britain and France would not have landed their troops at Saloniki had they believed that the Greek government intended to carry out the obligations incumbent upon it by the treaty of alliance with Servia. Finally, he adds that Venizelos and his adherents were far from considering the landing of the troops as an evil. On the contrary, they hailed them from the beginning as a benefit to Greece, because they reasoned that had it not been for the timely arrival of the Entente troops in Macedonia, the Austro-Germans would have firmly established themselves in Saloniki. See his article entitled "The Hellenic Crisis," Part IV, in the *Amer. Jour. of Int. Law.*, Vol. 12, pp. 562 ff.

[1] De Visscher, *Belgium's Case*, p. 11.

railway for the conveyance of troops for the assistance of Servia,[1] this on the principle that their ally Servia was by treaty
also an ally of Greece. That is to say, they demanded an
attitude of benevolent neutrality toward them in their effort
to rescue Servia. Whatever may be said in justification of
this demand, the Venizelos ministry promised to grant it, and
it was only the refusal of the "unconstitutional" ministries
which governed after his dismissal, to accord the benevolent
neutrality promised, that made necessary most of the subsequent extraordinary measures on the part of the allies. At
first the occupying authorities refrained from interfering with
the domestic affairs of the country, and it was not until it had
become evident that the Greek government, under the domination of the king and a small group of politicians, was working
in secret agreement with Germany, Austria, and Bulgaria that
the allies were compelled to resort to the extreme measures
detailed above.[2]

The territory of Greece, it was alleged, was being used as a
source of supplies for the enemy; German and Austrian submarines were using the coasts and territorial waters of the
country as bases of operations against the Anglo-French fleet;
an extensive German propaganda against the allied cause was
being carried on with the approval, if not the encouragement,
of the Greek government; demonstrations of insult against the
allied legations were openly permitted by the police; large
quantities of arms and munitions were furnished to the central
Empires; the strongest fortification in the country was surrendered to the Bulgarians with the consent of the Skouloudis
ministry; an entire army corps of forty thousand men with its
equipment was handed over to the Germans at Kavala for
"friendly internment" in Germany; and other similar acts
took place that were incompatible with the attitude of benevolent neutrality which the government had pledged itself to
observe.[3]

---

[1] Cf. Headlam, op. cit., p. 11.

[2] Professor Duggan, a well-informed student of the Balkan situation, thinks
that an overwhelming majority of the Greek people were in favor of Greece's
taking the side of the Entente allies at the outbreak of the war, but that this feeling gradually developed into resentment in consequence of various measures which
served to hurt their pride. Article cited above, p. 250.

[3] Cf. Headlam, p. 12. Sir Edward Grey in his statement referred to above,
adverting to the failure of the unconstitutional Skouloudis ministry to accord the

These reasons may not be a sufficient justification for all the extraordinary measures adopted by the Entente allies toward Greece, but they at least show that the alleged parellelism between them and the German invasion of Belgium breaks down at some of the most vital points. The purpose, the manner in which they were carried out, and the treatment which the inhabitants received at the hands of the occupying forces in the two cases were widely different.[1]

Allies the benevolent neutrality which had been promised by the Venizelos ministry, said: "But even this promise was not carried out. The Greek posts, telegraphs and wireless stations were being used to the prejudice of the allies. The police and so-called reservist associations were becoming centres of anti-Allied propaganda and the enemy legations had become an agency of an elaborate system of espionage. These dangers had to be averted, and it was also necessary to ask the Greek government to hand over to the Allies an amount of war material equivalent to that with which it had furnished the Central Powers by the pre-arranged surrender of Fort Rupel and Kavala. This the king had spontaneously offered to hand over to the Allies, and when the obligation was not fulfilled, the demand for the surrender of the material was the cause for the recent grave disturbances. Allied troops were landed to enforce this demand, and although a definite promise had been given by the king and government that order would be maintained and that the Greek royalist troops would in no case begin hostilities, the allied troops were treacherously attacked and suffered considerable losses. The royalists also took advantage of the situation to treat the adherents of M. Venizelos who are in the minority in Athens itself, with the grossest brutality, of which particulars are now beginning to arrive."

[1] Cf. an editorial on the subject in the New York *Times* of June 24, 1916. Professor Ion in the article referred to above (12 *Amer. Jour. of Int. Law*, pp. 796 ff.) reviews the conduct of the Allied powers in Greece and concludes that their measures may be considered as "acts of reprisals justified by the unneutral conduct of the government of Constantine." There is abundant unimpeachable evidence, he says, that Constantine's government was not only aiding secretly the Central powers, but was only waiting for an opportunity to attack the allied armies in Macedonia.

CHAPTER XXXI

DESTRUCTION OF NEUTRAL MERCHANT VESSELS

§ 474. Practice of the Past; § 475. Russian Practice in 1904–1905; § 476. Prize Regulations of Other States; § 477. English Opinion as to the Legality of Neutral Prize Destruction; § 478. English Judicial Authority; § 479. Views of Continental Publicists; § 480. Right of Destruction Affirmed; § 481. Discussion at the Second Hague Conference; § 482. Discussion at the International Naval Conference, 1908–1909; § 483. Rules of the Declaration of London; § 484. Practice during the Recent War; § 485. Case of the *Frye;* § 486. Case of the *Maria;* § 487. Case of the *Medea;* § 488. Losses of the Spanish Merchant Marine; § 489. Losses of Denmark and Sweden; § 490. Destruction of Norwegian Ships; § 491. Total Losses of Neutral Merchant Marines; § 492. The German Defence; § 493. Conclusion; § 494. Status of Neutral Property Destroyed on Enemy Merchantmen.

§ 474. **Practice of the Past.** The history of the naval operations of the recent war is without parallel not only by reason of the destruction of a large number of enemy merchant vessels and the drowning of thousands of persons who were aboard them as seamen or passengers, but also because of the sinking of some seventeen hundred neutral merchant vessels also with a heavy loss of life. Mr. Thomas Baty, a well-known English authority of high standing on international law, writing in 1911, thus stated the practice of the past:[1]

"It is surely very remarkable, that in all the history of war up to the twentieth century not a single instance can be adduced of a neutral ship's being destroyed on the high seas. Surely it is most significant that despite the utmost temptations and the fiercest stress of conflict, belligerents uniformly and scrupulously abstained from the least interference with neutral vessels, beyond ascertaining their characters and bringing them into port. French, Americans, Spaniards, Dutch, Danes — strict navy men and lax privateers — polished admirals and rough desperadoes — none of them dared send to the bottom a ship bearing the flag of a neutral State."[2]

During the Napoleonic wars four American merchantmen (the *Acteon*, the *Rufus*, the *Felicity*, and the *William*) were sunk by over-zealous British captains, but in fact they were not

---

[1] *Britain and Sea Law*, p. 2.   [2] *Ibid.*, p. 33.

neutral ships at all, but hostile vessels, because they flew the enemy's ensign and were *prima facie* liable to destruction. Not even the "corsair" Semmes was "imbecile" enough, Baty observes, to destroy neutral ships and alienate neutral sympathy. Semmes destroyed only enemy ships and then only after providing for the safety of their crews and passengers.[1] There is, it is believed, no record of the intentional destruction of a neutral ship on the high seas during the Crimean war, the American Civil war, or the Franco-German war,[2] the Spanish-American war,[3] the Boer war, the Turco-Italian war,[4] or the Balkan wars.

§ 475. Russian Practice in 1904-1905. The first war in which the right to destroy neutral vessels was asserted and exercised was that between Russia and Japan in 1904-1905. During this war Russian naval commanders sank eight neutral merchantmen: the *Knight Commander*, the *Hipsang*, the *Saint Kilda*, the *Oldhamia*, the *Ikhona*, the *Thea*, the *Tetartos*, and the *Princess Marie*. They were all English ships except the *Thea* and the *Tetartos*, which were German, and the *Princess Marie*, which was Danish. In every case, it appears, the crew, the passengers, and the mails were taken off, and there was no loss of life, except that several persons were killed by the gunfire directed against the *Hipsang* while she was attempting to escape. The destruction of this vessel may be distinguished from the destruction of the others for the reason that it was not a case of the sinking of a prize, but the destruction of a merchantman for refusing to stop after repeated warning shots and for attempting to escape. The case of the *Oldhamia* likewise belongs in a class by itself. It had been captured and was stranded while in charge of a prize crew; it being impossible to float it, the captor, fearing that delay might lead to its recapture, sank it. It

---

[1] Cf. Semmes' own testimony in his book *Service Afloat*, p. 535, the truth of which was confirmed by the solicitor of the United States navy, Bolles, in an article in the *Atlantic Monthly*, Vol. 30, p. 50.

[2] Six British ships were destroyed in the Seine by the Germans in 1870, but, as Baty adds (*ibid.*, p. 24), this was unobjectionable, because a neutral vessel venturing into France at the time was subject to the risks of war.

[3] There were a few cases of capture of neutral prizes during the American war with Spain, but none were destroyed. Benton, *International Law and Diplomacy of the Spanish-American War*, pp. 205-209.

[4] Coquet, *La Guerre Italo-Turque, Rev. Gén. de Droit Int. Pub.*, Vol. 20 (1914), p. 40.

was not, therefore, the destruction of a prize, but of a wreck. The other ships were sunk because their cargoes were alleged to have consisted, wholly or in part, of contraband, and owing to their proximity to enemy ports, the danger of recapture, and the lack of a sufficient supply of coal, it was regarded as dangerous or impossible to take them in for adjudication. In several cases, the Supreme Court of Russia held that the prizes destroyed were not liable to condemnation, and compensation was awarded.[1] In one case, that of the *Cilurmun*, the cargo was jettisoned and the ship spared from destruction.[2]

The Russian naval prize regulations prepared in 1895 [3] authorized the destruction of prizes in certain cases. Article 21 reads as follows:

"In exceptional cases, when the preservation of a captured vessel appears impossible on account of her bad condition or unseaworthiness, the danger of her recapture by the enemy, or the great distance, or the blockade of ports, or else on account of the danger threatening the ship which has made the capture, or the success of her operations, it is permissible for the commander, on his own responsibility, to burn or sink the captured vessel, after he has taken off all persons on board, and as much of the cargo as possible, and arranged for the safety of the vessel's papers and any other objects which may be necessary for throwing light on the case at the inquiry to be instituted in accordance with the procedure in prize cases."

It will be noted that no distinction was here made between enemy vessels and neutral vessels; both were liable to destruction under the same conditions. In consequence, however, of the protest of the English government against the destruction of neutral vessels the Russian government in August, 1905, gave instructions to its naval commanders that in the future neutral merchantmen laden with contraband were not to be sunk "except in case of direst necessity."

§ 476. **Prize Regulations of Other States.** The prize regulations of various other States likewise authorize destruction of

---

[1] Notably in the cases of the *Ikhona* and the *Tetartos*, the latter being destined to a neutral port and therefore not liable to capture, because Russia did not recognize the doctrine of continuous voyage.

[2] The facts concerning the destruction of neutral prizes by the Russians have been taken from the texts of the prize court decisions in each case, as printed in Hurst and Bray's *Russian and Japanese Prize Cases*, Vol. I (1912), and from Takahashi's *International Law Applied to the Russo-Japanese War*, pp. 310–330. There is also a summary in Baty, *op. cit.*, pp. 7–21.

[3] Text in Hurst and Bray, *op. cit.*, pp. 311–331.

prizes in exceptional cases, and some of them make no distinction between enemy and neutral vessels.[1] Thus the American instructions to blockading vessels and cruisers in 1898 (Article 28) provided that

"If there are controlling reasons why the vessels may not be sent in for adjudication, as unseaworthiness, the existence of infectious disease, or the lack of a prize crew, they may be appraised and sold; and if this cannot be done they may be destroyed. The imminent danger of recapture would justify destruction if there was no doubt that the vessel was good prize. But in all such cases all the papers and other testimony should be sent to the prize court in order that a decree may be entered."

As was the case with the Russian regulations, no distinction was made between enemy and neutral prizes. Whether it was intended to authorize the destruction of neutral merchantmen in any case may be doubted. In fact, no vessels of either class were destroyed during the war.

The Japanese regulations of 1904 (Article 91) authorized the destruction of "captured" vessels when it was "unavoidable" or when they were unseaworthy, when there was danger of recapture or when the captor was unable to spare a prize crew without endangering his own safety. But before destroying the ship the commander was required to transship all persons on board and, as far as possible, also the cargo, and to preserve all papers and documents.[2] No distinction was made between enemy and neutral vessels, but in fact no neutral ships were destroyed by Japanese naval commanders.[3] The prize regulations of France of 1870 likewise authorized the destruction of neutral vessels when their preservation endangered the safety or success of the operations of the captor, but naval commanders were directed to exercise the right of destruction with the greatest reserve.[4] The British naval prize manual of 1888, however, advised the destruction of *enemy* vessels only and directed naval commanders to release neutral prizes which,

[1] For the texts of the prize regulations of the more important States governing the destruction of neutral prizes cf. *International Law Situations*, 1905, pp. 64–68; and 1907, pp. 77 ff. For a full discussion of the whole subject see *ibid.*, 1911, pp. 51–98.

[2] The Japanese regulations are printed in Takahashi, pp. 778–789.

[3] See the list of vessels destroyed and captured during the Russo-Japanese war, Takahashi, pp. 75–283.

[4] Snow, *Cases on International Law*, p. 577.

owing to their unseaworthiness or the inability of the captor to spare a prize crew, could not be sent in for adjudication.

The French government by a decree of August 25, 1914, modified by a decree of November 6, 1914, put into effect the Declaration of London (Article 49 of which allows the destruction of neutral prizes when they cannot be taken in without danger to the captor ship or to the success of the military operations in which it is engaged) with certain modifications and additions, none of which, however, related to the disposition of prizes.[1] The British government put the Declaration of London into effect with substantially the same additions and modifications. Great Britain and France, therefore, bound themselves not to destroy neutral prizes except in the cases authorized by the Declaration. In no case, it is believed, did the naval commanders of either belligerent deliberately destroy a neutral merchantman during the recent war for carrying contraband or for other reason. The German prize code, promulgated on August 3, 1914, asserted the right to destroy neutral vessels for carrying contraband, for breach of blockade, or for unneutral service, if the taking of the ship into port would subject the capturing ship to danger or impede the success of its operations, for example, if the prize was unseaworthy or unable to follow the captor, lacked a sufficient supply of coal or was near the enemy's coast, or if the captor was unable to provide a prize crew (article 113). In all such contingencies it was assumed that the taking of the prize in would interfere with the success of the naval operations of the captor or would expose his ship to danger. The right of destruction recognized by the German code was, therefore, somewhat broader than that allowed by the Declaration of London, since the latter does not admit the right of destruction for inability to spare a prize crew, or for lack of a sufficient coal supply, or because of proximity to the enemy's coasts. Nevertheless, they could all be brought by a liberal interpretation within the purview of the Declaration, because it might fairly be claimed that the existence of these circumstances in any case would either involve danger to the captor or impede his operations, were an attempt made to take the ship into a home port. Article 116 of the German prize code provides, however, that before destroying a prize the

---

[1] Cf. 22 Rev. Gén. de Droit Int. Pub., pp. 23–35, for the text of the French decree.

commander shall take off the papers and crew, and that full provision shall be made for the safety of all persons on board. This humane requirement, found in all the prize regulations, was, with rare exceptions, disregarded by the commanders of German submarines during the recent war, apparently with the approval of the German government.

§ 477. **English Opinion as to the Legality of Neutral Prize Destruction.** The destruction of British merchantmen by Russian cruisers during the Russo-Japanese war aroused considerable indignation in England, and the legality of the sinking of the *Knight Commander*, in particular, was vigorously contested by English publicists and Statesmen. The Marquis of Lansdowne in the House of Lords referred to the act as "a very serious breach of international law" and as an outrage against which it was necessary to protest. Mr. Balfour, speaking in the House of Commons, described it as "entirely contrary to the accepted practice of civilized nations." Similar language was used by Mr. Thomas Gibson Bowles.[1]

Professor Holland stood almost alone among English publicists in maintaining that the destruction of neutral prizes was not absolutely prohibited by international law under any and all circumstances. In a letter of June 29, 1905, to the London *Times* he declared that "a *consensus gentium* to this effect will hardly be alleged by those who are aware that such sinking is permitted by the most recent prize regulations of France, Russia, Japan, and the United States," although he readily admitted that the practice should by further international agreement be absolutely forbidden.[2] While it is most desirable, he said, that neutral property should not be exposed to destruction without inquiry, cases might occasionally occur in which a belligerent could hardly be expected to permit the escape of such property when he was unable to send it in for adjudication.[3] At the time, however, the great preponderance of English opinion was against the right of destruction. Law-

[1] Holland, *Letters on War and Neutrality*, p. 161; Baty, *Britain and Sea Law*, p. 10, and *International Law Situations*, 1907, p. 82, and 1911, p. 57.

[2] The text of his letter is printed in his *Letters on War and Neutrality*, p. 168. Professor Holland's position was strongly attacked by Thomas Gibson Bowles in several letters to the *Times*.

[3] *Neutral Duties in Maritime War*, Proceedings of the British Academy, Vol. II, pp. 12–13, quoted by Moore, *Digest*, Vol. VII, p. 520.

rence, speaking of the sinking of the *Knight Commander*, declared
that it was not lawful to sink a neutral prize before taking
it in.[1] Hall likewise maintained that neutral ships or goods
cannot be destroyed until they have been condemned by a
prize court. Ownership of such goods, he held, does not rest
upon capture, but remains in the neutral until judgment of
confiscation has been pronounced by a competent court.[2] This
in substance is also the view of Phillmore,[3] Atlay,[4] Atherley-Jones,[5]
Bentwich, and most of the other English authorities.

§ 478. **English Judicial Authority.** English judicial authority,
like that of English text writers, has likewise denied the legality
of neutral prize destruction. Lord Stowell in the case of the
Felicity in 1819 said: "Where it is neutral, the act of destruction
cannot be justified to the neutral owner by the gravest importance of such an act to the public service of the captor's own
State; to the neutral it can only be justified under any circumstances by a full restitution in value. These rules are so
clear in principle and established in practice that they require
neither reasoning nor precedent to illustrate or support them."[6]
So during the Crimean war Dr. Lushington, while affirming the
right and duty of a captor in certain cases to destroy *enemy*
merchant vessels, declared that

"for wholly different reasons, which I need not enter upon, where a vessel
under *neutral colors* is detained she has the right to be brought to adjudication, according to the regular course of proceedings in the prize court;
and it is the very first duty of the captor to bring it in, if it be practicable."[7]

Baty, commenting on these decisions, remarks that they have
sometimes been represented as showing that Stowell and Lushington regarded it as permissible for a cruiser to sink any ship
it liked upon condition of making restitution and paying damages
and costs, but in fact, as he points out, they admitted no such

---

[1] *War and Neutrality in the Far East*, p. 455. In an article entitled *La Dés-
truction des Prises Neutres* in the *Rev. de Droit Int.*, 2d Ser., Vol. 8, p. 434 (1906),
Baty maintains that the recent practice of destroying neutral prizes has been
introduced without authority. The fact, he says, that no neutral prize had ever
been sunk in modern wars because of the impossibility of taking it in was proof
convincing.

[2] *Int. Law*, 5th ed., p. 735. [3] *Int. Law*, Vol. III, p. 432.
[4] See his edition of Wheaton, sec. 350e. [5] *Commerce in War*, p. 531.
[6] Dodson's *Admiralty Reports*, Vol. II, p. 381.
[7] The *Leucade* (1855), Spink's *Prize Cases*, p. 221.

principle; all they were concerned with was the remedy their own court could give the owner. They were not concerned with the question of the right to destroy a neutral vessel; "in fact, they scarcely contemplated the occurrence of such an outrage; it was and had been for centuries an unheard-of thing." [1]

§ 479. **Views of Continental Publicists.** Among continental publicists Kleen is a vigorous opponent of the right to destroy neutral prizes. The destruction of neutral property is never a "necessity of war," he says, and the captain of a cruiser who in open sea commits such an act arrogates to himself the powers of a judge, a quality which does not belong to him. [2] Other continental writers who do not admit the right to destroy neutral prizes are: Bluntschli, [3] Nippold, [4] and, apparently, de Boeck, [5] Gessner, [6] and Bonfils. [7] Taylor, [8] Woolsey, [9] and Wheaton, [10] among American writers, likewise deny the right to destroy neutral prizes.

§ 480. **Right of Destruction Affirmed.** There is, however, much authority in favor of the right to destroy in exceptional cases. [11] Oppenheim remarks that the practice of States does not recognize the English rule of absolute prohibition, and he cites Geffcken, Calvo, Fiore, Martens, Dupuis, and Perels — he might have added Rivier [12] and others — in favor of the

---

[1] *Britain and Sea Law*, p. 5. [2] *Lois et Usages de la Neutralité*, t. II, p. 532.

[3] *Droit International Codifié*, sec. 672.

[4] Cited by Huberich in an article on "Destruction of Neutral Prizes" in the *Illinois Law Review*, for May, 1915.

[5] *De la Propriété Privée Ennemie sous Pavillon Ennemi*, p. 302.

[6] *Le Droit des Neutres sur Mer* (1876), p. 348.

[7] *Droit Int. Pub.*, sec. 1415. There is some uncertainty as to the opinions of de Boeck, Gessner, and Bonfils, as they do not distinguish clearly between the destruction of enemy prizes and neutral prizes. It may at least be said, however, that they do not expressly recognize the right to destroy neutral ships.

[8] *Int. Law*, p. 573.

[9] *Int. Law*, sec. 184. "The right to destroy," he says, "is barbarous, and ought to disappear from the law of nations," and he makes no distinction between enemy and neutral prizes.

[10] Cited by Baty (*Britain and Sea Law*, pp. 5–6).

[11] *Int. Law*, Vol. II, p. 471, n. 2. Calvo, sec. 3019, states that as a general rule a neutral prize may not be destroyed, but that it is permissible in exceptional circumstances, as for example in case of "imperious military necessity" or *force majeure* resulting from pursuit of the enemy or inability to spare a prize crew. Cf. Martens, *Traité de Droit Int.*, Vol. III, p. 298; Perels, *Manuel de Droit Maritime* (French trans. by Arendt), p. 334, and Dupuis, *Le Droit de la Guerre Maritime d'après les Conférences de la Haye, etc.*, p. 368, to the same effect.

[12] *Principes du Droit des Gens*, Vol. II, p. 350.

right to destroy in certain cases. Westlake is one of the few
English writers who admits the right of destruction. A neutral,
he says, cannot justly complain if his property is destroyed
when, if it is brought in, it would be condemned under the law
of blockade or contraband.[1] Holland, as we have seen, took
the same view in 1905; and Moore,[1] commenting on Hall's
opinion, remarks that the authorities hardly sustain it as a rule
of unqualified or universal obligation.[2] At the time of the
controversy between the British and Russian governments over
the sinking of the *Knight Commander*, Mr. Loomis, acting
secretary of state of the United States, sent a telegram to Mr.
Choate (July 9, 1904) saying that the American government
considered that the sinking of the vessel was not justified by
the bare fact that there was contraband on board,[3] and on
July 30 the Russian government was informed that the government of the United States "views with the gravest concern the
application of similar treatment to American vessels and cargoes."[4] But in a subsequent telegram of August 6 to Mr.
Choate, Secretary Hay stated that he was "not prepared to
say that in case of imperative necessity a prize may not be
lawfully destroyed by a belligerent captor."[5]

§ 481. Discussion at the Second Hague Conference. In the
presence of this conflicting opinion regarding the right to destroy
neutral prizes, the Second Hague Conference entered upon a
discussion of the subject in the hope of reaching a general agreement in respect to the conditions under which the destruction
of neutral prizes should be admitted, if at all.[6] In the proposal
submitted by the British delegation the view was expressed
that the destruction of neutral prizes should be prohibited

---

[1] *Int. Law*, Vol. II, p. 309.   [2] *Digest of Int. Law*, Vol. 7, p. 523.
[3] *United States Foreign Relations*, 1904, p. 333.
[4] *Ibid.*, p. 734.   [5] *Ibid.*, p. 337.
[6] The matter had been considered by the Institute of International Law at its
meeting at Turin in 1882, and the prize *règlement* which it adopted recognized the
right to destroy prizes in certain exceptional cases. No distinction was made
between neutral and enemy prizes, and apparently none was intended to be made.
There was some opposition, especially by the English members, to the *règlement*
because of the failure to recognize this distinction, and at the session of 1883
the *règlement* was amended, and the right to destroy was expressly limited to
enemy prizes. The manual of maritime war adopted by the Institute at its Oxford
meeting in 1913 recognizes the right to destroy enemy vessels, but nothing is said
in regard to the right to destroy neutral prizes (cf. the *Annuaire* of the Institute,
Vol. 26, p. 348).

absolutely, and that every neutral prize which could not be taken in for adjudication should be released.[1] Sir Ernest Satow defended with much ability the British proposal.[2] The destruction of neutral prizes, he said, was contrary to international law, and the proposal to admit it was a dangerous innovation. The American delegation submitted a proposal identical in substance with that of the British delegation, and it was ably sustained by General Davis upon grounds of both humanity and practice. The present construction of ships of war, he said, offers few accommodations for persons taken from captured ships, and, besides, they would be exposed to the danger of battle in a much greater degree than when fleets were constructed of wood and propelled by sail.[3]

The Russian delegation proposed that the right of destruction be admitted in exceptional cases, for example, where the safety of the captor would otherwise be compromised or the success of his operations would be impeded. But in all such cases the right of destruction should be exercised with the greatest reserve and only after all papers had been preserved and provision made for the safety of the passengers and crew. The Russian proposal was also defended by the German delegate, Herr Kriege, who asserted that the right of destruction in exceptional cases was recognized by the existing rules and practice, and that it was indispensable from the point of view of military necessity.[4]

Count Tornielli of Italy sought to reconcile the conflicting views by a proposal allowing prizes to be taken into neutral ports pending sequestration by a prize court. This proposal, embodied in article 23 of the convention respecting the rights and duties of neutral powers in naval warfare, represents the only achievement of the Conference on the subject of prize destruction.[5] Its purpose, as M. Renault pointed out, was "to render more rare or to prevent entirely the destruction of prizes." Sir Ernest Satow strongly opposed the adoption of this article, because it made no distinction between enemy and

---

[1] *Deuxième Conférence Internationale de la Paix, Actes et Documents*, p. 1134.
[2] *Ibid.*, pp. 903-907.   [3] *Ibid.*, p. 1050.   [4] *Ibid.*, p. 903.
[5] The *Proceedings of the Second Hague Conference* in respect to the destruction of prizes are reviewed and analyzed by Dupuis in *Le Droit de la Guerre Maritime d'après les Conférences de la Haye et de Londres*, pp. 372-382, and by Lémonon in *La Seconde Conférence de la Paix*, pp. 685-694. The memoranda submitted to the Conference are analyzed in *International Law Situations* for 1911, pp. 61-68.

neutral prizes and allowed belligerents the right to make use of neutral ports to their peculiar advantage. The delegates of a number of the great powers, including those of Great Britain, Japan, and the United States, either voted against the proposal or abstained from voting, and their governments later reserved their ratification of the article as adopted. Undoubtedly, if neutrals could be induced to allow belligerents this privilege, the excuse or necessity for destruction would in many cases be removed, but there is little disposition to grant it.

§ 482. **Discussion at the International Naval Conference, 1908-1909.** The discussion of the question of the right to destroy neutral prizes was renewed at the International Naval Conference at London in 1908-1909. Sir Edward Grey in a letter of December 1, 1908, to Lord Desart, president of the British delegation, dwelt upon the desirability of an agreement which would place greater restrictions upon the right of belligerents to destroy neutral prizes. The discussions at the Hague conference, however, had evidently convinced the British government of the necessity of making some concessions to those who defended the right of destruction in exceptional cases, and it did not therefore insist as in 1907 on absolute prohibition. Adverting to the fact that it was universally admitted that all prizes ought, if possible, to be taken into a prize court for adjudication, Sir Edward admitted that the right to destroy *enemy* prizes in cases where the captor finds himself unable without compromising his own safety or without having the success of his operations impeded, or where, owing to his distance from a home port, the prize could not be taken in, was generally recognized. As to *neutral* prizes, Great Britain, he said, had always contended that if they could not be taken in, they should be released, and that no military necessity could justify destruction. His Majesty's Government, he said, could not admit the proposition that inability to spare a prize crew was sufficient justification to destroy a neutral vessel, for such an admission would probably be held to authorize destruction in the majority of cases where the captor had no convenient port of his own. However, the British government might be prepared, he added, to admit the right to sink neutral prizes in case of imperative military necessity, but it was not prepared to admit that inability to spare a prize crew or the mere remoteness of a convenient home port constituted a military necessity which would justify the sinking of a neutral prize.[1]

Nevertheless, the memorandum submitted by the British delegation, and also that of Japan, proposed that the destruction of neutral vessels be prohibited in all cases whatsoever.[2] The proposals submitted by the other delegations, while admitting the general principle that neutral ships ought to be taken in for adjudication, nevertheless affirmed the right of a belligerent to destroy them in exceptional cases. The German memorandum proposed to recognize the right in cases where the taking in would compromise the safety of the captor or the success of his operations.[3] The memorandum of the American delegation proposed the rules of the naval code of 1900, article 50 of which permitted destruction where there were controlling reasons why vessels should not be sent in for adjudication, such as unseaworthiness, the existence of infectious diseases, or the lack of a prize crew, or where there was imminent danger of recapture.[4] The French memorandum proposed to authorize destruction only when the taking of the prize in would compromise the safety of the captor or the success of his operations, as for example, where he could not spare a prize crew; but in every such case the right of destruction should be exercised with the greatest reserve.[5] The memoranda submitted by the delegations of the other powers proposed to recognize the right of destruction under essentially similar conditions.[6]

The discussion of the question was very full, especially by the delegates having technical knowledge of the methods of naval warfare. The British delegation reaffirmed the views of the British government in 1907, but, realizing that if any agreement was reached, the right to destroy in exceptional cases would have to be admitted, directed their efforts toward obtaining adequate safeguards against the abuse of the right and toward securing provision for due reparation to injured neutrals.[7]

---

[1] Proceedings of the International Naval Conference, House of Commons Sessional Papers, *Misc.*, No. 4, Vol. 54 (1909), p. 28.

[2] *Ibid.*, No. 5, p. 38.   [3] *Ibid.*, p. 6.

[4] *Ibid.*, pp. 8-16.   [5] *Ibid.*,

[6] The memoranda of the several delegations are analyzed by Dupuis, *op. cit.*, pp. 383 ff. Cf. also *Int. Law Situations*, 1911, pp. 73-77.

[7] Cf. the letter of the British delegates to Lord Desart, March 1, 1909, House of Commons Sessional Papers, *Misc.*, No. 4 (1909), p. 98.

§ 483. Rules of the Declaration of London. The rule finally adopted by the Conference affirmed the general principle that a neutral vessel cannot be destroyed, but must be taken in for adjudication by a prize court. Nevertheless, by way of exception the right of destruction was admitted in cases where conveyance of the prize ship into a home port would involve danger to the captor or to the success of the military operations in which he was at the time engaged (article 49).[1] The effort of the British delegation to obtain express recognition of the rule that mere inability to spare a prize crew did not constitute a danger to the captor failed to receive the approval of the Conference, it being regarded as unwise to undertake to specify the particular contingencies which should constitute danger.

Article 50 of the Declaration took care to provide, however, that before destruction in any case all persons on board must be placed in safety, and all the ship's papers likely to be of value to the prize court in determining the validity of the capture must be preserved.

While the rules adopted by the Conference represented a compromise between two conflicting views, they undoubtedly provided some safeguards against arbitrary destruction, and if they were strictly observed by belligerents, the cases in which neutrals would be exposed to wrong would probably be few. It is, of course, true that the Declaration has never been ratified in accordance with its own provisions and was not therefore legally binding upon the belligerents during the recent war. Nevertheless, it was put into effect with certain modifications and additions, none of which affected substantially its rules in respect to prize destruction, except that, as already stated, the German prize regulations expressly enumerate the contingencies which shall constitute danger to the captor, or which might impede his operations, among which are inability to spare a prize crew, shortage of coal, proximity to the enemy's coasts, etc. It may also be remarked that the Declaration affirmed at the outset that the rules contained in its various chapters "correspond in substance to the generally recognized law." To that extent, therefore, they were binding upon the several belligerents, even though the declaration was never ratified.

---

[1] Cf. the analysis and comment in Bentwich, *The Declaration of London*, pp. 94-95.

§ 484. **Practice during the Recent War.** The right of a belligerent to destroy neutral prizes in the exceptional cases and subject to the conditions mentioned above being generally recognized, we may now inquire whether the practice during the recent war was in conformity with these rules. In most of the cases in which neutral ships were destroyed, the destruction was wrought by German submarines, although in a very few cases there were doubts as to whether it was done by submarines or mines, and if by mines whether they were laid by Great Britain or by Germany. In a very few cases also, like that of the *Frye*, the destruction was wrought by a battle ship or cruiser. Regarding the procedure of destruction, the rule in respect to making provision for the safety of crews and passengers was rarely observed by the commanders of German submarines, and in most cases innocent persons on board lost their lives in consequence of the failure to give warning or, in case warning was given, to allow sufficient time for the passengers and crew to save themselves.

In the great majority of cases in which neutral merchantmen were destroyed, the reason alleged was the presence of contraband on board; but in a number of cases the destruction was alleged to have been due to the inability of the submarine commanders to distinguish the marking of the ships. It being impossible, it was claimed, for the commander to bring the vessel to, send a searching party aboard, or otherwise verify its nationality, the ship was destroyed upon suspicion. Thus in the case of the American steamer *Gulflight*, torpedoed on May 7, 1915, without warning and with the loss of three lives, all Americans, it was alleged that the ship was convoyed by an English merchant vessel, which it was assumed was armed, and being unable to distinguish the neutral markings of the *Gulflight* and considering it dangerous to approach the vessel for the purpose of verifying its nationality, in view of the presence of the convoying ship of the enemy, the submarine torpedoed it.[1] The destruction of the ship was, therefore, an "unfortunate accident" for which the German government expressed regret and declared itself ready to make full compensation.

[1] See the note of the German minister of foreign affairs to the American ambassador at Berlin, of June 1, 1915. The chief officer of the *Gulflight* in a sworn statement filed with the department of state declared that the ship at the time it was torpedoed was flying a large American ensign six by ten feet in size which was clearly visible.

Another similar case was the torpedoing on May 25, 1915, of the American vessel *Nebraskan* while proceeding in ballast from Liverpool to the United States. The commander of the submarine claimed to have mistaken it for an English vessel because of insufficient markings. The German government expressed regret for the act and offered to make compensation to the owners.[1] The captain, however, testified that the ship had painted on its side in large letters the words, "Nebraskan of New York," which must have been seen by the submarine commander.

§ 485. **Case of the *Frye*.** A case which attracted particular attention, and which was the subject of prolonged diplomatic controversy between the American and the German governments, was the sinking of the *William P. Frye* on January 28, 1915, by the German cruiser *Prinz Eitel Friedrich*. The *Frye*, while proceeding on a voyage from Seattle to Queenstown, Falmouth, and Plymouth with a cargo consigned "to order," was stopped, a searching party was sent aboard, and after examining the papers the commander directed that the cargo be thrown overboard. Subsequently, "after having tried to remove the cargo," the commander took the papers and crew aboard and sunk the ship.

In a note dated March 31, 1915, the secretary of state after reciting briefly the facts of the case and without entering into an argument concerning the illegality of the sinking, presented a bill to the German government for $228,059.54 to cover the value of the vessel, freight, travelling and other expenses of the captain and its agents, the personal effects of the captain, and damages on account of the loss of the ship. In a note dated April 5, the German government replied that the commander had "acted in accordance with the principles of international law as laid down in the Declaration of London and the German prize regulations." The ports to which the vessel was destined, it was asserted, were "strongly fortified" and were moreover serving as bases for the British naval forces; consequently the cargo was to be considered as destined for the use of the armed forces of the enemy, and since it was not possible to take the prize into a German port without exposing the captor to danger

[1] Memorandum of the German foreign office delivered to Mr. Gerard July 12, 1915.

or without impeding the success of his operations, he was justified in destroying it, and this he did after taking off the papers and the crew.

§ 486. **Case of the Maria.** The *Maria* was a Dutch vessel laden with a cargo of wheat, which had sailed from Portland, Oregon, before the outbreak of the war. Both the ship and cargo were sunk by the *Karlsruhe* in September, 1914. Part of the cargo was consigned "to order" to Belfast and part to Dublin. The legality of the sinking was upheld by the superior prize court at Hamburg on the ground that the cargo was conditional contraband destined for the use of the armed forces of the enemy, the captor being unable to take the prize into a home port owing to his inability to spare a prize crew and because of the risk of recapture due to the proximity of the enemy's war-ships. The Imperial prize court at Berlin affirmed the decision of the lower court. Article 113 of the German prize code authorizes the destruction of a neutral vessel which is liable to condemnation whenever the taking of it into port would subject the captor vessel to danger or would impede the success of the operations in which it is for the time engaged. Various circumstances are held to establish such a presumption, such as the proximity of the enemy's forces, lack of an adequate prize crew, etc.[1]

§ 487. **Case of the Medea.** Still another notable case which fairly illustrates German practice and interpretation of the law arose in connection with the sinking on March 25, 1915, by a German submarine of the Dutch steamer *Medea* laden with a cargo of oranges consigned to private parties in London. The government of the Netherlands formally protested against the sinking of the *Medea* on the ground "that the destruction of a neutral prize is an act which international law has never sanctioned." It was true, said the Dutch note, that the Declaration of London recognized it, but the Declaration had never been ratified. Even admitting that it was in force, the destruction of the *Medea* was unlawful, because the Declaration affirmed the general principle that a captor must take his prize in for adjudication, and it admitted the right of destruction only under exceptional conditions, such as were not present in

[1] Huberich and King, *The German Prize Code*, p. 66; Grotius *Annuaire*, 1917, pp. 73 ff.

the case of the *Medea*. The signatories of the Declaration, it was affirmed, never intended to sanction the employment of submarines against neutral commerce, because they do not possess the facilities for taking care of crews and passengers. In the present case the crews were put into small life-boats and abandoned in the open sea. Finally, the cargo of the *Medea* consisted of oranges, which could not be regarded as subsistence for armies and was not therefore contraband of war; in any case, they were destined for the use of the civil population of England and not for the armed forces. To this remonstrance the German government replied that the contention of the Dutch government that the right to destroy neutral prizes was not sanctioned by international law, was contrary to the facts. It called attention to the rule of the Declaration of London which admitted the right of destruction in certain cases and pointed out that, although it had never been ratified, the Declaration itself affirmed that the rules which it laid down corresponded in substance to the generally recognized principles of international law, and that practice in recent wars fully sustained the right of destruction under certain conditions. The conditions justifying destruction, it was added, were fully present in the case at issue. The capture took place in close proximity to the English coast and in the presence of superior naval forces of the enemy, so that an attempt to take the prize into a German port would have exposed the German submarine to grave danger and possible destruction. Regarding the character of the cargo, the German government denied the Dutch contention that oranges could not be regarded as "provisions" (*vivres*) and asserted that it had evidence that the British government was in fact furnishing its troops with fruits of this kind. As to the contention that the cargo was intended for the civil population, the German government replied that for the captor it was sufficient that its destination was an enemy fortified port which at the same time served as a base of supplies for the army. London was clearly such a place; its approaches were defended by mines and batteries; it possessed docks, arsenals, and warehouses, and it was surrounded by a ring of forts, redoubts, and batteries. The legality of the sinking of the *Medea* was upheld by the German prize court at Hamburg, and the decision was affirmed by the superior prize court of Berlin. The Dutch government continued to protest against the decision as contrary to international law and again affirmed that the destruction of a neutral prize is under all circumstances an illegal act. Finally, it proposed to submit the differences between the two governments to the decision of an international tribunal, but this proposal the German government declined to accept.[1]

§ 488. Losses of the Spanish Merchant Marine. During the first year of the war Spanish losses were rare, but with the inauguration of submarine warfare in the Mediterranean, the sinkings of Spanish ships became frequent, and in June, 1917, it was stated that one-seventh of the entire Spanish merchant marine had been sunk by Teutonic submarines. During the spring and summer of 1918 the German war upon Spanish commerce was carried to such lengths that a crisis in the relations of the two countries was precipitated, and for a time the Spanish government appears to have been on the point of breaking off diplomatic relations with Germany. In August, 1918, the cabinet issued a statement in which it asserted that German submarines had sunk more than 20 per cent of the Spanish merchant marine; that more than one hundred Spanish sailors

[1] The correspondence between the two governments regarding the sinking of the *Medea* may be found in a Dutch white book entitled *Oversicht der Voornaamste van July 1914 tot October 1915, etc.*, published by the Dutch ministry of foreign affairs (pp. 19 ff.), and a Dutch orange book entitled *Mededeelingen van den minister van Buitenlandsche Zaken aan de Staten-Generaal July–Dec. 1916*, pp. 11 ff. Cf. also the *Rev. Gén. de Droit Int. Pub.*, 1917, Docs., pp. 17, 90, 95, 98.

Other notable sinkings of Dutch ships were those of the *Batavier V*, the *Zaanstroom*, the *Sidney Albert*, the *Katwijk*, the *Rijndijk* and the *Blommersdijk*. In the three last-mentioned cases the German government admitted that the vessels were wrongfully torpedoed. In the case of the *Batavier V* the German prize court repudiated the doctrine of the "older literature that prize courts are bound to apply international law even when it is not in conformity with the municipal law," and asserted that the German prize courts must judge according to the law of their own State. This law was contained in the prize ordinance of September 13, 1909. "International law," said the court, "only, lays down rights and duties as between different States. The prize courts, when judging of the legality of prize actions, can take general international principles only into account when the prize regulations contain no instructions and, therefore, tacitly refer to the principles of international law. Therefore, the question whether an instruction of the prize regulations agrees with general international law is not for the prize court to decide. If a contradiction in this connection is asserted, the point in controversy is to be settled in another manner."

For a review of the German decisions in respect to the destruction of Dutch Merchant Vessels see the Grotius *Annuaire International*, 1916, pp. 104 ff., and 1917, pp. 68 ff.

had lost their lives in consequence of the sinkings, and that many others had been exposed to suffering from having been abandoned in life-boats at sea. "Ships needed exclusively for Spanish use," it added, "have been torpedoed without the slightest pretext." [1]

The Spanish government protested in a succession of notes to the German government and pointed out that Germany had derived special benefit from Spain's policy of neutrality, that the Spanish government had received and cared for numerous German refugees from the Cameroons, and that it had undertaken and faithfully performed the task of looking after German interests in various belligerent countries. In return for these services and evidences of friendship, Spanish ships were torpedoed in large numbers without reason and Spanish seamen drowned or left to endure tortures from exposure in small life-boats at sea.[2] As a last resort the Spanish government finally decided to seize a number of German merchant vessels which had taken refuge in the ports of Spain at the outbreak of the war [3] and use them in Spanish commerce to replace those destroyed by German submarines. There was no thought, however, of confiscating them; the government of Spain was actuated only by the necessity of finding vessels to carry on its commerce, and it informed the German government that the solution determined upon was intended to be only temporary, and at the conclusion of the war the vessels would be restored to Germany with adequate compensation for all damages.[4] The German government, however, threatened to take action against Spain in case

[1] Text in New York *Times* of August 22, 1918. The *Times* in an editorial of the same date stated that the Germans had sunk eighty-one Spanish ships.

[2] The United States war trade board in March, 1918, charged that the German policy of "ruthlessness" against Spanish ships was inaugurated for the purpose of preventing the United States from sending food to Switzerland. The sinking of the Spanish steamer *Sardinero* was cited as proof of this charge. The *Sardinero*, while carrying a cargo of grain intended for Switzerland and while en route to a port to which the German government had promised to leave open a safe passage, was torpedoed outside the barred zone. The vessel was sunk after the submarine commander had made an examination of the ship's papers and satisfied himself of the nature and destination of the cargo, so that the plea of "mistake" was not admissible. "The evident intent and result of the act," the war trade board declared, "was to prevent Switzerland, whose urgent and immediate need of food is well known to Germany, from receiving American grain."

[3] There were at the time ninety German ships in Spanish ports.

[4] Text in the New York *Times*, August 22, 1918, and the Paris *Journal*, same date.

this measure was put into effect, and apparently only one vessel was ever taken over.[1]

§ 489. **Losses of Denmark and Sweden.** The merchant marines of both Denmark and Sweden were heavy sufferers from German submarine warfare. The New York *Times* in an editorial of March 9, 1918, stated that German submarines had sunk 216 Danish ships, in consequence of which 234 Danish sailors had lost their lives. Many of the vessels were torpedoed without warning and in waters far removed from the so-called barred zone.[2]

According to an official report of the Swedish government made in September, 1917, 126 steam and sailing vessels belonging to its merchant marine had been destroyed by German submarines or sunk by German mines since the beginning of the war. In addition eight others had been captured and confiscated by the German government, making a total of 134, or about 12 per cent of the entire merchant marine.[3] Of all

---

[1] New York *Times*, September 3, 1918. In August, 1918, the German government offered to deliver safe-conducts to certain Spanish ships, which would protect them against destruction by German submarines. Whereupon the French ministry of marine issued an order to the effect that "every neutral ship which should place itself under the control of the enemy by receiving an enemy safe-conduct would not be recognized by the allies . . . and would be regarded as navigating in the interest of an enemy State and therefore subject to capture and confiscation." 25 *Rev. Gén.*, Docs., p. 45. It will be recalled that the *Gulflight* was alleged to have been convoyed by a British war vessel at the time it was attacked by a German submarine. Certain Scandinavian vessels are said to have been convoyed in the Baltic Sea by German war ships. There is no agreement among the authorities as to the legal status of neutral vessels under belligerent convoy. Some hold that it affords no protection to the neutral vessel against capture; others hold that the acceptance of such a convoy renders the vessel liable to condemnation on the ground that it amounts to constructive resistance or a violation of neutrality; while others still take the position that while it creates suspicion, it does not necessarily justify condemnation. The views of the authorities are reviewed by Huberich in an article in *International Law Notes* for January, 1916, pp. 5–8.

[2] A goodly number of the Danish ships sunk were torpedoed while voyaging between Iceland and Denmark, entirely outside the war zone. The United States war trade board charged that the German war upon neutral commerce was for the purpose of destroying possible neutral competitors after the war, and this charge was frequently made in neutral countries. It was also frequently asserted in the early part of the year 1918 that the German government was endeavoring by threats, intimidation, and attacks upon neutral vessels to prevent neutrals from receiving food and other supplies under relief agreements concluded with the United States. See the statement of the war trade board in United States *Official Bulletin* of March 15, 1918.

[3] New York *Times*, September 16, 1917.

the neutral powers of Europe, Sweden's neutrality toward Germany was probably the most benevolent and her friendship the most cordial. Great Britain was never able to blockade the Baltic coasts of Germany, and the Swedes carried on a profitable trade with the latter country from the beginning until the end of the war. Germany was especially indebted to the Swedes for large quantities of food-stuffs and iron ores, but this did not secure immunity to Swedish vessels which claimed an equal right to trade with Russia.

§ 490. **Destruction of Norwegian Ships.** Of all the neutral merchant marines that of Norway suffered the most from German submarines. At the outbreak of the war the Norwegian merchant marine ranked third among those of Europe and fourth among those of the world, and one-fifth of the population was dependent upon the shipping industry. During the war the total number of Norwegian vessels sunk by German torpedoes or mines is said to have amounted to 929 (aggregate tonnage 1,240,000) with a loss of more than a thousand lives.[1] Although less benevolent toward Germany in their neutrality, the Norwegians supplied her with large quantities of sorely needed nickel ore; but as in the case of the Swedes, the German government did not recognize their right to trade with enemy belligerents. Many charges were made by the Norwegians in respect to the barbarity of the submarine commanders who were accused of firing upon crews while leaving their ships or while in the life-boats.[2] Public opinion in Norway was stirred

[1] Report of the Royal Norwegian navigation bureau, quoted in the New York *Nation*, May 17, 1919, p. 818. Forty-seven per cent of the total tonnage of Norway was estimated to have been destroyed.

[2] Among the atrocities with which German submarine commanders were charged was the shelling of the Norwegian bark *Eglinton* in August, 1918, with the loss of all on board except one. No warning was given, the rigging and sails were shot away, and while the crew were endeavoring to escape to the life-boats, they were fired upon by the submarine. The sea was choppy, and the submarine circled around the raft upon which six of the men had escaped and looked on without offering any assistance. After drifting at sea for some hours, the sole survivor was rescued. New York *Times*, August 3, 1918. Another case which fairly illustrated the barbarity of German submarine methods was the sinking in mid-ocean of the Norwegian steamer *Augvoldon*, June 23, 1918. Three of the crew were drowned and thirteen others were unaccounted for. The survivors, after drifting at sea in small life-boats for eleven days and subsisting most of that time on sea-weed and rain water wrung from their clothes or caught in their caps, were rescued in an exhausted condition.

to indignation, and in November, 1917, the various shipping associations addressed a protest to the German people in which, after reciting various instances of cruelty and barbarity by German submarine commanders, they declared the conduct of the German navy to be "without parallel in the history of naval warfare and unworthy of a seafaring nation." [1] Norway, it was charged, was filled with German spies who kept German submarine commanders, who lay in wait outside the territorial waters, informed as to the movement of Norwegian vessels, and it was asserted that secret wireless stations were erected at various places along the Norwegian coast.[2]

In June, 1917, a German plot to blow up Norwegian ships while lying in the home ports of Norway was discovered. More than a ton of explosives was found in the baggage of a German foreign office courier, addressed to the German legation at Christiania.[3] The explosives, it was charged, were to have been placed upon Norwegian ships for the purpose of blowing them up when they got to sea.

Other neutral States were similarly treated. In the spring of 1917 the American government obtained possession of a despatch addressed by Count Luxburg, German chargé d'affaires in Argentina, to his government advising it not to make reparation for the sinking of Argentine merchant vessels and adding: "As regards Argentine steamers I recommend either compelling them to turn back, sinking them without leaving a trace (*spurlos versenkt*), or letting them through." [4]

§ 491. Total Losses of Neutral Merchant Marines. Accurate statistics concerning the total number of neutral merchant and fishing vessels torpedoed by German submarines or sunk by German mines are not available, but the following figures are offered as representing the approximate losses:

---

[1] Text of the protest in United States *Official Bulletin*, March 18, 1918.

[2] There was complaint in Norway that secret agents of the German government, who reported the sailings of Norwegian vessels, were tolerated by the Norwegian government, whereas similar agents had been expelled from Holland. New York *Times* despatch from Christiania (*Times*, October 11, 1916).

[3] New York *Times*, June 28, 1917.

[4] In another despatch Count Luxburg advised his government that two Argentine steamers, the *Oran* and the *Guazo*, were then nearing Bordeaux and recommended that they be spared if possible or else "sunk without a trace being left."

Norway.............................	929
Denmark............................	172
Sweden.............................	124
Holland............................	328 [1]
Spain..............................	83
United States......................	20
Greece.............................	60 [2]
Total.......................	1716 [3]

To this should be added at least a half dozen vessels belonging to South American merchant marines (Brazil, Argentina, Peru, and Uruguay). The total number of sailors drowned or killed on such vessels is said to have exceeded two thousand.[4]

§ 492. **The German Defence.** As has been said above, in the great majority of cases in which neutral merchantmen were destroyed by the Germans during the recent war, the offence alleged was the carrying of contraband. Is it lawful to destroy a neutral merchantman for carrying contraband, and if so, under what conditions and restrictions may the right be exercised? According to the Declaration of London, which the German government put into force at the outbreak of the war, neutral vessels *which are liable to condemnation by a prize court* for carrying contraband may be sunk if, for the reasons mentioned above, it is dangerous to attempt to take them in, and *if at least half the cargo* consists of contraband goods.[5] Vessels, there-

[1] These are the figures of Dutch losses as given by the New York *Times Current Hist. Mag.* (November, 1918, p. 256). According to the information there given fifty of the Dutch ships sunk were fishing vessels. The lives of 939 Dutch seamen were lost.

[2] According to an official report of the American state department in June, 1917, nearly one-fifteenth of the entire Greek tonnage had been sunk by Teutonic submarines during the preceding three months. New York *Times*, June 24, 1917.

[3] Most of the above estimates are those published by the New York *Times* (of September 4, 1918). The *Times* of March 9, 1918, however, placed the total Danish losses at 216 instead of 172. The Swedish government is reported to have placed its losses in September, 1917, at 126 vessels. Statistics of the losses of the various neutral powers from German submarines and mines down to April 26, 1917, together with the names of the vessels destroyed and the dates of destruction, are given in a booklet entitled *A List of Neutral Ships Sunk by the Germans*, published by Geo. H. Doran and Company (1917). This publication placed the total number of vessels mined and torpedoed by the Germans down to that time at 849 with an aggregate tonnage of 1,653,654. According to a Washington press despatch of March 2, 1917, twenty-three American ships had been attacked by German submarines since the outbreak of the war, and twelve had been destroyed by mines and submarines.

[4] New York *Times*, September 4, 1918.   [5] Art. 40.

fore, laden with contraband in smaller proportions cannot lawfully be sunk. Moreover, the burden of proving that he acted in the face of "exceptional necessity" is placed upon the captor, and in case he fails to produce such proof, his government is bound to indemnify the owners.[1] These rules, which are also those of the German prize code (articles 41, 113–115), were generally disregarded by German naval commanders.

In the first place, as stated above, only neutral vessels which are *liable to condemnation* as good prize may be destroyed. Manifestly, such liability can be determined only by stopping the suspected vessel and by sending aboard a searching party to verify its nationality, to inspect its papers, to examine the cargo, and to weigh the evidence from these and other sources very much as a prize court would do if the vessel were taken in for adjudication. But this was not the procedure of the German submarine commanders. In all the hundreds of cases in which they destroyed neutral merchantmen, they rarely stopped, visited, or searched the vessels sunk by them. They contented themselves with a long-distance view of the vessel through a periscope, and if it looked suspicious, the doubt was generally resolved against the ship, and it was torpedoed. With its sinking frequently went cargo, crew, passengers, evidence, and all to the bottom of the sea. The rule which allows destruction of vessels only that are liable to condemnation by a prize court means nothing if they may be destroyed on sight without any effort to verify their nationality, ascertain the character of their cargoes, or to determine the destination of the vessel or the use for which the cargo is intended. The whole procedure is very much like ambushing an accused person and assassinating him on suspicion without a hearing or a trial. The German prize code embodies the rule of the Declaration of London that the captor's government is bound to indemnify the owner of a vessel or cargo destroyed in case the captor fails to produce proof that the vessel was liable to destruction. But how can a captor produce proof of this kind when he torpedoes a vessel without taking off and preserving the papers or other evidence of its character? In fact, save in a few instances, as in the case of the sinking of the *Frye* where the sinking was for-

[1] Art. 51.

bidden by special treaty stipulations, no indemnities were paid to neutrals for the destruction of their vessels.

Furthermore, as stated above, the rule of the Declaration of London that only vessels carrying contraband are liable to condemnation and destruction when the contraband goods constitute at least half the cargo, is incorporated in the German prize code. But this rule, like the others, was generally disregarded. How a submarine commander, whose knowledge of the contents of the ship's cargo is limited to what he sees through the narrow slit of a periscope, can determine the proportion which the contraband goods bears to the entire cargo, it is difficult to see. According to the Declaration of London, (article 49) as well as the German prize code itself (article 32), *conditional* contraband is not liable to condemnation unless it is destined for the armed forces or the government of the enemy. To justify the destruction of a neutral vessel laden with conditional contraband, therefore, it is not sufficient for a belligerent to show that the vessel is destined to an enemy port; he must show that the goods are intended for the use of the government or armed forces of the enemy, and according to article 34 of the Declaration of London, such use may be presumed only when they are consigned to the public authorities or a government contractor, to an enemy fortified place, or to a place serving as a base for the armed forces of the enemy. In short, the right of condemnation because of mere enemy destination applies only to *absolute* contraband. As Professor John Bassett Moore justly remarks:

" When publicists have spoken of the presence of contraband as justifying or excusing the destruction of a neutral ship that should not be brought in, they have, no doubt, had in mind cargoes composed of things especially adapted to use in war and confessedly contraband, such as arms and ammunition, and cannot be assumed to have contemplated the subjection of neutral commerce to general depredation under an extension of the categories of contraband." [1]

The German government, however, did not act upon this principle. It recognized no distinction between absolute and conditional contraband, nor did it observe the provisions of its own prize code which distinguishes between the destination of the vessel and the use to which the goods are to be put. It

[1] *Digest of International Law*, Vol. VII, p. 527.

destroyed neutral vessels laden with conditional contraband equally with those carrying absolute contraband. It treated all towns on the English coasts as "fortified places" or as places serving as "bases" of supplies for the armed forces of the enemy, and consequently vessels laden with conditional or absolute contraband bound to any English port were, whenever possible, sunk. In consequence of the very wide extension of the list of contraband articles — an extension so wide as to amount almost to the assimilation of all goods to the category of contraband — practically all neutral vessels trading with the countries at war with Germany were liable to destruction by German submarines, and many hundreds of them were in fact destroyed.

§ 493. **Conclusion.** The record of German depredations upon neutral commerce during the late war was, of course, without precedent in the history of modern warfare. It resulted in the destruction of a large part of the merchant marines of some of the small States of Europe or in the paralysis of their commerce, — States which were so circumstanced that they dared not offer resistance or adopt adequate measures for the protection of their rights. It is hard to reconcile such a policy of depredation and destruction with the contention of the German government that it was fighting for the freedom of the seas, a freedom which, we are told, had been destroyed by Great Britain. In fact, Germany's record formed a striking contrast to that of Great Britain, for there appears to have been no instance in which a neutral ship was intentionally destroyed during the recent war by the British navy, and it has been stated by the British admiralty that not a single non-combatant life was ever lost on the high seas through the action of the British naval forces.[1]

Nevertheless, the very general character of the language of the Declaration of London in respect to the destruction of

[1] In view of German practice in respect to the sinking of neutral vessels it is interesting to note the view of Treitschke, who went to the length of denouncing Great Britain as the "unblushing representative of barbarism in international law" and of asserting that the right of a belligerent to capture enemy ships on the high seas was "an organized form of piracy." *Deutsche Kämpfe*, Vol. II, p. 362, quoted by Schmitt in his *England and Germany*, p. 161. If it is "organized piracy" and "privileged robbery" to capture enemy ships, what must be said of the sinking of neutral vessels?

neutral prizes undoubtedly leaves belligerents a very wide latitude, so that it is possible to turn the exception into the rule without a literal violation of the Declaration. With Germany's ports blockaded and her naval operations limited to those carried on by submarines, she could reasonably claim that whenever a prize was captured at sea, the taking of it in would have involved grave danger to the submarine, even if it had been possible for such craft to conduct it into a home port. German naval commanders were practically in the same situation as the Confederate naval commanders were during the American Civil war. Their home ports were blockaded, and neutral ports were not open to the reception of their prizes; they were obliged, therefore, to allow them to go free or destroy them. But in the recent war the Germans did what no Confederate naval commander ever assumed to do; they destroyed not only enemy prizes, but also hundreds of neutral vessels carrying contraband, this with little or no regard to whether the goods consisted of munitions of war or food-stuffs, usually without satisfying themselves as to the true nationality of the ship or the character of the cargo, and often without making any provision for the safety of the crew or passengers. If the existing rules of international law are susceptible of an interpretation which permits a belligerent to depredate upon neutral commerce in this fashion, they should be speedily altered. It is not to be assumed that it was the intention of the International Naval Conference to authorize general destruction by belligerents of neutral vessels carrying food-stuffs and other articles of conditional contraband, but the failure to specify precisely the contingencies under which a vessel may be sunk has had the effect of making each belligerent the judge of the conditions under which destruction is allowable. If this principle be admitted, the rights of neutral commerce must henceforth be at the mercy of belligerent naval commanders; they will be free to destroy any neutral vessel carrying goods which they may find inconvenient to take in for adjudication by a prize court.[1]

---

[1] Sir Graham Bower, a retired British naval commander, in the *Contemporary Review* for November, 1918, makes the suggestion that the right to destroy neutral merchant vessels be absolutely prohibited; that in return for this, the right to arm neutral vessels be abandoned, and that prizes which cannot be taken in by the captor to a home port may be interned in a neutral port. Somewhat similar

§ 494. **Status of Neutral Property Destroyed on Enemy Merchantmen.** In many instances enemy merchant vessels sunk by German submarines during the late war carried cargoes owned wholly or in part by persons of neutral nationality. Was Germany bound to compensate the owners of such property? In the case of the *Glitra*, a British merchantman carrying a cargo a part of which was Norwegian-owned, and which was sunk by a German submarine on October 20, 1914, the supreme prize court of the Empire declined to award compensation to the claimants.[1] In the case of the *Indian Prince*, a British vessel carrying a cargo owned by the nationals of various neutral States, the German prize court reached the same decision.[2]

The claimants relied mainly on article 3 of the Declaration of Paris, which declares that neutral property on enemy ships, contraband excepted, is exempt from capture. Being immune from capture, the belligerent destroying it is bound to make compensation to the owners. No decision had been reached by the London Naval Conference in regard to the obligation of belligerents to make compensation in such cases, but it was argued by the claimants that article 114 of the German prize code contemplated that compensation should be made. The German prize court, however, held that the obligation applied only to goods on *neutral* vessels, and that neutral owners of property on *enemy* ships destroyed as an act of war had no just claim to compensation. As to article 3 of the Declaration of Paris, that was intended to protect neutral property in enemy ships "which under the prize law as it existed prior to the Declaration were subject to capture." A naval commander, it was

suggestions were made by the British sailors' and firemen's union. But manifestly, to condition the immunity of neutral merchant vessels upon their abstention from carrying arms for purposes of defence involves a recognition of the preponderance of belligerent interest over that of neutrals. Would it not be more in accord with the rights of neutrals, to say nothing of the dictates of humanity, to observe strictly the existing rules which allow the destruction of neutral vessels under exceptional circumstances and permit such vessels to carry armament as in the past for the purpose of defence against unlawful attack? Cf. the comment of Scott in the *Amer. Jour. of Int. Law*, 12:371 ff.; and the memoranda of Sir John MacDonell and Sir Erle Richards in Grotius Society, Problems of the War, vol. iv, pp. xliv–xlviii.

[1] Text of the decision in the *Zeitschrift für Völkerrecht*, Bd. IX, pp. 399 ff. Eng. trans. in *Amer. Jour. of Int. Law*, Vol. X, p. 921. See also Grotius, *Annuaire*, 1917, pp. 70 ff.

[2] Eng. text of the decision in *Amer. Jour. of Int. Law*, Vol. X, p. 930.

said, is not bound to refrain from sinking a vessel which he has a legal right to destroy, merely because it would entail the destruction of neutral property. A neutral who intrusts his property to an enemy vessel which is liable to destruction takes a risk, and if he suffers loss, he is not entitled to compensation.

This doctrine does not appear to be in accord either with the German prize code or the generally recognized law of nations. An examination of articles 112, 113, and 115 of the prize code would seem to leave little doubt that it was the intention of the authors to recognize an obligation to make compensation for property destroyed on enemy as well as neutral vessels, and this intent is strengthened by the attitude of German text writers [1] and by the German delegation at the London Naval Conference.[2] It would seem to be a sound principle that if the destruction of an enemy merchant vessel is required by urgent military necessity, as the French claimed to have been the case when they sank the *Ludwig*, and the *Vorwaerts* in the Seine in 1871, there is no obligation to compensate neutrals for the losses which they may incidentally sustain in consequence of such destruction. But where merchant vessels of the enemy are systematically destroyed as a general practice of maritime war, and not in exceptional cases required by extraordinary military necessity, a failure to compensate owners of neutral property thereon is a clear violation of article 3 of the Declaration of Paris.[3] This principle is as old as the *Consolato del Mare*, and it has been affirmed by text writers almost without exception.

[1] For example, by Perels, *Das Int. Öff. Seerecht der Gegenwart*, 2d ed., p. 299.
[2] See their memorandum, House of Commons Sessional Papers, 1909, *Misc.*, No. 5, p. 99.
[3] See a learned discussion of the subject by Quincy Wright in *Amer. Jour. of Int. Law*, Vol. XI, p. 377.

CHAPTER XXXII

CONTRABAND, RIGHT OF SEARCH, AND CONTINUOUS VOYAGE

§ 495. Importance of the Question during the Recent War; § 496. British and French Policy; § 497. Protests against the Disregard of the Declaration of London; § 498. Cotton as Contraband; § 499. Food-Stuffs as Contraband; § 500. American Complaints regarding British Detentions; § 501. Extension of the Doctrine of Continuous Voyage to the Carriage of Conditional Contraband; § 502. History of the Doctrine of Continuous Voyage; § 503. Neutral Embargoes on Exportations to Belligerent Territory; § 504. British and American Practice Compared; § 505. Defence of the Doctrine of Continuous Voyage under Modern Conditions; § 506. The Case of the *Kim* and Others; § 507. French Cases; § 508. German Cases; § 508a. Conclusion.

§ 495. **Importance of the Question during the Recent War.** On account of the fact that all the principal maritime powers were belligerents, traffic in contraband goods naturally assumed an importance during the recent war hitherto unknown. Owing also to the fact that Germany, the chief belligerent on one side, was flanked by a group of neutral States most of which have seaboards and through whose ports trade, had it not been intercepted by her enemies, could easily have found its way to Germany, the whole problem of dealing with contraband traffic raised difficulties for England and France which could hardly have been met without infringing upon the well-recognized rights of neutrals. The difficulty was further increased by the existence of a situation in which it was practically impossible to distinguish between supplies intended for the civilian population of Germany and those intended for the armed forces. Finally, owing to the recent progress of invention and the extensive military use that was made of many articles which formerly were not adapted to such use, the distinction between contraband and non-contraband largely disappeared.

§ 496. **British and French Policy.** By a succession of orders in council beginning on August 4, 1914, the British government announced lists of articles which it proposed to treat as contraband. The first list was identical with that of the Declaration of London, except that air craft, which is listed as conditional contraband in the Declaration, was put on the list of absolute contraband by the order in council. On September 21 various articles, such as unwrought copper, iron ore, lead, glycerine, rubber, hides, and skins, which are either on the free list in the Declaration or are not mentioned at all, were placed on the list of conditional contraband. On October 29 this list was withdrawn and replaced by a new one which placed on the list of absolute contraband many articles which are either on the free list or on the list of conditional contraband in the Declaration of London. This list was superseded on December 23 by a new one which contained still further additions to the category of absolute contraband. On March 11 raw wool, worsted yarns, tin, castor oil, paraffine wax, ammonia, and other articles, none of which are used exclusively for war purposes, were declared to be absolute contraband.

Although food-stuffs had from the outset been regarded as conditional contraband, corn, wheat and flour were in effect treated as absolute contraband from February, 1915, in consequence of the German government's having taken over the control and distribution of these commodities. By a proclamation of May 27, 1915, maps, toluole, lathes and other machines or machine tools capable of being employed in the manufacture of munitions were added to the list of absolute contraband. By a proclamation of August 20, 1915, raw cotton was added; by a proclamation of January 27, 1916, cork, bones, soap, and vegetable fibres were declared to be absolute contraband, while caseine, bladders, guts, and sausage skins were placed on the list of conditional contraband; by a proclamation of April 13, 1916, gold, silver, paper money, and all negotiable instruments and realizable securities, metallic chlorides, starch, borax, boric acid, and sabadilla seeds were declared to be absolute contraband.[1] In the Declaration of London gold and silver bullion or coin and also paper money (but not checks or bills of exchange) are treated as conditional contraband, and they

[1] The British prize court at Malta in the case of the *Turkish Moneys Taken at Madras* condemned a quantity of Turkish coin and Ottoman bank notes which were being taken to Constantinople by two Greek money-lenders from Saloniki on the ground that the "moneys, having a commercial purpose in enemy territory, had a hostile commercial or trade domicile." Trehern, *British and Colonial Prize Cases*, Vol. II, p. 336.

were so treated in the early British proclamations. The reason given by the British government for putting these articles on the list of absolute contraband was the "unprecedented importance which the transfer of credit had taken on since the outbreak of the war."

It will be noted that in all these proclamations the distinction between absolute and conditional contraband was maintained, but so many articles were put on the list of absolute contraband which were in fact only conditional contraband when tested by former principles of classification, that the attempt to preserve the distinction became absurd, and accordingly, by a proclamation of April 19, 1916, the British government adopted the more logical course of formally abandoning the distinction. A single list of contraband articles embracing several hundred items arranged alphabetically, without distinction as to whether they were absolute or conditional contraband, was accordingly issued. In explanation of this action, the foreign office stated that

"The circumstances of the present war are so peculiar that His Majesty's government consider that for practical purposes the distinction between the two classes of contraband has ceased to have any value. So large a proportion of the inhabitants of the enemy country are taking part, directly or indirectly, in the war that no real distinction can now be drawn between the armed forces and the civilian population. Similarly, the enemy government has taken control, by a series of decrees and orders, of practically all the articles in the list of conditional contraband, so that they are now available for government use. So long as these exceptional conditions continue our belligerent rights with respect to the two kinds of contraband are the same and our treatment of them must be identical." [1]

The French government by a decree of August 11, 1914, proclaimed a list of contraband articles which included various articles as conditional contraband which are either on the free list of the Declaration of London, or which are not enumerated at all. Among them were iron and steel — including oxides, sulphides, and carbonates of iron — copper, lead, nickel, chrome

[1] The list of articles thus declared to be contraband may be found in the London weekly *Times* of April 28, 1916. Cf. also *European War*, No. III, pp. 109-113. In all of the proclamations the number of articles placed on the list of absolute contraband greatly outnumbered those on the list of conditional contraband so that in fact the distinction had already been largely abandoned. Thus in one of the proclamations of April, 1916, 299 articles and groups of articles are designated as absolute contraband and 78 designated as conditional contraband.

iron, hides, and automobile tires. By a decree of November 6, 1914, the lists of absolute and conditional contraband were largely extended, and by a further decree of January 2, 1915, the French lists were made identical with the British lists.

§ 497. Protests against the Disregard of the Declaration of London. The German government addressed a protest to neutral powers against the action of the British and French governments in thus modifying the Declaration of London, although German submarines from the outset sank neutral vessels laden with cargoes of conditional contraband destined to unfortified British ports and ports not serving as bases of military operation.[1]

In its note of December 28, 1914, to the British government, in respect to the detention of neutral ships and their cargoes, the American government refrained from discussing at that time the propriety of including certain articles in the contraband list, although it asserted that some of them were open to objection. The right of belligerents, said the note, to determine what they shall regard as contraband and to adopt such classification as they choose cannot be denied, but it is well established that their action must be in conformity with existing treaties and the generally recognized rules of international law. The right cannot therefore be arbitrarily exercised.[2] When the French government in 1895 announced its intention of treating rice as contraband when destined to Chinese ports north of Canton, Lord Granville stated that "His Majesty's government feel themselves bound to reserve their rights of protesting at once against the doctrine that it is for the belligerent to decide what is and what is not contraband of war, regardless of the well-established rights of neutrals."[3] During the Russo-Japanese war Lord Lansdowne in a communication of July 29, 1904, to secretary of state John Hay, apropos of the action of the Russian government in putting coal, naphtha, and other fuel on the list of absolute contraband, expressed substantially the same view, and so did Mr. Hay in his protest against the condemnation of the cargoes of the *Arabia* and the *Calchas*.[4]

[1] See the cases of the *Frye*, the *Maria*, the *Samanthe*, and the *Anita*. Cf. Pyke, *The Law of Contraband*, p. 185.
[2] Cf. on this point Oppenheim, *International Law*, Vol. II, p. 424.
[3] Quoted by Atherley-Jones, *Commerce in War*, p. 45.
[4] *Foreign Relations of the United States*, 1904, p. 760.

The distinction between absolute and conditional contraband is as old as Grotius, and as a principle of international law it had never been contested by the United States or Great Britain.[1]

§ 498. **Cotton as Contraband.** For some time the British government declined to treat cotton as contraband. In a letter of April 18, 1915, addressed to certain memorialists who urged that cotton be placed on the list of contraband, the attorney-general stated that cotton was being excluded from Germany and Austria under the blockade order in council of March 11 as effectively as if it were absolute contraband, and that nothing would be gained by putting it on the list of contraband. The order in council prevented access to German ports of all articles whether contraband or not; the effect of the order, he said, was virtually that of a blockade, and therefore to declare cotton contraband would not alter the situation. But public opinion in England continued to demand that cotton be formally placed on the contraband list, and this opinion was intensified by the belief, not to say the evidence, that large quantities of cotton were reaching Germany and Austria, especially through neutral ports, in spite of the blockade. The result of this pressure was an order in council of August 20, 1915, placing raw cotton, cotton linters, cotton waste, and cotton yarns on the list of absolute contraband. The British government defended its action on the ground that evidence had accumulated that cotton was being extensively used by the enemy in the manufacture of explosives, particularly those of a propulsive character, and that it had largely taken the place of saltpetre in the manufacture of gunpowder.[2] Under the circumstances "it was right and proper that cotton with an enemy destination

---

[1] This distinction, however, has been attacked by many continental publicists, and the Institute of International Law at its session of 1896 adopted a proposal for the abolition of what is called relative or accidental contraband. For a summary of the views of continental publicists on the subject cf. Hershey, *International Law and Diplomacy in the Russo-Japanese War*, pp. 162-163.

[2] At a public meeting held in London on August 11, 1915, to urge upon the government the necessity of declaring cotton contraband Sir William Ramsay stated that cotton was the only substance required for the manufacture of munitions which the Germans could not supply themselves. He asserted that no chemical products could take the place of cotton in the manufacture of propulsive ammunition, and that ammunition made from used cotton was not as effective as that made from unused cotton. He maintained that while substitutes for cotton could be used in making nitro-cellulose, none of them had what was called the "ballistic power" of cotton.

should be subjected to condemnation and not merely prevented from passing, and it was for this reason that it was declared to be contraband." [1]

Denial was made in Germany, however, that cotton was being used for the manufacture of explosives or other war materials, and it was asserted that owing to recent scientific discoveries it had been possible to dispense entirely with its use for such purposes. [2]

In the United States, especially among the Southern cotton growers, the action of Great Britain in putting cotton on the list of absolute contraband was the subject of vigorous protest. The great majority of the people of the world, it was said, were clothed with goods manufactured from cotton, and it had been uniformly treated by belligerents in the wars of the past as non-contraband. It was admitted that during the Russo-Japanese war Russia had declared cotton to be absolute contraband on the ground that it was capable of being used for the manufacture of explosives, but against this action the British government vigorously protested, as did the American government. [3]

But regarding only the equities of the case and taking into consideration the extensive use now made of cotton in the manufacture of explosives, there would seem to be no logical reason why, if various other articles used for similar purposes may be properly treated as contraband, cotton may not be equally so regarded. And since the distinction between con-

---

[1] Memorandum of Sir Edward Grey of April, 1916.

[2] Senator Hoke Smith in an address in the United States Senate on January 20, 1916 (*Cong. Record*, pp. 1451 ff.), undertook to answer the British assertion that cotton was being used by the Germans for the manufacture of explosives. He cited at length the opinions of various German scientists in support of his contention.

[3] Sir Chas. Hardinge to Count Lansdorff, October 9, 1904, Moore's *Digest*, Vol. VII, p. 693. Cf. also the criticism of Russia's action by Jones, *Commerce in War*, p. 63. Professor T. E. Holland in the London *Times* of August 6, 1904, declared that Russia's action in treating cotton as contraband was "wholly unprecedented, for the treatment of cotton during the American Civil war as contraband will be found on examination to have no bearing on the question under consideration." Mr. F. E. Smith at the time took the same view in an address before the Liverpool Chamber of Commerce. Smith and Sibley, *International Law as Interpreted during the Russo-Japanese War*, p. 445. The action of the American government, he said, was based on the view that cotton took the place of money. There was no comparison, therefore, between the action of the United States government and that of Russia.

ditional and absolute contraband has under modern conditions proved to be largely impracticable, it will have to be admitted that cotton will henceforth be treated on the same footing with munitions of war.

§ 499. **Food-Stuffs as Contraband.** Likewise in regard to the treatment of food-stuffs as contraband the policy of the British government during the recent war was contrary to the practice of the past. The former practice had been to regard food-stuffs as contraband only when destined for the use of the military or naval forces of the enemy,[1] and this view was embodied in the declaration of London. As has been said, the British government in 1885 protested against the announcement by the French government of its intention to treat rice as contraband when destined to Chinese ports north of Canton. On that occasion Lord Granville declared that the "British government could not admit that provisions could be treated as contraband of war merely because they were consigned to a belligerent port." Lord Salisbury at the time thus defined the position of His Majesty's government on the question of food-stuffs: "Food-stuffs with a hostile destination can be considered contraband of war only if they are supplies for the enemy's forces. It is not sufficient that they are capable of being so used; it must be shown that this was in fact their destination at the time of the seizure."[2]

A similar protest was made by the British government against the treatment of food-stuffs as absolute contraband by the Russian government in 1904, Lord Lansdowne declaring that His Majesty's government regarded such a step as "inconsistent with the law and practice of nations." This view was defended by the British royal commission appointed in 1904 to consider the question of the supply of food and raw material in time of war, and it was the view expressed in 1911 in the debates in the House of Commons during the consideration of the Declaration of London.

§ 500. **American Complaints regarding British Detentions.** The American government complained, however, not so much

---

[1] Cf. a review of the authority and practice in Moore's *Digest*, Vol. VII, pp. 679 ff.

[2] Quoted in Moore's *Digest*, *ibid.*, pp. 682, 685, 686. Cf. also Atherley-Jones, *Commerce in War*, pp. 44-45.

of the unprecedented extension of the doctrine of contraband of goods formerly regarded as innocent, as against the British practice of taking into distant ports American ships for the purpose of examining their cargoes, this, it was alleged, on mere suspicion rather than upon reasonable evidence. This practice, it was asserted, was not only contrary to the established rules of visit and search, but it exposed owners of perishable cargoes to ruinous losses from the long delays which resulted. In short, it was not the right of search, but rather the manner of its exercise against which the American government protested.[1] The American government also complained that the expense of detention had to be borne mainly by the owners, and that in some cases it amounted to large sums.[2]

"The authorities lay down the general rule that searches must be conducted with as much regard for the rights and safety of the vessel as is consistent with a thorough examination of the vessel and cargo, and that any detention beyond what is necessary is unlawful."[3]

The British naval prize regulations provided that "in exercising the right of search the commander should be careful not to occasion the neutral ship any delay or deviation from her course

---

[1] Note of December 28, 1914. In a note of October 21, 1915, Secretary Lansing complained that the detentions of American vessels were not "uniformly based on proofs obtained at the time of seizure" but that vessels were detained while search was being made for evidence of the contraband character of the cargoes or attempt to evade the non-intercourse measures of Great Britain. This evidence, he said, could properly be obtained only by search at sea before the vessel was taken in. This, he added, was the practice of the American government during the Civil war, the assertions of the British government to the contrary notwithstanding. Mr. Lansing's note contained a list of some three hundred American vessels that had been detained in British ports for one reason or another. See the list in *European War*, No. III, pp. 40–49. Representative Fess in an address in the House of Representatives on January 11, 1916 (*Cong. Record*, pp. 95 ff.), stated that 428 neutral ships had been detained by the British authorities up to that time. He appended to his remarks a list of 271 vessels carrying American cargoes which had been taken to Kirkwall for examination between March 11, 1915, and June 16, 1915. All neutral vessels bound to and from Scandinavian and Dutch ports were required to put into Kirkwall for examination.

[2] In the case of the *Baron Stjernblad* the British House of Lords held that a claimant is not entitled to any costs or damages in account of the detention of a neutral ship laden with contraband goods, seized on reasonable suspicion of an ultimate enemy destination, but which is subsequently released.
Trehern, *British and Colonial Prize Cases*, Vol. III, p. 17. Compare also the case of the *Stigstad*, *ibid.*, II, 179.

[3] Cf. the opinions on this point in Moore's *Digest*, Vol. VII, pp. 475–479.

that can be avoided and generally to cause as little annoyance as possible."

It would seem that if reasonable suspicion is a sufficient justification for taking in a vessel for prize adjudication, it may be taken in for further examination. In fact, American commanders appear to have followed this course during the Spanish-American war and during the Civil war.[1] And what amounts to "probable cause" is, as the British prize court said in the case of the *Kronprinz Gustaf Adolf* (1917), incapable of precise definition and must be ascertained by the court according to the circumstances of each particular case.[2]

The British government justified the detentions against which the American government complained on the ground that strong suspicion, if not evidence, indicated the concealment of contraband, particularly of copper, in or under bales of cotton, hay, etc., and that an "imperative necessity for the safety of the country" required a more thorough examination than was possible at sea under modern conditions, and hence the ships must be taken into port where the cargoes could be unloaded and the suspected bales weighed or opened.[3] It also called attention

[1] For example, Commander Frailey, in reporting to the secretary of the navy the capture of the British ship *Adela*, said: "I did not examine her hold, being under the impression at that time that I had no authority to open her hatches, but having a *suspicion* of her character, I deemed it my duty to send her into port and hand her over to the judicial authority for examination." Quoted by A. Maurice Low in New York *Times*, December 24, 1914. Likewise the Supreme Court in the case of the *Olinde Rodrigues* (174 U. S. 510) said: "Probable cause exists when there are circumstances sufficient to warrant *suspicion*, though it may turn out that the facts are not sufficient to warrant condemnation." Cf. also the opinion of Chief Justice Chase in the case of the *Peterhof*.

[2] Trehern, *British and Colonial Prize Cases*, Vol. II, p. 419.

[3] See especially Sir Edward Grey's notes of January 7 and February 10, 1915, and the memorandum of April, 1916 (*European War*, No. 3, pp. 64 ff.). Owing to the size of modern steamships, Sir Edward argued, it was often, especially during rough weather, a matter of extreme danger, if not impossible, even to board such ships without taking them into calm waters. Secretary Lansing, however, quoted a contrary opinion by a board of American naval experts. This report was submitted by the British government to Admiral Sir John Jellicoe, who expressed a different opinion and affirmed that the size of modern steamers made the task of search at sea very difficult, a difficulty which was enhanced by the practice of concealment. *European War*, No. 3, pp. 63–64. Cf. further, on the difficulties of search at sea under modern conditions, Pyke, *Law of Contraband of War*, p. 201. "Under modern conditions," says Pyke, "searches at sea are practically futile. Whenever real ground for suspicion exists, it is absolutely necessary to bring the ship into port for examination, as was done with the *General* in the Boer war."

in its second reply to the American note to the fact that during the Russo-Japanese war and during the Balkan wars "British vessels were made to deviate from their course and follow the cruisers to some spot where the right of visit and search could be more conveniently carried out," and that in both cases it acquiesced. To take a ship into port, it added, was not the assertion of a new belligerent right, but rather the adaptation of an existing right to modern conditions of commerce. Again, it was alleged by the British government that the evidence in some cases indicated other fraudulent acts, such as the painting of copper bars in imitation of pigs of iron, the labelling of rubber as gum, etc.[1] Finally it was claimed that in some cases the manifests were fraudulent or incomplete, and that the policy adopted by the American government of withholding from the public all information regarding the contents and destinations of outward cargoes until thirty days after the clearance of the vessels, increased the difficulty of ascertaining the presence of contraband and made necessary a general system of examinations and detentions which would otherwise have been unnecessary.[2] In the case of vessels bound to an enemy port at any rate, and where strong suspicion indicates the concealment of contraband under heavy cargoes, the difficulty of verification at sea would seem to justify the taking of the ships into port where a more thorough examination can be made; otherwise the right of search would in many instances be worthless; but in such cases the captor should be held liable in damages if the evidence does not reveal the presence of contraband.[3] Among the articles of the

[1] The British authorities were able to produce evidence of numerous examples of fraudulent concealment and smuggling. Some of the devices adopted for this purpose were the use of double bottoms, decks, bulkheads, and hollow masts for concealing guns and ammunition; copper keels, plates, and bottoms on sailing ships for smuggling copper; the simulation of rubber as onions, hammers, etc., concealment of rubber in coffee bags, copper in flour barrels, and other devices of a similar kind. In May, 1915, three Germans were convicted by the United States court of New York for conspiring to defraud the United States by making and filing false manifests in that they had not declared $50,000 worth of rubber which they had concealed in barrels of rosin, and thirty tons of rubber which they had done up in bales of cotton waste.

[2] In consequence of numerous complaints on the part of exporters the order forbidding customs officials from making public such information was revoked in February, 1915.

[3] Cf. Hershey (*Amer. Jour. of Int. Law*, Vol. X, p. 583), who remarks that the attitude of the United States in respect to the British methods of search appeared to be "needlessly obstructive, legalistic and technical" and was based on the

cargo found aboard the Swedish steamship *Urra*, bound from New York to Gothenburg and Copenhagen in January, 1915, were goods described in the bill of lading as fifteen cases of hammers sent from the United States to Danish forwarding agents. They were found on examination to consist of fifteen cases, each containing a bag of copper, brass, and apparently aluminum filings and turnings. In the cargo of the Norwegian steamer *Lyngenfjord*, which sailed from New York on April 4, 1916, were found 250 sacks of what appeared to be coffee, but which turned out to be rubber.

It would seem, however, that the necessity of detention (which sometimes proves ruinous to shippers) resulting from concealment and fraudulent manifests might be removed by some system of official certification whereby neutral vessels could carry, if they chose, satisfactory assurances that their cargoes consisted only of the goods described in their papers.[1] In some cases such certificates were in fact issued by the United States' custom officials under authority of the treasury department and in other cases by British consuls under whose supervision the vessels were loaded, but the British government declined to regard such certificates as conclusive on the ground that they afforded no assurance against subsequent augmentation of the cargo at sea. In several cases cargoes so certified were seized and taken into port for examination.

In 1916 an arrangement was made by which "letters of assurance" were granted by the British embassy at Washington to exporters of cargoes which upon inspection were found to be unobjectionable. The presence of such a letter on board the ship assured it against interference on the part of British cruisers upon arrival in the zone of blockade.

§ 501. **Extension of the Doctrine of Continuous Voyage to the Carriage of Conditional Contraband.** Another subject of complaint by the American government was the extension by the British government of the rule of continuous voyage to the

---

"letter rather than the spirit of our rights." Cf. also Allin in the *Minnesota Law Review*, April, 1917, pp. 19 ff.

[1] Suggestions have frequently been made that this expedient should be adopted, and the proposed code adopted by the American Institute of International Law at its Havana session in 1917 contained a provision that certificates of this kind should be furnished merchant vessels and that those carrying them should be exempt from search.

carriage of conditional contraband and the introduction of "new principles which create presumptions of guilt not recognized either by the Declaration of London or the existing usage of nations." Article 35 of the Declaration lays down the rule that conditional contraband is not liable to capture, except when found on board a vessel bound for an enemy port and for the use of the armed forces of the enemy, and when it is not to be discharged in an intervening port.[1] The British order in council of October 29, however, proclaimed that notwithstanding the provisions of article 35, vessels bound for neutral ports, if the goods were consigned "to order," or if the ship's papers did not show who was the consignee, or if they showed a consignee in territory belonging to or occupied by the enemy, should be liable to capture, and that in such cases the onus of proving an innocent destination should be upon the owners of the goods. The effect of this order in council was to extend the application of the rule of continuous voyage to the carriage of conditional contraband to neutral ports unless the consignment was to a specifically named person, and to reverse the established rule, which placed upon the captor, not upon the owner, the burden of proving a hostile destination.[2] The order in council, however, recognized the distinction between absolute and conditional contraband. But by an order in council of March 30, 1916, the distinction, as stated above, was declared to have ceased to have any real foundation in view of the German government's having taken over the control of many articles which were not munitions of war, so that such articles consigned to enemy territory had the same status as if they were consigned directly to the government or its armed forces. The order, therefore, announced that the doctrine of continuous voyage would be applied to all contraband whether absolute or conditional and whether consigned to order or to specifically named persons.

In July, 1916, following the decision of the British and French

---

[1] The intention of article 35 as shown by the general report of the committee was to prohibit the application of the doctrine of continuous voyage to the carriage of conditional contraband. Cf. Stockton, "The International Naval Conference of London, 1908-1909," *Amer. Jour. of Int. Law*, Vol. III, p. 608.

[2] This latter rule had formerly been vigorously maintained by Great Britain, notably during the Russo-Japanese war. Cf. Bentwich, *The Declaration of London*, p. 71.

governments to abandon *in toto* the Declaration of London and
to exercise their belligerent rights at sea in accordance with
"the existing law of nations," a new order in council was issued
laying down the rule that the doctrine of continuous voyage or
ultimate destination should henceforth be applicable both to the
carriage of contraband and blockade.

§ 502. **History of the Doctrine of Continuous Voyage.** To
enable belligerents to meet effectively the situation caused by
the proximity of neutral ports to enemy territory, the doctrine
of continuous voyage was developed and applied to the carriage
of contraband to such ports when it was evident that the ultimate destination was enemy territory. It appears to have
been first applied to the carriage of contraband by the French
courts during the Crimean war in the case of the *Frau Anna
Howina*, when a cargo of saltpetre bound from Lisbon to Hamburg was condemned on the ground that the real destination
was an enemy port in Russia.[1]

As is well known, the doctrine was applied by the United
States courts to the carriage of contraband, notably in the
cases of the *Dolphin*, the *Pearl*, the *Bermuda*, the *Stephen Hart*,
the *Circassian*, the *Springbok*, and others;[2] it was applied
during the Boer war by the British government[3] which had
acquiesced in the American practice during the Civil war, but
which, it is well known, did not recognize its validity;[4] it was

---

[1] Calvo, *Le Droit Int.*, Vol. V, secs. 1961, 2767.

[2] For an analysis of and comment on these cases cf. Elliott, "The Doctrine of
Continuous Voyages," *Amer. Jour. of Int. Law*, Vol. I, pp. 61 ff., and Woolsey,
"Early Cases on the Doctrine of Continuous Voyages," *ibid.*, Vol. IV, pp. 823 ff.

[3] Baty, *Int. Law in South Africa*, pp. 1-44; White, *Law Qu. Review*, Vol. 17,
p. 12; Hart, art. cited, p. 193, and Elliott, art. cited, p. 100.

[4] Sir Edward Grey, however, speaking of the continental opposition to American
practice during the Civil war, stated in his note of July 23, 1915, to the American
government that "the United States and the British government took a broader
view and looked below the surface at the underlying purpose." Baty (*Britain
and Sea Law*, p. 72) remarks that the British government did not "strenuously
object" to the novel doctrine enunciated in the *Springbok* and other cases, because
it "hoped to find it useful and it proved to be so in the South African war." The
theory of continuous voyage as enunciated and applied by the Supreme Court
in the case of the *Springbok* was criticised by the Institute of International Law in
1882 as "subversive of an established rule of the law of maritime warfare according to which neutral property on board a vessel under a neutral flag, while on its
way to a another neutral port, is not liable to capture or confiscation." *Revue de
Droit Int.*, Vol. XIV, pp. 329-331. This fairly represented the opinions of continental and English publicists. But at its session of 1896 the Institute reversed
itself and approved the *Springbok* doctrine. *Annuaire*, Vol. XV, p. 231.

also applied by the Italian government during its war with Abyssinia in 1896.[1]   Great Britain until recently had uniformly opposed the doctrine of ultimate destination, and in 1885, when the French government announced its intention of seizing neutral vessels carrying contraband goods to the English port of Hong Kong, on the ground that their ultimate destination was the armed forces of China, the English government protested vigorously and asserted the right of neutral vessels to trade freely between neutral ports.[2] During the Boer war, however, as has been said, Great Britain undertook to apply the rule which she had formerly condemned. Three German ships, the *Bundesrath*, the *Herzog*, and the *General*, bound for the neutral port of Lorenzo Marquez in Delagoa bay, were seized on the ground that portions of their cargoes consisted of contraband the ultimate destination of which was the Boer armies. The ships were released on account of the vigorous protest of the German government. Several vessels laden with cargoes of American flour bound to Portuguese ports in Delagoa bay were also seized by British cruisers during the same war. There was a strong protest in the United States, and the American government declared that it could not recognize the validity of "any right of capture by a belligerent of provisions and other goods shipped by American citizens in the ordinary course of commerce and destined to a neutral port." But it turned out that the ships were English and not neutral vessels, and were seized for transporting goods to enemy territory in violation of a municipal statute. The seizure of the cargoes was declared to be incidental to the seizure of the ships, and the British government agreed to liberate or purchase them. The controversy was not, therefore, one involving the question of contraband.[3]

[1] Notably in the Doelwick case which was identical with the case of the *Peterhof*. The *Doelwick* was a Dutch ship captured by an Italian cruiser while bound for the French-African port of Djibouta. But although the ship and cargo were condemned by the prize court, they were restored, the war having ended before the prize was condemned.   Brusa, *Rev. Gén. de Droit Int. Pub.*, Vol. IV, p. 157; Clunet, Vol. XXIV, pp. 268, 275; Bonfils, sec. 1707, and Pillet, *Les Lois Actuelles*, sec. 269. As thus applied by the Italian prize court it met the approval of the Institute of International Law. *Annuaire*, Vol. XV, p. 231.

[2] Cf. an article by Geffcken entitled *La France en Chine et le Droit International*, in the *Rev. de Droit Int. et de Lég. Comp.*, Vol. 17, p. 149 (1885).

[3] J. B. Moore, *La Contrebande de Guerre, Revue de Droit Int. et de Lég. Comp.*, Vol. 44, p. 239. The whole subject of these seizures is examined at length in Campbell's *Neutral Rights and Obligations in the Anglo-Boer War*, ch. III.

It was to meet such a situation as that presented by the Delagoa bay cases that the Declaration of London allows the rule of continuous voyage to be applied to the carriage of conditional contraband (as well as absolute contraband) when the enemy has no seaboard. When the recent war broke out, this doctrine was generally accepted by all maritime States. Both Germany and Austria, however, had seaports, and hence the rule of continuous voyage could not, if the Declaration had been observed, have been applied to the carriage of American cargoes of conditional contraband to neutral ports in Europe. But this feature of the Declaration was not acceptable to Great Britain, and it was modified by the orders in council of October 29 and March 30, 1916, and finally the entire Declaration was abrogated in July, 1916, after which she applied the rule which the British prize courts had always repudiated, and which British authorities without exception had condemned.[1]

§ 503. **Neutral Embargoes on Exportations to Belligerent Territory.** The British and French governments went farther and employed their power over neutral commerce to compel such neutral countries as Italy, the Netherlands, Norway, Sweden, and Denmark to place an embargo upon the exportation to enemy territory of many articles of both absolute and conditional contraband.[2] Confronted by the prospect of seeing their over-seas trade reduced to insignificant proportions, one after another of them were induced to prohibit the exportation or transportation through their territories of such goods as the British and French governments chose to regard as contraband, and which therefore they would not permit to be delivered from abroad without a pledge that they should not be allowed to go to Germany or Austria. The result was, com-

---

[1] As to the views of the British authorities cf., e.g., Westlake, Vol. II, p. 253; Atherley-Jones *op. cit.*, p. 257; Baty, *Int. Law in South Africa*, pp. 6, 19; Bentwich, *The Declaration of London*, pp. 18, 75, and Hall, *op. cit.*, p. 673. This view was also affirmed by the British government in its instructions to its delegates to the London Naval Conference in 1908. House of Coms. Ses. Papers, *Misc.*, No. 5 (1909), p. 95.

[2] Some of these embargo lists may be found in *International Law Situations* for 1915, pp. 33 ff. On the Danish list are some two hundred and fifty items, including such articles as drugs, bicycles, vegetables, and other food products, chemicals, oils, ores, grain, cloth, fertilizers, gasoline, lubricants, lumber, machinery, potash, rags, rubber, rosin, seeds, skins, steel, wool, etc. The Dutch list contains some 200 articles, that of Norway 250, that of Switzerland about 200, and those of Portugal, Roumania, Spain, and Sweden about 500 each.

merce between America and the neutral powers of Europe
was virtually carried on under the license of the British and
French governments.

§ 504. British and American Practice Compared.   The American government was reproached by the British government for
protesting against the exercise by Great Britain of a right which
the United States exercised in respect to the carriage of contraband during the Civil war.   Thus, in a communication to the
department of state in November, 1914, the British ambassador
said:

"As you are aware, the Supreme Court of the United States in 1863
considered vessels as carrying contraband, although sailing from one neutral
port to another, if the goods concerned were destined to be transported by
land or sea from the neutral port of landing into the enemy's territory.
It then decided that the character of the goods is determined by their ultimate and not their immediate destination, and this doctrine was at the time
acquiesced in by Great Britain, though her own trade was the chief sufferer."

But it was pointed out in the United States that the circumstances under which the rule of continuous voyage was applied
during the Civil war differed in important respects from those
under which it was applied by Great Britain and France during
the recent war.   During the Civil war the neutral ports to
which the intercepted cargoes were destined were really nothing
more than ports of call or transshipment where there existed
little or no local demand for the enormous quantities of goods
which were consigned thereto, and they were in addition well
known as notorious bases near the coast of the Confederacy
for blockade runners.   Upon delivery the cargoes did not
become a part of the common stock of the country, but were
immediately reladen on other vessels and reforwarded to belligerent territory.   As Judge Marvin said in the case of the
Dolphin, Nassau furnished no market for such a cargo as that
vessel contained.

"It is," he said, "a small town.   The adjacent islands possess but a
small population dependent upon it for supplies.   Probably not three
merchant steamers ever arrived at that port from any part of the world
until after the present blockade was established, except the regular government mail steamers.   The size of the country, the smallness of the population, and the absence of local demand, therefore, repelled the assumption
that goods of the character and quantity involved in these transactions
were intended for local consumption."

In the recent war the neutral ports to which the detained cargoes were consigned were the ports not of small islands, but of countries with extensive populations among whom there was a large local demand for the particular commodities in question, a demand which was increased considerably by the cutting off of the accustomed supply at the outbreak of the war, from the neighboring belligerent States. They were not mere ports of call or transshipment. In every case the cargoes were intended to be unloaded, after which they would become mixed with the common stock of the country, a transaction which interrupted the voyage; if a subsequent shipment took place, it would be an entirely new voyage and not a continuation of the initial voyage.[1]

Sir Edward Grey in his first note to the American government, January 7, 1915, produced statistics to show that there had been a large increase in the volume of exports, particularly of copper, from America to the neutral countries of Europe since the outbreak of the war.[2] " With such figures," he said, " the presumption is very strong that the bulk of the copper consigned to these countries has recently been intended not for their own use but that of the belligerent who cannot import it directly." But there had always been a large demand for copper in these countries, and, as has been said, it was increased by the cutting off of the supply from Germany and Austria at the outbreak of the war. Neutrals therefore refused to admit the validity of the British contention that the increase of imports from America by neutral States adjacent to Germany was conclusive as to enemy destination, all the more so because those countries had placed embargoes on the reëxportation of most of the goods so imported.

Sir Edward Grey in a memorandum of April, 1916, replied

[1] Cf. Secretary Lansing's note of October 21, 1915, *European War*, No. 3, pp. 25 ff., and Burgess, *America's Relations to the War*, p. 101.

[2] Sir Edward Grey submitted among other data the following exhibit of exports from New York to certain neutral countries for the months of November, 1913 and 1914, respectively:

	1913	1914
To Denmark	$558,000	$7,101,000
Sweden	377,000	2,858,000
Norway	477,000	2,318,000
Italy	2,971,000	4,781,000
Holland	4,389,000	3,960,000

at length to the American contention that goods consigned to neutral ports and intended to become a part of the "common stock" were not liable to seizure under the doctrine of ultimate destination. The statistics which he quoted concerning the vast increase of imports and other evidence repelled the presumption, he said, that these goods were intended to become a part of the common stock of the country.

"However sound the principle that goods intended for incorporation in the common stock of a neutral country should not be treated as contraband may be in theory," he said "it is one that can have but little application to the present imports of the Scandinavian countries. The circumstances of a large number of these shipments negative any conclusion that they are *bona fide* shipments for the importing countries. Many of them are made to persons who are apparently nominees of enemy agents, and who never figured before as importers of such articles. Consignments of meat products are addressed to lightermen and dock labourers. Several thousands of tons of such goods have been found documented for a neutral port and addressed to firms which do not exist there. Large consignments of similar goods were addressed to a baker, to the keeper of a small private hotel, or to a maker of musical instruments. Will it be contended that such imports ought to be regarded as *bona fide* shipments intended to become part of the common stock of the country? To press any such theory is tantamount to asking that all trade between neutral ports shall be free, and would thus render nugatory the exercise of sea power and destroy the pressure which the command of the sea enables the allies to impose upon their enemy." [1]

§ 505. **Defence of the Doctrine of Continuous Voyage under Modern Conditions.** It must be admitted that the circumstances under which the early doctrines relative to the seizure of contraband were applied, were radically different from those which exist today. At that time the lack of facilities for land transportation made it difficult for a belligerent to obtain over-seas supplies through the ports of neighboring neutral States. The question of ulterior enemy destination was therefore of relatively small importance. Under those circumstances Sir William Scott could say, as he did in the case of the *Immina*, that goods going to a neutral port "cannot be regarded as con-

[1] In a statement presented to the House of Commons in January, 1916, entitled: *Measures Adopted to Intercept the Sea-borne Commerce of Germany* (*Misc.*, No. 2, Cd. 8145), the British government contrasted the conditions in earlier wars, under which the old rule was practicable, with those of the recent war, when without the application of the doctrine of continuous voyage it would have been impossible to prevent illicit trade with Germany.

traband, but that they must be taken *in delicto* in the actual prosecution of a voyage to an enemy port." On this principle he was justified in refusing to condemn a cargo of cheese destined to Quimper on the opposite side of the peninsula from Brest, a port of naval equipment, because on account of the lack of land transportation facilities between the two places it was impossible to say that the ultimate destination of the cargo was the latter port.[1] But he was entirely justified in condemning, as he did the following day, a cargo destined to the port of Coruña, because it was situated in close proximity to the naval port of Ferrol to which the goods could be carried on in the same ship.[2] In other words, he applied the doctrine of continuous voyage whenever the means of transportation between the intermediate neutral port and the belligerent port were such that the goods could be easily reforwarded and transshipped to the enemy.[3] The old English rule, according to which the destination of the ship was primarily the test, was effective enough under the conditions of land transit then existing; but with the development of railway and other facilities for land transportation, which made it as easy for a belligerent to obtain over-sea supplies by land through the medium of adjacent neutral ports as through his own ports, the old rule no longer sufficed. Unless, therefore, a belligerent were allowed to apply the doctrine of ultimate destination to the carriage of contraband to such neutral ports, his power to intercept contraband would be of little avail in a war with a continental enemy. Accordingly, the prize courts of France, the United States, and Italy extended the old rule so as to make it conform to the altered conditions.[4]

§ 506. **Cases of the *Kim* and Others.** Naturally a large number of cases involving questions of contraband came before the prize courts of the various belligerents during the recent war. It is impossible to examine any considerable number of them here; it must suffice, therefore, to refer only to a few of the more important cases decided by the British, French, and German prize courts.

---

[1] The *Frau Margaretha*, 6 C. Rob. 92 (1805).
[2] The *Zelden Rust*, 6 C. Rob. 93 (1805).
[3] Compare Pyke, *The Law of Contraband of War*, pp. 144, 156.
[4] Compare Perrinjaquet in 22 *Rev. Gén. de Droit Int. Pub.*, p. 129. See also two articles entitled *Contrebande de Guerre dans le Conflit Actuelle* in 42 Clunet, pp. 453 ff. and 831 ff.

A series of cases which attracted widespread attention by reason of the great value of the cargoes seized, and which are important because they involved the question of the applicability of the doctrine of continuous voyage, were those of the *Kim*, the *Alfred Nobel*, the *Björnstjerne Björnson*, and the *Fridland*, all Norwegian and Swedish steamers laden with large cargoes of lard, meat, and other food products, wheat, oil, and rubber, the aggregate value of which was estimated at about $15,000,000, destined to Copenhagen and consigned " to order." They all sailed from New York in October, 1914, and were captured during the following month by British cruisers and taken in on the ground that their cargoes were conditional contraband destined ultimately for the government or armed forces of Germany.

After a long delay the cases were brought to trial before the British prize court in July, 1915. The owners, five American meat packing concerns, contended that since the goods were conditional contraband, it must be shown that they were intended for the government or armed forces of Germany, and that this intent existed from the first; also that the onus of proving the intent rested upon the crown. They contended, furthermore, that the doctrine of continuous voyage could not be applied, because this doctrine was applicable only where the destination was that to which the original consignor intended the goods to be sent, and in these cases that destination was a neutral port. To hold, as the crown insisted, that because the whole German nation was under arms, provisions going to Germany might be treated as if they were destined for the use of the government or the armed forces, would be to disregard the time-honored distinction between absolute and conditional contraband. The claim of the crown that in view of the practice of the German government of making requisitions upon merchants for food supplies, in consequence of which any goods going to Germany might be taken for the use of the military forces, the British government would be justified in treating them as absolute contraband, was denied. The mere fact that they were destined to enemy territory and might ultimately find their way to the armed forces did not render them confiscable. Adverting again to the doctrine of continuous voyage, the claimants argued that the test of a continuous voyage was, as Sir Edward Grey had instructed the British delegates to the London Naval Conference, "whether the whole transaction was made in pursuance of a single mercantile transaction, preconceived by the consignor from the outset." The doctrine of continuous voyage, they further argued, had never been applied to a case where the goods on arrival at a neutral port had been sold there, and it could not be applied where the evidence went no farther than to show that they were sent to the neutral port in the hope of finding a market there for delivery elsewhere. This view, they affirmed, was that taken by the United States Supreme Court in the cases of the *Stephen Hart*, the *Bermuda*, the *Springbok*, and the *Peterhof* during the American Civil war. The question was also raised as to whether it was competent for the crown by order in council to alter the rules of international law in such a way as to affect the rights of neutrals, and the opinion was expressed that the order in council of October 29, 1914, had so altered the law and was not binding on the prize court.

On September 16, nearly a year after the seizure of the vessels, the prize court rendered its decision. Adverting, in the first place, to the enormous increase of exports from the United States to the Scandinavian countries since the outbreak of the war, a fact which created a strong presumption that a large portion of such exports were intended for Germany, Sir Samuel Evans called attention to the fact that Denmark, the country to which the cargoes in question were consigned, was a small State, containing less than three million inhabitants, and one which, as regards food-stuffs, was an exporting rather than an importing country, yet whose proximity to Germany rendered it a convenient territory from which goods imported from America could be transported to Hamburg, Altona, Lübeck, Stettin, and Berlin. Sir Samuel then quoted statistics to show that vast quantities of lard, meat, bacon, etc., were being imported into Denmark, far in excess of the local demand. For example, the average annual quantity of lard imported into Denmark during the years 1911 to 1913 from all sources was 1,459,000 pounds, whereas the quantity of lard consigned on the four ships in question alone amounted to 19,252,000 pounds. In short, within a period of a month these vessels had transported more than thirteen times the quantity of lard which had been imported annually into Denmark for each of the three years prior to the war. Armour and Company alone shipped to Copenhagen in October and November, 1914, twenty times the amount of lard exported from the United States to all Scandinavia during the corresponding period of 1913. These facts, Sir Samuel observed, "give practical certainty to the inference that an overwhelming portion, so overwhelming as to amount to almost the whole, of the consignments of lard in the four vessels being dealt with, was intended for, or would find its way into Germany." These facts were important to bear in mind, although they were not conclusive as to the liability of the goods to confiscation as prize.

The evidence showed, or seemed to show, he said, that the goods in question were shipped to Copenhagen, in part to named consignees, but for the greater part to agents of the packers or to their order, who, instead of being genuine neutral buyers, were merely persons employed by the packers on commission or sent by them from their German branch houses for the purpose of insuring the immediate transportation of the consignments to Germany. Some of these agents sent to Copenhagen from Germany established themselves in hotels; two of them organized a Danish importing company with a capital of $600 and within five weeks imported $1,400,000 worth of lard. Some agents were found to be moving about from place to place in Europe, and in one case a German agent employed the innocent name of "Davis" in his cable despatches; a special cable code was invented; hastily devised arrangements were made for payment by the establishment of large credits in Scandinavian banks, etc. In spite of these facts it was pretended that the business was *bona fide* neutral trade, and that the packers had no interest beyond that of selling and consigning to neutral buyers. With some minor exceptions, there were no invoices, insurance policies, checks, or other proofs of sale or payments; their affidavits were in the most general terms, and no attempt was made to explain away the damaging evidence of various letters and telegrams disclosed by the crown.

Turning to the question of continuous voyage, Sir Samuel reviewed at length the history and development of the doctrine. There was no reported case, he said, in which it had been applied by the British courts to the carriage of contraband; but it had been so applied and extended by the American courts, it had received the approval of the British government, and was defended by Lord Salisbury during the South African war in connection with the Delagoa bay cases. Finally, the doctrine, so far as absolute contraband was concerned, had received the sanction of the London Naval Conference. The refusal of the Conference to admit it in the case of conditional contraband (except where the enemy country has no seaboard) was, like most compromises, not founded on reasons of logic.

"If," he added, "it is right that a belligerent should be permitted to capture absolute contraband proceeding by various voyages or transport with an ultimate destination for the enemy territory, why should it not be allowed to capture goods which, though not absolutely contraband, become contraband by reason of a further destination to the enemy government or its armed forces? And with the facilities for transportation by sea and land which now exist, the right of a belligerent to capture conditional contraband would be of a very shadowy value if a mere consignment to a neutral port were sufficient to protect the goods. It appears also to be obvious that in these days of easy transit, if the doctrine of continuous voyage or continuous transportation is to hold at all, it must cover not only voyages from port to port at sea but also transportation by land until the real, as distinguished from the merely ostensible, destination is reached."

The contention of the claimants that the order in council of October 29 was contrary to international law and therefore not binding on the court was, he said, unfounded. Article 35 of the Declaration of London, which excluded the application of the rule of continuous voyage to the carriage of conditional contraband, was itself an innovation in international law, and the effect of the order in council was to prevent that innovation. It was, therefore, not in contravention of, but in accordance with the existing law and practice. Then adverting to the state of things in Germany in consequence of the enrolment of the whole able-bodied portion of the male population in the military forces, he quoted a passage from the note of Sir Edward Grey of February 10, 1915, to the American government, where it was said that the reason for drawing a distinction between food-stuffs intended for the civil population and for the armed forces itself disappears, which must be the case in a country where the armed forces embrace so large a portion of the population, and where the power to requisition was used on a large scale to obtain supplies for the use of the government and the army. On this point he said:

"It was given in evidence that about ten millions of men were either serving the German army or dependent upon or under the control of the military authorities of the German government out of a population of between sixty-five and seventy millions of men, women and children. Of the food required for the population it would not be extravagant to estimate that at least one-fourth would be consumed by these ten million adults."

To hold, therefore, that the goods were not intended for German military and naval use "would be to allow one's eyes to be filled by the dust of theories and technicalities and to be blinded to the realities of the case." The cargoes (except certain insignificant portions) were therefore condemned.[1]

The owners filed a protest with the American department of state against the decision of the prize court and urged it to intervene diplomatically in their behalf, with a view to obtaining reparation for the losses which they had sustained. In their protest they alleged that "the judgment was unsupported by facts and proceeded upon inferences and presumptions." Not withstanding the condemnation of the cargo, the British government agreed to compensate the owners, and in due course the value of the goods was paid to the representatives of the owners, who expressed their appreciation of the fairness and friendly consideration with which they were treated.[2] Many other cases involving the carriage of contraband were decided by the English prize courts, but the limits of this chapter do not permit of their examination.[3]

---

[1] Trehern, *Brit. and Col. Prize Cases*, Vol. I, pp. 405–492.

[2] The *London Times* of September 17, 1915, commenting on the decision referred to as "one which will be memorable in the history of jurisprudence," said: "The result, if adverse to American shippers, may be said to be a compliment to American jurisprudence, as the judgment was influenced very much by the decisions of the United States courts during the Civil war and the precedents most in point were the judgments of Chief Justice Chase, and his colleagues in regard to British cargoes seized as contraband." Mr. H. R. Pyke, the author of a valuable treatise on the *Law of Contraband of War*, in an article in the *Law Quar. Review* for January, 1916 (pp. 60 ff.), on the *Kim* case expressed the opinion that the decision of the prize court was "fully justified as a reasonable application under modern conditions of the general principle of international law that neutral traders are bound to refrain from consigning directly or indirectly to the enemy of a belligerent who has sufficient command of the sea to prevent such consignment, any object intended to assist the enemy in his war operations." Mr. Pyke adds that the decision makes a refreshing contrast to the decision of the German prize court in the case of the *Maria* which sailed before the outbreak of the war. The decision however, is the subject of criticism by Mr. C. P. Anderson in 11 *Amer. Jour. of Int. Law*, pp. 251 ff.

[3] Among the more important were the *Sorfaren*, the *Lorenzo*, the *Alwina*, the *Jeanne*, and the *Marecaibo*, all of which may be found in Trehern's collection of *British and Colonial Prize Cases*.

In the case of the *Axel Johnson* (*ibid.* II, 532) the British prize court condemned a cargo of wool destined from Sweden to Germany where, the claimants alleged, it was being sent to be combed after which it was to be returned to Sweden, except the waste wool and by-products which were to be retained by the German spinners as a part of their payment. In the case of the *Balto* (*ibid.* II, 398) it condemned a cargo of leather destined for Sweden on the ground that there existed an intention to convert the leather into shoes after which they were to be exported to Germany. In the case of the *Bonna* (*ibid.* III, 163) which involved the liability to condemnation of a cargo of cocoanut oil destined to Sweden for the manufacture of margarine to be sent to Germany, Sir Samuel Evans said that the doctrine of continuous voyage would be applicable if there was evidence of an intent to export the manufactured article to Germany but he added that raw materials on their way to Sweden for conversion into manufactured articles for consumption in that country were not subject to condemnation "solely on the ground that the consequences might or even would necessarily be that another article of a like kind would be exported to the enemy by other citizens of that neutral country."

§ 507. **French Cases.** A large number of cases involving questions of contraband were decided by the French council of prizes. In the case of the *Nieuw-Amsterdam*,[1] which seems to have been the first French case involving a question of contraband, the council of prizes laid down a rule which it subsequently followed in many cases, namely, that in respect to *conditional* contraband destined to specific consignees in neutral ports, it was incumbent upon the captor to prove that the goods were intended for the use of the armed forces or governmental authorities of the enemy, but that the onus did not rest upon the captor when the consignments were "to order."[2]

---

[1] Text of the decision in the *Rev. Gén. de Droit Int. Pub.*, Vol. 22, 1915, *Jurisprudence*, pp. 13 ff.

[2] Cf. also the later case of the *Zoodochos-Pighi*, *ibid.*, 1917, No. 2, *Jurisprudence*, p. 33, and the case of the *Ellespontos* (*ibid.*, p. 38), where it was held that a cargo of conditional contraband for which there was no bill of lading or other papers naming a consignee, but only a manifest indicating neither weight nor destination, and which was claimed by a person in relation with a notorious supplier of contraband to the enemy and who could not establish an innocent destination, was liable to condemnation.

As to *absolute* contraband, however, the prize council held that when consigned to neutral European ports or an enemy agent in neutral territory, especially if consigned "to order" or if the papers did not indicate the consignee the burden of proof that the ultimate destination was not the enemy rested upon the claimants and not upon the captor.[1]

Many cases involved the liability to capture of goods consigned to firms in Switzerland. When absolute contraband, the prize council uniformly condemned the goods if the consignee was a firm in constant commercial relations with Germany, or if the goods were consigned "to order," or if they were not on the Swiss embargo list; otherwise they were released.[2] In such cases the fact that the final lap of the voyage was by land did not alter the situation.[3] In the case of consignments "to order" the prize council asserted the right to examine into all the circumstances with a view to ascertaining the real destination of the goods. The case of the *Nieuw-Amsterdam* involved the liability to capture of certain portions of a cargo of food-stuffs shipped from New York to Amsterdam and Rotterdam by various American milling and manufacturing companies. The ports of Holland, the prize council said, must be assimilated to German ports if, in virtue of the Rhine navigation convention of October 17, 1868, goods laden on vessels which touch at Dutch ports might be freely transported by way of the Rhine to German territory. There was therefore sufficient presumption that goods destined to such ports were destined ultimately to Germany. Moreover, the measures adopted by the German government for the control of the food supply within German territory had, it was said, destroyed the distinction between goods intended for the State or its agents and those consigned to private persons. Consequently consignments of contraband goods to such persons were subject to the same rules of capture as consignments to the government or its agents.[4]

[1] See, for example, the case of the *Canellopoulas*, 24 *Rev. Gén., Jurispr.*, p. 55.
[2] The *Peloponesos*, *ibid.*, 1917, p. 32. Cf. especially the cases of the *Rioja*, *ibid.*, 1916, *Jurisprudence*, pp. 30, 62; the *Achilleus*, *ibid.*, p. 32; the *Grao*, *ibid.*, p. 105, and the *Teresa-Fabregas*, *ibid.*, p. 36.
[3] The *Milano*, *ibid.*, p. 127. As to the introduction of contraband into Germany through Switzerland, see 45 Chunet, pp. 99 ff. See also *ibid.*, p. 126 for the measures of the Swiss government to suppress this traffic.
[4] A large number of other cases involving questions of contraband were decided by the French prize council, but it is impossible to consider them here. Among

§ 508. **German Cases.** Owing to the small number of captures made by the naval forces of Germany, the German prize courts had occasion to render very few decisions. There were, however, some captures during the early days of the war before the German fleet was driven to cover; occasionally captures were afterwards made by raiders, and in a few instances these prizes were taken in for adjudication. The most important case involving the question of contraband was that of the *Maria* the circumstances of the sinking of which are set forth in the preceding chapter (sec. 486). The claimants contended that the cargo was intended for the use of private mills in Ireland which operated for private purposes. They argued, furthermore, that the sinking of the *Maria* took place before Dublin, to which more than half the cargo had been consigned, had been declared a naval base, and consequently the ship could not be said to have been destined to a prohibited place at the time of its destruction.[1] The imperial prize court, however, asserted that while it had not been especially declared to be a naval base, it was in fact a base of operations and supply from the very beginning of the war, and inasmuch as the *Maria* intended to land first at Belfast, which had already been declared a naval base, the cargo was liable to condemnation, and for the reasons stated above both the cargo and ship were subject to destruction. The contention of the claimants that the cargo was intended for private mills was rejected on the ground that no proof was produced to show that the government authorities would not requisition the grain, after its delivery, for the use of the military or naval forces, and even if such proof had been furnished, there would have been nothing to prevent the public authorities from doing this. The fact that the cargo was consigned "to order" facilitated the free disposal of the cargo. In short, the court presumed from these facts not that the cargo was destined ultimately for the use of the armed or naval forces of the enemy, but that there was nothing to prevent its being taken by the

---

the more important may be mentioned the cases of the *Insulinde*, the *Jiul*, the *Eir*, the *Joannina*, the *Atlas*, the *Fortuna*, the *Boeroe*, the *Barcelo*, the *Karimata*, the *Apollonia*, the *Agliastra*, the *Oranje Nassau*, the *Banda*, the *Cotentin*, and the *Achilleus*. I have used the texts printed in the *Rev. Gén. de Droit Int. Pub.*

[1] Belfast had been declared a base for the British fleet in August, 1914, but Dublin was not so declared until November 25.

government for such use; i.e., possible use and not actual destination was adopted as the test for condemnation.

The burden of proof was placed upon the claimants to show not only that the cargo was not intended for the use of the military or naval forces, but also that the government would not have requisitioned it, had it reached its destination. This evidence, of course, they could not furnish, and such as was produced was treated by the court as mere assertion. What the court insisted on was a guarantee that in the end the grain would not be used for the military or naval forces. Manifestly, under this decision all contraband destined for enemy territory was liable to seizure and condemnation regardless of whether consigned to a naval base or not. Thus the rule which distinguishes between conditional contraband consigned to certain places of military or naval importance and that consigned to enemy territory in general was in effect swept aside.[1] The decision has been strongly criticised by high authority as being a virtual negation of the right of neutrals to transport conditional contraband to enemy territory for private consumption.[2]

The case was nearly identical with that of the *William P. Frye*, an American sailing vessel laden with grain and bound for English ports, which was sunk by a German cruiser in January, 1915.[3] In this case, however, the German government agreed

[1] The text of the decision may be found in the *Zeitschrift für Völkerrecht*, Bd. IX, Heft 3 (1916), pp. 408 ff. An English translation of the decision is printed in the *Amer. Jour. of Int. Law* for October, 1916, pp. 927 ff.

[2] Cf. H. R. Pyke in the *Law Quar. Review*, January, 1916, pp. 60 ff. In his judgment in the case of the *Kim*, Sir Samuel Evans, referring to the decision of the German prize court in the case of the *Maria*, said: "I refer to it, not because I look upon it as profitable or helpful (on the contrary, I agree with Sir Robert Finlay that it should rather be regarded as a 'shocking example), but because it is not uninteresting as an example of the ease with which a prize court in Germany hacks its way through *bona fide* commercial transactions when dealing with wheat which was shipped from America before the war, and which had also before the war been sold in the ordinary course of business to a well-known firm of British merchants." Trehern, *Brit. and Col. Prize Cases*, Vol. I, p. 490.

[3] The case also bears some resemblance to that of the *Wilhelmina* where the British government defended the seizure of a cargo of conditional contraband laden on board a neutral vessel and consigned to a private firm in Hamburg. The two cases, however, are by no means analogous. Hamburg, unlike Dublin, was a fortified place, and, besides, the German government had taken over the control of the grain supply, thus abolishing the distinction between the military and civil population. This, of course, had not been done by the British government. Moreover, instead of destroying the *Wilhelmina* and its cargo, the captor took them in for adjudication, and the owners of the cargo were paid by the British government for the goods taken.

to compensate the owners of both the ship and cargo in consequence of treaty stipulations, but there being no similar treaty between Germany and the Netherlands, the German government appears not to have made compensation to the Dutch owners. In the case of the *Elida*,[1] however, the Imperial prize court dealt more generously with the claim of a Swedish firm for compensation on account of the seizure by a German torpedo boat of a Swedish steamer laden with a cargo of wood which had been sold by a Swedish firm to an English firm in Hull. The prize court at Kiel had released the ship and cargo on the ground that the seizure took place within the "zone of neutrality" proclaimed by Sweden, i.e., within four miles of the coast of Sweden,[1] and further because the cargo of wood was "timber" and not "fuel" and therefore not contraband according to the German list then in force. Nevertheless, the lower court refused to allow compensation to the owner of the steamer for damages sustained by the seizure and detention of the ship and cargo. The Imperial supreme prize court, however, reversed the decision of the lower court so far as it related to compensation and ruled that the claim for compensation was fully justified. The commander of the capturing vessel was in error in considering the cargo as "fuel" rather than "timber," and an incorrect interpretation by naval commanders of prize regulations could never be regarded as a sufficient justification for seizure.

§ 508a. Conclusion. It is probably safe to say that the majority of the controversies between belligerents and neutrals to which every war gives rise are connected with trade in contraband. It has therefore been proposed by some writers that neutral governments should forbid their nationals to engage in such traffic, and some even maintain that they are under an obligation to do so.[2] In practice, the governments of certain States have occasionally undertaken to prevent the transportation to belligerents of contraband goods. Thus during

---

[1] Text in the *Zeitschrift für Völkerrecht*, Bd. IX (1915), pp. 109 ff.

[2] Among them may be mentioned Kleen (*Contrabande de Guerre*, p. 52), Hautefeuille (*Nations Neutres en Temps de Guerre*), and Field (*Outlines*, sec. 964). Woolsey (*Int. Law*, p. 320) thinks all innocent trade with the enemy should be free, but that neutrals should pass stringent and effectual laws against contraband trade. Phillimore (*Int. Law*, Vol. III, secs. 227–241) seems to hold the same opinion.

the Franco-German war of 1870 the governments of Austria, Denmark, Spain, the Netherlands, Belgium, Switzerland, and Japan prohibited the exportation of arms and munitions of war to either belligerent, those of Belgium, Switzerland, and Japan considering that it was their duty to do so.[1] During the same war the German government declared through its representatives at London and Washington that neutral governments were not permitted to allow their nationals to engage in such trade, but, on the contrary, it was their duty to prohibit it, because " the precepts of international law are binding upon States as well as upon individuals." During the Spanish-American war the governments of Brazil and Denmark likewise prohibited the exportation of war materials to either belligerent. These cases of prohibition, however, are exceptional, the general rule being that neutrals are under no obligation to forbid their nationals from engaging in contraband trade, whatever the character of the goods.[2]

Another proposal which goes to the other extreme is to remove all restrictions on trade in contraband and to exempt contraband goods from liability to capture. Such a proposal was made by the British delegation at the Second Hague Conference. In its memorandum it called attention to the lack of precise rules governing the question of what is and what is not contraband and the multiplicity of controversies to which trade in contraband goods gives rise. It also pointed out that the right of capture in such cases is out of harmony with modern conditions. In the days of sail boats, it was said, contraband consisted almost exclusively of articles used only for war purposes, and the

---

[1] In 1870 the German government contended that it was the duty of neutral governments to prevent their subjects from engaging in contraband trade. Bluntschli, sec. 766. For an argument against the prohibition of trade in contraband see Baty, *op. cit.*, pp. 33–35. The question was discussed by the Institute of International Law at its sessions of 1892, 1894, and 1896 (see the *Rev. Gén. de Droit Int. Pub.*, Vol. III, pp. 648–658 for a review of the discussions). The proposal to prohibit trade in contraband was opposed by Lardy, Stoerk, and General den Beer Poortugael, but defended by Brusa. At the session of 1896, the Institute agreed to a proposal to abolish conditional contraband, reserving to belligerents a right of sequestration or preëmption at their pleasure and to neutrals an equitable indemnity. *Annuaire*, t. XV, pp. 205 *et seq.*, and p. 231. At the Second Hague Conference of 1907 Admiral Sperry proposed in the name of the American delegation that the right of capture be limited to absolute contraband, and the Brazilian delegation made a similar proposal.

[2] This question is considered more at length in secs. 548–552.

destination of the ship sufficed ordinarily to indicate the hostile destination and character of the goods. Moreover, ships were small in size, and the right of search could be exercised easily and without the necessity of diverting the ship to a distant port for the purpose of verifying the character of the cargo, and thus subjecting the shipper to ruinous losses on account of long detention. Today these conditions no longer exist. The number and variety of contraband articles are vastly greater, and the increased size of ships makes search on the high seas much more difficult. Furthermore, with increased railroad facilities contraband easily finds its way to belligerents, so that prohibitions are usually ineffective. All these circumstances tend to render more difficult the exercise of the right of search, to multiply the number of controversies, and to inflict upon neutral commerce an inconvenience out of all proportion to the legitimate interests of belligerents.[1] It would be better, therefore, to abolish the right of capture and allow contraband to be carried freely, except where prevented by blockade.

It is interesting to note that of the thirty-five States voting on the British proposal, twenty-six voted for it.[2] Only five — Germany, the United States, France, Montenegro, and Russia — voted against it, although five others abstained from voting. This vote was very significant and indicated a general dissatisfaction with the present rule and practice in regard to trade in contraband and the desire for a less objectionable and more logical solution of the problem.[3]

[1] See the memorandum in *Deuxième Conférence de la Paix, Actes et Documents*, Vol. I, pp. 256–258. This proposal was advocated by Secretary Marcy in 1856; also by Lorimer, Coceje, Kluber, Rayneval, von Bar, and others at the meeting of the Institute of International Law in 1874. Cf. Pyke, *Law of Contraband*, p. 102.

[2] *Deuxième Conférence de la Paix, Actes et Documents*, t. III, p. 881.

[3] Professor J. B. Moore in an address before the National Foreign Trade Convention at St. Louis in June, 1915, pointed out the unsatisfactory character of the rules of the Declaration of London in respect to trade in contraband. The inferences which it creates in regard to hostile destination, he said, are so vague that "they would seem to justify in almost any case the presumption that the cargo, if bound to an enemy port, was 'destined for the use of the armed forces or of a government department of the enemy state.' Any merchant established in the enemy country, who deals in the things described, will sell them to the government; and, if it becomes public that he does so, it will be 'well known' that he supplies them. Again, practically every important port is a 'fortified place'; and yet the existence of fortifications would usually bear no relation whatever to the eventual use of provisions and various other articles mentioned. Nor can it be denied that, in this age of railways, almost any place may serve as a 'base,'

for supplying the armed forces of the enemy. And of what interest or advantage is it to a belligerent to prevent the enemy from obtaining supplies from a 'base,' from a 'fortified place,' or from a merchant 'well known' to deal with him in his own country, where, the entire community being subject to his authority, he can obtain by requisition whatever he needs, if dealers in commodities hesitate to sell voluntarily." The proper solution according to Professor Moore is to be found, if not in the abolition of the principle of contraband, at any rate (1) in the adoption of a plan embracing the abolition of conditional contraband, and (2) a single list having been agreed upon, in the coöperation of neutrals and belligerents in the certification of the contents of cargoes so that the risk of capture may be borne by those who may voluntarily assume it. "Harassing searches and detentions" he added, "will then be heard of no more."

CHAPTER XXXIII

BLOCKADES

§ 509. The German Submarine "Blockade" of England; § 510. Some Examples of Actual Blockades; § 511. The Anglo-French Blockade of Germany; § 512. Criticism of the Proposed Blockade; § 513. The Order in Council of March 11, 1915; § 514. Character of the Blockade thus Established; § 515. Neutral Protests; § 516. The British Defence; § 517. Legality of the Anglo-French Blockade; § 518. Criticism regarding the Discriminatory Features of the Blockade; § 519. Charge that the Blockade Applied to Neutral Ports; § 520. Extension of the Doctrine of Continuous Voyage to Blockade Running; § 521. Defence of the Doctrine; § 522. Popular Demand in England for a Real Blockade; § 523. German Criticism of the Blockade as a "Starvation" Measure; § 524. Attitude of the British and French Governments in Regard to the Admission of Hospital Supplies to Germany; § 525. Admission of Food Supplies to the Occupied Districts of Belgium, France, and Poland; § 526. The Problem of Preventing Commerce with the Enemy; § 527. The Netherlands Overseas Trust; § 528. The System of "Rationing" Neutrals; § 529. Neutral Protests; § 530. American Policy; § 531. Other Expedients.

§ 509. **The German Submarine "Blockade" of England.** During the early months of the war neither the British nor the German government proclaimed a blockade of the ports of the other. It is true that the German war zone decree of February 4, 1915, was frequently referred to as a blockade measure,[1] but it does not appear to have been so intended by the German government. If so, it possessed few if any of the elements of a lawful blockade as blockades have heretofore been understood, because no adequate naval forces were stationed off the coasts of England to make it effective, its enforcement being left entirely to submarines. In fact, several thousand ships arrived

---

[1] In the British diplomatic correspondence it was frequently so referred to. But Heilbronn in the *Zeitschrift für Völkerrecht* (Bd. IX, p. 58) denies that it was a "blockade," since no intention of interdicting neutral ships from entering British ports had been asserted by Germany. In short, the German measure was directed only against enemy ships. The German war zone decree of January, 1917, was even more frequently referred to as a "blockade." It was so characterized by Dr. Paul Ritter, Swiss minister at Washington, in a communication to the American government of March 23, 1917.

and cleared from British ports each week after the German decree was put into effect.[1]

§ 510. Some Examples of Legal Blockades. The first instance during the recent war of the institution of a real blockade, as the term is understood in international law, was that established by Austria-Hungary of the coast of Montenegro on August 10, 1914. Due notice was given to neutrals, and it was announced that the blockade would be made effective by means of naval forces.[2] A second example was that established by Great Britain and France in the latter part of February, 1915, of the coast of German East Africa. The British and French orders proclaiming the blockade announced that the area of the blockade would include the coast from latitude 4°, 41′ South to latitude 10°, 40′ South, a distance of 300 miles, and that four days' grace would be allowed for the departure of neutral vessels from the blockaded ports. It was also announced that a sufficient number of vessels would be stationed off the blockaded ports to make the blockade effective. Apparently the institution of both blockades was entirely in conformity with the rules of international law as embodied in the Declaration of London, and, so far as known, no complaints were made by neutrals either in respect to their legality or mode of execution.

Other blockades were those proclaimed on August 27, 1914, by Japan of the coast of Kiau-Chau; by Great Britain on June 2, 1915, of certain parts of the coast of Asia Minor;[3] by France on August 22, 1915, of the coasts of Asia Minor and Syria from the Island of Samos to the Egyptian frontier;[4] by the English and French fleets of the Œgean coast of Bulgaria, October 16, 1915;[5] by Italy of certain parts of the Austro-Hungarian

[1] Sir Edward Carson stated that during the first eighteen days after the German decree was announced an average of 607 ships of over 100 tons burden, not including fishing craft and sailing vessels, arrived in the ports of England each day, and that during this period 5873 vessels cleared therefrom. As to the ineffectiveness of the German "blockade" of England cf. also Villeneuve-Trans, *Le Blocus de l'Allemagne*, ch. III. I have considered in sec. 573 the question as to whether a legal blockade can be maintained by submarines. See also Fauchille in 25 *Rev. Gén.* p. 79 and 9 *Amer. Jour.* of *Int. Law*, 461.

[2] Text in 22 *Rev. Gén. de Droit Int. Pub.* (1915), p. 74.

[3] London *Gazette*, October 19, 1915.

[4] *Législation de la Guerre*, Vol. II, pp. 302–303.

[5] Clunet, 42:299.

coast and the coast of Albania, May 26, 1915,[1] and by Great Britain and France of Saloniki in June, 1916, and later of all the Greek coasts from the mouth of the Struma river to the Greco-Bulgarian frontier.[2] Greece being a neutral country, the blockade of its coasts under ordinary circumstances would, of course, have been unjustified; but the situation was anomalous, owing to the occupation of the country by British and French forces, who, their governments claimed, were there by invitation.[3] The legality of the blockade was, therefore, a subject of controversy.

Other blockades were proclaimed and established by the various belligerent governments from time to time. Most of them were in the customary form. They were expressly proclaimed as blockades; the extent of the coasts blockaded was specified; due notice was given as to when they would take effect, and in nearly every case days of grace were allowed during which neutral vessels in the blockaded ports would be allowed to depart.[4]

§ 511. The Anglo-French Blockade of Germany. The blockades mentioned above were, on the whole, of minor importance, and owing to the comparative commercial insignificance of the blockaded territories they did not seriously interfere with neutral trade, nor did they, except in the cases of the Albanian and the Greek blockades, evoke protest or controversy. It was otherwise, however, with the Anglo-French blockade of Germany. As stated above, the war had been in progress some seven months before Great Britain and France decided to have recourse to blockade as a means of cutting off trade with Germany. During this period such goods as had not been declared

---

[1] *Ibid.*, 42: 265; *Rev. Gén. de Droit Int. Pub.*, 1915, Docs., pp. 215, 220. There were some protests against the blockade of the coast of Albania because it was a neutral State. It was also complained that the blockade extended to arms of the open seas. Cf. the criticism of Professor Lammasch quoted in the *Continental Times* of July 3, 1915. Albanians in the United States protested that the blockade was unlawful and unprecedented. The Italian government appears to have defended the blockade on the ground that Austro-Hungarian forces were making use of certain of the Albanian ports for the purpose of revictualling the Austrian fleet.

[2] Press despatches of June 8, 1916. Text of the blockade proclamation, which took effect December 8, in 24 *Rev. Gén. de Droit Int. Pub.* (1917), p. 53.

[3] I have described this anomalous situation more at length, in ch. XXX.

[4] As to the character of these earlier blockades see Pchédecki, *Le Droit Maritime et la Grande Guerre*, p. 175.

contraband were allowed to go freely to Germany. On March 1, 1915, however, the British government announced that it was the intention of the allied governments "to seize all ships carrying goods of presumed enemy destination, ownership or origin." Adverting to the German war zone decree of February 4 as a measure "entirely outside the scope of international law," contrary to the humane practice of the past, and adopted against peaceful traders and non-combatant crews with the avowed object of preventing commodities of all kinds, including food for the civil population, from reaching or leaving the British Isles or northern France, the British announcement stated that

"Her opponents are therefore driven to frame retaliatory measures in order in their turn to prevent commodities of any kind from reaching or leaving Germany. These measures will, however, be enforced by the British and French governments without risk to neutral ships or to neutral or non-combatant life and in strict observance of the dictates of humanity. The British and French governments will therefore hold themselves free to detain and take into port ships carrying goods of presumed enemy destination, ownership, or origin. It is not intended to confiscate such vessels or cargoes unless they would otherwise be liable to condemnation."[1]

§ 512. **Criticism of the Proposed Blockade.** This announcement raised two questions of interest to students of international law. In the first place, it contained a declaration of an intention to establish what in effect was a blockade without designating it as such and without conforming it to the requirements heretofore recognized as essential to a valid blockade. In the second place, this non-conformity to recognized legal requirements was defended as a justifiable act of retaliation against the enemy for violation of the laws of war. The prime minister of England, in a speech in the House of Commons on March 1, announcing the measure, declared that it had been decided upon in the exercise of "an unquestionable right of retaliation." "In the retaliatory measures we propose to adopt," he said, "'blockade,' 'contraband' and other technical terms do

[1] A communication from the French ambassador at Washington in practically identical language was sent to the secretary of state at the same time. The German war zone decree, it may be remarked, was itself defended by the German government as a justifiable act of retaliation for various alleged violations of international law by Great Britain, notably the British measures in respect to contraband, disregard of the Declarations of Paris and of London, and the conversion of the North Sea into a military area.

not occur; and advisedly, in dealing with an opponent who has openly repudiated all the restraints of law and humanity, we are not going to allow our efforts to be strangled in a net-work of juridical meshes."

Both the form of the measure and the reason upon which it was sought to justify it were attacked in the United States as in other neutral countries as being contrary to the law of blockade and therefore without justification.[1] It was described by the American government as a "so-called blockade" and, being "admittedly retaliatory," was therefore "illegal in conception and nature."

Mr. A. J. Balfour, in an article published in the London *Times* of April 2, 1915, defended at length the Anglo-French measure as a justifiable act of retaliation against Germany. He said:

"Put shortly, the case is this. The Germans declare that they will sink every merchant ship which they believe to be British, without regard to life, without regard to the ownership of the cargo, without any assurance that the vessel is not neutral, and without even the pretence of legal investigation. The British reply that if these are to be the methods of warfare employed by the enemy, the Allies will retaliate by enforcing a blockade designed to prevent all foreign goods from entering Germany and all German goods from going abroad."

To hold, he argued, that Great Britain, in technically violating the law governing blockades in order to meet the measures of an adversary who openly disregarded the law of nations and of humanity, was equally deserving of condemnation was to apply rigid technical standards in a case where technical standards must be used with caution; it was appealing to the letter of international law but ignoring the spirit. After all, he added, it was the equity of the allied case rather than the law which mainly interested the thinking public in America and elsewhere. It was a question rather of international morality than of international law. To insist that the repudiation of the generally accepted rules of conduct by one belligerent does not impair in the least the obligations of the other is to confound international morality with international law, two closely related though not identical bodies of principles.

[1] Note of Secretary Lansing of October 21, 1915; cf. also his memorandum of April, 1916, *European War*, No. 3, pp. 77-78.

"The obligations of the former," he continued, "are absolute; those of
the latter are conditional, and one of the conditions is reciprocity. In the
present unorganized condition of international relations it could not well be
otherwise.   But let them remember that impotence, like power, has duties
as well as privileges; and if they cannot enforce the law on those who violate
both its spirit and its letter, let them not make haste to criticise belligerents
who may thereby be compelled in self-defence to violate its letter while
carefully regarding its spirit.   For otherwise the injury to the future development of international law may be serious indeed. If the rules of warfare
are to bind one belligerent and leave the other free, they cease to mitigate
suffering; they only load the dice in favor of the unscrupulous; and those
countries will most readily agree to changes in the law of nations who do
not mean to be bound by them."

The plea thus put forward in defence of a measure which was
avowedly retaliatory and which did not conform to the established rules raised a delicate question and one upon which strong
argument may be advanced on both sides. It involved the
whole question as to how far it is.permissible for a belligerent
to violate the laws of war as an act of retaliation against his
enemy, and to what extent the obligation to conform to the
law rests upon the principle of reciprocity.[1] Whatever may be
the differences of opinion on this point, there is a general agreement that a belligerent may not in his measures of reprisal
against an enemy disregard the rules of international law established for the protection of neutrals, and it was mainly on this
ground that the validity of the Anglo-French blockade was
attacked in neutral countries.[2]

[1] The right of retaliation against an enemy who refuses to conform to the law
of nations is recognized by most writers. Cf. Wheaton (Lawrence's ed.), pp. 605–
608; Taylor, op. cit., sec. 487; Rivier, op. cit., Vol. II, p. 298; Oppenheim, Vol. II,
p. 259; Spaight, p. 463; Westlake, Collected Papers, p. 260.   The whole matter is
considered by Wilkinson in an article on "Reprisals in Warfare," in the Law
Mag. and Review, May, 1915.

[2] Baty, an English writer criticising the British order in council of March 11,
remarks that it was avowedly a retaliatory measure, and he adds, "How, as Phillimore says, can you retaliate against neutrals who have never injured you?"   See
his article in the Pennsylvania Law Review, June, 1915, p. 717.   In 1918 the English prize court in the case of the Leonora considered at length the question as to
how far a belligerent may, in the exercise of the right of retaliation against an
enemy, interfere with the rights of neutrals, as those rights are recognized by the
existing rules of international law.   The court affirmed that the maritime commerce of neutrals may be restricted by belligerents if that commerce tends to assist
the enemy directly or indirectly in his warlike operations.   It also upheld the
British blockade measure as a legitimate act of retaliation against the illegal
methods of warfare pursued by the enemy.   The decision of the prize court was
affirmed on appeal by the judicial committee of the privy council (London Times,

§ 513. The Order in Council of March 11. By an order in council of March 11 the proposed measures against commerce with Germany were definitely proclaimed.[1] The order in council contained a long preamble denouncing the German war zone decree of February 4 as a violation of the usages of war and declaring that "such attempts on the part of the enemy give to His Majesty an unquestionable right of retaliation." The order then decreed that no merchant vessel which had sailed from her port of departure after March 1, 1915, to any German port would be allowed to proceed unless the vessel were provided with a pass authorizing her to proceed to some neutral or allied port, in which case the goods on board would be discharged in a British port and placed in the custody of a prize court. If non-contraband of war and if not requisitioned for the use of His Majesty, they would be restored under such conditions as the court might deem to be just. No merchant vessel which had sailed from any German port after March 1 would be allowed to proceed on her voyage with any goods laden at such port. All such goods would be put in the custody of the prize court and disposed of in the same manner as those found on board ships bound to German ports. Every merchant vessel which had sailed from her port of departure after March 1 to a port other than a German port, and carrying goods with an enemy destination or which were enemy property, *might* be required to be discharged in a British port and placed in the custody of the prize court and disposed

---

August 1, 1919). Adverting to the unlawful German onslaught on shipping generally, Lord Sumner concluded: "It is plain that measures of retaliation and repression would be fully justified in the interest of the common good even at the cost of very considerable risk and inconvenience to neutrals in particular cases." The decision is criticised by Yntema in an article in 17 *Mich. Law Review*, pp. 64 ff. This author attacks as unwarranted the principle laid down by the prize court that an enemy may be punished by way of retaliation "through the sides of a neutral" and asserts that the fact of non-conformity by one belligerent to a rule of international law does not justify the other in refusing to observe it. Cf. also the opinion of the English prize court in the case of the *Stigstad*, affirmed by the judicial committee of the privy council (Trehern, III, 181), upholding the right of reprisal even when it causes delays and inconveniences to neutrals. This case is analyzed and criticised by Borchard in the *Yale Law Journal*, 1919, pp. 583 ff. See also the opinion of Sir Samuel Evans in the case of the *Hakon*, Trehern, II, 201.

[1] By a decree of March 13, 1915, the French government put into effect a measure substantially the same as that of the British order in council of March 11.

of in a similar manner to those destined directly to or from a German port, as explained above, provided that the crown might release neutral property of enemy origin upon proper application.

§ 514. **Character of the Blockade thus Established.** It will be noted that the employment of the word "blockade" was deliberately avoided throughout the text of the order in council, nor was the order clothed in the form of a blockade proclamation, nor did it define the area blockaded, nor lay down any rules as to presumed knowledge of the existence of the blockade such as are required by the Declaration of London, nor was anything said in regard to measures for making the blockade effective by means of cruisers or other craft as was done in the proclamations establishing the blockades mentioned above. British officials, however, frankly admitted that the purpose of the order was to institute a blockade of all commerce with Germany, both incoming and outgoing. On March 13 this was definitely asserted by Sir Edward Grey in a memorandum placed in the hands of the American ambassador in London. In this memorandum Sir Edward stated that

"The government of Great Britain have frankly declared, in concert with the government of France, their intention to meet the German attempt to stop all supplies of every kind from leaving or entering British or French ports by themselves stopping supplies going to or from Germany for this end. The British fleet has instituted a *blockade*, effectively controlling by cruiser 'cordon' all passage to and from Germany by sea."

Thus all doubt as to the character and purpose of the measure was removed. It was avowedly to be a blockade differing in form and technique from the usual type of blockade and also differing in legal effect, inasmuch as not all goods destined to or from the blockaded ports in violation of the order would be confiscated, but, if non-contraband of war, they would be restored or paid for under such conditions as the prize court might deem just. The measure would therefore be more favorable to neutrals than the customary blockades of the past under which cargoes of non-contraband equally with contraband goods, as well as the ships which carry them (subject to certain exceptions), are confiscated when destined to a blockaded port.

§ 515. **Neutral Protests.** The British order in council and the French decree provoked vigorous protests by the governments of the United States, Denmark, the Netherlands, Norway, and Sweden. In a succession of notes addressed to the British government the American secretary of state declared that the measures of the allied governments constituted an encroach-. ment upon the rights of neutrals; that the effect was to establish a virtual blockade of the ports of neutral countries adjacent to Germany; that the right of retaliation against an enemy did not include the right to interfere with the lawful commerce of neutrals, etc. The measure was characterized as a "socalled" blockade which did not distinguish between enemy and neutral trade; it was ineffective even according to the admission of the British government as shown by its order placing cotton on the list of contraband as a means of effectually preventing the shipment of that commodity to Germany; it was illegal, because it was not applied impartially to the ships of all nations since German ports on the Baltic were "notoriously open" to traffic with the ports of Denmark, Norway, and Sweden, and also because it barred access to neutral ports and coasts in violation of the Declaration of London; finally, it was argued that the doctrine in the *Springbok* case was not applicable to the present situation, because the circumstances were different, the ports of the Confederacy having been effectually blockaded, though no neutral ports were closed.[1]

§ 516. The British Defence. In a note of July 24, 1915, Sir Edward Grey undertook to answer the criticisms made by the secretary of state of the United States. He began by asserting that the allies were bound "to take every step in their power" to overcome an enemy which had committed so many shocking violations of the recognized rules and principles of civilized warfare.

Regarding the American complaint as to the blockade of neutral ports, Sir Edward declared that His Majesty's government was unable to accept the contention that if a belligerent is so circumstanced that his commerce can pass through adjacent neutral ports as easily as through ports in his own territory, his opponent has no right to interfere and must restrict his measures of blockade in such a manner as to leave such channels of commerce still open to his adversary. Such a contention,

[1] These arguments are set forth in detail especially in the American note of October 21, 1915. Cf. also the note of March 30, 1915.

he said, could not be sustained upon principles either of international law or international equity. The British government was unable to admit that a belligerent violates any fundamental principle of international law by applying a blockade in such a way as to cut off the enemy's commerce with foreign countries through neutral ports, if the circumstances render such an application of the principles of blockade the only means of making it effective. The American government had intimated its readiness to take into account the great changes that had occurred in the conditions and methods of naval warfare and had admitted that it was no longer practicable to render a blockade effective by means of a cordon of ships in the immediate offing of the blockaded port. The only question then about which a controversy could properly arise was whether the measures adopted were "in conformity with the spirit and principles of the essence of the rules of war." Sir Edward then reviewed at some length the measures adopted by the government of the United States during the Civil war in the enforcement of the blockade of the Southern States. To meet the difficulties resulting from the proximity of neutral ports to enemy territory the old principles relating to contraband and blockade were, he said, extended by the American government, and the doctrine of continuous voyage was applied and enforced, under which goods destined to the territory of the enemy were intercepted before they reached the neighboring neutral ports from which they were to be reëxported. The difficulties which confronted the United States were similar in some respects to those which the allies then faced in dealing with the trade of their enemy, for, he said,

"Adjacent to Germany are various neutral countries which afford her convenient opportunities for carrying on her trade with foreign countries. Her own territories are covered by a network of railways and waterways, which enable her commerce to pass as conveniently through ports in such neutral countries as through her own. A blockade limited to enemy ports would leave open routes by which every kind of German commerce could pass almost as easily as through the ports in her own territory. Rotterdam is indeed the nearest outlet for some of the industrial districts of Germany."

If Germany, he added, may send her commerce through a neutral country without compromising its neutrality, Great Britain may fairly claim to intercept such commerce before it has reached, or after it has left, the adjacent neutral State, provided it is the commerce of the enemy and not commerce which is *bona fide* destined for or proceeding from the neutral State. If, therefore, it be recognized that a blockade is a legitimate method of intercepting trade with an enemy, and if the blockade can be made effective only by extending it to enemy commerce passing through adjacent neutral ports, such an extension is defensible and in accordance with the generally accepted principles of international law.

The methods of making a blockade effective, the degree of effectiveness, the rules as to public notification, the presumption of knowledge of the existence of the blockade, the penalty to which a blockade runner should be subjected, and other particulars in respect to the establishment and maintenance of a blockade were, he said, matters upon which different views had prevailed, and regarding which the practice of States had been altered from time to time. The one principle which was fundamental, and which had obtained universal recognition, was that a belligerent had a lawful right by means of an effective blockade to cut off the sea-borne commerce of the enemy, and this, and this only, Great Britain was endeavoring to do.

§ 517. **Legality of the Anglo-French Blockade.** Regarding the legality of the "so-called" blockade of Germany, there is, of course, ground for a difference of opinion. Unquestionably it did not conform to the technical rules heretofore recognized as essential to a valid blockade. Before the days of torpedoes, mines, submarines, and air craft the prevailing conception was that a blockaded port must be closed by a cordon of ships stationed in the immediate offing or as near as was compatible with safety from the enemy's defences (which in those days consisted of guns), to make ingress and egress dangerous if not impossible.[1] It can hardly be maintained, however, that since the introduction of the new agencies and methods of naval warfare referred to above, the old requirement of blockade by a cruiser cordon is now essential. The American government in its note of March 30, 1915, expressed a readiness to admit that the old form was no longer practicable in the face of an enemy possessing the means and opportunity to make an effect-

---

[1] Cf. the views of Julian S. Corbett in the *Nineteenth Century and After* Vol. 61, p. 926; also Bentwich, *The Declaration of London*, p. 16.

ive defence by the use of submarines, mines, and air craft. The long-range blockade must therefore be recognized as valid and blockading craft must be permitted to remain so far out as to be beyond the range of torpedo boats or mines, which means that they may be so completely 'out of sight of the blockaded port as to render ingress and egress no longer dangerous. If this is not recognized as an effective blockade, blockade under modern conditions is now impossible.[1]

Likewise the criticism of the British blockade that it was not legal because it was not effective can hardly be justified except on the theory that a blockade is legal only when it prevents absolutely access to the enemy's coasts. Tested by that rule, many of the blockades of the past were illegal, among them the blockade of the Southern States during the Civil war.[2] During the recent war over-seas trade direct with Germany was in fact more completely cut off than commerce with the Confederacy ever was during the Civil war.[3]

§ 518. Criticism regarding the Discriminatory Features of the Blockade. Another criticism directed against the Anglo-French blockade was that it did not conform to the rule of international law that a blockade to be legal must be impartially enforced against the commerce of all neutrals alike.[4] At first

[1] As to what constitutes a legal blockade under the new and changed conditions, see Alessandri, *Contribution à l'Étude des Blocus Nouveaux*. See also 43 Clunet, pp. 148 ff. for a defence of the legality of the Anglo-French blockade.

[2] On the "ineffectiveness" of the American blockade during the Civil war cf. Rhodes, *History of the United States*, Vol. V, pp. 396 ff., and Soley, *The Blockades and Cruisers*, pp. 44 ff. Soley remarks that the "absolute locking up of a well-fortified port, whose trade offers powerful inducements to commercial enterprise, is an absolute impossibility." This is, of course, much more true today with new instruments of naval warfare, such as submarines, aeroplanes, mines, and torpedoes. It appears that on July 25, 1861, the British consul at Charleston gave it as his opinion that the blockade was effective only as against large vessels, but one vessel having been stationed off the port of Charleston. The British consul at Wilmington expressed a similar opinion regarding the blockade of the Gulf ports. Cf. Atherley-Jones, *Commerce in War*, p. 164.

[3] Sir Edward Grey pointed out in his memorandum of April, 1916, that the number of ships stationed off a blockaded port or coast was not the only test of the effectiveness of a blockade. "The best proof of the thoroughness of a blockade," he said, "is to be found in its results. This is the test which Mr. Seward in 1863, when secretary of state, maintained should be applied to the blockade of the Confederate States."

[4] Art. 5 of the Declaration of London declares that "a blockade must be applied impartially to the ships of all nations." Cf. on this point Bentwich, *The Declaration of London*, p. 47.

the British and French governments made no attempt to send war ships into the Baltic Sea for the purpose of blockading the northern coast of Germany. The result was the development of an extensive trade between Sweden and Germany, whereas trade between America and Germany through the North Sea was barred by means of the blockade. American shippers therefore complained of the operation of the blockade in its effect upon neutrals and on this ground attacked it as illegal.[1] The British answer to this criticism was that the alleged discrimination was not in fact discrimination at all, and that the failure to blockade the Baltic ports of Germany resulted not from deliberate intention, but from a geographical situation which rendered it impossible to do so. It was not, therefore, due to any desire to favor Scandinavian trade as against American exporters.[2]

Manifestly, the equality required by international law does not mean that the advantage derived by one neutral on account of its geographical situation, which makes impossible a blockade of enemy ports to which it has access, must be compensated for when another neutral, differently circumstanced geographically, is cut off from trade with the same country by means of a blockade. It means nothing more than that the blockading power may not deliberately grant favors to one neutral which are not given equally to all. Furthermore, it is quite certain that the rule as to the impartial application of a blockade to the ships of all neutral nations was never intended to impose upon belligerents an obligation when they institute a blockade to blockade

[1] See Mr. Lansing's note of October 21, 1915.
[2] Cf. the following defence by Mr. A. J. Balfour in a letter published in the London *Times* (weekly edition) of April 2, 1915: "Now the object of this rule (which forbids discrimination as between neutrals) seems clear. It is designed to prevent the blockading power from using its privileges in order to mete out different treatment to different countries; as for instance, by letting ships of one nationality pass the blockading cordon while it captures the ships of another. Such a procedure is, on the face of it, unfair. It could have no object but to assist the trade of one neutral as against the trade of another and arbitrarily to redistribute the burden which war unhappily inflicts on neutrals as well as on belligerents. Now I submit that if there be discrimination inflicted by the British blockade, it is not discrimination of this kind. It does no doubt leave the German trade with Sweden and Norway in the same position as the German trade with Holland and Denmark, and in a different position from the German trade with America or Africa. But the discrimination (if it is to be so described) is not the result of a deliberate policy, but of a geographical accident."

the whole of the enemy's coasts. Blockade is a belligerent right which may be exercised or not at the discretion of the belligerent, and it is optional whether he shall blockade all or some of the enemy's ports or coasts. Having once proclaimed a blockade, a belligerent may extend or contract the blockaded area at will. In practice this right has often been exercised.[1] Blockades have been confined to a single port or to a portion of the enemy's coast. The first blockade proclaimed by President Lincoln (April 19, 1861) applied only to the States of the lower South. Virginia and North Carolina were not blockaded until April 28, and it was not considered that the leaving of the ports of these States open during the interval, involved any discrimination against certain neutrals. President McKinley by a proclamation of April 22, 1898, declared a blockade of the ports of the northern coast of Cuba from Cárdenas to Bahía Honda and the port of Cienfuegos on the south. Subsequently, by a proclamation of June 27 the blockade was extended to include all the ports on the southern coast from Cape Frances to Cape Cruz. As to Porto Rico, only the port of San Juan was blockaded. But there was no complaint on the part of neutrals that the leaving open of certain ports violated the rule of impartiality. Several of the minor blockades referred to above, proclaimed during the recent war, applied only to particular ports and coasts of the enemy and not to all of them. But there was no criticism that they were for that reason unlawful.

§ 519. **Charge that the Blockade Applied to Neutral Ports.** The principal criticism directed against the Anglo-French blockade, however, was not so much its non-conformity to the technical requirements in respect to its form, nor its ineffectiveness, nor its alleged discriminatory features, as that it "barred access to neutral ports and coasts in violation of the Declaration of London."[2] This situation was brought about by the extension of the doctrine of continuous voyage to the transportation by sea of goods to and from the ports of neutral countries adjacent to Germany whenever the ultimate destination of the goods was enemy territory, or when they were of enemy origin. It is incontestable that, as a general principle, a belligerent has no lawful right to blockade directly or indirectly the ports and

[1] Cf. Atherley-Jones, *Commerce in War*, pp. 125 ff.
[2] American note of October 21, 1915.

coasts of a neutral State; but if the enemy is wholly or partially surrounded by neutral territory through whose ports he may draw supplies from over the seas, and through which he may send his goods abroad, has the opposing belligerent no right to intercept such trade through the exercise of his power to prohibit commerce altogether by means of a blockade? Manifestly, if he has no such right, the power which international law gives him in respect to blockade must in many cases be ineffective, if not illusory. Under such circumstances the right of blockade could be exercised effectively only against insular States. "It would," as Lawrence remarks, "be absurd to suppose that a powerful fleet would rock idly on the waves off a great neutral port, while cargo after cargo of arms and munitions of war were poured in under its eyes and taken from the quays by a short railway journey to the arsenals of a foe whose navy it had swept from the seas, and whose ports it was keeping under strict blockade. Justice demands that no such perversion of neutrality should be allowed." Germany was flanked by a group of neutral States, some of them geographically separated from her only by a surveyor's line, others only by narrow seas. In the case of the former States, extensive railway connections made it as easy — in some cases easier — to transport goods from certain neighboring neutral ports to points in Germany where they were needed, as it was to move them to Hamburg or Bremen.

§ 520. **Extension of the Doctrine of Continuous Voyage to Blockade Running.** As was pointed out in the preceding chapter, the doctrine of continuous voyage was developed in order to enable belligerents to meet effectively the situation caused by the proximity of neutral ports to enemy territory, through which the enemy might draw supplies from over seas, and this doctrine was given an important extension by the Supreme Court of the United States during the Civil war. Those who attacked the legality of the Anglo-French blockade measure of 1915, however, argued that the American decisions extended the doctrine of continuous voyage only to the carriage of contraband and not to the transportation of non-contraband goods to non-blockaded ports, as Great Britain and France undertook to do during the recent war. They pointed out that in the case of the *Peterhof* [1] the United States Supreme Court

[1] 5 Wall, 28 (1866).

definitely refused to extend the rule of continuous voyage to blockade running, by declining to condemn goods shipped from England to Matamoras, a non-blockaded port, although the evidence indicated that the goods were to be transported by land from Matamoras to the Confederacy. In short, the doctrine of continuous voyage did not apply when the last lap of the voyage was by inland transportation from a neutral port to enemy territory, although it did apply when the second part of the voyage was by sea.[1] The voyage of the *Peterhof*, it was said, was exactly parallel to a voyage during the recent war from New York to Rotterdam or Copenhagen, whereas those with which the Supreme Court was dealing in the *Springbok* and other similar cases were not. Finally, it was pointed out that whatever may have been the practice in the past, the Declaration of London, while sanctioning the rule of continuous voyage generally in respect to the transportation of absolute contraband and also the carriage of conditional contraband in case the enemy had no seaboard, made no such concession in respect to blockade. On the contrary, it expressly declared that "whatever may be the ulterior destination of a . . . vessel, or of her cargo, she cannot be captured for breach of blockade if at the moment, she is on her way to a non-blockaded port."[2] This rule embodied the view which the British delegation to the London Naval Conference was instructed to insist upon.[3] But by an order in council of March 30, 1916, this rule was abrogated, and the doctrine of continuous voyage or ultimate destination was made applicable to blockades as to the carriage

---

[1] Cf. the comment of Burgess, *America's Relations to the Great War*, pp. 108 ff., and Holtzoff, "Some Phases of the Law of Blockade," *Amer. Jour. of Int. Law*, Vol. X, pp. 53 ff. There is no offence, Holtzoff contends, if the goods are to be unloaded at a neutral port and are to be introduced into the blockaded country from the interior by means of land, canal, or river transportation. Cf. also Perrinjaquet, a French writer, in the *Rev. Gén. de Droit Int. Pub.* (1915, pp. 225–226), who maintains that the doctrine of continuous voyage in respect to blockade can be applied only where there are two voyages, the second of which, like the first, is by sea, but unlike the first, is between a neutral port and a blockaded port, as was the case with the *Springbok*. In the case of neutral ships destined to Dutch ports during the recent war, there was but one maritime voyage, and it was between ports both of which were neutral. If there was a subsequent transshipment to the belligerent, it was by land and could not, therefore, be reached by a maritime blockading measure.

[2] Art. 19.

[3] Bentwich, *Declaration of London*, p. 56; also *House of Coms. Ses. Papers*, 54 (No. 4, 1909): 27.

of contraband.[1] Ships on their way to neutral ports were therefore liable to capture if their cargoes were destined to enemy territory.

§ 521. **Defence of the Doctrine.** Although the action of the British government was severely criticised in neutral countries, there is good ground for arguing that the extension of the rule of continuous voyage to blockade running is a logical consequence of the admitted right of a belligerent to cut off the over-seas commerce of the enemy. To hold that the doctrine of continuous voyage may be applied when both laps of the voyage are by sea, but not when the second is by land, is to introduce distinctions which seem to be neither logical nor reasonable under modern conditions.[2] It would seem that the better test is not whether the voyage is continuous by sea, but whether the real destination of the goods is enemy territory. The distinction between the two situations tends to render the right of blockade illusory in many cases and makes the means of transportation rather than the intent or effect the real test.

It is equally questionable whether the distinction between blockade running and the transportation of contraband, so far as the applicability of the doctrine of continuous voyage is concerned, rests upon any sound principle. In fact, both operations are closely connected, and they were so inextricably mixed during the recent war that it was practically impossible to separate them.[3] The effort of the Supreme Court of the United States during the Civil war to maintain the distinction in the application of the doctrine of continuous voyage was not

---

[1] Text in *European War*, No. 3, pp. 62–63. By a decree of April 12, 1916, the French government followed the action of the British government and abrogated art. 19 of the Declaration of London.

[2] Cf. the following observations of Sir Edward Grey in his memorandum of April, 1916: "It must be remembered that the passage of commerce to a blockaded area across a land frontier or across an inland sea has never been held to interfere with the effectiveness of the blockade. If the right to intercept commerce on its way to or from a belligerent country, even though it may enter that country through a neutral port, be granted, it is difficult to see why the interposition of a few miles of sea as well should make any difference. If the doctrine of continuous voyage may be rightly applied to goods going to Germany through Rotterdam, on what ground can it be contended that it is not equally applicable to goods with a similar destination passing through some Swedish port and across the Baltic or even through neutral waters only?"

[3] Cf. on this point Sir John McDonell in the *Pubs. of the Grotius Society*, Vol. I, p. 93.

a success, and passages are occasionally to be found in its decisions which indicate that it did not always in fact differentiate between blockade running and the transportation of contraband.[1] It is obvious that if a belligerent is not allowed to capture a vessel proceeding to a neutral port in close proximity to the territory of the enemy when the evidence is conclusive that the goods are intended to be forwarded to the enemy, the right of blockade as against an enemy whose territory is partly flanked by neutral states, as a belligerent weapon can be of little value.[2]

§ 522. **Popular Demand in England for a Real Blockade.** Notwithstanding the protests of the American and other neutral governments against the Anglo-French blockade, complaints were widespread in England that it was not enforced with sufficient rigor, in consequence of which large quantities of goods were alleged to have found their way through neutral ports to Germany. A number of English newspapers published statistics to show that the order in council of March 11 was far from being effective, and they demanded that a blockade in the strict technical sense of the term be established and rigorously enforced.[3] It was urged that the substitution of "an actual legal blockade," properly proclaimed and notified as such, would not only remove the foreign office restrictions which, it was alleged, had hampered the naval forces, but it would answer the chief American objection to a blockade which Americans had never recognized as legal. Had this been done at the outset, the irritating controversy with the United States regarding the legality of the order in council would have been avoided, and illicit trade with Germany would have been reduced to a minimum.[4]

---

[1] Such passages may be found in the opinions delivered in the cases of the *Bermuda*, the *Springbok*, and the *Stephen Hart*.

[2] Cf. Sir John McDonell, article cited, p. 101; J. E. G. Montmorency, *ibid.*, Vol. II, p. 29, and Sir Gilbert Murray, *Great Britain's Sea Policy*, p. 17. Cf. also the observations of Sir H. Erle Richards to the effect that "blockade in the form in which it has been sanctioned in the past by international law has ceased to exist." *International Law: Some Problems of the War*, p. 10.

[3] In the course of a debate in the House of Lords in February, 1916, Lord Charles Beresford described the existing measure as "a sort of blockade carried on by proclamation and orders in council." London weekly *Times*, March 3, 1916.

[4] Mr. A. Maurice Low in an article entitled "The Law of Contraband," New York *Herald*, March 12, 1916, says the British government made a serious mistake in "refusing to proclaim a blockade" instead of attempting to accomplish the same purpose by means of an order in council which to many Americans seemed to be

It may be seriously doubted, however, whether the substitution of a "legal blockade" for the measure instituted by the order in council would have removed the objections raised in neutral countries, so long as the rule of ultimate destination was applied. But it would have altered the legal situation in one important particular. Under the order in council of March 11, ships carrying contraband were not liable to confiscation, nor was the non-contraband portion of their cargoes; but had a "legal" blockade been instituted, contraband and non-contraband goods alike would have been liable to confiscation, and so would the vessels carrying them. The temptations of traders, therefore, to violate the blockade would have been less strong.

The government, however, refused to change its policy. The measure instituted by the order in council of March 11 therefore remained in force, and no blockade in the technical sense was ever established against Germany. Regarding the substance rather than the form, one is not convinced how the substitution of such a blockade in the place of the order in council would have inured to the benefit of neutrals. On the contrary, it is difficult to see why the reverse would not have been the case, since, as has been said, had a blockade in the usual sense been established, the rights of the blockading powers over neutral commerce would have been considerably enlarged, for in that case all goods, non-contraband and contraband alike, destined for the enemy directly or through neutral ports would have been liable to capture and confiscation without any obligation to make compensation.[1] It would seem, therefore, that neutral criticism of the blockade, so far as it related to its non-conformity to the formal and technical requirements, was a contention for

---

a mere subterfuge. "Why, then," he asks, "did not England proclaim a blockade? Simply because a blockade would have brought incalculable injury and loss to America and all other neutrals. Had a blockade been in force from the fourth of August, 1914, England would have been strictly within her legal rights in taking into her ports every ship under any neutral flag — those of the United States as well as Italy, for instance, who at that time was a neutral and not a belligerent — and if there was the smallest quantity of contraband in the cargo, the whole, contraband and non-contraband as well as the ship, would have been lawful prize. Had Great Britain applied the same rule of law that the United States did, had Great Britain held that the ultimate destination of the cargo was sufficient ground for condemnation, there could be no escape."

[1] Cf. on this point the remarks of Lord Haldane in an interview published in the London *Daily Chronicle* of April 1, 1915.

the lesser and narrower right against the larger and broader right; it was a plea for the observance of the form rather than the spirit of international law.

§ 523. **German Criticism of the Blockade as a "Starvation" Measure.** The Anglo-French blockade was fiercely attacked in Germany and by German sympathizers in neutral countries on the ground that its purpose was to reduce the civil population of Germany to starvation. The Imperial Chancellor in a speech of April 5, 1916, declared it to be contrary to international law, because it seeks " to starve us out and to extend the war to the entire German nation, to our women and our children." "It should not be forgotten," he said, "that in this war England set out to starve over 65,000,000 people; directly, by cutting off their food; indirectly, by closing the arteries of their commerce." This charge was repeated by the Chancellor in a speech of February 28, 1917. Great Britain, he said, desired "to make victims of the women and children, the aged and the ill of a nation numbering 70,000,000 people in order to force them into submission."[1] It was many times reiterated by other officials of the German government, by German newspapers, and by German propagandists in America.[2]

---

[1] Text in New York *Times*, February 28, 1917. Cf. also the German note of January 31, 1917, to the American government announcing the resumption of unrestricted submarine warfare. Whether any of the German civilian population actually died of starvation in consequence of the blockade would, of course, be difficult to prove. It was stated by the German government in January, 1919, that more than five hundred thousand deaths in Germany had resulted from malnutrition or under-nutrition] due to the blockade between the autumn of 1916 and the end of the year 1918. Associated Press despatch from Berlin, New York *Times*, January 24, 1919. Count Brockdorff-Rantzau, head of the German delegation at the Peace Conference, asserted in his address of May 7, 1919, at the opening session that "hundreds of thousands of non-combatants who have perished since November 11 (the date of the signing of the armistice) by reason of the blockade were killed with cold deliberation after our adversaries had conquered and victory had been assured them." Text of his address in New York *Times*, May 8, 1919. The German delegation at the Peace Conference, it may be added, submitted a claim for compensation on account of the suffering and death occasioned by the blockade, but it was not accorded.

[2] Cf., for example, von Mach, *Germany's Point of View*, pp. 288, 363 ff., and Burgess, *America's Relations to the Great War*, ch. I. The Germans attempted to justify in part their methods of submarine warfare as an act of reprisal against Great Britain for her "inhuman attempt to starve the women and children of the Empire." The Chancellor in his speech of April 15, 1916, referred to above, said: "No fair-minded neutral, no matter whether he favors us or not, can contest our right on our part to take measures of defence against this war of starvation,

But the right of a belligerent to cut off the food supply of his enemy by means of a siege or blockade and to starve him if possible into submission has always been recognized as a legitimate belligerent right, and it has been exercised in all wars where it was possible to do so. As is well known, Metz and Paris were reduced to submission in 1870 partly by bombardment and partly by starvation,[1] and Bismarck, adverting to representations from London to the effect that the capitulation of Paris ought to be brought about by hunger rather than bombardment, stated that it was debatable whether the one was more humane than the other; both, he argued, were perfectly legitimate methods for overcoming the enemy and compelling him to surrender.[2] In reply to a memorial from a number of Hamburg merchants regarding the announcement of the French government in 1885 of its intention to treat rice as absolute contraband Bismarck made the following statement:

"Any disadvantage our commercial and carrying interests may suffer by the treatment of rice as contraband of war does not justify our opposing the measure which it has been thought fit to take in carrying on a foreign war. . . . The measure in question has for its object the shortening of the war by increasing the difficulties of the enemy and is a justifiable step in war if impartially enforced against all neutral ships."

In 1892 Count Caprivi, then Imperial Chancellor, thus defended starvation as a legitimate belligerent weapon:

"A country may be dependent for her food, or for her raw produce upon her trade; in fact it may be absolutely necessary to destroy the enemy's trade. . . . The private introduction of provisions into Paris was prohibited during the siege, and in the same way a nation would be justified in preventing the import of food and raw produce."[3]

---

which is contrary to international law. No one can expect us to permit the arms of defence at our disposal to be wrested from us. We use them, and must use them. We respect the legitimate interests of neutrals in trade and commerce, but we expect that this respect be appreciated and that our right and our duty be recognized to use all means possible for retaliating against this policy of starvation which sets at defiance not only international law but the plainest duties of humanity."

[1] Cf. Spaight, *War Rights on Land*, pp. 174 ff.

[2] *Bismarck, The Man and the Statesman* (English trans. by Butler, Vol. II, p. 125).

[3] Quoted in Pyke, *The Law of Contraband*, p. 99. The legitimacy of blockade as a measure for cutting off the food supply of the enemy is defended by the German writer Perels, *Manuel de Droit Maritime* (French trans. by Arendt), pp. 270, 280.

Obviously, if a siege or a blockade which intercepts the food supply of the enemy is illegal for that reason, the right of siege and of blockade would be of little value to a belligerent. As is well known, both the effect and the purpose of the blockade of the Southern Confederacy was to deprive the civil as well as the military population of food and other supplies. Not only was the food supply cut off, but even materials for the manufacture of Red Cross supplies, as well as drugs and medicines of every kind.[1] It may be safely assumed that if the positions of the contending belligerents in the recent war had been reversed and the German navy had been in control of the seas, with the British Isles commercially isolated, the German government would never have permitted a stream of food supplies to pour into Great Britain for the sustenance of the civil population. The German military authorities showed no such solicitude for the women and children of the enemy in 1870-1871, nor did they show it during the recent war. Lord Robert Cecil, replying in the House of Commons on March 19, 1916, to the German charge of inhumanity against the British government for cutting off the milk supply for the starving babies of Germany, stated that within the occupied districts of France when the Germans arrived, there were half a million of cattle.

"Hardly one is now left," he said, "and today Mr. Hoover's commission is sending into that district 3,000,000 tins of condensed milk monthly to keep alive the thousands of French babies whose source of supply has been taken from them by the Germans. This milk is being paid for by French money. Without this fund and the work of a neutral commission, these French babies would be dying of starvation today." "Belgium," he added, "had 1,500 000 cattle; we know that practically half of these have gone to Germany."

Finally, it may be added that the right of Germany's enemies to cut off by means of a blockade over-seas supplies for the civil population was strengthened by the impossibility of distinguishing between the civil and military population. The Germans had long insisted that their army was the nation in arms; if it was such in the past, it was doubly so during the recent war.[2] Under the circumstances it is difficult to see how the application of the blockade could have been limited to the interdiction of

[1] See Rhodes' *History of the United States from the Compromise of 1850*, Vol. V, pp. 396–410.
[2] This was admitted by the Chancellor in his speech of February 28, 1917.

supplies to the military population alone, even if the allies had
desired to so limit it.

§ 524. Attitude of the British and French Governments in
Regard to the Admission of Hospital Supplies to Germany.
The refusal of the British and French governments to permit
the shipment to enemy countries of hospital supplies was also
the subject of strong criticism, particularly in Germany. It
appears that at the outset shipment to the enemy country of
hospital supplies generally, except rubber goods such as gloves
worn by surgeons and nurses, blankets, tubing, and similar
articles, was exempted from the order in council establishing
the blockade. The allied governments took the position that
the admission of the articles mentioned to the enemy country
would release an equivalent amount of the domestic stock for
the manufacture of automobile tires and other articles of military necessity. Later, it appears, further restrictions were
introduced the effect of which was to debar the shipment of
practically all hospital supplies to Germany. At the insistence
of the American Red Cross society the department of state made
representations to the governments of Great Britain and France
with a view to inducing them to consent to a modification of
their policy regarding the exclusion of hospital supplies. Thereupon the allied governments, in July, 1916, agreed to allow the
American Red Cross society to ship hospital supplies of all
kinds to the enemy countries, provided they were consigned
directly to the units of the Red Cross society operating in such
countries, and provided further that the society would give
an undertaking that such supplies would be used exclusively
by the American Red Cross, and that they would be destroyed
after being once used. This guarantee the society could not
give in consequence of its units having been withdrawn in
October, 1915, from Germany for lack of funds.[1]

[1] In June, 1916, Mr. Taft, chairman of the central committee of the American
society, proposed to the British government that the society be allowed to send
a commission to Germany and Austria to receive and distribute Red Cross supplies,
the commission to guarantee that they would be used exclusively for hospital
purposes. He pointed out that under art. 16 of the Geneva convention the materials of relief societies admitted to the benefits of the convention were exempt
from capture as contraband, and that this implied the right to ship hospital
supplies to the Red Cross organization of Germany. He also added that it was
a humanitarian duty which would in no way inure to the military advantage of
Great Britain's enemies. The British government, however, took the position

In consequence of the attitude of the allied governments the German government as a measure of retaliation announced in August, 1916, that it would no longer allow the free passage of hospital supplies to enemy countries, and that the naval forces would receive instructions to confiscate such articles for their own use whenever captured.

§ 525. **Admission of Food Supplies to the Occupied Regions of Belgium, France, and Poland.** A somewhat similar question related to the admission of food supplies to the occupied territories of Belgium, France, and Poland. The allied governments insisted on a guarantee from the German government not only that it would not requisition the supplies imported by neutral agencies into those territories for the relief of the civil population, but also that it would not requisition the domestic food crops.[1]

The attitude of the British and French governments was the subject of strong complaint in Germany, but in view of the wholesale policy of requisition which the German authorities carried out in Belgium and Poland, both governments were quite aware that raw materials and food-stuffs imported into these territories for the use of the native population or, what amounted to the same thing, an equivalent of the domestic stocks which

---

that unless the distribution of such articles were under the strict control of neutral agencies, they would be requisitioned by the German authorities for military purposes. Moreover, there was no evidence for believing that the domestic supply in Germany was inadequate, and high German authority was quoted in support of this view. If there was any real scarcity, it must be due to the fact that the governments of the Central powers preferred to use such materials for other than Red Cross purposes, and the admission of supplies from America would only set free larger quantities of the domestic stock for belligerent uses. See Sir Edward Grey's reply of July 12 to Secretary Lansing's communication, New York *Times*, July 18, 1916.

[1] See the British parliamentary paper, *Correspondence respecting the Relief of Allied Territories in the Occupation of the Enemy, Misc.*, No. 32 (1916), Cd. 8348; also *ibid.*, No. 24 (1916), Cd. 8295. Cf. also an article by Vernon Kellogg, a member of the American relief commission, in the *World's Work* for August, 1917; pp. 405 ff.; also his *Headquarters Nights*, pp. 85 ff. Mr. Kellogg says that the Germans considered that in agreeing to refrain from requisitioning the Belgian crops they were making a great concession in view of their feeling that under international law an occupying army has a right to maintain itself on the produce of the territory occupied. He states also that the Germans seemed to have been under the impression that the Americans were deriving financial profit from the business of feeding the Belgians, so strong was their belief that money-getting was the sole object of all American enterprise. He was frankly asked by a member of von Bissing's staff, "What do you Americans get out of this business?"

would be released by the importations from abroad, would be taken by the German military authorities for their own use. To have allowed such importations would therefore have put Great Britain in the position of aiding her own enemies.

The controversy between the Entente governments and those of Germany and Austria-Hungary regarding the admission of food supplies into Poland was even more irritating. After repeated efforts to secure a pledge from the German government that it would cease its systematic policy of draining Poland of its food supplies under the guise of requisitions, the British government on May 11, 1916, responding to the appeal of the American government, proposed a scheme by which the importation of food-stuffs into Poland would be allowed, subject to reasonable guarantees to insure that the domestic stocks released by such importations would not be requisitioned by the Germans, but to this proposal the German government never made any reply.[1] On July 29, 1916, the German foreign office issued a statement regarding the British proposal in which it asserted that the British proposal was "nothing more than an attempt to include the territories occupied by Germany and Austria-Hungary into the system for the starvation of Germany which has been proclaimed by the British government contrary to all international law." It is clear that the German government feared that the effect of the British scheme would be to give the Poles a share of the produce of their crops, which the Germans claimed rightly belonged to them in consequence of their contribution to the increased output, and that it would place the Poles on a more favorable footing in respect to rations than it would the occupying forces. The German contention was quite in accordance with their theory of occupation, that the occupant has a lawful right to take the produce of the occupied territory for his own subsistence, even if it reduces the civil population to destitution, or at least he is entitled to an equal share of it with the inhabitants. On October 17, 1916, President Wilson issued a statement from Long Branch in which, adverting to his efforts to bring about an agreement among the belligerent nations under which supplies might be admitted to

[1] See the British white paper, *Correspondence respecting the Relief of Allied Territories in the Occupation of the Enemy, Misc.,* No. 32 (1916), Cd. 8348.

Poland for the relief of the destitute civil population, he announced that they had resulted in failure[1].

§ 526. **The Problem of Preventing Commerce with the Enemy.** The Problem of blockading effectively the ports of Germany, flanked as she was by a group of neutral countries several of which were separated from her by only a surveyor's line and others by only a few miles of sea, without at the same time blockading the ports of these countries was a difficult one indeed. Sir Robert Cecil, speaking at a meeting at the Mansion House on August 7, 1916, thus stated the problem: "We had to do something never before done in the history of the world: blockade our enemy through neutral countries which surrounded him. We had, therefore, to sift out that part of the trade which belonged to the enemy and deal with it, while leaving trade to be carried on as far as possible without interference." [2] Under the doctrine of ultimate destination Great Britain and France clearly had a right to seize contraband goods consigned to neutral ports when the evidence was conclusive that their ultimate destination was the enemy, and whether or not, under the law of nations, they had a right to prevent non-contraband goods from reaching the enemy through neutral ports, by applying the doctrine of continuous voyage to blockade running, they proceeded on the theory that they did have such a right. But whatever may have been their lawful rights in this matter, they clearly had no right to intercept trade in goods, whether contraband or not, intended for use or consumption in the neutral countries to which they were consigned. The difficulty of determining in many cases whether such goods were intended for local use or consumption or for reëxportation to the enemy country naturally led to many arbitrary seizures and unjust interferences with legitimate neutral trade, against all of which neutrals vigorously protested.

§ 527. **The Netherlands Over-seas Trust.** In the beginning, the Dutch government undertook the responsibility of guaranteeing that imported goods allowed to pass the blockade would not be reëxported to Germany, but the burden becoming intolerable, it was taken over by an extraordinary association known as the Netherlands Over-seas Trust, organized on No-

[1] Text in New York *Times* of October 18, 1916.
[2] *Solicitors' Journal and Weekly Reporter*, Vol. 60, p. 684.

vember 24, 1914. The object of the association, as stated in its statutes, was "to act as an intermediary for Dutch merchants and trading companies with a view to enabling the unmolested conveyance from oversea, merchandise which has been or may be declared contraband — either absolute or conditional — by belligerent States." The definition was subsequently altered to read, "the unmolested import and export of merchandise as much as possible," an alteration which was more in accord with the new conditions. Under this arrangement importers and consignees gave a pledge that goods received by them would not be reëxported to belligerent territory. For the observance of this pledge they furnished a bond to the Over-seas Trust, the amount of which at first was fixed at the value of the cargo, but was subsequently raised to three times its value. Thereupon the Trust undertook to guarantee that the merchandise so imported would not be shipped to Germany or Austria-Hungary, in return for which over-seas consignments to it were allowed to pass the blockade.[1] Thereafter practically all commerce between the Netherlands and countries beyond the seas was carried on through the intermediary of this association.[2]

The extraordinary high prices offered in Germany afforded a great temptation to neutral importers to violate their agreements, and cases were not lacking where this was done, the prices being sufficient to cover the cost of forfeiting the bond, still leaving the importer a handsome profit. The Netherlands Over-seas Trust, however, appears to have made an honest attempt to prevent reëxportations to Germany, and in some cases it took drastic action to prevent violations of its agreement with the British government.

A somewhat similar organization was formed in Switzerland under the name of the *Société Surveillance Suisse*. In Denmark the Danish merchants' guild performed a similar function, although the Danish government appears never to have entered

---

[1] Cf. an article on The Netherlands Overseas Trust" by Alexander Nicol-Speyer in *International Law Notes* for August, 1916, pp. 120-122; also the *London Solicitors' Journal and Weekly Reporter*, February 5, 1916, p. 249; and the Grotius *Annuaire International*, 1915, p. 70.

[2] Originally estabished in offices of three rooms and with a staff of less than half a dozen men, it occupied before the end of the year 1916 eighteen buildings and employed a staff of over one thousand persons.

into an agreement with the British government not to export goods to Germany. In most neutral countries adjacent to Germany and Austria-Hungary importers showed a willingness to enter into such arrangements out of sheer necessity, and their governments, while unwilling themselves to guarantee that the terms of such agreements would be observed, appear to have countenanced the organization of private associations of merchants or importers for the purpose. In the absence of such an arrangement no contraband goods were allowed to pass the blockade.

§ 528. The System of "Rationing" Neutrals. Another and somewhat more arbitrary expedient adopted by the Entente allies for cutting off the enemy's over-seas trade through neutral ports was a system of "rationing." It was discovered that at the outset neutral countries adjacent to Germany were importing goods, mainly from America, vastly in excess of their customary importations before the war and far beyond their normal requirements.[1] The conclusion drawn by the British government from this fact was that the greater part of the excess was being reëxported, mainly to Germany. The statistics produced by the allied governments in proof of this were in some cases attacked by the neutrals concerned as being exaggerated, but it would be a very credulous person who should refuse to be convinced by the evidence adduced that when due allowance was made for exaggeration, a very large quantity of goods imported from America ultimately found their way to Germany.[2] A large amount of the exportations to Germany, to be sure, con-

---

[1] Thus statistics were produced to show that the exports from the United States to Norway during the fiscal year ending June 30, 1916, were valued at $53,675,000 as against $9,067,000 for the year ending June 30, 1914. For Sweden the figures were: 1913, $12,104,366; 1916, $48,353,387; for Switzerland: 1913, $826,549; 1916, $13,654,256; for Denmark: 1913, $18,687,791; 1916, $56,335,596. Sir Samuel Evans stated in the case of the *Kim* that more lard was imported into Copenhagen in three weeks in 1915 than had been imported into all Denmark during the previous eight years.

[2] The New York *Times* of July 2, 1917, printed a Washington despatch in which it was asserted on the basis of "figures obtained by the British government after careful investigation" that fats in sufficient quantities to supply the rations of 7,700,000 soldiers, "practically the entire army of effectives in Germany," were then going to Germany from neighboring neutral countries. The chief of the Bureau of foreign commerce estimated in August, 1917, that Germany had obtained from neutrals meat enough to support all her armies for a period of 275 days.

sisted of domestic products with the export of which no belligerent government had any lawful right to interfere. This was, in fact, a necessity in some cases in order to enable neutral countries adjacent to Germany to obtain from the Central powers commodities such as coal and iron which were indispensable to their economic life, since they were dependent upon Germany in particular for these commodities and she would not allow them to draw on her for them except in return for a certain portion of their surplus products. An agreement, for example, was entered into between the Dutch and German governments by which the former bound itself to allow Germany to have 75 per cent of all Dutch exports of butter, vegetables, eggs, and fruit; 50 per cent of all exports of flax, and as much of all kinds of meat as the total of such exports to all other countries.[1] In return for this concession Germany agreed to allow coal and iron to be exported to the Netherlands. The necessity of such arrangements was recognized by the governments of the Entente allies, but they complained that in certain instances the quantity allowed to go to Germany was more than was necessary to preserve the balance, and they denied *in toto* the right of the countries in question to expose their own populations to starvation through the exportation of their domestic supplies and then to replace them by means of importations from America. In short, there was no difference in principle between furnishing Germany with supplies imported from America and furnishing her with supplies of domestic production when the deficit thus produced had to be made up by importations from America.

Under these circumstances Great Britain and France, as has been said, adopted the system of rationing, under which importations into those countries were limited to the estimated amount of their domestic requirements. Goods in excess thereof were seized under the application of the principle of ultimate destination.

§ 529. **Neutral Protests.** Neutrals thus affected naturally protested against the application of a measure which from the very nature of the case could not be enforced without arbitrariness and without infringements upon their right to trade with one another. They complained that in determining the extent

[1] An English translation of this agreement may be found in the New York *Times* of September 30, 1917. It was concluded on December 1, 1916.

of their local needs the allied governments did not take into consideration the fact that their German, Austro-Hungarian, and Belgian sources of supply had been largely cut off by the war, and that consequently larger importations from America were necessary. Before the war, for example, Norway imported her flour from Germany and Russia; Holland obtained her supply of coal and iron from Germany; Switzerland drew her raw materials, metals, and iron largely from the same country, and so on. They were therefore reduced to the necessity of importing more heavily from America, and it did not follow that the excess of importations over those of peace times necessarily meant that it was being reëxported to Germany. Some of the neutral governments, indeed, complained that the allied governments in the enforcement of the rationing system limited the amount of importations to a point far below the urgent local needs of the population.

§ 530. American Policy. With the entrance of the United States into the war in 1917 the task of Great Britain and France in dealing with the shipments from America to neutral countries in Europe of goods which ultimately went to Germany was greatly simplified. Since the greater proportion of these supplies came from the United States, the American government had only to place an embargo on their exportation, after which Great Britain and France would be largely relieved from the difficult and more or less arbitrary task of sifting out goods which they suspected were intended for Germany. In pursuance of authority conferred by the Espionage Act the President in July, 1917, proclaimed an embargo on the shipment of some six hundred commodities to the neutral countries of western and northern Europe, except upon license granted by his authority. Furthermore, an order was issued requiring every steamship leaving an American port to obtain a license before it would be allowed to take on a supply of bunker coal. Statistics having been produced to show that a large proportion of exports from America to the neutral countries of Europe had been going to Germany, there was a widespread popular demand that the embargo should be rigorously applied, and that no licenses should be granted for the exportation of any goods which there was reason to believe would ultimately find their way to enemy country. The President promptly adopted this policy. Commissions from the various neutral countries affected soon arrived in the United States, supplied with statistics to show that the charges concerning the reëxportation of American goods to Germany had been greatly exaggerated, and that the rigid enforcement of an embargo on shipments from America to those countries would paralyze their industries and reduce their populations to the verge of destitution. While their appeals for relaxation were carefully considered, the President was firm in his determination not to grant any licenses except upon sufficient guarantees, which would insure that no supplies exported from America would find their way to Germany. For many months, in fact, no licenses were granted. In September, 1917, eighty-four Dutch vessels laden with grain and other supplies were lying in American ports and could not depart for lack of licenses. The American government declined to issue licenses so long as the Dutch agreement with Germany referred to above, under which the Dutch government was bound to allow Germany to have a large proportion of the native produce of Holland, remained in force.

As the American government had an unquestionable right to prohibit the exportation from its territory of goods which it had reason to believe would ultimately find their way to the enemy, no question of international law could arise between it and neutral countries, such as had arisen between them and Great Britain, since the United States was merely restricting its own trade, whereas Great Britain had interfered with trade between neutrals.

The assertion was made in some quarters that the American embargo policy against the neutral powers of Europe was inconsistent with its former protest, when it was a neutral, against the British claim to intercept trade with Germany through neutral ports. This charge, however, was without foundation. What the American government had complained of was the British practice of intercepting commerce between neutral countries on the ground that the ultimate destination was enemy territory. It never protested against the right of the British government to restrict its own trade with neutrals.

§ 531. Other Expedients. Another device adopted by the British government to cut off trade with Germany through neutral ports took the form of agreements with neutral shipping

lines, under which their vessels were allowed to proceed without
molestation to their destinations upon their undertaking to
return to England, for adjudication by the prize courts, any
goods whose destination was suspected of being enemy country,
or to store them until the end of the war in the neutral country
to which they were consigned, and to comply with the other
regulations of the British government in regard to such trade.
Agreements of this kind were entered into with most of the
leading steamship lines, the vessels entitled to this favored
treatment being known as "white ships."

Another expedient was the policy of the British government
of refusing bunker coal at British ports to neutral merchant
vessels whose owners declined to comply with certain regulations
intended to prevent cargoes from going to Germany. Neutrals
complained of this measure, but the British government maintained that it had an undoubted right to refuse coal to any
vessel which it had reason to believe was engaged in carrying
supplies to the enemy.[1] It was stated in the press despatches
from Sweden that Great Britain was able by refusing bunker
coal to control absolutely all commerce carried on in Danish
and Norwegian steamers.[2]

Still another device was the so-called "Skinner scheme,"
suggested by the American consul-general at London, Mr.
Skinner, under which the British embassy at Washington upon
application of American exporters investigated the particulars
regarding proposed consignments and cabled the facts to the
contraband committee in London, which in turn notified the
embassy at Washington whether the consignment would be
permitted to pass the blockade. If the report was favorable,
a "letter of assurance" was issued and carried by the steamer
which bore the privileged cargo. No steamship sailing from
an American port would accept a shipment to a neutral port
in northern Europe unless it was accompanied by such a letter.
Aside from the more or less humiliating position in which neutral

---

[1] The American government was one of those which complained of this policy;
but in 1917 when the United States had become a belligerent and was itself endeavoring to cut off trade with Germany through neutral ports, it was announced
from Washington that one of the weapons at the disposal of the government was
its power to refuse bunker coal to neutral vessels carrying goods with a suspected
ultimate enemy destination, and that it would be employed if necessary.

[2] New York *Times*, July 24, 1916.

shippers were thus placed in being obliged to apply to the British government for permits to trade with one another, there was much complaint that permits were frequently delayed or even refused when the goods were on the embargo lists of the countries to which they were consigned.[1] Through these and other measures the German over-seas supply through European neutral ports was gradually reduced to insignificant proportions.[2] Loud complaints were made by neutrals against the alleged arbitrariness of these measures which, it was said, not only interfered with their lawful right to trade with belligerents in non-contraband goods, but also reduced their own supply for domestic consumption in many cases below their actual necessities. The British government, on the other hand, asserted that it was only exercising its lawful rights, and that most of the measures in question were adopted for the convenience of neutrals and with a view to relieving their vessels from the delays and inconveniences to which they would otherwise have been subjected.

[1] A detailed description of the British procedure of dealing with vessels bound for neutral ports in Europe by Sir Frank Newnes may be found in the New York *Times* of July 23, 1916.

[2] In September, 1916, the British government estimated that over 92 per cent of German exports to the United States had been stopped. As to goods imported into Germany, it was estimated that some of the most important commodities, such as cotton, wool, and rubber, were totally excluded. But throughout the year 1916 and a part of 1917 a considerable quantity of fats, oils, and other commodities from America "leaked" through the blockade, and it was not until the establishment of the American embargo in the autumn of 1917 that this trade was reduced to insignificant proportions.

CHAPTER XXXIV

INTERFERENCE WITH MAILS AND PERSONS OF ENEMY NATIONALITY ON NEUTRAL· VESSELS

§ 532. German Exploitation of the Postal Service for Belligerent Purposes; § 533. Early Measures of the British and French Governments; § 534. Neutral Protests; § 535. Provisions of the Hague Convention regarding Postal Correspondence; § 536. Attitude of the American Government; § 537. Views of the British and French Governments; § 538. Removal of Enemy Persons from Neutral Vessels; Case of Piepenbrink; § 539. Cases of Garde and Others; § 540. Seizures on the *China;* § 541. What Persons are Liable to Seizure on Neutral Vessels?; § 542. Views of the Authorities; § 543. Practice of the Past; § 544. Case of the *Frederico;* § 545. Status of Despatch Bearers on Neutral Vessels.

§ 532. **German Exploitation of the Postal Service for Belligerent Purposes.** During the first year of the war the British and French governments in the enforcement of their measures against commerce with Germany did not interfere with the transportation of mails on neutral vessels. When, however, their measures had succeeded in almost completely putting an end to over-sea trade with Germany,[1] the Germans undertook through the agency of the international postal service to evade the allied restrictions in respect to blockade and contraband, and also to exploit the postal service for military purposes. These efforts took several forms: (1) An attempt was made to import through the medium of the postal service supplies from abroad which, on account of the blockade and contraband restrictions, could not be imported through the regular channels of commerce; (2) an attempt was made to export through the same agency goods which otherwise were not allowed to leave Germany; (3) an attempt was made to establish credits in

[1] It was stated in a London press despatch of April 7, 1916, based on information furnished by the foreign office, that the total over-sea exports of Germany at that time amounted only to five or six per cent of those of peace times, and that such goods were being transported exclusively through the mails, except those shipped as freight under licenses granted by the British government for goods purchased before March 1, 1915.

foreign countries by sending abroad through the mails money orders, drafts, bills of exchange, bonds, stock certificates, and instrumentalities of finance; (4) by the organization of a system of incendiarism and sabotage in countries from which the Entente allies were drawing supplies of arms and munitions, and (5) by organizing and carrying on a propaganda in foreign countries by means of the distribution of literature with a view to inciting the people of India to insurrection against the British government.

§ 533. **Early Measures of the British and French Governments.** Toward the end of the year 1915 these activities had assumed such proportions and seemed to be such a manifest perversion of the purposes of the international postal service in violation of the rights of belligerents in respect to blockade and contraband, that the British and French governments determined to adopt measures to prevent the further evasion of what they considered their rights, under the cover of the postal service. Accordingly, beginning in December, the allied governments proceeded to examine the mails found on neutral steamers bound for Scandinavian and Dutch ports, and to detain postal parcels containing merchandise destined to the enemy country. The first instance of the kind to attract attention appears to have been the seizure of 734 bags of mail on the Danish steamer *Oscar II*, which was *en route* from the United States to Norway, Denmark, and Sweden. About the same time 58 bags were removed from the Swedish steamer *Stockholm* while *en route* from Gothenburg to New York. Five thousand packages of merchandise were taken from the Danish steamer *United States;* 597 bags of parcels from the Danish steamer *Frederik VIII;* 300 bags from the Danish steamer *Hellig Olav*, and later 800 bags from the same ship; 185 bags from the Danish steamer *Lyngenfjord;* 130 bags from the Dutch liner *Noordam*, etc. Throughout the year 1916 this policy was continued, practically all mails destined to or from the neutral countries of northern Europe being removed, taken to London for examination, and those portions containing merchandise originating in Germany or intended for delivery there being detained. The character of a large portion of the mails so destined fully justified, according to the view of the British government, its policy of examination and detention. Among

the articles discovered were thousands of parcels of rubber.[1]
Other large quantities of such articles as jewellery, chemicals,
platinum, laces, tea, cotton lint, pictures, toys, cereals, coffee,
cocoa, sausages, condensed milk, soap, lard, dried fruit, chocolate,
bacon, woollens, seeds, chromos, engravings, violin strings,
scissors, needles, files, cigarette cases, revolvers, skins, military
boots, etc., were found in the mails. Most of these articles
were being imported from America or the Dutch Indies, but
in some instances they consisted of exports originating in Germany. Many were found in the first-class mails the postage
on which exceeded their normal value.[2]   In this way a consider-

[1] Among the parcels taken from the *Oscar II* were 55 bags of rubber destined
for Germany, the aggregate weight of which was estimated to be about 4000 pounds.
Among the parcels taken from the mails on the *Frederik VIII* were 125 packages
of rubber weighing not less than 1375 pounds. Of the 300 bags taken from the
Hellig Olav, 109 contained rubber consigned to a well-known forwarding house
in Sweden. One thousand two hundred and sixty-five parcels of rubber were
taken from the Dutch steamer *Holandia* in February, 1915, and 1390 parcels
from the *Gelria*, both bound from South America to Rotterdam. These parcels
were said to have been destined to Germany. On the *Gelria* were also found 400
revolvers intended for Germany. The parcels from the *Gelria* were condemned
by the prize court in May. In the mails of the *Tubantia* were found 174 pounds
of rubber marked "samples without value." In the mails of the *Ryndam* was
found a large quantity of propagandist literature of German origin addressed to
firms with German names in the United States.

The Dutch government in a note of March 31, 1916, addressed to Sir Edward
Grey, asserted that not only had parcels containing absolute contraband been
removed from the Dutch steamers *Goenter*, *Insulinde*, and *Rembrandt*, but that
parcels of non-contraband had been similarly removed from the *Jan Preters*, the
Coen, the *Goentoer*, the *Tubantia*, the *Rembrandt*, the *Insulinde*, the *Orange*, the
Tubanan, and the *Tambara*, even when destined for persons in the Netherlands
and the Dutch Indies.

[2] One hundred and fifty packages of food mailed as first-class matter and
addressed to persons in Germany were taken from the *Kristianiafjord*, each package
of which weighed about seven pounds and each bearing postage stamps amounting
to $3.48. One parcel contained twelve pounds of dried meat sent by a German
in the United States and on which $9.60 in postage stamps had been affixed. Many
ingenious devices were resorted to for the purpose of evading the consequences
of the allied restrictions. Thus some articles were marked "samples of no value";
others were labelled "reading matter"; rubber was mailed under the disguise
of onions, narcissus bulbs, golf balls, and the like. Slices of bacon were sent in
letters; sheets of metal were sent between photo-cardboards; rubber gloves in
bundles of newspapers; parcels were wrapped in duplicate covers and addressed
to persons in neutral countries who only had to tear off the outer cover and repost
the parcel to a German address; copper and bronze were mailed under the innocent
form of medals, etc.

The office of the censor at London became a veritable museum of curiosities of
this kind. Cf. an article by Syndey Brooks in the New York *Times Magazine*
of November 12, 1916.

able trade, which the allied governments regarded as an evasion of their blockade and contraband measures, was carried on between Germany and America as well as other neutral countries.

Among the articles seized were large quantities of securities and instruments for the transfer of money, which were being sent to America for the establishment of German credit. The aggregate value of the securities thus seized and in the custody of the British prize court in March, 1916, was said to have been ten million dollars. In addition, a vast number of checks, drafts, and money orders, representing a value of $250,000,000, were similarly seized. These securities appear to have been taken from neutral steamers while *en route* from Dutch ports to America. They were said to have been of German ownership, representing in part the offerings of German banks and individuals to American investors, and had been sold through Dutch bankers under financial pressure.[1] Some are alleged to have consisted of Belgian and French securities which had been seized and confiscated by the German military authorities.

§ 534. Neutral Protests. Against these proceedings the governments of the United States, the Netherlands, Denmark, Norway, Switzerland, and Sweden protested, and the Swedish government went to the length of retaliating by refusing to allow British mails to be transported through Sweden to or from Russia and by prohibiting the exportation to England of wood pulp, upon the Norwegian and Swedish supply of which Great Britain was mainly dependent for the manufacture of paper.[2]

[1] In the early days of the war Germany is said to have provided herself with large sums through the sale of American securities to bankers in Holland who subsequently sold them at a large profit in America. Gold and silver bullion as well as paper money are on the list of conditional contraband in the Declaration of London. Nothing, however, is said of drafts, stocks, and other securities. In the general report attached to the Declaration it is declared that paper money includes only inconvertible paper, i.e., bank notes, whether legal tender or not. Bills of exchange and checks are specifically excluded. By a British order in council of April 12, 1916, gold, silver, paper money, and all negotiable instruments, and realizable securities, including checks, drafts, letters of credit, and other documents relating to the transfer of money or credit, were declared to be contraband. Only these securities of German ownership were placed in the custody of the prize court; all others were forwarded to the consignees.

[2] On February 18, 1916, it was reported in the press despatches that approximately fifty thousand parcels of British mail were being held in Sweden. The

In a memorandum of January 10, 1916, addressed to the British foreign office, the secretary of state of the United States declared that the American government was "inclined" to regard parcels-post articles as being "subject to the same treatment as articles sent by express or freight in respect to belligerent search, seizure and condemnation"; but on the other hand, they were entitled to "the usual protection of neutral trade." There was, therefore, no difference of opinion between the two governments regarding the status of mails in the form of parcels containing merchandise. Such mails were subject to the same belligerent

---

controversy between Great Britain and Sweden in regard to the seizure and detention of mails on Swedish steamers at one time threatened to bring about a rupture of friendly relations between the two countries. The British government justified the seizures on the ground that the mails so detained consisted of contraband; that the vessels from which they were taken were visited and searched in accordance with the well-established rules regarding visit and search; that the remaining mails were reforwarded as speedily as possible, and that the postal immunity guaranteed by the eleventh Hague convention did not extend to parcels post merchandise. The Swedish government readily admitted the last-mentioned proposition, but nevertheless contended that the contents of parcels "as a rule are of a more personal character than consignments of goods in general" and were not therefore liable to the same treatment; that the amount of merchandise in the objectionable parcels was not considerable enough to warrant their seizure for military reasons, and that rubber was on the free list in the Declaration of London, the rules of which were declared in its preamble "to correspond in substance with the generally recognized principles of international law." Therefore the parcels were not liable to seizure as contraband. Furthermore, since the exportation of rubber from Sweden had been prohibited, and since no lawful blockade had been established by Great Britain, they could not be seized on the ground of being destined to a blockaded port. In a note of January 3, 1916, Sir Edward Grey replied to each of these contentions. The Swedish government, he said, having declared that it did not recognize the Hague conventions to be operative, could not consistently invoke their provisions in the present controversy. As to the Declaration of London, its provisions in respect to contraband had been modified by the British government, as it had a legal right to do. The claim of a special sanctity for post parcels because of their "more personal character" was, to say the least, novel and unprecedented. Finally, the mails in question had been seized because they were contraband and in application of the doctrine of continuous voyage, and the fact that the exportation to Germany of merchandise of the kind which they contained had been prohibited by the Swedish government did not operate as a bar to their seizure by a belligerent. The right to seize contraband destined ultimately to the enemy could not, he said, be taken away by the action of a neutral government in laying an embargo on the exportation of such contraband. See the correspondence between the British and Swedish governments in a parliamentary paper, *Relating to the Detention of Mails, Misc.*, No. 28 (1916), Cd. 8322. The correspondence between the Dutch Government and that of Great Britain relative to British interference with mails on Dutch steamers may be found in 24 *Revue Générale de Droit Int. Pub.* (1917) docs., pp. 79 ff. See also the Grotius *Annuaire International*, 1916, p 107.

right of search, seizure, and capture as ordinary freight or express.

§ 535. Provisions of the Hague Convention regarding Postal Correspondence. The eleventh Hague convention of 1907 relative to certain restrictions on the exercise of the right of capture in maritime war contains the following provisions in regard to *correspondence postale:*

> The postal correspondence of neutrals or belligerents, whatever its official or private character may be, found on the high seas on board a neutral or enemy ship, is inviolable. If the ship is detained, the correspondence is forwarded by the captor with the least possible delay.
>
> The provisions of the preceding paragraph do not apply, in case of violation of blockade, to correspondence destined for or proceeding from a blockaded port. (Art. I.)
>
> The inviolability of postal correspondence does not exempt a neutral mail ship from the laws and customs of maritime war as to neutral merchant ships in general. The ship, however, may not be searched except when absolutely necessary, and then only with as much consideration and expedition as possible. (Art. II.)

These provisions embody in substance a proposal made by the German delegate, Herr Kriege, who in presenting it to the Conference said it was to be intended to be a sort of annex to the *projet* on contraband.[1]   So many private and commercial interests, he said, were dependent upon the regular service of the mails that it was indispensable that this service should be protected from the disturbances of maritime war. On the other hand, the benefit to belligerents from interference with the postal service was no longer in proportion to the injury which such control would inflict upon inoffensive commerce, for the reason that cable and telegraphic communication offered to belligerents a more rapid and certain means of communication.[2] In short, the new and more rapid means of telegraphic communication had largely eliminated the danger from surreptitious use of the mails for the transmission of military information, and therefore belligerents would have little or nothing to gain from interfering with postal correspondence. During the discussion of the proposal Captain Otley, one of the British delegates, stated that the British delegation was prepared to accept

[1] *Actes et Documents, la Deuxième Conférence de la Paix*, Vol. III, p. 173.
[2] *Ibid.*, Vol. I, p. 266, and Vol. III, p. 861.

it, but he wished it to be understood that the inviolability of postal correspondence on board mail packets was not to be construed as implying that such boats were not liable to capture.[1] Herr Kriege replied that this was his understanding of the intent of the proposal.[2] Count Tornielli then asked whether the immunity contemplated by the German *projet* applied to parcels-post packages (*colis postaux*) as well as to postal correspondence (*correspondence postale*). Herr Kriege replied that the former were certainly excluded from the privileged treatment accorded to postal correspondence. The proposal was thereupon unanimously adopted. It would seem, therefore, from the text of article 1 of the convention and from the express understanding of those who participated in the discussion of it that the immunity which it was designed to establish was intended to apply only to mails which may be comprehended under the term *correspondence*, and not to parcels of merchandise, and this irrespective of whether they were sent as first-class matter or otherwise.[3] Moreover, the benefit of the immunity was expressly withheld from all mails, whether *correspondence* or *colis postaux*, when destined to or proceeding from a blockaded port.[4] It is, of course, true that the British government had not proclaimed a technical blockade of Germany, and it could not lawfully blockade the ports of Holland and Scandinavia, but it contended that postal parcels of merchandise were subject to the same treatment as goods shipped by express or freight, and having established a blockade in fact, if not technically, of Germany, it could treat them as goods destined ultimately

[1] *Int. Law Topics*, Naval War College, 1906, p. 3.

[2] *Actes et Documents*, Vol. III, p. 1122.

[3] Technically, of course, the convention was not binding since it was not ratified by several belligerents in the recent war (Bulgaria, Italy, Montenegro, Russia, Servia, and Turkey). In its correspondence with the British government the German foreign office recognized the binding force of the convention and invoked its provisions, but in its controversy with Norway regarding the seizure of mails by the German naval authorities, it argued that the convention, not having been ratified by all the belligerents, had no force. *Brit. Parl. Paper, Misc.*, No. 28 (1916), Cd. 8322, p. 9.

[4] The British prize court in the case of the *Simla* (May, 1915) so interpreted the meaning of the Hague convention. The mails condemned contained a quantity of elephant tusks, leopard and snake skins, and curios shipped by parcels post from German East Africa to various persons in the German Empire. Trehern, *Brit. and Col. Prize Cases*, Vol. I, p. 281.

to a blockaded port,[1] or treat them as contraband, and in either case apply the doctrine of ultimate destination to their carriage.

§ 536. **Attitude of the American Government.** As already stated, the American government agreed to the Anglo-French interpretation of the meaning of article 1 of the convention and did not, therefore, deny their right to seize and detain postal parcels containing contraband goods destined for the use of the enemy. It was also "inclined to the opinion" that the class of mail which included stocks, bonds, coupons, and similar securities was to be regarded as of the same nature as merchandise and therefore subject to the exercise of the same belligerent rights, and so were money orders, checks, drafts, notes, and other negotiable instruments.

What the American government did contest, however, was the manner in which the belligerent right of search and detention was exercised. It admitted that "genuine correspondence" was inviolable, but it did not admit that belligerents had a lawful right "to search other private sea-borne mails for any other purpose than to discover whether they contained articles of enemy ownership carried on belligerent vessels or articles of contraband transmitted under sealed cover as letter mail" except mail coming in and going out of effectively blockaded ports, of which there were none under the "so-called British blockade."

"The government of the United States," said the secretary of state in his memorandum of January 4, 1916, "is unable to admit the right of His Majesty's authorities forcibly to bring into port neutral vessels plying directly between American and neutral European ports without intention of touching at British ports and there to remove or censor mails carried by them. Modern practice generally recognizes that mails are not to be censored, confiscated, or destroyed on the high seas, even when carried by belligerent mail ships, and it seems certainly to follow that to bring mail ships within British jurisdiction for purposes of search and then to subject them to local regulations allowing a censorship of mails cannot be justified on the ground of national jurisdiction. In cases where neutral mail ships merely touch at British ports the government of the United States believes

[1] Cf. Hershey, *Amer. Jour. of Int. Law*, Vol. X, p. 581, and Allin, *Minnesota Law Review*, April, 1917, p. 9. The British government did not in express terms attempt to justify the seizures complained of on the ground that the goods in question were destined ultimately to blockaded territory. Nevertheless, there are certain passages in Sir Edward Grey's note of January 1, 1916, to Count Wrangel, Swedish minister at London, which would indicate that the right of blockade was relied upon.

that His Majesty's authorities have no right in international law to remove the sealed mails or to censor them on board ship, since mails on such ships never rightfully come into the custody of the British mail service, which is entirely without responsibility for their transit or safety."

In a note of May 24 the American government, referring to assurances given by the allied governments in February previous that they would refrain from confiscating "on the high seas" genuine correspondence, asserted that the allied governments proceeded to deny neutral governments the benefit of these assurances by forcibly taking their vessels into port and confiscating their mails there instead of on the high seas. There was no distinction, it was argued, between the seizure of mails at sea, which the allied governments had renounced, and their seizure of them upon vessels voluntarily or involuntarily in British ports. Forcing or inducing neutral vessels to enter British ports added nothing to the belligerent right in respect to the mails which they had on board. Such a procedure, it was declared, was arbitrary and contrary to the practice of the past, was a violation of the spirit of the assurances given on February 15, and was in violation of the eleventh Hague convention. Moreover, it had resulted "most disastrously" to citizens of the United States through the loss of important papers which could not be duplicated. Other losses and inconveniences had been sustained through delays in receiving shipping documents. Checks, drafts, money orders, and similar property had been lost or detained for weeks and even months, and international money-order lists for Germany after a lapse of months had not reached their destination, although the property belonged in the category of "genuine correspondence." [1]

[1] The American government contrasted the practice of the allies with that of the United States during the Civil war when Secretary Seward announced that "the public mails of any friendly or neutral power, duly certified or authenticated as such, shall not be searched nor opened, but will be put as speedily as may be convenient on the way to their designated destinations"; with the practice of France in 1870; with that of the United States in 1898; with that of Great Britain during the Boer war; with that of Japan and Russia in 1904, and even with that of Germany during the recent war. It may be seriously doubted, however, whether the practice in those wars would have differed materially from that of the Entente allies in the recent war had the circumstances been the same. In none of those wars was an attempt made on a large scale by one of the belligerents to use the postal service to carry on a trade which they could not have carried on through the ordinary channels of commerce. In fact, during the Civil war neutral mails were examined to determine the character of vessels suspected of being blockade

The "improper methods" thus employed by the British and French authorities in seizing and detaining mails passing between the United States and the enemies of Great Britain could no longer be tolerated; to submit to a "lawless practice" of this character would open the door to repeated violations of international law by the belligerent powers on the ground of military necessity, and the government of the United States confidently expected it to cease.[1]

§ 537. Views of the British and French Governments. The position of the British and French governments was set forth in a succession of notes and memoranda.[2] Replying in the first place, to the American criticism in regard to the practice of taking mails into British ports for examination, the allied governments asserted that this was an absolute necessity, since it could not be done on board the vessels which carried them, without "involving a great deal of confusion, without causing serious delay to the mails, passengers and cargo and without great risk of error, loss or miscarriage." For these reasons mail bags must be taken into ports where there was a

runners. Cf., e.g., the case of the *Adela*, 6 Wall, 266. It hardly seems permissible to compare German practice during the recent war with the practice of the allies. The large number of mail steamers with their mails sunk by German cruisers and submarines did not indicate any particular solicitude on the part of Germany for the inviolability of the mails. The only reported case in which they took off the mails before destroying a ship was that in connection with the *Floride*. In this case the letter mail was forwarded to its destination without examination, but it may be safely assumed that if any military purpose would have been subserved by searching or detaining it, this would have been done. In fact, the parcels mail on board was sunk with the ship. This was an illegal act, because it should have been made the object of prize proceedings, as was done in the case of parcels mail seized as contraband by the British and French authorities.

[1] The Dutch government protested against the measures of the allied governments quite as vigorously as did that of the United States, and especially against the seizure and censure of mails on neutral steamers in British ports or territorial waters. Like the United States government it did not contest the right of the British and French governments to seize parcels post mail containing contraband on board neutral ships on the high seas. The destruction of mails by the Germans in connection with the sinking of prizes was, it was added, a consequence of the destruction of the ships which bore them and constituted no justification for the measures of the allied governments. See the Dutch notes of January 12, 1916, March 31, 1916, and April 11, 1916, in 24 *Rev. Gén. de Droit Int. Pub.*, 1917, Docs., pp. 79. As to the protests of the Norwegian government see its Orange Book issued in 1916, pp. 28 ff.

[2] Most of the correspondence may be found in the white book, *European War*, No. 3, issued by the American government in August, 1916, pp. 145 ff.

sufficient staff [1] and other facilities for insuring the rapid and effective examination of their contents. Regarding the American contention that the practice of the allied governments was contrary to their own early assurances in that they had disclaimed any intention of seizing or confiscating *bona fide* correspondence on the high seas, but were in fact accomplishing the same purpose by inducing or compelling neutral ships to touch at British ports, where they were subjected to the local jurisdiction, and where a wider belligerent right was exercised over them than was allowable on the high seas, the allied governments replied that they had never in fact differentiated between their treatment of mails on the high seas and those on board neutral ships compulsorily diverted to British or French ports. As to merchant vessels voluntarily touching at such ports, the case was different, for it was a well-settled principle of international law, which had been recognized by the United States Supreme Court [2] that they were under the jurisdiction of the local law, and consequently the authorities had a lawful right before granting clearances to satisfy themselves that the ships carried nothing hostile to the interests of the national defence. Moreover, the provisions of the Hague convention applied only to mails found on the "high seas" and not to those on ships within the local jurisdiction. The allied memorandum of October 12 reviewed at length the past practice of belligerents in respect to the treatment of mails on neutral ships, and it asserted that there was nothing in their procedure during the existing war that was contrary to the methods employed by belligerents in previous wars. The American government was

---

[1] The enormous work entailed by the examination of mails may be inferred from the fact that the staff of the censor's office in London consisted of more than one thousand persons.

[2] *United States* v. *Dikeelman*, 92 U. S. 520 (1875). But neutrals complained that the distinction which the British authorities made between ships voluntarily touching at British ports and those "involuntarily" entering was not warranted, since practically all those bound for Dutch and Scandinavian ports entered British ports not "voluntarily" but "involuntarily," because if they took the southern route, they could not, in view of the mine fields in the English Channel, avoid passing through the territorial waters of. Great Britain. Consequently, it was specious to consider that they had voluntarily placed themselves within the jurisdiction of the local law and thereby subjected their mails to a censorship to which they were not liable on the high seas. The British government replied to this contention by saying that such vessels were free to take the northern route if they wished and thereby avoid coming within British territorial jurisdiction.

also reminded that between December 31, 1914, and December 31, 1915, German and Austro-Hungarian naval commanders had destroyed without warning or preliminary visit thirteen mail steamers, together with the mail bags on board, while they were proceeding to or from neutral or allied ports, "without troubling themselves any more about the inviolability of the despatches and correspondence they contained than about the lives of the inoffensive persons on board these vessels," and the allied governments were not aware that any protest regarding the destruction of the mails had ever been addressed to the governments of Germany or Austria-Hungary. Moreover, the German naval authorities had seized and censored the mails of all origins and destinations on the neutral mail steamers *Iris, Haakon VII*, and *Germania* in August, 1915. The British and French governments therefore would not have been entirely without justification had they insisted on the right to seize mails destined to Germany, as an act of reprisal against Germany for destroying their mails, though in fact this plea had not been put forward. Regarding various specific complaints of the American government in respect to unreasonable detentions and the losses and inconveniences to which American citizens had been subjected, the allied governments replied that in every case innocent mails had been reforwarded with the least possible delay, and only those which were suspected of enemy origin or destination were put into the custody of the prize court. Diplomatic mail pouches had never been interfered with, German charges to the contrary notwithstanding. As to shipping documents, assurances were given in the allied memorandum of October 12, 1916, that in the future they would, whenever possible, be forwarded by the vessel from which they were taken. As to money order lists, which the American government regarded as falling within the category of ordinary correspondence, the allied governments took the contrary view. Those sent from the United States to Germany and Austria-Hungary, it was pointed out, "correspond to money deposited in the United States, the equivalent of which was payable by the German and Austrian postal administrations," and were therefore in reality genuine money orders forwarded *en bloc* in favor of several payees. The allied governments could not therefore allow funds to be transmitted to the enemy under this form. Finally, the allied governments affirmed that they were sincerely endeavoring to avoid any encroachment on the legitimate rights of neutral commerce, but they considered that they were within their rights in preventing the transportation to their enemies of any goods calculated to increase or maintain their power of resistance.

Looking at the equities of the case one can hardly avoid the conclusion that the general principle which the allied governments asserted was not unreasonable, and that the contention put forward by the American government rested mainly on the narrow technical aspects of the case.[1] If we regard the spirit rather than the form and take into consideration the extensive facilities which the postal service offers today as a medium for the transportation of merchandise and the enormous scale on which the Germans and their sympathizers in neutral countries attempted to exploit it for the purpose of circumventing the belligerent rights of the enemy in respect to blockade and contraband, we cannot justly claim for such traffic an immunity which was originally intended to protect the transportation of mails under different conditions and circumstances.

As time passed, the organization of the censorship machinery was perfected, so that the despatch of detained mails was expedited, the injuries from delays and losses became fewer,[2] and the complaints of neutrals were less numerous and serious. Finally, with the entrance of the United States into the war · in March, 1917, the controversy between that country and the allies came to an end.

§ 538. Removal of Enemy Persons from Neutral Vessels: Case of Piepenbrink. The stopping of neutral vessels on the high seas and the removal therefrom of persons of enemy nationality by British and French cruisers in a number of instances in the latter part of the year 1914 and the early part of 1915, like their interference with the mails, raised an important ques-

---

[1] Cf. Hershey in *Amer. Jour. of Int. Law*, Vol. X, p. 583.

[2] Lord Robert Cecil, minister of blockade, referring to the criticism regarding delays and losses, stated in the summer of 1916 that with the enormous staff in the censor's office the British government was able to guarantee that within forty-eight hours after delivery to the censor all mails were ready to be reforwarded. Losses, he said, had been reduced to a minimum, and when delays had occurred, they were due generally not to the fault of the cruiser, but to infrequent and uncertain sailings of mail steamers.

tion of international law and led to some diplomatic controversy with neutral governments and particularly with that of the United States.[1] The first case of the kind was the removal from the American steamer *Windber* by officers of the French cruiser *Condé* on November 13, 1914, of August Piepenbrink, a waiter or steward on the ship. At the time he was taken off, the vessel was on the high seas about 250 miles south of Kingston, Jamaica, and was proceeding to a neutral port. Piepenbrink was of German birth, but he had some years before filed his declaration of intention to become an American citizen. The department of state in a brief communication to the American ambassador at Paris on December 7, 1914, instructed him to ask the French government for the release of Piepenbrink, who was then being detained as a prisoner of war by the British authorities at Kingston. Similar instructions were communicated to the American ambassador at London. The communication did not enter into a discussion of the law of nations governing such cases, and no reasons were given in support of the request, it being assumed that the illegality of the seizure was incontestible.[2] On January 4, 1915, the British government replied that although Piepenbrink had declared his intention of becoming an American citizen, legally he was still a German subject, and under the circumstances it was not possible to release him. To this communication the department of state replied on March 2, 1915, calling the attention of the British government to the fact that Piepenbrink had, since declaring his intention of becoming an American citizen, been employed in the American merchant marine, and that by section 2174 of the revised statutes of the United States "every foreign seaman employed on board an American merchant vessel who had declared his intention of becoming an American citizen should for all purposes of protection be deemed an American citizen after the filing of his declaration of intention to become

---

[1] In the memorial of the German Imperial government of February 4, 1915, "respecting retaliatory measures rendered necessary by the means employed by England contrary to international law," she was charged with various lawless acts, among which was the "causing of numerous German subjects capable of bearing arms, to be taken from neutral ships and made prisoners of war."

[2] On the same date a telegram was sent to the vice-consul at Kingston demanding the release of Piepenbrink on the ground that "his arrest and detention are deemed to be without right."

such citizen." Moreover, independently of the question of Piepenbrink's citizenship, the American government insisted that his removal from an American vessel on the high seas was "without legal justification." Article 47 of the Declaration of London provides that "any individual embodied in the armed forces of the enemy who is found on board a neutral merchant vessel may be made a prisoner of war, even though there be no ground for the capture of the vessel," but the American government contended that Piepenbrink was not "embodied in the armed forces of the enemy" in the sense of the rule of the Declaration. Apart from the Declaration, which the American government did not recognize as being legally in force, there was no justification, it was said, for the removal of an enemy subject from a neutral vessel on the high seas bound to a neutral port, even if he could properly be regarded as a military person. This position had been assumed by the British government in the case of the *Trent* during the American Civil war.

In a communication to the French government of the same date the above-mentioned reasons for the release of Piepenbrink were repeated, and the attention of the French government was called to the similar attitude taken by the French minister of foreign affairs in the case of the *Trent*.[1]

In April, 1915, the British and French governments decided to liberate Piepenbrink as "a friendly act," while reserving the question of principle involved.[2] In view of the fact that he was by the municipal law of the United States a citizen, for the purposes of protection, the taking of him from a neutral ship could not of course be justified. The contention of the American government, however, that even if he had been an enemy subject and a "military person," there would have been no justification for removing him from a neutral vessel bound for a neutral port, may be questioned. The Declaration of London expressly affirms, as already said, that such persons, if incorporated in the armed forces of the enemy, may be made prisoners of war, and it makes no distinction between those found on neutral vessels bound to enemy ports and those on vessels bound to

---

[1] As to the attitude of the British and French governments in the *Trent* affair See Moore, *Digest*, Vol. VII, p. 772.

[2] The correspondence relating to the case of Piepenbrink is printed in the American white book, *European War*, No. 2, pp. 133-136.

neutral ports. Such persons have usually been treated as analogues of contraband and therefore liable to seizure, even when the vessel was proceeding to neutral ports.

§ 539. The Cases of Garde and Others. At various times in December, 1914, the American steamships *San Juan*, *Coamo*, *Carolina*, and *Barinquen* were stopped by the French cruiser *Descartes* on the high seas, and a number of Germans and Austrians were removed and sent to Martinique, where they were detained as prisoners of war. Among the passengers removed from the *Barinquen* was a civilian named Garde, the purser of the steamship, who, it appears, was a German by birth, but had formally declared his intention of becoming an American citizen. His case was therefore identical with that of Piepenbrink referred to above, and upon the demand of the American government he was released. The release of the other Germans and Austrians was also demanded by the American government on the ground that the removal from a neutral vessel plying between neutral ports, of any person, whether of enemy nationality or not, was a violation of international law. As in the Piepenbrink case, it was asserted that the men removed were not "embodied" in the armed forces of the enemy in the sense of the Declaration of London, and again it was asserted that even if they could have been properly regarded as military persons, their removal from a neutral vessel bound for a neutral port was unjustifiable. In consequence of the American representations the French government in January, 1915, released the persons removed from the American vessels and delivered them over to the American consul at Fort de France, Martinique, where they had been detained. Inasmuch as the vessels from which they had been taken were plying between ports of the United States, it is doubtful whether under the circumstances the French government would have been justified in treating them as analogues of contraband, even had they been "embodied" in the military forces of the enemy. But had they been taken from a vessel bound to an enemy port or to the port of a neutral country geographically adjacent to Germany, and had they been of military age, whether "embodied" in the armed forces of the enemy or not, a different question would have been presented, for under such circumstances the doctrine of ultimate destination could have been applied with much more reason than would have been possible in the case of a voyage between two American ports.

§ 540. Seizures on the *China*. On February 18, 1915, the British cruiser *Laurentic* stopped the *China*, an American steamship bound from Shanghai to San Francisco, and took off some thirty-eight Germans, Austrians, and Turkish subjects and conveyed them to Hongkong where they were placed in military barracks. The American government protested against the seizure and again reaffirmed the view that the removal of enemy subjects, even if they could be regarded as military persons, from a neutral vessel on the high seas proceeding to a neutral port was an invasion of the sovereignty of American vessels on the high seas and therefore contrary to the rules of international law. In a reply of April, 1916, to the American protest the British government alleged that the persons in question were an "integral part of a plot" organized in Shanghai for the purpose of making Manila a base for the perpetration of unneutral acts against the Entente allies. It had been definitely established from "actual occurrences and reliable information," the British note stated, that Germens resident in Shanghai had been en6aged for some time in the collection of arms and ammunition both for clandestine transmission to India and if possible for the arming of a ship to play the part of a Far Eastern *Möwe*. Persons of this description, it was asserted, belonged to the class of individuals who may without any infraction of the sovereignty of a neutral State be removed from a neutral vessel on the high seas.[1]

At the beginning of the war, Sir Edward Grey added, the British government adhered to the interpretation of article 47 of the Declaration of London that it was not to be considered as permitting the arrest of passengers on neutral vessels who were not yet attached to their military units, but when the German government began to remove able-bodied persons of

[1] It is evident, however, said the British note, from the foregoing observations that the principle (often contended for in the past by certain continental nations) that there are certain classes of persons who are not protected by a neutral flag on the high seas and may therefore, without any invasion of the sovereign rights of the neutral, be removed from a neutral ship, is now generally admitted. The carriage of such persons may in some cases amount to unneutral service rendering the ship liable to condemnation; but even when this is not so, the removal of such persons from a neutral ship by a belligerent does not justify any complaint by the neutral state concerned.

military age from the occupied portions of Belgium and France, the British government then notified neutral powers that it could no longer accept the restrictive interpretation placed for practical reasons on article 47, and that it would in the future arrest all enemy reservists found on board neutral ships on the high seas, no matter where they might be met.[1] It was of the greatest importance, he added, for a belligerent power to intercept not only mobilized members of the opposing army who might be found travelling on neutral ships, but also agents sent by the enemy to injure his opponents abroad.

It appears that subsequently the British government released such of the persons taken from the *China* as were found to be over military age or who were not in any sense reservists, but all others were detained as prisoners of war.

§ 541. **What Persons are Liable to Seizure on Neutral Vessels?** The right of a belligerent to remove from neutral vessels military persons (*militaires*) has long been recognized and in practice exercised, and it was finally sanctioned by the Declaration of London, although article 47 limits the right to persons who are "embodied" in the armed forces of the enemy, that is, those who actually constitute a part of the military forces. This limitation would therefore seem to prohibit the seizure of so-called "noxious persons," other than those actually incorporated in the army.[2]

Military persons were assimilated by the older writers to the character of contraband and were often referred to as "analogues of contraband." Some writers, however, held that the conveyance of contraband is a different thing and is governed by different rules.[3] But the great majority of writers treat the

---

[1] This note was dated November 1, 1914, and reads as follows: "In view of the action taken by the German forces in Belgium and France of removing, as prisoners of war, all persons who are liable to military service, His Majesty's Government have given instructions that all enemy reservists on board neutral vessels should be made prisoners of war."

[2] Dana (ed. of Wheaton, 656, note) doubted whether the right to take "noxious persons" from neutral vessels existed apart from treaty right. But even in the absence of treaty stipulations a strong argument can be made in favor of the right to take off such persons (cf. Atherley-Jones, *Commerce in War*, p. 310), and this right was affirmed by the Declaration of London.

[3] The analogy between the transportation of military persons and the carriage of contraband goods is pronounced false by Dupuis (*Le Droit de la Guerre Maritime*, sec. 172) and by Kleen (*Lois et Usages de la Neutralité*, p. 455). The transportation of contraband goods, says Dupuis, is different in purpose and in effect from the

transportation of persons in the military service of the enemy either as the carriage of contraband or as analogous thereto. Whether there is any real analogy between the two acts would seem to be of little practical consequence, for the effect is largely the same. Indeed, says Phillimore, the consequences of the transportation of military persons and despatches may extend far beyond those resulting from the exportation of any contraband that can be conveyed to the enemy, since manifestly by the carriage of despatches the most important operations of a belligerent may be promoted or obstructed. Whereas in the case of the transportation of contraband goods the quantity of the articles carried may be a material circumstance, still the smaller despatch may suffice to turn the fortune of war in favor of a particular belligerent.[1] If therefore it is permissible for a belligerent to intercept contraband goods going to the enemy, it is all the more important that he should be allowed to intercept military persons and despatches.

§ 542. **Views of the Authorities.** The Declaration of London, as stated above, expressly recognizes the right to take off persons "embodied in the armed forces" of the enemy, but there is a difference of opinion as to the meaning of this phrase. Referring to the doubt concerning its meaning, the general report of the drafting committee of the International Naval Conference expressed the opinion that reservists, i.e., individuals who are returning home in response to a summons to fulfil their military obligations, are not to be considered as being *embodied* in the sense of articles 45 and 47 in the armed forces. Apart from provisions of municipal law to the contrary, this opinion, it was added, was "more in accordance with practical necessity and

---

transportation of persons, the purpose of the former being commercial gain, whereas the effect if not the purpose of the latter is direct assistance to one of the belligerents. Secretary Seward in his defence of the seizure of Mason and Slidell stated that all writers and judges considered "naval and military persons in the service of the enemy as contraband of war." Hall, criticizing Seward's statement, remarks that he produced no proof in support of his assertion. It is to be regretted, says Hall, that Lord Russell did not address himself to the refutation of the doctrine that persons can be contraband of war. *Int. Law*, 3d ed., p. 684. Montague Bernard was of the same opinion. "It is incorrect," he said, "to speak of the conveyance of persons in the military or civil employment of a belligerent as if it were the same thing as the conveyance of contraband of war, or as if the same rule were applicable to it. It is a different thing and the rules applicable to it are different." *Neutrality of Great Britain during the American Civil War*, p. 224.

[1] *Int. Law*, Vol. III, sec. 271.

has been accepted by all in a spirit of conciliation." [1] Bentwich,[2] Higgins,[3] Dupuis [4] Bluntschli,[5] Perels,[6] Marquardsen,[7] Lawrence,[8] Kleen,[9] Montague Bernard,[10] and many others take the same view, namely, that the subjects of an enemy State at the outbreak of the war who have been summoned to join the colors, but who have not yet actually done so, and who are travelling as ordinary passengers without uniform or organization, cannot lawfully be taken from a neutral vessel, and such carriage does not incriminate the vessel, unless the voyage is undertaken especially for their transport. The Institute of International Law at its session of 1896 adopted a resolution denying the right of neutral vessels to transport troops for the benefit of a belligerent, but expressly excepted from the operation of the rule those "who were not yet in the military service of a belligerent even though their intention is to enter it, or who make the voyage as simple passengers without manifest connection with military service." [11] This rule was ultimately embodied in the *Manuel des Lois de la Guerre Maritime* adopted by the Institute in 1913.[12] According to this view, therefore,

---

[1] *House of Commons Sessional Papers*, Vol. 54, No. 4 (1909), p. 53.

[2] *The Declaration of London*, p. 89.

[3] *The Hague Peace Conferences*, p. 594.

[4] *Le Droit de la Guerre Maritime d'après les Conférences de la Haye et Londres*, p. 339.

[5] *Le Droit Int. Cod.*, sec. 815.

[6] *Droit Maritime Int.* (French trans. by Arendt), sec. 47. Perels holds that all individuals who are returning home with the intention of engaging in military or naval operations are not liable to seizure, but only those who are already in the strict sense of the word a part of the army.

[7] *Der Trent Fall*, ch. 10.

[8] *Principles of Int. Law*, 4th ed., p. 728. This interpretation, says Lawrence, is important in view of the large number of emigrant reservists who will be returning to the colors in the event of the outbreak of war.

[9] *Lois et Usages de la Neutralité*, Vol. I, p. 463. Kleen emphasizes the fact that intention to enlist does not confer the military character. The individual must be an actual part of the military forces in order to justify his seizure as a prisoner of war. Moreover, the number of such persons is irrelevant, and it would be impracticable to prescribe a maximum.

[10] *Neutrality of Great Britain During the American Civil War*, p. 223.

[11] *Annuaire*, Vol. XV, pp. 231-232.

[12] M. Fauchille, however, wished to have the rule applied to reservists, but upon the request of certain members of the Institute who pointed out that such an extension would not be in harmony with the Declaration of London, he withdrew his proposal. See *ibid.*, pp. 104 and 297; also Vol. XXI, pp. 116, 304. The question of what persons were liable to seizure as *militaires* on neutral vessels was discussed at the Second Hague Conference in connection with the subject of con-

it is not lawful for a belligerent to take off persons known as reservists and make prisoners of war of them.

§ 543. Practice of the Past. In 1870 large numbers of French and German subjects left the United States and returned to their respective countries in order to perform their military obligations. In one instance as many as twelve hundred Frenchmen embarked in two vessels sailing from New York, but inasmuch as they travelled as ordinary passengers, unarmed and not under military discipline, secretary of state Fish took the position that they were not a part of the armed forces, and consequently there was no violation of American neutrality in permitting them to depart. Neither belligerent made any attempt to intercept their return, although Lawrence thinks they could have been made prisoners of war had they been captured by the enemy during the course of the voyage.[1]

In the controversy between Great Britain and Germany over the detention by British cruisers of the *Bundesrath*, the *General*, and the *Herzog* during the Boer war, it appears that one of the grounds alleged by Great Britain in justification of the seizure of the *Bundesrath* was that she carried a number of Dutch, Austrians, and Germans, all believed to be intending combatants. Replying to the request of the German government for the release of the vessel, Lord Salisbury stated among other things that "she had on board a number of passengers believed to be volunteers for service with the Boers."[2] The *Bundesrath*, like the *China* in the recent war, it may be added, was plying between neutral ports, the only difference between the two cases being that the *Bundesrath* was bound for a neutral port in close geographical proximity to the territory of the enemy, so that

---

traband. An article was proposed providing that a ship which had on board *formations de troupes* should be liable to condemnation if the owner or captain had knowledge of their military character. Like penalty was to be inflicted on ships which carried individual passengers who belonged to the armed forces of the enemy if the voyage was especially undertaken for their conveyance. During the course of the discussion of the proposed article Captain Otley asked what was meant by *formations de troupes*. Professor Renault replied that they were bodies of men bound by discipline and subject to the authority of a commander (*Actes et Documents*, Vol. III, p. 1123). General Amourel then inquired whether reservists, returning home to be incorporated in the army were included. Herr Kriege replied in the negative. They were, he said, simple passengers and not military persons. Count Tornielli agreed with Renault and Kriege that *formations de troupes* did not include reservists travelling as individual passengers.

[1] *Op. cit.*, p. 621.   [2] Moore, *Digest*, Vol. VII, p. 765.

the application of the doctrine of continuous voyage would have been more justifiable than in the case of the *China*. Nevertheless, it was not alleged that any of the suspected persons were soldiers in the actual service of the enemy; their seizure rather appears to have been based on the theory that they were contraband by analogy. Professor Holland at the time expressed the opinion that "the carriage by a neutral ship of enemy troops or even of a few military officers and also of enemy despatches was an "enemy service of so important a kind as to involve the confiscation of the vessel concerned, a penalty which under ordinary circumstances is not imposed upon carriage of contraband properly so called." [1]

§ 544. **The Case of the *Fredrico*.** The question of the liability to capture of a neutral vessel carrying military persons arose during the recent war in the case of the *Fredrico*, decided by the French prize council in May, 1915.[2] The *Fredrico* was a Spanish steamer captured on the high seas October 10, 1914, by a French torpedo destroyer and taken to Toulon. It had on board a number of German and Austro-Hungarian *mobilisés*, the exact number of whom is not stated, who were returning home to join the colors of their respective regiments. The owner of the steamer asked for its release on the ground that the passengers in question were not "incorporated" in the armed forces of their respective countries, and that the voyage of the vessel had not been undertaken with a view to the transportation of such persons. The prize council, however, condemned the ship as good prize on the ground that a neutral vessel engaged in the transporting of "numerous passengers" of this nature, even when proceeding from one neutral port to another, is liable to capture and confiscation. The passengers in question, the prize council held, must be considered as being "incorporated," within the meaning of article 47 of the Declaration of London, in the armed forces of their respective governments. Finally, the Declaration of London never having been ratified by the powers and the French government having put it into effect with certain modifications and additions, it must

---

[1] London *Times*, January 3, 1902.
[2] Text in 22 *Rev. Gén. de Droit Int. Pub.* (1915), *Jurisprudence*, pp. 17 ff. Cf. also the decree of the President of the French Republic rejecting an appeal from the decision of the prize court, *ibid.*, 1917, *Jurisprudence*, p. 11.

be considered as a unilateral act, the interpretation of which belonged to the French prize council.

It is generally admitted that a neutral vessel engaged in the carriage of military persons is liable to condemnation when the vessel has been hired as a transport, or when the persons are such in number, importance, or destination, and at the same time when the circumstances of their reception are such as to create a reasonable presumption that the owner or his agent intended to aid the belligerent in his war.[1] But it does not follow from this admitted principle that neutral vessels engaging in the ordinary course of trade, and which carry military persons as regular passengers and without any intention of aiding one of the belligerents, are equally liable to condemnation. Hall remarks that when "belligerent persons, whatever their quality, go on board a neutral vessel as simple passengers, the ship remains neutral and covers the persons on board with the protection of her neutral character."

The line of demarcation between the transportation of persons for the aid of a belligerent and their transportation in the ordinary course of commerce is not always easy to draw. In any case, from the point of view of the belligerent, the importance of the act consists not in the manner in which it is done, nor in the motive which may animate the carrier, but in the effect. Whether the circumstances of the transportation may or may not be such as to render the vessel liable to confiscation, it is reasonable to hold that it is the right of a belligerent to take proper measures to prevent the enemy from receiving military aid under the protection of a neutral flag. No rule can be laid down as to the number of military persons on board which may be necessary to render the vessel liable to confiscation. The transportation of a single general or admiral might under some circumstances be a more noxious act than the conveyance of a large number of ordinary soldiers.[2] It would seem, however, that the confiscation by the French prize council of the *Fredrico* was a somewhat extreme application of the rule. It does not

---

[1] Hall, *Int. Law*, 4th ed., p. 701. Cf. also Smith and Sibley, *Int. Law as Interpreted during the Russo-Japanese War*, p. 249, who says the liability of the vessel to capture depends on whether it is hired by the belligerent for the purposes of a transport. Montagne Bernard (*Neutrality of Great Britian during the American Civil War*, p. 223) held the same opinion.

[2] Cf. Moore, *Digest*, Vol. VII, p. 756, and Lawrence's *Wheaton*, ed. of 1863, p. 802.

appear that the vessel was hired as a transport by the enemy government; on the contrary, it was engaged in the regular course of trade and carried the German and Austrian *mobilisés* as ordinary passengers. They were unorganized reservists and were not incorporated in the armed forces in accordance with article 47 of the Declaration of London, as that article has usually been interpreted. Nevertheless, as the Declaration of London was not binding on the prize council, it was free, as it asserted, to place its own interpretation on the meaning of the article in question.

It is certain that Great Britain and France in taking from neutral vessels persons of enemy nationality who were not actually incorporated in the armed forces, and who in some cases appear not even to have been reservists returning home in response to a summons from their governments, and detaining them as prisoners of war, did not conform to the general usage of the past nor to the terms of the Declaration of London.[1] As already stated, they conformed their action in the beginning to the general interpretation that has been placed on article 47 and confined their seizures to persons actually incorporated in the armed forces of the enemy; but in November, 1914, in consequence of the German policy of deporting able-bodied men of military age from the occupied regions of Belgium and of Northern France, this policy was altered, and enemy reservists and apparently, indeed, all persons subject to military service were declared liable to seizure. This decision was avowedly an act of reprisal against Germany and was not without justification, although its enforcement involved infringements on the rights of neutrals, like various other acts of reprisal during the recent war.

§ 545. Status of Despatch Bearers on Neutral Steamers. In December, 1914, a German or Austrian submarine stopped a Greek steamer near Messina and took off Colonel Napier and Captain Arthur Wilson, the latter a member of the British Parliament, and detained them as prisoners of war. At the time of their seizure they were conveying letters of a military or naval character from the eastern Mediterranean to London. The views of text writers as well as judicial authority seem to

---

[1] Their action in this respect is criticised by the French writer Perrinjaquet in 22 *Rev. Gén. de Droit Int. Pub.* (1915), p. 184.

be in agreement that diplomatic despatches written for a belligerent purpose and addressed to the civil or military authorities of the enemy are analogous to contraband, and they, with the persons bearing them, may be taken from a neutral steamer on the high seas.[1] In the above-mentioned case the steamer was allowed to continue her voyage unmolested, and no proceedings were instituted looking toward her condemnation. Sir Edward Grey in reply to a question addressed to him by a member of the House of Commons admitted that the removal of Colonel Napier and Captain Wilson from the steamer was not in contravention of the generally accepted rules of international law.[2]

[1] Cf. Hall, *op. cit.*, 3d ed., p. 678, and Rivier, *Principes*, Vol. II, p. 389; also the review of the cases of the *Atalanta*, the *Constantia*, the *Susan*, the *Hope*, the *Caroline*, the *Madison*, and *Rapid* in Moore's *Digest*, Vol. VII, pp. 761–763; also Atherley-Jones, *Commerce in War*, p. 79, and pp. 304–309, where most of these cases are analyzed.

[2] Sir Edward had stated the view of the British government in his instructions to Lord Desart, president of the British delegation to the International Naval Conference in 1909, when he said: "The carriage of enemy despatches and the conveyance of military detachments or of individual officers or civil agents of the enemy have generally been admitted to render the ship liable to seizure and possibly to confiscation. But," he added, "it would be desirable to arrive at some understanding that in admitting conveyance by neutral vessels of a few individuals having the character of analogues of contraband it should not entail on such vessels more than the minimum amount of interference necessary for preventing the contraband persons from reaching their destination." *House of Commons Sessional Papers*, Vol. 54, No. 4 (1904), p. 30.

CHAPTER XXXV

THE EXPORTATION OF ARMS AND MUNITIONS TO BELLIGERENTS

§ 546. Policy of the United States; § 547. Are Neutrals Bound to prohibit such Trade?; § 548. Views of German Writers before the Late War; § 549. Practice in Former Wars; American Policy; § 550. British and French Practice; § 551. German Practice; § 552. Instances of Embargoes on the Exportation of Arms and Munitions; § 553. Protests of the German and Austrian Governments in 1915; § 554. Their Contentions Analyzed; § 555. The Question of Moral Obligation to Forbid such Trade; § 556. Analysis of the Arguments; § 557. Practical Difficulties in the Way of Prohibition; § 558. Legality of the Alteration of the Rule during War.

§ 546. **Policy of the United States.** The Policy of the United States government in permitting the exportation of arms, munitions, and other war supplies for the use of belligerents during the war was the subject of much discussion in Congress and in the press and provoked diplomatic remonstrances from the governments of Germany and Austria-Hungary. As a general proposition it was admitted by those who complained of the extensive traffic which went on between American manufacturers and the Entente powers that neutral governments are not by the existing rules of international law bound to prevent their nationals from engaging in such traffic; but it was argued that special circumstances, to which the recent war gave rise, gave a "new conception to the aspect of neutrality," and that an abnormal and unprecedented situation was created which made the continued furnishing of arms and munitions to the belligerents on one side, when their adversaries were unable to avail of the American markets, a violation of the spirit of strict neutrality.

In consequence of the unexampled magnitude of the war and the huge demand which it created for American arms, munitions, and other supplies, a demand which was augmented by the closing of the markets of the neutral States of Europe to the various belligerents, the arms and munitions industries

375

of the United States quickly "soared to unimagined heights."
Existing establishments were promptly enlarged and were
operated night and day to the full limit of their capacity, two
and sometimes three shifts of workingmen being employed for
the purpose.[1] In some instances establishments for the manufacture of clocks, typewriters, locomotives, and other articles
were converted into manufactories for the production of war
supplies. So enormous were the demands, and so alluring were
the profits, that new industries were quickly organized, and in
several instances populous cities sprang into existence as if by
magic, the entire populations of which were engaged in the
manufacture of supplies to meet the necessities of the war.[2]
The governments of Germany and Austria-Hungary, as well
as large numbers of their sympathizers in the United States,
protested and asserted that in permitting the territory of the
United States to become the seat of such a traffic, in fact for
the benefit of the Entente powers alone, the government was
violating the spirit if not the letter of the law of neutrality.

§ 547. **Are Neutrals Bound to Prohibit Such Traffic?** Do the
established rules of international law impose on the governments
of neutral States an obligation generally to prevent their nationals
from selling and transporting arms and munitions to any belligerents who may wish to buy? If not, are there conceivable
special circumstances which may make it their duty to do so
in order to preserve the spirit as well as the form of neutrality?
And if so, may it be done at any time during the progress of
the war when the effect would be to alter the existing situation
to the advantage of one belligerent and to the detriment of the
other?

The first question can be answered only in the negative. A

[1] The Remington Arms Company is reported to have added eleven new buildings at a cost of approximately three million dollars to its plant during the early
months of the war.

[2] It is impossible to give even approximately correct figures of the volume of this
trade. The daily press frequently contained reports of contracts with agents of the
British, French, and Russian governments for fifty-million and hundred-million
dollar orders. According to information given out by the department of com-
merce on May 31, 1916, the total purchases of arms and munitions in the United
States during the first twenty months of the war amounted to $388,000,000. By
July 16 the amount had gone up to $446,000,000. According to the New York
Journal of Commerce the export of munitions and acccessories from the United
States in 1913 was valued at $49,701,000; in 1916 it amounted to $944,919,000.
Quoted in the New York *Times*, March 11, 1917.

neutral government is not legally bound to forbid its nationals from selling and transporting for the use of belligerents, arms, munitions, or any other supplies which they may wish to buy. Fully nine-tenths of the text writers on international law who have expressed opinions on the question have pronounced in favor of this view. It is the view on which States have generally acted in the past; and it is the view formally embodied in two international conventions adopted by the Second Hague Conference.[1]

It would be a work of supererogation to cite all the text writers and jurists of repute from Albericus Gentilis to the present [2] who have affirmed this view. The opinion expressed by Jefferson as secretary of state in 1793, when the British government complained of the sale by American citizens of arms and munitions to an agent of the French government, that "our citizens have always been free to vend and export arms; that it is the constant occupation and livelihood of some of them;" that "to suppress their callings, the only means perhaps of their subsistence, because a war exists in foreign and distant countries in which we have no concern would scarcely be expected;" and that "it would be hard in principle and impossible in practice,"[3] has been affirmed and reaffirmed by nearly all American writers, judges, secretaries of state, and Presidents who have had occasion to pronounce opinions on the

---

[1] This is expressly affirmed by art. 7 of the Hague conventions Nos. V and XIII of 1907. The latter convention has been ratified by twenty-five and adhered to by three non-signatory powers, including Germany and Austria-Hungary, and none of them reserved their ratification to art. 7. It can hardly be maintained that because several of the belligerents in the recent war never ratified the conventions, art. 7 of either convention was not binding. This, because the rule laid down by art. 7 is declaratory, not amendatory, of the existing law of nations. The discussions of the subject at the Second Hague Conference show very clearly that art. 7 of the two conventions was not intended to impose on neutral governments an obligation to forbid such trade. Cf. especially the remarks of Herr Kriege (*Actes et Documents*, Vol. III, p. 859) and of M. Renault (*ibid.*, p. 867), and the report of Colonel Borel (*ibid.*, Vol. I, p. 141).

[2] When England complained in the sixteenth century of the sale by neutral merchants of munitions to Spain, says Gentilis, the complaint was probably well founded in equity but not in law. Quoted by Nys, *Le Droit International*, Vol. III, p. 637.

[3] Letter to the minister of Great Britain, May 15, 1793, quoted by Moore, *Digest*, Vol. VII, p. 955. The views of a large number of text writers are given by Calvo in his *Le Droit International*, Vol. IV, sec. 2625. Many pages in Moore's *Digest* (Vol. VII, pp. 955-975) are devoted to setting forth the views of American writers, presidents, secretaries of state, and judges on the subject.

subject.   Field [1] and Woolsey [2] appear to be the only American writers of note who have questioned the morality of the existing rule.   Likewise, the opinion of Jefferson and his successors has been that almost unanimously held by British writers, the only dissenting voice apparently being that of Phillimore, who holds that it is contrary to neutrality for a government to permit the sale within its territory of munitions of war to a belligerent.[3] Among French jurists the right of neutrals to engage in such traffic has been denied by only a few, the best known of whom are Hautefeuille,[4] Pistoye and Duverdy.[5]   Kleen, a Swedish jurist and writer of high repute, also holds the view that it is the duty of neutrals to prevent their subjects from engaging in contraband traffic,[6] Brusa, an Italian writer, takes the same view.[7]

§ 548. Views of German Writers Before the War.   Among German writers, there was, prior to the late war, almost the same unanimity of view in favor of the right of neutrals to sell arms and munitions to belligerents.   Perels, at one time legal adviser to the German Admiralty, referring to the "oft-discussed question" as to whether a neutral government is *obliged* to pre-

---

[1] *Outlines of an International Code*, Sec. 964.

[2] Referring to the opinion of Story in the case of the *Santissima Trinidad* (7 Wheaton, 340) that "there is nothing in our laws or in the law of nations that forbids our citizens from sending armed vessels as well as munitions of war to foreign ports for sale; that it is a commercial venture which no nation is bound to prohibit," Woolsey (*Int. Law*, p. 320, n. 1) expresses regret that Judge Story should have said this, if it be true.   Such trade, Woolsey says, is "immoral and tends to produce lasting animosities."   "A juster and more humane policy," he adds, "would make all innocent trade with the enemy valid and require a neutral to pass stringent and effectual laws against contraband trade."

[3] "If," says Phillimore (*Int. Law*, Vol. III, sec. 230), "the foundations of international justice have been correctly pointed out in a former volume of this work (Vol. I, Pt. I, ch. 3), and if it be the true character of a neutral to abstain from every act which may better or worsen the condition of a belligerent, the unlawfulness of any such sale is a necessary conclusion from these premises."

[4] *Droits et Devoirs des Nations Neutres en Temps de Guerre*, Vol. II, p. 424.

[5] *Traité des Prises Maritimes*, Vol. I, p. 394.

[6] "Every neutral State," says Kleen (*Lois et Usages de la Neutralité*, Vol. I, sec. 93), "must not only itself abstain from furnishing to either belligerent contraband articles, but must watch over (*surveiller*) its subjects and other individuals who find themselves within its territory, to see that they do not furnish belligerents with such articles; it must prohibit by law such traffic and must prevent it as far as possible and punish such acts wherever it exercises sovereign authority."   Cf. also his *Contrebande de Guerre*, pp. 52, 67.

[7] *Rev. de Droit Int.*, Vol. XXVI (1894), p. 404.

vent its subjects from loaning money to belligerents or furnishing them with war materials, etc., says: "It cannot be doubted in fact that unless there is a notorious favor shown towards one of the belligerents there is no obligation to forbid the assistance.[1] Kluber likewise holds that "ordinarily a belligerent does not have the right to require a neutral State to abstain from trade with his enemy" and that "the law of nations does not prohibit neutrals from trading in articles of merchandise which serve the immediate military needs of belligerents, provided there is no design to favor one of the belligerents as against the other." [2]

Geffcken, who considers the subject of trade in arms and war material at greater length than most German writers, concludes that "it is well-established by international law that the sale and exportation of contraband by the subjects of neutral States is no violation of their neutral duties." [3] After reviewing at length the opinions of the text-writers, the vast majority of whom pronounce in favor of the legitimacy of such trade, Geffcken remarks that, in view of this array of authority, the contention of the German government in 1870 that England was bound to prohibit the sale of arms and munitions of war to agents of the French government naturally excited astonishment.

Among German jurists who have defended most strongly the right of neutrals to engage in contraband trade may be mentioned Professor von Bar of Göttingen.[4] He criticises Kleen's *projet* for prohibiting such trade as one which, if made a rule of international law, would injure incalculably not only the commerce of neutrals, but even their manufacturing industry and in a large measure the production of their agriculture, forests and mines, and reduce a considerable part of their population to famine. It would, moreover, he asserts, entail a necessity of surveillance and control over the sale and transportation of merchandise in neutral countries which would be intolerable, necessitate numerous searches by customs officials and impose upon neutral governments obligations and duties

---

[1] *Manuel de Droit Maritime International* (French trans. by Arendt), p. 270.

[2] *Droit des Gens Moderne de l'Europe* (French trans. by Ott), sec. 287.

[3] *Handel mit Waffen und Kriegsmaterial* in Holtzendorff, *Handbuch des Völkerrechts*, Bd. IV, sec. 152.

[4] In an article entitled *Observations sur la Contrebande de Guerre*, in the *Rev. de Droit Int.*, Vol. XXVI (1894), pp. 401 ff.

which they would find it impossible to enforce. He goes on to say:

"What a belligerent may lawfully demand, is only that the relations between a neutral and his adversary shall remain as they were before. Consequently, the subjects of neutral States may continue to maintain commercial relations with belligerents as formerly, and if they manufacture arms and munitions, and have before the war, sold them to everybody, they may continue to do so after the war, even to belligerents."

True progress, says von Bar, consists not in prohibiting trade in contraband, as Kleen and Brusa would do, but in abolishing the right of belligerents to interfere with such traffic, leaving to them only the right of blockade.[1]

Turning to the argument sometimes advanced that the sale of arms and munitions to belligerents serves only to prolong the evils of war and that a trade the profits of which are drawn from bloody combats which the interests of humanity require to be stopped as promptly as possible is immoral, von Bar pronounces it to be specious as Lorimer had pointed out

"with his usual sagacity when he remarked that the object of war is not a temporary cessation of hostilities but a durable peace, and it is quite unreasonable that a nation should be forced to make peace by refusing to furnish it with the means of continuing the war. If the end of the war is brought about by the sole reason that one of the belligerents has been prevented from obtaining arms and munitions by purchasing them with its own money, it is not really vanquished and in a later time the quarrel and the war will be renewed."

Among other German and Austrian writers who have considered the subject, the following admit that neutral States are not bound to prohibit their subjects from selling or exporting arms and munitions of war to belligerents: von Liszt,[2] Martens,[3] Lehman,[4] Schmalz,[5] Marquardsen,[6] Schramn,[7] Einicke,[8] Hold

---

[1] *Ibid.*, p. 408. This suggestion, he said, had already been advocated by Kluber and Lorimer.

[2] *Das Völkerrecht*, 4th ed., p. 362.

[3] *Précis du Droit des Gens*, Vol. II, sec. 315.

[4] *Die Zufuhr von Kriegskontrebanden Waren*, p. 53.

[5] *Das Europäische Völkerrecht*, pp. 286–287.

[6] *Der "Trent" Fall*, p. 37. "If a neutral sells arms or munitions within his own land to agents of a belligerent, the doctrine of contraband does not apply. A neutral State may forbid such traffic through anxiety or the fear of a powerful belligerent, but there is no legal obligation (*Vorschrift*) to do it."

[7] *Das Prisenrecht in Seiner Neuesten Gestalt*, sec. 10.

[8] *Recht und Pflichten de neutralen Mächte im Seekriege*, p. 99.

von Ferneck [1] and Saalfeld.[2] The German official view was expressed by Herr Kriege at the Second Hague Conference during the discussion of the British proposal to abolish contraband, when he said, "neutral States are not bound to prevent their subjects from engaging in a commerce which from the point of view of belligerents must be considered as illicit," [3] and the German delegation was one of the five which voted against the proposal.

Gessner is one of the very few German authorities who have pronounced an opinion against the existing practice. The sale of contraband articles to a belligerent is, he contends, a violation of the law of nations, for which the injured belligerent has a right to damages and against which he may resort to reprisals, or even war, in case of persistency.[4] The toleration by the British government in 1870 of the sale of arms to the French was, he says, such a violation, although it was in a measure excusable for the reason that during the Crimean War the Prussian government had allowed the transit of arms through Prussian territory to Russia.

Bluntschli distinguishes between the exportation of arms in large quantities and exportation in small quantities (*zwischen Sendungen im grossen und kleinen*), the former of which a neutral is bound to prevent "when it results from the circumstances that the sending of these articles constitutes a subsidy of war." [5] The German general staff in the *Kriegsbrauch im Landkriege* makes the same distinction.[6] But as Geffcken has pointed out, no valid distinction between the furnishing of arms in large

---

[1] *Die Kriegskontrebande.* See p. 155 for the text of a proposed *projet* concerning the rights and duties of neutral States regarding trade in contraband, art. I, sec. 2 of which declares that "neutrals are not bound to prohibit their citizens from trading in these articles," i.e., articles of a contraband character.

[2] *Handbuch des Positiven Völkerrechts*, sec. 133.

[3] *Actes et Documents*, Vol. III, p. 859.

[4] *Le Droit des Neutres*, p. 126.

[5] *Droit Int. Cod.* (ed. by Lardy), sec. 766. A neutral State, says Bluntschli, is not required to prohibit the exportation *en détail* of arms and munitions, because such trade is of little importance in the relations between belligerents and neutrals, and the responsibility of preventing it would be very difficult if not impossible and would subject the citizens to innumerable vexations. But it is otherwise, he says, in regard to *expéditions en gros*, since they give one of the belligerents a real advantage and often amount to a veritable subsidy.

[6] Pt. III, sec. 3, par. b.

quantities and the furnishing of them in small quantities can be made, both acts being the same in principle.[1]

But one conclusion is possible from this review of the opinions of the leading writers, namely, that the sale by citizens of neutral States of arms and munitions to belligerents has not in the past been regarded as contrary to the accepted notions of neutrality. Only a very few jurists of repute have ever maintained the contrary, and it may be added that most of them are to be found among the older writers. There appears to be no authoritative text writer of the present day except Brusa and Kleen, who advocates the latter view.

§ 549. Practice in Former Wars — American Policy. The practice of neutrals in the past has for the most part been in accordance with the views of the text writers. In all the wars since the United States achieved its independence, its markets have been open to belligerents to purchase without restriction such supplies as they wished. During the Napoleonic wars the French purchased arms and munitions in the United States, and the well-known answer of the secretary of state to the complaints of the British government has been quoted above.

President Pierce in his annual message of December 3, 1854, adverting to the neutrality policy of the United States during the Crimean War, stated that

"During the progress of the present war in Europe, our citizens have without national responsibility . . . sold powder and arms to all buyers regardless of the destination of those articles. . . . The laws of the United States do not forbid their citizens to sell to either of the belligerent powers articles contraband of war or to take munitions of war or soldiers on board their private ships for transportation; and, although in so doing the individual citizen exposes his property or person to some of the hazards of war, his acts do not involve any breach of national neutrality."[2]

President Grant in his proclamation of neutrality of August 22, 1870, issued at the outbreak of the war between Germany and France, stated that American citizens might

"lawfully and without restriction by reason of the aforesaid state of war manufacture and sell within the United States arms and munitions of war

[1] Holtzendorff, *Handbuch*, Bd. IV, p. 690. Cf. also his note on page 351 of Heffter. Numerous other writers have criticised as impracticable if not impossible the attempt to draw a distinction between large and small commercial transactions in respect to the sale of contraband goods. Cf., for example, Lawrence, p. 699; Oppenheim, Vol. II, p. 377, and Snow, *Int. Law*, p. 134.

[2] Richardson, *Messages and Papers of the Presidents*, Vol. V, p. 331.

and other articles known as 'contraband of war,' although," he added, "they could not carry such articles upon the high seas for the use of belligerents without incurring the risk of captn re and the penalties denounced by the law of nations in their behalf." [1]

President Wilson in his neutrality proclamation of August 4, 1914, upon the outbreak of the recent war, reaffirmed, in the identical words of President Grant, the right of American citizens to manufacture and sell arms and munitions of war to belligerents, subject to the same conditions.

But while adopting this view the government of the United States took the position that the sale of arms, munitions and other war supplies did not include the right to transport supplies to belligerent warships on the high seas. In consequence of rumors during the early months of the war that certain vessels were transporting fuel and other supplies from American ports to certain belligerent cruisers at sea, the department of state issued a circular on September 19, 1914, declaring that vessels engaging in such transactions would not be allowed to depart for the reason that such use of American territory would make it a base of operations for belligerent warships. [2]

Likewise the American government took the position that the right of citizens of the United States to sell and export arms and munitions did not include the exportation of weapons the use of which is forbidden by international law. In reply to a communication from the German Ambassador that he had received "information the accuracy of which was undoubted" that eight million cartridges "fitted with mush-room bullets" had been delivered by the union metallic cartridge company for the use of the British army, the secretary of state said:

"If, however, you can furnish the department with evidence that this or any other company are manufacturing and selling for the use of the contending armies in Europe cartridges whose use would contravene the Hague convention, the government would be glad to be furnished with

[1] *Ibid.*, Vol. VII, p. 88.
[2] In a note of the Austro-Hungarian government of June 29, 1915, it was complained that the policy of the American government in preventing the delivery of supplies to German and Austro-Hungarian war vessels on the high seas, while Great Britain and France were free to buy in the United States without restriction, was a departure from the spirit of true neutrality. To this charge of inconsistency Secretary Lansing replied in a note of August 12, 1915, that the prohibition of supplies to ships of war rested on the principle that a neutral power must not permit its territory to become a base for either belligerent.

the evidence, and the President directs me to inform you that in case any American company is shown to be engaged in this traffic, he will use his influence to prevent, so far as possible, sales of such ammunition to the powers engaged in the European war without regard to whether it is the duty of this government upon legal or conventional grounds to take such action."

Similarly, upon complaint of the German ambassador that submarines were being built in the United States by a concern in Seattle for the use of the Entente powers, the government made an investigation and took steps to prevent further deliveries during the war. Finally, when it was found that the Schwab companies were manufacturing submarines to be shipped in parts to Canada where they were to be assembled and put together, the President decided that such transactions constituted a violation of the spirit of neutrality and a promise was obtained from the president of the company that none of the submarines built in his establishments would be delivered until the close of the war.[1]

The policy of the United States, when it was a belligerent, in respect to the right of neutrals to sell and export munitions of war, has uniformly been in accordance with the view which it has defended as a neutral, and it does not appear that in any war in which it was a belligerent formal protest by the government against the furnishing of war supplies to the enemy was ever made. During the Civil war, large quantities of arms, munitions, and other supplies were purchased by both belligerents in England and on the Continent.[2] It is true that the case of the United States before the Geneva Arbitration Tribunal

[1] Upon reports that hydro-aeroplanes were being built in the United States for the use of the Entente powers, the German ambassador in a communication dated January 19, 1915, took the position that they were to be regarded as war vessels, the sale of which to belligerents was contrary to art. 8 of the thirteenth convention of the Second Hague Conference. They were not mentioned by name in the convention, he said, because there were none in existence at the time. Secretary Bryan in a note of January 29, 1915, dissented from the view that hydro-aeroplanes were vessels merely because they rise from and alight upon the sea. They were, he said, essentially air craft, and could be used for military purposes in the air only. Mr. Bryan also took occasion to call the attention of the ambassador to the fact that air craft had been placed by the German government on its list of conditional contraband, "for which no special treatment involving neutral duty . . had been provided by treaty to which the United States was a signatory or adhering power." Cf. the correspondence in *Amer. Jour. of Int. Law*, Special supp., July, 1915, pp. 366–368.

[2] The facts relating to these transactions are fully narrated in the British and American cases submitted to the Geneva Tribunal. Cf. also a summary in Moore,

of 1872 asserted that "a neutral ought not to permit a belligerent to use the neutral soil as the main if not the only base of its military supplies, during a long and bloody contest, as the soil of Great Britain was used by the insurgents," [1] but this fact was alleged along with numerous others merely as particular evidence of the general unfriendliness and laxity of the British government in the observance of its obligations of neutrality.

It is of course true that there have been a few embargoes laid by the United States on the exportation of arms and munitions. Such prohibitions were laid in 1862 and 1898 when the United States was a belligerent, in the interest of national defence. In 1905 the exportation of arms and munitions to San Domingo was prohibited and, as is well known, a similar embargo in 1912 was placed on shipments of arms and munitions to Mexico, but neither was in fact a neutrality measure.

§ 550. **British and French Practice.** The practice of Great Britain has been similar to that of the United States. Prohibitions on the sale of arms and munitions have occasionally been laid in pursuance of treaty stipulations, as in 1822 during the war between Spain and her South American colonies and in 1848 during the war between Denmark and Prussia; [2] or when Great Britain was herself a belligerent, as during the Crimean War and at the outbreak of the recent war. The only instance of a departure from the general practice appears to have been the order in council of September 30, 1825, issued at the outbreak of the war between Greece and Turkey [3] forbidding for a period

---

History and Digest of International Arbitrations, Vol. I, p. 620. Montague Bernard in his *Historical Account of the Neutrality of Great Britain during the American Civil War* (pp. 330–332) states that the export of arms and military stores from Great Britain to both Northern and Southern ports "went on freely without intermission as long as the contest lasted." The British case before the Geneva Arbitration Tribunal states that "extra supplies of small arms, percussion caps, cannon and other ordnance, saltpeter, lead, clothing, and other war-like stores, representing a value of not less than £2,000,000 of which £500,000 were for muskets and rifles alone, were exported from England to the Northern parts of the United States during the Civil War." Moore, I, 620.

[1] Alabama Claims, Case of the U. S., Part V, p. 125.

[2] The embargo of 1822 was laid in pursuance of an old treaty with Spain by which it was stipulated that neither party would in case of war permit the exportation of arms to the enemy of the other; that of 1848 was laid in consequence of treaties concluded between Great Britain and Denmark in 1670, 1780, and 1814. Calvo, Vol. IV, sec. 2627, and Gessner, p. 129.

[3] In pursuance of an Act of Parliament passed in the 29th year of George II.

of six months the exportation of arms and warlike stores to any port beyond the seas, except by leave of the Crown. No reason for the prohibition was given further than that it was "judged necessary." [1] Notwithstanding the urgent plea of the Duke of Wellington in 1826 that it should be renewed in the interest of neutrality, the government declined to do so. George Canning, minister of foreign affairs, in a letter dated August 4, 1826, explaining the reason for the refusal of the government to renew the order, declared that

"Neutrality that is as completely observed by *permitting* export to the belligerents as by *prohibiting* it to both; but to *allow* it to one and to *refuse* it to the other may be very wise, or very courteous, or very praiseworthy, but it certainly would not be neutral. But whatever be the merit of the case, my business was to state the law as it is; and I must authorize Stratford so to say, if he is to state the case of his country truly." [2]

During the Franco-German war of 1870-1871 Count Bernstorff called the attention of Earl Granville to the act of 1853 authorizing the crown in its discretion to prohibit the exportation of war materials and urged the government to prohibit the sale and exportation of arms and munitions which were being supplied in large quantities to the French government. There was no question, he asserted, but that

"France had wantonly made war on Germany. The verdict of the world and especially the verdict of the statesmen as well as of the public of England has unconsciously pronounced the Emperor of the French guilty of a most flagitious breach of the peace. Germany, on the other hand, entered into the contest with the consciousness of a good cause. She was therefore led to expect that the neutrality of Great Britain, her former ally against Napoleonic aggression, however strict in form, would at least be *benevolent in spirit* to Germany, for it is impossible for the human mind not to side with one or the other party in a conflict like the present one. What is the use of being right or wrong in the eyes of the world if the public remains insensible to the merits of a cause? Those who deny the necessity of such a distinction, forego the appeal to public opinion which we are daily taught to consider as the foremost of the great powers."

" In the face of the continuous export of arms, munitions, coal, and other war material from Great Britain to France," Count Bernstorff went on to say, "in the face of facts openly made a boast of by the French minister of war and not denied by the

[1] Cf. the text in *British and Foreign State Papers*, Vol. XII, p. 529.
[2] Wellington, Despatches, Vol. III, 3d Series, p. 364, cited by Gessner, *Droit des Neutres*, p. 131.

British government, it is not necessary to prove that the neutrality of Great Britain, far from being impartial to that party which has been pronounced to be in the right, is, on the contrary, such as it might possibly have been if that party had been wrong in the eyes of the British people and government." The nation would be morally responsible for the blood which was being shed through the agency of rapacious individuals who were making fortunes out of a trade which was condemned by the nation. England was "feeding" a war which would have ended sooner had France been left dependent on her own resources; hence the policy of the British government was if not intentionally, at least practically, benevolent to France, notwithstanding the fact that the verdict of popular opinion was against the cause for which France was fighting.

To this communication Earl Granville replied on September 15,[1] saying that the propositions of the Prussian Ambassador amounted to a demand that British neutrality should be both in spirit and in practice benevolent toward Prussia and consequently, as it would seem, unfavorable toward France. The idea of "benevolent neutrality," he added, was new and its meaning and practical effect would have to be explained.

"The Prussian ambassador could not be understood as laying down a principle applicable only to the present war; rules of international law could not be confined to exceptional cases, they must be of general application to all wars. If the Prussian proposition were admitted, it would be the duty of every neutral government at the beginning of a war to determine which belligerent was favored by public opinion of its subjects and then assume an attitude of benevolent neutrality toward that belligerent. Such a policy would lead to insuperable difficulties. Where could the line be drawn between a departure from the usual practice, in order to confer material advantages on one belligerent state to the exclusion of the other, and a participation in hostilities? It seems hardly to admit of doubt that neutrality when it once departs from strict impartiality, runs the risk of altering its essence, and the moment a neutral allows his proceedings to be biassed by a predilection for one of two belligerents, he ceases to be neutral. The idea, therefore, of benevolent neutrality can mean little less than the extinction of neutrality."[2]

---

[1] Text in *Briish and Foreign State Papers*, Vol. 61, pp. 759 ff.

[2] Commenting on this proposition of the Prussian ambassador, Westlake, in an article on the "Export of Contraband of War" (*Collected Papers*, p. 374) remarks: "He assumes that the cause of Germany is just, that the public opinion, and even the statesmen of England have recognized its justice and that therefore we should furnish not a strict neutrality; but one which should be calculated to give effective

Earl Granville then turned to the conduct of the Prussian government during the Crimean War, during the whole of which war "arms and other contraband of war were copiously supplied to Russia by the States of the Zollverein, regular agents for the traffic in which being established at Berlin, Magdeburg, Thorn, Königsberg, Bromberg and other places." No restraint was put upon their operations, notwithstanding the fact that the Prussian government had issued a decree in March, 1854, prohibiting the transit of arms from other countries through Prussia, and another decree in March, 1855, prohibiting also the transit of other contraband. When the attention of the Prussian government was called by the government of Her Majesty to its negligence in enforcing these decrees to the injury of Great Britain, which was then at war with Russia, the Prussian government replied, not that it was justified in permitting these exports on the principle of "benevolent neutrality," but that it could not interfere with the course of trade,— an answer, said Earl Granville, which would "seem to have been based rather on the principle that the first duty of Prussia as a neutral, was to consider the interests of her own subjects, not those of the subjects of a country which had engaged itself in a war with which Prussia had no concern."

Many German writers maintain that the conduct of the British government during the Franco-Prussian War was not in accord with the spirit of neutrality,[1] but others like Geffcken [2] and von Bar [3] do not consider that the German complaint was well founded. The policy of the British government was ably defended by Sir William Harcourt under the pseudonym of *Historicus* in a series of letters to the *Times;* but public opinion

---

expression to our real or supposed sentiments in favor of his country." Westlake adds that considering the circumstances, the first elements of the act of persuasion would have dictated an appeal in the name of strict neutrality rather than in that of a benevolent neutrality.

[1] For example, Bluntschli, *Droit Int. Cod.*, p. 442; Gessner, *Kriegsführende und Neutrale Mächte*, p. 77; also his *Le Droit des Neutres sur Mer*, p. 133; Kusserow, *Les Devoirs d'un Gouvernement Neutre, Rev. de Droit Int.*, Vol. VI (1874), p. 64, and Gotha, *La Question des Exportations d'Armes Anglaises* (1871). Perels, *Droit Mar. Int.*, discusses the question but expresses no opinion.

[2] *Der Handel mit Waffen und Kriegsmaterial* in Holtzendorff's *Handbuch*, Bd. IV, pp. 692 ff.; also his edition of Heffter, p. 350, note.

[3] *Observations sur la Contrebande de Guerre, Rev. de Droit Int.*, Vol. XXVI (1894), p. 405.

in England was by no means unanimous in support of the government. During the wars since 1870 British policy has been substantially the same.[1]

French practice has been substantially the same as that of Great Britain and the United States. By an act of the French Parliament of April 13, 1895, the government was authorized to prohibit the exportation of arms by individuals whenever it should judge such a measure to be necessary to the interests of the country. But apparently the authority thus conferred has not been exercised during any of the wars since that date.[2]

§ 551. German Practice. In view of the Austrian and German attacks upon the policy of the American government in permitting the sale and exportation of arms and munitions during the late war, a review of their own practice in some of the more important recent wars will not be inappropriate. The open toleration by the Prussian government during the Crimean War of the transportation through Prussian territory of large quantities of war supplies from Belgium to Russia, notwithstanding that such traffic had been forbidden by two decrees of the

---

[1] In a petition addressed to the President and Congress of the United States during the recent war and alleged to have been signed by 1,000,000 American citizens, the statement was made that "on April 23, 1898, after the Spanish-American war had begun, the British government placed an embargo on munitions of war." This statement, like many others made by the embargo propagandists, was erroneous. The queen's neutrality proclamation of April 23 warned British subjects that if any of them presumed to do any acts in derogation of their duty as neutral subjects or in violation or contravention of the law of nations, and more especially by breaking a blockade, or by carrying officers, soldiers, despatches, arms, munitions, military stores, or articles deemed contraband according to the law of nations, for the use of either belligerent, all such persons so offending, together with their ships and goods, would rightfully incur and be justly liable to hostile capture and to the penalties denounced by the law of nations. (Cf. the text in *Proclamations and Decrees of Neutrality in the War with Spain*, published by the United States government, p. 35.) It will be noted that the proclamation did not prohibit British subjects from transporting contraband to either belligerent, and no penalty was prescribed for doing such acts. There is merely the customary warning usually found in neutrality proclamations that those who engage in contraband trade are exposed to the loss of their ships and goods through capture and confiscation by one of the belligerents. The English colony of Jamaica in fact is said to have become the chief source of supply for the Spanish army in Cuba, and except for a mild protest from the American consul at Kingston, no complaint was made by any official of the United States. Benton, *International Law and Diplomacy of the Spanish-American War*, pp. 195-196.

[2] See Bonfils, *Droit Int. Pub.*, p. 891. "During the Russo-Japanese war of 1904–1905," says Bonfils, "the exportation of arms from France to Russia took place freely."

Prussian government, has already been referred to. During the American Civil War both belligerents bought supplies in Germany and Austria. Soon after the outbreak of the war the Confederate government sent Major Caleb Huse to Europe to buy and make contracts for arms and munitions.[1] Major Huse subsequently published a pamphlet entitled "The Supplies for the Confederate Army; How they were obtained in Europe and How Paid For,"[2] in which he described his purchases in various countries of Europe, and particularly in Austria where he purchased "100,000 rifles of the latest Austrian pattern, ten batteries of field artillery and a quantity of ammunition all to be delivered on a ship at Hamburg."[3]

It was widely asserted by German sympathizers in the United States that during the war between Spain and the United States Germany forbade the exportation of arms and munitions to Spain.[4] This assertion was based on a passage in the Autobiography of Andrew D. White,[5] but the facts show that the contrary was the case. Dr. White in a recent letter explaining the incident to which he refers in his Autobiography, stated that the particular vessel which he requested the German foreign office to search, although laden with contraband "after a brief wait proceeded on her way" (to Spain), and that "our agents at Hamburg informed me later that during the entire war, vessels freely carried munitions from German ports both to Spain and to the United States, and that neither of the belligerents made any remonstrance."[6] When the department of state learned of the incident, it instructed the American Ambassador

---

[1] Jefferson Davis, *Rise and Fall of the Confederate Government*, Vol. I, p. 311. Speaking of the purchase of arms in Europe during the Civil war, Bernard (*British Neutrality during the American Civil War*, p. 331) says, "Many rifles were also imported from Prussia." The British case before the Geneva Arbitration Tribunal in 1872 stated that "large quantities of arms were purchased by the United States in France, Austria, and other neutral countries." Moore, *History and Digest of International Arbitrations*, Vol. I, p. 620.

[2] Boston, T. R. Marvin and Son, 1904.

[3] Pp. 26–27.

[4] This assertion was made by Mr. Vollmer in the House of Representatives on March 4, 1915 (*Cong. Rec.*, App., p. 736). Cf. also the New York *Evening Mail* of January 27, 1916, and the petition of 1,000,000 American citizens (*Cong. Rec.*, January 27, 1916, p. 1743).

[5] Ch. XIV, pp. 168–169.

[6] This letter is dated October 6, 1915, and was addressed to W. B. Blake of New York City. It was printed in the New York *Times* of January 29, 1916.

to ascertain whether or not there were "any laws or regulations in force in Germany forbidding the shipment of contraband of war," in order that if there existed such laws or regulations the American government might be so informed so as to avoid the embarrassments which might arise if it should decide to protest against the action of neutral governments in permitting contraband articles to be shipped from their ports. The Ambassador reported that there were no such laws or regulations in force, and the matter was therefore dropped.[1] It appears that the German government never issued any proclamation of neutrality, that it never took any steps whatever to prevent the sale and exportation of arms and munitions to either belligerent, and that in fact German manufacturers sold such articles freely to the Spanish government.

During the Boer War large quantities of war material were sold to the British government by manufacturers and merchants of both Austria and Germany. Although the sympathies of the people of Austria and Germany were overwhelmingly on the side of the Boers, that did not "prevent England from obtaining in Germany the quick-firing guns which she needed so badly and from Austria the big howitzers which it was thought would be required for the siege of Pretoria."[2]

German and Austrian dealers were of course quite willing to sell to the Burghers of the South African Republics, although the situation of the Boers was almost identical with that of Germany and Austria in 1915; that is to say, they were commercially isolated by the British navy and were prevented from buying arms from neutrals. The German and Austro-Hungarian governments did not then consider that "parity of treatment" required them to prohibit the sale and export of war supplies for the use of the British forces. They proceeded on the principle which the government of the United States then laid down[3]

---

[1] Cf. extracts from the correspondence relating to the incident and appropriate comment by William C. Dennis in the *Annals of the American Academy of Political and Social Science*, July, 1915, pp. 13-14; cf. also an official statement of the secretary of state regarding the matter, published in the daily press of April 23, 1915.

[2] Spaight, *War Rights on Land*, p. 478.

[3] It appears that in November, 1899, Dr. Hendrick Müller, envoy extraordinary of the Orange Free State at The Hague, complained to the American minister to The Netherlands that the shipment of war materials from the United States on a large scale to Great Britain was contrary to the law of nations and urged him to

and upon which it subsequently acted under identical circumstances. Likewise during the Russo-Japanese war there were large exportations of arms, artillery, munitions and coal from Germany to Russia, and it was charged that the German government failed to prevent, if it did not directly or indirectly encourage, the sale to Russia of a number of transatlantic steamers belonging to its auxiliary navy, and that it permitted the exportation overland of torpedo boats to Russia, the several parts of the vessels being exported as half-finished manufactures and put together in Libau, Russia, — this for the purpose of disguising the real nature of the transactions and thus avoiding the charge of non-conformity to the technical rules of neutrality relating to the sale of war vessels to belligerents.[1]

During the Turco-Italian War, German arms and munitions were sold and exported in large quantities to the Ottoman government, and during the Balkan Wars German and Austrian markets were the principal sources of supply for all the belligerents. It is probably safe to say that no other country had developed such an extensive system of industries for the manufacture of war material as Germany, or had supplied the needs of belligerents on such a large scale. Indeed, there appears to be no instance in which the German government ever prohibited the sale and exportation of such articles to belligerents,[2] and but one instance in which Austria-Hungary had done so.[3]

Finally, it is well known that Germany purchased military and other supplies in the United States during the early weeks of the recent war and until the American supply was cut off by Great Britain. Moreover, it may be added that after the entrance of Turkey into the war, large quantities of German-made war supplies were shipped through the neutral territory

---

remonstrate with the American government against the continuance of the traffic. Secretary Hay on December 15, 1899, replied to the communication of the American minister, saying that in view of the fact that the law and practice of the United States was then settled in favor of the right of neutrals to sell and export contraband goods to belligerents, it was not considered necessary to investigate the charges of Dr. Müller.

[1] These charges were made by certain socialist members of the *Reichstag* and were widely published in the newspapers of the time. Cf. Hershey, *International Law and Diplomacy of the Russo-Japanese War*, pp. 91–92.

[2] The embargo during the Crimean war, referred to above, applied only to the transit through Prussia of arms from foreign countries.

[3] This was during the Franco-German war of 1870–1871.

of Roumania for the use of the Ottoman government, and when in the middle of the year 1915 the Roumanian government, in pursuance of the Hague convention respecting the rights and duties of neutrals (Arts. 2–5), issued an order prohibiting the transit of arms and munitions through its territory for the use of belligerents, the German government complained that the embargo was an unneutral act resorted to with a view to aiding the Allies, under whose pressure (after the entrance of Italy into the war) the Roumanian policy of benevolent neutrality toward Germany had been abandoned.

§ 552. **Instances of Embargoes on the Exportation of Arms and Munitions.** Thus it will be seen that the general practice of neutral States has been to permit their nationals to sell and export arms and munitions to belligerents, and this privilege has been freely exercised during most of the wars of the past. There have, however, been a few departures from this general practice. Thus, during the Franco-German War of 1870, Belgium, Switzerland, Austria-Hungary, Denmark, Spain, Italy, the Netherlands, and Japan are said to have issued proclamations forbidding the transportation of arms and munitions to both belligerents.[1]

Upon the outbreak of the war between Spain and the United States in 1898, the government of Brazil "prohibited absolutely" the exportation of war material from Brazilian ports to those of either belligerent, under the Brazilian flag or any other flag.[2] Likewise the King of Denmark, by a proclamation of April 29, forbade Danish subjects "to transport contraband of war to either of the belligerent Powers," although it did not prohibit the sale thereof.[3] The governor of Curaçao, acting on the instructions of the Dutch government, published a decree forbidding the exportation of arms, munitions, or other war materials to either belligerent.[4] The Portuguese government by a decree of April 29, declared that articles of lawful commerce belonging to the subjects of belligerent Powers might be

---

[1] Bluntschli, sec. 766, and Rivier, *Droit des Gens*, Vol. II, p. 412. Rivier says all the States mentioned above issued such prohibitions, but Kleen does not include Austria-Hungary, Denmark, Spain, Italy, or the Netherlands in the list which he gives. *Lois et Usages*, Vol. I, p. 382, and *Contrebande de Guerre*, pp. 52, 68. Bonfils, secs. 1472 and 1474, mentions only Belgium, Switzerland, and The Netherlands.
[2] *Proclamations and Decrees during the War with Spain*, p. 13.
[3] *Ibid.*, p. 22.　　　　[4] *Ibid.*, p. 27.

transported under the Portuguese flag, and that such articles belonging to Portuguese subjects could be transported under the flag of either belligerent, but "goods which could be considered as contraband of war" were expressly excluded from this privilege.[1]

Upon the outbreak of the recent war, embargoes on the exportation of arms were laid by a number of States, although Brazil appears to have been the only one outside Europe that adopted such a policy.[2] The other embargoes were laid by various neutral States of Europe, notably Denmark, Norway, Sweden, Switzerland, Spain, and the Netherlands. They were, however, erroneously regarded by some persons as neutrality measures. In fact, they were laid partly under pressure from Great Britain, with a view to protecting their over-sea commerce from the measures adopted by the British government, and partly for the purpose of conserving their own supply of arms, munitions, and other commodities, with a view to the eventual possibility of their being forced into the war.[3]

It is clear, therefore, that no argument in favor of an embargo on the sale and exportation of arms, as a measure of neutrality, can be drawn from these precedents.

§ 553. Protests of the German and Austrian Governments in 1915. But it was argued that the situation to which the recent war gave rise was wholly different from that in any preceding war, and hence the same standards of neutrality could not be applied. Thus in a memorandum delivered by the German Ambassador at Washington, on April 4, 1915, to the secretary of state, it was said that,

"The situation in the present war differs from that of any previous war. Therefore any reference to arms furnished by Germany in former

[1] *Ibid.*, p. 61.

[2] It appears that Brazil has general rules of neutrality governing trade in contraband, art. IV of which "absolutely forbids" the exportation of arms and munitions of war from Brazil to any belligerent under the Brazilian or any other flag. Cf. an article by Señor Da Gama, Brazilian ambassador to the United States, in the *Annals of the American Academy of Political and Social Science*, July, 1915, pp. 147 ff.

[3] Cf. the remarks of Prof. J. B. Moore, who, referring to the above-mentioned embargoes, says: "In reality they are essentially regulations of a domestic nature, employed for the purpose of preserving a proper supply of articles, even arms and munitions of war, in the countries concerned." *Annals of the American Academy of Political and Social Science*, July, 1915, p. 146.

wars is not justified, for then it was not a question *whether* war material should be supplied to the belligerents, but *who* should supply it in competition with other nations. In the present war all nations having a war material industry worth mentioning are either involved in the war themselves or are engaged in perfecting their own armaments, and have therefore laid an embargo against the exportation of war material. The United States is accordingly the only neutral country in a position to furnish war materials. The conception of neutrality is thereby given a new purport, independently of the formal question of hitherto existing law. In contradiction thereto, the United States is building up a powerful arms industry in the broadest sense, the existing plants not only being worked but enlarged by all available means, and new ones built. The international conventions for the protection of the rights of neutral nations doubtless sprang from the necessity of protecting the existing industries of neutral nations as far as possible from injury in their business. But it can in no event be in accordance with the spirit of true neutrality if, under the protection of such international stipulations, an entirely new industry is created in a neutral state, such as is the development of the arms industry in the United States, the business whereof, under the present conditions, can benefit only the belligerent powers."

The willingness of American manufacturers and merchants to sell to Germany, said the Ambassador, did not alter the case. The fact was that sales and deliveries were being made to but one side, that a new and vast industry had suddenly sprung into existence under the artificial stimulus of the English, French, and Russian demand for arms and munitions, and that the United States had been transformed into a veritable arsenal for the supply of the armed forces of Germany's enemies, a supply upon which Germany and her allies could not draw.

The Austro-Hungarian government likewise, in a note of June 29, 1915, complained that the industry of manufacturing arms and munitions in America had "soared to unimagined heights."

"In order to turn out the huge quantities of arms, ammunition, and other war material of every description ordered in the past months by Great Britain and her allies from the United States, not only the full capacity of the existing plants, but also their transformation and enlargement, and the creation of new larger plants, as well as a flocking of workmen of all trades into that branch of industry; in brief, far-reaching changes of economic life encompassing the whole country, became necessary."

§ 554. **Their Contentions Analyzed.** It must of course be admitted that the situation to which the recent war gave rise was quite different from that created by the smaller wars of the past, but in fact the difference was not one of principle, but rather one of degree. If the legal right of neutrals to sell arms and munitions to belligerents be admitted, and apparently neither the German nor the Austro-Hungarian government denied the existence of this right as a general principle of law,[1] it would seem difficult in practice to introduce a distinction between the right to sell and export in small quantities and the right to sell and export in large quantities. Likewise the distinction between the sale of supplies produced by establishments already in existence at the outbreak of the war and the sale of those produced by newly created industries is not a sound principle for distinguishing between neutral and unneutral conduct. In effect, the distinction is similar to that made by Bluntschli and the German General Staff in the *Kriegsbrauch im Landkriege* between sales *en gros* and sales *en détail*. Like most quantitative distinctions, it is more or less arbitrary, rests upon no juridical principle, and the attempt to apply a rule based on such a distinction would in practice lead to insuperable difficulties, as the German writers Geffcken and von Bar, as well as many others in England and America, have pointed out.

Likewise, the contention put forward by the German and Austro-Hungarian governments that the conception of neutrality was given a "new aspect" by the fact that in the recent war the markets of but a single State became the chief, if not the sole, source of foreign supply for the belligerents, cannot be admitted to be sound. Such a contention rests on the assumption that traffic in arms and munitions is legitimate, so long as the markets of other neutral Powers are open to belligerents, but that it ceases to be consistent with the spirit of neutrality the moment the number of such States is reduced to one. It is tantamount to maintaining that while all or several neutral Powers may permit the sale and exportation of war materials, one alone may not do so.

[1] The German government, in a note of December 15, 1914, had already stated that "under the general principles of international law no exception can be taken to neutral states letting war material go to Germany's enemies from or through neutral territory."

Cf. also the remarks of Dr. Dernburg before the American Academy of Political and Social Science in the *Annals* of the Academy, July, 1915, p. 195: "I want to state here most emphatically that Germany at no time has disputed the right to ship and sell arms."

Similarly, the view advanced that since the quantity of arms and munitions sold to belligerents in former wars was comparitively small, the practice in those wars cannot be regarded as precedents to justify a traffic of such proportions as that which the business assumed in the late war, ignores the difference in the magnitude of those wars and that of the recent conflict. It was stated by the British minister of munitions that less ammunition was used by the British forces during the entire Boer War than was consumed in a single well-known battle during the late war.

In a note of July 16, 1915, the German Imperial government made a plea for an equalization of advantages as between the Entente allies and the Central powers:

"While a trade in arms existed between American manufacturers and Germany's enemies estimated at many hundred million marks, the German government had not made any charge of a *formal breach of neutrality*. The German government could not, however, do otherwise than to emphasize that they were placed at a great disadvantage through the fact that the neutral powers have hitherto achieved little or no success in the assertion of their lawful right of trade with Germany, whereas they make unlimited use of their right to tolerate trade in contraband with England and Germany's other enemies. Admitting that it is the express right of neutrals not to protect their lawful trade with Germany, and even to allow themselves knowingly and willingly to be ordered by England to restrict such trade, it is on the other hand not less their good right, although unfortunately not exercised, to stop trade in contraband, especially the trade in arms, with Germany's enemies. . . . In regard to the latter point (contraband trade especially in war materials by neutral merchant vessels), the German government ventures to hope that the American government upon reconsideration will see their way clear to a measure of intervention in accordance with *the spirit of true neutrality*."

Again in the memorandum of April 4, 1915, the German Imperial government observed that, "It is necessary to take into consideration not only the formal aspect of the case, but also *the spirit in which the neutrality is carried out*"; and further that "If it is the will of the American people that there shall be *a true neutrality* the United States will find the means of preventing this *one-sided* supplying of arms, or at least of utilizing it to protect legitimate trade with Germany, especially that in food-stuffs." Likewise the Austro-Hungarian government in a note of June 29, 1915, raised the question whether in view of the "absolute exclusion" of Germany and Austria-Hungary from the markets of America, it "would now seem possible, even imperative, that appropriate measures be adopted toward bringing into full effect the desire of the Federal government to maintain an attitude of strict parity with respect to both belligerent parties."

It will be seen from these extracts that the German and Austro-Hungarian governments did not allege any violation of the letter of the law governing the rights and duties of neutrals, but they contended that the sale of arms to one belligerent when the fortunes of war had deprived the other of access to neutral markets was contrary to the spirit of neutrality, and the inequality of opportunity thus resulting should have been removed by the neutral through an embargo on sales to all belligerents; that is, a "strict parity" should have been restored and the disadvantages of one eliminated by depriving the other of the fruits of a victory which he had won through his superior naval power. To this somewhat extraordinary contention, Secretary Lansing replied in a note of August 12, 1915, that the American government could not accede to such a proposition:

"The recognition of an obligation of this sort, unknown to the international practice of the past, would impose upon every neutral nation a duty to sit in judgment on the progress of a war and to restrict its commercial intercourse with a belligerent whose naval successes prevented the neutral from trade with the enemy. . . . Manifestly the idea of strict neutrality now advanced by the Imperial and Royal government would involve a neutral nation in a mass of perplexities which would obscure the whole field of international obligation, produce economic confusion and deprive all commerce and industry of legitimate fields of enterprise, already heavily burdened by the unavoidable restrictions of war."

As has been said, the situation of the South African Republics during the Boer War was practically identical with that of Germany and Austria-Hungary during the late war. Great Britain had succeeded in commercially isolating those republics and depriving them of access to neutral markets, but the German government at the time did not consider it a violation of the spirit of neutrality to permit German manufacturers to sell and export arms to one of the belligerents when the fortunes of war had deprived the other of access to German markets. As Secretary Lansing in his reply to the Austro-Hungarian remonstrance pertinently remarked,

"If at that time Austria-Hungary and her present ally had refused to sell arms and ammunition to Great Britain, on the ground that to do so would violate the spirit of strict neutrality, the Imperial and Royal government might with greater consistency and greater force urge its present contention."

§ 555. The Question of Moral Obligation to Forbid Such Trade. But apart from the special circumstances of the late war, which it was urged, made it desirable to alter the existing rule, it was argued that there were general considerations of morality and public policy which condemned the present practice. The furnishing of arms and munitions to belligerents, it was contended, was contrary not only to the spirit of genuine neutrality, but also to the best standards of international ethical conduct as well as to sound principles of national and international policy. Thus Senator Works of California in a speech in the Senate on January 27, 1916 said:

"I believe the trade to be immoral and demoralizing to the people of the United States. I believe that most of the complications that have grown up between this and foreign nations now at war have been the result of the trade in munitions of war. I believe that if it had not been for the fact that we are dealing in that nefarious trade, the people upon the *Lusitania* would not have lost their lives. We have in effect made our country a party to the war across the ocean. It is our ammunition, our shot and shell, that are taking the lives of the citizens and subjects of friendly nations in Europe. We cannot justify ourselves in that position or in that trade by saying that it is allowed by the laws of neutrality. There is something higher that should control the people of the United States than the mere strict law of neutrality." [1]

It was the veriest cant and hypocrisy, it was said, for a people to pray for peace on Sunday and during the rest of the week devote their energies and resources to the manufacture of the instruments of death for the perpetuation of a struggle in which millions of lives were being sacrificed. Besides prolonging

[1] *Cong. Rec.*, 64th Cong., 1st sess., p. 1797. Cf. also the remarks of Senator Kenyon to the same effect, *ibid.*, p. 1793; of Senator LaFollette, *ibid.*, p. 1800; of Senator Ashurst, *ibid.*, p. 1796; of Senator Robinson, *ibid.*, p. 1797; of Representative Ricketts, *ibid.*, pp. 2657–2658; of Senator Hitchcock, *ibid.*, 63d Cong. 3d sess., p. 3938; of Representative Porter, *ibid.*, App., pp. 583–585; of Representative Vollmer, *ibid.*, App., pp. 735–736. Cf. also a pamphlet entitled *Private Property and the Nation's Honor*, by Aked and Rauschenbuch; Burgess, *The European War*, ch. VII; an article by von Mach, "The German View Point," Boston *Transcript*, April 14, 1915, and Butte, *Proceedings of the American Society of International Law*, 1915, p. 129.

the duration of the war and swelling the volume of the rivers of blood, the effect of such traffic was to array citizens of a common country against one another, arouse animosities, provoke the enmity of foreign nations, and lay the foundations for future international controversies.[1]

Furthermore, it was asked, why should it be regarded as unneutral for a government to sell arms and munitions to belligerents, but entirely consistent with neutrality for a government to allow its citizens to do so? Why maintain a double standard of conduct, one for the State and another for the citizens who compose it? "International law," said Senator Hitchcock in the Senate on February 17, 1915,[2] "is entirely out of harmony with the spirit of the age in permitting this traffic. . . . It relates to a time and has its roots in an age when war was the legitimate method of settling international disputes."

§ 556. **Analysis of the Arguments.** Space does not permit an extended discussion of all these points, but I venture to offer a few observations on some of them.

First of all, it is submitted that the presumption must be largely in favor of the morality of a rule of international conduct which has been approved by the leading jurists and text writers from Gentilis to the present time, with only a few exceptions, and which has been generally followed in practice by States and sanctioned by international agreement to which practically all the States of the world are parties. If authority, practice, and convention count for anything in determining the general consensus in respect to the validity of a rule of conduct, the present rule rests on solid foundations of morality and public policy, national and international.

I venture also to raise the question whether ethically there is any substantial ground for a distinction between the sale of arms and munitions in time of war to be used immediately by a belligerent for killing his enemies, and sales in time of peace for the purpose of putting him in readiness for killing possible

---

[1] "I believe," said Senator Hitchcock in the Senate on February 17, 1915 (*Cong. Rec.*, p. 3939), "the United States should put a stop to this horrible traffic, not because of the effect it may have upon the European war, but because of the effect that it is having among our own people, the effect it is having in stirring up hate, in arousing prejudices, in destroying neutrality, and in dissipating the American spirit, which before the war was welding us into a common people."

[2] *Cong. Rec.*, p. 3938.

enemies at some future time. If war is admitted to be a legitimate mode of settling international controversies, it seems difficult to deny the morality of making and selling the instruments by which it is carried on; and if it is not immoral to furnish them before an army takes the field, it is not immoral to do so afterwards.[1]

Moreover, if it is ethically permissible to furnish a belligerent with cloth for making uniforms, cotton and other materials for making explosives, coal for supplying warships, mules for drawing artillery, and other materials without which war cannot be carried on, why is it any more reprehensible morally to sell him arms and munitions? Ethically there is no sound basis for such a distinction; yet most of the proposed embargo measures introduced in Congress in 1915 proposed to prohibit only the sale and exportation of arms and munitions.

No line of distinction, as the late Professor Westlake declared, can be drawn between the sale of munitions, on the one hand, and other articles, which, though not directly employed for killing men, are essential to belligerents in the carrying on of war. "No principle can turn on the degree of utility of the article sold, or on the degree of proximity in which its employment contributes to the physical act of killing or wounding."[2] If the principles of morality or considerations of neutrality require prohibition of the sale of the one class of articles they require equally a prohibition of the sale of the other; but if both classes should be prohibited, where is the line between prohibited and innocent goods to be drawn? As Earl Granville pointed out in his note of September 15, 1870, to Count Bernstorff:

"In the American Civil war no cargoes would have been more useful to the Southern States than cloth, leather, and quinine. It would be difficult for a neutral and obviously impossible for a belligerent to draw the line. Moreover, articles invaluable to a belligerent at one time may be valueless at another, and *vice versa*. Is the neutral to watch the shifting phases and vary his restrictions in accordance with them?"[3]

In view of the German attack upon the trade in arms and

[1] Cf. on this point the remarks of Prof. T. S. Woolsey in an article entitled "Case for the Munitions Trade," *Leslie's Weekly*, July 29, 1915.

[2] *Collected Papers*, pp. 379-380.

[3] *British and Foreign State Papers*, Vol. 61, p. 765.

munitions, it may be interesting to quote the views of a highly respected German jurist, and one of the most eminent authorities on international law, Professor von Bar, of Göttingen. After dwelling at length upon the serious injuries which an embargo would inflict upon the industries of neutral nations, as well as the difficulties which would be encountered in the enforcement of such a measure, he proceeds to consider the moral aspects of the question. On this point he says:

"It is wrong, therefore, to denounce, as has often been done, the sale of arms by neutrals to belligerents, as a business which pollutes the hands and honor of neutral countries. This phrase has no more force than a tirade launched against a fire insurance company, on the ground that it is engaged in a miserable business which draws its profits from the misfortunes of others." [1]

§ 557. Practical Difficulties in the Way of Prohibition. Admitting, however, that the present practice is objectionable on moral grounds, as well as for reasons connected with the maintenance of a policy of strict neutrality, there are several practical difficulties which stand in the way of the proposed change. The first of these is the difficulty of enforcing prohibitory trade measures. As Earl Granville in his reply to Count Bernstorff in 1870 pointed out, if the exportation of arms and munitions were prohibited by law, they would be exported clandestinely, to prevent which it would be necessary "to establish an expensive, intricate, and inquisitorial customs system, under which all suspicious packages, no matter what their assumed destination, would be opened and examined." "Moreover," he said, "it would cause infinite delay and obstruction to innocent trade." [2]

The difficulty of preventing such trade, Earl Granville went on to say, had been abundantly shown during the Crimean War. The Prussian government had by decree forbidden the transit through Prussian territory to Russia of arms and munitions, but the customs authorities were powerless to prevent violations of the law. If the Prussian authorities could not

---

[1] These views of von Bar are set forth in an article entitled, *Observations sur la Contrebande de Guerre*, published in the *Rev. de Droit Int. et de Lég. Comp.*, Vol. XXVI (1894), pp. 401 ff.
[2] *British and Foreign State Papers*, Vol. 61, p. 674.

prevent such traffic across a land frontier, it would be still more difficult for Great Britain, which has no land frontier, since a ship leaving her ports may go where she please.[1] Geffcken and von Bar condemned the proposal to prohibit the exportation of arms and munitions largely for this reason. Geffcken[2] remarks that to attempt such a measure would be to impose upon neutrals impossible responsibilities. Von Bar[3] says it "would not only injure incalculably the commerce of neutrals, but it would necessitate a system of surveillance and control by neutrals over the sale and transportation of merchandise which would be intolerable."[4]

The obligation to prohibit such traffic being once recognized, legal responsibility for failure to enforce the prohibition follows as a consequence and the neutral is exposed to liability for damages to an injured belligerent for neglect to exercise due diligence. As Lawrence observes, a nation "after having dislocated its commerce and aroused the anger of its trading classes, might possibly find itself arraigned before an international tribunal and cast in damages because a few cargoes had slipped through the cordon it maintained against its own subjects."[5] "No chain of mountains and no coast line," says Lorimer, "has ever been or really could be guarded, and a State which

---

[1] Westlake remarks (and his views apply with equal force to the United States) that if the exportation of contraband were prohibited, England would be the country in which, with the best intentions and greatest activity on the part of the government, such a rule would be the worst observed, and which would suffer most from international difficulties to which the breach of it would give rise. *Collected Papers*, p. 391. The Zulus, says Spaight (*War Rights on Land*, p. 478), who fought at Isandlewana and Rorke's Drift in 1879 were armed with rifles which had been smuggled into Zululand by English traders who knew perfectly well for what purpose the arms were to be used. Spaight also remarks that the sword-bayonets for the French *chassepots* used in the Franco-German war of 1870, though sold at Birmingham, were first imported from Germany and thus employed to kill Germans.

[2] *Der Handel mit Waffen und Kriegsmaterial* in Holtzendorff, *Handbuch*, Bd. IV, sec. 152.

[3] *Op. cit.*, p. 401.

[4] The proposal to prohibit trade in contraband has also been criticised on the above-mentioned grounds by Creasy, *First Platform of Int. Law*, p. 608; by Calvo, *Droit Int. Pub.*, Vol. V, sec. 2774; by Davis, *Elements of Int. Law*, p. 403; by Lawrence, *Principles*, p. 712 (who remarks that the effective enforcement of such a policy would require an army of spies and informers), and by many jurists at various sessions of the Institute of International Law, notably by Westlake and Lorimer at the meeting of 1875 (*Rev. de Droit Int.*, Vol. VII, pp. 605 ff.) and by General den Beer Poortugael and M. Lardy in 1894 (*ibid.*, Vol. XXVI, pp. 323 ff.).

[5] *Principles of Int. Law*, 4th ed., p. 702.

undertakes to do it would be exposed to the accusation of having
failed in its engagements." [1]

The practical result of such a policy would be to shift the
responsibility which now rests upon belligerents themselves to
intercept shipments of contraband destined for the use of the
enemy, to the shoulders of the neutral who would become
liable to damages for failure to do it. Instead, therefore, of
removing what is admitted to be one of the chief sources of
controversy between belligerents and neutrals, it is believed that
such a rule would by imposing impossible duties upon neutrals,
greatly augment the already serious inconveniences to which
they are subjected, and lay the foundations for international
claims and controversies. [2]

Another practical objection to a rule of law which would
prohibit merchants of neutral States from selling arms, munitions
and other war materials to belligerents, and one which was often
pointed out during the recent war, is to be found in the necessity
which it would impose upon States which do not maintain large
and fully equipped military establishments, or which do not
possess extensive industries for the manufacture of military
armament, of purchasing and storing in time of peace adequate
quantities of such supplies, or of establishing new industries
of their own upon which they could rely in case of war. In
short, "unprepared" nations would be compelled to put themselves in a war posture in time of peace, to be in readiness at
all times to meet any emergency; otherwise, in the event of
attack by a powerful military State, they would find themselves
embarrassed by the lack of arms and munitions and by the
means of producing them in sufficient quantities for the purposes
of national defense. As Westlake aptly observes,

"The manifest tendency of all rules which interfere with a belligerent's
power to recruit his resources in the markets of the world is to give the
victory in war to the belligerent who is best prepared at the outset; therefore, to make it necessary for States to be in a constant condition of preparation for war; therefore, to make war more probable." [3]

[1] *Revue de Droit Int.* etc., Vol. VII (1875), p. 609.
[2] Cf. the remarks of William C. Dennis in the *Annals of the American Academy
of Political and Social Science*, July, 1915, p. 173.
[3] *Collected Papers*, pp. 391-392. Cf. also the remarks of Wm. C. Dennis, Esq.,
in the *Annals of the American Academy of Political and Social Science*, July, 1915,
p. 175, and a letter of ex-President Taft of January 24, 1916, to E. von Mach.
published in the press at that time.

The tendency, if not the effect of such a rule would be to compel non-military nations which devote their wealth and energies to the peaceful industrial arts to divert their resources and activities to the manufacture of munitions of war and the upbuilding of military and naval armaments. Such a policy, instead of diminishing the eventualities of war would on the contrary probably multiply certain influences which promote wars, unless the manufacture of arms and munitions were made a government monopoly.[1]

The attacks that were made upon the existing rule, so long approved by the jurists and text writers of all countries, and so generally followed in practice by States, were, as is well known, not made in the interest of neutrality, but in the interest of a particular belligerent. The purpose of the proposed alteration of the rule was not to maintain equality of treatment in respect to all belligerents, but to nullify the advantage which one of them had won through its superior naval strength. Nowhere was the case against the proposed alteration of the existing rule more cogently summarized than in Secretary Lansing's note of August 12, 1915, in reply to the Austro-Hungarian protest, where he said:

"The principles of international law, the practice of nations, the national safety of the United States and other nations without great military and naval establishments, the prevention of increased armies and navies, the adoption of peaceful methods for the adjustment of international differences, and, finally, neutrality itself are opposed to the prohibition by a neutral nation of the exportation of arms, ammunition, or other munitions of war to belligerent powers during the progress of the war. "

§ 558. Legality of the Alteration of the Rule during War. But admitting that considerations of morality and the spirit of neutrality outweigh the inconveniences and dangers to which certain neutral States would be exposed by an abrogation of the

---

[1] Mr. Lansing, in his note of June 29, 1915, to the Austro-Hungarian government, thus stated the practical objection to such a policy: "The general adoption by the nations of the world of the theory that neutral powers ought to prohibit the sale of arms and ammunition to belligerents, would compel every nation to have in readiness at all times sufficient munitions of war to meet any emergency which might arise and to erect and maintain establishments for the manufacture of arms and ammunition sufficient to supply the needs of its military and naval forces throughout the progress of a war. Manifestly the application of this theory would result in every nation becoming an armed camp, ready to resist aggression, and tempted to employ force in asserting its rights rather than appeal to reason and justice for the settlement of international disputes.".

existing rule, the question arises when and how should the rule be altered? The right of a neutral Power to prohibit at the outbreak of a war the exportation of arms and munitions from its territory is universally admitted; but may it do so during the progress of the war, after one of the belligerents by means of his superior naval strength has succeeded in commercially isolating his adversary and cutting off his access to neutral markets?

If a neutral government upon the outbreak of war announces that its markets will be open on equal terms to all belligerents, and subsequently when one belligerent has driven the naval forces of his enemy from the seas and blockaded his ports, the neutral decides to close its markets to all belligerents, would not the effect be to nullify in large degree the victory achieved by the one belligerent by depriving him of an advantage honestly won? Has the latter not a right to expect, as von Bar says, that the relations between the neutral and his adversary shall not be changed to his own disadvantage? The general opinion of the authorities is that such a change would not only not be consistent with the maintenance of an attitude of neutrality, but, on the contrary, it would in effect amount to giving assistance to the belligerent who in consequence of the fortunes of war has been excluded by his enemy from recourse to neutral markets. The true principle was stated by Secretary Lansing in his communication to the Austro-Hungarian government. In this communication the Secretary said:

"This government holding, as I believe Your Excellency is aware, and as it is constrained to hold in view of the present indisputable doctrines of accepted international law, that any change in its own laws of neutrality during the progress of a war which would affect unequally the relations of the United States with the nations at war would be an unjustifiable departure from the principle of strict neutrality, submits that none of the circumstances urged in Your Excellency's memorandum alters the principle involved. The placing of an embargo on the trade in arms at the present time would constitute such a change and be a direct violation of the neutrality of the United States. It will, I feel assured, be clear to Your Excellency that, holding this view and considering itself in honor bound by it, it is out of the question for this government to consider such a course." [1]

[1] Professor Burgess (*The European War*, p. 181) pronounces this argument as "manifest sophistry" and says: "If it is advanced by the neutral it is only a pretext for favoring one belligerent. It is one of the most fundamental rules of international law that indirect consequences are not to be taken into account."

This view is that held by the leading jurists and text writers. To cite only one of many, Westlake, adverting to Earl Granville's statement to Count Bernstorff in 1870 that "Her Majesty's government would be prepared to enter into consultation with other nations as to the possibility of adopting in common a stricter rule," observed that

"at least, whether or not such a consultation may follow the conclusion of the present war, it must be allowed that to change an existing rule to the prejudice of one belligerent during the war, and that in compliance with the express request of the other belligerent that our neutrality should be more favorable to him, would be a clear breach of neutrality, even although there might be the most excellent reasons for giving a general preference to the new rule on future occasions." [1]

But, it was asserted by those who argued that an alteration of the rule by a neutral during the progress of the war would constitute no violation of neutral duty, most of the neutral Powers of Europe had in fact prohibited the exportation of arms, munitions, and other commodities of war from their territories. The answer to this argument is that those embargoes, as has already been stated, were not intended as neutrality measures, but measures of conservation and defense, and there was therefore, no analogy between them and the proposed American embargo. Moreover, as was pointed out by Senator Lodge in the course of a debate in the Senate, the effect of the European embargoes was in no case to alter the existing situation as between the several belligerents by depriving one of an advantage already gained, whereas the proposed American embargo would in fact have cut off the supply of but one belligerent and its allies without affecting the other. In the language of the Senator, it would have been "worth more than a million men to Germany." The argument that the action of President Wilson in 1914 in lifting an embargo which had been laid in 1912 on the exportation of arms to Mexico constituted a precedent in support of the contention that the rule may be changed during the progress of a war was without weight because the situation in the two cases was not analogous.

[1] *Collected Papers of John Westlake*, p. 378.

CHAPTER XXXVI

MISCELLANEOUS QUESTIONS OF NEUTRALITY

§ 559. Loans to Belligerent Governments; § 560. Submarine Cables and Wireless Telegraphy; § 561. Procuring Supplies in Neutral Ports; § 562. Violation of Neutral Waters by Belligerent War Ships; § 563. Internment of Belligerent War Ships with Their Officers and Crews in Neutral Ports; § 564. Treatment of Submarines in Neutral Waters; § 565. Commercial Submarines, Case of the *Deutschland;* § 566. Taking of Prizes into Neutral Ports; § 567. Case of the *Appam;* § 568. Hovering of War Ships off Neutral Ports; § 569. Submarine Operations off the American Coast; § 570. Transit across Neutral Territory of Materials Susceptible of Military Use; § 571. Navigation of the River Scheldt by Belligerents.

§ 559. **Loans to Belligerent Governments.** In nearly every war of the past belligerents have borrowed money freely in neutral countries and the practice has rarely been considered as contrary to the accepted principles of neutrality so long as the loans were made by private individuals and not by neutral governments. "A modern belligerent," as Hall remarks, "no more dreams of complaining because the markets of a neutral nation are open to his enemy for the purchase of money than because they are open for the purchase of cotton."[1] This is the view generally held by the authorities and the text writers,[2] and the practice of the past has been in accord with it. At the outbreak of the recent war however, the government of the United States adopted a somewhat stricter view in respect to the duties of neutral governments regarding loans. In September, 1914, the department of state in reply to certain inquiries as to the attitude the government would take in case American bankers should be asked to make loans to any of the belligerent

[1] *Int. Law,* p. 598.
[2] A few of the older writers, however, adopted a different view and maintained that it was contrary to the spirit of true neutrality for a neutral government either to make loans to belligerent governments or to permit them to be made by their nationals. Cf., e.g., Bluntschli, *Droit Int. Cod.,* sec. 768; Phillimore, *Int. Law,* Vol. III, sec. 151; Calvo, *Droit Int.,* secs. 1060, 2628–2630; and Halleck, *Int. Law* (Baker's ed.), Vol. II, p. 195. But this view is not in conformity with the practice. Cf. Lawrence, *Principles,* p. 631; Hershey, *Int. Law and Diplomacy of the Russo-Japanese War,* p. 84, and Westlake, *Int. Law,* Vol. II, p. 207.

governments involved in the European war, stated thát "there is no reason why loans should not be made to the governments of belligerent nations, but in the judgment of this government loans by American bankers to any foreign nation which is at war is inconsistent with the true spirit of neutrality." This announcement contained no intimation that such loans would be forbidden; it was merely an expression of opinion as to what the spirit of true neutrality required, and as such it undoubtedly represented advanced ground in regard to the duties of neutrals. The attitude of the government appears to have been based partly on the ground that the sending of large quantities of American gold out of the country might seriously embarrass the government in case it needed to borrow money itself, and partly because of the belief that if the loan were offered for popular subscription it would be taken chiefly by those who were in sympathy with the belligerent seeking it, with the result that large numbers of the American people might "become partisans with a material interest in the success of the particular belligerent whose bonds they held." [1] The effect therefore would tend to "jeopardize the neutrality of the country." [2] Later, however, when various belligerent governments undertook to establish credits in the United States for the payment of supplies purchased there, the government refused to interpose objection, and in fact Great Britain, France, Russia and Germany negotiated large loans of this character in the United States. They were regarded as unobjectionable because they did not require the sending of American gold abroad and not being offered to the public in the form of bonds there was less opportunity for dividing the sympathies of the American people as between the several belligerents. Charges were made in some quarters that the attitude of the American government was inconsistent with the view expressed in regard to loans at the outbreak of the war, but manifestly the distinction between general popular loans, when the amount raised is sent abroad, and the establish-

[1] Cf. Secretary Bryan's letter of January 20, 1915, to Senator Stone. *Dip. Cor. with Belligerent Governments Relating to Neutral Rights and Duties, Dept. of State, European War*, No. 2, p. 61.

[2] Subsequently Mr. Lansing, who had in the meantime become secretary of state, stated that "There was no legal obstacle to loans being made by bankers in this country." The only objection was that which " from an idealistic point of view might lie against such transactions on the ground that by enabling nations at war to prolong the conflict they were not in strict accordance with the spirit of neutrality."

ment of credits for the payment of supplies purchased in the neutral country, is a reasonable one, and the former may be discouraged and the latter approved without inconsistency.

Certain German sympathizers in the United States, however, charged the government with unfairness and inconsistency in disapproving war loans and at the same time permitting the exportation of arms and munitions to belligerent countries. Secretary Bryan, in replying to this charge, pointed out that there was a clearly defined difference between a war loan and the purchase of arms and munitions. The policy of disapproving war loans, he said, affects all governments alike, so that the disapproval is not an unneutral act; whereas to prohibit the exportation of arms and munitions might not, and in the present case, would not, operate equally upon the nations at war. Contracts for, and sales of, contraband were mere matters of trade; the manufacturer ordinarily would sell to one belligerent as readily as to another, so that no general spirit of partisanship would be aroused and no sympathies excited.[1]

§ 560. **Submarine Cables and Wireless Telegraphy.** In the early days of the war German sympathizers in the United States complained at the action of the American government in establishing a censorship of wireless communication between the United States and Germany while permitting unrestricted communication by cable between America and Great Britain. Soon after the outbreak of the war the two German cables connecting Europe and America were cut near the Azores by order of the British government.[2] One British cable near Fanning Island was likewise cut by the Germans, but the other British cables connecting with America were unmolested. It resulted therefore that while British communication by cable

---

[1] Letter to Senator Stone, *loc. cit.*

[2] Several German cables in the Pacific Ocean were also seized by the British naval forces. At the Peace Conference the question of the disposition of the German cables that had been cut by order of the British government was a subject of controversy. Representatives of the British government are reported to have put forward the contention that the cables thus cut were prizes of war and were not to be returned to their German owners. The American delegates are said to have argued that the cables were unlawfully cut, since they connected with the United States, which was then a neutral power, and should not be retained by Great Britain. But, as pointed out below, the United States cut during the Spanish-American war cables connecting enemy territory with neutral territory and refused to make compensation therefor.

with America was uninterrupted, German communication by this method was entirely cut off, leaving to the Germans only the resource of communication by wireless. This in itself was a serious handicap to them and it was still further increased when the American government established a rigid censorship of all communications sent out from wireless stations in the United States.[1] At first, the owners of the stations were permitted to remain in possession and they continued to be operated by agents of the companies owning them, subject only to the oversight of the government censors. It soon transpired, however, that the censorship regulations were being evaded, and it was even asserted that the station at Sayville was nothing more than an "adjunct to the German spy system" that had been organized in the United States. Under the cover of innocent commercial messages and by means of a secret code, valuable information of a military character was alleged to have been sent to Germany and it was even asserted that communication was established with German submarines in the eastern Atlantic. Under these circumstances the American government took over entire control of the station at Sayville in July, 1915.[2] The reason assigned was that it was considered necessary to preserve the neutrality of the United States. Thereafter messages accepted for transmission were to be forwarded by government naval operators instead of by agents of the company owning the stations.[3]

The action of the American government called forth strong protest from German sympathizers, who denied the charge that

[1] There were two wireless stations in the United States upon which the Germans depended for communication with America. One was at Tuckerton, N. J., and the other at Sayville, Long Island. Both were private stations, and both appear to have been German-owned.

[2] Already earlier in the war it had taken over the control of the station at Tuckerton, N. J. In consequence of the action of the wireless station at Honolulu in giving publicity to the news of the arrival of the German war ship *Geier*, the naval commander was instructed to close the station unless a satisfactory explanation was made within twenty-four hours. It being discovered that the message was sent while the censor's back was turned, the operator was severely reprimanded.

[3] By another order the ships of all belligerent countries entering the waters of the United States were prohibited from using their radio apparatus while within the jurisdiction of the country, the apparatus being sealed to prevent its use. Other neutral governments issued similar regulations. Cf. the "Neutrality Declarations and Regulations" in *Int. Law Topics* for 1916 (*Pubs. of the Naval War College*).

the neutrality of the United States had been violated by the use of the wireless stations for military purposes and asserted that since this was Germany's only means of communication with America it was an act of discrimination against Germany, all the more so because no restrictions had been placed upon cable communication with England.

In answer to this charge the American government called attention to the very different character of the two methods of communication. Communications by cable, it was pointed out, could not be sent from neutral territory to belligerent warships on the high seas as wireless messages could. Furthermore, cables connecting neutral and belligerent territory could be lawfully cut by the opposing belligerent and thus the enemy prevented from receiving information from neutral sources. The right of belligerents to cut such cables is well established, and it was in pursuance of this right that both Germany and Great Britain had in the early days of the war cut the cables referred to above.[1] In short, belligerents have a lawful right to protect themselves against the sending of messages to their enemies from neutral territory by cutting the cables over which they are transmitted, and if they cannot or do not exercise the right, as Germany did not during the recent war, the neutral cannot be held responsible for any advantage the opposing belligerent may derive from such inability or failure. The receiving of information by this method is analogous to the carriage of contraband; it is lawful subject to the right of the injured belligerent to prevent it; in short, the responsibility for preventing it is on him and not upon the neutral.

In the case of wireless communication, however, the situation is different. Messages transmitted from neutral territory by

[1] As is well known, the United States cut the cables connecting Cuba and the Philippines with neutral countries during the Spanish-American war. Benton, *Int. Law and Diplomacy of the Spanish War*, p. 151; Hershey, *Int. Law and Diplomacy of the Russo-Japanese War*, pp. 121, 124; Rolland, *Journal de Droit Int. Privé*, 1898, p. 651, and Lawrence, *Principles*, pp. 612–616. The international cable convention of 1884 for the protection of submarine cables had reference only to the protection of cables in time of peace. It expressly stated that belligerents should be free to act in time of war as if the convention did not exist. The Institute of International Law in 1902 adopted a rule that cables connecting belligerent with neutral territory could be cut by belligerents only if there was an effective blockade and provided the cable were restored with the smallest possible delay at the close of the war. *Annuaire*, 1902, p. 301.

this method can be received by all stations and vessels within a certain radius and they cannot be interrupted by either belligerent. If sent to belligerent warships and if they contain information of military value, the neutral territory from which they are sent manifestly becomes a base of naval operations.[1] In order to avoid responsibility therefor the neutral must prevent the despatch of such messages either through a censorship or the total prohibition of wireless communication of any kind. The action of the American government, therefore, in assuming control of the wireless stations within its jurisdiction and of preventing their use for sending communications of military value was not only not unneutral but was a necessary measure for the maintenance of a policy of strict neutrality. In the exercise of this duty the American government treated all belligerents alike and there was no just ground for complaint on the part of any of them.

Several complaints were made by the British and French governments that the neutrality of various Latin-American countries was being violated by the action of wireless stations in sending messages to German warships in the South Atlantic and Pacific oceans. The most notable instance of the kind

---

[1] Cf. Secretary Bryan's letter to Senator Stone, referred to above. Since all cables between America and northern Europe passed through the British isles, the British government was in a position to control cable communication between America and that part of Europe, and it did so by means of a rigid censorship. This was a source of some irritation in the neutral countries of northern Europe, and it was reported that the government of Sweden intimated a desire that the United States should join with it in a protest against British interference. Clearly, however, a British censorship would have afforded no ground for a protest. Naturally all cable communication with Germany was subjected to such control. Official messages from Berlin to America were not allowed to be sent over the British cables. Nevertheless, the German government was permitted to communicate by cable with the government of the United States as well as with the German ambassador at Washington — provided it were done through the medium of the American ambassador at Berlin and under his own cipher — without being censored by the British authorities. It was not, therefore, true, as was asserted, that the German government could not communicate directly with the American government or with the German ambassador in the United States without having the contents of the communication known to the British government. The German government could also communicate with its ambassador in Washington by means of wireless and in a private code known only to the American government. The demand made by certain German sympathizers that the German government should be allowed to communicate directly with its representative in Washington by means of the British cable and in its own secret code was one, of course, which the British government could not concede.

was the charge that messages were sent from wireless stations in Ecuador and Colombia informing the Germans of the position and movements of British warships. It was stated in the press despatches that an appeal was addressed to the American government by the British government to use its good offices with the two governments mentioned to induce them to observe more strictly their obligations as neutrals. The diplomatic and consular representatives in the two countries were therefore directed by the secretary of state to make an investigation and report to the United States government the results. The governments of both countries denied the charge and asserted that there had been no such violations of their neutrality.[1]

Some charges were also made in the United States that certain British warships while in the Panama Canal used their wireless installations in violation of the neutrality regulations governing the use of radio instruments within the jurisdiction of the United States. The acts complained of, however, appear to have been committed under a misapprehension as to what the regulations prohibited.[2]

An incident involving the neutrality of the Netherlands was the action of the Belgian government in October, 1915, in installing a radio-telegraphic station in the Belgian commune of Bar-le-Duc, which is an *enclave* entirely surrounded by Dutch territory. The Hague conventions Nos. V and XIII forbid belligerents from erecting on the territory of neutral powers wireless telegraph stations for the purpose of communicating with belligerent forces on land or sea. Although the place where the station in question had been erected was politically a part of the Belgian State and therefore the installation of the wireless outfit there did not involve the neutrality of the Netherlands, the Dutch government was not indifferent to the novel situation

---

[1] The Colombian government stated that the particular wireless station complained of had been placed under strict government censorship, although it admitted that in spite of its efforts to maintain a strict neutrality one of the belligerents may have succeeded in erecting a secret station somewhere on the Colombian coast. None, however, had been found, although a diligent search had been conducted. Later the high-power wireless station at Cartagena, Colombia, was removed in consequence of British protests. Rumors were afloat from time to time of hidden wireless stations on the coast of the United States, but none appear to have been discovered.

[2] Cf. the cases of the *Mollino* and the *Protesilaus*, the facts regarding which are set forth in *Dip. Cor. of the United States, European War*, No. 2, pp. 23-24.

resulting from the fact that the place was a Dutch *enclave*. It accordingly prohibited the transportation from Dutch territory to the *enclave* commune of any supplies considered necessary in the operation of the wireless installation and in one instance detained at the Dutch frontier a quantity of petroleum shipped from England and addressed to the mayor of the commune. In order to insure the strict enforcement of the measure thus adopted the Dutch government went to the length of erecting a barbed-wire stockade around the *enclave* and created a commission composed of both Dutch and Belgian representatives to determine what necessary supplies should be admitted for the sustenance of the population.[1]

§ 561. **Procuring Supplies in Neutral Ports.** Numerous charges were made by both the British and German authorities that the war ships of the enemy procured supplies in one way or another from the ports of certain neutral countries. The British government complained that neutral steamers took on cargoes of coal and other supplies in the port of Manila (Philippines) and cleared for another neutral port to which they merely called, after which they proceeded to an unknown point and delivered their supplies to German war ships. One such steamer was captured by a British cruiser and put into the custody of a prize court. Charges were also made that certain German merchant vessels refugeeing in ports of the United States were guilty of carrying coal to German war ships on the high seas, and various rumors of plots on the part of German vessels to leave the United States with supplies of coal for German war ships caused the British government much concern and the attention of the department of state was called to the reports. At the same time the American government was urged to limit the amount of coal which German steamers in American ports should be allowed to take on. The British

---

[1] Dutch orange book, *Ministère des Affaires Etrangères, Recueil de Diverses Communications, etc.* (The Hague, 1916), pp. 168–170. The conduct of the Dutch government in permitting German troops to traverse Dutch territory on the day following the conclusion of the armistice, was criticised in allied quarters as being inconsistent with the high standard of neutrality set in the above-mentioned instance. The Dutch explanation appears to have been that they regarded the armistice as virtually the conclusion of peace. The conduct of the Dutch authorities was contrasted with that of Belgium and Switzerland in 1870 in refusing to permit recruits and even wounded to pass through their territory.

government also appears to have adopted the expedient of placing an embargo on the shipment of coal from Great Britain to the Philippines. The American government declined to adopt the suggestion of the British government regarding the limitation of the coal supply of German merchant vessels, but it took more stringent measures to prevent such vessels from leaving American ports with large supplies of coal. At the time, there appears to have been no law under which the owners of such vessels could be punished for such acts, but in March, 1915, a joint resolution was passed by Congress which authorized the President to direct the customs collectors to withhold clearance papers from any vessel, American or foreign, which he had reason to believe was about to carry fuel, arms, men or supplies to any war ship or tender of a belligerent nation in violation of the neutrality obligations of the United States, under penalty of a heavy fine or imprisonment. Through the activity of German agents fraudulent manifests were procured in a good many instances, under which German vessels in American ports carried supplies to German war ships. The managing director of the *Hamburg-American Line*, with a number of its other officials, were indicted for procuring such manifests, and in December, 1915, were convicted and sentenced to terms of imprisonment. At the trial they confessed that they had sent out twelve ships which were proved to have had fraudulent papers. All, however, were captured before reaching their destination. Similar activities took place on the Pacific Coast, where the steamers *Sacramento* and *Mazatlan* were systematically engaged in this illicit traffic.[1]

The task of preventing the belligerents from obtaining coal for war purposes was one which occupied the serious attention of the government of Chili. As is well known, the southern portions of the Atlantic and Pacific oceans in the neighborhood of Chili and Argentina were the theatre of extensive operations by British and German naval forces during the first year of the war. Under article 19 of the 13th Hague Convention of 1907 belligerent war ships are allowed to take on in neutral ports only sufficient fuel to enable them to reach the nearest port in

[1] Cf. the pamphlet *German Plots and Intrigues in the United States during the Period of Our Neutrality* (pp. 38–39), issued by the United States Committee on Public Information.

their own country. Since the nearest home ports of Germany and Great Britain were thousands of miles distant from Chili it was possible for the war ships of either belligerent to take on a large supply of coal in a Chilian port and remain for weeks in the waters of the southern Pacific and Atlantic engaging in operations of war, after which they could return for a new supply. To stop this practice, which it regarded as contrary to the spirit if not the letter of the Hague convention, the Chilian government adopted rigorous measures. By a decree of December 15, 1914, the amount of coal which belligerent ships of war were permitted to take in Chilian ports was limited to what was necessary to enable them to reach the nearest port of a neighboring neutral country having a coal depot. It was also found that merchant vessels of belligerent nationality, particularly those of the Kosmos Line (German) and the Pacific Steam Navigation Company (British) which were engaged in the coasting trade of South America were guilty in many cases of taking on large supplies of coal on the pretext of making voyages to Europe but which in fact delivered their coal to war ships in the neighboring waters of the Pacific. This raised a somewhat perplexing question for the Chilian authorities, since the restrictions imposed by the Hague convention in respect to supplies of coal apply only to war vessels and not to merchantmen. Nevertheless the Chilian authorities considered this practice to be a violation of the spirit of true neutrality and accordingly by the decree referred to above the quantity of coal allowed to merchant vessels of belligerent nationality was limited to their ordinary needs except where they desired to make a voyage to a European port, in which case guarantees would be required that the coal furnished would be used exclusively for such voyage,[1] and it was further provided that in case any merchant vessel were guilty of violating any of the neutrality regulations issued by the Chilian government, no coal would be furnished to any of the merchant vessels of the company to which the offending ship belonged. Against the terms of this decree the British government protested and

---

[1] The particular guarantee required consisted of a deposit of five pounds sterling for each ton of coal taken on board by a merchant vessel of belligerent nationality bound for a European port.

urged the Chilian government to modify the decree, but without success.[1]

Practically all merchant ships of the German Kosmos Line systematically carried coal from Chilian ports to German war ships on the high seas.[2] The Chilian government took the position that such vessels were auxiliaries of the German fleet and they were treated as such. Some English merchant vessels were charged with the same offence and the German government demanded that they should be treated as auxiliaries of the English fleet. By an order of November 26, 1914, it was directed that all the vessels of the Kosmos company should be interned in case they did not leave the ports of Chili within twenty-four hours in accordance with article 12 of the 13th Hague convention. Naturally the company protested, but the Chilian government refused to modify its order. The captains of these vessels, it was said, had made false declarations, had abused the privileges accorded them, had deliberately misunderstood the regulations of the government and had committed numerous violations of the neutrality of the country. Finally, it was added that their internment was none the less a source of injury to the people of Chili who were largely dependent upon the ships of the company for carrying their commerce, but their systematic violation of the neutrality laws could no longer be tolerated.

[1] Alvarez, *La Grande Guerre Européenne et la Neutralité du Chili*, ch. V.   Various regulations of the Chilian government regarding this and other matters of neutrality may be found in the *Rev. Gén. de Droit Int. Pub.*, Vol. 23, Docs., pp. 7 ff., and in English in *Int. Law Topics* for 1916, pp. 15 ff. In a note of February 4, 1915, the British minister to Chili addressed a note to the Chilian government requesting to be informed whether British merchant vessels which had served as colliers to British war ships under the orders of the admiralty would, after having ceased to perform such service, continue to be treated by the Chilian government as auxiliary cruisers. The Chilian government replied that since neither the second Hague Conference nor the London Naval Conference had reached an agreement on all points regarding the conversion of merchant vessels into war ships, it was within the rights of neutral governments to apply such rules as they saw fit, to cover the points not regulated by the international conventions, and that the Chilian government was prepared to admit to its ports and waters and to treat as merchant vessels ships which had served as auxiliaries to belligerent war vessels, but which had resumed their normal commercial operations, provided that they had committed no violation of Chilian neutrality, provided that the transformation had taken place in the jurisdictional waters of the country to which the ships belonged, and provided that their government would engage that the vessels would not in the future serve as auxiliaries to an armed fleet. Communication of March 15, 1915, to the British minister; text in Alvarez, pp. 254–256.

[2] Cf. Alvarez, pp. 216–219, for a long list of such infractions.

§ 562. Violations of Neutral Waters by Belligerent War Ships.
The 13th Hague Convention, as is well known, contains various
rules regarding the entry, sojourn and departure of war ships into
and from neutral ports and regarding the making of repairs,
revictualling, taking of supplies, and the like. The rules of
this convention were supplemented by municipal regulations
issued by the various governments [1] prior to the outbreak of the
late war and by the neutrality proclamations promulgated after
the commencement of the war.[2] Naturally many charges and
counter-charges were made of the violations of these rules by
the war ships belonging to one or other of the belligerents.
The Norwegian authorities complained that German submarines
systematically made use of the territorial waters of the country,
in consequence of which regulations were issued excluding such
craft from traversing Norwegian waters. Charges were also
occasionally made that both war ships and neutral merchant
vessels were sunk in Norwegian waters. Similar charges were
made by the Swedish government from time to time. As
already stated, both Norway and Sweden went to the length of
excluding war ships from their territorial waters except in cases
of emergency. The government of the Netherlands did likewise, although the prohibition did not prevent various violations
of its neutrality.[3] The Spanish government, in July, 1917,
also went to the length of excluding belligerent submarines of
enemy nationality from its ports and waters. The government
of Chili, as stated above, complained that British and German
war ships violated the neutrality of the country by taking
supplies of coal and revictualling, in contravention of the Hague
rules and sometimes in violation of specific engagements.[4] It

[1] Cf. the texts of these regulations in Supp. to the *Amer. Jour. of Int. Law,*
Vol. X, No. 3 (1916), pp. 121 ff.
[2] The neutrality declarations and regulations issued by the governments of
most of the neutral powers may be found in *Int. Law Topics* for 1916.
[3] The territorial waters of the Netherlands were again and again violated by
the war ships or submarines of both England and Germany. Among other instances complained of was the action of the British submarine L-55 in pursuing
the German steamer *Batavier II* into Dutch waters where it was captured. A
prize crew was then placed aboard the vessel, and it was taken outside Dutch
jurisdiction. As to measures adopted by the government of the Netherlands for
the enforcement of its neutrality see the *Rev. Gén.* for Jan., 1919, pp. 177 ff.
[4] On October 26, 1914, the German cruiser *Leipsig* took provisions in the Isle
of Juan Fernandez (Chili) and in the middle of November requested to be permitted to revictual at Valparaiso. Against the granting of the request the British

also complained of the violation of the twenty-four-hour rule by the British cruiser *Bristol* in leaving the port of Punta Arenas following the departure of the German cruiser *Dresden*, less than twenty-four hours earlier. A number of German war ships were also charged with systematically using the ports of the island of Juan Fernandez as a base of operations and with sojourning more than twenty-four hours in the ports of the Isle de Pâques. It was also a subject of complaint that the German battle ship, *Prinz Eitel Friedrich*, without notifying the authorities, entered a Chilian port and landed the crew of an English ship which had been sunk on the high seas. Against this act the Chilian government lodged a protest on the ground that the act did not show proper respect toward the local authorities. The same cruiser remained in the port of the Isle of Pâques for eight days, engaged in transshipping coal from the French steamer *Jean*, which had been brought to the harbor as a prize.

The most flagrant violation of Chilian neutrality was the attack by two British cruisers, the *Kent* and the *Glasgow*, upon the German cruiser *Dresden* in the territorial waters of Chili in March, 1915. It appears that the *Dresden* arrived in Cumberland Bay on the 9th of March and asked to be allowed to remain there for a period of eight days in order to repair her engines. This request was refused and the *Dresden* was ordered to leave within twenty-four hours under pain of internment. At the expiration of the period the port authorities notified the captain of the *Dresden* that he had incurred the penalty imposed and the fact was immediately reported to the governor of the Republic. Meanwhile, on March 14, the British cruisers, *Kent* and *Glasgow*, arrived in the bay and opened fire on the *Dresden*. Thereupon the *Dresden* hoisted a flag of truce and despatched one of her officers to inform the *Glasgow* that she was in neutral waters. This circumstance was disregarded by the British squadron, which summoned the *Dresden* to surrender, warning her that if she refused she would be destroyed. Thereupon the captain of the *Dresden* gave orders to blow up the powder

---

minister protested on the ground that under art. 20 of the thirteenth Hague convention a belligerent war ship which has shipped fuel in a neutral port may not replenish its supply within three months. But the Chilian government pointed out that this restriction was limited to fuel and did not apply to revictualling. Other similar cases occurred. Cf. Alvarez, *op. cit.*, p. 205.

magazine and sink the ship. In reply to a protest against this act of hostility [1] in the territorial waters of Chili, Sir Edward Grey expressed deep regret that "any misunderstanding should have arisen which should be a cause of complaint to the Chilian government" and stated that His Majesty's government was "prepared to offer an ample apology." At the same time, he stated that the information at hand pointed to the fact that the *Dresden* had not accepted internment and at the time of the attack still flew her colors and had her guns trained. If this were so and there were no other means available at the time for enforcing the decision of the Chilian authorities to intern the *Dresden* she might have escaped again to attack British commerce had not the British squadron taken the measures it did. To this argument the Chilian government responded that the notification by the local authorities that the vessel had incurred the penalty of internment was equivalent to internment and that at the time of the attack the *Dresden* was as effectually interned as the circumstances permitted, so that it was not liable to attack. There was therefore no excuse for the serious offence committed against the sovereignty of the Chilian government.[2]

[1] The Chilian government also addressed a protest to the German government against the action of the *Dresden* for remaining longer than twenty-four hours in the territorial waters of Chili and for not having obeyed the order to intern. To this protest the German government replied that the sojourn of the *Dresden* for more than twenty-four hours in Chilian waters constituted no violation of the law of nations, since under art. 14 of the thirteenth Hague convention a belligerent war ship may prolong its stay in a neutral port beyond twenty-four hours when it is necessary to repair injuries received. The order of internment at the expiration of twenty-four hours was not, therefore, justified. Furthermore, the German government did not recognize the twenty-four-hour rule as a rule of the law of nations, but considered it as contrary to the existing law, and, in fact, the German government had reserved its ratification to the article of the Hague convention in which it is incorporated. Text in Alvarez, pp. 232 ff.

[2] As to the facts regarding the affair and the diplomatic correspondence cf. Alvarez, *op. cit.*, pp. 227 ff., and Supp. to *Amer. Jour. of Int. Law*, Vol. X (1916), pp. 72 ff. Cf. a criticism of the British defence by Baty in the *Pennsylvania Law Review*, 1915, p. 716. Baty remarks that Sir Edward Grey "had the temerity to hint that where there is no effective neutral force on the spot, the belligerent may take his own forcible measures in neutral territory." The action of the Chilian authorities in interning the crew of the *Dresden* after its destruction provoked a protest by the German government. The Chilian authorities took the position that the internment of the crew of a belligerent war ship which had taken asylum in a neutral port was in conformity not only with the general principles of international law but also with arts. 15 and 19 of the tenth Hague convention of 1907. The German government combated this view and demanded that the crew should

§ 563. **Internment of Belligerent War Ships with their Officers and Crews in Neutral Ports.** During the late war as during the Russo-Japanese war there were numerous instances in which belligerent war vessels sought refuge in neutral ports or entered them for the purpose of making repairs or obtaining supplies. Such acts are somewhat analogous to the entrance of an army into neutral territory, although of course there are certain differences. During the Russo-Japanese war the practice was adopted by neutrals of interning such vessels provided they were unable to complete the repairs necessary to render them seaworthy and to depart within a certain time prescribed by the neutral.[1] This practice was followed in the recent war and

be set at liberty. The basis of the German contention was that the *Dresden* had been attacked by enemy cruisers in neutral waters in violation of the law of nations, and that by reason of this circumstance the crew was obliged to debark in Chilian territory. Under these conditions their internment was inadmissible. To this argument the Chilian government replied that if the *Dresden* had been regularly interned, there could be no doubt that the crew also must be interned. Likewise, supposing that the internment was not legitimate because the commander had not accepted it, the internment of the crew was none the less justifiable according to the law of nations. It was clearly established by the letter and spirit of the Hague conventions that the armed forces of a belligerent who set foot on neutral territory must be interned. Text of the correspondence in Alvarez, pp. 229-231.

[1] Takahashi (*Int. Law as Applied to the Russo-Japanese War*, pp. 411-418) gives the names of thirty Russian war vessels that were interned in neutral ports during the war. A well-known case was that of the *Lena*, interned in the port of San Francisco. Cf. Hershey, *Int. Law and Diplomacy of the Russo-Japanese War*, p. 207. Three Russian vessels were also interned at Manila. The practice of interning belligerent war ships is a new one in international law having, as stated above, been first resorted to on a large scale during the Russo-Japanese war of 1904-1905. The internment of land forces, however, is a much older practice, and it was regularized by the First Hague Conference which provided that belligerent troops who are received in neutral territory shall be interned. This provision was readopted by the Conference in 1907 and is embodied in arts. 11 and 12 of the convention respecting the rights and duties of neutral powers and persons in war on land. The convention respecting the rights and duties of neutral powers in naval war contains various restrictions upon the rights of belligerent war ships in neutral ports, and art. 24 provides that in case such a ship after notification does not leave a port in which it is not entitled to remain, the neutral power is entitled to take such measures as it considers necessary to render the ship incapable of taking the sea, and that when the ship is detained, the officers and crew are likewise detained. The latter may be left in the ship or on land and may be subjected to such measures of restriction as may seem necessary. Officers may be left at liberty on giving their word not to leave the neutral territory without permission. By art. 25 the neutral power is bound to exercise such surveillance as its means may allow to prevent any violations of the duties prescribed by the convention. It will be observed that the word "interned" which is used in the convention relative to combatants in land warfare is not employed in this convention, the word "detained"

it appears to be in accord with modern ideas of neutrality. The neutrality proclamation issued by the President of the United States at the outbreak of the war in Europe limited the stay of war ships in American ports to twenty-four hours, except in case of stress of weather, the necessity of procuring supplies for the subsistence of the crew, or the need of repairs. A similar rule was adopted by other neutral governments.[1] In the United States it is the practice of the port authorities to determine the time required to complete the necessary repairs; the war ship is then allowed twenty-four hours after the expiration of this period to depart, failing which the vessel is interned.

The first case of internment during the recent war was that of the *Geier*, a German war vessel which put into the port of Honolulu on October 15, 1914. The captain requested permission to make the necessary repairs to render the vessel seaworthy. He estimated that one week would be necessary for this purpose. The naval constructor at the port, after an examination, recommended that the time be extended eight days. Subsequently the German consul requested from eight to ten days' additional time. The vessel was evidently in very bad condition and the government, believing that it did not comport with a strict neutrality or a fair interpretation of the Hague convention to allow such a vessel to complete unlimited repairs in an American port, caused the captain of the *Geier* to be informed that he would be allowed three weeks to make repairs, after which the vessel would be interned in case it were not able to leave. In the meantime the British ambassador at Washington was protesting against the continued presence of the *Geier* in an American port as being in contravention of article 17 of the 13th Hague convention of 1907. Complaint was also made of the presence in Honolulu of the German ship *Locksun*, which it was charged had been engaged in furnishing supplies

being used instead. It is admitted, however, that the status of war ships so "detained" is analogous to that of the troops of a belligerent power who enter neutral territory and are "interned," and that both cases are controlled by the same rule. Cf. the observations of M. Renault in *Actes et Documents, Deux. Conf.*, Vol. I, p. 322.

[1] Cf. the texts of the regulations of the various governments governing the visits of men of war to foreign ports, in Supp. to *Amer. Jour. of Int. Law*, Vol. X (1916), pp. 121 ff. Cf. also the texts of the neutrality declarations and regulations of various neutral powers in *Int. Law Topics*, 1916.

to German war ships and that under the general rules of international law and the neutrality regulations of the United States there was ground for detaining it also. After an investigation of the activities of the *Locksun* the secretary of state notified the German embassy, on November 7, 1914, that the vessel had in effect served as a tender to the *Geier*, that its status was therefore the same, and that it would therefore be interned if it did not leave the port of Honolulu immediately. To this communication the German ambassador replied that the *Locksun* could not be considered as a man-of-war or even as an auxiliary vessel, but simply as a merchant ship, and that there was no rule of international law which stamps a merchant vessel serving as a tender to a war ship with a belligerent character. On November 8 both vessels were interned.[1]

On December 15, 1914, the German cruiser *Cormoran*, at the request of its commander, was interned at Guam with twenty-two officers and three hundred and fifty-five men. Another case of internment was that of the German cruiser *Prinz Eitel Friedrich*, which entered the port of Newport News, Virginia, on March 10, 1915, and asked for permission to make repairs. The naval authorities, after an examination of the vessel, came to the conclusion that fourteen days would be necessary to complete the necessary repairs. The government thereupon notified the commander that he would be allowed until midnight of April 6 to complete the repairs, and in addition twenty-four hours to leave the territorial waters of the United States, failing which the ship would be interned until the end of the war. Not leaving within the time thus prescribed, the vessel was interned on April 7.

Still another case was that of the German cruiser *Kronprinz Wilhelm* which arrived at Newport News on April 11, 1915,

---

[1] The German ambassador also complained that two officers of the *Geier* with their orderlies, who had been granted sick leave before the internment of the ship, were interned with the rest of the crew. The government, however, declined to modify its decision, on the ground that the officers in question were not only duly incorporated in the armed forces of Germany, but were also in a sense a part of an organized body of such forces entering a neutral port. The fact that they had been granted sick leave did not divest them of their military character. Their status was different from that of Major Robertson, a British army officer who, having arrived in the United States as an individual, was not treated as subject to internment. Cf. the correspondence regarding the cases of the *Geier* and the *Locksun*, in *European War*, No. 2, pp. 49–52.

and asked permission to land sixty-one persons belonging to the
crews of enemy vessels sunk by the cruiser and to make the
repairs necessary to render the ship seaworthy. The naval
authorities reported that six working days would be necessary
to complete the repairs; thereupon the commander was notified
that he would be allowed until midnight of the 29th of April
in which to make the repairs and an additional twenty-four
hours in which to leave, failing which it would be necessary to
intern the vessel. Not leaving within the period prescribed,
the ship was interned. An incident connected with the internment of the two vessels mentioned above was the escape of a
number of officers and men belonging to their crews. Each
commanding officer had given a pledge for himself, officers and
crews not to commit any unneutral acts and not to leave the
limits prescribed in their paroles.[1] Some of them were recovered
but others succeeded in escaping from the country and probably
returned to Germany. The secretary of state, in a communication to the German government, complained that the action
of the German officers in violating their paroles was not only
contrary to express instructions, but was also in violation of the
standard of honorable conduct expected under the circumstances, in consequence of which the United States was compelled to discontinue the practice of paroling interned officers
and men on their honor and to restrict the liberal privileges
that had previously been allowed. The secretary of state also
took occasion to call the attention of the German government
to the fact that when, during the Russo-Japanese war, three
Russian officers had escaped from the *Lena*, which had been

---

[1] The right of a neutral power to accord a certain liberty to interned officers
upon their giving a parole not to leave the country is recognized by art. II of the
Hague convention of 1907 respecting the rights and duties of neutral powers and
persons in case of war on land, and by art. 24 of the corresponding convention
relative to naval warfare. As a part of its internment policy the Dutch government notified officers interned in its ports that this privilege would be accorded
them. When subsequently several of the belligerent governments forbade their
officers to give such paroles, the Dutch government, although taking the position
that such a prohibition did not affect its right to accept paroles, recognized that in
giving it, an officer would be confronted by a conflict of duties. Accordingly, in
such cases it refrained thereafter from inquiring of such officers liable to internment whether they desired to give a parole in a permanent form. But a certain
liberty of movement was accorded temporarily to all officers who would give their
promise to conform to the law. Orange book, *Recueil de Diverses Communications*,
etc., pp. 175-176.

interned in the port of San Francisco, the Russian government, being informed of the fact, immediately caused the escaped officers to return to America, where they were interned for the remainder of the war. The action of the Russian government, the secretary added, was in accord with the best practice of nations, and he intimated that the German government should follow the Russian example and see that the German officers and seamen were returned to the United States for internment with their respective ships. The German foreign office expressed regret that the officers and seamen had escaped and suggested that the terms of the parole did not bind them to remain within American jurisdiction. Only one of the officers in question, it was added, had returned to Germany and he would be instructed to return to his vessel as soon as the American government had obtained a safe conduct for him from the enemy governments.[1] He was never returned and the others who had succeeded in escaping appear never to have been discovered.[2] After the outbreak of the war between the United States and Germany the remaining officers and seamen were confined in internment camps at Forts McPherson and Oglethorpe.[3]

---

[1] The correspondence regarding the matter is published in *European War*, No. 3, pp. 347–356; cf. also *Int. Law Notes* for February, 1917, pp. 24 ff.; the *Amer. Jour. of Int. Law*, Vol. X, pp. 877 ff., and the New York *Times*, of August 18, 1916.

[2] Except one who was captured by the British naval authorities in the North Sea.

[3] In several instances German war ships made attempts to escape from neutral ports in which they were interned or to leave in violation of the port regulations. Thus in February, 1915, a German war ship interned at Para, Brazil, made a dash for the sea, but was prevented by Brazilian war ships from escaping. Other similar attempts to escape from the ports of Rio de Janeiro, Buenos Aires, and Punta Arenas were reported in the press despatches. In April, 1915, a controversy took place between the American and German governments in consequence of the action of the port authorities of San Juan, Porto Rico, in firing upon the German steamer *Odenwald*, which undertook to leave the port without clearance papers in violation of the navigation laws of the United States. The German ambassador protested against the "reckless action of the harbor authorities in opening fire on the steamer without warning," thus endangering the lives of the crew. The secretary of state after reviewing the facts concerning the conduct of the vessel stated that no less than six distinct warnings were given to the captain of the *Odenwald* that force would be used in case he attempted to leave the port without clearance papers, and that none of these warnings were heeded by the captain, who persisted in his determination to leave the port in violation of the customs laws. None of the shots fired were aimed at the vessel, and none in fact struck it. Cf. the correspondence regarding the affair in *European War*, No. 2, pp. 111–113.

The status of the crew of a shipwrecked submarine who were rescued and taken into a neutral port was the subject of a controversy between the British and Dutch governments during the summer of 1916. The crew of the British submarine E-17 having been rescued by the Dutch cruiser *Noord-Brabant* were taken into a port of the Netherlands, where they were interned. Against this action the British government protested. The Dutch government argued that according to the law of nations shipwrecked or wounded seamen belonging to the armed forces of a belligerent power who fall into the hands of the enemy may be made prisoners of war. They were bound therefore to intern such persons without regard to whether the shipwreck was the result of injuries received in battle or from other causes.

The British government contested this reasoning and maintained that article 13 of the tenth Hague convention did not impose on neutral Powers the obligation to intern the members of shipwrecked crews rescued by their war vessels and taken into their jurisdiction. It only required that "every possible precaution" should be taken to insure that such persons do not again take part in the operations of the war, thus leaving the neutral free to act in each case according to the special circumstances existing. But in reply to this contention the Dutch government pointed out that the obligation created by the said article applied not to neutral powers but to the commanders of the neutral war ship by which such persons were rescued. This was the plain language of the article and it was clear from M. Renault's report that it was the intention of the conference that such persons should be interned, since their situation was entirely analogous to that of combatants in land warfare who take refuge in neutral territory.[1]

The British government further maintained that the provisions of the tenth Hague convention could not be invoked in the present case since it had not been ratified by all the belligerent powers in accordance with the general participation article. To this contention the Dutch government replied that the provisions of the convention were not new rules of law but were merely declaratory of the existing customary law of nations and as such were binding irrespective of the status of the con-

[1] *Actes et Documents*, Vol. III, pp. 76, 345.

vention. Almost all the States of the world had by their acts
of ratification expressed the opinion that the rules adopted by
the second Hague conference were in conformity with the
existing law of nations; neutral powers were therefore bound
to observe those rules. The British government was also reminded that the Dutch government, acting in accordance with
these rules, had in October, 1915, released the shipwrecked
persons rescued from the British war ships, ·Cressy, Hogue and
Aboukir, by Dutch merchant vessels and taken into ports of
the Netherlands.[1]

Finally, the British government asserted that there were no
precedents in support of the position of the Dutch government.
It called attention to the cases of the Korietz and Variag, two
Russian ships of war, the shipwrecked crews of which were
rescued by English, French and Italian cruisers during the
Russo-Japanese war and who in pursuance of an arrangement
with the Japanese government were delivered over to the Russian government in a neutral port. Regarding this precedent
the Dutch government pointed out, however, that the surrender
of the shipwrecked Russians to their government was made only
under the condition that they should not again take part in
the operations of the war, the neutral powers concerned having
evidently recognized that it was their duty to take measures
to insure that the persons in question would not again take
part in the war, the agreement of both the Japanese and Russian governments rendering it unnecessary for the neutral
power to resort to the measure of internment.[2]

[1] As to the facts regarding these cases, cf. the Dutch orange book, Dip. Cor.
from October, 1915, to July, 1916, p. 27. Again in June, 1916, the crew of the
German war ship Elbing, which was brought into a Dutch port under similar circumstances, were set at liberty. In October, 1914, the crew of the French torpedo
destroyer Mousquet, the members of which had been transferred by the Emden to
an English merchant ship by which they were debarked in a port of the Dutch
East Indies, were likewise set at liberty. Cf. the Dutch orange book, Recueil de
Diverses Communications, etc., p. 175. Also the Grotius Annuaire for 1915, p. 65,
and for 1916, pp. 98, 102.

[2] Cf. the communication of M. Loudon, Dutch minister of foreign affairs, to
the British foreign office, March 18, 1916. Text in Dutch orange book, Correspondence between October, 1915, and July, 1916, pp. 31–32. On January 19, 1916, the
English submarine H-6 as a result of error ran aground within Dutch territorial
waters, a number of the members of the crew who were rescued having debarked
in a Dutch port. The ship not having entered Dutch waters in consequence of
injuries or stress of weather, the crew were interned. Orange book cited above,
p. 24.

The action of the Dutch government in interning the German submarine C–8 which entered the territorial waters of the Netherlands on November 4, 1915, was the subject of protest by the German government which contended that its action was neither in accord with its declaration of neutrality nor the existing law of nations. The Dutch government in reply called the attention of the German government to article 4 of its declaration of neutrality which provided that no ship of war belonging to a belligerent power would be permitted in the territorial waters of the country except when forced therein by injuries or stress of weather and to article 3 which prescribed internment for any such ship which should find itself within Dutch waters in misapprehension of the prohibition of article 4. The prohibition prescribed by article 4, it contended, was in no sense contrary to the law of nations. When article 10 of the 13th Hague convention, which declares that the neutrality of a State is not compromised by the simple passage of belligerent war ships through the territorial waters of neutral States, was under discussion, it was admitted that the question as to whether a neutral State might forbid such passage was left under the empire of the general law of nations. This law allowed neutral powers to take in their territorial waters such measures as they judged proper to safeguard their rights of sovereignty. They were therefore free to prohibit belligerent war ships from traversing their territorial waters if they saw fit, and this liberty was affirmed by various contemporary authorities on the law of nations.[1] The submarine had suffered no injury which necessitated its entrance into Dutch waters. If it lacked an efficient electric compass, as the German commander alleged, which caused him to run aground in Dutch waters, that was no valid excuse, since in view of the well-known difficulties of navigation in those parts the commander should have taken the necessary precautions to avoid entering the jurisdiction of the Netherlands.[2]

[1] Wehberg, *Das Seekriegsrecht*, was cited as an example.

[2] Communication of M. Loudon to the German foreign office November 22, 1915, Dutch orange book containing the correspondence of the minister of foreign affairs from October, 1915, to July, 1916, pp. 18, 19; also the Dutch orange book entitled *Ministère des Affaires Etrangères, Recueil de Diverses Communications, etc.*, pp. 148 ff. As to the controversy between Chili and Germany regarding the internment of the crew of the *Dresden* sunk by British war ships in the territorial

The Spanish government likewise adopted the policy of internment of belligerent war ships and submarines which entered its ports in violation of the decree referred to above, and a number of German submarines incurred the penalty imposed by the decree. The internment in July, 1917, of the U-23, which entered the port of Corunna in a seriously damaged condition, was the subject of protest by the German government, which argued that the act was contrary to the Hague convention. It is difficult, however, to see any foundation for the contention.

§ 564. **Treatment of Submarines in Neutral Waters.** The right of belligerent war vessels which navigate the surface of the ocean to enter neutral ports for certain purposes and to remain there for a limited period is well established. The Hague convention, however, prescribes certain rules which such vessels must observe in neutral waters and it seems clear that neutrals may if they judge proper prescribe additional restrictions and they may undoubtedly prohibit absolutely the entrance of such vessels into their ports if they fail to conform to the neutrality regulations which have been issued.[1] In practice they have usually been allowed to enter, although occasionally neutral governments have excluded them from all or certain of their territorial waters.[2]

---

waters of Chili and also as to what constituted internment, see sec. 562. Who shall bear the expense of internment? When the Chilian government interned the ships of the German Kosmos line, the Company insisted that the interning power must bear the expense and also assume the risk which the ships incur. The government of Chili took the position, and justly, it would seem, that the company whose vessels committed the infractions which caused them to be interned should bear the expense and assume all risks. Alvarez, *La Grande Guerre Européenne et la Neutralité du Chili*, p. 284. May a merchant vessel demand to be interned in a neutral port? Certain ships of the above-mentioned company finding themselves in Chilian ports and not wishing to incur the risk of being captured, in effect declared themselves to be interned. The question is not dealt with by the Hague convention. Article 24, which deals with the matter of internment, applies only to war ships, and even as to these it contains no rule as to the right of a ship to demand that it be interned.

[1] Convention of 1907 concerning the rights and duties of neutral powers in naval war, art. 9.

[2] In 1834 Austria closed the port of Cataro to the war ships of belligerents. During the same war the Danish government closed the port of Christiansand to all belligerent war ships. In 1870 the Swedish government similarly closed five of its ports to belligerent men of war. By a decree of December 20, 1912, belligerent war submarines were forbidden to navigate or sojourn in Swedish territorial waters. Its decision was notified to the powers, and no protest was made by

What is the duty of a neutral government·in respect to submarines of belligerent nationality? Do the rules which govern the entrance and stay of war vessels which navigate the surface of the ocean apply to submarines which navigate below the surface? This question was raised for the first time during the late war and the decisions reached by neutral governments were not uniform.

In August, 1916, the governments of Great Britain and France sent a memorandum to the various neutral governments urging them "to take effective measures if they have not already done so, with a view to preventing belligerent submarine vessels, whatever the purpose to which they are put, from making use of neutral waters, roadsteads and ports." The memorandum went on to say that as regards submarines "the application of the principles of the law of nations is affected by special and novel conditions: first, by the fact that these vessels can navigate and remain at sea submerged and can escape all control and observation; second, by the fact that it is impossible to identify them and establish their national character, whether neutral or belligerent, combatant or non-combatant, and to remove the capacity for harm inherent in the nature of such vessels." It was further added that any place which provides a submarine far from its base with an opportunity for rest and replenishment of its supplies thereby furnishes such addition to its powers as to give the place the character of a base of operations. In conclusion the memorandum expressed the opinion that "submarine vessels should be excluded from the benefit of the rules hitherto recognized by the law of nations regarding the admission of vessels of war or merchant vessels into neutral waters, roadsteads or ports and their sojourn in them." Any belligerent submarine entering a neutral port should therefore be detained.[1]

The allied memorandum appears not to have made a very favorable impression on the government of the United States.

any of them. By a royal order of the Danish government concerning the neutrality of Denmark in case of war between foreign powers, promulgated December 20, 1912, war vessels of belligerent powers were prohibited from entering the harbor and roadstead of Copenhagen and from entering inner-territorial waters whose entrances were closed by mines or other means of defence. The right was also reserved to prohibit entrance to other Danish ports or waters.

[1] Text of the memorandum in New York *Times*, October 10, 1916.

In a communication of October 11 the secretary of state sent a reply in which he expressed "surprise" that there appeared to be an endeavor on the part of the allied powers to "determine the rule of action governing what they regard as a 'novel situation' in respect to the use of submarines in time of war and to enforce acceptance of that rule, at least in part, by warning neutral powers of the great danger to their submarines in waters that may be visited by belligerent submarines." [1]   No circumstances, it was added, had been set forth by the allied governments concerning the use of submarines which would render the existing rules of international law inapplicable to them. The government of the United States would therefore reserve its liberty of action in all respects and would treat such vessels as in its opinion "becomes the action of a power which may be said to have taken the first steps toward establishing the principles of neutrality, and which for over a century has maintained those principles in the traditional spirit and with the high sense of impartiality in which they were conceived." The note concluded:

"In order, however, that there should be no misunderstanding as to the attitude of the United States, the government of the United States announces to the Allied Powers that it holds it to be the duty of belligerent Powers to distinguish between submarines of neutral and belligerent nationality and that responsibility for any conflict that may arise between belligerent warships and neutral submarines on account of the neglect of a belligerent to so distinguish between these classes of submarines must rest entirely upon the negligent Power."

Shortly thereafter the American policy was put to the test by the arrival in the harbor of Newport of the German war submarine U-53.   During its voyage across the Atlantic the submarine had sunk a number of British merchantmen and several neutral vessels.   The submarine, however, was allowed to enter American waters, to remain there for some hours, and to depart freely, after which it resumed its attacks upon enemy merchant vessels off the American coast.   The submarine appears not to have taken on any supplies while in American waters or to have committed any unneutral acts.   Its purpose in

---

[1] In the concluding paragraph of the memorandum the allied governments took occasion "to point out to the neutral powers the grave danger incurred by their submarines in the navigation of regions frequented by belligerent submarines."

entering an American port was not clear and was the subject of more or less conjecture. It was suggested that it came in with a view to seeking information which might be of value to it and other submarines in the prosecution of their operations against enemy merchantmen, but whether it succeeded in obtaining any such information is not known. The decision of the American government to accord hospitality to the submarine was the subject of considerable criticism in the English and French press, although neither the British nor French government appears to have made a formal protest against the action of the American government. The matter, however, was brought up for discussion in the British House of Lords, and it was evident that the action of the American government did not meet the approval of the British authorities.

Regarding the merits of the allied contention that the rules of international law concerning the admission to neutral ports of war ships which navigate on the surface of the ocean were inapplicable to submarines, it must be admitted that there was ground for the distinction. The existing rules were undoubtedly framed upon the theory of surface navigation, and the ability of a submarine to submerge and traverse neutral waters below the surface and thus evade the port regulations would certainly justify the neutral in subjecting it to different rules or even to exclude it from entering altogether. This, however, is a matter between the neutral government and the belligerent in whose service the submarine is operating. Nevertheless, as the allied memorandum pointed out, to allow a submarine operating far from its base to enter a neutral port for the purpose of resting and replenishing its supplies would clearly give the port the character of a base of operations. But since the U-53 did not make use of the port for these purposes it is doubtful whether the enemy belligerents had good ground for protest. Had its acts been otherwise, a different question would have arisen. In that case the duty of the American government would have been to refuse the hospitality of its ports to such craft and the German government could not have justly complained.

Unlike the policy of the American government, which was to deal with each case as it arose and according to the facts of the particular case, certain other neutral governments announced general rules which they proposed to apply to submarines in their ports. Thus the Norwegian government, by a decree of October 13, 1916, forbade armed belligerent submarines from traversing Norwegian waters except in case of *force majeure*, resulting from stress of weather or unseaworthiness, and in the latter case they were required to navigate the surface of the water and to fly the national flag.[1] By the same decree commercial submarines were allowed in Norwegian waters only during daylight and on condition that they refrained from submerging and that they carried the national flag. The Norwegian decree was the subject of bitter attack by the German press and the German government is reported to have addressed a protest to the Norwegian government in which it attacked the decree as being contrary to the Hague convention and incompatible with an impartial neutrality. The Norwegian differentiation between submarines and other war ships, it was said, was not justified, and it was contrasted with the attitude of the American government in the case of the U-53, which represented the "true spirit of a neutral." Threats are said to have been made by high German officials that the German government would not tolerate the Norwegian policy of differential treatment and that the terms of the decree would be ignored, as they appear in fact to have frequently been. The geographical proximity of Norway to Germany and the character of its coast line gave the question an aspect entirely different from that which confronted the United States. It was notorious that German submarines made use of Norwegian waters for rest and recuperation and perhaps for conferring with German spies, with which Norway was overrun.[2] As is well known, German submarines also stationed themselves outside the marginal waters and sank large numbers of Norwegian merchant vessels as they emerged from their home ports, and there appear indeed to have been a good many instances in which they sank vessels well within the territorial waters of Norway. Under these circumstances the Norwegian government was clearly within its rights. Not-

---

[1] Text in 44 Clunet, p. 322.

[2] *American Scandinavian Review*, March–April, 1917, p. 118. As to German submarine activities in Norwegian waters and the measures adopted by the Norwegian government cf. 45 Clunet, pp. 323 ff. Regarding the use of Norwegian ports by belligerent war ships cf. the Norwegian orange book, issued in 1916, pp. 2 ff.

withstanding the German protest, the Norwegian decree was never modified, although by way of reprisal the German policy of sinking Norwegian vessels is said to have been greatly extended after the adoption of the new rules.[1]

The Swedish government adopted substantially the same policy as that of Norway and excluded belligerent war submarines from passing through and remaining in Swedish territorial waters (Decree of July 19, 1916). The frequent use by war ships of both Great Britain and Germany of the territorial waters of Sweden, which greatly added to the Swedish burden of patrolling those waters, led the government to mine the waters of Kogrund Channel and to close them to all except Swedish vessels. Against this measure the governments of the Entente powers protested, as the German government had protested against the Norwegian decree respecting submarines, this on the ground that the Swedish order closed the only route by which allied vessels could pass into and out of the Baltic without being exposed to destruction by German war ships. The protest also added that the Swedish government had left open a route accessible only to Swedish and German vessels, thus discriminating against the Entente powers.[2] The Swedish

[1] Cf. an article by Dr. A. F. Frangulis entitled *le Cas de la Norvège et le Droit des Gens*, 45 Clunet, pp. 563 ff. The *Norddeutsche Zeitung* of October 20, 1916, published an official *communiqué* which charged that the decree of the Norwegian government was directed mainly against Germany and as such was in contravention of the spirit of true neutrality, and the German minister at Christiania was instructed to make "express reserves in respect to the attitude of the Norwegian government."

[2] Text of the note in 24 *Rev. Gén. de Droit Int. Pub.*, pp. 232–233. The protest also complained that the Swedish government made a distinction between commercial and war submarines, a distinction which, it was said, was not well founded, since it was difficult to distinguish the one from the other at sea. The Swedish authorities would therefore hesitate to attack a German submarine of any character found in its waters, through fear of committing a mistake, whereas they would never hesitate to attack a British or French war submarine, for the reason that it was well known that neither Great Britain nor France possessed any commercial submarines. In effect, therefore, the decree would result to the advantage of Germany. But, as M. Perrinjaquet remarks (24 *Rev. Gén. de Droit Int. Pub.*, p. 233), the allied position in regard to the identity of the two classes of submarines was not well founded. Their contention, however, in regard to the closing of the waters of the Kogrund Channel rested on a sounder basis, since the result was to discriminate against the allies in favor of Germany, and it is doubtful whether the Swedish government was within its rights in virtually closing a strait connecting two open seas, even if the strait comprises the territorial waters of the neutral. Cf. Perrinjaquet, *op. cit.*, p. 234, Despagnet-de Boeck, p. 630, and 43 Clunet, p. 1716.

government sharply denied the allied charge of partiality toward Germany and declared that it must refuse to enter into a discussion as to the sincerity and impartiality of its neutrality policy.[1]

The Dutch neutrality declaration of August 4, 1914, prohibited all war ships and ships assimilated thereto from entering Dutch territorial waters except when forced to enter by stress of weather or damages, and this was interpreted to include submarines.[2] The king of Spain in June, 1917, issued a decree forbidding all submarines of whatever kind belonging to belligerent powers from navigating Spanish territorial waters or from entering Spanish ports upon pain of being interned until the end of the war. Submarines of neutral powers, however, were allowed to enter on condition that they navigated on the surface with their colors visibly displayed.[3]

There is a growing opinion in favor of the view that neutrals should be required to prohibit belligerent war vessels of enemy character from entering their ports or making use of their waters except where considerations of humanity require such entry or use, and the results of the recent war will probably strengthen the opinion.[4] Had this measure been adopted at the outbreak of the recent war by all neutrals, as it was subsequently adopted by a few of the powers, many irritating controversies would

[1] Text of the Swedish note of September 9, 1916, in 24 *Rev. Gén. de Droit Int. Pub.*, pp. 233–234, n. 2.

[2] Text of the Declaration in *Int. Law Topics*, 1916, pp. 61 ff. See also Grotius *Annuaire* for 1916, p. 101, and 24 *Rev. Gén.*, Docs., pp. 110–114, 186.

[3] The decree was intended to prevent a repetition of such acts as that which occurred at Cadiz where a German submarine took refuge and was later escorted out of the port by Spanish torpedo boats. Text in Supp. to *Amer. Jour. of Int. Law*, Vol. XI, p. 177.

[4] Cf. the French writer M. Perrinjaquet in 24 *Rev. Gén. de Droit Int. Pub.*, p. 230. Prior to the recent war, however, the majority of French jurists looked with disfavor on the proposition to forbid belligerent war ships from revictualling, taking supplies of coal, and making repairs necessary to enable them to put to sea, regardless of what may have been the cause of the injuries received. Cf. the report of M. Lapradelle to the Institute of International Law in 1910 (*Annuaire*, 23, pp. 100 ff.) and the discussion on the same (p. 397). Cf. also Lapradelle's article entitled *La Nouvelle Thèse du Refus de Charbon au Belligérants dans les Eaux Neutres*, in the *Rev. Gén. de Droit Int. Pub.*, Vol. XI, pp. 531 ff.; Dupuis, same *Revue*, Vol. XVI, p. 581, and Despagnet-de Boeck, pp. 1215 ff. Cf. also the stringent rules adopted by the American Institute of International Law at Havana in 1917 (arts. 12–15). Cf. also an article entitled *Du Régime à imposer aux Sous-Marins dans les Eaux Territoriales et Ports Neutres*, in 44 Clunet, pp. 96 ff.

have been avoided and the requirements of a true neutrality would have been more fully met.

§ 565. Commercial Submarines, Case of the *Deutschland*
The visit of the German commercial submarine *Deutschland* to the United States in July, 1916, raised the question as to the status of such craft in neutral ports.[1] A thorough examination of the build and equipment of the submarine was made by order of the department of state, and it was found that it was not constructed with a view to conversion into a war vessel, that it carried no torpedoes or rapid-fire guns or weapons of any kind even for defensive purposes, and that its voyage was purely a commercial venture. Under these circumstances the government ruled that the submarine was an inoffensive merchant vessel and as such was entitled to the usual privileges accorded belligerent merchant vessels in neutral ports. It was accordingly permitted to remain in port without restriction, to discharge its cargo and take on a new cargo and to clear when it was ready to depart. The question thus presented was unique and without precedent. The only circumstance which distinguished the submarine from a merchant ship, strictly speaking, was its ability to navigate below the surface, thus enabling it, if it chose, to evade the customs laws and the port regulations. Since, however, it conformed strictly to those laws and regulations, the American government saw no reason for treating it differently from regular merchant craft. In its ruling, however, the government took occasion to announce that its decision in this particular case was not to be regarded as a precedent and that each such case arising in the future would be decided on the basis of the facts. The decision appears to have been a correct one under the circumstances, although it caused some irritation in England and France. It is understood that the British and French embassies at Washington made *pro forma* representations against treating the submarine as a merchant vessel, this on the ground that it was alleged to be potentially a war vessel, although designed and used as a merchant ship. But the investigation showed that this contention

---

[1] Subsequently the *Deutschland* made another visit to the United States and took back to Germany a cargo of 360 tons of nickel, 180 tons of rubber, and a quantity of other goods which were on the British list of contraband, and which were said to have been purchased in the United States by agents of the German government.

was unfounded. It will be recalled that the allied memorandum referred to above (communicated to neutral governments a month later) urged them to exclude from their ports all submarine vessels *whatever the purpose to which they are put;* that is, they should forbid entrance to commercial as well as war submarines.[1] But the American government, as stated above, refused not only to recognize any distinction between commercial submarines and regular merchant vessels but also to apply any different rules to war submarines than were applicable to other war vessels.[2] The Dutch government also appears to have adopted the same course and treated commercial submarines as it treated regular merchantmen.

§ 566. **Taking of Prizes into Neutral Ports.** In several instances neutral governments found themselves embarrassed by the action of belligerent men-of-war in bringing prizes into their ports. In March, 1915, the German cruiser *Prinz Eitel Friedrich* brought the French sailing vessel *Jean* into a Chilian port as a prize of war and held it there for eight days, during which time the captor was engaged in trans-shipping coal from the vessel to his own ship. The government of Chili protested against this violation of its neutrality and offence against its sovereignty as being contrary to articles 12 and 21 of the 13th Hague convention.[3] A like protest was made against the conduct of several German men-of-war in bringing into the

---

[1] As already mentioned in the preceding section, the British and French governments in their protest against the Swedish ordinance excluding war submarines from its waters complained that it made a distinction between war and commercial submarines, a distinction which, it was argued, was not justified in view of the difficulty of distinguishing between the two types of submersibles.

[2] Judge Atherley-Jones in a paper read before the Grotius Society of London on March 20, 1917, argued that the attempt to distinguish between commercial and war submarines is "from the belligerent's point of view wholly impracticable." The ability of a submarine to submerge, he says, makes it impossible for a naval commander to visit and search it with a view to verifying its nationality or determining the nature of the service in which it is engaged. Moreover, its ability to run a blockade would make it impossible for a belligerent to maintain an effective and therefore legal blockade. As to the *Deutschland* it was, he contends, in fact a public vessel in the service of the German government, and its voyage to the United States was in the interest of the State and was undertaken at the instance of the executive. It should, therefore, have been treated by the American government as a war vessel. *Pubs. of the Grotius Society*, Vol. III, p. 40.   But compare Reeves in XI *Amer. Jour. of Int. Law*, 149 who maintains that the status of a commercial submarine and an ordinary merchant vessel is the same, although the neutral may require the former to navigate its waters on the surface.

[3] Alvarez, *op. cit.*, pp. 231–232.

Chilian port of Juan Fernandez the French steamer *Valentine*, the Norwegian steamer *Helicon*, and the American steamer *Sacramento* as prizes and holding them there for a period of seven days, during which time their cargoes of coal and provisions were transferred to the vessels of their captors. This act was denounced by the Chilian government as a flagrant violation of the neutrality of the country, all the more reprehensible because it was committed with premeditation in the waters of an island over which, by reason of its distance from the mainland, the Chilian authorities were unable to exercise the surveillance which they were able to exercise over their continental ports. The ships were brought in for other purposes, it was asserted, than sequestration, the real end being to make the ports of the island a depot of prizes and a base of naval operations in violation of articles 5 and 23 of the 13th Hague convention. The French government on its part addressed a note to the Chilian government demanding reparation for damages sustained on account of the capture and loss of the *Valentine*, this on the ground that the government of Chili was responsible, since it had tolerated the bringing in and the holding of the ship as a prize of war in its territorial waters. The Chilian government, in a reply of July 19, 1915, to the French demand, stated that it had conformed strictly to the provisions of article 25 of the 13th Hague convention by the heavy sacrifices which it had made in exercising a strict surveillance over its ports and waters in order to prevent violations of its neutrality, and it called attention to the distance of the island from its coasts, the lack of communications therewith, and the consequent difficulties that were encountered in compelling the war ships of the contending belligerents to respect the neutrality of the island. The Chilian government, it was asserted, had exercised due diligence to prevent the acts complained of and it could not, therefore, be held responsible for infractions which it had been unable to prevent.[1]

§ 567. **Case of the *Appam*.** A more notable and more widely discussed case was that of the *Appam*, a British merchantman which had been captured off the African coast by a German "raider" and brought into the port of Newport News, Virginia, in February, 1916, by a prize crew which had been put aboard

[1] Alvarez, ch. 9.

by the captor and which was assisted by the passengers and
crew of the *Appam* who were compelled to aid in keeping guard
and in navigating the ship. Upon the arrival of the *Appam*
the German ambassador at Washington informed the secretary
of state of the intention of the German prize master to remain
with his prize in American waters until further notice, claiming
the right to do so under article 19 of the Prussian-American
treaty of 1799. He also requested the internment in the United
States during the remainder of the war of certain of her passengers on the ground that they had offered resistance to the
captors.[1] This request was refused by the American authorities,
and the ship's crew and passengers were set at liberty. The
German prize crew, however, were retained on board the ship
virtually as prisoners and the prize-master was required to
give his parole not to leave the vessel except for the transaction
of official business with the customs authorities. The British
ambassador at Washington in the meantime had made a formal
demand upon the American government that instructions be
given for the release of the *Appam* to the British owners, on
the ground that the status of the vessel was determined not by
the Prussian-American treaty but by article 21 of the 13th
Hague convention which lays down the rule that "a prize may
be brought into a neutral port only on account of unseaworthiness, stress of weather or want of fuel or provisions." This
demand was shortly followed by the filing of a libel against the
Appam in the United States district court by the British owners.
Thereupon the German ambassador addressed a communication
to the secretary of state denying that the court had any jurisdiction of the case; this denial was based on article 19 of
the Prussian treaty and the inoperation of the 13th Hague
convention in consequence of its non-ratification by the British
government. The communication further added that since the
Appam was flying the naval flag of the German government and
belonged to its captors as a lawful prize, no neutral court could
lawfully take cognizance of the case with a view to wresting
the prize from its captors. In a communication of March 2
which was not made public until May 17 out of respect to the

---

[1] The *Appam* had on board 116 of her own passengers, a crew of 155 persons, a
German prize crew of 22 persons, and 138 seamen who had been taken from other
vessels captured or sunk by the *Appam's* captor.

court which had already taken jurisdiction of the case, the secretary of state informed the German ambassador that in his opinion article 19 of the treaty of 1799 as revived in 1828 applied only to prizes brought into American ports by vessels of war and not to those like the *Appam* which were brought in by a prize master and crew, unaccompanied by a ship of war. Furthermore the *Appam* did not fall within the evident meaning of article 19, which contemplated only temporary asylum for vessels of war accompanying prizes while en route to places named in the commander's commission and not the deposit of spoils of war in an American port. The *Appam* therefore was entitled "only to the privileges usually granted by maritime nations to prizes of war, namely to enter neutral ports only in case of stress of weather, want of fuel and provisions, or necessity of repairs, but to leave as soon as the cause of their entry has been removed." [1]

This view of the status of the *Appam* was reached by the district court. The court held that the case was governed by articles 21 and 22 of the 13th Hague convention of 1907 and not by the Prussian-American treaty. These articles, the court added, did not embody new rules, but were merely declaratory of the existing law of nations and as such were binding independently of the status of the convention of which they formed a part. True, Great Britain had not ratified the convention, but most of the other powers, some forty-three in number, including Germany and the United States, had ratified it. Moreover, the principle embodied in the two articles was entirely in accord with the policy of both the United States and Germany. The court declared that it was now the generally accepted doctrine among enlightened nations that their ports could not be allowed as places of asylum or permanent rendezvous for the prizes of belligerents. To do so would be to involve them in conflict with nations with whom they were at peace. The conclusion of the court was

"that the manner of bringing the *Appam* into the waters of the United States, as well as her presence in those waters, constitutes a violation of the

---

[1] The correspondence between Secretary Lansing and the British and German ambassadors regarding the status of the *Appam* may be found in *Dip. Cor. with Bellig. Gov'ts relating to Neutral Rights and Duties, Dept. of State, European War*, No. 3, pp. 331–344.

neutrality of the United States; that she came in without bidding or permission; that she is here in violation of the law; that she is unable to leave for lack of a crew, which she cannot provide or augment without further violation of neutrality; that in her present condition she is without a lawful right to be in and remain in these waters; that she, as between her captors and owners, to all practical interests and purposes, must be treated as abandoned and stranded upon our shores, and that her owners are entitled to restitution of their property, which this country should award irrespective of the prize court proceedings of the Court of the Imperial Government of the German Empire, and it will be so ordered." [1]

Upon appeal to the United States Supreme Court the decision of the lower court was affirmed.[2]

The decision was entirely in accord with the letter and spirit of the Hague convention, as well as the policy of modern nations, especially the United States and Great Britain.[3] It is clear that the Hague Conference intended to prohibit the taking of prizes into neutral ports except in cases of unseaworthiness, stress of weather, or lack of fuel or provisions, and that when taken in for any of these reasons they were bound to leave as soon as the necessity for their entrance had passed.[4] No such necessity

---

[1] Already on May 11 the German Imperial prize court at Hamburg had rendered a decision in the case of the *Appam* holding that it had been legally captured, although of course the court expressed no opinion on the question as to the right of the captors to take it into a neutral port and lay it up until the end of the war.

[2] *Hans Berg, Prize Master, etc.,* v. *British and African Steam Navigation Co.,* decided March 6, 1917. In its opinion Mr. Justice Day, speaking for the Supreme Court, said: "The principles of international law recognized by this government, leaving the treaty aside, will not permit the ports of the United States to be thus used by belligerents. If such use were permitted, it would constitute of the ports of a neutral country harbors of safety into which prizes, captured by one of the belligerents, might be safely brought and indefinitely kept."

[3] As to the authority and practice cf. Dana's *Wheaton,* § 391; Bernard, *History of British Neutrality,* pp. 137-141; Hall, *Int. Law,* 5th ed., p. 618; Risley, *Laws of War,* p. 176; Westlake, *Int. Law,* Pt. II, p. 215; Bluntschli, *Droit Int. Cod.,* note to § 778; Stockton, *Outlines of Int. Law,* p. 408, and Scott, *The Peace Conferences of 1899 and 1907,* Vol. I, pp. 645-646. The practice of the past and the opinions of the authorities are reviewed by Mr. F. R. Coudert in his brief for the libellants in the case of the *Appam,* pp. 17 ff. As to the case of the *Appam* cf. an article by C. D. Allin in the *Minnesota Law Review* for January, 1917, a paper by H. H. L. Bellot in the *Pubs. of the Grotius Society,* Vol. II, pp. 11 ff. An article by F. R. Coudert in 11 *Amer. Jour. of Int. Law,* pp. 302 ff., and an article by E. M. Borchard, *ibid.,* pp. 270 ff.

[4] Art. 23 of the thirteenth Hague convention permits neutrals to allow prizes to be brought into their ports and roadsteads to be sequestrated pending the decision of a prize court. Both Great Britain and the United States, however, reserved their ratification of this article, and the German prize code, although embodying textually arts. 21 and 22, makes no mention of art. 23. It is clear

caused the *Appam* to enter à port of the United States; its entrance therefore was a violation of the neutrality of the country and the captor could not hold it there until the end of the war. It remained the property of the original owners.

§ 568. **The Hovering of War Ships off Neutral Ports.** During the early years of the war Great Britain maintained a somewhat elaborate naval patrol off the principal ports of the Atlantic coast of the United States for the purpose of intercepting German war ships which might attempt to enter such ports and of preventing the escape of enemy merchant vessels laid up therein. The patrolling ships, in general, scrupulously kept outside the three-mile limit and rarely molested neutral vessels. In several instances, however, complaint was made in the United States that neutral vessels were followed within the three-mile limit by British war ships and that in other instances they were subjected to an annoying surveillance. One such case was that of the Danish merchantman *Vinland*, which was alleged to have been followed by a British war ship for some distance down the coast within American territorial waters. In reply to a representation of the department of state the British ambassador denied that the war ship in question ever came within the territorial waters of the United States and asserted that the commanders of British war vessels had explicit instructions to keep outside such waters. In a communication of December 16, 1915, to the British ambassador, Secretary Lansing stated that the American government had "always regarded the practice of belligerent cruisers patrolling American coasts in close proximity to the territorial waters of the United States and making the neighborhood a station for their observations as inconsistent with the treatment to be expected from the naval vessels of a friendly power in time of war and has maintained that the consequent menace of such proceedings to the freedom of American commerce is vexatious and uncourteous to the United States." The British ambassador replied that the objection raised by the secretary of state appeared to rest on a claim to distinguish between different parts of the high seas,

that these and other powers regarded the article as contrary to the spirit of true neutrality, and so far as is known, no such permission has ever been granted by any neutral government to a belligerent. Cf. a review of the practice in Coudert's brief referred to above, pp. 10 ff.

in one of which it was legitimate to carry on belligerent operations, while in the other it was not, a distinction which was unknown to the law of nations. The ambassador took occasion also to remind the secretary of state that during the Civil War in the United States the American naval forces maintained a system of patrol and surveillance in the neighborhood of Bermuda which was no different in character from that against which the secretary was complaining; and indeed American war ships were charged with having maintained "a system of cruising" within the territorial waters of Bermuda. Extracts from the official records of the navy were submitted in support of the charge. The ambassador further called attention to the presence of the large number of enemy merchant ships sheltering in American ports, to prevent the escape of which it was necessary for the British government to maintain cruisers in a position where they would be able to intercept any vessels that might attempt to leave. Finally, it was added that neutral ships were known to have carried supplies from American ports to enemy war ships on the high seas. This was another reason why British cruisers were bound to keep a close and constant watch over ships departing from American ports. The secretary of state did not deny that British war ships which were engaged in cruising off the American coast outside the three-mile limit were within their legal rights, but his objections to the practice were based upon the "irritation which it naturally causes to a neutral country"; it was an "inevitable source of annoyance and offence." As to the charges that American cruisers were guilty of a similar practice off the coast of Bermuda during the Civil war, the secretary asserted that the circumstances were very different and the acts alleged were far less offensive. The cruising complained of then took place in the vicinity of small islands near the American coast which were being used as a rendezvous for vessels notoriously engaged in running the blockade, whereas in the present case the British cruisers were patrolling off the great commercial ports of the United States from which routes diverge to all parts of the world. As to the circumstance that enemy merchant vessels in large numbers were refugeeing in American ports and had to be closely watched, the secretary reminded him that the duty of preventing them from escaping had been successfully discharged by the American government.

Finally, the secretary, adverting to the analogy of land warfare, called the attention of the ambassador to the fact that in time of peace the mobilization of an army near the frontier had often been regarded as ground for serious offence and made the subject of protest. As was well known, it had been the ground for Germany's declaration of war against Russia in August, 1914. On the same principle the "constant and menacing presence of cruisers on the high seas near the ports of a neutral country may be regarded according to the canons of international courtesy as a just ground for offence, although it may be strictly legal." [1]

§ 569. Submarine Operations off the American Coast. In October, 1916, considerable excitement was aroused in the United States by the action of the German war submarine U-53, which had been allowed to enter and depart freely from the port of Newport, in sinking off the coast of Massachusetts four British, one Dutch and one Norwegian merchant vessel. [2] The acts took place well without the territorial waters of the United States, but so near the coast line as to cause no little irritation and widespread criticism in the United States. It was variously asserted that if it was a violation of the canons of good friendship for British cruisers to hover off the ports of the United States for the purpose of keeping watch over incoming and outgoing German vessels, it was still more offensive for German submarines to bring the war to the American coast and to sink neutral as well as enemy merchant vessels within sight of the American coast, and this in the barbarous manner in which German submarines were accustomed to destroy such vessels. In the minds of many persons the acts were all the more offensive for the reason that, a few hours before, the U-53 had enjoyed the hospitality of an American port and had been allowed to depart freely. It was variously asserted that a virtual blockade of American ports had been created by the appearance of the U-53 in the western Atlantic, that American neutrality had been grossly violated, that the U-53 would be followed by others, that American waters would be converted into a war zone, that secret submarine bases would be established on the American

---

[1] The correspondence between the secretary of state and the British ambassador may be found in *Diplomatic Correspondence, European War*, No. 3, pp. 131-141.
[2] New York *Times* of October 9, 1916. •

coast, that American merchant vessels entering and leaving port would be exposed to destruction, and the like.

The situation seemed to raise a serious problem for the government of the United States, but fortunately no other acts of the kind took place near the American coasts. The incident was the subject of deliberation by the President and the secretary of state, but they finally reached the conclusion that since the operations of the submarine took place on the high seas there was no legal ground on which a complaint could be based. It would seem to be a sound principle of international law that the destruction by a belligerent of enemy merchant vessels and also of neutral vessels when destruction is legitimate, on the high seas, even if near the coast of a neutral, is as lawful as if done in the middle of the ocean. It may be offensive and irritating to the neutral near whose coast the act takes place, but it can hardly be said to be a violation of the legal rules of neutrality. The question of the legality of such operations is, however, entirely different from the question as to whether neutrals should admit such craft to their waters on an equal footing and subject to the same conditions under which war ships which navigate the surface of the ocean are admitted. Whatever may be said against the right of a neutral to protest against the conduct of submarine warfare in the neighborhood of its coasts, their right to exclude such craft from entering their ports is scarcely arguable.

§ 570. Transit across Neutral Territory of Materials Susceptible of Military Use. A long-drawn-out controversy took place between the British and Dutch governments over the action of Dutch authorities in permitting certain metals to be shipped through the Netherlands from Belgium to Germany and in allowing sand and gravel to be shipped through Dutch territory from Germany to Belgium, then under the occupation of the German military forces. Early in the war the British government protested against the permission thus accorded the German authorities, on the ground that since the metals were used in Germany for the manufacture of instruments of war and the sand and gravel sent to Belgium were employed in the construction of military roads and defences, the action of the Netherlands government was a violation of its duties as a neutral. As to the transit of metals the Dutch government maintained

that it was bound, on the one side by the Rhine convention of
1868 which guarantees a free passage for all merchandise up and
down the river, and on the other, by the 5th Hague Convention
of 1907, which does not allow the transit of convoys either of
munitions or provisions through neutral territory. Being
obliged to reconcile the two somewhat conflicting obligations,
the Netherlands government adopted the policy of limiting the
obligatory free passage through its territory of goods from
Belgium to Germany, to those which, it asserted, had no connection with military operations in Belgium. No metals which
had been requisitioned by the German government were therefore allowed to pass through. But non-requisitioned metals,
including those produced in Belgium by the melting of ore
imported for that purpose from Germany, the Dutch government was bound under the Rhine Convention and article 2 of
the 5th Hague convention to allow to pass through. The
threat of the British government to discontinue all facilities for
the transmission of Dutch commercial cable messages in case
the Dutch government did not modify its decision would therefore, if actually resorted to, be an act of reprisal against the
Netherlands and an abuse of power by a belligerent toward a
neutral government which had observed in the most scrupulous
manner its duties of neutrality. The contention of the Dutch
government that its obligation extended only to the prohibition
of the transit of requisitioned goods was rejected as unsound
by the British government, which in turn maintained that it
was a general principle of international law that a neutral
State must not allow its territory to be made use of by a belligerent for military operations, as the Dutch government was
in fact doing. If Germany found it necessary to send commodities containing copper to Belgium to be smelted in order
to extract the metal and then to return the metal to Germany
for use in her ammunition factories, the transportation of these
commodities back and forth by way of neutral territory was
affording direct relief to the military transport system of Germany and constituted the use by Germany of Netherlands
territory for military purposes. Neither articles 2 nor 7 of the
5th Hague convention sanctioned the permission thus granted.
Article 7, which relieves neutrals from the obligation of preventing the export or transport on behalf of belligerents of

arms, munitions, and military supplies, has reference to the transport of goods which have been acquired by a belligerent as a result of commercial transactions with private persons in foreign countries and not to the transit through neutral territory of war materials between a belligerent State and enemy territory. Finally, there was nothing in the Rhine convention which made it obligatory upon the Dutch government to permit the passage of such materials. That convention dealt with the right of passage of goods up and down the Rhine between the riverain States and the sea, and had as its general purpose the freedom of commerce in time of peace on the Rhine and could not be interpreted to justify, still less to compel, violation of the obligations of neutrality.[1]

As to the transit of sand and gravel through Netherlands territory from Germany to Belgium, the Dutch government contended that it had taken all possible measures to assure itself that these materials were being used by the Germans only for non-military purposes such as the repair of highways, railroads, the strengthening of canal embankments, quays, and the like, and that as early as July, 1916, in consequence of British remonstrances, the Dutch government had taken measures to restrict materially the amount which might be transited through its territory with a view to limiting its use to ordinary civil purposes.[2] The British government, on its part, took the

[1] The Rhine Convention of October 7, 1868, was a treaty between France, Baden, Bavaria, Hesse, the Netherlands, and Prussia, entered into for the purpose of revising the earlier treaty of March 31, 1831, between the same parties (including Nassau). Both treaties were intended to assure to the riverain states of the Rhine that freedom of navigation of rivers passing through several states on which the Congress of Vienna had determined, and to protect them against the levying of taxation or the imposition of restrictions by particular states through whose territory the commerce of others had to pass. The British government contended and rightly, it would seem, that the stipulations related only to commerce in its ordinary sense and could have no bearing on the measures which a State is bound to take or may be justified in taking, to defend its neutrality in time of war. Text of the convention in Supp. to *Amer. Jour. of Int. Law*, Vol. X, p. 195.

[2] In a memorandum of February 12, 1916, to the German government the Dutch minister at Berlin called attention to the fact that during the months of August and December of the preceding year the quantity of sand and gravel exported from Germany to Belgium exceeded by four or five times the quantity exported during the entire year of 1913. It was clear, therefore, that the larger part of these materials were being used by the Germans for military purposes in Belgium. Under these circumstances the government of the Netherlands felt obliged to restrict the quantity of materials allowed to pass, to what was deemed

position that the Dutch government was required by the neutrality convention to prohibit the transit of all such materials and not merely to restrict the amount. Furthermore, it was reasonable to suppose that the construction and repair of railways, canal embankments, quays and the like was being undertaken by the Germans not for the benefit of the Belgian people, because it was notorious that the German authorities in Belgium had not only shown no disposition to improve their economic condition, but on the contrary had carried off their live stock, machinery, raw materials and otherwise destroyed their industrial and economic resources. It was clear, therefore, if they were improving roads, embankments, quays, etc., it was for no other purpose than to subserve their own military ends.[1] It would seem that the position of the British government was well founded. According to the admission of the Dutch government itself, the importation by the Germans of sand and gravel into Belgium was far in excess of the quantity imported in peace times, and all the evidence, circumstantial and other, pointed strongly to the conclusion that a large part of these materials was being used by the Germans for the construction of military defences or the improvement of the military transportation system. There was little or no difference between the transportation of such materials through neutral territory and the transportation of arms and munitions. The spirit of the Hague convention clearly condemns such transactions and it was the duty of the Dutch government to refuse to allow its territory to be made the medium of such traffic.[2]

---

necessary for ordinary civil purposes. Accordingly, the German government was notified, on July 5, 1917, that after August 1 the transit of sand and gravel through the Netherlands to Belgium would be prohibited unless the Dutch government was convinced in the meantime that the materials were necessary for the construction or repair of non-military works and were intended for such purposes.

[1] The entire correspondence between the Dutch and British governments regarding this matter and that between the Dutch and German governments may be found in a Dutch white paper entitled *Doorvoer Door Nederland uit Duitschland Naar Belge, en Omgekeerde Richting* (s'Gravenhage, 1917). A part of the British-Dutch correspondence may be found in a British white paper entitled correspondence respecting the Transit Traffic Across Holland of Materials Susceptible of Employment as Military Supplies, *Misc.*, No. 17 (1917), Cd. 8693; and Supp. *Amer. Jour. Int. Law*, Vol. X, pp. 175 ff. See also an article by De Visscher in the *Rev. Gén.*, 1919, pp. 142, ff.

[2] The attitude of the Dutch government in respect to its obligations as a neutral has been contrasted with that of the United States, which went to the length of

§ 571. Navigation of the River Scheldt by Belligerents.
At the outbreak of the war a number of German and Austrian
ships which were lying in the port of Antwerp were seized by the
Belgian government. On September 2, 1914, the British
minister at the Hague notified the Dutch government of the
intention of his government to transfer these vessels with their
English crews to England by way of the Western Scheldt.
The right to do this, he affirmed, was based on the free navigation
of the river guaranteed by the treaty of London of 1839, and
the view was expressed that the Dutch government would not
object to the passage of these unarmed merchant vessels through
Dutch territory to the sea.   The Dutch government in its reply
to this communication, however, stated that it could not permit
the right of passage requested, since the vessels in question had
fallen into the power of the Belgian government as the result
of an act of war and the observance of a strict neutrality forbade
it from allowing its territory to be used for the continuation of
the act of war. It was further added that the freedom of
navigation guaranteed by the treaty of 1839 had reference only
to commerce and not to the passage of ships seized as an act of
war by a belligerent. Notice was therefore given that if an
attempt were made to take the ships through the Scheldt they
would be seized upon entering Dutch territory and would be
interned until the end of the war. Upon the subsequent occupation of Antwerp by the German forces the ships in question
fell into the possession of the German government, which was
thereupon notified by the Dutch government that they would
not be allowed to pass through the territory of the Netherlands.
Several of them later entered Dutch territory and were seques-
tered, with the understanding that their ultimate disposition
would be determined at the close of the war. Boats for internal
navigation belonging to German subjects and which found themselves in Belgian jurisdiction at the outbreak of the war were
treated differently, however, from ocean-going vessels such as
those for which the British government demanded the right

---

refusing to allow wounded or disabled Canadian soldiers who had been discharged
from passing through the State of Maine as individuals on the way from Europe
to their homes in Canada. See the correspondence between the American and
British governments regarding the matter, in Supp. to *Amer. Jour. of Int. Law*,
October, 1917, pp. 231–232.

of passage, and they were freely admitted within the jurisdiction of the Netherlands.[1]

When, however, the British government, in October, 1914, requested permission for a hospital ship, the *China*, flying the British flag to pass through the Scheldt to Antwerp and to take on board a number of sick and wounded and return with the same to England, the request was granted subject to the conditions mentioned in article 14 of the Hague convention concerning the rights and duties of neutral persons and powers in case of war on land and also subject to the condition that the ship should transport neither personnel nor material of war.[2]

[1] Dutch orange book, *Ministere des Affaires Etrangères, Recueil de Diverses Communications*, etc., pp. 170–172.

[2] *Ibid.*, pp. 172–174. In consequence of the early capture of Antwerp by the Germans, the *China* was unable to avail herself of the permission thus accorded.

CHAPTER XXXVII

EFFECT OF THE WAR ON INTERNATIONAL LAW

§ 572. Imperfections of International Law Revealed by the War; § 573. Effect of the War on the Laws of Maritime Warfare; Blockade and Contraband; § 574. Other Unsettled Questions of Maritime Law; § 575. The Freedom of the Seas; § 576. The Need of New Regulations; § 577. Necessity for an International Conference.

§ 572. Imperfections of International Law Revealed by the War. It was inevitable that the recent war, embracing as it did so large a number of the States of the world, conducted to a great extent by new instrumentalities and according to new methods and carried on under conditions widely different in many respects from those of previous wars, should not only have revealed many imperfections in the existing rules governing the conduct of war, but that the whole system of international law itself should have been rudely shaken to its very foundations. It was equally inevitable that such a war should have brought to light many divergencies of view as to what the law allows and what it forbids, both to belligerents and neutrals, and that there should have been many irritating controversies between neutrals and belligerents concerning their respective rights.

In the first place, the war demonstrated in a striking manner that many of the rules which had been agreed upon by the body of States for the conduct of war were inadequate, illogical, or inapplicable to the somewhat peculiar and novel conditions under which they had to be applied during the late war. In the second place, the war brought out the fact that the existing rules did not by any means cover the whole field; that they were wholly silent in regard to the employment of various agencies and instrumentalities for waging war, and that they did not deal at all with certain conditions and circumstances which were unforeseen at the time the rules were formulated.[1]

[1] Dr. J. de Louter, Professor of International Law in the University of Utrecht, in an article entitled *La Crise du Droit International*, published in the *Revue Générale*

§ 573. Effect of the War on the Laws of Maritime Warfare; Blockade and Contraband. The recent invention and employment on a large scale, for the first time during the recent war, of the submarine mine, the submarine torpedo boat, the wireless telegraph and the air ship have largely transformed the methods of war on the sea and upset some of the rules that had been formulated to govern the conduct of naval warfare under different conditions. Thus the old form of blockade, with its cordon of ships stationed in the immediate offing of the blockaded port, has been rendered impossible. and this was admitted by the American secretary of state in a note of March 5, 1915, to the American ambassador at London. The " long range " blockade in which the blockading cruisers are permitted to remain far enough out to be beyond the reach of mines planted by the blockaded belligerent will therefore have to be recognized. The employment by a blockaded power of submarines for defence still further increases the difficulty of the enemy's maintaining an " effective " blockade by means of surface plying craft. The old rule as to " effectiveness " will therefore have to be modified if both mines and submarines are to be used by the blockaded power for this purpose.[1] The powers will have to determine also whether a blockade maintained by submarines shall be recognized as a lawful blockade, when it is notoriously ineffective.[2] A more important question still is

---

de Droit-Int. Pub. (Jan.–Feb. 1919), observes that the existing body of international law, although by no means destroyed, as well as the old organization of international relations, have proved to be inadequate to prevent war or to curb its violence. It is now passing through a period analogous to a pathological crisis in the case of a sick man and its foundations and content must be reformed. The content of the reformed law of nations should be enlarged so as to embrace within its scope the larger domain of international commerce, communication, finance, instruments of exchange, public health and the like. Among the bases of the new law should be justice, the maintenance of a juridical order among States, respect for the principle of nationality, abolition of the right of conquest, no cession of territory without the consent of the inhabitants thereof, liberty of commerce, freedom of the seas, abolition of secret treaties, etc.

[1] This is the thesis of M. Alessandri in his treatise *Contribution à l'Étude des Blocus Nouveaux* (Paris, 1919). This writer contends that in consequence of the use of mines and submarines "fictitious" blockades will now have to be looked upon with less disfavor.

[2] Alessandri, in the book referred to in the preceding note, maintains that a lawful blockade may be maintained by submarines provided the old rule as to "effectiveness" is modified though he admits that if they ply beneath the surface it will be difficult to verify the fact of effectiveness. In short, a belligerent might

whether belligerents shall be allowed to apply the doctrine of
continuous voyage or ultimate destination to blockade, so that a
belligerent may intercept the transportation of non-contraband
goods to his enemy, through neutral ports. The Declaration
of London expressly forbade the application of the rule to
blockade, but the Entente powers declined to abide by it.
Much may be said on both sides of the question; an endeavor
should be made to find some rule by which the just rights of
both belligerents and neutrals may be reconciled, and this will
involve the determination of the large question as to whether
the rights of belligerents shall be recognized as paramount to
those of neutrals, the affirmative of which was asserted by
more than one high authority during the recent war. Another
question which should receive the careful consideration of a
future conference is whether commercial blockades shall be
abolished and belligerents left merely the resource of military
blockade. There has been some demand in the past for this
change, and the conduct of the belligerents during the late war
served to accentuate it.

As was pointed out in a preceding chapter of this work, the
old rules in respect to contraband, especially those regarding
the test of its liability to capture, have been shown to be unsatisfactory, illogical, and to some extent out of harmony with
present-day conditions. The distinction which the Declaration
of London makes between consignments to fortified places,
military bases, and government contractors, on the one side,
and those to commercial ports and private merchants, on the
other, is, for all practical purposes, illogical and arbitrary.

---

proclaim a blockade, declare it to be effective, and yet it might be impossible for
neutrals to ascertain whether it was so or not. He thinks the right of belligerents
to employ submarines for purposes of blockade will have to be recognized, although
they should be required to conform to the same rules that apply to cruisers that
are employed in maintaining a blockade. But since they are hardly fitted for
capturing and taking in vessels charged with violating the blockade, what resource
will they have except to destroy them? Fauchille, on the contrary, maintains
that a legal blockade cannot be maintained by submarines. There is no means,
he points out, of determining whether such a blockade is effective, if the blockading
submarines choose to remain below the surface. Neutrals, therefore, cannot know
whether the blockade is effective or not. When a neutral vessel approaches the
blockade zone it is entitled to notice, yet if the blockading submarines are beneath
the surface, how are they to be notified? See his article, *La Guerre Sous-Marine
Allemande*, 25 *Rev. Gén.* 79.

As has also been pointed out, the distinction between absolute and conditional contraband has, under modern conditions, ceased to have any real basis in fact, and the attempt of the belligerents during the early part of the recent war to respect the distinction broke down in practice. Whether all restrictions on the carriage of contraband, or at least upon everything except arms and munitions should be removed, as was proposed by the British delegation at the second Hague Conference, and belligerents left only the weapon of blockade, is a question on both sides of which much may be said. In any case the question is one which should be carefully reëxamined at a future conference. One thing is clear, if the right to seize contraband is to be retained the right of search should be defined with more precision, and the question of the right of a captor to take neutral vessels into his home ports and to detain them for the purpose of search should be removed from the domain of controversy. Under modern conditions it would seem that this right will have to be recognized. Neutrals may and should, however, be spared the ruinous delays which must often result from this practice, by some form of certification under which vessels carrying innocent cargoes shall be exempt from search or detention.[1] But it would seem that the retention of the doctrine of continuous voyage under modern conditions is a necessity.[2] The interpretation of the existing rules in regard to the status of mails and of so-called "noxious" persons on neutral merchant vessels was the cause of much irritating controversy between belligerents and neutrals; the uncertainties should be cleared up and the right of belligerents to interfere with their transportation should be more specifically defined.[3]

§ 574. Other Unsettled Questions of Maritime Law. The law in respect to the places where and the conditions under which merchant vessels may be converted into naval auxiliaries was left unsettled by the Declaration of London and there is

[1] The proposed code of the American Institute of International Law, adopted at its session at Havana in January, 1917, abolishes the right of search and provides that merchant vessels shall carry papers certifying to the character of their cargoes, which papers shall be viséed by the local authorities of the ports from which they sail.

[2] Cf. Perrinjaquet, La Guerre Européenne, etc., 22 Rev. Gén. 129.

[3] The proposed American Institute code for neutrals declares that official or private postal correspondence of neutrals or belligerents found in the open sea on board a neutral or enemy vessel shall be inviolable.

a divergence of view and of practice among States in regard to the matter. During the late war Germany claimed and exercised the right to so convert merchant vessels on the high seas; Great Britain vigorously contested the right and demanded that neutrals should not recognize such vessels as lawful belligerent craft. This question like the others mentioned above should be definitely settled by a future conference.

As was pointed out in a previous chapter, the rules of the Declaration of London in regard to the transfers of flag are imperfect and unsatisfactory. The failure of the powers to ratify the Declaration has left the law in a chaotic state, each State being free to follow whatever rule it chooses. The question raised by the transfer to American registry of the Wagner ships and the refusal of the British and French prize courts to recognize the legality of the transfers should be settled by the adoption of a rule definitely determining whether the nationality of the owner or the flag shall be conclusive as to the character of the ship. The question also whether neutrals circumstanced as were the United States, Chili and other countries during the late war, which found themselves without ships for carrying on their commerce should not be allowed to purchase and transfer to their own merchant marines, belligerent ships lying idle in their ports, is one which deserves the favorable consideration of a future conference. Their right to requisition such ships upon payment of compensation ought to be clearly affirmed so as to remove all doubt and to avoid irritating controversies such as occurred during the late war between several neutral and belligerent powers. The whole matter of prize destruction should be regulated with more detail. The circumstances under which neutral prizes may be destroyed, if it is to be allowed at all, should be more precisely defined. Under no circumstances should belligerent ships which do not possess accommodations for taking care of passengers and crews be permitted to sink merchant vessels, either of enemy or neutral nationality, and the setting of crews and passengers adrift in small life boats should not be recognized as a compliance with the rule in respect to the obligation of the captor to provide for their safety. Since submarines in their present state of development do not possess such facilities, they should be prohibited absolutely from attacking merchant vessels, except in case of attempted escape or resistance.[1] No distinction should be recognized between the obligations of submarine commanders and the commanders of cruisers to provide for the safety of crews and passengers and this should be definitely affirmed by the new international law.

The right of merchant vessels to carry armament for the purpose of defence against unlawful attacks of submarines or other belligerent craft should be definitely affirmed and made a rule of the conventional law of nations. The proposal that they should surrender this right in return for an abandonment on the part of submarines of their claim to attack such vessels should be rejected.[2] The status of vessels so armed should be definitely fixed and it should include the right to enter and use neutral ports on equality with unarmed merchant vessels. The status of commercial submarines should also be defined. The British and French contention that no distinction should be made between commercial and war submarines does not appear to be warranted; but the question should be settled by a positive rule of the law of nations.

§ 575. The Freedom of the Seas. The unprecedented assertions of belligerent authority over the high seas and the grave infringement upon the rights of neutral commerce during the late war provoked a widespread discussion concerning the nature and limits of what is popularly known as the freedom of the seas. Throughout all the years of the war the Germans professed to be fighting, among other things, for this freedom which it was asserted Great Britain had destroyed.[3] The

---

[1] Compare the recommendations of a committee of British jurists appointed by the Grotius Society. Transactions of the Grotius Society, vol. IV, p. xli.

[2] The committee of English jurists referred to in the preceding note recommends that the destruction of enemy merchantmen before adjudication by a prize court should be entirely prohibited, in return for which belligerents and their subjects should be forbidden to arm merchantmen for purposes of offence or defence against submarines or other war vessels. From this recommendation, however, Sir John Macdonell vigorously dissented, on the ground that it would take away an immemorial right of self-defence; that it would be a concession to "militarism"; that it was contrary to the unanimous conclusions of the Institute of International Law; that there was no likelihood that nations, especially those with small navies, would surrender the right; that the contention that it is impossible to distinguish between acts of offence and defence is not well founded, etc. Ibid., pp. xlii, xiv.

[3] The German government, in one of its notes to the American government, enumerated among the objects for which Germany was fighting: "definite rules and safeguards, limitation of armaments on land and sea, as well as the freedom and community of high seas." Count Czernin, Austrian foreign minister, in a note to the American government, stated that "the high seas which rightfully

British government, on the other hand, asserted that the only real encroachments upon the principle of the freedom of the seas had been made by the Germans through the planting of mines in the open seas, by treating vast areas of the ocean as war zones within which commerce of every description and nationality was destroyed and by their ruthless methods of submarine warfare against merchant vessels of both belligerent and neutral nationality. Their professed solicitude for the maintenance of the freedom of the seas was therefore more hypocritical than sincere. Juristic discussion of the question was precipitated by a proposal of the President of the United States in January, 1918. One of the fourteen conditions of peace which he laid down in his address of January 8 to Congress was as follows:

" Absolute freedom of navigation upon the seas, outside territorial waters, alike in peace and in war, except as the seas may be closed in whole or in part by international action for the enforcement of international covenants."[1] Since no contention had been made that the seas were not free in time of peace the President's proposal could in fact therefore have had reference only to their freedom in time of war.

Under the established rules of international law the restrictions upon the freedom of the seas in time of war consist of the right of belligerents to cut off by means of a lawful blockade all trade and intercourse by seas with the enemy, to intercept the carriage of contraband of war to the enemy, and to prevent

---

belong to all the nations of the earth must be freed from domination or paramountcy and opened equally to all." In a note of July 21, 1915, to the British government the American secretary of state observed that "Germany and ourselves are both contending for the freedom of the seas." Professor A. S. Hershey, in an article entitled "The German Conception of the Freedom of the Seas" (13 *Amer. Jour. of Int. Law*, pp. 206 ff.), reviews the opinions that have been put forward by German writers and jurists. He points out that there is no agreement among them concerning the essentials of a program. Some like Schücking favor internationalization of the high seas; some like Meurer advocate the abolition of commercial blockade, contraband, and the capture of private property at sea; while others like Triepel and Stier-Somlo consider the proposal to do away with contraband and blockade as utopian.

[1] A year earlier, while the United States was still a neutral power, the President had in an address to the Senate declared that "the paths of the sea must alike in law and in fact be free. The freedom of the seas is the *sine qua non* of peace, equality, and coöperation." The Pope in a peace message of August 1, 1917, also made an appeal for the recognition of the principle of the freedom of the seas.

certain unneutral acts such as the carriage of dispatches, noxious persons, etc. The President's proposal for " absolute " freedom of the seas literally interpreted would therefore require belligerents to surrender these long-recognized methods of putting stress upon their enemies.[1] Naturally the proposal did not meet with favor at the hands of the British and French governments and in their reply they called attention to the fact that the language employed by the President was open to various interpretations, some of which they could not accept. They stated, therefore, that they must reserve to themselves complete freedom on this subject when they entered the peace conference. The President's proposal does not appear to have been pressed at the peace conference and had it been, there is little likelihood that it would have found favor. There are of course and have long been writers who have advocated the abolition of commercial as contra-distinguished from purely military blockades, but they are greatly in the minority.[2] In any case if it were desirable to prohibit the former, belligerents could not be justly deprived of the latter weapon unless the right of siege in land warfare were also taken away. The abolition of blockade and the taking away from belligerents of the right to seize contraband going to the enemy would place naval powers at a disadvantage in comparison with the great military land powers. It would, especially if it were accompanied by the abolition of the right of capture of private property at sea, virtually put an

[1] Some of the more advanced advocates, especially Germans, would extend the principle of the freedom of the seas to include even the abolition of the right to capture enemy private property on enemy ships. See Hershey's article cited above.

[2] See an article by A. G. Hays in 12 *Amer. Jour. of Int. Law*, 283, where it is argued that freedom of the seas means abolition of the doctrine of contraband, of commercial blockades and immunity of private property from capture at sea. The American Institute of International Law at its session at Havana in January, 1917, adopted a code of rules of maritime neutrality which went to the length of abolishing commercial blockade, of proclaiming the immunity of private property (except contraband) at sea, of forbidding the sinking of merchant ships of both belligerent and neutral nationality under any pretext whatever, the search of properly certified neutral merchant vessels, and the seizure on the high seas of mails on neutral or enemy steamers under any pretext. Text in New York *Times*, June 23, 1917.

Meurer, a German jurist, declares that the right of commercial blockade is " rotten; it is a defiance of neutrality; it is the legal form for brutal acts against neutrals and their trade." *Das Program der Meers-freiheit*, p. 60. But Triepel and Stier-Somlo think there is no likelihood that the nations will agree to abolish it. (Quoted by Hershey, *loc. cit.*, p. 225.)

end to naval warfare. Absolute freedom of the seas, therefore, is largely incompatible with the existence of naval warfare. Under these circumstances naval powers can hardly be expected to surrender willingly their chief means of carrying on war. The reform of naval and land warfare must go hand in hand; it would obviously be discrimination to draw the teeth of strong naval powers and leave the great military powers free to employ the right of siege and other analogous weapons.[1] It has been many times pointed out that a freedom of the seas which would exclude the right of blockade and the right to prevent the transportation of contraband to the enemy would have made difficult if not impossible the defeat of the Confederacy during the Civil war and it would probably have insured the triumph of Germany during the recent war.

The seas should, however, be free in the sense that no belligerent should be permitted to plant mines in them outside his own territorial waters, to assert control over portions of them under the guise of war zones, to blockade directly neutral ports, to conduct unlawful searches, to extend the doctrine of contraband beyond reasonable limits, or to interfere generally with the transportation of letter mail on neutral steamers.

§ 576. The Need of New Regulations. As has been stated above, the recent war demonstrated not only that many of the existing rules of international law are inadequate and to some extent out of harmony with present-day conditions, but that new rules have been made necessary largely in consequence of the invention of new instrumentalities and methods of warfare. Aside from the prohibition of the Hague convention in respect to the bombardment of undefended places, the conduct of aerial warfare is unregulated by convention;[2] and since the

[1] Cf. Woolsey, Freedom of the Land and Freedom of the Sea, 28 *Yale Law Journal*, 153; Corbett, The League of Peace and a Free Sea; Baty, The Supposed Chaos in the Law of Nations, *Penn. Law Review*, June, 1915, p. 78; Fenwick, The Freedom of the Seas, 11 *Amer. Pol. Sci. Review*, 387; Coudert, Neutral Rights upon the Seas, *Annals of the Amer. Acad. of Pol. and Soc. Sci.*, July, 1917, 58 ff; Anderson, Freedom of the Seas, *ibid.*, pp. 65 ff.; Hurd, Freedom of the Seas, *Fortnightly*, 108 (New Ser. 102), pp. 685 ff.; Balfour, The Freedom of the Seas, London *Weekly Times*, May 26, 1916 (interview). Mr. Balfour observes that to "paralyze naval power and leave military power uncontrolled is surely the worst injury which international law can inflict upon mankind."

[2] The proposed convention for the regulation of international air navigation prepared by a subcommittee of the Peace Conference deals only partially with the conduct of aerial warfare, many questions raised during the late war not being touched upon at all.

late war was the first in which the air ship was employed as an instrument of combat, there is no body of customary law governing the conduct of this mode of warfare. The above-mentioned prohibition lays down no test for determining what constitutes defence. The test applied in land and naval warfare, namely the presence of troops, the existence of fortifications, and the like, is not a proper test in aerial warfare, and the matter should receive the attention of a future conference. The employment of air craft for dropping bombs on peaceful towns situated far behind the lines, whether they are defended in the sense of possessing fortifications or not, should be forbidden and aerial activities confined to the zone of military operations. There is no difference in principle between torpedoing a merchant vessel without warning and drowning the non-combatant crews and passengers and the indiscriminate dropping of bombs by air craft upon towns and villages inhabited only by non-combatants. The proposal made in the Institute of International Law in 1911 and seriously advocated by a large number of distinguished jurists to so restrict the use of air craft was one which should receive the careful consideration of the next conference. It seems quite illogical to ban the submarine and leave the aviator free to launch his bombs upon private houses and upon unoffending peaceful non-combatants hundreds of miles behind the battle lines.

The introduction and employment of the air ship on a large scale has also given rise to a host of questions involving the rights of neutrals, the more important of which have been referred to in Chapter XIX. There are as yet no international regulations dealing with these questions except in so far as the rules of land and naval warfare can be interpreted to apply to them. In view of the important part which the air ship seems destined to play in the wars of the future the adoption of a convention regulating the conduct of aerial warfare would seem to be one of the necessary tasks of the next conference.

The submarine torpedo boat, like the air ship, is largely a new instrument of warfare, and the conditions under which it may be employed should be precisely defined. Like the air ship, it is a lawful instrument only when it is employed against legitimate objects of attack. Its operations should be restricted by international convention and its employment for the sinking of merchant vessels should be absolutely forbidden.

The invention of other agencies of destruction, notably asphyxiating and poisonous gases, has provoked much discussion as to the means that may be employed by a belligerent for injuring his enemy. This latter question is an old one, — one which has come to the front with the invention of every new instrumentality of destruction, and there is little likelihood that there will ever be an agreement as to what instruments are and what are not legitimate. The Hague convention deals to some extent with the means of injuring the enemy, but, as is so often the case with these conventions, the generality of the language employed leaves belligerents a large discretion. Most persons are agreed that if war cannot be conducted in a civilized manner it can at least and should be conducted with some regard to the principles of humanity. The progress of inventive science and the certainty that the wars of the future will be carried on by more powerful and destructive agencies than ever before known, make it important that the next conference should endeavor to define with more precision the means that may be employed against those whose unhappy lot it will be to participate actively in such wars.

Aside from the need of new regulations governing the employment of newly invented instrumentalities and agencies of destruction the existing rules of international law should be supplemented by regulations covering various matters now unregulated either by convention or custom. The right of reprisal so often resorted to or threatened during the late war is not touched upon by any of the international conventions. An effort should be made to define the acts for which resort to this doubtful expedient shall be recognized as legitimate and some limit set to the conduct of belligerents in the choice of the means they may adopt in carrying out their measures of reprisal. Likewise, the right of hostage-taking so greatly abused by the Germans during the late war is not dealt with by any of the international conventions. It should either be forbidden outright or the purposes for which hostages may be taken and the treatment to which they may be subjected should be precisely defined. The whole doctrine of military necessity should likewise be carefully considered and an effort made to define its limits. As interpreted by the Germans during the late war it virtually reduced the Hague conventions to a nullity.

These conventions recognize that the law may be overridden whenever considerations of military necessity require it, but they make no attempt to define the term or set limits to the power of belligerents. As the law now stands therefore, belligerents are left largely to their own arbitrary discretion.

§ 577. **Necessity of an International Conference.** In respect to these and other matters the existing conventions are either silent, inadequate, or out of harmony with present-day conditions. There is hardly one of the Hague conventions that cannot be greatly improved in the light of the experience of the recent war. The whole body of international law needs thorough revision and amplification; so far as possible, its rules ought to be precisely stated and embodied in a written code and they should embrace not only regulations governing the conduct of war and the customary relations of peace, but in a larger degree also the whole domain of international commerce, trade, navigation, labor, finance, international waterways, and the like.[1] To this end there should be assembled at as early a date as possible a conference representing the powers, to which should be sent as delegates their leading international jurists and statesmen for the purpose of carrying out this large and necessary task. Mr. Elihu Root has expressed regret that the covenant of the League of Nations does not mention international law at all except in its preamble and that " no method is provided and no purpose is expressed to insist upon obedience to law, to develop the law and to press forward agreement upon its rules and recognition of its obligations." Among the amendments which he proposed to the draft of the covenant was that the executive council should call a general conference to meet not less than two years not more than five years after the signing of the covenant, for the purpose of " reviewing the conditions of international law and of agreeing upon and stating in authoritative form the principles and rules thereof." He also suggested that regular conferences for this purpose should be held at stated times.[2] This task may be said to be one of the

---

[1] Cf. Alvarez, *Le Droit International de l'Avenir*, p. 126, and De Louter, *La Crise du Droit International*, 26 *Rev. Gén. de Droit Int. Pub.* (1919).

[2] N. Y. *Times*, March 31, 1919. Lord Bryce also remarks that "the first duty of the allies is to call a conference for revising the laws and usages of war on land and sea." He suggests that the Hague conventions and the Declaration of London might form the basis of the revision; that the new international law should enumer-

legacies left by the war and it should be entered upon at the
earliest possible date and with the seriousness of purpose com-
mensurate with the magnitude of its importance.

ate in more detail the acts which shall be forbidden and that appropriate penalties
should be prescribed for the violations of the same. See his address on the "Outlook for International Law," Proceedings of the American Society of International
Law, 1915.

CHAPTER XXXVIII

ENFORCEMENT OF INTERNATIONAL LAW; OUTLOOK FOR THE FUTURE

§ 578. The Problem Stated; § 579. Lack of Effective Sanctions; § 580. Indemnity for Damages; § 581. Penal Clauses of the Treaty of Peace; § 582. The Principle of Personal Responsibility of Soldiers for Criminal Acts; § 583. Provisions of Military Manuals; § 584. Difficulties of Application; § 585. Punishment of Crimes Committed in Foreign Territory; § 586. Jurisdiction of Crimes on the High Seas; § 587. Trial of Offenders in their Absence; § 588. The Plea of Superior Command; § 589. Responsibility of Chiefs of States; § 590. Decision of the Peace Conference regarding the Trial of the German Emperor; § 591. Decision of the Peace Conference Considered; § 592. Precedents for the Trial of Chiefs of States; § 593. Immunity of Chiefs of States; § 594. New Attitude toward Violations of International Law; § 595. Outlook for the Future.

§ 578. **The Problem Stated.** More important than the task of reconstructing international law is the problem of making it more effective, that is, of devising means for compelling respect for its commands and prohibitions. As Mr. Root has aptly remarked, the civilized world must now determine whether what we call international law is to be continued as a mere code of etiquette or whether it is to be a real body of laws imposing obligations much more definite and inevitable than they have been heretofore.[1]

It hardly seems possible that international law can ever be made effective in the sense in which municipal law is effective. Nevertheless, there would seem to be several ways by which its binding force can be materially strengthened and its value as a body of law enhanced. In the first place, as stated above, the body of law itself must be reconstructed and elaborated, and to this end there should be provided a more efficacious machinery for making international law and for revising it, from time to time, as changing conditions require. In the second place, an effort should be made to establish an international organization with appropriate agencies for enforcing its prescriptions. Third,

[1] See his address on "The Outlook for International Law," in the *Proceedings of the Amer. Soc. of Int. Law, 1915*.

provision should be made for the compulsory investigation of international disputes of a political character and the compulsory arbitration of those of a justiciable character. Finally, there should be an agreement among the powers to employ their moral and economic, and if necessary their armed, strength to compel disputing nations to have recourse, except in cases of self-defence, to the one or the other of these expedients, depending on the nature of the controversy.[1] In short, the making of war, except in case of self-defence, should be declared illegal and the disputants should be restrained by the joint action of the body of States from attacking each other and thereby disturbing the general peace, until they have made a sincere attempt to settle their disputes by conciliation or arbitration.

The realization of this scheme will necessarily involve the assumption of new and unprecedented obligations on the part of States as well as the loss of a certain portion of what is commonly described as their sovereignty. But there is really nothing new in this principle, since all States by entering into treaties and by becoming parties to general international conventions assume thereby new obligations and at the same time relinquish in the common interest a portion of their own liberty of action. Civil society was founded on this principle, many political unions have been organized in this way, and whatever progress has thus far been achieved in the direction of international organization and administration, and it is much larger than it is generally supposed, has come through the common assumption of new obligations and the mutual relinquishment by States of their own freedom of action in certain particulars. The only possible way by which a real society of States can be formed and a system of law and justice substituted in the place of force is through the further extension of this sound and necessary principle. The body of States must consent to give up the barbaric right to be their own judges in controversies with other States and to make war upon their neighbors for any reason which may seem to them sufficient, and those which refuse to

[1] Compare the suggestions of Professor J. B. Moore in the *American Political Science Review*, vol. 9, pp. 1 ff. See also the observations of Dr. Alvarez in his book *Le Droit International de l'Avenir*, chapters 14 ff. Dr. De Louter, in the article referred to above, makes the suggestion that war should be regarded not as a result of law but as an attack upon the law and that its benefits should be denied to those who by provoking an unjust war are aggressors against the law.

do so voluntarily,[1] in the general interest of civilization, must be compelled by the joint action of the rest, in accordance with the principle that was adopted in the organization of civil society itself. The proposed League of Nations unfortunately meets the situation only in a partial degree. It provides for the investigation of disputes, it undertakes to guarantee the territorial integrity and political independence of States against external aggression, it provides for the use of joint force against a member which disregards its covenants; but instead of providing for the compulsory arbitration of justiciable disputes it creates an obligation to arbitrate only disputes which the parties " recognize to be suitable for submission to arbitration." There is, therefore, no obligation to arbitrate anything, but merely an agreement to arbitrate whenever the parties choose to do so.[2]

§ 579. Lack of Effective Sanctions. The want of effective sanctions has always been and remains the chief weakness of international law, and one of the necessary tasks of the future is to provide such sanctions. Heretofore, so far as there has been any sanction at all, it has been the force of public opinion:

[1] Compare on this point the interesting book of Mr. David Jayne Hill, entitled the *Rebuilding of Europe*, in which he attacks the "monstrous" and "wicked" dogma of absolute sovereignty as the "real enemy that must be destroyed." The world, he says, must be freed from this sinister inheritance through a modern reconstruction of the State; States must be brought under the dominion of the law and their conduct regulated by obligatory rules and their legal right to make war for any or no reason must be taken away from them. M. Alvarez, in his suggestive treatise, *Le Droit International de l'Avenir*, dwells upon the necessity of a reorganization of society on juridical bases rather than on the basis of force, but unlike Mr. Hill, he maintains that the existing sovereignty of States must be respected (p. 73). If sovereignty be interpreted to mean the absolute freedom of States to do what they will, it is difficult to see how that freedom can be maintained under the proposed reorganization. It is safe to assume, however, that M. Alvarez does not interpret the term in this unrestricted sense. Professor De Louter, in the article cited above, argues against a form of international reorganization that will destroy the existing sovereignty of States. The retention of their sovereignty, he contends, is not only not an obstacle to the progress of international law but is a necessary instrument. The difficulty rather lies in the false conception of sovereignty which is interpreted to include the right of States to determine their own standards of international conduct, to be the judges of their own controversies with other States, and to pursue policies that are subversive of the rights and interests of their neighbors. It is this view of sovereignty that should be abandoned and not the right of each State to determine for itself its own internal policies which is all that true national sovereignty embraces (p. 88).

[2] Compare the incisive analysis and criticism of Mr. Root in a letter published in the N. Y. *Times* of March 31, 1919.

the national sensitiveness to the disapprobation of the civilized world, the regard for what Jefferson called "a decent respect for the opinions of mankind," the unwillingness to incur the odium and the obloquy which follow non-conformity to the standards of international conduct set by the civilized world, and the like. In the past this feeling has often proved a powerful deterrent to national wrong-doing and has exerted a potent influence in causing States to respect their international obligations.[1] But the numerous and shocking violations of international law and breaches of treaty engagements during the late war have rudely shaken the faith of us all in the potency of this force and have accentuated the demand for the creation of more effective sanctions. The rules of international law, as is well known, are devoid of penal sanctions. Like the rules of the criminal law they lay down commands and prohibitions, but unlike the criminal law, they do not prescribe penalties for their violation. Thus the Hague convention respecting the laws and customs of war on land forbids certain acts such as the maltreatment of prisoners, the use of poison or poisoned weapons, the use of projectiles which diffuse asphyxiating gases, the refusal of quarter, the bombardment of undefended towns, assassination, pillage, violations of family honor, and the like, but they prescribe no penalties for the commission of such acts, nor do they even affirm the obligations of belligerents to punish the members of their armed forces for committing such acts or recognize the right of belligerents to try and punish the soldiers of the adversary for having committed them.[2] Professor Renault stated shortly before his death that the draft of the *règlement* was hastily passed over by the Conference, a few changes of detail being made here and there, and that the question of penal sanctions was overlooked. He expressed the opinion, however, that the silence of the *règlement* on this point afforded no basis for the claim that the criminal law cannot be

[1] Compare the address of Mr. Root entitled "Sanctions of International Law," *Amer. Jour. of Int. Law*, vol. II, pp. 451 ff.

[2] The Geneva convention of 1906, however, affirms the principle of penal responsibility by a declaration that in the event the military penal laws of the contracting parties are insufficient they "engage to take or to recommend to their legislatures, the necessary measures to repress, in time of war, individual acts of pillage, and ill treatment of the sick and wounded of the armies." (Art. 28.) The Hague convention of 1907 for the adaptation of the principles of the Geneva convention to maritime warfare repeated this recommendation. (Art. 21.)

applied to acts of war that are in fact crimes and he added that it was the right and duty of each belligerent not only to punish infractions committed by his own troops, but also those committed by persons belonging to the forces of the enemy.[1]

§ 580. **Indemnity for Damages.** The second Hague Conference undertook to provide a form of civil sanction for the violation of the laws of war by establishing an obligation on the part of belligerents to indemnify individuals for injuries done them in contravention of the prohibitions of the Hague convention respecting the laws and customs of war on land. Article 3 of this convention provides that " a belligerent party which violates the provisions of the regulations annexed to the said convention shall, if the case demands, be liable to pay compensation. It shall be responsible for all acts committed by persons forming part of its armed forces." By a singular irony this article was proposed by the German delegation and it afforded a legal basis for the decision of the peace conference to exact an indemnity from Germany for the injuries committed by her armed forces in violation of the regulations annexed to the convention. The responsibility created by the article is clearly civil and not penal in character, that is, it is to be satisfied by the payment of compensation for the injuries committed; it does not contemplate the trial and punishment of individuals who commit acts in violation of the law nor the commanders who are responsible for them. It would also seem that the responsibility is not directly to the injured individual, but to the State of which he is a national. It is therefore for the victim's State to make the demand of the offending belligerent and to collect the damages due.[2] The adoption of this provision marks an important

---

[1] *De l'Application du Droit Pénal aux Faits de Guerre*, 25 *Rev. Gén. de Droit Int. Pub.* (1918), pp. 15–17; also 39 *Rev. Pén.*, p. 413.

[2] See the interpretation of Professor Weiss of the University of Paris in the *Temps* of May 1, 1915, and of M. Lémonon in an article entitled *La Sanction de Droit des Gens*, published in *Le Parlement et l'Opinion*, May, 1915. Professor Weiss, in an address before the Société Générale des Prisons on May 19, 1915 (39 *Revue Pénitentiare et de Droit Pénal*, p. 461), made the suggestion that the amount of compensation for damages claimed by the Allied powers of Germany under the above-mentioned provision of the Hague convention should be determined by the Hague Tribunal of Arbitration. He thought such a stipulation should be inserted in the treaty of peace and in case Germany refused to agree to submit the matter to the Hague Tribunal, the Allies alone should do it and the Tribunal should render judgment, fix the amount of the indemnity, and even publish the names of the guilty offenders, "for the enlightenment of the public

step toward making international law something more than a code of etiquette, by expressly affirming the principle of civil responsibility for injuries committed by belligerents or members of their armed forces in violation of the commands and prohibitions of the Hague convention and by creating a legal liability upon the basis of which the injured belligerent may demand compensation.[1] In accordance with this provision the treaty of peace required Germany not only to make compensation for injuries sustained on account of violations of the laws of war but for " all damage done to the civilian population of the Allied and Associated powers and to their property." Nine categories of acts were enumerated for which compensation might be claimed. They include damages or injuries to civilians caused by acts of war, cruelty, violence, maltreatment of prisoners, forced labor without remuneration, the seizure or carrying away of or destruction of property (except military and naval works or materials), and damages in the form of levies, fines, and other similar exactions imposed on the inhabitants of occupied territory.[2] This is the first instance in which an attempt has been made to enforce the above-mentioned rule of the Hague convention. Happily it is an easy matter to enforce it against a defeated belligerent, but there appears to be no way by which it can be enforced against a victorious belligerent whose armed forces may also have committed violations of the convention. The remedy which it provides, however,

---

conscience." "Humanity," he added, "would be placed in the presence of veritable international decisions which would create a precedent and a jurisprudence, which would give to the law of nations and to the Hague conventions, so impudently violated, a commentary and a sanction very energetic."

In consequence of the overwhelming defeat of Germany, the suggestion does not appear to have been considered by the peace conference and the duty of determining the amount of the indemnity was devolved upon a reparations commission composed entirely of representatives of the Allied and Associated powers which is to notify the German government on or before May 1, 1921 of the amount due. (Art. 233.)

[1] The American Institute of International Law at its session at Havana in January, 1917, in its proposed code affirmed this principle. Art. 32 provides that belligerents who violate the rights of neutrals as they are set forth in the code shall pay to the injured State a pecuniary indemnity, the amount to be determined by a conference to neutrals.

[2] Article 232 and Annex I. It appears from the language of the treaty (Annex I, Par. 10) that the compensation for damages in the form of fines and levies is not limited to those which were not imposed in the exercise of a lawful belligerent right, but embraces all levies whether lawful or unlawful.

is only partial. Without it the victorious belligerent would still be free to exact reparation from his vanquished adversary while with it the latter will be in no position to exact compensation for injuries committed by the former.

§ 581. Penal Clauses of the Treaty of Peace. The treaty of peace between Germany and the Allied and Associated powers, signed at Versailles on the 28th of June, 1919, formally sanctioned the principle that individuals belonging to the armed or naval forces of the adversary, as well as his civil functionaries, are responsible under the criminal law for offences against the laws and customs of war and may be tried and punished for such acts. The treaty declared that Germany recognizes " the right of the Allied and Associated powers to bring before military tribunals persons accused of having committed acts in violation of the laws and customs of war." It added: " Such persons shall, if found guilty, be sentenced to punishments laid down by law. This provision will apply notwithstanding any proceedings or prosecution before a tribunal in Germany or in the territory of her allies." The treaty further required Germany to hand over to the Allied and Associated powers or to such of them as shall so request, all persons accused of having committed any act in violation of the laws and customs of war who are specified either by name or by the rank, office or employment which they held under the German authorities and to furnish " all documents and information of every kind, the production of which may be considered necessary to the full knowledge of the incriminating acts, the discovery of offenders and the just appreciation of responsibility." [1] This appears to be the first treaty of peace in which an attempt has been made by the victorious belligerent to enforce against his defeated adversary the application of the principle of individual responsibility for criminal acts committed during war by members of the latter's armed forces against the persons or property of the other party. [2]

[1] Articles 228, 230. Identical provisions are contained in the treaty with Austria (Arts. 173, 175), but there appear to be no such stipulations in the treaty with Bulgaria.

[2] The late Professor Renault, speaking before the French General Prison Society in 1915, referred to a suggestion that he had received, to the effect that in the treaty of peace a clause should be inserted requiring the delivery up of the principal offenders against the laws of war. Regarding the suggestion M. Renault said: "I do not see how a government, even if conquered, could consent to such a clause; it would be the abdication of all its dignity; moreover, almost always, it is upon

§ 582. The Principle of Personal Responsibility of Soldiers for Criminal Acts. The principal that the individual soldier who commits acts in violation of the laws of war when those acts are at the same time offences against the general criminal law should be liable to trial and punishment by the courts of the injured adversary in case he falls into the hands of the authorities thereof has long been maintained by some writers, and in 1880 it was expressly affirmed by the Institute of International Law. Article 84 of its manual of the laws of war on land adopted at Oxford in that year declared that if any of the rules thereof were violated, "the offending parties should be punished, after a judicial hearing, by the belligerent in whose hands they are." It was further added that "offenders against the laws of war are liable to the punishments specified in the penal or criminal law," whenever the person of the offender could be secured.[1]

The many shocking acts committed by German soldiers in Belgium and France during the late war in violation of the laws and customs of war revived interest in the subject, and already there is an extensive literature dealing with it.[2] All writers who

---

superior order that infractions of the law of nations have been committed. I have found the proposal excessive, though I understand the sentiment that inspired it. I cite it because it shows well to what point men animated by justice and shocked by what has taken place desire that the monstrosities of which French and Belgians have been victims should not go unpunished." 25 *Rev. Gén. de Droit Int. Pub.* p. 25; also 39 *Rev. Pénitentiaire*, p. 425.

[1] *Annuaire de l'Institut*, 1881–1882, p. 174.

[2] See especially Renault, *De l'Application du Droit Pénal aux faits de Guerre* 25 *Rev. Gén. de Droit Int. Pub.* (1918), 5 ff.; also his address before the Société Générale des Prisons, 39 *Rev. Pénitentiaire*, pp. 406 ff. (1915); Pic, *Violations des Lois de la Guerre, Les Sanctions Nécessaires*, 23 *Rev. Gén.* 261 ff. (1916); Feraud-Giraud, *Recours en Raison des Dommages Causés par la Guerre;* Dumas, *Les Sanctions Pénales des Crimes Allemands* (1916); Merignhac, *Sanctions des Infractions au Droit des Gens Commisés au Cours de la Guerre Européenne, Rev. Gén. de Droit Int. Pub.*, 1917, pp. 10 ff.; Bellot, *War Crimes, Their Prevention and Punishment*, Grotius Soc'y Pubs. II, 46; Fauchille, *L'Evacuation des Ters. Occupés par l'Allemagne dans le Nord de la France;* Tchernoff, *Revue Politique et Parlementaire*, July, 1915; Nast, *Les Sanctions Pénales de l'Enlèvement par les Allemands du Matériel Industriel en Territoires français et Belges occupés par leurs troupes*, 26 *Rev. Gén. de Droit Int. Pub.* (1919), pp. 111 ff.; L. D., *Des Sanctions à établir pour la Répression des Crimes commis par les Allemands en violation du Droit des Gens et des Traités Internationaux*, 44 Clunet, pp. 125 ff., and the report of MMs. Larnaude and Lapradelle entitled *Examen de la Responsabilité pénale de L'Empereur Guillaume II d'Allemagne*, 46 Clunet, pp. 131 ff. The subject was discussed by a group of distinguished French jurists at several sessions of the Société Générale des Prisons in 1915 and 1916. See especially the addresses of Garraud, Larnaude, Garcon, Renault, Clunet, Pillet, and Weiss. English and American authorities,

have discussed the subject are in agreement that certain acts committed by soldiers are none the less criminal because they are committed during war. Such are acts of pillage, theft, incendiarism, violence, rape, robbery, assassination, maltreatment of prisoners and the like.[1] The late Professor Renault aptly remarked that most acts of war, when the element of intent is discarded, contain all the essentials of criminal acts and if they are forbidden by the law of nations they are analogous to ordinary crimes and may be punished as such. What deprives such acts of the element of criminality is their conformity to the rules of international law. That is to say, the killing by a soldier of a person belonging to the enemy's forces or the taking of private property in occupied territory are lawful acts of war only when they are done in the manner and subject to the conditions prescribed by international law, otherwise they are murder or theft as the case may be and their authors are liable to punishment as criminals.[2] In short, soldiers as well as civilians may commit crimes during war and it would be extraordinary to hold that they are protected by their uniform against punishment. As a general rule, a soldier cannot be held criminally responsible for acts committed by him in the line of duty during war when those acts are authorized by the generally accepted laws of war; but if they are forbidden by such laws they are not legitimate acts of war and they may be crimes under the common criminal law. The United

---

of course, are not lacking who have supported the doctrine of individual criminal responsibility. Both prime ministers Asquith and Lloyd George publicly declared that Germans guilty of committing criminal acts against British soldiers would, in case they fell into the hands of the authorities, be tried and punished. Sir Frederick Smith, while attorney general of England, also advocated the trial and punishment of such persons. See also the remarks of Mr. E. P. Wheeler, an American lawyer, in the *Proceedings of the American Society of International Law*, 1917, p. 36.

[1] See, for example, Pic, Art., cited p. 29; Feraud-Giraud, *op. cit.;* Merignhac, Art. cited p. 29; and Renault, Art. cited p. 8.

[2] Art. cited p. 10. Compare also the following observations of M. Garcon, a distinguished French jurist: "The legal justification of acts committed during war is found in the customs of the law of nations. In time of war, therefore, all acts committed in the course of hostilities are justified if they are in conformity to its customs. But at the same time, all those which are contrary to the rules of international law, written or traditional, are crimes, which as regards French law are punishable under the common law. The authors of these crimes, as well as their accomplices, French and foreigners alike, may be punished." 39 *Revue Pénitentiare*, p. 479.

States Supreme Court has affirmed that soldiers are not liable for acts done by them in accordance with the usages of civilized warfare and by military authority. It would seem to follow logically that the authors of acts in violation of those usages may be held personally responsible.[1] Most of the war manuals and military criminal codes recognize that certain acts committed by soldiers in time of war are ordinary crimes and they provide for the punishment of such acts whenever the offenders fall into the hands of the authorities. Article 249 of the French code of military justice, for example, declares that "every individual who in the zone of operation despoils a wounded, sick or dead soldier shall be punished by *réclusion* and every individual who commits violence on such a soldier shall be put to death." The provisions of the criminal code relative to murder, assault, and assassination are declared to be applicable to such cases. The term "every individual" is certainly broad enough to include members of the enemy's forces who commit such acts in the zone of operations.

§ 583. **Provisions of Military Manuals.** The American *Rules of Land Warfare* (1914) provide for the punishment of acts of pillage and maltreatment of the dead and wounded,[2] for inflicting intentionally additional wounds upon an enemy already disabled or for killing such an enemy, *whether he belongs to the army of the United States or is an enemy captured after having committed the misdeed,*[3] for the wanton destruction of property,[4] for committing any one of a long list of acts such as the use of poison, refusal of quarter, killing of wounded, maltreatment of dead bodies, ill treatment of prisoners and of inhabitants of occupied territory, and many other acts.[5] Crimes punishable by all criminal codes, such as arson, murder, theft, burglary, rape, and the like, if committed by an American soldier in a hostile country against its inhabitants are declared to be punishable not only as at home, but in all cases in which death is not inflicted, the severer punishment shall be preferred.[6] Except as to the wounding of disabled soldiers no express mention is made, how-

---

[1] Compare the views of Mr. C. A. H. Bartlett in an article entitled "Liability for Official War Crimes," 35 *Law Quar. Review* (1919), p. 186.

[2] Art. 112.

[3] Art. 181. Compare also Art. 71 of Lieber's Instructions for the Government of the United States Armies in the Field.

[4] Art. 340.   [5] Art. 366.   [6] Art. 378.

ever, of the punishment of offenders belonging to the enemy's forces, but there is little doubt that every person guilty of committing such acts against American soldiers, would if apprehended be punished equally with those belonging to the American army.[1] American practice during the Civil war was in accordance with this view.[2]

The British Manual of Military Law likewise enumerates a long list of war crimes which may be punished as such irrespective of whether they are committed by British soldiers or those belonging to the enemy's forces, except that those may not be punished for such violations of the recognized rules of warfare, as are ordered by their government or commander.[3] The German *Kriegsbrauch im Landkriege* is none the less explicit on this point. It declares that the inhabitants of occupied territory must not be injured in life, limb, honor, or freedom; that every unlawful killing, every bodily injury due to fraud or negligence, every insult, every disturbance of domestic peace, every attack on family honor, or morality, and generally, every unlawful and outrageous attack or act of violence are just as strictly punishable as though they had been committed against the inhabitants of one's own land. It expressly prohibits all aimless destruction, devastation, burning, and ravaging of the enemy's country, and declares that the soldier who does such acts is "an offender according to the appropriate law." Finally, it declares that the seizure and carrying away of money, watches, jewelry, and other objects of value is considered to be criminal theft and is punishable as such.[4]

§ 584. **Difficulties of Application.** It being recognized that certain acts committed by soldiers during war in violation of the rules of international law are assimilable to ordinary crimes and may be punished as such, several questions are presented

---

[1] Art. 71 declares in fact that "a prisoner of war remains answerable for his crimes against the captor's army or people, committed before he was captured and for which he has not been punished by his own army."

[2] As is well known, William Wirz, commandant of the Confederate prison at Andersonville during the Civil War was tried by a military commission of the United States on the charge of brutal treatment of Federal prisoners. He was convicted and hanged November 10, 1865. Rhodes, History of the United States, vol. V, p. 506.

[3] Art. 443.

[4] Morgan, *War Book of the German General Staff*, pp. 148, 162, and Carpentier, *Les Lois de la Guerre Continentale (Kriegsbrauch im Landkriege)*, pp. 104, 121, 131.

as to the practical application of the principle. May, for example, the courts of one belligerent try and punish offenders belonging to the forces of the enemy, and if so, shall it be the ordinary criminal courts or the military tribunals.[1] Practically all the authorities are agreed that soldiers belonging to the enemy army may be tried by the courts of the opposing belligerent for crimes committed in violation of the laws of war in the latter's territory against the persons or property of nationals of the injured belligerent if they fall into his hands.[2] And this is the view laid down in the military manuals and military penal codes. But in countries which follow the personal theory of jurisdiction their nationals are also punishable for crimes committed abroad. Thus, according to German law, a German soldier who committed a crime in the occupied regions of Belgium and France was liable to trial and punishment by the German courts. Could he also be tried and punished by a Belgian or French court? Renault, Pic, Garcon, Merignhac, Feraud-Giraud, and other French jurists maintain that jurisdiction in such cases is concurrent, that is to say, the courts of either belligerent may take jurisdiction, and the fact that the offender may already have been tried and punished by a German court does not deprive a Belgian or French court from trying him.[3] Otherwise, offenders would often be insufficiently punished or not punished at all. It is well known that the German authorities during the late war not only approved the commission of various acts committed by German soldiers in violation of the laws of war, but even encouraged them, and the instances in which such offenders were tried and punished by the German courts were distressingly rare. The treaty of peace expressly declares that trial by a German court of Germans charged with violation of the laws of war shall be no bar to their prosecution before the courts of the allied powers.[4]

[1] The treaty of peace provides that the military tribunals of the country of which the injured victim is a national shall have jurisdiction. Professor T. S. Woolsey thinks the trial of such offenders should be before a neutral or international court, *Procs. Amer. Soc. of Int. Law*, 1915, p. 67. Merignhac, however, advocates trial before a special court composed of judges representing only the victorious belligerents, Art. cited p. 55.

[2] Beling, a German writer, in the *Deutsche Juristen-Zeitung* of February 1, 1915, however, denies that one belligerent may lawfully punish offenders belonging to the armed forces of the adversary. Cited in 43 Clunet, p. 72.

[3] Renault, Art. cited p. 17; Pic, Art. cited p. 262; Merignhac, Art. cited p. 32.

[4] Art. 228.

The right of the belligerent in whose territory, even if it be at the moment under the military occupation of the enemy, crimes are committed by enemy soldiers, to try and punish the offenders must be admitted in the interest of justice. The fact that the territory in which the offence is committed is at the time under hostile occupation would not seem to constitute a legal impediment to the assumption of jurisdiction by the courts of the country occupied, since under the modern conception of occupation there is no extinction of sovereignty but only its temporary displacement.[1] In practice France has proceeded on the assumption that its courts may take jurisdiction of crimes committed by German soldiers within French territory under German military occupation. Some cases occurred after the close of the war of 1870–71 [2] and there were many instances during the late war.[3] The treaty of peace, as stated above, required Germany to deliver up to the Allies such offenders as they might designate. In accordance therewith a list of 890 persons or groups of persons was addressed to the German government and their surrender demanded. The British list contained the names of 97 persons against whom charges were preferred; the French list, 344; the Belgian, 334; the Polish, 51; the Roumanian, 41, and the Italian, 29. Among the accused were Dr. von Bethmann-Hollweg, former imperial Chancellor, field marshall von Hindenburg, generals von Ludendorff and Mackensen; Crown Prince Rupprecht of Bavaria, the Duke of Wurtemberg, and a number of other persons belonging to the

[1] Nevertheless it may be remarked that the German International Society of Comparative Law and Political Economy maintains the exclusive jurisdiction of the military occupant. A soldier in enemy territory, it insists, is under the exclusive jurisdiction of the laws of his own country, and he cannot be punished by the courts of the opposing belligerent. *Berliner Tageblatt*, February 10, 1915, quoted by Merignhac, Art. cited p. 37.

[2] Renault, Art. cited p. 18; Merignhac, Art. cited p. 35.

[3] On February 26, 1915, a German soldier was sentenced to death by a French military court at Rennes for pillage, incendiarism, and assassination of a wounded soldier on the field of battle in Belgium. Other cases are mentioned by Merignhac, Art. cited p. 35. In May, 1919, a former German captain committed suicide while being held for trial by a French court on the charge of looting in France during the war. In November, 1919, five officers of the German army were arrested by the French military authorities in Germany and returned to France for trial on the charge of pillage and robbery in French territory during the German occupation thereof. A press dispatch from Lille, dated November 20, 1919, stated that allied officers were searching for one hundred and fifty other Germans who were charged with similar offences.

royal families; twelve admirals and many other army and
navy officers of high rank including von Tirpitz, von Capelle,
von Trotha, von Müller, and von Schroeder. The publication
of the list evoked strong protest in Germany and Baron von
Lersner, head of the German delegation to the Peace Conference, refused to transmit the list to his government and
declared his intention of resigning. In the face of an opposition which threatened to render impossible the execution of the
treaty provision, the Supreme Council agreed to a modification
of its original terms and to allow the accused to be tried in
Germany by the *Reichsgericht* at Leipsig.

§ 585. Punishment of Crimes Committed in Foreign Territory. If there is no doubt that a belligerent has jurisdiction
over crimes committed by enemy troops in his own territory,
even though it be under hostile occupation, what shall we say
as to his right to try and punish persons belonging to the enemy's
forces who commit criminal acts against the soldiers of the
former in a foreign country? Take, for example, the case of
maltreatment by the Germans of a French soldier in a German
prison or the receiving by persons in Germany of stolen property taken from France. There were many cases of this kind
during the late war. Would a French court be competent to
try the offenders in case they should subsequently fall into the
hands of the French authorities? Renault distinguishes between
offences of this kind committed within the zone of operations
of the French army and those committed without such zone.
The former fall within the jurisdiction of the French criminal
courts, although they are committed in foreign territory; the
latter do not.[1] Under the French code of criminal instruction
(Art. 7) offences committed outside French territory are punishable in France only when they constitute attacks against
the safety of the state.[2] Belgian law is the same (code of criminal instruction, Art. 10). M. Clunet thinks crimes committed
by the enemy against French prisoners in foreign territory violate the public order of France and amount to an attack upon
its authority; they might therefore be treated as crimes against

[1] 26 *Rev. Gén. de Dr. Int. Pub.* (1918), p. 28.
[2] See the recent case of Wechsler, in which a French court took jurisdiction
of an offence committed against the safety of the State by a Roumanian subject
in Roumania. 44 Clunet (1917), p. 1745.

the safety of the State and the offenders tried and punished by the French courts if they should fall into the hands of the French authorities.[1] Obviously, however, this would be an unwarranted interpretation of the term "safety of the State," elastic as it is, and M. Clunet himself admits that it is a "bit subtle."[2] Merignhac expresses the opinion that an interpretation which forbids the French courts from taking jurisdiction of crimes committed in foreign territory against French nationals (except those which constitute attacks upon the safety of the State) is reasonable enough in time of peace, but that in time of war, especially war conducted in the manner in which it was carried on by the Germans, a belligerent whose nationals (especially prisoners and hostages) are maltreated by the enemy should have the same right to punish such offences when committed in foreign territory that he has to punish offences against the safety of the State. Article 7 of the French code of criminal instruction should therefore be interpreted during war to apply to all crimes committed against French nationals in foreign territory.[3] This question was recently raised in France under the form of the right of the French courts to take jurisdiction of certain Germans who were charged with having received in Germany stolen property carried away from France.

As is well known, the Germans during their occupation of Belgium and the north of France despoiled many factories and other industrial establishments of their machinery and equipment, and sold it to German manufacturers who in turn utilized it in their own establishments for the manufacture of war materials and articles for civilian use. After the occupation by the allied troops of the Rhine province of Germany, following the Armistice, they found large quantities of this machinery and arrested, with a view to their trial in France, a number of German manufacturers in whose plants the machinery was found. The German government protested against the arrests on the ground that the seizure and transportation of the property in question to Germany was a lawful act of war entirely in accord with Article 23 (g) of the Hague convention respecting the laws and customs of war on land, which allows a belligerent

[1] 40 *Revue Pénitentiaire* (1916), p. 37.
[2] M. Garraud thinks, and it would seem, properly, that M. Clunet's reasoning cannot be defended. *Ibid.*, p. 38.
[3] 24 *Rev. Gén. de Dr. Int. Pub.* (1917), pp. 42-45.

to appropriate enemy private property whenever it is "imperatively demanded by the necessities of war." This plea of necessity, however, can hardly be defended.[1] What was intended, and this alone, was to authorize the seizure or destruction of private property only in exceptional cases when it was an imperative necessity for the conduct of his military operations in the locality where it was situated or for the execution of measures of occupation.[2] This interpretation is further strengthened by Article 46 of the convention which requires belligerents to respect enemy private property and which forbids confiscation, and by Article 47 which formally prohibits pillage. The *Kriegsbrauch im Landkriege* itself declares that the carrying away of enemy private property from occupied territory must be "regarded as criminal robbery and be punished accordingly."[3]

It would seem therefore that the acts complained of were not lawful acts of war but that they constituted the crime of theft which is punishable by the criminal law of all countries and the crime having been committed within French territory, though under hostile occupation, all persons participating directly or indirectly in the seizure and transportation to Germany of the said machinery were liable to trial and punishment by the French criminal courts.[4] But among those arrested were a number of German manufacturers who had purchased the French machinery of others but who had not participated themselves directly or indirectly in its removal from France. Could they also be tried by the French courts on the charge of having received stolen property (*recel*)? The answer is no, since the act of receiving the property in question took place not in France but in Germany, and under Article 7 of the French code of criminal instruction the French courts are not competent to take jurisdiction of offences committed outside French territory except where they constitute attacks upon the safety of the State.[5]

[1] See *Supra*, § 396.
[2] Compare an article by Professor Nast of the University of Nancy entitled *Les Sanctions Pénales de l'Enlèvement par les Allemands du Matériel Industriel*, etc., 26 *Rev. Gén. de Droit Int. Pub.* (1919), pp. 111 ff.
[3] Morgan, *War Book of the German General Staff*, p. 170.
[4] M. Nast thinks, however, that those persons who were forced by the German authorities to assist in the removal of the machinery could not be held responsible. Art. cited p. 123.
[5] This is the conclusion of M. Nast in the article cited p. 123.

§ 586. Jurisdiction of Crimes on the High Seas. Another question which arises in connection with the application of the criminal law to individual acts committed in violation of the laws of war is whether the criminal courts of a belligerent may take jurisdiction of offenders charged with the unlawful destruction of their merchant vessels on the high seas and the drowning of their crews and passengers or with attacks upon hospital ships, of which there were many cases during the late war. The names of many German submarine commanders guilty of such acts were known to the British and French authorities, and there is a general agreement that these acts were not lawful belligerent acts, but crimes under the common law of nations. The coroner's jury at Kinsale which held an inquest upon the death of the victims of the *Lusitania*, and the United States district court at New York both came to the conclusion that the sinking of the *Lusitania* was such a crime. The act having been committed without the territorial jurisdiction of Great Britain, would a British court be competent to try the commander of the submarine which torpedoed the vessel in case he should fall into the hands of the British authorities? It would seem that on the legal fiction that a merchant vessel is assimilable to floating territory of the country whose flag it flies, an unlawful attack upon it, on the high seas or elsewhere, which resulted in the death of the nationals of the State whose nationality it bears would fall within the jurisdiction of such State.[1]

§ 587. Trial of Offenders in their Absence. Still another question has arisen in connection with the attempt to apply the criminal law in the case of individual violators of the laws of

[1] Compare the opinions of Coleridge, C. J., and Denman, J., in the case of *Queen* v. *Keyn*, 2 H. of L. Cases, 1; also the Report of Larnaude and Lapradelle, in 46 Clunet, p. 139. In May, 1919, the captain of the German submarine which sank the British hospital ship *Glenart Castle* was arrested by the British authorities, placed in the tower of London and held for trial. The legal department of the government is said to have ruled that the authorities had no right to detain him during the life of the Armistice, article 6 of which provided that in territories evacuated by the enemy no persons should be prosecuted for offences or participation in war measures prior to the signing of the Armistice, but the admiralty took the position that they had the right to arrest such offenders at any time and hold them for trial after peace was declared. The prisoner was released, however, on the ground that he was not liable to arrest until peace had been officially declared, but there was considerable criticism of the action of the government, especially by admiralty officials who had done much to trace the perpetrators of German submarine atrocities. N. Y. *Times*, May 10, and November 30, 1919.

war, namely, whether an offender may be tried and condemned
in his absence (*condemnation par contumace*, as French law
terms it). As stated above, the names of many of the most
flagrant offenders on the German side, especially among the
higher commanders (e.g., Generals Stenger, Manteuffel, Von
Bülow, Klauss and Mackensen, Prince Eitel Friederich, Crown
Prince Rupprecht of Bavaria, the Duke of Brunswick and the
Duke of Gronau) were well known to the British, Belgian and
French authorities. The proclamations which they issued
(e.g., General Stenger's order directing his soldiers to take no
prisoners) or the towns which were destroyed by their orders
constitute unimpeachable evidence of their guilt and their acts
were so obviously contrary to the laws and customs of war that
no legitimate defence could be pleaded if they were to appear
in person at the trial. Some French jurists during the late war
advocated this procedure and in several instances German
offenders were indicted, though it does not appear that any of
them were actually tried and condemned *par contumace*. In
favor of this procedure it was argued that the evidence of guilt
in many instances was so abundant in quantity and conclusive
in character that there would be no injustice in pronouncing
condemnation against the guilty parties in their absence; that
the putting *en lumière* by means of a trial and condemnation, of
the facts concerning atrocities committed would have a certain
moral effect in that the condemned would henceforth stand
before the world as convicted criminals; and that in the event
of their conviction if they should subsequently come within the
jurisdiction of the country they could be arrested and compelled to undergo the punishment imposed by the court.[1] It
is hardly likely that an American or English court could be
induced to take jurisdiction of a case in which the accused
was not present, even if it had the constitutional power, and in
any case it may be seriously doubted whether anything would

---

[1] Cf., e.g., Pic, 23 *Rev. Gén. de Droit Int. Pub.* (1916), p. 261. Renault (25
ibid., p. 24) and *Merignhac* (24 *ibid.*, p. 47) think condemnation *par contumace* is
rather a question of expediency than of law and Merignhac doubts whether it
would ever be expedient. Trial under such circumstances would be difficult,
witnesses would hesitate through fear to tell what they know, etc. See also the
remarks of Commandant Jullien before the General Prison Society (40 *Rev. Pénitentiaire*, p. 110), who says the French law of contumacy never contemplated the
trial *in absentia* of enemy soldiers charged with committing acts in violation of
the laws of war. It is therefore inapplicable to such cases.

be gained, since if the accused were convicted he would avoid the consequences by remaining outside the jurisdiction of the court.

§ 588. **The Plea of Superior Command.** The most perplexing question, perhaps, of all those likely to arise in connection with the attempt to punish individual violators of the laws of war is whether the plea of command by a superior officer shall be admitted as a defence against the prosecution of a soldier charged with a crime committed by him while under arms. During the late war German soldiers again and again asserted in the presence of their victims that they had been ordered by their commanders to commit the acts against which the inhabitants protested, and which they themselves committed with reluctance. Some of the men who took part in the deportation of the civilian population of Belgium and France are said to have broken down under the strain of the scenes which they were compelled to witness and were arrested and punished by the higher military authorities for refusing to execute the orders which they had received.[1] After the devastation of the Somme region in France certain diaries of German soldiers were found in which the writers recorded that they carried out the work of destruction with reluctance, knowing that it was not lawful warfare, and that they did it only because they had been ordered to do so.[2] In July, 1915, a French council of war sitting at Rennes sentenced to death a Saxon soldier for pillage, incendiarism and assassination of wounded enemy soldiers on the field of battle. When arraigned before the council he pleaded the formal orders of his commander and he named the general from whom the order emanated and the lieutenant who compelled him to execute it. The court, having every reason to believe that the facts alleged by him were true, made a report of the same to the minister of war in order that he might recommend clemency in case he desired to do so.[3] Another German soldier having been traduced before a council of war at Toulouse and condemned to twenty years of forced labor on the charge of having, in September, 1914, burned a house in the Oise and

---

[1] Cf. Cyril Brown in the N. Y. *Times* of August 19, 1916.
[2] *Les Nouvelles* (a Dutch Journal) of April 13, 1917, published a diary of this kind. See also Wythe Williams in the N. Y. *Times* of March 28, 1917.
[3] 24 *Rev. Gén.*, p. 53.

wounded one of the inmates, who died the following evening, alleged that he acted under the orders of his captain.[1] M. Renault related before the General Prison Society the case of a German officer who, when reproached for having committed certain acts in a Belgian village, replied: "Yes, I know it was contrary to the law of nations for I am a doctor of law; I did not wish to do it, but I did it in obedience to the formal order of the governor-general of Brussels."[2] Who should be punished in such cases? The soldier who commits the crime or the officer who gives the order and directs its execution, or the commander from whom it emanates in the first instance, or all of them and any others to whom any share of the responsibility, immediate or ultimate, may be attributed? It is argued by some that it would be manifestly unjust to punish the soldier, who is compelled by his superior officer to commit the act and who does it only because he would himself be severely punished for disobedience of orders in case he refused. Obedience to orders is the first duty of a soldier, and it is absolutely necessary to military discipline. He cannot discuss or question the commands that are given him; he is not the judge of their legality or illegality; and if he were, his ignorance of the laws of war would in many cases make him an incompetent judge. A French officer speaking before the *Société d'Economie Sociale* of Paris in February, 1915, related that an intelligent young German soldier, when placed on trial before a council of war at Paris on the charge of pillage, alleged that the general in command had given the order to shoot civilians and to pillage the town, and the prisoner added gravely: "With us it is not good when the chief gives an order to refuse to execute it."[3] Had he refused he probably would have been shot by his own commander. In such cases therefore justice, it is said, requires the punishment of the officer who is responsible for the order rather than the simple soldier who acts by constraint and who has no power of judgment or discretion. But there are practical procedural difficulties in the application of this principle, since it is not easy to determine the motives which animate a soldier in committing such an act. The mere allegation that he committed it because he was ordered to do so is not evidence. In fact

[1] *Ibid.*, p. 36. [2] 39 *Revue Pénitentiaire* (1915), p. 427.
[3] *Réforme Sociale*, 1915, p. 202.

he may have felt no scruples that it was wrong or contrary to the laws of war. The probabilities are that every soldier who commits such an act would, if put on trial, plead the superior command of his officer as a defence, although he may have done it voluntarily and without any feeling of repugnance. Moreover, it would be impossible in many cases to establish the fact of a superior command. Where commands are issued in the form of written orders or proclamations there would not necessarily be any difficulty, but many military orders are verbal. Should the allegation of the accused that he acted under verbal orders be accepted when no proof is adduced? If the rule of the criminal law which puts the burden of proof on the State were followed in such cases, there would probably be few convictions, for the accused would usually allege that he acted under verbal orders and the prosecution would find it difficult to show the contrary. It is an axiom, at least of English and American law, that the plea of superior order is no defence to an illegal act.[1] But is the rule applicable in the case of acts committed by soldiers during war, when those acts have been ordered by their commanders?

The British Manual of Military Law enumerates a list of acts which it denominates as war crimes and for the commission of which the authors shall be punished, but it adds that "members of the armed forces who commit such violations of the recognized rules of warfare *as are ordered by their government or commander* cannot be punished by the enemy."[2] But the officers

[1] See the early English case of *Mostyn* v. *Fabrigas*, 1 Cowper 180, decided by Lord Mansfield, and the American cases of *Little* v. *Barreme*, 2 Cranch, 170, 179, and *Mitchell* v. *Harmony*, 13 How. 115. In the first-mentioned American case Chief Justice Marshall said it was the duty of a soldier to execute the *lawful* orders of his superiors, but that he was personally liable for the execution of an illegal order. In the case of *Mitchell* v. *Harmony* the Supreme Court repudiated the doctrine that an officer may take shelter under the plea of superior command. Referring to an order given to a military officer by his commander to commit an illegal act, the court declared that the order was no justification to the person by whom it was executed. It added: "Upon principle, independent of the weight of judicial decision, it can never be maintained that a military officer can justify himself for doing an unlawful act by producing the order of his superior."

[2] Art. 443. This qualification is criticised by Bellot (Grotius Soc'y Pubs. II: 46) as one which "makes waste paper for the whole chapter" and he points out that it was not in any previous edition of the manual. It is also criticised by a writer in the *Jour. of the Soc'y of Comparative Legislation and Int. Law* (18: 154) as contrary to the rule of Anglo-American jurisprudence that an individual is responsible for his acts whether committed under order or not.

or commanders responsible for such orders may, if they fall into the hands of the enemy, be punished.

This provision also appears in the American *Rules of Land Warfare*,[1] but English authority generally is hardly in accord with this view. A belligerent, says Hall, "possesses the right to punish persons who have violated the laws of war, if they afterwards fall into his hands,"[2] and he makes no reservation in the case of those who have committed the violation by order of their commanders. Holland adopts the same view.[3] Phillipson asserts that "the contention that a combatant's acts, no matter how heinous, outrageous, or abominable do not possess a criminal character if they are committed under orders from superior officers — carried to its logical conclusion would lead to ineptitude and absurdity; the successive shifting of responsibility would exculpate every one until he reached the ultimate cause."[4] Sir Frederick Smith, attorney general of England, was also of the opinion that the guilty offenders should not be permitted to plead the orders of their superiors and thus shift the responsibility ultimately to the head of the State. But Oppenheim approves the rule of the American and British manuals.[5]

Article 64 of the French criminal code lays down the rule that an act committed by a person who has been constrained by force is neither a crime nor a misdemeanor (*délit*). Professor Nast of the University of Nancy has expressed the opinion that this immunity would cover the case of a soldier who is compelled to commit an act in violation of the laws of war and that

[1] Art. 366. "Individuals of the armed forces will not be punished for these offences in case they are committed under the orders or sanction of their government or commanders. The commanders ordering the commission of such acts, or under whose authority they are committed by their troops, may be punished by the belligerent into whose hands they may fall."

[2] *International Law*, 6th ed., p. 410.

[3] *Laws of War on Land*, §§ 117–118.

[4] *International Law and the Great War*, p. 260. Compare also the following from Bartlett, an English writer in 35 *Law Quar. Review*, p. 191: "The great principle of national justice, which, while casting its cloak of immunity over the officer for acts committed while in the line of his duty does not strip him from the consequences of wanton, cruel, and unnecessary crime. Human justice is not blind to intentional and wilful wrongdoing because the offender may happen to wear a uniform or claim exemption under the orders of a superior. That would amount to the defence of duress — compulsion — and no rule of law is better established than that the defence of duress is unavailing whenever the danger was not urgent or immediate."

[5] *International Law*, Vol. II, Sec. 253.

therefore German soldiers who were compelled by their commanders to participate in the spoliation of French industrial establishments and the removal of their machinery to Germany, although the acts were contrary to the Hague convention, were not liable to arrest and trial by the French courts.[1] Professor Merignhac of Toulouse, however, adopts a contrary view and maintains that Article 64 of the penal code was never intended to shield soldiers who in time of war commit atrocities and who afterwards seek refuge under the plea that they were ordered by their commanders to commit them. "Article 64 of the French penal code," he says, " is a law for civilized people; it assumes a constraint exercised in isolated cases, and in fact its application is rare in the courts of criminal repression; it cannot therefore apply to the totality of punishable acts committed in war entire, because the public action would find itself paralyzed in case its exceptional character were transformed into a general rule. It would mean that all prosecutions against German prisoners would immediately cease, and at the conclusion of war no action could be taken against those who had not been captured, because they could invoke the excuse of constraint; and, as we have indicated, all subordinates and all chiefs, great and small, would escape punishment."[2] This is the view adopted by the great majority of French jurists who have discussed the question.[3] They maintain that every person who has any share in the commission of a criminal act during war — the private soldier who commits it, the officer who delivers the order to him, the commander from whom it emanates and even the chief of State who is ultimately responsible — may be tried and punished if found guilty. And the French military courts acted on this principle in all the cases that came before them during the late war. In every case where the plea of superior command was invoked the courts made short shrift of it and if the evidence established the guilt of the accused he was condemned, even when he produced conclusive proof that he acted under orders.[4]

[1] 26 *Revue Générale de Droit Int. Pub.* (1919), p. 123.
[2] 24 *Revue Générale de Droit Int. Pub.* (1917), p. 53.
[3] Renault, however, expressed no positive opinion on the question and he appears to have been in doubt as to whether the individual soldier should be held responsible for criminal acts committed under orders. 25 *Rev. Gén.*, p. 27.
[4] Some cases are cited by Merignhac in 24 *Rev. Gén.* (1917), p. 53.

Whether or not the individual soldier should be held responsible and punished in such cases there will always, perhaps, be a
difference of opinion; but concerning the general proposition
that commanders upon whom the responsibility for criminal
acts in violation of the generally recognized laws of war
should be held accountable and punished by the adversary in
case they fall into his hands, there ought to be no dissent.[1] If
it were generally understood in the future that commanders
would be so held responsible, it is probable that such orders as
that issued by general Stenger directing his men to take no
prisoners would be rarer. Provision might well be made for
collecting information concerning acts in violation of the laws
of war and for keeping registers of the names of officers guilty
of issuing orders under which such acts are committed, and the
victorious belligerent should require in the treaty of peace the
surrender of such persons for trial and punishment.

§ 589. Responsibility of Chiefs of State. The principle that
military officers should be held personally responsible for orders
in violation of the laws and customs of war, if pushed to its
logical limits, would render commanders-in-chief, that is, heads
of States, liable for illegal acts for which they are responsible,
directly or indirectly. Very early during the late war jurists
in both France and England advocated the holding of the German Emperor, in case Germany were defeated, responsible for
acts committed by his military and naval forces in violation
of the criminal law and the laws of war. A French officer,
speaking before the French Society of Social Economy in 1915,
asserted that "it was necessary to go beyond the individual, the
actual author of the act complained of; it was necessary to
search for the chiefs; from chief to chief we must go to the
top. In the German army there is one supreme chief, the
Emperor. Let us know, for example, whether the act of general Stenger, who was accused of having issued a proclamation

---

[1] Some writers, however, think it would be preferable to defer the trial of commanders, chiefs of State, and high functionaries charged with such crimes to an
international criminal court rather than to try them before a national court, and
it has been suggested that the Hague tribunal of arbitration might be organized
into a court for this purpose. This procedure, it is argued, would insure greater
impartiality and would be more in accord with the principles of justice, but the
realization of the proposal would not be without practical difficulties. Compare
the remarks of Professor Pic in 23 *Rev. Gén.* (1916), p. 267.

ordering his troops to give no quarter, was ever disavowed. We do not know whether it was or not; but it is certain that this proclamation reached the ears of the Kaiser and it is he who is responsible."[1] Professor Merignhac approved the suggestion. "It is evident," he said, "that the Kaiser knew it, and perhaps one may even say, ordered it. Of course he did not give directly all the barbarous orders issued by his generals, but the latter knew that their acts had his approval; they were only the executors, high or low, of measures decreed by their master, who felicitated, decorated, or promoted those who distinguished themselves by their ferocity."[2] Professor Weiss, an eminent member of the law faculty of the University of Paris, took the same view in an address before the General Prison Society of France in 1915. " I think," he said, "that not only the direct immediate offenders should be held responsible, but that we must go to the top; we must pass over the heads of the primary offenders, to the chiefs, to those of whom the soldiers and officers have been only the servants and valets."[3] Professors Larnaude and Lapradelle, in an elaborate report to the French government on the question of the penal responsibility of the ex-Emperor, advocated that he be held personally responsible for the crimes committed by his armed and naval forces in violation of the laws and customs of war and that he be placed on trial before an international tribunal. "Modern

---

[1] *Réforme Sociale*, 1915, p. 203.

[2] 24 *Rev. Gén. de Droit Int. Pub.*, p. 51. As evidence of the Emperor's responsibility, Merignhac quotes the following from a letter written by William to Francis Joseph early in the war: "My soul is torn; it is necessary to put everything to fire and blood; to slaughter men and women, the children and the aged; not to leave standing a tree or a house. By means of these measures of terrorism, the only ones capable of striking a people so degenerate as the French, we may finish the war before two months. If I respect humanitarian considerations, the war may be prolonged for several years. In spite of my repugnance I have therefore chosen the first system, which will spare much blood, although in appearance the contrary may seem to be the case." This letter was published in No. 318 of the *Bulletin de l'Œuvre des Ecoles d'Orient.*

[3] 39 *Revue Pénitentiaire* (1915), p. 457. The commission of the French Chamber of Deputies which was charged with reporting on the bill for the ratification of the treaty of peace with Germany declared in its report that "among the responsibilities incurred, none is higher and more grave than that of the German Emperor. He should be judicially prosecuted for having violated the laws and customs of war. Supreme chief of the armed forces on land and sea, the 'lord of war' not only knew but tolerated and encouraged the crimes which his troops committed on land and sea. History will demand that he be held responsible for these acts." Text of the report in Barthou, *Le Traité de Paix*, p. 49.

law," they declared, "does not recognize irresponsible authorities, even at the summit of hierarchy. It brings a State down from its pedestal and makes it submit to the rule of the judge. There can therefore be no question of saving from the judge a man who is at the summit of hierarchy either by the application of internal law or of international law."[1] Jurists and statesmen in England also demanded the trial of the ex-Emperor, who, it was asserted, was not only responsible for starting the war, but also for many of the worst atrocities committed by his officers, soldiers and sailors. Judicial authority both in England and the United States, it may be remarked, placed upon the Emperor the responsibility for such acts as the torpedoing of the *Lusitania*, which resulted in the drowning of more than one thousand unoffending non-combatants, — men, women and children.[2]

§ 590. Decision of the Peace Conference Regarding the Trial of the German Emperor. The question of the responsibility of the authors of the war, the facts as to the breaches of the laws and customs of war by the forces of the German Empire and their allies and the degree of responsibility for offences committed by persons belonging to the enemy forces, regardless of their rank or station, was made the subject of an elaborate report by a commission of the Peace Conference.[3] The commission reported that the war was "premeditated by the central powers together with their allies, Turkey and Bulgaria, and was the result of acts deliberately connected in order to make it unavoidable "; and that the war was carried on by these powers by "barbarous methods in violation of the established laws and customs of war and the elementary laws of

[1] Their report is published in 46 Clunet (1919), pp. 131 ff.
[2] The coroner's jury which held the inquest over the victims of the *Lusitania* at Kinsale declared in its verdict that "this appalling crime was contrary to international law and the conventions of all civilized nations and we therefore charge the officers of the said submarine and the Emperor and government of Germany under whose orders they acted with the crime of wilful and wholesale murder before the tribunal of the civilized world." In the case of the *Lusitania* Judge Mayer of the United States District Court for the Southern District of New York (251 Fed. 715, August 24, 1918) declared that "the cause of the sinking of the *Lusitania* was the illegal act of the imperial German government acting through its instrument, the submarine commander, and violating a cherished and humane rule, observed until this war by even the bitterest antagonists."
[3] Printed in English by the Carnegie Endowment for International Peace; Div. of Int. Law, pamphlet No. 32.

humanity." Regarding the personal responsibility of individual offenders against the law of nations, the commission declared: "In these circumstances the commission desires to state expressly that in the hierarchy of persons in authority, there is no reason why rank, however exalted, should in any circumstances protect the holder of it from responsibility when that responsibility has been established before a properly constituted tribunal. This extends even to the heads of States." There was little doubt, the commission added, that "the ex-Kaiser and others in high authority were cognizant of and could at least have mitigated the barbarities committed during the course of the war. A word from them would have brought about a different method in the action of their subordinates on land, at sea and in the air." To hold that the head of the State is not liable to trial for such offences when the responsibility can be traced directly to him "would involve laying down the principle that the greatest outrages against the laws and customs of war and the laws of humanity, if proved against him, could in no circumstances be punished. Such a conclusion would shock the conscience of civilized mankind. The vindication of the principles of the laws and customs of war and the laws of humanity which have been violated would be incomplete if the ex-Kaiser were not brought to trial and if other offenders, less highly placed, were punished." Moreover, the trial of the lesser offenders might be seriously prejudiced if they attempted and were able to plead the superior orders of a sovereign against whom no steps had been or were being taken. The conclusion of the commission was that "all persons belonging to enemy countries, however high their positions may have been, without distinction of rank, including chiefs of States, who have been guilty of offences against the laws and customs of war or the laws of humanity are liable to prosecution."

As to acts which provoked the war, although the responsibility could be definitely placed, the commission advised that the authors be not made the object of criminal proceedings. The same conclusion was reached in respect to the violation of the neutrality of Belgium and Luxemburg. No criminal charge could be brought against the Kaiser or other persons responsible for these acts. Nevertheless, "in view of the gravity of these outrages upon the principles of the law of nations and upon international good faith" they should be made the subject of a formal condemnation by the Peace Conference. It was further recommended that as to these acts, as well as those by which the war was provoked, "it would be right for the Peace Conference in a matter so unprecedented to adopt special measures and even to create a special organ in order to deal as they deserve with the authors of such acts." Finally, it was suggested that "for the future it was desirable that penal sanctions should be provided for such grave outrages against the elementary principles of international law."[1]

The Peace Conference adopted in principle the recommendations of the commission in respect to the trial of the ex-Emperor. Article 227 of the treaty with Germany is as follows:

The Allied and Associated Powers publicly arraign William II of Hohenzollern, formerly German Emperor, for a supreme offence against international morality and the sanctity of treaties. A special tribunal will be constituted to try the accused, thereby assuring him the guarantees essential to the right of defence. It will be composed of five judges, one appointed by each of the following Powers: namely the United States of

---

[1] The two American members of the commission, Messrs. Lansing and Scott, dissented from certain conclusions and recommendations of the commission. They declared that they were as earnestly desirous as the other members that those persons responsible for causing the war and those responsible for violations of the laws and customs of war should be punished for their crimes, moral and legal, and that the perpetrators should be held up to the execration of mankind, but they did not consider that a judicial tribunal was a proper forum for the trial of offences of a moral nature and they objected to the proposal of the majority to place on trial before a court of justice persons charged with having violated the "principles of humanity" or the "laws of humanity." They also objected to the "unprecedented proposal" to put on trial before an international criminal court the heads of States not only for having directly ordered illegal acts of war but for having abstained from preventing such acts. This would be to subject chiefs of State to "a degree of responsibility hitherto unknown to municipal or international law, for which no precedents are to be found in the modern practice of nations." It was contrary to the doctrine of immunity of sovereigns from judicial process as laid down by Chief Justice Marshall in the case of the *Schooner Exchange* v. *McFaddon* (7 Cranch 116). "The head of a State is responsible only to the law of his own country and he cannot be subjected to trial and punishment by a tribunal to whose jurisdiction he was not subject when the alleged offences were committed."

The reasoning of the American members was in accord with the somewhat technical conceptions of American criminal law and procedure, but there are doubtless American jurists who will not concur in their line of reasoning or in their conclusions.

The two Japanese members of the Commission also dissented from certain of the conclusions of the majority and expressed doubt whether under the law of nations offenders against the laws of war, belonging to the forces of the adversary, could be tried before a court constituted by the opposing belligerents.

America, Great Britain, France, Italy and Japan. In its decision the tribunal will be guided by the highest motives of international policy, with a view to vindicating the solemn obligations of international undertakings and the validity of international morality. It will be its duty to fix the punishment which it considers should be imposed. The Allied and Associated· Powers will address a request to the government of the Netherlands for the surrender to them of the ex-Emperor in order that he may be put on trial.

§ 591. **Decision of the Peace Conference Considered.** It will be noted that the accused was to be tried not for an offence against the criminal law nor for violation of the laws and customs of war by his subordinates, for which he might perhaps have been held responsible, but only for offences against morality and for breaches of treaty faith. In fact, the Dutch government refused to surrender him. By a note of January 15, 1920, the allied powers requested his surrender in accordance with Article 228 of the treaty of Versailles. The note called attention to "the premeditated violations of international treaties as well as a systematic disregard of the most sacred rules of the rights of man," for which the ex-Emperor was responsible and expressed the opinion that "Holland would not fulfill her international duty if she refused to associate herself with them (the Allies) within the limit of her ability, to pursue, or at least not to impede, the punishment of crimes committed." The note emphasized "the special character of their demands, which contemplate, not a juridical accusation, but an act of high international policy and they make an appeal to Holland's respect for law and justice not to cover with her moral authority violation by Germany of the essential principles of the solidarity of nations." To this request the Dutch government returned a prompt refusal. It "rejected with energy all suspicion of wishing to cover with its sovereign right and its moral authority violations of the essential principles of the solidarity of nations," but it could not "recognize an international duty to associate itself with this act of high international policy of the powers." The government, it was added, could not "admit any other duty than that imposed upon it by the laws of the kingdom and national tradition." According to these laws and traditions Holland had always been regarded as "a refuge for the vanquished in international conflicts," and the government could not refuse to the former Emperor their benefit and thus "betray

the faith of those who have confided themselves to their free
institutions." Had he been surrendered and placed on trial, it
is not clear what punishment could have been imposed. Since
he was not charged with a crime, he would hardly seem liable
to the penalties prescribed for violations of the criminal law,
and since the law of nations prescribes no penalties for offences
against international morality or the sanctity of treaties, it
would seem that the judgment of the court would have been
limited to a formal pronouncement, stigmatizing him perhaps
as a treaty-breaker primarily responsible for the war and holding
him up to the execration of mankind. But the Peace Conference
as well as the public opinion of the greater part of the world
had already pronounced him guilty of these acts and it is not
quite clear what would have been gained by having a court
try him on moral charges for which he had already been convicted and to have pronounced a condemnation which he had
already received. It may be questioned therefore whether the
decision of the Peace Conference was the best solution of the
problem.

If the Conference believed that he deserved to be punished,
would it not have been more logical and more in accord with the
principles of criminal law and procedure to have extended the
theory of responsibility for criminal acts one degree higher
than it actually did, declared that the ex-Emperor was as much
responsible for a criminal act which he sanctioned or permitted
as a general who gave the order to commit it, and having laid
down this principle, provided for the creation of a court to
try him on criminal charges instead of for moral offences? But,
as was pointed out by the American members of the commission
on responsibilities, it is a well-established rule of the law of
nations that heads of States are exempt from the jurisdiction
of foreign courts [1] and in the United States this immunity has
even been interpreted to apply to ex-sovereigns.[2] The latter
interpretation of the immunity, however, can hardly be said
to be a rule of international law, and it may be argued with

[1] See the cases of *Mighell* v. *the Sultan* of Johore, 1 Q.B. 149 (1894); *de Haber* v.
The Queen of Portugal, 17 Q.B. 196 (1851); *Schooner Exchange* v. *McFaddon*,
7 Cranch 116 (1812); and Moore, Digest of International Law, vol. II, sec. 250.
[2] *Hatch* v. *Baez*, 7 Hun. 596; and *Underhill* v. *Hernandez*, 26 U.S. App. 573
(1895). This matter is learnedly discussed by Quincy Wright in 13 *Amer. Political
Science Review* (1919), pp. 120.

reason that the exemption accorded to reigning sovereigns was never intended to shield and protect from punishment heads of States responsible for such crimes and offences against the rights of nations as those with which the German Emperor was charged. The immunity referred to was founded on considerations of international comity and public policy and was introduced for the purpose of preventing the courts of one State from interfering with the discharge by the heads of other States of their high and important duties. It may be confidently asserted that it was not intended to lay down the principle that an abdicated or deposed chief of State cannot be arraigned before an international tribunal for high crimes committed by him against other nations while he was in power. The fact is, cases like that of the former German Emperor are not governed by the established rules of international law; whether he should have been tried by an international tribunal and punished, if convicted, was rather a matter of expediency and of international policy than of municipal or international law.

§ 592. **Precedents for the Trial of Chiefs of States.** Precedents for the trial and punishment of ex-sovereigns are not entirely lacking. Napoleon I appears to have been regarded as liable to trial by the British courts after his abdication.[1] In fact, he was never put on trial before a national or international court, although the congress of Vienna declared that in consequence of his violations of the convention establishing him on the Island of Elba he had "placed himself without the pale of civil and social relations and that as an enemy and a disturber of the tranquillity of the world, he had rendered himself liable to public vengeance." In August, 1815, a convention was concluded between Great Britain, Austria, Prussia, and Russia declaring him to be a prisoner of the signatory powers; he was entrusted to the custody of the British government, by which he was exiled to the Island of St. Helena.

As is well known, Jefferson Davis, ex-President of the Southern Confederacy, was indicted after the close of the Civil war, in a

---

[1] Lord Rosebery says the admiral who had the custody of Napoleon "was chased around his own fleet through an entire day by a lawyer with a writ on account of Napoleon." *Napoleon, The Last Phase*, p. 59, edited by Wright, *loc. cit.*, p. 122.

United States court for treason and the "murder of union prisoners of war and other barbarous and cruel treatment toward them." After having been held in custody for more than two years, he was admitted to bail. The case came up in December, 1868, before chief justice Chase and Judge Underwood sitting in the United States circuit court for Virginia, who heard arguments on a motion to quash the indictment. The two judges disagreed and the matter was certified to the Supreme Court. While the case was still pending Davis was released under the general amnesty of December 25, 1868.[1] His case was analogous in essential respects to that of the ex-Emperor, the principal difference being that Davis was indicted for criminal acts, whereas the ex-Emperor was to have been arraigned only for offences against international morality and the sanctity of treaties; and the tribunal before which Davis was arraigned was a national court, while that which was to have tried William was an international court. The cases of Napoleon I and Jefferson Davis therefore constitute precedents which do not differ in fundamental principle from that upon which the decision of the Peace Conference was based in respect to the trial of William of Hohenzollern.

The contention of the American members of the commission on responsibilities that the proposal to set up "an international criminal tribunal" was "unprecedented" and that it "subjects chiefs of States to a degree of responsibility hitherto unknown to municipal or international law," was only true in part.[2] In any case, even if there were no precise precedents for traducing former heads of States before international tribunals, that in itself would constitute no valid reason for not putting the former German Emperor on trial, for the reason that the offences with which he was charged were without precedent, and it may be remarked also that the American members of the commission on responsibilities did not hesitate to give their approval to other pro-

[1] Rhodes, *History of the United States*, vol. VI, p. 57.

[2] There have, of course, been a number of cases in which chiefs of State have been held personally responsible for their criminal acts and put on trial before specially created courts or other extraordinary bodies of their own country. Mary Queen of Scots was tried for conspiracy against the life of Queen Elizabeth by an extraordinary commission created by special act of Parliament. Charles I was tried by a similar commission for "traitorously and maliciously levying war against the English Parliament and people," and Louis XVI of France was tried by the convention and executed.

visions of the treaty relating to penalties and reparations that were equally "without precedents in the modern practice of nations."

§ 593. Immunity of Chiefs of States. There is room, of course, for a difference of opinion regarding the expediency of placing the ex-Emperor on trial, whether for criminal acts or moral offences. It may be said and has been said that he was no more culpable than the German people, that he was merely their representative and that the acts with which he was charged were approved by the great majority of his people. "This prosecution of the Emperor," said Professor Zitelmann of the University of Bonn, "is an iniquitous thing. From the juridical point of view the accusation has nothing to stand on. The entire nation was back of the Kaiser when we entered the war. He had the unanimity of the national conscience. The prosecution goes beyond his personality. If any one ought to be judged, it is all Germany. One cannot separate William II from his people."[1] The latter statement may have been and probably was true, but one is tempted to ask why, if the principle of personal responsibility should be extended to generals, admirals, members of the general staff and others high in command of the armed and naval forces, and they put on trial for criminal acts for which they were directly or indirectly responsible, the principle should not be pushed to its logical limits, extended to him who sits at the top of the hierarchy and applied to the commander-in-chief? If the principle of personal responsibility is once introduced, the attempt to draw a line between those to whom it should be applied and those to whom it should not apply must necessarily be more or less arbitrary and lead to injustice.

The Peace Conference, as stated in the early part of this chapter, set a new precedent, one that is to be highly commended in affirming the principle that individual offenders against the laws of war, whenever their acts are criminal in character, are personally responsible and liable to punishment, and in endeavoring to give practical effect to this principle by requiring German offenders during the recent war to be delivered up for trial and punishment. In relieving the chief offender, the ex-Kaiser,

[1] Interview in the *Journal des Débats*, March 12, 1919, reproduced in 46 Clunet (1919), p. 528.

from responsibility for criminal acts which he permitted if he did not directly approve and encourage, the conference failed, in the opinion of many persons, to go to the limit which logic, consistency, and considerations of equal justice required. Had it affirmed the elementary principle that no man, however high his station, is above the law and that heads of states who are commanders-in-chief who permit, approve, and even encourage the commission of crimes by their subordinates in the field are equally guilty and that they cannot escape responsibility by taking refuge under the plea of an immunity which was really never intended to shield them from the consequences of their crimes, the moral effect in the wars of the future would have been most salutary. It would have been tantamount to the serving of notice on chiefs of State that he who provokes an unjust war, who wages it according to cruel and barbarous methods, who permits and sanctions atrocities by his troops, who approves and even encourages shocking violations of the most elementary and long-established laws and usages of war, and who rewards by decorations and promotions their authors, does so with full knowledge that if he is defeated he will be brought to the bar of justice and punished equally with the humblest soldier who has been compelled to violate the law and who for this and other reasons may be a thousand times less responsible.

§ 594. **New Attitude Toward Violations of International Law.** Whatever may be the result of the attempt to enforce greater respect for international law through the application of penal sanctions, it would seem that the time has arrived when the body of States should adopt a different attitude toward violations of international law by particular States. The traditional view and practice in the past has generally been to regard violations of international law by a particular belligerent as of no concern to other States not immediately injured. In short, breaches of international law have been regarded as analogous to torts under the civil law, that is, as wrongs against only the victim who suffers the specific injury. Other States are regarded as strangers to the affair; they not only have no right to intervene for the purpose of preventing the act or for compelling reparation, but it is not even considered proper for them to protest, since it would be tantamount to a claim to sit in judgment on the merits of a controversy between other parties than themselves. A good illustration of this view was afforded during the recent war by the attitude of neutral powers toward the German invasion of Belgium. It does not appear that any of them formally protested or expressed a word of denunciation of this flagrant violation of a great international convention to which they were all parties. When a commission representing the Belgian government waited on the President of the United States, on September 10, 1914, and told him how the Germans, in brutal violation of the convention, had invaded their country and committed numerous shocking atrocities against the Belgian people, the President responded in a brief address in which he thanked the Commission for the documentary evidence which they had placed in his hands, promised that it should receive his thoughtful attention, expressed the opinion that where wrongs had been committed the consequences and responsibility would be assessed, and added in conclusion: "You will, I am sure, not expect me to say more."[1] No word of condemnation or protest was uttered either by the President or the Congress and the President even went to the length of addressing an appeal to the American people to remain neutral in thought as well as in action, in the presence of this and other conduct in shocking violation of the international conventions and customs.[2] This attitude of official silence on the part of neutrals was quite in accord with the traditional practice; but as Germany's violations of the law of nations and of humanity multiplied, it was abandoned and the governments of the United States, Holland, Spain, Switzerland, and other neutral powers found themselves addressing formal protests against such acts as the deportation of the civilian population from Belgium. The federal council

[1] N. Y. *Times*, September 17, 1914.

[2] Americans, however, were by no means lacking who did not approve this attitude of official silence in the presence of flagrant and inexcusable violations of international law. Ex-president Roosevelt declared that the United States should never have ratified the Hague conventions if it was not prepared to maintain them and to seal them if necessary with American blood. To stand by and allow them to be flagrantly violated without even so much as a word of protest was "the cult of cowardice and the betrayal of a solemn trust" (see the *Independent*, January 4, 1915). Judge Holt of the United States district court of New York took the same view (the *Independent*, November 23, 1914). Ex-president Eliot of Harvard University even went to the length of suggesting that the United States would have been justified in joining the Allies in a war against Germany, on the ground that it was the duty of powerful neutral States to defend small and defenceless States like Belgium against the aggressions of Germany.

of Switzerland in its protest disclaimed any intention of setting itself up as a judge of the acts of the warring powers, but it felt obliged to protest against such acts because they were not only in violation of the laws of humanity but of the Hague conventions. Switzerland, it added, had no thought of departing from her policy of neutrality but she did not consider neutrality and indifference to be synonymous.[1]

As Mr. Root has justly observed, the view heretofore acted upon is illogical and does not prevail in the criminal law of any country. An offence against the criminal law is regarded as an attack upon the rights not merely of the individual victim, but upon the rights of the entire community, and it is punished as such. If the law of nations is to be respected, he adds, the theory upon which the criminal law is founded must be adopted in respect to offences against international law. That is to say, violations of international law which threaten the peace and order of the community of States must be treated as a violation of the rights of all, for the law which has been broken is the law of all; it is their protection as well as the protection of the State immediately attacked; they may be strangers to a controversy between two nations as to what the law requires in the particular controversy, but they cannot be strangers to a dispute as to whether the law which is applicable to the circumstances shall be observed and respected.[2] The whole body of civilized nations is concerned in the observance of the great international conventions which they have formulated and ratified,[3] they cannot be indifferent to acts committed in deliber-

[1] Texts of the protests in Van den Heuvel's article cited above, pp. 290 ff. The United States and other neutral powers also protested against the German methods of submarine warfare, on the ground that they were in contravention of the "sacred rights of humanity." Protests were also made against the deportation of the civilian population from Belgium and France.

[2] See his address on the "Outlook for International Law," referred to above. See also his address in the Senate, February 19, 1916, Cong. Record, p. 3256.

[3] Cf. Dampierre, German Imperialism and International Law, p. 10. This author remarks that it is not only the right but the duty of neutrals to take notice of violations committed by belligerents, and he suggests that governments, jurists, and learned societies of neutral countries should undertake to investigate all charges in respect to such acts and to give full publicity to the findings. They ought to express their condemnation of crimes committed by belligerents and pronounce a curse on the authors. The civilized world should feel a joint responsibility for their punishment, and if the belligerent guilty of committing them should win the war, the other signatory powers to the violated conventions should, so far as possible, prevent him from enjoying the fruits of his victory. Compare also

ate and flagrant violation of them; a violation of the right of one is a violation of the rights of all, for the injury consists in the violation of the law which is the protection of all.[1]

§ 595. **Outlook for the Future.** It was frequently asserted during the course of the late war that the Hague conventions had been reduced to "scraps of paper," that international law had been destroyed, and the like. It is quite true that practically every one of the Hague conventions, to say nothing of many of the customary rules of international law, were violated, some of them many times, deliberately and flagrantly. Germany was of course the chief offender, although the other belligerents were by no means guiltless.[2] The German government and its

the observations of Dr. Alvarez, who remarks that today violations of international law are denounced only by the enemy. He adds that neutrals should take notice of them and adopt joint measures to compel respect for the law. He suggests that the Hague court should appoint commissions composed of neutral representatives to sit in belligerent territory with power to investigate and make reports as to how the laws of war are respected and observed. *Le Droit International de l'Avenir*, pp. 120-121.

Referring to German violations of the Hague conventions, as well as the rules of honor and of humanity, M. Fauchille remarks that justice, to say nothing of the interests of neutrals, gives them the right and makes it their duty to protest against violations of the law of nations, 22 *Rev. Gén.*, p. 410. Renault expressed the same opinion.

[1] Compare the observations of Scott in the *American Journal of International Law*, April, 1916, pp. 341-3.

[2] The commission on the responsibility of the authors of the war and on the enforcement of penalties, in its report to the peace conference, submitted the following list of crimes and violations of the laws of war committed by Germany and her allies:

   (1) Murders and massacres; systematic terrorism.
   (2) Putting hostages to death.
   (3) Torture of civilians.
   (4) Deliberate starvation of civilians.
   (5) Rape.
   (6) Abduction of girls and women for the purpose of enforced prostitution.
   (7) Deportation of civilians.
   (8) Internment of civilians under inhuman conditions.
   (9) Forced labor of civilians in connection with the military operations of the enemy.
   (10) Usurpation of sovereignty during military occupation.
   (11) Compulsory enlistment of soldiers among the inhabitants of occupied territory.
   (12) Attempts to denationalize the inhabitants of occupied territory.
   (13) Pillage.
   (14) Confiscation of property.
   (15) Exaction of illegitimate or of exorbitant contributions and requisitions.
   (16) Debasement of the currency, and issue of spurious currency.

apologists denied most of the charges in respect to violations committed by Germany or pleaded the excuse of military necessity or the right of reprisal in defence of those which it admitted. The German foreign office, in a note of June 10, 1916, to the British government relative to the *Baralong* affair, went to the length of asserting that the "German army and navy have observed all the principles of international law and of humanity and the authorities have taken care that all violations will be carefully investigated and punished.[1] Professor Zitelmann tells us that "Germany in this war has observed international law in all its vital aspects and has daily proven its validity." And he adds, "Our conscience is clear."[2] Whenever violations of the law were committed by Germany, he says, they were justifiable for one reason or another. Professor Von Liszt found that in Belgium international law was held "in the highest esteem"; there the German military and civil authorities were "observing

---

(17) Imposition of collective penalties.
(18) Wanton devastation and destruction of property.
(19) Deliberate bombardment of undefended places.
(20) Wanton destruction of religious, charitable, educational, and historic buildings and monuments.
(21) Destruction of merchant ships and passenger vessels without warning and without provision for the safety of passengers or crew.
(22) Destruction of fishing boats and of relief ships.
(23) Deliberate bombardment of hospitals.
(24) Attack on and destruction of hospital ships.
(25) Breach of other rules relating to the Red Cross.
(26) Use of deleterious and asphyxiating gases.
(27) Use of explosive or expanding bullets, and other inhuman appliances.
(28) Directions to give no quarter.
(29) Ill-treatment of wounded and prisoners of war.
(30) Employment of prisoners of war on unauthorized works.
(31) Misuse of flags of truce.
(32) Poisoning of wells.

This exhibit, the report added, constituted "the most striking list of crimes that has even been drawn up, to the eternal shame of those who committed them. The facts are established. They are numerous and so vouched for that they admit of no doubt and they cry for justice." The German government in a communication to the Swiss government charged the Allies with having committed thirty-seven specific violations of international law.

[1] The German foreign office in a note of July 8, 1915, to the American government asserted that "Germany had always been tenacious of the principle that war should be conducted against the armed organized forces of the enemy only and that the civil population must be spared as far as possible of the measures of war."

[2] See his article *Haben wir Noch ein Völkerrecht*, in the *Preussische Jahrbücher*, Oct.-Dec., 1914, pp. 472 ff; see also his chapter in *Modern Germany*, p. 605.

with meticulous care every provision of the law of war." Instead of finding international law in a state of collapse, he had never seen it in so "high repute and so dominating the public conduct of the administration."[1] With a few honorable exceptions, German jurists found nothing in the conduct of the German government or of its military and naval forces to criticise; every violation of the laws of war was denied or defended on some ground or other.[2] "The Germans," says Professor Schmoller, "are the nation capable of doing most for the advancement of international law and international arbitration."[3] If this be true, their conduct during the late war was all the more regrettable and inexcusable and it is to be hoped that they will now join with the other nations in reconstructing it upon permanent bases and infusing new life and vitality into its weakened body.

The late Mr. W. E. Hall, in the preface to the third edition (1889) of his treatise on international law, foresaw with the vision of a prophet how during the next war the strength of international law would be sorely tried. Whole nations, he said, would be in the field; the commerce of the world would be on the sea to win; national existences would be at stake; men would be tempted to do anything which would shorten hostilities and tend to a decisive issue; and in all probability the conduct of belligerents would be unscrupulous. But he added that if this were the case, the war would be followed by a reaction toward increased stringency of law, just as in the community periods of lawlessness are succeeded by renewed efforts to strengthen the law and insure its enforcement.

It is of course idle to say that the system of international law has been destroyed. Its prestige has suffered; it has been discredited in the minds of some persons; its weaknesses have

---

[1] Article "How Germany Works Through the War to Build up International Law," *Frankfürter Zeitung* of Oct. 29, 1916. French trans. in Clunet, 1917, pp. 911 ff., and summary in N. Y. *Times* of Nov. 19, 1916.

[2] Among the German and Austrian jurists who refused to follow their colleagues in defending all the violations of law committed by their governments or armed forces were Wehberg, Schücking, and Lammasch. See Schücking, *Die Deutschen Professoren und der Weltkrieg.* Wehberg withdrew from the editorial staff of the *Zeitschrift fur Volkerrecht* because of the views of its managing editor, Joseph Kohler. See the details in 10 *Amer. Jour. of Int. Law*, 925. As to the attitude of the German jurists, see also de Visscher, *La Belgique et les Juristes Allemands* (1916), and Nippold, *La Science du Droit des Gens pendant et après la Guerre,* in 24 *Rev. Gén.* 523.

[3] See his chapter in *Modern Germany,* p. 217.

been demonstrated as never before, but as a system it was no more destroyed by the recent war than outbreaks of crime in a community destroy the criminal law.[1] As Sir Frederick Pollock has aptly remarked: "Law does not cease to exist because it is broken or even because for a time it may be broken on a large scale."[2] No, international law never can be destroyed so long as civilization endures. Francis Lieber, himself a German, hardly exaggerated its value when he said it was the "greatest blessing of modern civilization and every settlement of a principle in the law of nations is a distinct, plain step in the progress of humanity."[3] It is as Lord Bryce observes, "the only thing which stands between us and primitive savagery." That it will be preserved, revitalized, and more generally respected in the future may be confidently assumed.

[1] Cf. Scott in 10 *Amer. Jour. of Int. Law*, p. 475; Hill, *Rebuilding of Europe*, p. 57; and De Louter, 26 *Rev. Gén.* 76.
[2] Introduction to Phillipson's ed. of Wheaton's *International Law*, p. lx.
[3] Perry, *Life and Letters of Francis Lieber*, quoted by Greene in his brochure, *Lieber and Schurz*, p. 17.

BIBLIOGRAPHY

THE following is a list of the more important books, brochures, official documents, and other publications that have appeared since the outbreak of the war, most of which have been used in the preparation of this work. The list does not include books published prior to the year 1914, nor does it include articles published in periodicals or in the proceedings of learned societies.

I

BOOKS

AJAX, The German Pirate, His Methods and Record, New York, 1918.
ALESSANDRI, J., *Contribution à l'Étude des Blocus Nouveaux*, Paris, 1919.
ALLIER, R., *Les Allemands à Saint-Dié*, Paris, 1919.
ALVAREZ, A., *La Grande Guerre Européenne et la Neutralité du Chili*, Paris, 1915.
ALVAREZ, A., *Le Droit International de l'Avenir*, Washington, 1916.
ARCHER, W., The Pirates' Progress, A Short History of the U-Boat, New York, 1918.
AUBRY, A., *Ma Captivité en Allemagne*, Paris, 1916.
BARBOUR, R. H., For the Freedom of the Seas, New York, 1919.
BARCLAY, T., Law and Usage of War, London, 1914.
BARCLAY, T., Collapse and Reconstruction, Boston, 1919.
BARRÈS, M., *La Lorraine dévastée*, Paris, 1919.
BARTHÉLEMY, J., *Le Droit Public en temps de Guerre*, Paris, 1915.
BARTHOU, L., *Le Traité de Paix*, Paris, 1919.
BASILESCO, N., *La Roumanie dans la Guerre et dans la Paix*, Paris, 1915.
BATEMAN, C. H., U-Boat Deviltry, London, 1918.
BATY, T., Prize Law and Continuous Voyage, London, 1915.
BATY, T., and MORGAN, J. H., War: its Conduct and Legal Results, New York, 1915.
BAUDRILLART, Mgr., The German War and Catholicism, Paris, 1915.
BECK, J. M., The Evidence in the Case, New York and London, 1914.
BECK, J. M., The War and Humanity, New York, 1916.
BREWER, D. C., Rights and Duties of Neutrals. A Discussion of Principles and Practices, New York, 1916.
BROWN, L. F., The Freedom of the Seas, New York, 1919.
BROWN, P. M., International Realities, New York, 1917.
BRUCY, J., *Les Traités et la Règlementation du Droit de la Guerre*, Paris, 1917.
BRUNEAU, *L'Allemagne en France*, Paris, 1914.
BRYCE, JAMES, and Others, The War of Democracy: The Allies' Statement, New York, 1915.
BUCHAN, J., Nelson's History of the War, 23 vols., London, 1914–18.
BULLARD, A., The Diplomacy of the Great War, New York, 1915.

BURGESS, J. W., America's Relations to the Great War, Chicago, 1916.
BURGESS, J. W., The European War of 1914, Chicago, 1915.
CALIPPE, A. C., La Somme sous l'Occupation Allemande, Paris, 1918.
CAMPBELL, H. C., The Law of War and Contract, Oxford, 1918.
CARILLO, G. E., Among the Ruins, London, 1915.
CARLÉS, M. W. R., La République Argentine et la Guerre Européenne, Paris, 1915.
CARSTEN, L., Maatregelen ter handhaving onzer onsijdigheid in den huidegen oorlog. (Measures taken by the Netherlands for the Maintenance of their Neutrality during the Present War.) London, 1916.
CATELLANI, E., Le Droit Aérien, Paris, 1915.
CHAMBRY, R., The Truth about Louvain, London, 1915.
CHAPTAL, M., Rapatriés, 1915–1918; Paris, 1915.
CHARLTON, R., and LASCOT, F. R., Edith Cavell, London, 1915.
CLAPP, E. J., Economic Aspects of the War, Neutral Rights, Belligerent Claims and American Commerce in the Years 1914–15, New Haven, 1915.
CLAUSEWITZ, C. VON, On War. New and revised edition, with introduction and notes by F. N. Maude, New York, 1915.
CLEMENTS, A. F., and WATERSON, H. G., Commercial Law in War Time, New York, 1916.
COHEN, L., The Ruhleben Prison Camp, New York, 1917.
"Cosmos," The Basis of a Durable Peace, New York, 1917.
DAMPIERRE, J. M., German Imperialism and International Law, London, 1917.
DAMPIERRE, J., L'Allemagne et le Droit des Gens d'après les Sources Allemandes et les Archives du Gouvernement François, Paris, 1915.
DAMPIERRE, J., Carnet de Route de Combattants Allemands. (Publication authorized by the French Minister of War.) Paris, 1916.
DAVIS, G. B., Elements of International Law, 4th ed., New York, 1916.
DAVISON, C. S., The Freedom of the Seas, New York, 1918.
DEMBOSKI, N., Europe and the New Sea Law: A Manual of International Politics and Maritime Law, London, 1914.
DESSON, G., A Hostage in Germany, London, 1917.
Deutschland und der Weltkrieg, various German authors. (English translation under title "Modern Germany" by W. W. Whitelock.) New York, 1916.
DILLON, E. J., A Scrap of Paper, London, 1914.
DUCKWORTH, L., Principles of Marine Law, 3d ed., London, 1916.
ECCARD, F., L'Alsace sous la Domination Allemande, Paris, 1919.
ECCARD, Biens et Intérêts Français en Allemagne et en Alsace-Lorraine pendant la Guerre, Paris, 1917.
EDWARDS, G. W., Vanished Towers and Chimes of Flanders, Philadelphia, 1916.
EDWARDS, G. W., Vanished Halls and Cathedrals of France, Philadelphia, 1917.
EVANS, L. B., Leading Cases on International Law, Chicago, 1917.
FAGE, A., Lille sous la Griffe Allemande, Paris, 1917.
FAVRAUD, Y., Contrebande de Guerre, Blocus, Droit de Visite, Paris, 1916.
FAYLE, E. C., The Great Settlement, New York, 1915.
FERRAND, Des Réquisitions en Matière de Droit International Public (Deuxième edition), Paris, 1917.
FRANÇOIS, J. P. A., Duik boot en Volkenrecht (Submarines and International Law), Leyden, 1919.
FRANK, R., Die Belgische Neutralität, Tübingen, 1915.
FRANK, R., Das Seekriegsrecht, Tübingen, 1916.
FRIED, A. H., The Restoration of Europe, New York, 1916.
FROST, W., German Submarine Warfare, New York, 1918.

FUEHR, A., The Neutrality of Belgium, New York and London, 1915.

GERARD, J. W., My Four Years in Germany, New York, 1917.

GIBSON, H., A Journal from our Legation in Belgium, New York, 1917.

GOMERY, G. DE, Belgium in War Time, New York, 1916.

GORE-BROWNE, Effect of War on Commercial Relations and the Position of Corporations during the War, London, 1918.

GRASSHOFF, R., The Tragedy of Belgium, New York, 1915.

GREEN, H., The Log of a Non-combatant, Boston and New York, 1915.

GRONDYS, L. H., The Germans in Belgium, Experiences of a Neutral. (English translation.) London, 1915.

GROTIUS, *Annuaire International pour les Années 1914, 1915, 1916, 1917*, etc., The Hague, 1914-1919.

GROTIUS SOCIETY, Problems of the War, 4 vols., Papers by various authors, London, 1916-1919.

GRUET, P. L., *Réquisitions Militaires (Armées de Terre et de Mer)*, Paris, 1915.

GUEULLETTE, *Des Effets Juridiques de la Guerre sur les Contrats*, Paris, 1918.

GUYOT, YVES, *Les Causes et les Conséquences de la Guerre*, Paris, 1915.

HALL, W. E., International Law. (Seventh edition by A. P. Higgins.) Oxford, 1918.

HAMILTON, C., Senlis, London, 1917.

HART, A. B., The War in Europe, Its Causes and Results, New York and London, 1914.

HEADLAM, J. W., The History of Twelve Days, London, 1915.

HEDIN, S., With the German Armies in the West, New York and London, 1915.

HÉLYS, M., *Les Provinces Françaises pendant la Guerre*, Paris, 1918.

HENNEBOIS, C., In German Hands. (The diary of a severely wounded soldier.) London, 1916.

HENNING, R., *Les Déportations de Civils Belges en Allemagne et dans le Nord de la France*, Brussels, 1919.

HILL, D. J., The Rebuilding of Europe, a Survey of Forces and Conditions, New York, 1917.

HILLIS, N. D., The Blot on the Kaiser's Scutcheon, New York, 1918.

HÖCKER, P. O., *An der Spitze meiner Kompagnie* (Three Months of Campaigning), Berlin, 1914.

HÖLYER, O., *La Théorie de l'Équilibre et le Droit des Gens*, Paris, 1917.

HOOGHE, E. D., *Droit Aérien*, Paris, 1914.

HUBERICH, C. H., *Das Englische Prisenrecht in seiner neuesten Gestalt*, Berlin, 1915.

HUBERICH, C. H., The Law Relating to Trading with the Enemy, New York, 1918.

HUBERICH, C. H., and KING, R., The Development of German Prize Law, New York, 1918.

JITTA, D. G., The Renovation of International Law, The Hague, 1919.

JOHNSON, O., The Spirit of France, New York, 1916.

JONES, J., The Fall of Tsingtau, Boston and New York, 1915.

JULLIET, *Les Aéronefs Sanitaires et la Guerre de 1914*, Paris, 1918.

KELLOGG, V., Headquarters Nights, Boston, 1917.

KIPLING, R., Sea Warfare, New York, 1917.

KRAUEL, W., *Neutralität, Neutralisation und Befriedung im Völkerrecht*, Munich and Leipzig, 1915.

LABALLE, J. B. DE, *El Peru y la Gran Guerra*, Lima, 1919.

LAINEL, G., *La Propriété Industrielle et la Guerre*, Paris, 1917.

LANGENHOVE, F., The Growth of a Legend, a Study based upon the German accounts of *Francs-Tireurs* and "atrocities" in Belgium. (English translation by E. B. Sherlock.) New York, 1916.

508 BIBLIOGRAPHY

LANESSAN, J. L., *Les Empires Germaniques et la Politique de la Force*, Paris, 1915.
LAURENTIE, J., *Les Lois de la Guerre*, Paris, 1917.
LAWRENCE, T. J., The Society of Nations, Oxford, 1919.
LE FUR, L., *Des Représailles en Temps de Guerre*, Paris, 1919.
LEMOINE, A., *Les Conventions Internationales sur le Régime des Prisonniers de Guerre*, Paris, 1917.
LETTENHOVE, H. K., *La Guerre et les Œuvres d'Art en Belgique*, Brussels and Paris, 1917.
LISZT, F. VON, *Das Völkerrecht*, 11th ed., Berlin, 1918.
LODGE, H. C., War Addresses, 1915-1917, New York, 1917.
MACCAS, L., German Barbarism, a Neutral's Indictment. (English translation from the French.) London, 1916.
MACCAS, L., *Ainsi parla Venizelos*, Paris, 1916.
MACH, E. VON, What Germany Wants, Boston, 1915.
MACH, E. VON, Germany's Point of View, Chicago, 1915.
MAHONEY, H. C., Sixteen Months in Four German Prisons, New York, 1917.
MAHONEY, H. C., Interned in Germany, New York, 1918.
MALNOURY, L., *L'Etat de Guerre et ses Conséquences Juridiques*, Besançon, 1915.
MARÈS, R., *La Belgique Envahie*, Paris, 1915.
MARGUERITTE, P., *Contre les Barbares 1914-15*, Paris, 1915.
MARGUILLER, *La Destruction des Monuments sur le Front Occidental*, Paris, 1919.
MARINO, F., *Corso di diritto internazionale pubblico*, Naples, 1917.
MARTIN, H., and BAKER, J. R., Laws of Maritime War Affecting Rights and Duties of Belligerents as Existing August 1, 1914, Washington, 1918.
MASSART, J., Belgians under the German Eagle, New York, 1916.
MASSART, J., *Comment les Belges résistent à la Domination Allemande*, Paris, 1917.
MASSART, J., The Secret Press in Belgium, New York, 1919.
MATOT, JULES, *Almanach de la Guerre, Reims et la Marne, 1914-15*, Reims, 1916.
MAUSBACH, *Naturrecht und Völkerrecht*, Freiburg, 1918.
MAYERS, E. C., Admiralty Law and Practice in Canada, London, 1916.
McCARTHY, D. J., The Prisoner of War in Germany, New York, 1918.
McCLELLAN, G. B., The Heel of War, New York, 1916.
MEARS, E. G., The Destruction of Belgium, a Reply to the German White Book, London, 1916.
MERCIER, CARDINAL, The Voice of Belgium, London, 1917.
MEURER, C., *Die völkerrechtliche Stellung der vom Feind besetzen Gebiete*, Tübingen, 1915.
MEURER, C., *Das Program der Meeresfreiheit*, Berlin, 1917.
MEURER, C., *Der Lusitania-Fall*, Tübingen, 1915.
MICHEL, A., *Les Villes Martyres*, Paris, 1915.
MIKHAILOW, P., *Le Rôle de la Russie dans de Droit International*. Preface by M. Renault, Paris, 1915.
MOKVELD, L., The German Fury in Belgium, Experiences of a Netherlands Journalist during Four Months with the German army in Belgium. London and New York, 1917.
MORGAN, J. H., The War Book of the German General Staff, being "the Usages of War on Land," issued by the Great General Staff of the German army. New York, 1915.
MORGAN, J. H., German Atrocities: an Official Investigation, London, 1916.
MORGANTHAU, H., Ambassador Morganthau's Story, New York, 1918.
MOULIN, *La Guerre et les Neutres*, Paris, 1915.
MÜLLER-MEININGEN, Der Weltkrieg und der Zusammenbruch des Völkerrechts, Berlin, 1915.

NIEMEYER, T., *Privateigentum im Seekriege*, Munich, 1915.

NEWBOLT, H., Submarine and Anti-Submarine, New York, 1919.

NIPPOLD, O., *Die Gestaltung des Völkerrechts nach dem Weltkriege*, Zurich, 1917.

NOEL, L., Louvain 891–1914, Oxford, 1915.

NOTHOMB, P., *Les Barbares en Belgique*, Paris, 1915.

NOTHOMB, P., *La Belgique Martyre*, Paris, 1915.

NOYES, A., Open Boats, New York, 1917.

NYROP, *L'Arrestation des Professeurs Belges et l'Université de Gand*, Paris, 1917.

OPPENHEIM, L., The League of Nations, London, 1919.

OTLET, P., *Problèmes Internationaux et la Guerre*, Geneva, 1916.

PAGE, A., War and Alien Enemies, The Law Affecting their Personal and Trading Rights, 2d ed., London, 1915.

PALMER, F., My Year of the Great War, New York, 1915.

PALMER, F., My Second Year of the War, New York, 1917.

PARKER, SIR GILBERT, The World in the Crucible, An account of the Origins and Conduct of the Great War, New York, 1915.

PASSELECQ, F., *Les Déportations Belges à la Lumière des Documents Allemands*, Paris and Nancy, 1917.

PASSELECQ, F., *La Question Flamande et l'Allemagne*, Paris and Nancy, 1917.

PASSELECQ, F., *La Vérité sur les Déportations Belges*, Paris and Nancy, 1917.

PASSELECQ, F., *Le Second Livre Blanc Allemand*, Paris, 1917.

PCHÉDECKI, E., *Le Droit International Maritime et la Grande Guerre*, Paris, 1916.

PETRE, M. D., Reflections of a Non-combatant, New York and London, 1915.

PHILLIPSON, C., International Law and the Great War, London, 1915.

PIGGOTT, F., The Neutral Merchant in Relation of the Law of Contraband of War and Blockade under the Order in Council of March, 1915, London, 1915.

PILLET, A., *La Guerre Actuelle et le Droit des Gens*, Paris, 1916.

PILLET, A., *Les Conventions de la Haye, Etude Juridique et Critique*, Paris, 1918.

PLATER, C., A Primer of Peace and War, the Principles of International Morality, New York and London, 1915.

POHL, H., *Deutsches Seekriegsrecht*, Berlin, 1915.

POTEZ, H., *Villes Meurtries de France* (Arras), Paris, 1919.

POWELL, A. E., Fighting in Flanders, New York, 1914.

PRATT, S. C., Military Law: its Procedure and Practice, 19th ed., London, 1915.

PULLING, A. (Editor), Manual of Emergency Legislation (comprising all the acts of Parliament, proclamations, orders, etc. passed and made in consequence of the war). With 4 supplements, London, 1914–16.

PYKE, G., To Ruheleben and Back, Boston, 1916.

PYKE, H. R., The Law of Contraband of War, Oxford, 1915.

RECOULY, J., *M. Jonnart en Grèce et l'Abdication de Constantin*, Paris, 1918.

REDSLOB, R., *Das Problem des Völkerrechts*, Leipzig, 1917.

REULOS, A., *Manuel des Séquestres*, Paris, 1916.

ROBIDA, A., *Les Villes Martyres*, Paris, 1915.

ROGERS, LINDSAY, America's Case against Germany, New York, 1917.

ROHRBACH, P., *Der Krieg und die deutsche Politik*, Weimar, 1915.

ROLLAND, L., *Les Pratiques de la Guerre Aérienne dans le Conflit de 1914 et le Droit des Gens*, Paris, 1916.

ROSENTHAL, E., *Deutsches Kriegsrecht*, Berlin, 1915.

ROTHERY, H. C., Price Droits. (A Report of H. M. Treasury on Droits of the Crown and of Admiralty in times of war. Revised and Annotated by E. S. Roscoe.) London, 1915.

ROUSSEAU, A., *Sous-Marins et Blocus*, Paris, 1917.

ROXBURGH, R. F., The Prisoners of War Information Bureau in London, Preface by L. Oppenheim, London, 1915.

SAINT-AYMOUR, COMTE DE G., *Autour de Noyon, sur les Traces des Barbares*, Paris, 1917.

SAINT YVES, P., *Les Responsabilités de l'Allemagne dans la Guerre de 1914*, Paris, 1915.

SANGER, C. P., and NORTON, H. J., England's Guarantee to Belgium and Luxemburg, London, 1915.

SAROLEA, C., How Belgium saved Europe, London, 1915.

SAYOUS, A. E., *Blocus Economique de l'Allemagne*, Paris, 1915.

SCHÜCKUNG, W., *Die deutschen Professoren und der Weltkrieg*, Berlin, 1915.

SCHÜCKUNG, W., *Die völkerrechtliche Lehre des Weltkriegs*, Leipzig, 1918.

SCHULTE, A., *Von der Neutralität Belgiens*, Bonn, 1915.

SCHVEITZER, M., *L'Interdiction du Commerce avec l'Ennemi*, Paris, 1918.

SCOTT, J. B., A Survey of International Relations between the United States and Germany, New York, 1917.

SCOTT, LESLIE, Trading with the Enemy; the Effect of War on Contracts, 2d ed., London.

SEYMOUR, CHARLES, The Diplomatic Background of the War, New Haven, 1916.

SEIGNOREL, J., *Le Droit Français pendant la Guerre, Le Statut des Sujets Ennemis*, Paris, 1916.

SHIEL, M. P., Contraband of War, London, 1914.

SMITH, SIR, F. E., The Destruction of Merchant Ships under International Law, New York, 1917.

SMITH, SIR, F. E., International Law, fifth ed., by C. Phillipson, New York, 1919.

SMITH, MUNROE, Militarism and State Craft, New York, 1918.

SMUTS, J. C., War Time Speeches, New York, 1917.

SOMVILLE, G., *Vers Liège, le Chemin du Crime*, Paris, 1915. (English translation, by B. Maill under the title The Road to Liège.) London, 1916.

SOUTTAR, H. S., A Surgeon in Belgium, London, 1915.

SPAIGHT, J. M., War Rights on Land, 2d ed., London, 1915.

STEEN, F. E., *Négociations pour les Prisonniers de Guerre*, Paris, 1918.

STEINUTH, H., *England und der U-Boat Krieg*, Stuttgart, 1915.

STIER-SOMLO, F., *Die Freiheit des Meeres und das Völkerrecht*, Leipzig, 1917.

STILKE, VON G. (Editor), *Die Belgische Neutralität*, Berlin, 1914.

STOCKTON, C. H., Outlines of International Law, New York, 1915.

STOWELL, E. C., The Diplomacy of the War of 1914, Boston and New York, 1915.

STOWELL, E. C., and MUNRO, H. F., International Cases (2 vols.), Boston, 1916.

STRUPP, K., *Das internationale Landkriegsrecht*, Frankfurt, 1914.

STRUYCKEN, A. A. H., *De Oorlogen het Volkenrecht*, The Hague, 1914.

STRUYCKEN, A. A. H., The German White Book on the War in Belgium, A Commentary, London, 1916.

SUAREZ, S. P., *Tratado de derecho internacional público*, Madrid, 1916.

TAILLEFER, A., and CLARO, C., *Les Brevets, Dessins, Marques et la Propriété Littéraire et Artistique pendant la Guerre*, Paris, 1918.

Times Documentary History of the War, 8 vols., London, 1917–19.

TIVERTON, VISCOUNT, The Principles and Practice of Prize Law, London, 1914.

TOYNBEE, A. J., Armenian Atrocities; the Murder of a Nation, London, 1915.

TOYNBEE, A. J., The Destruction of Poland, a Study in German Efficiency, London, 1917.

TOYNBEE, A. J., The German Terror in Belgium, New York, 1917.

TOYNBEE, A. J., The German Terror in France, London, 1917.

TOYNBEE, A. J., The Belgian Deportations, with a statement by Viscount Bryce, London, 1917.

TRIEPEL, H., *Die Freiheit der Meere und der künftige Friedensschluss*, Berlin, 1917.

TROIMAUX, E., *Séquestres et Séquestrés; Les Biens Austro-Allemands pendant la Guerre*, Paris, 1916.

TROTTER, W. F., Supplement to the Law of Contract during War, London, 1915.

QUIGLEY, H. F., The Immunity of Private Property from Capture at Sea, Madison, 1916.

VACHON, M., *Les Villes Martyres de France et de Belgique*, Paris, 1915.

VALENTINE, V., *Belgien und die grosse Politik der Neuzeit*, Munich, 1915.

VALERY, J., *Les Crimes de la Population Belge*, Paris, 1916.

VALLOTTON, B., *Au Pays de la Mort*, Paris, 1917.

VAN DER ESSEN, The Invasion and the War in Belgium, London, 1918.

VENIZELOS, Politis, and others, *Cinq Ans d'Histoire (1912-1917) Grecque*. (French translation by L. Maccas.) Paris, 1917.

VERHAEREN, E., *La Belgique Sanglante*, Paris, 1915. (English translation under title "Belgium's Agony," by T. H. Sadler.) London, 1915.

VERMOND, E., *Manuel de Droit Maritime*, 4th ed., Paris, 1917.

VERZIJL, J. H. W., *Het Prijsrecht Tegenover Neutralen in den Wereld Oorlog van 1914 en Volgende Jaren*, The Hague, 1917.

VESNITCH, R., *Le Devoir des Neutres et le Droit International Moderne*, Nîmes, 1917.

VEUILLOT, F., *La Guerre Allemande et le Catholicisme*, Paris, 1915.

VILLENEUVE-TRANS, R., *La Liberté des Mers; Le Blocus de l'Allemagne; La Guerre Sous-marine*, Paris, 1917.

VISSCHER, CHARLES DE, Belgium's Case, A Juridical Inquiry, London, New York, 1916.

VISSCHER, CHARLES DE, *La Belgique et les Juristes Allemands*, Paris and Lausanne, 1916.

VOLLENHOVEN, C., *Trois Phases du Droit des Gens*, The Hague, 1919.

WAMPACH, G., *Le Dossier de la Guerre* (3 vols.), Paris, 1915-16.

WAMPACH, G., *Le Grand-duché de Luxembourg et l'Invasion Allemande*, Paris, 1915.

WASHBURN, S., The Russian Campaign, London, 1915.

WASHBURN, S., The Russian Advance, New York, 1917.

WAXWEILER, E., Belgium Neutral and Loyal, the War of 1914, New York, 1915.

WAXWEILER, E., Belgium and the Great Powers; Her Neutrality Explained and Vindicated, New York, 1916.

WEHBERG, H., *Das Seekriegsrecht*, Berlin, 1915.

WHITE, C. and HARPER, H., Aircraft in the Great War, London and Chicago, 1915.

WHITE, J. M., A Textbook of the War for Americans, Philadelphia, 1915.

WHITLOCK, BRAND, Belgium (2 vols.), New York, 1919.

WIJNVELDT, J., *Neutraliteitsrecht te Land*, The Hague, 1917.

WILLIAMS, A. R., In the Claws of the German Eagle, New York, 1917.

WILLIAMS, V., With our Army in Flanders.

WILLIAMS, WYTHE, Passed by the Censor, New York, 1917.

WOOD, E. F., The Note-book of an Attaché; Seven Months in the War Zone, New York, 1915.

ZOLLER, O., *Das Völkerrecht und der Krieg, 1914-15*, Zurich, 1915.

ZURLINDEN, S., *Der Weltkrieg, vorläufige Orientierung von einem Schweizerischen Standpunkt aus.* (2 Vols.), Zurich, 1917-18.

Z., *La Belgique sous la Griffe Allemande*, Paris, 1915.

Z., *Les Monuments Français Détruits par l'Allemagne*, Paris, 1918.

Z., *Les Allemands Destructeurs de Cathédrales et de Trésors du Passé*, Paris, 1915.

An Eye Witness, The Horrors of Louvain, Introduction by Lord Halifax, London, 1916.

Neutralité du Grand-Duché de Luxembourg pendant la Guerre de 191.;-18, Luxembourg, 1919.

Der Lusitania-Fall im Urteile von Deutschen Gelehrten, Various Authors, Breslau, 1915.

II

BROCHURES, PAMPHLETS, REPRINTS, ETC.

ANDLER, C., "Frightfulness" in Theory and Practice as compared with the Franco-British War Usages. Edited and translated by B. Miall, London, 1915.

ANDLER, C., and LAVISSE, E., German Theory and Practice of War. (English translation by L. S.), Paris, 1915.

ANDLER, C. H., *Usages de la Guerre et la Doctrine de l'Etat-Major Général Allemand*, Paris, 1915.

BALFOUR, A. J., The British Blockade, London, 1915.

BALFOUR, A. J., The Freedom of the Seas, London, 1916.

BEDIER, J., German Atrocities from German Evidence. (English translation by B. Harrison.) Paris, 1915.

BEDIER, J., How Germany seeks to Justify her Atrocities. (English translation by J. S.), Paris, 1915.

BISSING, GENERAL VON, Political Testament: A Study in German Ideals, New York and London, 1917.

BISSING, GENERAL VON, *Belgien unter deutschen Verwaltung*, München, 1915.

BURGESS, J. W., and others, Germany's Just Cause, New York, 1914.

BUYENS, BARON, *L'Allemagne avant la Guerre, Les Causes et les Responsabilités*, Bruxelles et Paris, 1915.

CAMMAERTS, E., Through the Iron Bars, London, 1917.

CHARRIANT, H., *La Belgique, Le Droit contre la Force*, Paris, 1915.

COOK, J. A., Kaiser, Krupp and Kultur, New York, 1915.

CORBETT, J., The League of Peace and A Free Sea, London, 1917.

DEJONGH, C., *L'Allemagne et les Conventions de la Haye*, Lausanne, 1915.

DERNBURG, B., Germany and England, the Real Issue, Publications of the Germanistic Society, Chicago, 1914.

DERNBURG, B., Germany and the War, New York, 1915.

DICKINSON, G. L., The European Anarchy, London, 1916.

DOUMERGUE, E., *Le Droit et la Force d'après les Manuels des Etats-Majors Allemands et Français*, Paris, 1915.

DUMAS, J., *Les Sanctions Pénales des Crimes Allemands*, Paris, 1916.

EBERS, G. J., *Der Krieg und das Völkerrecht*, Münster, 1915.

FAUCHILLE, P., *Les Attentats Allemands contre les Biens et Contre les Personnes en Belgique et en France*, Paris, 1915.

FAUCHILLE, P., *L'Evacuation des Territoires Occupés par l'Allemagne dans le Nord de la France*, Paris, 1917.

FLACH, J., *La Déviation de la Justice en Allemagne, La Force et le Droit*, Paris, 1915.

FRANKE, K., Germany's Fateful Hour, Chicago, 1914.

GROSSE, J., *Les Mines sous-Marines*, Paris, 1914.

GRUBEN, H., *Les Allemands à Louvain: Souvenirs d'un Témoin, Paris*, 1915.

HEADLAM, J. W., Belgium and Greece, London and New York, 1917.

HELFERICH, Karl, Germany's Case in the Supreme Court of Civilization, New York, 1915.

HIGGINS, A. P., Defensively Armed Merchant Ships and Submarine Warfare, London, 1917.

HIGGINS, A. P., The Law of Nations and the War, Oxford, 1914.

HILL, G. F., The Commemorative Medal in the Service of Germany, New York and London, 1917.

HURD, A., Submarines and Zeppelins in Warfare and Outrage, London, 1916.

KRAUS, H., *Der gegenwartige Krieg vor dem Forum des Völkerrechts*, Berlin, 1915.

LESAGE, C., *Cables sous-Marins Allemands*, Paris, 1915.

MASSON, A., *L'Invasion des Barbares en 1914*, Paris, 1915.

MEURER, C., *Der Volkskrieg und das Strafgericht über Löwen*, Breslau, 1914.

MILHAUD, E., *Du Droit de la Force et de la Force du Droit*, Geneva, 1915.

MILNER, VISCOUNT, Cotton as Contraband, London, 1915.

MUIR, RAMSEY, *Mare Libernum*, The Freedom of the Seas, London, 1917.

MURRAY, GILBERT, Great Britain's Sea Policy, London, 1917.

REISS, R. A., *Comment les Austro-Hongrois ont fait la Guerre en Serbie*, Paris, 1915.

RICHARDS, SIR H. E., Does International Law Still Exist? Oxford, 1915.

RICHARDS, SIR H. E., International Law, Some Problems of the War, Oxford, 1915.

RENAULT, L., *Les Premières Violations du Droit des Gens par l'Allemagne, Luxembourg et Belgique*, Paris, 1917.

SAROLEA, C., The Murder of Nurse Cavell, London, 1916.

SCHULTE, F., *Von der Neutralität Belgiens*, 1915.

SOHR, F., *Le Culte de la Violence, Notes à propos du Manuel Allemand "l'Interprète Militaire" du Capitaine von Scharfenort*, Le Havre, 1918.

STILKE, G., *Belgische Neutralität*, Berlin, 1914.

THIESING, T. H., Trading with the Enemy, Washington, 1917.

TRIANA, S. P., How to Enforce Laws of War, London, 1915.

VAN DER ESSEN, L., A statement about the Destruction of Louvain and Neighborhood; also Some More News about the Destruction of Louvain, Chicago, 1915 (privately printed).

VAN DEN HEUVEL, J., *De la Violation de la Neutralité Belge*, Paris, 1914.

WEHBERG, H., *Der Deutsch-Englische Handels- und Unter See Boot-krieg*, Vienna, 1915.

WEHBERG, H., *Der Lusitania-Fall*, Vienna, 1915.

WEHBERG, H., *Von Tirpits und das Seekriegsrecht*, Bonn, 1915.

WEISS, A., The Violation by Germany of the Neutrality of Belgium and Luxemburg. (English translation by W. Thomas.) Paris, 1915.

WISE, B. R., The Freedom of the Sea, London, 1915.

The Violation of the Neutrality of Belgium. Preface by M. Paul Hymans, London, 1915.

The Mails as a German War Weapon (memorandum on the Censorship of Mails carried by Neutral Ships), London, 1916.

The Murder of Captain Fryatt, London, 1916 (Hodder and Stoughton).

Les Prisonniers au Maroc; La Campagne de Diffamation Allemande; Le Jugement Porté par les Neutres; Le Témoignage des Prisonniers Allemands, Paris, 1917.

Censorship and Trade, London, 1916.

Why Mail Censorship is Vital to Britain, An Interview with the Rt. Hon. Lord Robert Cecil, Minister of Blockade, London, 1916.

Great Britain's Measures against German Trade. A Speech by the Rt. Hon. Sir Edward Grey in the House of Commons, Jan. 26, 1916. London, 1916.

The War on Hospital Ships, from the Narrative of an Eye Witness, London, 1917.

Why we are at War, by Members of the Oxford University Faculty of Modern History, Oxford, 1914.

Frightfulness in Retreat, London, 1917.

An Eye Witness at Louvain, London, 1914.

The Horrors of Louvain, by an Eye Witness, with an introduction by Lord Fairfax, London, 1915.

Lille sous le Joug Allemand, Paris, 1917.

III

DOCUMENTARY COLLECTIONS AND REPORTS, OFFICIAL AND UNOFFICIAL

AMERICAN

Diplomatic Correspondence with Belligerent Governments Relating to Neutral Rights and Duties: European War Nos. 1-3. Three White papers published by the United States Government, Washington, 1915-1916.

Diplomatic Correspondence between the United States and Belligerent Governments Relating to Neutral Rights and Commerce. Three volumes. Special Supplements to *Amer. Jour. of Int. Law* for July, 1915, October, 1916, and October, 1917. New York, 1915, 1916, 1917.

Documents Regarding the European War — Blue, Red, Orange, Yellow, etc. — White Books issued by the various governments. Reprinted by the American Association for International Conciliation. New York, 1915, 1916.

Documents, Official, Concerning Neutral and Belligerent Rights. Reprinted by the World Peace Foundation, Boston, 1915.

SCOTT, J. B. (Editor), Diplomatic Documents Relating to the Outbreak of the European War. Published by the Carnegie Endowment for International Peace. 2 vols., New York, 1916.

SCOTT, J. B. (Editor), Reports to the Hague Conferences of 1899 and 1907. Publication of the Carnegie Endowment for International Peace, New York, 1917.

SCOTT, J. B. (Editor), Resolutions of the Institute of International Law Dealing with the Law of Nations. Carnegie Endowment for International Peace, New York, 1916.

VON MACH, E., Official Diplomatic Documents Relating to the Outbreak of the European War. With photographic reproductions of official editions of the documents (Blue, White, etc., books), published by various belligerent governments, New York, 1916.

The War Message and Facts behind it. Issued by the United States Committee on Public Information, Washington, 1918.

The President's Flag Day Address, with Evidence of Germany's Plans, issued by the United States Committee on Public Information, Washington, 1917.

FESS, S. D., The Problems of Neutrality when the World is at War. A history of our relations with Germany and Great Britain as detailed in the Documents, etc., H. of R. Doc. No. 2111, 64th Cong. 2nd Sess., Washington, 1917.

Institut Américain de Droit International, Acte Final de la Session de la Havane. Jan. 22-27, 1917, New York, 1917.

MUNRO, D. C., SELLERY, C. S., and KREY, A. C., German War Practices, Issued by the United States Committee on Public Information, Washington, 1917.

NOTESTEIN, W., and STOLL, E., Conquest and Kultur, Aims of the Germans in their own Words, Pubs. of United States Committee on Information, Washington, 1917.

PAXON, F. L., CORWIN, E. S., and HARDING, S. B., War Cyclopedia, A Handbook for Ready Reference on the Great War. Issued by the United States Committee on Public Information, Washington, 1918.

SPERRY, E. E., and WEST, W. M., German Plots and Intrigues in the United States during the Period of our Neutrality. Issued by the United States Committee on Public Information, Washington, 1918.

Rules of Land Warfare, United States War Department, Washington, 1914.

Naval War College, International Law. Topics and Documents, 1915, 1916, 1917. Texts of Neutrality proclamations, declarations of war, and other documents, Washington, 1915, 1916.

BELGIAN

Arrêtés et Proclamations de Guerre Allemands du 20 Août 1914 au 25 Janvier 1915. Docs. Hist. *Affichés à Bruxelles pendant l'Occupation*, London, 1915.
L'Armée Allemande à Louvain en Août 1914 et le Livre Blanc Allemand du 10 Mai 1915. Publié par le gouvernement Belge, Paris, 1917.
Les Cahiers Belges, a series of documents issued by the Belgian government relative to German conduct in Belgium, Brussels and Paris, 1917, 1918.
Réponse au Livre Blanc Allemand du 10 Mai 1915, "Die völkerrechtswidrige Führung des belgischen Volkskriegs." Publication of the Belgian government, Paris, 1917.
Correspondance Diplomatique Relative à la Guerre de 1914-1915. Grey Book, Paris, 1915.
Rapports sur la Violation du Droit des Gens en Belgique. Pub. off. du gouv. belge. Préf. de J. Van den Heuvel (2 vols.), Paris, 1916.
Reports of the official commission of the Belgian Government on the Rights of Nations and the Laws and Customs of War. English Translation of the previously mentioned *Rapports*, published on behalf of the Belgian Legation, by H. M., Stationery Office, London, 2 vols.
DAVIGNON, H., Belgium and Germany, Texts and Documents, London, 1915.
HUBERICH, C. H., and NICOL-SPEYER, H., German Legislation for the Occupied Territories of Belgium, 16 vols., The Hague, 1915-1919.
SIMON, A., *Recueil des lois, Arrêtés Royaux et Mesures Diverses, Nécessités par l'État de guerre. Royaume de Belgique*, Havre, 1915.
Case of Belgium in the Present War. An Account of the violation of the neutrality of Belgium and of the Laws of War on Belgian Territory. Published for the Belgian Delegates to the United States, New York, 1915.
Scraps of Paper: German Proclamations in Belgium and France, London, 1917.
The Martyrdom of Belgium. Official Report of Massacres of Peaceable Citizens, Women and Children by the German Army. Testimony of Eye Witnesses. Baltimore, 1915.

ENGLISH

Collected Diplomatic Documents Relating to the Outbreak of the European War. Includes the British White, French Yellow, Russian Orange, Belgian Grey, Servian Blue, German White and Austro-Hungarian Red Books, with documents published subsequently. Published by the British Government, Misc., No. 10 (1915), Cd. 7860.
Correspondence between His Majesty's government and the United States Government respecting the Rights of Belligerents. Various Parliamentary papers issued by the British Government, London, 1915-1916.
Correspondence Respecting the European Crisis (known as the British White Paper, Cd. 7467). London, 1914.
Great Britain and the European Crisis. London, 1914.
Proclamations, Orders in Council and Documents Relating to the European War (4 vols). Compiled by the Dept. of the Sec'y of State of Canada. Ottawa, 1916-1917.
Report of the Committee on Alleged German Outrages, appointed by His Majesty's Government and presided over by Right Hon. Viscount Bryce, with Evidence and Documents. New York and London, 1915.

The Treatment of Prisoners of War in England and Germany during the First Eight Months of the War, London, 1915.

Turkish Prisoners in Egypt, a Report by the Delegates of the International Committee of the Red Cross, London, 1917.

Prisoners, Treatment of. Various Parliamentary papers issued by the British Government. Cited in the chapters on the treatment of prisoners.

German Prisoners in Great Britain, London, 1917.

German Atrocities and Breaches of the Rules of War in Africa. Parl. paper issued by the British Government, London, 1916.

German Breaches of the Laws of War. (English translation from the French Official Report and Evidence.) London, 1915.

Germany's Violations of the Laws of War, 1914–15; compiled under the Auspices of the French Ministry of Foreign affairs, translated into English with an introduction by J. O. P. Bland. London, 1915.

PULLING, A., Manual of the Emergency Legislation, comprising all the acts of Parliament, proclamations, orders, etc., passed and made in consequence of the war. Four Supplements to the above. London, 1914.

TREHERN, E. C. M. (Editor), British and Colonial Prize Cases. 3 vols., London, 1916–1919.

FRENCH

Recueil de Documents Intéressants de Droit International. Avant-propos par P. Fauchille, 2 vols. Imprimerie Nationale, Paris, 1918.

DALLOZ, *Guerre de 1914. Documents Officiels, Textes Législatifs et réglementaires.* 24 Vols. to January, 1918. Imprimerie Nationale. Paris, 1914–1918.

Décisions du Conseil des Prises et Décrets Rendus en Conseil d'Etat en Matière de Prises Maritimes. Paris, 1916.

FAUCHILLE, P., *Jurisprudence Française en Matière de Prises Maritimes; Recueil de Décisions*, Paris, 1916.

FAUCHILLE, P., and BASDEVANT, J., *Jurisprudence Britannique en Matière de Prises Maritimes.* Paris, 1918.

FAUCHILLE, P., and BASDEVANT, J., *La Guerre de 1915. Jurisprudence Italienne en Matière des Prises Maritimes.* Paris, 1918.

Instructions sur l'Application du Droit International en Cas de Guerre, Addressées par le Ministre de la Marine à des Officiers Généraux, etc., Paris, 1916.

CARPENTIER, P. (Translator), *Les Lois de la Guerre Continentale; Publication de la Section Historique du Grand Etat-Major Allemand (Kriegsbrauch im Landkriege).* Paris, 1916.

JACOMET, R. (Editor). *Les Lois de la Guerre Continentale, Préface de M. Louis Renault; Publié sous la Direction de la Section Historique de l'Etat-Major de l'Armée.* Paris, 1913.

Rapports et Procès-Verbaux d'Enquête de la Commission Instituée en Vue de Constater les Actes Commis par l'Ennemi en Violation du Droit des Gens (5 vols). Paris, 1916.

Les Prisonniers Allemands au Moroc. Paris, 1917.

Législation Française depuis la Guerre. Recueil des Lois, Décrets, Arrêtés, etc. Parus au Journal Officiel depuis la Mobilisation. Paris, 1915.

Législation de la Guerre de 1914. Lois, Décrets, Arrêtés, etc. (4 vols.) Paris, 1915–1918.

Les Violations des Lois de la Guerre par l'Allemagne. Publication Faite par les Soins du Min. des Affrs. Etrongs. Paris, 1915.

Le Régime des Prisonniers de Guerre en France et en Allemagne au Regard des Conventions Internationales 1914–1916. Preface by M. Renault. Paris, 1916.

The Deportation of Women and Girls from Lille. Translation of note addressed by the French government to neutral powers with extracts from documents, New York, 1916.

PHILY, F., *Jurisprudence et Législation de la Guerre 1914-1915*. Paris, 1916.

GERMAN AND AUSTRO-HUNGARIAN

Die Kriegs-Notgesetze; Sammlung der wichtigsten Gesetze, Verordnungen und Erlasse für das Reich und Preussen. 14 vols. Berlin, 1914-16.

Deutschland und der Weltkrieg: die Entstehung und die wichtigsten Ereignisse des Kriegs unter Abdruck aller wichtigen Dokumente, dargestellt von deutschen Völkerrechtslehren. Breslau, 1914.

The Case of Belgium, in the Light of Official Reports found in the Secret Archives of the Belgian Government after the Occupation of Brussels. Publication issued by the German Government, 1915.

The Innocence of Belgium, established by the Military Documents published by Germany, Washington, 1914.

Greueltaten russischer Truppen gegen deutsche Zivilpersonen und deutsche Kriegsgefangene, Berlin, 1915.

European Politics during the Decade before the War as described by Belgian Diplomats. Documents issued by the German Imperial Foreign Office, Berlin, 1915.

Die Beschiessung der Kathedrale von Reims, Berlin, 1915.

Die völkerrechtswidrige Führung des belgischen Volkskriegs. Publication of the German Foreign Office, Berlin, 1915. A part of this document was translated and published in English under the title "The Belgian People's War." London, 1915.

Denkschrift der deutschen Regierung über die Ermordung der Besatzung eines deutschen Unterseeboots durch den Kommandanten des britischen Hülfskreuzers "Baralong." Publication of the German Foreign Office, Berlin, 1915.

Völkerrechtswidrige Verwendung farbiger Truppen auf dem Europäischen Kriegsschauplatz durch England und Frankreich. Publication of the German Foreign Office, Berlin, 1915.

Employment Contrary to International Law of Colored Troops upon the Arena of War by England and France. Publication issued by the German Foreign Office. (English translation of the previously mentioned publication.) Berlin, 1916.

Ausnahmegesetz gegen deutsche Privatrechte in England, Frankreich und Russland. Publication issued by the German Foreign Office, Berlin, undated.

Widerlegung der von der französischen Regierung erhobenen Anschuldigungen. Official publication of the German Ministry of War. Berlin, 1915.

Violation of the Geneva Convention of July 6, 1906, by French troops and *Francstireurs.* An undated pamphlet apparently issued by the German government.

Die Lügentaktik des französischen amtlichen Berichts über angebliche deutsche Plunderungen. Berlin, 1915.

Denkschrift der deutschen Regierung im Sachen der Beschlagnahme des Hilfslazarettschiffs "Ophelia" durch britische See Streitkräfte, Berlin, 1915.

German White Book on Armed Merchantmen, with facsimiles of the secret orders of the British admiralty. Issued by the German government. 1916.

Denkschrift über die Behandlung der deutschen Konsuln im Russland und die Zerstörung der deutschen Botschaft in Petersburg. White paper issued by the German government.

SOERGEL, T., *Kriegsrechtssprechung und Kriegsrechtlehre*, Berlin, 1916.

Austria-Hungary and the War. Publication issued by the Austro-Hungarian
  Consulate-General. New York, 1915.
Diplomatic Documents Concerning the Relations of Austria-Hungary with Italy
  from July 20, 1914, to May 23, 1915. Published by the Austro-Hungarian
  Ministry of Foreign Affairs, Vienna, 1915.
*Sammlung von Nachweisen für die Verletzungen des Völkerrechtes durch die mit
  Österreich-Ungarn kriegführenden Staaten.* Published by the Austro-Hun-
  garian Foreign Office, Vienna, 1915.

OTHER COUNTRIES

*Recueil de Diverses Communications du Ministre des Affaires Etrangères aux Etats-
  Généraux par rapport à la Neutralité des Pays-Bas et au Respect du Droit des
  Gens.* The Hague, 1916.
Netherlands Orange and White Books:
  (1) *Overzicht van Einige in Het Tijd Vak Oct. 1915 tot Juli 1916 Door Het
      Ministerie van Buitenlandsche Zaken Behandelde Aangelegenheden.*
  (2) *Overzicht der Voornaamste van Juli 1914 tot Oct. 1915.*
  (3) *Mededeelingen van den Minister van Buitenlandsche Zaken Aan de Staten-
      Generaal Juli-Dec., 1916.*
  (4) *Opbrenging van de Nederlandsche Schepen "Eloe" en "Bernisse."*
  (5) *Diplomatieke Bescheiden Betreffende de Vaart in die Noordzee en Het Kanaal
      in Verband met den Oorlagstoestand.*
Norwegian Orange Book: *Oversigt over de vigtigste av udenriks-departementet under
  krigen indtil Mai 1916 behandlede saken, som egner sig for offentliggjørelse.*
  Kristiania, 1916.
Diplomatisk skriftvedxling i anledning av visse postbeslag. Stockholm, 1916.
Chinese White Paper: The Claim of China for Direct Restitution to Herself of the
  Leased Territory of Kiaochow, the Tsingtao-Chinan railway and other German
  Rights in Respect of Shantung Province. Paris, 1919.
The Shantung Question. A Statement of China's Claim, together with important
  Documents Submitted to the Peace Conference in Paris, New York, 1919.
Questions for Readjustment Submitted by China to the Peace Conference. Paris,
  1919.
Publications de l'Institut Nobel Norvégien, Vol. III. *Das Völkerrecht nach dem
  Kriege.* Christiania, 1917.
Recueil de Documents Diplomatiques: Négociations ayant précédé la Guerre. Petro-
  grad, 1914. (English translation, London, 1914.)
The Italian Green Book. London, 1915.

INDEX

Adela, case of the, II, 359.

Aerial warfare. *See* Warfare, aerial.

Aerial domain, right of navigation of, I, 478; jurisdiction of subjacent states over, I, 479.

Aeroplanes, legality of, as instruments of combat, I, 483.

Aghios Gorghios and *Vassilios*, cases of, I, 191.

Albania, status of during the war, I, 38; blockade of, II, 319.

Alessandri, on blockades, II, 453.

Aliens, enemy, treatment of, Chs. III–IV; former practice, I, 56 ff.; opinions of the authorities, I, 58; problem of, during recent war, I, 59; definition of, I, 61; early British measures in respect to, I, 64; proposed exchange of, I, 66 ff.; internment of in England, I, 69 ff.; measures against in France, I, 74; exchange of between Germany and France, I, 76; German policy in respect to, I, 78; Italian policy, I, 80; Japanese policy, I, 82; policy of the United States, I, 82 ff.; British policy, I, 86; French policy, I, 89; German policy, I, 93 ff.; measures in respect to patents, I, 107 ff.; in respect to copyrights, I, 113; right of access to the courts, Ch. V.

Alliances, may neutralized states enter into, II, 209.

Alvarez, A., views on transfers of flag, I, 204; on international reorganization, II, 467.

Ambassadors, British, treatment of after outbreak of war, I, 40, 45; German, treatment of by English, I, 44; American, treatment of by Germans, I, 45; French and Russian, treatment of, I, 41.

American Institute of International Law, proposed code of, II, 455, 459, 470.

Analogues of contraband, II, 367.

Angary, right of, I, 173, 179.

Antwerp, finding of by Germans, II, 148.

Appam, case of, I, 21; II, 439.

Argentina, government of, protests against seizure of *President Mitre*, I, 200.

Armez, French consul at Stuttgart, treatment of, I, 47.

Armitage and Batty v. *Borgemann*, case of, I, 250.

Armed merchant vessels, *see* Merchant vessels.

Arms and munitions, exportation of to belligerents. *See* Exportation of arms and munitions to belligerents.

Arnold, Karberg and Company v. *Blythe*, case of, I, 247.

Aviators, captured, treatment of, I, 494.

Axel Johnson, case of, II, 308.

BALFOUR, A. J., defence of British blockade of Germany, II, 321, 329.

Ballo, case of, II, 308.

Balloons, use of in war, I, 458.

Baltica, case of, I, 189.

Banks, in Belgium, treatment of by Germans, II, 129.

Bar, von, on air craft as instruments of combat, I, 484; on sale of munitions to belligerents, II, 3, 79, 402.

Bar-le-Duc, radio-telegraph station in, II, 414.

Barenfels, case of, I, 160.

Baron Stjernblad, case of, II, 292.

Barthélemy, J., defends right of enemy aliens to sue, I, 139.

Baty, T., on trade with the enemy, I, 210; on effect of war on contracts, I, 242, 252; on right of passage in time of war, II, 222; on destruction of neutral merchant vessels, II, 256, 262; on the British blockade of Germany, II, 322; criticism of policy of

British government in respect to the
Dresden, II, 422.
Belgian relief ships, torpedoing of, I,
519.
Belgian towns and cities, German contributions on, II, 108.
Belgium, invasion of, Chs. XXVIII-
XXIX; neutralization of, II, 186;
treaties of 1870, II, 187; British inquiry of July 31, 1914, II, 187; German ultimatum to Belgium, II, 188;
reply of Belgian government, II, 189;
German troops enter Belgium, II,
190; questions of international law involved, II, 190, 198; German pretext
of military necessity, II, 191; German theory of military necessity, II,
195; *Kriegsraison*, II, 196; German
argument of military necessity analyzed, II, 201; alleged French violations of Belgian neutrality, II, 203;
charges against Belgium, II, 206;
effect of treaties of 1870, II, 210; was
neutralization treaty of 1839 binding
on Germany in 1914, II, 212; provisions of Hague Convention in
respect to violation of neutral territory, II, 214; *rebus sic stantibus*
argument, II, 217; evacuation of
German arguments, II, 221; right of
passage in time of war, II, 221; duty
of Belgium to refuse German demand,
II, 225; duty of guarantors of neutralization treaty, II, 227; military
government in, *see* Military government in Belgium; contributions and
requisitions in, *see* Contributions and
requisitions; deportation of civilians
from, *see* Deportations.
Bellas, case of, I, 183.
Belligerents, list of in recent war, I,
36 ff.; care of interests of by neutral
representatives, I, 53; right of to
requisition neutral ships, I, 172.
Beneto Estenger, case of, I, 188.
Berne International Copyright Convention, status of during the war, I,
113.
Bernstorff, Count, urges British government in 1870 to prohibit sale of
arms and munitions to the French,
II, 386.
Bethmann-Hollweg, interview with Sir

E. Goschen, II, 192; speech in Reichstag in defence of invasion of Belgium,
II, 193; declares 1913 that Germany
would respect neutrality of Belgium,
II, 213.
Beveridge, A. J., views on employment
of uncivilized troops, I, 296.
Bigelow, Major, J., on methods and instruments, I, 282.
Birkhimer, on rights of military occupants, II, 87.
Bismarck, declares 1870 that Germany
would respect neutrality of Belgium,
II, 213; on starvation as a belligerent
measure, II, 337.
Bissing, General von, on methods and
instruments, I, 281; defence of German deportation policy, II, 181 ff.
"Black list" measures, I, 228 ff.
Blockades, Ch. XXXIII; German submarine "blockade" of England, II,
317; examples of legal blockades
during the late war, II, 318; Anglo-
French blockade of Germany, II, 319;
criticism of, II, 320; order in council
of March 11, 1915, II, 323; character
of the blockade, II, 324; neutral protests against, II, 324; the British
defence, II, 325; legality of, II, 327;
criticism regarding discriminatory
features of, II, 328; charge that it
applied to neutral ports, II, 330;
popular demand in England for a
"real" blockade, II, 334; German
criticism of British blockade as a
"starvation" measure, II, 336; controversy over admission of hospital
supplies to Germany, II, 339; controversy over admission of foodstuffs
to occupied territories, II, 340; problem of enforcing the blockade, II,
342; Netherlands Over-seas Trust, II,
342; system of "rationing" of neutrals, II, 344; neutral protests against
British measures, II, 345; American
policy, II, 346; other expedients, II,
347; effect of the war on law of, II,
453.
Bluntschli, on requisitions, II, 126; on
military necessity, II, 198; on right
of passage in time of war, II, 223; on
duty of guarantors of Belgian neutralization, II, 227, 228; on exporta-

tion of arms and munitions to belligerents, II, 381.

Bombardments, aerial, Ch. XIX, II, 461.

Bombardments, land and naval, Ch. XVII; examples of, I, 417; charges against entente powers, I, 419; provisions of Hague conventions, I, 419, 427; provisions of military manuals, I, 422; bombardment without notice, I, 423, 471; naval bombardments, I, 425; the German contention, I, 436.

Bonfils, on requisition of guides, II, 136; on collective penalties II, 158.

Bonna, case of, 308.

Boussmaker, ex parte, case of, I, 130.

Botha, General, correspondence with Colonel Franke regarding use of poison in wells, I, 279.

Bowles, T. G., on need of a British naval code, I, 9; on Declaration of Paris, I, 13; on planting mines in open seas, I, 344.

Bower, Sir Graham, on destruction of neutral vessels, II, 282.

Brazil, government of, requisitions German ships, I, 179.

Breslau and *Goeben*, cases of, I, 205.

Brindilla, case of, I, 184.

British manual of military law, I, 7; provisions in respect to requisition of guides, II, 137, 138; in respect to punishment of war crimes, II, 485.

Bruges, requisitions on, II, 120.

Brussels, German fines on, II, 144 ff., 160.

Brussels Conference, 1874, I, 15.

Bryan, W. J., letter to Senator Stone regarding American neutrality, II, 413.

Bryce, James, on value of international law, II, 504.

Buena Ventura, case of, I, 150.

Bullets, forbidden, use of, I, 262.

Bülow, General, threatens destruction of château of Prince of Monaco, II, 152.

Bundesrath, case of, I, 9; II, 298, 370.

Burgess, J. W., on invasion of Belgium, II, 212, 217; on sale of munitions to belligerents, II, 406.

Buzzati, on requisition of railway employés, II, 139.

CABLES, submarine, II, 410.

Calvo, Carlos, on contributions, II, 115.

Cambon, Jules, ambassador, treatment of by Germans, I, 41.

Canning, George, views as to sale of munitions to belligerents, II, 386.

Caroline, case of, II, 194, 198.

Cater, Judge, on Hague conventions, I, 27.

Cavell, Miss Edith, execution of by the Germans, II, 97; observations on case of, II, 105.

Cecil, Lord Robert, on German policy in respect to contributions, II, 113; on requisition of live stock in Belgium and France, II, 124; on German starvation measures in France, II, 338; on difficulties of enforcing the blockade, II, 342; on the British censorship, II, 362.

Charost, bishop of Lille, protest against deportations, II, 167.

Château de Coucy, destruction of, I, 449.

Chiefs of state, responsibility of for war crimes, II, 488; precedents for trial of; II, 495; immunity of, II, 497.

Chili, case of, I, 156.

Chili, government of, announces purpose to treat Hague conventions as binding during late war, I, 22.

Chili, controversy of, with Great Britain regarding transfers of flag, I, 203; attitude in respect to armed merchantmen, I, 387; use of ports of by belligerents, II, 416; measures of to protect neutrality, II, 417, 420; protest in case of the *Dresden*, II, 421.

China, seizure of enemy persons on, II, 366.

China, territory of violated by Japan, II, 237; Chinese concession of a "war zone," II, 238; seizure of Chinese railways, II, 239; Japanese conduct criticised, II, 240; German pillaging in, 1900, I, 437.

Civilians, deportation of by Germany from Belgium and France, Ch. XXVII; employment of by Germans as screens, I, 311.

Clausewitz, K., on methods of warfare, I, 278.

Cloth Hall at Ypres, destruction of, I, 448.

Chunet, E., defends right of enemy aliens to sue, I, 141.

Coal, procuring of in neutral ports by belligerents, II, 415.

Coal mines, destruction of by Germans in France, I, 323.

Cohen, I, author of book on Ruheleben prison camp, II, 17.

Colombia, charge against in respect to wireless messages, II, 414.

Colonia, case of, I, 183.

Community responsibility, Ch. XXVI.

Concadoro, case of, I, 161.

Consuls, treatment of in enemy countries, I, 47 ff.

Consuls, enemy, in Greece, deportation of, I, 50.

Continental Tyre and Rubber Case, I, 218, 226.

Contraband, Ch. XXXII; effect of war on law of, II, 455.

Contracts, effect of war on, Ch. IX; Anglo-American doctrine, I, 241 ff.; judicial decisions on, I, 244 ff.; effect on shares and debentures, I, 252; effect on debts, I, 253; French law and practice, I, 254 ff.; German doctrine and practice, I, 259 ff.

Contributions, Ch. XXV; German policy in wars of 1866 and 1870, II, 106; during recent war, II, 108; general contribution on Belgium, II, 112; provisions of Hague convention in respect to, II, 113; purposes for which may be levied, II, 114; decuple assessment on Belgian refugees, II, 116.

Conventions, see Hague conventions.

Converted merchantmen, I, 385; II, 455.

Copyrights, measures in respect to, I, 113.

Cormoran, internment of, II, 424.

Corporations under enemy control, status of, I, 217 ff., 223.

Courts, right of access to by enemy aliens, Ch. V; British and American doctrine and practice, I, 117 ff.; views of continental publicists, I, 121; English interpretation during late war, I, 123 ff.; American practice, I,

134 ff.; French practice, I, 137 ff.; German practice, I, 144 ff.

Courts, military, in Belgium, II, 81.

Criminal code of France, provision in respect to punishment of war crimes, II, 486.

Custodian, English, of enemy property, I, 86; American, I, 103.

Czar, Nicolai II, case of, I, 165.

Czar of Russia calls conference of 1874, I, 15.

Czecho-Slovaks, recognized as a belligerent power, I, 39.

Dacia, case of, I, 185, 194.

Dampierre, J., on the Kriegsbrauch, I, 6; on duty of neutrals to take notice of violations of international law by belligerents, II, 500.

Davis, G. B., interpretation of article 23 (h), I, 120; on destruction of merchant vessels, II, 265.

Days of grace for enemy merchant vessels to depart, I, 149.

Debts, effect of war on, I, 253.

Declaration of London, I, status of during recent war, I, 29 ff.; provisions regarding transfers of flag, I, 192; abrogation of art. 57 of, I, 197; disregard of provisions relating to contraband, II, 288; rules of relating to prize destruction, II, 268; as to liability of reservists on neutral vessels to seizure, II, 367; as to transfers of flag, II, 456.

Declarations of war, list of, I, 37.

Delbrück law, I, 62.

Denationalization of French citizens of German origin, I, 77.

Denmark, sinking of vessels of, II, 275; violation of neutrality of by aviators, I, 477.

Dernburg, Dr., on use of uncivilized troops, I, 297; on sale of arms and munitions to belligerents, II, 396.

Derfflinger, case of, I, 251.

Despatch bearers on neutral vessels, status of, II, 374.

Detention of neutral vessels by British, II, 292.

Deportation of civilians from Belgium and France, Ch. XXVII; Early German policy, II, 163; deportations from France, 1916, II, 164; manner of execution of, II, 166; protests against, II, 167; treatment of déportés, II, 168; the German defence, II, 169; deportations from Belgium, II, 171; manner of execution, II, 172; treatment of Belgian déportés, II, 175; allied protests against, II, 176; neutral protests, II, 177; German defence of, II, 178, 180 ff.; power of military occupant over inhabitants, II, 181; German policy criticised, II, 183.

Deutschland, case of, II, 437.

Devastation, Ch. XIII; in France, 1917, I, 315; the German defence, I, 319; rules of international law in respect to, I, 320; devastation in France, 1918, I, 323; the German defence, I, 327.

Diplomatic representatives, treatment of following outbreak of war, I, 29; care of belligerent interests by, I, 53.

Diplomatic and consular representatives in occupied territory, status of, I, 51.

Disfurth, General, on methods and instruments, I, 281.

Doelwick, case of, II, 298.

Dolphin, case of, II, 300.

Doyle, Sir C., advocates reprisals, I, 489.

Dresden, case of, II, 420.

Duchess of Sutherland, case of, I, 136, 214.

Dumba, C., Austrian ambassador at Washington recalled, I, 46.

Dutch vessels, requisition of by United States and Great Britain, I, 174. *See* also Netherlands.

EDUCATION, German interference with in Belgium, II, 72.

Eglinton, torpedoing of, II, 276.

Elida, case of, II, 313.

Ellespontos, case of, II, 309.

Embargoes, neutral, on exportations to belligerent countries, II, 299, 393, 407.

Embassy, German at St. Petersburg, destroyed by Russians, I, 45.

Emmich, General von, proclamation charging French with having violated Belgian neutrality, II, 203.

Emperor, German, demand for trial of, II, 489; provision of treaty of peace relative to, II, 490.

Enemy, trade with, *see* Trade with the enemy.

Enemy aliens, *see* Aliens, enemy.

Enemy cargo, sale of in expectation of war, I, 206.

Enemy character, test of, I, 212.

Enemy houses in neutral territory, I, 228.

Enemy persons on neutral vessels, seizure of, II, 362; case of Piepenbrink, II, 363; case of Garde and others, II, 365; seizures on the *China*, II, 366; what persons are liable to seizure, II, 367; views of the authorities, II, 368; practice of the past, II, 370; case of the *Fredrico*, II, 371; status of despatch bearers on neutral vessels, II, 373.

Enemy shareholders, rights of, I, 221.

Epernay, requisitions on, II, 119; fining of by Germans, II, 153.

Esposito v. *Bowden*, case of, I, 209.

Evans, Sir S., on binding force of Hague conventions, I, 25, 26. *See* also *Kim*, case of.

Exchange of enemy alien prisoners, I, 66, 76. *See also* Prisoners.

Exequaturs, revocation of, I, 51; II, 59.

Exportation of arms and munitions to belligerents, Ch. XXXV; policy of United States, II, 375, 382; are neutrals bound to prohibit such traffic, II, 376; views of German writers prior to late war, II, 378; practice in former wars, II, 382; British and French practice, II, 385; German practice, II, 389; embargoes on such traffic, II, 393; protests of German and Austrian governments in 1915 against American policy, II, 394; their contentions analyzed, II, 395 ff.; question of moral obligation to forbid such trade, II, 399; analysis of the arguments, II, 400; practical difficulties in the way of prohibition, II, 402; legality of alteration of sale during war, II, 405.

FASBENDER, COLONEL, requisitions on Lunéville, II, 119.

Fauchille, P., on aerial bombardments, I, 470; on legal nature of aerial domain, I, 480, 483; on status of reservists on neutral vessels, II, 369.

Fenix, case of, I, 26, 166.

Fines, collective, Ch. XXVI; German theory and practice as to, 1870–71, II, 141; British policy in South Africa, II, 143; German fines on Belgian towns and cities during late war, II, 144; German proclamations threatening fines, II, 150; fines on French towns and cities, II, 151; views of German writers, II, 154; rules of Hague convention, II, 156; interpretation of, II, 157; German policy criticised, II, 159.

Fire, liquid, use of by Germans, I, 287.

Flag, transfers of, I, Ch. VII; rules of Declaration of London, II, 456.

Flanders, Council of, II, 79.

Floride, case of, II, 359.

Foodstuffs, treated as contraband, II, 291.

Force majeure, I, 161.

Forests, cutting of by Germans in Belgium and France, II, 128.

Frédrico, case of, II, 371.

French, Sir John, report on use of poisonous gases by Germans, I, 271.

French manual, of land warfare, I, 6; of maritime warfare, I, 10; rules as to contributions, II, 116; as to requisitions, II, 123, 126; as to requisitions of guides, II, 137.

French towns and cities, German contributions on, II, 108.

Fryatt, Captain, shooting of, I, 407.

Frye, case of, II, 270, 312.

GARCON, M., on criminal acts committed during war, II, 473.

Garde, case of, II, 365.

Gases, asphyxiating and poisonous, use of, I, 271 ff., 284.

Geffcken, on rights of passage in time of war, II, 223; on sale of munitions to belligerents, II, 379.

Geneva convention, status of, I, 13; violations of Ch. XX; purpose of, I, 497; German violations of in Belgium, I, 498; in France I, 499; bombing of hospitals, I, 500; German and

Austrian charges, I, 502; the charges analyzed, I, 503; torpedoing of hospital ships, I, 505; German charges as to misuse of Red Cross flag, I, 508; British reply, I, 509; protest of international Red Cross Committee, I, 512; British and French countermeasures, I, 513; torpedoing of Belgian relief ships, I, 519; the German defence, I, 521; conclusion, I, 523; provisions of relative to hospital supplies, II, 339; relative to repression of criminal acts, II, 468.

Georgia, case of, I, 206.

Gerard, J. W. American ambassador at Berlin, treatment of, I, 46; assists Japanese subjects, I, 78; urged to negotiate new treaty, I, 83; efforts to secure arrangement for inspection of prison camps, II, 6; report on prison camp at Ruhleben, II, 17; on treatment of prisoners, II, 22, 25, 26, 31, 32, 33; on deportations from Belgium, II, 167.

Germania, case of, I, 162.

German prize code, I, 9.

Germany, government of, attitude toward Hague conventions, I, 22 ff.

Gessner, on sale of munitions to belligerents, II, 381.

Ghent, University of, transformed into a Flemish-German institution, II, 74.

Gibson, Hugh, intervention in behalf of Miss Cavell, II, 98.

Gier, internment of, II, 423.

Gladstone, W. E., on neutralization of Belgium, II, 229.

Glitra, case of, II, 283.

Goltz, General C. von der, views on methods and instruments, I, 281; appointment as governor-general of Belgium, II, 58; powers of, II, 62; threats of collective fines, II, 150.

Goschen, Sir E., treatment of by Germans, I, 40; interview with Herr von Jagow, II, 192.

Graevenitz, General, proclamation of, II, 109; defence of deportations from Lille, II, 165.

Granville, Earl, views as to benevolent neutrality, II, 387, 402.

Grasshoff, Richard, charges French with violating Belgian neutrality, II,

204; criticises Belgium for refusing German demand for right of passage, II, 226.

Great Britain, government of, attitude toward Hague conventions, I, 22.

Greece, occupation of by English and French, II, 241; acts of the entente powers in, II, 242; the Greek protest, II, 243; conflict between king and parliament, II, 244; attitude of guaranteeing powers, II, 245; allied demands on Greece, II, 246; abdication of the king, II, 249; comparison of occupation of Greece with invasion of Belgium, II, 250; conduct of the entente powers reviewed, II, 253 ff.

Grey, Sir Edward, on England's duty to Belgium, II, 230; on destruction of neutral prizes, II, 266; defence of British blockade, II, 326, 333; instructions to Lord Desart regarding status of despatch bearers on neutral vessels, II, 374.

Grotius, on right of passage in time of war, II, 222.

Guides, requisition of, II, 135.

Gulflight, torpedoing of, II, 269.

Gutenfels, case of, I, 159.

Haarsticher v. Baerselmann, case of, I, 245.

Habeas corpus, writ of, denied to interned enemy aliens, I, 128.

Hague conventions and declarations of 1899 and 1907, status of during recent war, I, 17 ff.; rules of, regarding enemy merchant vessels in past, I, 150; interpretation of, by Court of Siam, I, 171; provisions in respect to planting mines in open seas, I, 341; in respect to bombardments, I, 419; in respect to historic monuments, I, 434; in respect to aerial bombardments, I, 465; in respect to contributions, II, 113; in respect to requisitions, II, 122, 126; in respect to collective fines, II, 156; in respect to violation of neutral territory, II, 216; in respect to immunity of mails on neutral steamers, II, 354, 355; in respect to sale of arms and munitions to belligerents, II, 377; regarding erection of telegraph stations in neutral territory, II, 414; regarding taking supplies in neutral ports, II, 416; lack of penal sanctions, II, 468; provision regarding indemnity for damages, II, 469.

Hakan, case of, I, 34.

Haldane, J., on use of poisonous gases, I, 274.

Hall, W. E., on transfers of flag, I, 190; on right of passage in time of war, II, 223; on duty of guarantors of Belgian neutralization, II, 228; on analogues of contraband, II, 368; on punishment of military offences, II, 486; on effect of next war on international law, II, 503.

Hamborn, case of, I, 199.

Harcourt, Sir W., defends policy of British government 1870 in respect to sale of munitions to French, II, 388.

Hartmann, J., on methods and instruments, II, 279.

Hautefeuille, on right of passage in time of war, II, 223.

Hays, A. G., on freedom of the seas, II, 459.

Heilbronn, P., defence of submarine warfare, I, 376.

Hershy, A. S., on German conception of freedom of seas, II, 458.

Higgins, A. P., on transfers of flag, I, 190; on planting mines in open seas, I, 344; on status of armed merchantmen, I, 390.

Hill, D. J., on international reorganization, II, 467.

Hindenburg, General, on methods and instruments, I, 281.

Hipsang, destruction of, II, 257.

Holland, T. E., prepares Laws and Customs of War on Land, I, 7; on United States naval code, I, 9; on art 23 (h) of Hague convention, I, 121; views on naval bombardments, I, 426; on aerial bombardments, I, 468; on reprisals, I, 494; on rights of military occupants, II, 85; on usufruct, II, 128; on requisition of guides, II, 135, 137; on destruction of neutral prizes, II, 261; on cotton as contraband, II, 290; on transportation of enemy troops by neutral vessels, II, 371; on punishment of military offences, II, 486.

Hoop, case of, I, 118, 200.

Hospitals, bombing of, I, 500.

Hospital ships, torpedoing of, I, 505, 517; German charges against England and France, I, 508; the British reply, I, 509.

Hospital supplies, refusal of British and French governments to admit to Germany, II, 339.

Hostages, taking of, Ch. XII; seizures in Belgium, I, 298; shooting of at Dinant, I, 299; seizures in France, I, 301; treatment of, I, 304; former practice, I, 305; purposes for which they may be taken, I, 308; punishment of, I, 309.

Hostile proclamations, punishment for dropping, I, 495.

Hovering of warships off neutral ports, II, 443.

Hugh Stevenson and Sons v. *Aktiengesellschaft*, case of, I, 251.

Hut, General, fines city of Brussels, II, 145.

Hydro aeroplanes, status of, II, 384.

Indian Prince, case of, II, 283.

Ingle v. *Mannheim Insurance Co.*, case of, I, 215.

Institute of International Law, views on right of merchant vessels to arm, I, 402; on bombardments, I, 427; on reprisals, I, 494; on contributions, II, 114; on destruction of neutral prizes, II, 264; on transportation of troops on neutral steamers, II, 369; on responsibility of soldiers for criminal acts, II, 472.

Instructions of 1863 for government of United States armies, I, 2.

Internment of enemy aliens in England, I, 69 ff.; in France, I, 75; in Germany, I, 79.

Internment of warships in neutral ports, II, 422, 429.

International law. *See* law, international.

Invasion. *See* Belgium, invasion of.

Italy, government of, requisitions German and Austrian ships, I, 177.

JAEQUEMYNS, R., defence of German conduct in France, 1870, I, 5.

Jagow, Herr von, interview with Sir E. Goschen, II, 192; declares (1913) that Germany would respect neutrality of Belgium, II, 213; defence of invasion of Luxemburg, II, 233.

Janson v. *Dreifontein*, case of, I, 215, 243, 248.

Japan, violation of Chinese territory, II, 237.

Japanese subjects, arrested in Germany, I, 78.

Japanese treatment of Germans, I, 82.

Judges, Belgian, treatment of by Germans, II, 89.

Kankakee, Hocking, and *Genesee* cases of, I, 199.

Kellogg, Vernon, on requisitions in Belgium, II, 121, 340.

Kent, chancellor, on trade with the enemy, I, 210.

Kim, case of, I, 34; II, 303.

Kitchener, Lord, punishes South African towns by fines, II, 143.

Knight Commander, sinking of by Russians, 1904, II, 261, 264.

Kleen, on sale of arms and munitions to belligerents, II, 378.

Kluber, on sale of munitions to belligerents, II, 379.

Kohler, J., views as to effect of war on contracts, I, 259; defends invasion of Belgium, II, 199, 200, 226.

Korea, violation of by Japanese, 1904, II, 194.

Kriege, Herr, views on immunity of postal correspondence, II, 355; on exportation of arms and munitions to belligerents, II, 381.

Kriegsbrauch im Land Kriege, character of, I, 3 ff.; views as to methods and instruments, I, 280; views as to contributions, II, 115; as to requisitions, II, 122; on use of enemy railways, II, 128; on treatment of forests, II, 129; treatment of banks, II, 131; on requisition of guides, II, 136; on collective fines, II, 155; on responsibility of soldiers for criminal acts, II, 475, 480.

Kriegsraison and Kriegsmanier, I, 5; II, 195 ff.

Kronprinzessin Cecilie, case of, I, 161.

Kronprinz Gustaf Adolph, case of, II, 293.

Kronprinz Wilhelm, internment of, II, 424.

LABBERTON, PROFESSOR, defends invasion of Belgium, II, 226.

Labor, compulsory, of prisoners, II, 42; of déportés, II, 168.

Laborers, requisition of services of, by Germans, II, 132.

Lancken, Baron von der, execution of Miss Cavell, II, 98.

Lansing, Robert, address of, I, 54; on exportation of arms and munitions to belligerents, II, 398.

Larnaude, F., on trial of the German Emperor, II, 489.

Laval, Maître de, on German measures in Belgium, II, 84.

Law, international, growth of, I, 1; questions of, involved in invasion of Belgium, II, 190; effect of the war on, Ch. XXXVII; enforcement of, Ch. XXXVIII; imperfections of revealed by the war, II, 452; need of new regulations, II, 460; of an international conference to revise, II, 463; lack of effective sanctions, II, 465; provision relative to compensation for damages, II, 469; new attitude toward violation of, II, 498; violations of during late war, II, 501.

Lawrence, T. J., on destruction of merchant vessels, I, 373; on requisition of services, II, 137; on collective penalties, II, 157; on Japanese violation of Korea, II, 194; on continuous voyage, II, 331, on prohibition of trade in arms, II, 403.

Lémonon, on bombardments, I, 429.

Leonora, case of, II, 322.

Leutwitz, General, fines city of Brussels, II, 144.

Lieber, Francis, prepares instructions for government of United States armies, I, 2; on value of international law, II, 504.

Liebmann, ex parte, case of, I, 63.

Licenses to trade with the enemy, I, 216.

Liège, fining of by Germans, II, 146.

Lille, requisitions on, II, 120; fining of by Germans, II, 152; deportation of civilians from II, 165.

Lisle, Alice, execution of 1685, II, 102, 105.

Liszt, F. von, on Hague conventions, I, 23, 24.

Live stock, German requisition of in Belgium, II, 123.

Loans to belligerents, II, 408.

Lockism, internment of, II, 424.

Loder, J. C. B., views on effect of war on contracts, I, 242.

Lodge, H. C., on sale of munitions to belligerents, II, 407.

Loening, on requisitions, II, 122; on community punishments, II, 155.

London, liability to aerial bombardment, I, 468.

London Naval Conference, 1908–1909, I, 28. See also Declaration of London.

London & Northern Estates Co., v. *Schlesinger*, case of, I, 247.

Louter, J. de, on effect of the war on international law, II, 453, 466, 467.

Louvain, burning of, I, 437; requisitions on, II, 118.

Low, A. M., on the British blockade, II, 334.

Ludwig and Vorwaerts, case of, I, 364.

Lunéville, requisitions on, II, 119.

Lusitania, sinking of, I, 356; the German defence of, I, 357; illegality of, II, 481, 490.

Luxemburg, invasion of, Ch. XXX; neutralization of, II, 231; German troops enter, II, 233; Germany's defence, II, 234; the German defence analyzed, II, 234; invasion of Belgium and Luxemburg compared, II, 235; other German defences, II, 235.

MACHINERY, German transportation of from Belgium and France, II, 124.

McCarthy, D. J., on treatment of prisoners in Germany, II, 18, 21, 33.

Mails on neutral steamers, interference with, Ch. XXXIV; German exploitation of postal service for belligerent purposes, II, 350; early measures of

British and French governments, II, 351; provisions of Hague convention, II, 355; attitude of American government, II, 357; views of British and French governments, II, 359.

Marcy, W. L., views on transfers of flag, I, 187.

Maria, case of, II, 271, 311.

Marie Glaesser, case of, I, 157, 215.

Maritime law, status in 1914, I, 27.

Maritime warfare, effect of the war on the law of, II, 453.

Martens, G., advocates codification of laws of war, I, 15; on Brussels Act, I, 17.

Medea, sinking of, II, 271.

Merchant vessels, enemy, in port at outbreak of war, treatment of, Ch. VI; number in port at outbreak of war, I, 147; the old practice, I, 148; modern practice, I, 149; rules of Hague convention, I, 150; British and French policy, I, 154; policy of other governments, I, 156; status of refugee vessels, I, 161; status of yachts, I, 162; decisions of French prize council, I, 164; German policy I, 166; policy of the United States, I, 167; right of confiscation, I, 168; decision of peace conference, I, 171; liability of to destruction, I, 361; opinions of the authorities, I, 362; practice in former wars, I, 363, 371; restrictions on, I, 366; German practice during late war, I, 371; the German defence, I, 374; merchant vessels armed for defence, status of, Ch. XVI; early questions as to, I, 384; right to enter neutral ports, I, 386; attitude of American government, I, 388, 390; attitude of German government, I, 389, 398; policy of Dutch government, I, 391; decree of February, 1916, I, 394; German charges, I, 395; practice of the past, I, 399; views of Schramm, Oppenheim and Triepel, I, 403-404; shooting of Captain Fryatt, I, 407; right to carry armament, II, 457.

Merchant vessels, neutral, right to arm and resist attack, I, 413; American policy as to, I, 414; destruction of, Ch. XXXI; practice in former wars,

II, 256; Russian practice, 1904-1905, II, 257; prize regulations in respect to, II, 258; English opinion in 1904-1905, II, 261; English judicial authority, II, 262; views of continental publicists, II, 263; discussion at London Naval Conference, II, 266; rules of Declaration of London, II, 269; German practice during late war, II, 269; case of the *Frye*, II, 270; case of the *Maria*, II, 271; case of the *Medea*, II, 271; sinking of Spanish vessels, II, 273; of Danish and Swedish vessels, II, 275; of Norwegian vessels, II, 276; total losses of neutral merchant marines, II, 277; German defence, II, 278; conclusion, II, 281; status of neutral property on, II, 283.

Merignhac, Professor, on punishment of war criminals, II, 487; on trial of the German Emperor, II, 489.

Messages, cable and wireless, II, 410.

Meurer, C., on commerical blockade, II, 459.

Military government in Belgium, Chs. XXIII-XXIV; appointment of von der Goltz as governor-general, II, 58; revocation of consular exequaturs, II, 59; powers of the governor-general, II, 62; powers of the local authorities taken over, II, 63; German legislation in Belgium, II, 63; decrees and penalties, II, 65; restrictions on liberty of inhabitants, II, 68; on patriotic demonstrations, II, 70; in respect to education, II, 72; reorganization of the University of Ghent, II, 74; administrative division of, II, 78; German military courts in Belgium, II, 81; special tribunals, II, 83; rights of military occupants, II, 85; German practice criticised, II, 88; measures against Belgian judiciary, II, 89; Germans take over administration of justice in Belgium, II, 91; régime of criminal repression in Belgium, II, 92; war treason, II, 93; condemnations by German tribunals, II, 96; execution of women, case of Nurse Cavell, II, 17; German defence, II, 99; past practice as to execution of women, II,

102; observations on execution of Miss Cavell, II, 104.

Military manuals, character of, Ch. I; provisions in respect to responsibility of soldiers for criminal acts, II, 474.

Military necessity, German excuse of, as defence for invasion of Belgium, II, 191; German theory of, II, 195.

Military occupants, rights of, over inhabitants, II, 182; *see also* contributions; deportation of civilians; fines; hostages; labor, compulsory; and military government.

Minerva, case of, I, 205.

Mines, submarine, Ch. XIV; planting of in open seas by Germans, I, 329; counter-measures of British government, I, 331, 345; neutral protests against, I, 339; provisions of Hague convention in respect to, I, 341.

Mob outbreaks against enemy aliens in Great Britain, I, 69.

Mollard, French minister to Luxemburg, treatment of by Germans, I, 44.

Moltke, General, H. von, on methods and instruments, I, 279; on requisitions, II, 122.

Mons, fining of by Germans, II, 146.

Monuments, historic, and institutions devoted to science, etc., destruction of, Ch. XVIII; rules of Hague convention, I, 434; early practice, I, 435; recent examples, I, 435; University of Louvain, I, 437; Cathedral of Rheims, I, 441; other edifices and historic monuments, I, 446; destruction of in Italy, I, 451, 462; criticism of German practice, I, 453.

Moore, John Bassett, on sinking of neutral vessels, II, 290; on contraband, II, 315; on embargoes, against exportation of arms and munitions, II, 394.

Morgan, J. H., criticism of war treason, II, 93.

Möwe, case of, I, 25, 133, 158.

NAPOLEON, policy as to collective fines, II, 140.

Naval Codes, I, 8.

Naval conference of London, 1908–1909, I, 28. *See also* Declaration of London.

Neale, deportations from, II, 170.

Netherlands, government of, protests against interference with mails, II, 352, 359; policy of in respect to use of neutral territory, II, 414, 415; exclusion of warships from ports of, II, 419, 436; controversy with British government regarding internment of submarines, II, 429; regarding transit of materials across, II, 446.

Netherlands, violation of neutrality of by aviators, I, 374, 476; destruction of vessels of, II, 273, 275.

Netherlands Over-seas Trust, II, 342.

Neukamp, E., on binding force of Hague conventions, I, 24.

Neutral ports, procuring of supplies in, I, 415; taking of prizes into, II, 438; hovering of war ships off, II, 443; submarine operations off, II, 445.

Neutral protests against mine-laying, I, 339; against British and French contraband measures, II, 292; against blockade measures, II, 324; against interference with mails, II, 353; against deportation of civilians, II, 499.

Neutral registers, transfers to, Ch. VII.

Neutral territory, acts in violation of, II, 191; invasion of, Chs. XXIX–XXX; policy of Dutch government regarding Bar-le-Duc, II, 414; transit of materials across, II, 446.

Neutral vessels, right of belligerents to requisition, I, 172; destruction of, by the Germans, Ch. XXXI. *See also* Merchant vessels, destruction of; removal of mails from, Ch. XXXIV; removal of enemy persons from, II, 362; detention of, II, 292.

Neutrality, miscellaneous questions relating to, Ch. XXXVI; violations of by air craft, I, 471; by belligerent war ships, II, 415, 419; *see also* Belgium, invasion of; and Submarines and submarine warfare.

Neutralization, *see* Belgium, invasion of; *also* Luxemburg, invasion of.

Niemeyer, Professor, on military necessity as a defence for invasion of Belgium, II, 198.

Nieuw-Amsterdam, case of, II, 309.

Noord-Brabant, case of, II, 427.

Norway, sinking of vessels, II, 276; German plot to blow up ships of, II, 277; violation of waters of by belligerents, II, 419; exclusion of war ships from ports of, II, 419, 433.

Noyon, deportations from, II, 171.

Nys, E., on collective penalties, II, 158.

OCCUPIED TERRITORY, status of enemy diplomatic representative in, I, 51; trade with enemy houses in, I, 222; government of, Chs. XXIII–XXIV; rights of occupants over inhabitants, II, 182; admission of food supplies to, II, 340. *See also* Military government; contributions; fines and deportation of civilians.

Odenwald, case of, II, 426.

Oldhamia, destruction of, II, 257.

Ophelia, case of, I, 517.

Oppenheim, L., prepares chapter for British manual of military law, I, 7; addresses inquiry to British foreign office, I, 121; on transfers of flag, I, 190; on right of merchant vessels to arm for defence, I, 404; on rights of military occupants, II, 87; on war treason, II, 93; on requisition of guides, II, 135, 139; on right of self-preservation, II, 103; on right of passage in time of war, II, 223; on duty of guarantors of Belgium neutralization, II, 228; on punishment of military offences, II, 486.

Oriental, case of, I, 162.

Otley, Captain, on inviolability of postal correspondence, II, 356.

Paklat, case of, I, 517.

Panariellos, case of, I, 211.

Paris, Declaration of, I, 12; interpretation of by British prize court, I, 13.

Parole, violations of, by Germans, II, 425.

Partnerships, effect of war on, I, 249.

Pass of Balmaha, case of, I, 201.

Passage, right of in time of war, II, 221 ff.

Passengers and crews of merchant vessels, German treatment of, I, 380.

Patents, British policy in respect to, I, 107 ff.; French policy, I, 109; German policy, I, 109; American policy, I, 111.

Perels, on sale of munitions to belligerents, II, 378.

Pershing, General J. J., issues proclamation to inhabitants of Luxemburg, II, 237.

Peterhof, case of, II, 332.

Phillimore, Sir R., on sale of arms to belligerents, II, 378.

Pic, P., on enemy controlled companies, I, 224.

Piepenbrink, case of, II, 363.

Pillet, A., on rights of military occupants, II, 85; on war treason, II, 94; on requisition of guides, II, 136.

Pirenne and Frédéric, Professors, treatment of by Germans in Belgium, II, 76.

Poison, use of in wells, I, 288. *See also* Gases.

Poland, requisitions in, II, 121.

Politis, N., on right of enemy aliens to sue, I, 123.

Pollock, Sir F., on effect of the war on international law, II, 504; on destruction of Louvain, *see* Louvain.

Polseath, case of, I, 219.

Poona, case of, I, 222.

Poortugael, Gen. den Beer, prepares book entitled *Het Oorlagsrecht*, I, 15.

Pope, letter to Emperor of Austria regarding bombardments, I, 463.

Porter v. *Freudenberg*, case of, I, 123, 125, 131, 209, 214.

Porto, case of, I, 164.

Portugal, government of, requisitions, German vessels, I, 177.

Postal correspondence. *See* Mails.

Post offices, in Belgium, seizure of funds of by Germans, II, 129.

Premier Oil and Pipe Line Co., case of, I, 211, 221.

President Mitre, case of, I, 200.

Press, German restrictions on in Belgium, II, 69.

Princess Thurn and Taxis v. *Moffitt* case of, I, 125, 314.

Prins Adalbert, case of, I, 161.

Prinz Eitel Friedrich, internment of, II, 424.

Prisoners, treatment of, II, Chs. XXI–XXII; problem of caring for during late war, II, i; information bureaus, II, 2; inspection of camps, II, 5; methods of inspection, II, 7; pay of officer prisoners, II, 8; officers' quarters, II, 12; quarters for men, II, 13; prison camp of Ruheleben and Wittenberg, II, 17-18; Gerdelegen and other bad camps, II, 20; mixing of prisoners of different nationalities, II, 23; regulations as to clothing, II, 24; regulations as to food and diet, II, 28; dependence of British and French on parcels post packages, II, 32; British and French complaints, II, 34; regulations and practice as to letter writing, II, 36; employment of as laborers, II, 40; employment of behind the firing line, II, 44; payment of prisoners for labor, II, 45; punishment of, II, 46; treatment of prisoners captured on submarines, II, 50; exchange of, II, 53; transfer of to Switzerland, II, 55; repatriation of those in long captivity, II, 56.

Prize courts, attitude toward Hague conventions, I, 25.

Prize regulations in respect to sinking of merchant vessels, II, 258.

Prizes, destruction of, I, 362; duty of captors to take in, I, 368; practice in former wars, I, 370; German practice in late war, I, 371; taking of into neutral ports, II, 438; case of the *Appam*, II, 439.

Property, enemy, measures in respect to, Ch. IV; sale of in United States, I, 104.

Property, neutral, on enemy vessels, status of, II, 283.

Proton, case of, I, 199.

Pyke, R. H., comment on *Kim* case II, 309.

RAILWAY EMPLOYÉS, requisition of, II, 133; compulsory labor of, 139.

Railway material, German requisition of in Belgium, II, 127.

Rathenau, Dr., plan for exploitation of occupied territories, II, 117.

rebus sic stantibus, II, 217.

Red Cross, *see* Geneva convention.

Renault, L., on American instructions of 1863, I, 3; on invasion of Bel-

gium, II, 216; on destruction of neutral prizes, II, 265; on status of reservists on neutral ships, II, 370; on responsibility of soldiers for criminal acts, II, 471, 472.

Reprisals, in aerial warfare, I, 488, 494; on account of treatment of prisoners, II, 38, 49 ff., 51 ff. *See also* Blockade.

Requisitions, II, 117 ff.; German policy, II, 118; examples of, II, 119 ff.; provisions of Hague convention in respect to, II, 122; of live stock, II, 123; of machinery, II, 124; of railway material, II, 127; of timber and wood, II, 128; seizure of funds of private banks and of post offices, II, 129; treatment of Belgian banks, II, 130; requisitions of laborers, II, 132; treatment of Belgian towns, II, 133; requisition of guides, II, 135; views of the authorities, II, 137; German policy criticised, II, 139.

Requisition of neutral ships, I, 172; of belligerent vessels, I, 176.

Reservists, status of, I, 59; *see* Enemy persons on neutral vessels, seizure of.

Responsibility of soldiers for criminal acts, II, 472; provisions of military manuals relative to, II, 474; difficulties of application, II, 475; for crimes committed in foreign territory, II, 478; trial for offences on the high seas, II, 481; trial of in absentia, II, 481; plea of superior command, II, 483; responsibility of chiefs of state, II, 488; of the ex-German Emperor, II, 490; decision of peace conference reviewed, II, 493.

Rheims, cathedral of, destroyed, I, 441; fining of, II, 152.

Rio Tinto Co., cases of, I, 246.

Rivier, on right of self-preservation, II, 193.

Roberts, Lord, punishes South African towns by fines, II, 143.

Robinson and Co. v. *Cont. Insurance Co. of Mannheim*, case of, I, 130.

Root, Elihu, on covenant of League of Nations, II, 463; on need of sanctions for international law, II, 465; on new attitude toward violations of international law, II, 500.

Roscoe, E. G., on the case of *Porter* v. *Freudenberg*, I, 132.

Rothschild, Baron Lambert, contribution levied on, II, 115.

Roumania, case of, I, 222.

Roumania, pillage of, II, 122; deportation of civilians from, II, 164.

Ruheleben, prison camp, II, 16.

Rules of land warfare, American, character of, I, 3, 8; regarding collective punishments, II, 157; regarding punishment of war crimes, II, 474.

Russell, Lord John, on neutralization of Belgium, II, 227.

St. Petersburg, Declaration of, I, 14, 282.

Satow, Sir E., on planting mines in open seas, I, 343.

Schaffenius v. *Goldberg*, case of, I, 126, 243.

Scheldt, navigation of, II, 450.

Schmidhuber, Colonel, threatens to punish city of Lille, II, 151.

Schoenborn, Professor, defends invasion of Belgium, II, 199, 216, 217, 220.

Schramm, G., views on right of merchant vessels to arm, I, 403.

Schuster, E. J., on trade with the enemy, I, 210; on effect of war on contracts, I, 242, 243, 252.

Scott, J. B., views on shooting of Captain Fryatt, I, 409.

Scott, Leslie, views on effect of war on contracts, I, 241.

Search, right of, II, 292.

Seas, freedom of, I, 338; II, 457.

Self-preservation, right of, II, 193.

Seligman, v. *Eagle Insurance Co.*, case of, I, 245.

Semmes, Admiral, treatment of merchant vessels, II, 257.

Sequestrators of enemy property, in France, I, 90 ff.; in Germany, I, 95; in Belgium, I, 98.

Ships engaged on philanthropic missions, torpedoing of, I, 519. *See also* Merchant vessels.

Ship purchase bill, American, I, 201.

Shot guns, German protest against use of, I, 270.

Siam, prize court of, confiscates German ships, I, 171.

Sieveking, Dr., on right of enemy aliens to sue, I, 118, 122; on effect of war on contracts, I, 241.

Simla, case of, II, 356.

Society for Propagation of Gospel, case of, I, 226.

Solvay, M., contribution levied on, II, 115.

Solveig, case of, I, 199.

Spaight, J. M., on air craft as instruments of combat, I, 486; on rights of military occupants, II, 85; on requisition of guides, II, 136; on collective penalties, II, 158; on Japanese violation of Korea, II, 194; on sale of arms to belligerents, II, 403.

Spain, destruction of vessels of, II, 273; government of excludes submarines from its ports, II, 419.

Springbok, case of, II, 332.

Stein, Professor, on treatment of enemy railways, II, 128; on requisition of railway employés, II, 139.

Stigstad, case of, II, 323.

Stockton, Admiral, prepares naval code, I, 9.

Story, J., on sale of munitions to belligerents, II, 378.

Submarines, status of shipwrecked crews of, II, 427; treatment of in neutral waters, II, 430; distinction between commercial and war submarines, II, 432; exclusion of from neutral waters, II, 434; case of the *Deutschland*, II, 437; operations off American coast, II, 445.

Submarine warfare, Ch. XIV.

Suez Canal, status of during the war, I, 159.

Surratt, Mrs., execution of during American Civil War, II, 103.

Sweden, sinking of vessels of, II, 275; exclusion of warships from, II, 419, 435; controversy with Great Britain relative to interference with mails on neutral vessels, II, 354.

Switzerland, neutrality of violated by aviators, I, 472.

Taft, W. H., urges admission of hospital supplies to Germany, II, 339.

Tarnowski, Count, Austrian ambassador to United States given safe conduct, I, 46.

Telegraphs, wireless, II, 410.

Théodor, *bâtonnier*, treatment of by the Germans, II, 84.

Tingley v. *Müller*, case of, I, 212, 249.

Tommi and Rotherstand, cases of, I, 181.

Tournai, fining of by Germans, II, 146.

Trade with the enemy, Ch. VIII; subject not regulated by international law, I, 208; Anglo-American rule, I, 209; test of enemy character, I, 212; English decisions, I, 211 ff.; relaxations from the common law rule, I, 216; British legislation in respect to, I, 217; *Continental Tyre and Rubber Case*, I, 218; case of Premier Oil and Pipe Line Co., I, 221; case of the *Poona*, I, 222; trade with house in occupied territory, I, 222; French practice, I, 224; American judicial authority, I, 226; trade with enemy houses in neutral territory, I, 228 ff.; French legislation and practice, I, 235 ff.; German policy, I, 238 ff.

Transfers of flag, Ch. VII; before outbreak of war, I, 181; the French rule, I, 186; American view and practice, I, 186; British authority and practice, I, 188; views expressed at London Naval Conference, I, 191; case of Wagner ships, I, 198; German law and practice, I, 200; controversy between Chili and Great Britain regarding, I, 203; of war ships, I, 205.

Treaty of peace with Germany, provision regarding indemnities, II, 470; penal clauses of, II, 471, 477; provision relative to trial of the ex-Emperor, II, 492.

Treitschke, H., on "honest subjects" as spies, I, 57; on sinking of neutral merchant vessels, II, 281.

Trent, case of, II, 364.

Triepel, H., views on right of merchant vessels to arm, I, 402.

Troops, uncivilized, use of, I, 292.

UNDEFENDED TOWNS AND CITIES. See bombardments.

United States v. *Lapens*, case of, I, 243.

VAN DER ESSEN, on requisition of horses in Belgium, II, 123.

Vattel, on treatment of enemy aliens, I, 58; on right of passage in time of war, II, 222.

Visscher, Ch. de, criticism of doctrine of *Kriegsraison*, II, 197.

Walküre, case of, I, 165.

War, effect of on contracts, Ch. IX; methods and instruments employed for conduct of, Chs. X-XI; effect of on international law, Ch. XXXVII.

Warfare, aerial, Ch. XIX; employment of air craft in former wars, I, 458; operations during the late war, I, 459; raids over England, I, 460; over Italy, I, 462; over Germany, I, 463; views of Professor Holland, I, 468; when is a place defended against, I, 469; duty of aviator to give notice of attack, I, 471; violations of neutrality, I, 471; aeroplanes as instruments of combat, I, 483; German defence, I, 487; reprisals, I, 488; treatment of captured aviators, I, 494; bombing of hospitals, I, 500; need of new rules, II, 461.

War manuals, I, 1 ff.; value of, I, 11.

War ships in neutral ports, II, 415 ff.; exclusion of by certain neutral governments, II, 419; internment of, II, 423 ff.; hovering of off neutral ports, II, 443.

War treason, conception of, II, 93.

War zones, Ch. XIV; of Great Britain, I, 333; of Germany (1915), I, 335; of Germany (1917), I, 336; neutral protests against, I, 339; British war zone of 1914, I, 345; American protest, I, 346; Dutch protest, I, 350; legality of, I, 351.

Weapons and instruments, Chs. X-XI; forbidden bullets, I, 262 ff.; shot guns, I, 270; gases, I, 271 ff.; German theory in respect to means and instrumentalities, I, 278 ff.; use of gas shells, I, 284; liquid fire, I, 287; poisoned wells, I, 288; employment of uncivilized troops, I, 292.

Weber, ex parte, case of, I, 63.

Weiss, Professor, on compensation for damages committed by belligerents,

II, 469; on trial of the German Emperor, II, 489.

Westlake, J., views on transfers of flag, I, 196; on rights of military occupants, II, 85; on war treason, II, 93; on right of self-preservation, II, 194; on *Kriegsraison*, II, 197; on destruction of neutral prizes, II, 264; on sale of munitions to belligerents, II, 401, 404, 407.

White, Andrew D., explains German policy regarding sale of munitions to Spain, 1898, II, 390.

Whitlock, B., minister to Belgium, treatment of by Germans, I, 52; intervention in behalf of Miss Cavell, II, 98; on German policy of requisition in Belgium, II, 119; on German policy of deportations, II, 185.

Wilhelmina, case of, II, 312.

Wittenberg, prison camp at, II, 18.

Women, execution of in war, II, 97, 102.

Woolsey, T. D., on sale of munitions to belligerents, II, 378.

Woolsey, T. S., on trial of military offences, II, 476.

YACHTS, enemy, treatment of, I, 162.

Zamora, case of, I, 173.

Zimmermann, Herr, defence of execution of Miss Cavell, II, 99.

Zinc Corporation v. *Skipworth*, case of, I, 246.

Zitelmann, Professor E., on Hague conventions, I, 23; defence of submarine warfare, I, 375.

Zoodochos-Pighi, case of, II, 309.